INDIANA

Covin

Critte

Williamstown

Cynthiana

La Grange

Shelbyville
Louisville
Frankfort
Georgetown
Versailles
Paris
Lexington

Lawrenceburg
Bloomfield
Bardstown
Springfield
Mackville
Perryville
Harrodsburg
Bryantsville
Danville
Camp
Dick Robinson
Richmond
Kingston

Lebanon
Big Hill Mt.

OHIO RIVER
JEFFERSONVILLE R.R.
KENTUCKY CENTRAL

BARREN RIVER
K E N T U C K Y
Munfordville
Green River
Campbellsville
Crab Orchard

LOUISVILLE R.R.
NASHVILLE R.R.

Bowling Green
Cave City
Columbia
Logan's Cross Roads

Glasgow
Jamestown
Barboursville

Hopkinsville
Scottsville
Burkesville
Cumberland Gap
VA

Tompkinsville
CUMBERLAND RIVER
Gallatin

CUMBERLAND PLATEAU
Big Ct. Gap
Wilson Gap

CLINCH RIVER

Lebanon
Knoxville
TENNESSEE RIVER

Nashville
STONE'S RIVER
Nolensville
Franklin
Triune
College Grove
Murfreesboro
McMinnville

Thompson's Station
Spring Hill
Columbia
New Fosterville
Bell Buckle
Wartrace
Hoover's Gap
Liberty Gap
Fairfield

TENNESSEE
SEQUATCHIE RIVER
WALDEN'S RIDGE
CUMBERLAND
EAST TENNESSEE & GEORGIA R.R.
HIAWASSEE RIVER

Shelbyville
Normandy
Tullahoma
Estill Springs
Dechard
Winchester
Cowan
University
Manchester

Charleston
Harrison
Tyner's
Cleveland

NO. CAROLINA

Pulaski
Fayetteville
Bridgeport
Shawn
Perry
Trenton
Chattanooga
Chickamauga Sta.

NASHVILLE & DECATUR R.R.
ELK RIVER
CHATTANOOGA R.R.
Jasper

Stevenson
Graysville
Ringold
Tunnel Hill

HUNTSVILLE
NASHVILLE & CHARLESTON R.R.
Racoon River
Sand Mt.
Lookout Mountain
West Chickamauga Creek
Pigeon Mt.
Snake Creek Gap
Dalton
Dug Gap
La Fayette
Villanow

MPHIS
Decatur
TENNESSEE RIVER
McLemore's Cove
Sugar Valley
Resaca
WESTERN & ATLANTA R.R.
Calhoun

Guntersville
Alpine
Adairsville
Kingston
ETOWAH RIVER

Gaylesville
Rome
Cassville
Cassville Sta.

L A B A M A
Gadsden
COOSA RIVER
Allatoona
Acworth
G E O R G I A

Pickett's Mill
New Hope Church
Dallas
Pine Mt.
Gilgal church
Kenesaw
Marietta
Smyrna
PEACHTREE CREEK

Powder Springs
Ezra Church
Sandtown
Atlanta
Decatur
East Point
Rough & Ready
GEORGIA R.R.
Fairburn
Palmetto
Jonesboro

PAT CLEBURNE
CONFEDERATE GENERAL

MAJOR GENERAL PATRICK RONAYNE CLEBURNE
Provisional Army of the Confederates States of America
1828-1864

Photograph of General Cleburne Taken in Mobile, Ala.,
January 1864. The Only Known Picture of Him Made During the War.

PAT CLEBURNE

CONFEDERATE GENERAL

And Treasured Tales of Victory,
Midst Loud Triumphant Cheers,
Bring Richmond's Name and Cleburne's Fame
Re-echoing Down the Years.

A Definitive Biography
by
Howell and Elizabeth Purdue

Hill Jr. College Press   •   Hillsboro, Texas   •   1973

Library of Congress Catalog Card No.
73-76245
I.S.B.N. No.
912172-18-5

Printed by

Waco, Texas

Bound by
Library Binding Co.
Waco, Texas

To
Brigadier General Branner Pace Purdue
1900-1952
United States Military Academy Class Of 1925
Commander 120th. Infantry Regiment, W.W. II

PREFACE AND ACKNOWLEDGMENTS

The reader will find that this biography sets out substantially in toto the reports of battles and of military operations written by Maj. Gen. P. R. Cleburne. There are two reasons for rehearsing these documents: (1) According to Maj. Calhoun Benham, Cleburne's assistant adjutant-general, "it was the earnest wish of the General" that his reports "should be made public as a testimonial which he conceived his duty required him to give of the conduct of his officers and men"[1] (2) In the words of Wilbur G. Kurtz, authority on the Dalton to Atlanta campaign and fighting around Atlanta, "Cleburn's reports in all the thousands in the *Official Records* possess the rare quality of vividness."[2] Included in the biography are all of the personal letters of Cleburne which are extant, most of them hitherto unknown to historians. Hence, part of the book is in the nature of a journal.

During the war years, our focus is on Cleburne and his troops. We do not attempt to write another history of the Army of Tennessee or treat of the campaigns in detail. We assume that the reader is generally familiar with the campaigns and strategies of the Army of Tennessee, with those of the armies whom it fought, and with the battles as a whole.

Miss Anna Brooke Allan, curator, Southern Historical Collection, The University of North Carolina Library, was obliging in locating and mailing the writers reproductions of letters and documents in the Collection.

Edwin C. Bearss, Supervisory Historian, National Park Service, rendered expert assistance in depicting the position and movement of troops on several of the maps.

---

[1]Calhoun Benham to Robert Tarleton, June 5, 1867, in Tarleton Family Collection, Yale University Library.
[2]Wilbur G. Kurtz to T. R. Hay, June 23, 1953, in possession of T. R. Hay, Locust Valley, New York.

Charles M. Brown and Mrs. Gardner Wright, Jr., of Marietta, Georgia, grandchildren of Joseph M. Brown, former governor of Georgia, provided copies of cuts by A. R. Waud of scenes from Cleburne's battles in north Georgia. These illustrations originally appeared in Joseph M. Brown, *The Mountain Campaigns in Georgia or War Scenes on the W. & A.* (5th ed.; Buffalo, N. Y., 1890).

Harold H. Bull, Lt. Gen. U. S. A. (Rtd.), Washington, D. C., permitted the unlimited use of an excellent military study, "Campaign of Franklin and Nashville," written by him in 1927, when a major in the advanced course at the Infantry School, Fort Benning, Georgia. General Bull explained to the authors the violation by Hood at Franklin of principles of war and allied tactical principles. He also read the chapters of the manuscript on Spring Hill and Franklin.

The late Monroe Cockrell, Evanston, Illinois, supplied useful material and information relative to the battle of Shiloh, permitted the reproduction of a portion of his map of the battle of Franklin, and read the first six chapters of the manuscript.

Dr. E. Merton Coulter, Athens, Georgia, gave permission for the quoting of two short excerpts from his *The Confederate States of America, 1861-1865*, and informed the writers of a helpful authority.

The late Miss Georgia Cowan, Chief of the Biography Division, District of Columbia Public Library, was resourceful, helpful, and obliging in many ways.

Dr. John L. Ferguson, State Historian, Arkansas History Commission, promptly and efficiently complied with requests for information.

Lt.-Cmdr. M. Godfrey, Royal Navy (Rtd.), late of the Public Record Office i/c Naval and Military Records, London, interpreted in detail the records of Cleburne's service in the British Army, related pertinent facts regarding British Regiments of Foot in the 1840's, and cited military treatises and histories covering this period.

Dr. Gilbert E. Govan of Lookout Mountain, Tennessee, historian, took the writers on a tour of McLemore's Cove, Chickamauga battlefield, and Missionary Ridge; explained the geographic conditions of the area around Chattanooga at the time of the War between the States; and collaborated in the preparation of the portion of the manuscript dealing with the fiasco at McLemore's Cove.

Dr. Herschel Gower, Associate Professor of English, Vanderbilt University, read the entire manuscript and made valuable suggestions.

Mrs. Virginia R. Hawley, General Reference Supervisor, The Western Reserve Historical Society, gave of her knowledge of the Braxton Bragg Papers and the William P. Palmer Collection.

Thomas Robson Hay, historian, of Locust Valley, New York, made his entire files dating from 1921 of material about Cleburne available to the writers and assisted in other ways. In 1929 he treated of General Cleburne in his *Hood's Tennessee Campaign*; and in 1959, edited the reprint of Irving A. Buck, *Cleburne and His Command*, and wrote the "Introduction" thereto. Mr. Hay's extensive files on Cleburne contain valuable material available in no other source. In discussions, Mr. Hay advanced sound thinking about the fiasco at Spring Hill. He read the chapter of the manuscript on Spring Hill.

The late Robert Selph Henry, author and historian, Alexandria, Virginia, was the inspiration for this book. He extended encouragement and advice, and read a number of the chapters. He also gave permission for short quotations from his *The Story of the Confederacy*.

William Hogan and Dr. Denis Wilson, local historians of County Cork, Ireland, supplied invaluable information concerning Cleburne's boyhood and young manhood. In anticipation of the writers' coming to Ireland, they had located sites pertinent to the Cleburne story, to which they took the writers. These gentlemen also assisted in research.

John W. Hunt, Head, Reader Service Section, Stack and Reader Division, Library of Congress, located out-of-print books and periodicals for the writers.

Miss Dorothy James, title abstracter, Helena, Arkansas, was invaluable in locating records in the courthouse.

The late Wilbur G. Kurtz of Atlanta shared with the writers his vast knowledge of the battles and campaigns in north Georgia and around Atlanta, insofar as it pertained to

Cleburne and his men. Recognized as the leading authority on these campaigns, Mr. Kurtz's ground study began in 1916, and continued as an avocation over a period of fifty years. He served as technical adviser for the motion pictures, *Gone with the Wind* and *The Great Locomotive Chase*. Mr. Kurtz assisted the writers in various ways: in personal interviews; a field trip to the battlefields of Pickett's Mill and Atlanta, and other points; numerous informative letters respecting the campaigns; and reading the chapters on the Dalton to Atlanta campaign, the battles around Atlanta, and the Jonesboro campaign. Four maps, drawn by him especially for *Pat Cleburne: Confederate General* are a feature of the book. Mr. Kurtz wished to be of service in developing the Cleburne story because of his great admiration for the General.

Warren Lambert, Berea, Kentucky, pointed out to the writers the exact spot of the initial phase of the battle of Richmond, Kentucky, and went with them to Bighill Mountain and other points in the vicinity.

The late Hugh D. Miser, Washington, D. C., geologist U. S. Geological Survey, explained the geography of Phillips County, Arkansas; and interpreted geological maps of the battlefields of Shiloh and Perryville, and Bighill Mountain.

Mrs. Frank L. Owsley, former Director of Manuscript Section, Tennessee State Library and Archives, informed the writers of manuscripts and papers including General Cleburne's original report of the battle of Chickamauga. She also permitted the writers to quote a passage from Frank Lawrence Owsley (her late husband), *Plain Folk of the Old South*.

Elmer O. Parker, Assistant Director, Old Military Records Division, National Archives of the United States, supplied special information and documents and informed the writers of items of information in the Archives, heretofore unknown, concerning General Cleburne and his division.

The late John R. Peacock, High Point, North Carolina, supplied material pertaining to McLemore's Cove, Spring Hill, and Franklin.

Mrs. Dorothy E. Powers, Curator, Inland Rivers Library, The Public Library of Cincinnati and Hamilton County, assisted in securing information about Cleburne relatives in the Cincinnati area.

Van F. Pruitt, New York City, retired architect and son of a Confederate veteran, drew the map of the theater of Cleburne's military operations, which appears on the end sheets; and the map, "Portions of Helena, Arkansas in 1856."

The late C. H. Purvis, Helena, County Surveyor of Phillips County, Arkansas, acquainted the writers with information about the city and county in the early days.

Ralph V. Righton, Stone Mountain, Georgia, aided in the study of the fighting in north Georgia and informed the writers as to the present ownership and location of the sword given to Cleburne by the 15th Arkansas Regiment.

The late Dr. Daniel M. Robison, State Librarian and Archivist, Emeritus, Tennessee State Library and Archives, suggested sources of material. Mrs. Joseph Waggener, senior archivist, supplied two special items.

Timothy Seaton, Park Historian, Kennesaw Mountain National Battlefield Park, drew a map, for the writers' information, of a portion of the battlefield, based on the National Park Service's Master Plan; and supplied a copy of a map drawn by a Union soldier.

Col. Harold B. Simpson, Director, The Hill Junior College Press, carefully and knowledgeably edited the manuscript.

Allan Sloan, Columbia, Tennessee, guided the writers over the back road which the Army of Tennessee, led by Cleburne's division, traveled from Davis Ford to the vicinity of Spring Hill.

The late C. Eugene Smith, Secretary, Ancient and Accepted Scottish Rite of Freemasonry, Southern Jurisdiction of the United States, Little Rock, Arkansas, supplied information concerning P. R. Cleburne and the Masonic Order.

The late Ray D. Smith, Evanston, Illinois, and his secretary, Miss Helen Reynolds, provided references to Cleburne from his personally prepared index of the *Confederate Veteran.*

Dr. Winston Smith, Demopolis, Alabama, assisted in research in Marengo County with emphasis on sites and customs.

Edward E. Tinney, Park Historian, Shiloh National Military Park, accompanied the writers over the battlefield of Shiloh and located the position of Cleburne's troops at certain stages of the battle.

James W. Watterson, Jonesboro, Georgia, directed the writers on a tour of the battlefield of Jonesboro.

Dr. Denis Wilson. See William Hogan and Dr. Denis Wilson, *supra*.

Other acknowledgements appear in the footnotes.

The biography is being published by The Hill Junior College Press of Hillsboro, Texas, located only thirty miles from the city of Cleburne, Texas, named for the General.

Arlington, Virginia
October 1972   Howell and Elizabeth Purdue

CONTENTS

ILLUSTRATIONS

Gen. Patrick Ronayne Cleburne (Frontispiece)
Cleburne Coat of Arms (xvi)

Follow Page 32

Cliburn Hall, Westmorland County, England
Parish Church of Cliburn, Westmorland County, England
Bridepark Cottage, Ovens Township, County Cork, Ireland
Grange, Ovens Township, County Cork, Ireland
Annebrook, Home of Patrick Ronayne
St. Mary's Church, Parish of Athnowen, County Cork, Ireland
Mary Anne Ronayne Cleburne, Mother of General Cleburne

Follow Page 202

Ambrotype of P.R. Cleburne, Aged 21
Portion of Helena, Arkansas in 1856
Battle Flag of 1st. Arkansas Infantry, Cleburne's Division
Key's Battery Moving Out Peachtree Road-Kurtz Drawing
Gen. Joseph E. Johnston's Headquarters, Dalton, Ga.
Brig. Gen. James Deshler
Brig. Gen. Lucius E. Polk
Brig. Gen. M.P. Lowrey
Brig. Gen. D.C. Govan
Brig. Gen. H.B. Granbury
Cleburne's Repulse of Sherman at Missionary Ridge
Battle of Ringgold, Ga.
Battle of Pickett's Mill
The Truce in the Midst of the Battle of Kennesaw Mountain
Miss Susan Tarleton

Follow Page 434

Christopher S. Cleburne
Grave of Capt. Christopher S. Cleburne
General Cleburne's Saddle
Sword Presented to General Cleburne by 15th. Arkansas Infantry
General Cleburne's Pistol
The Pat Cleburne Cemetery, Jonesboro, Ga.
Steamboat Pat Cleburne
Officers of Pat Cleburne Camp, U.C.V., No. 222, Waco, Texas
General Cleburne Grave and Monument, Confederate Hill, Phillips
    County, Ark.

MAPS

Theater of Cleburne's Operations (Endsheets)

Follow Page 78

Moves of Cleburne's Brigade at Shiloh, April 6, 1862
First Engagement, Battle of Richmond, Kentucky, August 30, 1862
Central Kentucky
Moves of Cleburne's Brigade at Perryville, October 8, 1862
Advance of Cleburne's Brigades at Murfreesboro, December 30, 1862
McLemore's Cove, September 11, 1863

Follow Page 320

Cleburne's Map of Chickamauga
Cleburne's Defense of Ringgold Gap, November 27, 1863
Operations in Northwest Georgia
Pickett's Mill, May 27, 1864
Battle of Atlanta, July 22, 1864
Battle of Jonesboro, August 31-September 1, 1864
Cleburne's and Forrest's Attack, Spring Hill, November 29, 1864
Portion of Monroe F. Cockrell's Map of Franklin

FORWARD

CLIBBOR NE SCEAME

CLEBURNE COAT OF ARMS

CHAPTER I

FAMILY HISTORY – EARLY LIFE IN IRELAND

Forward Clibbor Ne Sceame
– Heraldic motto on Cleburne coat of arms.

Gen. Patrick Ronayne (rōw-nŭn[1]) Cleburne (clāy-bŭrn[2]) was one of the Confederacy's greatest military leaders. After the battle of Chickamauga, he was widely known as "the Stonewall Jackson of the West." This sobriquet was indeed a rare compliment, considering the veneration in which the memory of Lee's great lieutenant was held throughout the South.

Born in Ireland, Cleburne came to America in 1849, at the age of twenty-one, and soon thereafter settled in Helena, Arkansas. Prior to leaving Ireland he had served in an English regiment for three years and four months as a private and three months as a corporal. In 1860, when the War between the States was imminent, he volunteered as a private to fight for the Southern cause. In less than two years after the war began, Cleburne rose to the rank of Major General, in command of a division in the Army of Tennessee. At only thirty-six years of age, he was killed near the end of the war in the battle of Franklin, Tennessee.

2

The Cleburnes, an "ancient and knightly family," originated in Westmorland County, England. The family name was derived from the manor of "Cliburn," which was held by the Cleburne family (with variant spellings of the name) for more than 400 years, from early in the thirteenth century to the middle of the seventeenth century.

Cliburn Hall stands today, near the small village of Cliburn, six miles southeast of the town of Penrith, in historic Westmorland County, high above the rivulet Leith. The grand old stone building with a three-story "pele tower" was erected in the fourteenth century by Robert de Cliburn,

1

knight of the shire for Westmorland. Two hundred years later, the original structure was altered and enlarged by Richard Cleburne. On the Tudor estate were a large deer park, beautiful pleasure grounds, and terraced walks.

Cliburn Hall has undergone changes, the battlements, have been removed, the outer fortifications have disappeared, and some of the extensions have been destroyed. The old three-story building and one of the two-story wings now constitute a modern farm house.[3] But the spacious state room with a vaulted ceiling, a capacious fireplace at one end, and remnants of a minstrel loft at the other end, signify gracious living in days of yore. On a stone slab above the main entrance to the Hall, this couplet is inscribed:

RYCHARD . CLEBURN . THUS . THEY . ME .
CAWL . WCH . IN . MY . TYME . HATH . BEALDED .
YS . HALL . THE . YEARE . OF . OWRE . LORDE .
GOD . WHO . LYST . FOR . TO . NEAM . 1567 .[4]

Across the road from Cliburn Hall is the Parish Church of Cliburn, a Norman structure built in the twelfth century. On the north wall of the chancel in a small memorial window of "one round-headed light,"[5] is inscribed the Cleburne coat of arms, with the heraldic motto *Forward Clibbor Ne Sceame.* The cryptic Latin phrase means "Forward! The Cleburnes do not know otherwise," or "The Cleburnes do not know how to do anything else."[6] Below the window a bronze tablet reads:

IN . MEMORY
OF . MAJOR . GENERAL
PATRICK . RONAYNE . CLEBURNE
C . S . A .
BORN . 17TH . MARCH . 1828
KILLED . AT . THE . BATTLE . OF . FRANKLIN . TENN
30TH . NOVEMBER . 1864

This memorial was placed in the 1870's by Dr. Christopher James Cleborne, a first cousin of the General.[7] Dr. Cleborne, born in Edinburgh, Scotland, came to America and was a lieutenant commander in the medical corps of the Federal navy during the War between the States. He was a rear admiral when he retired in 1899.

The founder of the Cleburne family, Hervey de Cliburne

(Hervey meant "strong in war") and his descendants held the manor of Cliburne by "knight service." Early in the fifteenth century, one of Hervey's descendants, John Cleburne, married Elizabeth Curwen, whose blood was "darkly, deeply, beautifully blue." Her ancestor, the "great" Gospatrick, was a descendant of the Saxon King Ethelred II, and King Malcolm II of Scotland. Gospatrick's father was Maldred, the younger brother of the "Gracious Duncan," whom Macbeth murdered. John Cleburne fought in the bloody battles of Barnet, Tewksbury, and Bosworth; and died from wounds received in the skirmish of Kirtlemore. John Cleburne and his wife, Elizabeth Curwen, were direct ancestors of Patrick Ronayne Cleburne.[8]

About the middle of the seventeenth century, following the English reconquest of Ireland, William Cleburne, the second son of Thomas the fourteenth Lord of the manor of Cliburne, went to the City of Kilkenny, Ireland. He later settled in County Tipperary on the banks of the River Shannon. Cleburne kinsmen had preceded him to the general area, but William founded the Anglo-Irish line — the ancestors of Patrick Ronayne — the Cleburnes of Bally-collaton in Tipperary. William acquired "the castles, towns and lands of Ballycollitan," and "the villadge and lands of Bunnadubber." At that time, the Irish "hated" the English settlers, but the Cleburnes were an exception; because they had obtained their lands by purchase, not by confiscation. William was distinguished for kindness and unostantatious generosity to the distressed Gaels. ". . . it was said that 'a Cleburne might ride in safety from one end of the county to the other.'" William devoted much time to the study of "Philosophy and Physic." Known as "Wise William," he became arbitrator of disputes among his tenants and neighbors.[9]

John Cleburne (the eldest great grandson of "Wise William") divided all his lands between his two daughters by "legal hocuspocusing," leaving no lands to the male heirs. John's younger brother Edward (great grandfather of Patrick Ronayne Cleburne) spent all his means in an unsuccessful law suit trying to recover the estates for the male heirs. Hence Edward's son William of Rock Cottage (grandfather of

Patrick Ronayne Cleburne) did not live in a castle.[10]

Nevertheless, William of Rock Cottage was sufficiently affluent to send his eldest son, Joseph (father of Patrick Ronayne Cleburne), to the Royal College of Surgeons of England, in London. After graduating in 1822, Joseph began the practice of medicine in County Cork. The following year, he married Mary Anne Ronayne of that county and took her to live at Bridepark Cottage in Ovens Township.[11]

Patrick Ronayne Cleburne's mother, Mary Anne Ronayne, came from one of the oldest and most prominent Celtic families in Ireland, with many leaders and warriors. In Ossian's poems, a Ronan is one of the heroes of Irish legend. In 610 A. D., Ronans (the Gaelic spelling was "Ronain") were bishops, abbots, and chieftains. As tribal chiefs, Ronans and O'Ronans fought throughout the Danish wars; and in the twelfth century, after the Norman conquest, were formidable foes of the Normans. The name, however, became Frenchified to Ronayne.[12]

The habitat of the Ronains was the coastal area east of Cork extending from the walled seaport town of Youghal southwestward past the Great Island, in Cork Harbour. At the time of the Norman invasion, the Ronans possessed large landholdings in this section. For approximately a hundred years, beginning in 1558, almost consecutively, the mayor of Youghal was a Ronayne.[13]

In the fifteenth century, an ancestor of Patrick Ronayne Cleburne, Maurice Ronayne, a landowner in Youghal and Kinsale districts, wrung from King Edward IV "a grant of the Rights of Englishmen." Maurice's grandson, Thomas Ronayne, was Mayor of Cork in 1537 and again in 1549; and James, son of Thomas (ancestors of Patrick Ronayne Cleburne), was Mayor of Cork in 1575. This branch of the family were large landowners in the Great Island, the area between Youghal and Kinsale, and also in Cork and its environs.[14]

Annebrook, the home of Mary Anne Ronayne Cleburne, on the Great Island, just north of Cobh, was built late in the eighteenth century. Her branch of the family had prospered, but most of the Ronayne lands had passed to lateral relatives who were first sons.[15] Annebrook, a Georgian mansion,

4

remains today, on a scenic curve of the main road from Cobh to Cork, but unoccupied and in a bad state of repair. From the broad iron entrance gate between large stone pillars, an old road winds to the ruins of auxiliary buildings and tall garden walls.

Mary Anne Ronayne was described by a nephew as "a woman of strong, independent character, a radical in politics, a defender of the oppressed, a friend to liberty and equality."[16] "Radical in politics" indicates that she was an opponent of the political status quo in Ireland and England, and a firm supporter of all liberal thought. Indicative of his innate modesty, Patrick Ronayne Cleburne "never breathed" to his most intimate friends in America the distinguished lineage from which he sprang.[17]

3

On the bank of the sparkling River Bride in Ovens Township is Bridepark Cottage, a handsome residence of early nineteenth century architecture. Here,[18] on March 16, 1828, was born Patrick Ronayne Cleburne,[19] the third child of Joseph and Mary Anne Ronayne Cleburne. His being born on St. Patrick's Eve was a coincidence, since his parents had planned, if their child were a boy, to name him Patrick Ronayne, for his maternal grandfather.[20] Moreover, the date of birth was an auspicious omen. For this infant was to become a man of great energy and unbending determination, qualities which were outstanding attributes of the patron saint of Ireland.

In Ireland, Patrick Ronayne Cleburne was called Ronayne, the name by which he was always known to his family.[21] In America, to many friends he was "Cleburne" and he signed his name P. R. Cleburne. But to the Confederate soldiers, he became "Pat Cleburne," and thus he is known in history.

Anne Ronayne Cleburne died in 1829, when Ronayne was only nineteen months old. The other children were William aged five years, Anne aged three years, and Joseph, five months of age. Fourteen months later, Dr. Cleburne married Isabella Jane Stuart, aged nineteen, the daughter of a Scottish clergyman. The young Mrs. Cleburne was a kind, intelligent woman of strong character. She became a real mother to her stepchildren, and Ronayne was deeply devoted to her all of his life.[22]

Ronayne's half sister, Isabella, was born in 1832; and his half brother Edward Warren, in 1833. In 1836, the growing family moved from Bridepark Cottage to Grange, also in Ovens Township. Dr. Cleburne, now an eminent physician, leased for a long term this 205 acre estate at an annual rental of 230 pounds.[23]

Grange was on the site of an ancient abbey, some of which structure was utilized as part of the large two-story dwelling. Only one other residence in the township was of comparable size. Traces remained of the old fortification wall with four towers, formerly protected by a moat and drawbridge.[24] The Cleburne children no doubt enjoyed living in this historic atmosphere.

Dr. Cleburne was a vestryman in St. Mary's, the Parish Church of Athnowen, Church of Ireland (Episcopalean), in Ovens Township, where Ronayne was baptized. In addition to his private practice, conducted from his residence, he served as the attending physician at the dispensary in Ballincollig, a town three miles from Grange. In a land rampant with poverty and destitution, Dr. Cleburne was notably kind and charitable in assisting people in distress. He was known in the community as "The Poor Man's Friend."[25]

The Cleburne farm was worked by tenants and "labourers," in dairy farming and raising money crops, such as wheat, barley, and oats. But the operation suffered from lack of personal supervision which Dr. Cleburne was unable to give. Also, under the economic conditions in Ireland at the time, one who had earned the sobriquet, a "poor man's friend," could not be a successful farmer.[26]

As a child, with strangers Ronayne was shy and reserved; but with his family and friends, he was mischievous and merry. In his youth, he enjoyed nature and the solitude of the woods. He fished in the River Bride; and with dogs and gun, hunted for pheasants, woodcocks, and rabbits in woods bordering the River Lee. Along these scenic rivers near Grange, he found "tongues in trees, books in the running brooks, sermons in stones, and good in everything." On the other hand, he spurned the fox-hunting "set" of the period;[27] and was an indifferent horseman.

It is likely that Ronayne first viewed military parades at Ballincollig, where a field battery of the Royal Artillery was stationed at barracks. In blue and gold uniforms, the troops drilled on the large parade grounds. Each limber and gun was drawn by six horses with gunners on the limbers and astride some of the horses, followed by mounted artillerists as escorts. In Ballincollig, he probably also visited the Royal Gunpowder Mills Company, with its big furnaces and machinery covering four square miles.[28]

There were visits to his maternal grandparents at Annebrook, seventeen miles east of Grange. The Cleburnes probably traveled the eight miles to Cork by coach, over rolling hills, past fertile fields, and green pastures. From Cork, by boat on the River Lee, they passed handsome villas, artistic cottages, and ancient ruins. How exciting it must have been when Cobh and the harbor came into view!

> And doesn't old Cove look charming there,
>   Watching the wild waves' motion,
> Leaning her back against the hills,
>   And the tips of her toes in the ocean?[29]

At Cobh, Grandfather Ronayne's coach was likely waiting to take them to Annebrook. There were occasional visits to Ronayne relatives in County Cork and rugged County Waterford; and no doubt to their relative Christopher Cleburne, a flour factor in Cork.[30]

Ronayne's education, until twelve years of age, was furnished by a private tutor. He then attended an expensive private school for boys, near Ballincollig, where his brother William had graduated. The Reverend W. Spedding, a curate of the Established Church, was the headmaster. A "Prospectus" described the school as an "Establishment . . . for the education of a limited number of young gentlemen." "The Pupils are carefully prepared," the prospectus stated, "on the most improved plan for the several Universities, Naval and Military Colleges, &c. Also in Drafting Maps and the several departments of English Literature, in which Mathematics and Composition hold a prominent place."

Special courses were offered in "Drawing, French, Music, and Drill Masters."[31]

Ronayne enjoyed history, geography, and literature — especially poetry; but had a seeming ineptitude for Latin, Greek, and French. The prospectus read, "The Pupils are treated with paternal affection, and an anxious concern for their improvement." The latter feature apparently dominated the thinking of the Reverend Mr. Spedding, a man of small stature and stern countenance, who believed in applying the birch switch freely to his charges. This method used in trying to force Ronayne into mastering languages resulted in his developing a strong dislike for the teacher and these subjects.[32]

After moving to Grange, two more Cleburne children were born: Robert Stuart in 1837; and Christopher S. in 1841, when Ronayne was thirteen years old.[33] This little brother Christopher, whom Ronayne especially loved, was also destined to fight for the Confederate States of America.

Dr. Cleburne died less than two years after Christopher's birth, leaving the family in "moderately comfortable" circumstances. They continued living at Grange, although upon six months' notice the lease could have been surrendered, in March of any year, without penalty. However, some financial adjustments were necessary. William, then past eighteen, withdrew from Trinity College at Dublin after three years of study, two of which had been in engineering. As the eldest son, he likely took over supervision of the farm and other responsibilities. Ronayne, fifteen years of age, withdrew from Spedding school, which he had attended for three years. By his father's decision, Ronayne was destined for the medical profession. Although he had little desire to be a doctor, he became an apprentice under Dr. Thomas H. Justice, a physician and surgeon in the thriving town of Mallow, twenty miles north of Grange. Dr. Justice also owned and operated an apothecary shop, where young Cleburne acquired basic skills in tending shop and mixing medicines.[34]

Not having graduated from preparatory school, Ronayne hoped through the apprenticeship to qualify for admission to the medical school of Apothecaries' Hall at Dublin. In the fall of 1844, he applied for admission by mail but was "rejected."[35] He continued in the apprenticeship under Dr. Justice until February 1846. At this time, he traveled 165 miles by stagecoach to Dublin to take the entrance examination at the medical school. He failed the examination, which included Latin, Greek, and French.

Proud and sensitive, Ronayne felt that he had disgraced himself and his family by failing the examination. Without returning to Mallow or communicating with relatives or friends, he decided to disappear by joining the British 41st Regiment of Foot, stationed in Dublin, which he understood was under orders to embark for India.[36] On February 27, 1846, he enlisted as a private with pay of a shilling a day. The length of his enlistment does not appear in records now extant; but since most enlistments were "unlimited," *i. e.*, for life, presumably Ronayne's was for life. Concealing his identity, he gave his "Trade" as "Laborer," the occupation of the typical recruit; and stated his "Place of Birth"as "Desertmore," which was a parish adjoining that of his birth, Athnowen. According to measurements roughly taken upon enlistment, his height was then five feet, nine inches.[37]

The new recruit was issued a glamorous uniform — a red coateé with white facings; a high white collar trimmed with lace; blue trousers with narrow red welt seamings; and, for his head, a tall, black shako surmounted by a four-inch feather. With this splendor came arduous training — the "Manuel and Platoon Exercises" in use of the musket and bayonet; instruction in keeping of arms "in a serviceable state, clean, and regularly marked"; and instruction in maintenance of clothing and accoutrements.[38]

The regiment was not sent to India but remained in Ireland, as part of the strong garrison maintained there. Ironically, nearly one-half of the regiment was made up of Irishmen. When the "Great Famine" began in the spring of 1846, the British Government dispersed the regiment, with detachments scattered at different encampments in central and south central Ireland to protect property, keep order, and curb riots. As a soldier subject to orders, the only record of Cleburne's part in these activities is that on numerous occasions he marched from twenty to thirty miles to posts of duty, and was on guard patrol at one post.[39]

Also, various detachments of the regiment were engaged in regular training — the prescribed platoon, company, and battalion drill, musketry and field training; and outpost and patrol duties; as well as the "System and Discipline of the Regiment." Cleburne zealously applied himself to this training; and became a well drilled and disciplined soldier, skilled in the use of arms.[40]

Seventeen years later, when Cleburne was a division commander in the Confederate Army, he applied the knowledge of the minutiae of arms gained while in the British 41st Regiment of Foot. During Cleburne's first inspection of his regiments as a Confederate major general, a man in the ranks submitted a spotlessly clean rifle and the General instantly said, "Don't take those bands off again" — an act prohibited by the regulations. When the soldier was about to deny having removed the bands, General Cleburne pointed out that the U, a small mark on each band, was wrong side up. The soldiers witnessing the occurrence were awed by their General's knowledge and keen observation.[41]

A few months later, Lt. Col. James Arthur Lyon Fremantle of the Coldstream Guards, on military leave from the British Army, visited the Army of Tennessee and was entertained by General Cleburne. In discussing the difference between the British and Confederate infantry in drill and exercise of arms, Cleburne evinced much interest in his old outfit, the 41st Regiment. Colonel Fremantle recorded in his diary: "[General Cleburne] told me that he ascribed his advancement mainly to the useful lessons which he had learnt in the ranks of the British Army, and he pointed with a laugh to his general's white facings, which he said his 41st experience enabled him to keep cleaner than any other Confederate General."[42]

Cleburne had been in the British regiment eighteen months before his family learned of his whereabouts. He was unaware that an officer in the regiment was Capt. Robert Pratt, a grandson of the former Rector of Athnowen, and a son of the Rector of Desertmore — both rectors being close friends of the Cleburnes. Doubtless due to the dispersal of the 41st, Captain Pratt did not learn that Cleburne was in the regiment until July 1847, when Cleburne's detachment returned to regimental headquarters at Mulingar for a brief period. During a parade Captain Pratt recognized Cleburne, and notified the latter's family. The Captain had Cleburne transferred to his company, and showed him many acts of consideration and kindness. Years later in Arkansas, Cleburne said that he would have enlisted under an assumed name had he known that Captain Pratt was with the regiment.[43]

In December 1847, while his company was part of a detachment at Tarbert, Cleburne, in excess devotion to duty, disregarded exposure to freezing weather during long hours of guard patrol. As a result he was stricken with acute rheumatism; and confined for thirteen days in the hospital at regimental headquarters, then at Clare Castle. During the next fifteen months, the ailment recurred intermittently, requiring him to spend two months in hospitals in Cobh, Cork, and Dublin.[44]

During his forty-three months in the British regiment, Cleburne did a great deal of general reading, availing himself of the garrison library when stationed at regimental head-quarters. While convalscing in the hospitals, in addition to reading history and poetry, he studied Blackstone's *Commentaries*, thereby furthering an early interest he had acquired for the law.[45] From his knowledge of history and observation of the suffering of the downtrodden people of Ireland, he was imbued with ideals of personal liberty and hatred of tyranny in all forms.

In 1848, the famine having become less acute, the companies of the regiment reunited, with regimental head-quarters established at Buttevant in County Cork; and early in 1849 the 41st foot was transferred to the city of Cork. Thus young Cleburne, who had joined the regiment to go to India, now found himself stationed eight miles from his home. The following spring, he was transferred to a barracks on Spike Island, at the mouth of Cork Harbour — an island which had been owned by his ancestor Maurice Ronayne. Spike Island was less than three miles from Annebrook, his mother's birthplace, which had been inherited by an uncle following the death of Cleburne's maternal grandparents.[46]

4

In 1848 and early 1849, Cleburne obtained leave to visit

Grange at least twice; and found his family faced with critical economic problems because of the famine, with their resources nearing exhaustion. In 1847, the English Parliament had enacted legislation whereby, instead of the government continuing to conduct public works, the landlords and occupiers of land in Ireland were taxed for the relief of the destitute myriads. This taxation, "accompanied by low prices and bad produce," financially ruined one-third of the landlords and a large portion of the lessees. "By the end of 1849 it was said the Irish tenants looked as if they had just come out of their graves, and the landlords as if they were going into theirs." Obviously, the Cleburnes could not continue living at Grange, and plans had to be made for their future.[47] The courageous Mrs. Cleburne proposed that the family emigrate to the United States.

On June 28, 1849, from Spike Island Ronayne wrote his half-sister Isabella:

Dear Sister Isey

The manner in which a soldier lives but ill suits him for a correspondent; and you will allow that a state of society where duty is paramount to every consideration & kindred ties but very little respected, where every feeling of a softer nature is accounted a contemptible weakness, that every one subjected to such a discipline if he does not disregard them altogether will eventually contract a habit of concealing them from outward observation. The face of a soldier is in general but a very poor indication of the state of his feelings, and if on my last parting from home and friends I alone apeared [sic] callous it was from the before mentioned circumstances and not from a total insensibility to the kindness manifested on that and every other occasion.

If Mamma persists in her intention of going to America I will then have it more in my power to show that actions rather than words suit my temper. Situated as you have been up to the present time, my connection has been rather discreditable than otherwise, and my presence at home (in whatever light you might have regarded it) would in reality have been little else than an incumberance; but now as a change in circumstances are [sic] likely to make me somewhat more useful (though I do not consider myself competant [sic] to advise on that subject) if it should be ditermined [sic] on I will become both a willing & perservering agent towards its final accomplishment and success. I think if Mamma has made up her mind to go the best

12

plan would be to go as soon as possible, but not without sending some of us in advance so as not to be wholly ignorant of the manner of business in that country. All I can say at present is this: that if we should go & our hopes of prosperity be fulfiled I will be happy in the happiness of all; or if on the contrary disapointment & advirsity *[sic]* await us, I will endeavour by every means in my power to aleviate *[sic]* it. However, though I have not advised the following of my plan, still I will say that the prospects in this country are anything but good; and experiance *[sic]* goes very far to prove that they will not be better. If I get a pass I will come home in a few days time. I know that your kind disposition will prevent you from retaliating by an equally long silence.

And with affectionate love I remain your affectionate brother

Patrick Ronayne Cleburne

P. S. Tell Mamma & William that my presence at Grange in a few days will cancel the obligation I am under to them for their kind & to *[sic]* long unanswered letters.[48]

Three days after writing this letter, on July 1, 1849, Private Cleburne became a corporal. Some fourteen years later, speaking of this promotion, Cleburne said, "I was prouder of my corporal's commission than that of Major-General."[49] He held to his decision, however, to quit the army once definite plans were made for his family to go to America.

When he told Captain Pratt of his intention, the latter tried to persuade Cleburne to change his mind and remain in the army. Captain Pratt, who had been through the campaign of 1842 in Afghanistan, and later was to serve with distinction in the Crimea, ultimately rising to the rank of Lieutenant General, had perceived in Cleburne outstanding potential as a soldier. Cleburne realized that his chances for promotion would be limited. Under the system then prevailing in the British Army, field grade commissions were purchased at large sums. A man in the ranks could hope for advancement only to quartermaster, adjutant, or possibly captain.[50]

Four years later, from Arkansas, Cleburne was to write to his stepmother in Ireland:

I do not know what advantages Ireland now offers. I left it, however, under the impression that it was a hopeless case.

13

The elements of decay and destruction seemed to me to be so deeply seated in the heart of the body social or politic that to stay would only be to witness a lingering dissolution. I am not vain enough to expect you to take my thoughts for facts. You must judge yourself upon these matters. Had I been lead by Wm. Golins'[51] judgment (though I do not doubt for a moment his sincerity), I would now be a poor, servile mercenary without a will or thought of my own, in some soul cramping fortress or barracks instead of being as I am, a free man, knowing no superior, acknowledging no aristocracy except that of intellect or moral worth. Instead of being in a situation to aspire (were I so inclined) to office and honorable preferment, I should at best in my old age hold the commission of a petty officer, detested by inferiors and looked down on by superiors.[52]

In March 1849, becoming twenty-one, Cleburne received a small legacy. In all probability the money was his portion of a balance due the issue of Mary Anne Ronayne from the marriage settlement made by her father at the time of her wedding. Cleburne used twenty pounds of the sum to purchase his discharge from the British army on September 22, 1849.[53]

NOTES

CHAPTER I

[1]"R͞ow-nûn" is the pronunciation of the surname in Counties Cork and Waterford, Ireland.

[2]"Cl͞ay-bûrn" is the invariable pronunciation in County Cork, Ireland, the county of the General's birth; and throughout the Province of Munster, Ireland. In northern England, where the family originated, variant spellings were "Cleborne" and "Claiborne." Col. I. W. Avery of the Confederate Army, a personal friend, who wrote a sketch of Cleburne's life, noted variations in the early spelling of the name and pointed out that in the north of England *e* has the sound of *ai*. — I. W. Avery, "Patrick Ronayne Cleburne," *Kennesaw Gazette*, II (May 15, 1887), 1.

In Helena, Ark. where Cleburne resided, "Cl͞ay-bûrn" is the invariable pronunciation; the residents include persons who grew up knowing men and women who had known the General. Numerous written instances indicate that he pronounced his name "Cl͞ay-bûrn." Thus, the 1850 United States Census for Phillips County, Ark., lists him as "Patrick Claiborn." — Sch. I, Vol. IV, p. 250-R Census Schedules, 1850, Phillips County, Ark., Records of the Bureau of the Census, Record Group 29, National Archives Building. (Hereinafter, Census Schedules will be cited as CS; and Record Group___, National Archives Building, as RG___, NA.) In General Cleburne's Compiled Service Record in the National Archives (copies of the original Confederate records), the first entry is "Claiborne"; the spelling is correct in all subsequent entries. — Compiled Service Record of Patrick R. Cleburne in National Archives Microfilm Publication 317, roll 139. (Hereinafter, Compiled Service Records will be cited as CSR; and National Archives microfilm publication and roll numbers, as M___/___, NA.) ". . . Major-General Cleburne is frequently confounded with the Tennessee *Claibornes*, ..." — Ora, "Our Army Correspondence" (from Tullahoma, Tenn.), Mobile *Advertiser and Register*, Jan. 21, 1863, p. 1. "Cl͞ay-bûrn" is the pronunciation given in John Hugh Reynolds, *Makers of Arkansas History* (New York, 1918), 244.

[3]John O'Hart, *Irish Pedigrees* (New York, 1915), II, 100, 103, 106, 109; Michael Waistell Taylor, *The Old Manorial Halls of Westmoreland & Cumberland: Publications of the Cumberland and Westmoreland Antiquarian and Archaeological Society* (Kendal, Eng., 1892) VIII, 105, 107, 112. The present owner, Joseph Bowness, recently modernized the interior, and restored the outside, of Cliburn Hall.

"The pele tower was always an oblong rectangular building, and almost invariably contained three stories, having a vaulted basement; above this was the principal apartment, or the 'solar'; on the second floor was the special sleeping place, and over it was the roof and battlements." — Taylor, *Old Manorial Halls*, 42.

[4]The stone slab is reset, having originally been over the former main entrance. — Royal Commission on Historical Monuments, England, *An Inventory of the Historical Monuments in Westmorland* (London, 1936), 68. The phrase "Who lyst for to neam," is cryptic. "Lyst" is a variant of "list," one meaning of which is "To desire, like, wish *to do* something." — *The Oxford English Dictionary"* (Oxford, 1933), VI, 337. "Neam" is a variant of "nim," which is translated, "To take, in various senses of that verb" *(ibid.*, VII, 151) — *i. e.*, to grasp, to understand. The translation, therefore, would appear to be, "Who wishes to understand."

[5]Royal Commission, *Historical Monuments*, 67-68.

[6]Interpreted by Dr. Louis B. Wright.

[7]Records, Parish Church of Cliburn. "Cleborne" and "Cleburne" are different spellings of the same family name. — O'Hart, *Irish Pedigrees*, II, 100. Of the same family was William Claiborne, Secretary of State for the colony of Virginia, 1625-37, 1652-60. — O'Hart, *Irish Pedigrees,* II, 110; "Claiborne, William," *Dictionary of American Biography,* IV, 114. Another member was William Charles Coles Claiborne (descended from William Claiborne), Governor of Louisiana, 1804-16. — "Claiborne, Nathaniel Herbert," and "Claiborne, William Charles Coles," *Dictionary of American Biography*, IV, 113, 115.

[8]O'Hart, *Irish Pedigrees*, II, 101-03, 105, 107-08, 112, 117-18; John F. Curwen, *A Pedigree of the Family of Curwen of Workington and Kindred Branches* (Kendal, Eng., 1904 ?), Pt. 1, folding pedigree chart facing p. 1.

[9]O'Hart, *Irish Pedigrees*, II, 103, 112-14; Taylor, *Old Manorial Halls*, 106.

[10]O'Hart, *Irish Pedigrees*, II, 115-16.

[11]Records, Royal College of Surgeons of England; Cleburne family *Record Book* of marriages, births, and deaths, in possession of Charles Cleburne Jordan, Minneapolis, great-grandnephew of General Cleburne, hereinafter cited as Cleburne Family Record Book; note 18, *infra.*

[12]Frederick W. Knight, "Notes on the Family of Ronayne or Ronan, of Cos. Cork and Waterford," *Journal of the Cork Historical & Archaeological Society*, XXII, 2nd Ser. (1916), 57, 58, 63; E. C. R., "Some Desmond Incidents and Notes on the Ronayne Family," *ibid.*, XXIII, 2nd Ser. (1917), 104; John Noel Ronayne Macnamara,

· descendant of the Ronaynes of D'Loughtane, to authors, Nov. 12, 1964.

13E. C. R., "Ronayne Family," 104; Knight, "Family of Ronayne," *Journal of Cork Society*, XXII, 2nd Ser. (1916), 59, 61; Anthony Edwards, *Cork Rembrancer* (Cork, Ire., 1792), 295. These Ronaynes, collateral kinsmen of Patrick Ronayne Cleburne (Knight, "Family of Ronayne," *Journal of Cork Society*, XXII, 2nd Ser. (1916), 59, 178, 183), who lived at D'Loughtane, a large estate in County Waterford four miles northeast of Youghal, were known as Ronaynes of D'Loughtane. Beginning about 1700, when a Ronayne of D'Loughtane died, the town bell was tolled at hourly intervals until the burial. This custom was continued until 1933, following the death of Col. Louis Ronayne, the last resident bearing the name Ronayne of D'Loughtane. — Macnamara to authors, Nov. 12, 1964, Jan. 18, Feb. 4, 1965; Frank Moloney, Town Clerk of Youghal, to authors, July 20, 1964.

The tolling of the town bell was instituted as a tribute to Thomas Ronayne, mayor of Youghal from 1688 to 1690, during and following the brief reign of King James II, a Catholic. In 1689, a number of Protestants charged with various crimes against Catholics, while awaiting trial were imprisoned in Tynte's Castle, a fortress in Youghal. The townspeople became impatient when the trial was delayed, particularly since several of the accused were charged with murder. A mob, bent on lynching the prisoners, tried to enter the fortress. A messenger was sent to Mayor Thomas Ronayne at D'Loughtane, who immediately mounted his horse and rode to the castle. The beloved mayor addressed the crowd and convinced his Catholic brothers that they should not stain their hands with murder, and promised a speedy trial for the prisoners. The prisoners were tried shortly thereafter. In 1690, when a Protestant body was installed as the Corporation of Youghal, in gratitude to Thomas Ronayne, the resolution regarding the tolling of the bell was passed. — Macnamara letters, *supra*; John Gough Nichols (ed.), *The Annals of Youghal* (Youghal, Ire., 1847), 55.

14Knight, "Family of Ronayne," *Journal of Cork Society*, XXII, 2nd Ser. (1916), 59, 60, 183; "General P. R. Cleburne," *Kennesaw Gazette*, V (Apr. 15, 1890), 1.

15Knight "Family of Ronayne," *Journal of Cork Society*, XXIII, 2nd Ser. (1917), 144, 146, 150; *ibid.*, XXII, 2nd Ser. (1916), 184.

16"General P. R. Cleburne," *Kennesaw Gazette*, V (Apr. 15, 1890), 1.

17L. H. Mangum, "General P. R. Cleburne," *Kennesaw Gazette*, II (June 15, 1887), 2.

18"[Patrick R. Cleburne] was born at Bridgepark [*sic*] Cottage in the county of Cork, ten miles west from the city of Cork, ..." — L. H. Mangum, "General Patrick Cleburne," Little Rock *Arkansas Gazette*, May 30, 1886, p. 2. General Cleburne's brother William and sister

Anne furnished facts concerning the General's early life for this article. — *Ibid.* Mr. Henry Reid, whose handsome old residence is twenty-five feet from Bridepark Cottage, recalls his father (born in 1842) stated that the Cleburnes had lived next door, in Bridepark Cottage. — Conversation with authors, Apr. 26, 1964. By a marriage settlement dated Sept. 13, 1823, "Patrick Ronayne of Anne Brook Co Cork Esq" conveyed certain lands in trust as security for the payment of six hundred pounds, in annual installments of thirty-six pounds, to "Joseph Cleburne of Bride Park Cottage said county, member of the Royal College of Surgeons, London." The settlement recites that "a marriage" is "intended shortly" between Mary Anne Ronayne, daughter of Patrick Ronayne, and Joseph Cleburne. — Vol. 785, p. 64, Deed No. 530999, Registry of Deeds, Dublin. A lease of another property, dated Apr. 16, 1836, recites that it is "made between John Hawkes . . . in the County of Cork Esquire of the One Part and Joseph Cleburne of Bride Park in the said County of Cork Surgeon of the Other Part." — Transcript Book No. 7, 1836, Memorial No. 119, Registry of Deeds, Dublin.

[19] Cleburne Family Record Book.

[20] Mangum, *Arkansas Gazette.*

[21] "Uncle Ronayne (as the family called him) was . . . ." — Isabella C. Connelly, niece of General Cleburne, to T. R. Hay, May 1, 1918, in Thomas Robson Hay Collection of P. R. Cleburne Material, Locust Valley, New York. ". . . Ronayne . . . was never called Patrick by his family." — Statement by "a relative" of General Cleburne, quoting the General's stepmother, in "General P. R. Cleburne," *Kennesaw Gazette,* V (Feb. 1, 1890), 6. Albert J. Connelly, husband of Isabella Cleburne, spoke of the General as "Uncle Ronayne." — Conversation with authors, July 17, 1962.

[22] Cleburne Family Record Book; CS, 1860, Campbell County, Ky., Sch. I, Vol. IV, p. 439-R, RG 29, NA; Mangum, *Arkansas Gazette;* Mangum, *Kennesaw Gazette,* II (June 15, 1887), 2; Isabella C. Connelly to Hay, May 1, 1918, in Hay Collection.

[23] Cleburne Family Record Book; lease cited note 18, *supra.* The lease was for the term of 100 years or the life of the lessor and his brothers. Samuel Lewis, *A Topographical Dictionary of Ireland* (London, 1837), I, p. xvii, lists as one of the subscribers to the publication, "Joseph Cleburne Esq. M. D., Grange, Ballincollig, co. Cork."

[24] "Athnowen," in Lewis, *Topographical Dictionary of Ireland,* I, 89; I. C. Hawkes (son of John Hawkes) to John Reid, July 31, 1869, typescript in possession of Henry Reid (grandson of John Reid), Ovens, County Cork.

[25] Cleburne Family Record Book; John Francis Maguire, *The Irish in*

America (New York, 1873), 581-82; O'Hart, *Irish Pedigrees*, II, 117.

[26]Lease cited note 18, *supra*; William Cleburne to his cousin Patrick R. Cashman, July 8, 1849, in possession of Mrs. Otto (nee Ruth Cashman) Duemler, Fresno, Calif; Mangum, *Arkansas Gazette*.

[27]F. W. Knight, "General Patrick Ronayne Cleburne," *Journal of Cork Society*, XXI, 2nd Ser. (1915), 13; Sheets 73, 85, County Cork Ordnance Survey, 1845, National Library of Ireland, Dublin; Mangum, *Arkansas Gazette*.

[28]Ordnance survey cited note 27, *supra*; "Ballincollig," in Lewis, *Topographical Dictionary of Ireland*, I, 111.

[29]John Locke, "Dawn on the Irish Coast," in George Kyle and Mary Kyle Dallas (comps.), *Werner's Readings and Recitations* (New York, 1891), No. 3, p. 146.

[30]Knight, "General Cleburne," 13; William Cleburne to Cashman, July 8, 1849, in possession of Mrs. Otto Duemler; Marriage settlement cited note 18, *supra*.

[31]Mangum, *Arkansas Gazette*; "Clibborn, William" [*sic*] in George Dames Burtchaell and Thomas Ulick Sadleir (eds.), *Alumni Dublinenses* (Dublin, 1935), 157; John Carlisle D. Spedding, *The Spedding Family* (Dublin, 1909), 31. "Terms, L50 per Annum. — Parlour Boarders, L60, ..." — Printed "Prospectus" of the Spedding school dated October 1840, in possession of John N. Bank, Cobh, County Cork.

[32]Spedding, *Spedding Family*, portrait opp. p. 32; Mangum, *Arkansas Gazette*.

[33]Cleburne Family Record Book.

[34]Date of death, Nov. 27, 1843 — Headstone, grave of "Joseph Cleburne, M. D." in churchyard of Parish Church of Athnowen; Statement by "a relative" of General Cleburne; lease cited note 18, *supra*; Mangum, *Kennesaw Gazette*, II (June 15, 1887), 2; Isaac Slater (comp.), *Slater's National Commercial Directory of Ireland* (Manchester, Eng., 1846), 284, 286, 287. Dr. Cleburne died intestate. — Prerogative Grants Index, 1844-46, p. 13, Public Record Office of Ireland, Dublin. There is no record of the assets of his estate because the papers pertaining to the probate of the estate were destroyed in 1922 by an explosion and fire which wrecked the Four Courts in Dublin. Records, Trinity College, show that William entered July 1, 1840, and attended until Oct. 20, 1843. — College *Calendar* for 1841, 1842, and 1843; Junior Bursar's Books, 1843; W. O'Sullivan (Keeper of MSS, Trinity College) to authors, Apr. 7, 1965. William apparently withdrew attendant upon his father's last illness.

[35]J. D. H. Widders (Librarian, Royal College of Surgeons of Ireland, Dublin), "A Note on the Apothecaries' Hall" (dated Dec. 1964, MS in possession of Dr. Denis Wilson, Cork City, Ire.). Fragmentary

entries in the records of the Apothecaries' Hall in "Apprentices Book" are as follows:

"Name	Res.	Cnty.	
Sept. 28th, 1844			
Ronayne Clibborn	Mallow	Cork	Apprentice Rejected
Oct. 25th, 1844			
Ronayne Cliburne	Mallow	Cork	16-1/2 years
May 1845			
Patrick Ronayne Cleburne	Mallow	Cork	age 17"

36Mangum, *Arkansas Gazette*; Statement by "a relative" of General Cleburne.

37War Office Pay-Lists and Muster Rolls, 12/5444, Her Majesty's 41st Regiment of Foot, Jan. 1, 1846 to Mar. 31, 1846, Forms 6 and 8, Public Record Office, London. (Hereinafter, War Office Pay-Lists and Muster Rolls, 41st Foot, will be cited as W. O. 12.) W. O. 12/5446, July 1, 1849 to Sept. 30, 1849, Form 24; War Office Confidential Report of the Half-Yearly Inspection of the 41st Regiment of Foot, 1st Half Year 1849, 27/389, "General Return," Public Record Office, London. (Hereinafter, War Office Confidential Reports of Inspection, 41st Foot, will be cited as W. O. 27.) The attestation papers, on file in the Public Record Office, listing the names of recruits whose term of service was not "unlimited," were destroyed by enemy bombing in World War I. In practice, service for life meant about twenty years, a small pension being given at the time of discharge. — Michael Godfrey, "300 Years of the Marines," (London) *Daily Telegraph and Morning Post*, Apr. 24, 1964, p. 15.

38 A. C. Whitehorne, *The History of the Welch Regiment* (Cardiff, Wales, 1932), 65, 154-55; W. O. 27/355.

39W. O. 27/389, "General Return"; W. O. 12/5443; W. O. 12/5444; W. O. 12/5445; W. O. 27/360, "General Observations"; W. O. 27/366, "General Observations"; W. O. 27/371, "General Observations"; W. O. 12/5444, July 1, 1846 to Sept. 30, 1846, Form 6; W. O. 12/5445, Apr. 1, 1847 to June 30, 1847, Form 6; *ibid.*, July 1, 1847 to Sept. 30, 1847, Form 6; *ibid.*, Oct. 1, 1847 to Dec. 31, 1847, Form 6; *ibid.*, Apr. 1, 1848 to June 30, 1848, Form 6; *ibid.*, Oct. 1, 1848 to Dec. 31, 1848, Form 6; *ibid.*, Jan. 1, 1849 to Mar. 31, 1849, Form 6; Avery, "Patrick Ronayne Cleburne," 2.

40W. O. 27/360; W. O. 27/366; W. O. 27/371; W. O. 27/378; W. O. 27/383; Avery, "Patrick Ronayne Cleburne," 2.

41Calhoun Benham, "Major-Gen. P. R. Cleburne," *Kennesaw Gazette*, IV (Jan. 1, 1889), 2.

42Walter Lord (ed.), *The Fremantle Diary* (Boston, 1954), 122-23; Irving A. Buck, *Cleburne and His Command* (Reprint; Jackson,

Tenn., 1959), 127.

[43]War Office Commander in Chief's Memoranda, 31/761, 41 Foot, Mr. Robert Pratt, Public Record Office, London; John Pratt, *Pratt Family Records* (Millom, Eng., 1931), 73; Mangum, *Arkansas Gazette*; W. O. 12/5445, Apr. 1, 1847 to June 30, 1847, Form 6; *ibid.*, July 1, 1847 to Sept. 30, 1847, Form 6; Statement by "a relative" of General Cleburne.

[44]W. O. 12/5445, Oct. 1, 1847 to Dec. 31, 1847, Form 6; Avery, "Patrick Ronayne Cleburne," 2; W. O. 12/5445, Apr. 1, 1848 to June 30, 1848, Form 6; *ibid.*, July 1, 1848 to Sept. 30, 1848, Form 6; *ibid.*, Jan. 1, 1849 to Mar. 31, 1849, Form 6.

[45]Avery, "Patrick Ronayne Cleburne," 2; Statement by "a relative" of General Cleburne; Benham, *Kennesaw Gazette*, IV (Jan. 1, 1889), 2; References to the "Garrison and Barrack Library" in W. O. 27/360 and subsequent "Confidential Reports."

[46]W. O. 27/378, "General Observations"; W. O. 27/383, "General Observations"; W. O. 12/5445, Apr. 1, 1848 to June 30, 1848, Form 6; *ibid.*, July 1, 1848 to Sept. 30, 1848, Form 6; *ibid.*, Oct. 1, 1848 to Dec. 31, 1848, Form 6; *ibid.*, Jan. 1, 1849 to Mar. 31, 1849, Form 6; W. O. 12/5446, Apr. 1, 1849 to June 30, 1849, Form 6; Knight, "Family of Ronayne," *Journal of Cork Society*, XXII, 2nd Ser. (1916), 59; *ibid.*, XXIII, 2nd Ser. (1917), 144, 147.

[47]R. Barry O'Brien (ed.), *Two Centuries of Irish History: 1691-1870* (London, 1907), 413, 366, 403-04, 406-07, 410-11; William Cleburne to Cashman, July 8, 1849, in possession of Mrs. Otto Duemler.

[48]Patrick Ronayne Cleburne to Isabella Cleburne, June 28, 1849, in possession of Charles Cleburne Jordan. As was the custom in Ireland at that time, Cleburne's letters contain almost no paragraphs and very little punctuation. In this book, they have been edited to the extent of indenting an occasional paragraph and inserting some punctuation. Otherwise, they are reproduced exactly as written, including misspelling, which occurs with particular frequency in his earlier letters. (Hereinafter, footnote references to "Cleburne" are to P. R. Cleburne.)

[49]W. O. 12/5446, July 1, 1849 to Sept. 30, 1849, Form 6; Avery, "Patrick Ronayne Cleburne," 2.

[50]Mangum, *Arkansas Gazette;* Mangum, *Kennesaw Gazette,* II (June 15, 1887), 2; Michael Godfrey, "The Price of Glory Extracted from War Office Records," (British) *Army Quarterly and Defence Journal*, LXXXVI (1963), 51-53; Godfrey, conversation with authors, May 6, 1964.

[51]Identity unknown.

[52]Cleburne to Isabella Jane Cleburne, Oct. 27, 1853, in possession of Charles Cleburne Jordan.

53W. O. 12/5446, July 1, 1849 to Sept. 30, 1849, Forms 4 and 25. "Inheriting some property [Cleburne] purchased his discharge . . . ." — Benham, *Kennesaw Gazette,* IV (Jan. 1, 1889), 2. Mangum, *Arkansas Gazette,* referred to Cleburne's obtaining "means . . . from his mother's fortune." By the terms of the marriage settlement, cited note 18, *supra,* the payments thereunder were to go to Mary Anne Ronayne Cleburne if she should survive her husband, and likewise to their issue.

CHAPTER II

TO HELENA, ARKANSAS

He came to the Southland, she welcomed the stranger
As one of her own, as a well beloved son; . . . .
—Arthur Louis Peticobas, "Patrick Ronayne Cleburne."

On November 5, 1849, from the Port of Cork, the bark
Bridgetown set sail for New Orleans. With stones as ballast,
she carried 6 cabin and 258 steerage passengers. Four of the
cabin passengers were Cleburnes, listed thusly:

"Miss Anne Cleburne		23
Wm	"	25
Patr	"	21
Joseph	"	19."

After fifty days at sea, the *Bridgetown* sailed into New
Orleans Harbor on Christmas Day 1849, the passengers
remaining aboard until the 26th.[1] The gay city of New
Orleans, in the midst of holiday festivities, was the Cleburnes'
first glimpse of America.

Patrick Ronayne's baggage was a weather-beaten small
cowhide trunk, containing some well-worn clothing, an old
Damascus sword, and a pair of English boxing gloves. This
young man was about 5 feet 10 inches in height, and weighed
under 150 pounds. Muscular, lithe and erect, he possessed
great physical strength for his size. His military carriage, high
wide forehead, large expressive gray eyes, thick dark-brown
hair, and even features gave him a handsome appearance;
while his resolute countenance revealed strong character.[2]

Before the Cleburnes left Ireland, Sir Thomas Tobin, a
family friend, owner of the gunpowder mills in Ballincollig,
had given them a letter of introduction to Mr. George Currie
Duncan of New Orleans, president of the Carrollton Railroad. The goal of the enterprising young people, however,
seems to have been Cincinnati. A progressive city and, next
to New Orleans, the largest metropolis in the west, Cincinnati

offered a variety of opportunities. Desiring to succeed on his own, Cleburne chose not to linger in New Orleans with his brothers and sister to present the letter to Mr. Duncan; but boarded the first steamboat for Cincinnati.[3]

As the boat steamed up the Mississippi, main artery of travel and commerce in the heart of America, the young passenger no doubt contrasted this mighty river with the River Lee, considered large in Ireland. He likely wondered what lay beyond the dark forests bordering the river bank. Undoubtedly he was awed by the activities on this immense waterway. Occasionally, big side-wheelers splashed by, belching black smoke from their twin smokestacks; and long heavily-laden rafts floated past. The boat docked at busy wharfs, where burly Negro roustabouts unloaded and loaded heavy cargo, singing as they worked. After about a nine-day journey up the Mississippi and Ohio Rivers, young Cleburne reached the busy city of Cincinnati. Across the river in Kentucky were the small twin cities of Covington and Newport.

Two days later, William, Anne, and Joseph arrived at Cincinnati.[4] Little is known about the Cleburnes' stay in this city, which for the brothers was for only a few months. The city directory of 1850 lists P. R. Cleburne as a "clerk" in a drug store at 60 Broadway, owned by Thomas Salter; and as a boarder at "Mrs. Hanson's." William, Anne, and Joseph are not listed in the directory. William and Joseph must have left Cincinnati before the directory was compiled, and in the 1850's women were rarely listed. During William's stay in Cincinnati, Patrick Ronayne's political thinking was influenced by his older brother, whose business friends were Whigs.[5] William's entree into this group was probably through letters of introduction from Mr. Duncan.

It is believed that William became a surveyor in the construction of one of the railroads then being built in Ohio, Indiana, and Illinois; but the specific railroad is unknown. All that is known of Joseph is that he went to live in La Porte, Indiana. Anne remained in Cincinnati working as a milliner.[6]

2

Helena, the county seat of Phillips County, was located in southeastern Arkansas, on the Mississippi River, ninety-three miles by water below Memphis. Founded in 1820, the town had by 1850 grown to a flourishing little community of over 600 inhabitants, eighty percent of whom were white.

The circumstances leading Cleburne to Helena, a move that was to determine his whole future, were economic. In May of 1850, two young Helena physicians, Dr. Hector M. Grant, a native of Kentucky, and Dr. Charles E. Nash, a native of Missouri, formed a partnership in the practice of medicine. Dr. Grant had recently acquired half interest in a drug store and a new one-story frame building where the store was located. Dr. Nash purchased the other half interest in the enterprise. The two doctors had their office at the drug store. Not having time to run the store, they asked one of the previous owners, Mr. Freeman, to assist in procuring a manager. Upon returning to his former home in Cincinnati, Freeman contacted Mr. Salter, Cleburne's employer. The latter recommended Cleburne unqualifiedly, describing him as just the man for the job if he could be induced to leave Cincinnati. When the matter was discussed with Cleburne, he was interested in the proposition and agreed to depart for Helena within a few days.

After about a four-day voyage down the Ohio and the Mississippi, Cleburne, in June 1850, disembarked at Helena, with only a few dollars in his pocket. He had a letter from Freeman vouching for his character and ability as reported by Salter.[7] The newcomer made a favorable impression upon Drs. Grant and Nash. They explained that they wanted a person who could compound prescriptions competently and take over the complete operation of the store. Cleburne replied that he had had little business experience but was a fully qualified pharmicist and thought he would be equal to the job. He suggested that he be taken on trial for a month; and as to his salary, he said, "I will leave that to you." As part of his compensation he would have a room in the rear of the store, and would take his meals at Dr. Grant's home. His salary would be determined later, and he would be instructed in bookkeeping and buying by Mr. Freeman's former partner.

The store carried a variety of articles — "Drugs & Medicines, Chemicals, Perfumery, Fancy Articles, Surgical Instruments, Oils, Paints, Dye Stuffs, Pure Wines and Liquors [medicinal], Window Glass, Glass Ware, Stone Ware, Putty, &c." Drawing upon his experience in Ireland as an apothecary's apprentice and a clerk in the Cincinnati drug store, the new manager began his job with zeal and proficiency. He created the appearance and dignity of a city apothecary shop and was gratified by his employers' praise. At the end of the month, Drs. Grant and Nash assured Cleburne that his services had been highly satisfactory and that his employment would be permanent. He would begin with a salary of fifty dollars a month in addition to room and board, and as the business grew his salary would be increased. This arrangement was agreeable to Cleburne.[8] Thus began eleven eventful years of his life in the little town of which he became a part and grew to love.

3

Helena, a thriving river town, had been laid out to cover one square mile. At the southeast corner of the town was the busy steamship landing. The main streets and all of the alleys ran north and south.

Nearest and parallel to the river was Front Street, or Front Row. From the steamboat landing westward through the town was Rightor Street. A half block from Front, on the north side of Rightor at the corner of an alley, was located the drug store. All this area is now covered by a large levee.

Ohio, or Main Street, a north-south street, was one block west of Front. Another important east-west street was Porter, one block north of Rightor. The courthouse, a two-story frame building, stood at the southeast corner of Ohio and Porter.[9]

The town's business section was located on relatively high ground and also was protected by a small levee. On a gradually rising terrain the town stretched westward to Crowley's Ridge, an undulating highland three to five miles wide. Bordering the town on three sides were scenic hills.

Helena, the only town and the county seat, was the hub of Phillips County, an area of 755 square miles. The county was roughly triangular in shape, with the base on the north. On the east the Mississippi River was the hypotenuse, fifty-five miles long. Helena was located twenty miles from the northern end.

The annual flood of the river began in March, sometimes rising to an increased depth of fifty feet and covering over twenty miles of land. This vast periodic inundation was "among the grandest features of the western continent."[10] Because of the floods settlers in the county sought high lands for home sites. The highest of these areas was Crowley's Ridge, beginning three miles south of Helena, curving slightly to the west and continuing northward. West of Crowley's Ridge were many low ridges and terraces. Another high area was a natural levee on the bank of the Mississippi, south of Helena, some twenty miles in length.

The population of the sparsely settled county, including Helena, was 4,350 white inhabitants and 2,600 Negro slaves. Scarcely any of those over twenty-one years of age were natives. Almost all adults had pioneered to Arkansas, attracted by virgin land and navigation on the Mississippi. The great majority of the settlers came from Southern states proportionally in this order: Tennessee, North Carolina, Georgia, Kentucky, Alabama, Mississippi, Virginia, and South Carolina. Some were from Northern states, and a few from foreign countries.[11]

The top social stratum in the town was composed of professional men and substantial merchants, some of whom also owned plantations or farms. Dr. Grant had a plantation a few miles west of Helena; and Dr. Nash, a plantation just across the river in Mississippi. Helena's bar of about twenty lawyers included some of the ablest advocates in the state. Transactions and litigation involving real property accounted for the large number in the legal profession. Next in the social order were owners of small businesses, clerks, craftsmen, and artificers. On a lower level were a few "laborers"; and, at the bottom, were the riffraff, part and parcel of a river town.[12] Out in the county, the people lived on farms and plantations, except for a few scattered "settlements" and the tiny village of Marianna at the far north. Some of the land had been cleared but primeval forests covered a large portion of Phillips County. Dense canebrakes dotted the flood plains.

The overflows of the Mississippi and other streams in the lowlands had produced wide flood-plains of black alluvial soil of great fertility. Cotton grown in this soil, unusually long and of strong staple, brought a high market price. With rapidly rising values, land "speculation" could be very lucrative. A "land speculator" owned one of the two mansions in Helena.

There were twenty large planters, owning generally from 3,000 to 17,000 acres and 30 to 86 slaves. About 45 small planters owned 160 to 5,000 acres with 10 to 30 slaves. The crops raised by the planters were cotton and corn. Clearing and draining the land and constructing levees were expensive undertakings. Even the large planters chose to improve their land rather than to build pretentious residences. The planters, as a rule, lived in one- and two-story frame houses, some combined with brick, and in one- and two-story "double log houses."

There were about 180 "large farmers" living in the county. They differed from the small planters in that they owned few or no slaves. Their farms were of equivalent acreage to those of the small planters, and with substantial improvements. More than half of these farmers owned one to eight slaves, the rest owning none. The large farmers without slaves used "hired labor." Plantation owners, as well, utilized hired labor — Irish and German workmen — in land drainage and flood control.

There were also the "plain country folk" in the county, numbering some 315 householders. This group consisted of owners of small farms (or farms of little value), herdsmen, and the more thrifty tenant farmers. About ninety percent of this group were non-slaveholders, the remaining ten percent having one to five slaves. Most of the small farmers owned 40 to 160 acres; and a few, between 160 and 480 acres. With their acreage largely in woods, they cleared small tracts for tilling. The herdsmen tended droves of hogs, and occasionally herds of cattle. Also, there were a few plain country folk in miscellaneous occupations, such as "store keeper" and blacksmith.

There were about 150 farm and levee laborers, and some 70 shiftless tenant farmers. Scattered around in the county were a few squatters, idlers, and drifters.[13]

Living in a semi-frontier society, many citizens of the

town and county went about armed. Some men prided themselves on a "code of honor" whereby they settled disputes at knife- and pistol-point.[14]

Despite class differences the society was unified, and in a sense democratic. Generally the planters and large farmers were of plain bearing, and cordial in their associations. A friendly relationship existed between the middle class and the planters. The former admired the planter class, and some anticipated their children attaining that level. Some planters or their immediate forebears, and many professional men, were from the "plain folk."

There was an atmosphere of friendliness and respect for one's neighbors. All had common interests in their churches, love of the land, and mastery of hunting. They shared a strong sense of patriotism, followed national and local politics, and admired oratory.[15]

4

Cleburne arose before daybreak each morning, and from his room at the drug store walked three blocks up Rightor Street to the Grant's residence for breakfast. He was back in the store carrying on business before the other establishments opened.[16] At noon and the end of the day, Cleburne returned to the Grant home for "dinner" and "supper."

Because of the shortage of housing and the dearth of restaurants, many families in Helena had paying guests. Dr. and Mrs. Grant's family consisted of their two-year old daughter; two nieces twelve and six years of age; and Mrs. Grant's younger sister and her mother from North Carolina. Paying guests were a lawyer who was a relative of Dr. Grant, and a young couple, the man of whom was studying medicine under Drs. Grant and Nash.[17]

Modest and soft-spoken, Cleburne was a welcome addition to the family circle.[18] The children loved him and regarded him as an "uncle." He was especially fond of the Grant's little daughter, Mary. After supper she would climb on his lap, while he told the children stories about Ireland, his boyhood, and his trip across the ocean and up the river to Cincinnati. He delighted the children with humorous original jingles.

Cleburne liked the warm-hearted, genial people of the

community and made pleasant acquaintances through his work at the drug store. Being an adept chess player, he organized and became president of a chess club composed of several young men in the town. Readily recognized as a gentleman, Cleburne was invited into the best social circles. Life of the gentry in Helena was in many ways comparable to his family's social circle in Ireland.[19]

Cleburne and Dr. Nash, bachelors of about the same age, spent much time together. Occasionally Cleburne would bring out his treasured old sword and for exercise and amusement would practice fencing with an imaginary opponent. His boxing gloves went unused, as boxing was not a sport in Arkansas. Dr. Nash observed in his priceless book, *Biographical Sketches of Gen. Pat Cleburne and Gen. T. C. Hindman, etc.* (1898), that "Cleburne soon found that our bowie knife was far superior to his Damascus blade in close engagement, and our hard fists more effective than boxing gloves."[20]

Because of their close friendship, Cleburne aided Dr. Nash in his courtship of Mary Epps, Mrs. Grant's nineteen-year-old sister. In April 1851, Dr. Nash and Miss Epps were married at the residence of Dr. Grant and doubtless Cleburne was present.[21]

In the fall of 1851, little Mary Grant was stricken with an illness which proved to be fatal. Cleburne worked with the physicians in trying to save the little girl, and sat by her bed night after night. When she died in October, Cleburne wrote a poetic epitaph for her grave marker.[22]

For pleasure and edification Cleburne read poetry, memorizing many favorite passages and occasionally penning original verse. He pursued his keen interest in history and biography and joined a literary and debating society. Members of the society were young professional and businessmen who were to become prominent in the county, particularly two lawyers, James C. Tappan and Mark W. Alexander. Cleburne developed his talent for debating and oratory, and held his own in friendly competition.

His ideals of personal liberty and hatred of tyranny were furthered by earnest study of English history, the Declaration of Independence, and the Constitution of the United States.

These convictions were the foundation for Cleburne's becoming an ardent champion of states' rights.

Cleburne's military hero in English history was Wellington, and he disliked eulogies of Napoleon. He spent many hours reading and rereading *Plutarch's Lives.*[23] Careful study of the campaigns of Alexander and Caesar and the tactics and stratagems of Hannibal unquestionably contributed to Cleburne's brilliant military career.

About six months after Dr. and Mrs. Nash married, Cleburne went to live with them in their house on Porter Street, four blocks west of the drug store. Cleburne was regarded as a member of the family and when little Mary Nash was born, he loved her as though she were his niece.[24]

Cleburne was a good sport and enjoyed participating in popular recreational activities. Soon after arriving in Helena, when hiking with a group of men he attempted to follow his companions in leaping across a broad ditch, but landed waist deep in the mire. To the merriment of the group he continued jumping with the same result, until finally he cleared the ditch. Through practice he became the champion ditch jumper.

Although a skilled rifleman, Cleburne had had no experience in pistol shooting before coming to Helena. He purchased a pistol and practiced regularly until he became an expert in use of the weapon.[25]

In 1852 a Mormon "priest," accompanied by six wives, came to Helena; and was permitted by the sheriff to hold evening meetings in the courthouse. Hearing that some women were being impressed by the Mormon's harangues advocating polygomous marriages, Dr. Nash protested about the use of the courthouse; and the sheriff ordered the meetings discontinued. The angry Mormon went to the drug store and threatened Dr. Nash with reprisals. Standing across the counter from Dr. Nash and Cleburne, the "priest" reached for a concealed pistol. Vaulting over the counter Cleburne seized the man; and, with angry eyes ablaze, kicked him out of the store, saying, "If you ever come in again, I will serve you worse."

Aroused by this episode, the citizenry of Helena threatened to treat the Mormon to a coat of tar and feathers.

The ladies were to prepare the treatment and the gentlemen apply it if the troublemaker had not left town by a given time. The Mormon with his wives departed in short order; and Dr. Nash observed, "This was the rise and fall of the Mormon empire in Arkansas."[26]

A gang of levee workers on their pay day regularly got drunk in a room above John Smith's saloon, located across the street from the drug store. On such an occasion one of the men was seized with a "drunken fit," and Dr. Nash was summoned. Applying the accepted medical treatment, the physician drew a small amount of blood from the patient's temple. Seeing the blood, one drunkard, a powerful man, knocked Dr. Nash to the floor. Another kicked the doctor part way down the stairs, shouting, "That bloody butcher wants to kill my buddy!" Hearing the disturbance, Cleburne rushed to his friend's rescue. When the commotion quieted Cleburne and Dr. Nash went back and bandaged the drunkard's head. The next morning, the levee workers, having sobered up, went to Dr. Nash and apologized.[27]

One afternoon in 1852, as a "sporting event," a fight was arranged between a tame bear and a bear hunting dog. The owners, a butcher and bear hunter, wagered on the outcome. A large group of men including Cleburne gathered for the event on a hilltop at the edge of town. When it became apparent that the dog was losing, his owner attempted to pull him out of the ring. The butcher and the bear hunter began fighting and a riot broke out. Realizing the seriousness of the situation, Cleburne took charge; at his command quiet fell and order prevailed. Because of the unfairness of the match, the butcher did not claim the wager.[28]

On another occasion in 1852, friends invited Cleburne to ride with them through the hills. Not owning a horse, Cleburne went to Dr. Nash to borrow one. The doctor questioned the advisability of Cleburne trying to ride his horse, which had been a racehorse. But Cleburne insisted and set out on the lively steed. The road to the hills led across a marsh spanned by a plank bridge. As they approached the bridge, Cleburne's friend tapped his mount with the whip, and the horse began to run. Cleburne's horse thinking that a race was in order, quickly passed the other steed. Cleburne's

Cliburn Hall, Westmorland County, England
Photograph Taken About 1960

Parish Church of Cliburn, Westmorland County, England
Photograph Taken in 1964

Bridepark Cottage, Ovens Township, County Cork, Ireland
Birthplace of Patrick Ronayne Cleburne
Photograph Taken in 1964

Grange, Ovens Township, County Cork, Ireland
P.R. Cleburne's Boyhood Home
The Third Story Was Added Later

Annebrook, Home of Patrick Ronayne,
Maternal Grandfather of General Cleburne,
On the Great Island, County Cork, Ireland
Photograph Taken in 1964

—Courtesy Dr. Denis Wilson
St. Mary's Church, Parish of Athnowen, County Cork, Ireland
Where P.R. Cleburne Was Baptized
The Grave of His Father, Dr. Joseph Cleburne,
is in the Foreground

Portrait of Mary Anne Ronayne Cleburne,
Mother of General Cleburne

hat flew off as the racehorse sped across the bridge. In a futile effort to gain control, Cleburne leaned forward and gripped the bridle near the bit. In Dr. Nash's words, Cleburne, "always composed," decided to grasp the horse's nose to turn him toward the marsh. According to the rider's plan, as the horse halted at the edge of the marsh, Cleburne was to leap off. The plan worked — except that Cleburne was plunged in mire up to his waist. He accepted the discomfiture and laughter of his friends with good grace. "I can't tell which got the best of it, the horse or I," humorously yet seriously he said, "I shall part company with him; he wants his way and I, mine. I am satisfied to let him have it in the future, as I never wish to make a laughing stock of myself again."[29] Needless to say, Cleburne soon became a proficient horseman.

In spite of his accomplishments, Cleburne was quite shy and self conscious in the presence of young ladies. He would blush when waiting upon young female customers in the drug store. After he went to live with the Nashs, he was reluctant to enter the parlor when Mrs. Nash was entertaining ladies. But after a while Cleburne showed that he actually enjoyed feminine society. He particularly liked two attractive young women who were frequent dinner guests of the Nashs and escorted one of them to several social functions.

At a social one evening Cleburne attempted to dance in a quadrille without knowing the calls, and the group became confused. Some of the girls laughed and one called him, "a raw, gawky Irishman." Cleburne, embarrassed, dropped out of the dance; but shortly afterward took dancing lessons from a teacher newly-arrived from Memphis. Cleburne learned readily, and was soon a popular dancing partner. To many of the socials and dances he escorted two of the belles of the town, the beautiful daughters of the Episcopal rector.[30]

NOTES

CHAPTER II

[1]Passenger List and Cargo Manifest, Barque *Bridgetown,* Arrived Dec. 26, 1849, Port of New Orleans, RG 36, NA; New Orleans *Daily Picayune,* Dec. 26, 1849, p. 3; Mangum, *Arkansas Gazette.*

[2]Charles Edward Nash, *Biographical Sketches of Gen. Pat Cleburne and Gen. T. C. Hindman* (Little Rock, 1898), 10-11; Buck, *Cleburne,* 80; W. J. Hardee, "Biographic Sketch of Major General P. R. Cleburne," in Maguire, *Irish in America,* 651.

[3]J. Windele, *Historical and Descriptive Notices of the City of Cork and Its Vicinity* (Cork, Ire., 1839), 218; Mangum, *Arkansas Gazette;* Mangum, *Kennesaw Gazette,* II (June 15, 1887), 2.

[4]Mangum, *Arkansas Gazette.*

[5]Nash, *Gen. Pat Cleburne,* 87.

[6]*Infra,* p. 69; Anne Sherlock Jordan, granddaughter of Anne Cleburne and her husband James L. Sherlock, to authors, Oct. 17, 1963.

[7]H. M. Grant to Editor, Helena (Ark.) *World,* June 29, 1891, quoted in undated clipping from *World* in Scrapbook Belonging to Seven Generals Chapter, United Daughters of the Confederacy, Helena, Ark. (in Helena and Phillips County Public Library and Museum); Nash, *Gen. Pat Cleburne,* 7-9. (Hereinafter, the Scrapbook will be cited as Scrapbk, U.D.C., Helena; and the Library and Museum, as Helena Library.)

[8]Nash, *Gen. Pat Cleburne,* 9-10, 25, 27; Helena (Ark.) *Southern Shield,* Sept. 28, 1850, p. 2.

[9]Nicholas Rightor, Surveyor, *A Map of the Town of Helena, 1820* (copied from original by L. R. Parmelee, Civil Engineer, in 1924), Official Records of Phillips County, Ark.; deed, Jonas D. Smith to Hector M. Grant, recorded in Record Book "J," p. 377, Official Records of Phillips County, Ark.; advertisement of Nash & Cleburne, "Rightor Street, . . . Near the Steamboat Landing," in Helena (Ark.) *Southern Shield,* Jan. 10, 1852, p. 2; The Goodspeed Publishing Co. (pub.), *Biographical and Historical Memoirs of Eastern Arkansas* (Chicago, 1890), 739. The following evidence establishes that the post office was at the northeast corner of Ohio and Porter Streets: There being no post-office building, the practice was for the post office to be on the business premises of the postmaster. William D. Hornor was postmaster from July 28, 1848, to Oct. 9, 1855. — Records of the Appointment of Postmaster in Phillips County, Ark., Record of the Post Office Department, XIV, RG 28, NA. Lot 63, at

the northeast corner of Ohio and Porter, was owned by William Dunn Hornor and his two sisters, heirs of William B. R. Hornor, who died in 1838. — Estate of William B. R. Hornor, Dec'd, in Phillips County, Ark., Probate Court. In the Helena (Ark.) *Democratic Star,* Jan. 4, 1855, p. 3, James Erwin advertised his store as being, "One door east of the Post-office, north side of the public square." Manifestly, "the public square" was the area surrounding the courthouse.

The 1820 map of Helena, *supra,* shows the street nearest the river as "Water Street"; however, this street was uniformly called "Front Street" or "Front Row." — See advertisements of business establishments on "Front Street" and "Front Row" in Helena newspapers, 1850-58, 1860. The 1820 map depicts a prospective location of the public square in the north-central part of the town, but the square was never located at such site. — C. H. Purvis, County Surveyor of Phillips County, Ark., conversation with authors, Aug. 2, 1962.

[10]Joseph C. G. Kennedy, Superintendent of Census (comp.), *Population of the United States in 1860; Compiled from the Original Returns of the Eighth Census* (Washington, 1864), p. xliii.

[11]Helena (Ark.) *Southern Shield,* Jan. 4, 1851, p. 2; CS, 1850, Phillips County, Ark., Sch. I, Vol. IV, RG 29, NA; J. D. B. DeBow, Superintendent of Census (comp.), *The Seventh Census of the United States: 1850* (Washington, 1853), p. c.

[12]Ted R. Worley, "Helena on the Mississippi," *Arkansas Historical Quarterly,* XIII (1954), 3-4, 12, 14; CS, 1850, Phillips County, Ark., Sch. I, Vol. IV, pp. 121-129R, 137-143R, RG 29, NA; *ibid.,* Sch. II, Vol. II.

[13]CS, 1850, Phillips County, Ark., Sch. I, Vol. IV, RG 29, NA; *ibid.,* Sch. II, Vol. II; CS, 1850, Phillips County, Ark., Sch. IV (Arkansas History Commission, Little Rock, hereinafter cited as Ark. Hist. Comm.); *Tax List: Phillips County, Arkansas: 1850-51* (Ark. Hist. Comm.); C. H. Purvis, conversation with authors, Aug. 2, 1962; Advertisements of plantations and farms for sale or rent in Helena newspapers, 1849-52, 1855, 1858, 1860.

The small farms enumerated above do not include seven owned by professional and business men. One landowner classified as a small farmer had 160 acres and 7 slaves; 2 tenant farmers had 7 and 8 slaves, respectively. Unclassified herein are 11 persons of little means, but who owned unimproved and uncleared tracts of from 500 to 1,000 acres.

[14]John Hallum, *Biographical and Pictorial History of Arkansas* (Albany, 1887), I, 34.

[15]Mangum, *Arkansas Gazette;* Frank Lawrence Owsley, *Plain Folk of*

the Old South (Baton Rouge, 1949), pp. 90, 142; John Crowe Ransom, "Reconstructed but Unregenerate," in Twelve Southerners, *I'll Take My Stand: The South and the Agrarian Tradition* (Reprint; New York, 1951), pp. 12, 14.

16Nash, *Gen. Pat Cleburne*, 38. Location of Grant residence, depicted on accompanying map, per Mrs. John Sidney Hornor, conversation with authors, Oct. 4, 1961.

17CS, 1850, Phillips County, Ark., Sch. I, Vol. IV, p. 250, RG 29, NA.

18W. F. Randle, "Pat Cleburne's Early Career," *Confederate Veteran*, XIX (1911), 212.

19Nash, *Gen. Pat Cleburne*, 25, 37; Mangum, *Kennesaw Gazette*, II (June 15, 1887), 2; Ransom, "Reconstructed but Unregenerate," 3.

20CS, 1850, Phillips County, Ark., Sch. I, Vol. IV, p. 282, RG 29, NA; Nash, *Gen. Pat Cleburne*, 11.

21Nash, *Gen. Pat Cleburne*, 38; Helena (Ark.) *Southern Shield*, Apr. 19, 1851, p. 2.

22Nash, *Gen. Pat Cleburne*, 27-28.

23*Ibid.*, 28; Mangum, *Arkansas Gazette;* Benham, *Kennesaw Gazette*, IV (Jan. 15, 1889), 2.

24Nash, *Gen. Pat Cleburne*, 38, 39. Location of Nash residence depicted on map per Mrs. John Sidney Hornor, conversation with authors, Oct. 4, 1961.

25Edwin L. Drake, "General Patrick R. Cleburne," in Drake (ed.), *The Annals of the Army of Tennessee and Early Western History* (Nashville, 1878), I, 247.

26Nash, *Gen. Pat Cleburne* 15-18. "His eyes ... blazed fiercely in moments of excitement." — Hardee, "Major General Cleburne," 651.

27Nash, *Gen. Pat Cleburne* 18-19. Location of saloon shown by deed of property to John C. O. Smith, dated Mar. 21, 1851, recorded in Record Book "J," pp. 593-94, Official Records of Phillips County, Ark.

28Nash, *Gen. Pat Cleburne*, 22-24.

29*Ibid.*, 19-22.

30*Ibid.*, 15, 30, 36, 38-39; Mangum, *Arkansas Gazette*.

CHAPTER III

A CITIZEN OF HELENA

*I have some really kind and disinterested friends here and on
the whole I like the place and the people very much, and to
leave now would be like leaving a second home*
— From letter, Cleburne to his stepmother, October 26, 1853.

In December 1851 Cleburne bought Dr. Grant's interest
in the drug store. He paid $350 cash and executed a deed of
trust on his half interest as security for payment of the
$1,150 balance within twelve months.[1] On January 1, 1852,
the firm became Nash & Cleburne but Dr. Grant continued to
have his office in the drug store. Soon thereafter the new
partner went to Philadelphia to purchase supplies and
equipment. On January 10, Nash & Cleburne advertised
having, "constantly, a large and well selected stock . . . our
store has been newly fitted up, and new fixtures added . . .
prompt attention to shipment of goods."[2]

Early in 1852 Cleburne was made a member of Lafayette
Lodge, No. 16, Ancient York Masons. Leading citizens of
Helena and vicinity were members of this lodge. One of the
younger members was the County Clerk, Edward H.
Cowley,[3] who nine years later when war clouds were
gathering became an officer in an infantry company organized in Helena. Cleburne mentions Captain Cowley in his
report of the battle of Shiloh.

The Masonic Hall with bare floors and wooden benches
comprised the second story of a small building. A wooden
box draped in white cloth served as the altar, and a split
bottom chair for the Oriental chair. Cleburne attended every
meeting and studied Masonry diligently. In due course he
received the three degrees of Entered Apprentice, Fellow
Craft, and Master Mason.[4]

Late in 1852 Cleburne joined a division of the Sons of
Temperance. The order advocated prohibition of "spirituous

37

liquors," its members taking a pledge of abstinence except for medicinal purposes.[5]

During this time Cleburne's sister Anne continued to live in Cincinnati. His brother William pursued work as a surveyor for railroad construction in Ohio, Indiana, or Illinois. Late in 1850 William married Eliza Thomasina Rose, daughter of Wellington A. Rose of Foxhall, County Tipperary. Miss Rose, who had known William in Ireland, had recently come to America.[6]

In 1852 Anne went by steamboat to visit William and his wife. As Anne was returning aboard the *John Sherlock*, an Ohio River steamboat, she met James L. Sherlock of Cincinnati, an officer on the boat. The steamboat was owned by Rogers & Sherlock, Cincinnati commission merchants, Thomas Sherlock of the firm being an older brother of James. In March 1853 Anne and the younger Sherlock were married at Cincinnati.[7]

A year after becoming a Mason, in 1853, Cleburne was elected Worshipful Master of the lodge. His fellow members must have recognized him as an exceptional person. The new Master performed the duties of his office with honor and dignity. In conferring the three degrees he committed the "work" of the lengthy ritual to memory, and bestowed the degrees proficiently.[8]

That summer, another honor was bestowed on Worshipful Master Cleburne. Lafayette Lodge No. 16 and neighboring lodges of Austin and Friar's Point, Mississippi, decided to hold in Helena a joint celebration of the festival of St. John the Baptist. Delegates from the three lodges met to formulate plans and to select the orator of the occasion. The neighboring Mississippi lodges nominated two prominent members, one of whom was an experienced orator. Lafayette Lodge No. 16 nominated Cleburne and after several ballots, he was elected to be the orator. On the afternoon of the celebration, June 24, 1853, members of the three lodges marched in an "imposing procession" from the lodge hall to the Presbyterian Church, [9] the largest church in Helena, where Cleburne gave the Masonic address. Forty years later, in his reminiscences of Cleburne, Dr. Nash recalled the gist of the address:

> "I am proud that our order reaches above all contending parties in our land; that its members are free and untrammelled in all that lies between their God and themselves. We are glad that it meddles not with any duty which we of conscience owe to our Maker or to our country; and now may the camp fires which have increased so much in brilliancy, be rekindled in great strength, to the end that their lives may lead the world to study our motto, 'Brotherly love, friendship, charity and truth,' and may the principles of our order forever prevail."[10]

The following day Cleburne for the first time was the subject of a news account in a Helena paper. The *Southern Shield* reported:

> The Masonic Address delivered by our townsman, J. C. *[sic]* Cleburne, on yesterday, would have done credit to one of maturer years. Mr. C. we believe hails from over the water, but he is thoroughly Americanized. The eloquent bursts of patriotism that fell from his lips on yesterday stamps him as a patriot in the broadest sense of the term. The order were fortunate in their selection of an orator . . . . The diction of Mr. C. was chaste and elegant; his illustrations were very happy.[11]

Also in 1853, Dr. Grant, Dr. Nash, and Cleburne formed a class of candidates for the sublime degree of Royal Arch Mason. The degree was conferred by Albert Pike of Little Rock, Grand High Priest of the Grand Royal Arch Chapter of Arkansas. A native of Massachusetts, Pike lived for a number of years in Arkansas, where he achieved considerable fame and made a substantial fortune in practicing law. He became a brigadier general of the Confederacy, and later achieved world-wide renown for his contribution to the ritual of the Scottish Rite of Freemasonry and as an authority on Masonic law and symbolism.[12]

During Cleburne's tenure of office as Master, the membership of Lafayette Lodge No. 16 increased to fifty-four. He and other members took a firm stand against a decree of the Grand Lodge of Arkansas for the payment by the Helena lodge of stipends to support a college. Cleburne and other Helena Masons believed the decree to be contrary to the Masonic constitution.[13]

Cleburne infrequently wrote lengthy letters to his stepmother in Ireland.[14] The only extant letter was written when he learned that his half brother Edward, a seaman, had died of yellow fever on the west coast of Africa. The letter warrants quoting practically in its entirety for it gives an insight as to Cleburne's character and philosophy.

> Helena Arkansas
> 26th October '53

Dear Mamma

A day or two ago I received a note from Anne containing the sad and unlooked for news of brother Edward's death under painful circumstances, far away from his home and the kind attention of those who loved him. The life I have lead, constantly mingling with strange people and making few attachments, has been well calculated to blount the feelings and harden the heart; but this intelligence caused me a deep pang of sorrow. I knew Edward only as I saw him last. For near four years before that period, I had not seen his face even for a day; and since then it is four years more since I have heard his voice. I remember him only as a healthy, growing, fearless boy; independent as a republican; generous; and seemingly well calculated to make his own way through this bustling world. But now he is cut down ere half his race was run. This is a sad reflection indeed, but it bears a consolation with it that should in some sort reconcile the sorrowing parent for the loss of her child. It is this: that no son of Adam finishes his destine here. I care not what work we set our hearts upon, the grave is between us and its complete realization. This world is but the opening scene. Yourself and Edward and the re-mainder of us will meet in immortality. The present separation is small if we be not separated then. But he sleeps far off near the lonely sea. This is but an imaginary bereavement. Though we had all followed him to the grave, though we had seen him laid there and heard the earth sound hollow over all that remained of our brother, we would have learned nothing — we would have gained no consolation from this fact. He would be still as far as though the blue waves of the Atlantic rolled between us. In the tomb, whether it be on land or ocean, all is still and cold and lifeless. The only voice of comfort that issues from the grave is that true firm faith which tells of the not distant future when the tombs shall be burst and mothers shall take again their children to their arms. Afflictions, bitter as they seem at the moment, are often of inestimable value to the afflicted. They soften the heart; they humble our pride; they prepare us to look impartially upon ourselves and more charitably on others.

This affliction of our family has had the affect on me of making me think more seriously upon the subject of religion than I have been in the habit [of] doing of late. In this part of the world, local or individual attachments hang on a very slender thread and in breaking give but a momentary jar. Death, even in its more revolting forms, is an every day common place occurence on this great highway, the Mississippi River. It is looked lightly on by this busy people, who regard it as by no means the greatest evil. There are hundreds here who have no regard for religion — in fact who openly revile it. But yet under all these disadvantages I believe this mighty valley could furnish more sincere self sacrificing Christians than any spot on earth. In this town of a thousand inhabitants, we have three protestant churches and one more about to be built. I would like much [if] you could witness one of our Camp meetings in the woods in the country, where churches are few and far between. They erect an altar and desk in the forest. Rude tents and benches are prepared, and the surrounding inhabitants come there and worship God beneath his own ethereal roof. They kneel beneath the old forest trees; while the gay paroquet shrilly cries in the lofty branches above them and the delicate humming bird, like a fragment of the rainbow, glances from flower to flower. Oh! These old weird woods! They are standing now as they probably stood thousands of years ago. Festoons of grape vines are dangling from every tree and the playful squirl *[sic]* is jumping amongst them. Fifty years ago the war shoop and the war dance rang through these forest glades, but now these Indian mounds are all that remain of the stately sullen red man. How small seem individual greefs *[sic]* when we consider the unutterable woes that this once haughty race have endured, driven before the mighty machinery of civilization to the foot of the Rocky Mountains; and yet at no far distant day to be driven still farther to the general burial ground of their race!

I have lived in this small town going on 4 years and great changes have taken place. At that time there was one church (Methodist) and 4 drinking and gambling houses. Now there are 3 churches, one more about to be built, and the drinking houses are not making any thing. We have a lodge of the Sons of Temperance here (a secret society who's *[sic]* object it is to prevent the use of intoxicating liquors as a beverage), and it has worked wonders for the morality of Helena. A few years ago, and our town was known as the haunt of the most reckless, desperate characters in the Mississippi Valley. Pistol and Bowe Knife decided every quarrel. I, myself, have witnessed how low some men regarded their own and other peoples' lives; and narrowly escaped being shot in [a] fight which occured near our store. But now these old scenes are passing away; and there have been only three fights in which deadly weapons were used this year; and the principals in these

41

disgraceful rows were made to feal *[sic]* the full indignation of the laws they violated. Their *[sic]* is some probability of my being chosen orator at the next meeting of the Sons of Temperance for public procession next December. If I am and can fulfill it, I will send you a copy.

I am still driving away at the Drug business. In going into this business I incurred a considerable debt, which I have been paying off ever since. This time twelve months [ago] ¾ths of Helena were consumed by fire; and we suffered considerably by a very heavy and sudden rain that followed the fire and damped a great many of our things, which we had carried to the bank of the river for safety. But yet I have no reason to complain.

William & Anne I have not seen for near two years. Wm. & Anne have been married some time (but I suppose you know the particulars from themselves). I have nearly as little means of knowing any thing about them as you have, living as I do more than 700 miles from them . . . . William had a very good offer as Engineer in this state but did not accept it.

I am not married yet nor have any intentions of being just now. I paid some little attention to two or three young ladies here. Told one I loved her, which did not seem disagreeable; but did not propose to any of them. I have some really kind and disinterested friends here and on the whole I like the place and the people very much, and to leave now would be like leaving a second home.

Helena 27th Octor 1853

I often worder why Issy [Isabella], brother, or yourself have never written to me. I wrote you a letter on my return from Philladelphia *[sic]* near two years ago, but never received any answer to it. If there was any thing offensive in its language there was certainly none intended. I do not now recollect what I said, but am sure there was nothing in it that need have disturbed for a moment the affectionate relationship that subsists between us here in this new wild country, where we are as free from the enslaving trammel of passion as the trees of the forest, where aim or method in appearance of language is never consulted, where the heart is the only prompter and the conscience the only judge, where the sickly sentimentality of cities is despised. People do not mean the same or lay the same stress on words and sentences as in other communities. Their words convey no double meaning and carry no allusions. Tell Issy I would much like to hear from her. I have often in my day dreams wished I had her here with me. I have often thought how proudly I would feal *[sic]*. Every homage and attention her goodness and accomplishments would exact from our young men. I have often recollected with pain that she was beyond the protecting power of her older brother's arms, and I have prayed to God that he would shape her mind after the many great and glorious examples which her sex affords. And finally, I would say to you and give it to you as my advice, that you raise up Robert and Chris to be independent, self dependent fellows. Let them have good English Educations. Teach them to be practical in every thing. Let them bow knee to nothing but their creator, and teach them to look to America as their future home. In fact, I think you ought to send one of them out here at once. Any of us would be glad to have them with us if they come to any of these states. Stout of heart and strong of hand, they must succeed . . . . [The rest of this letter was quoted page 40, *supra.*]

I remain your affectionate son
P R Cleburne[15]

In December 1853, "Bro. P. R. Cleburne" delivered the address on the first anniversary of the Helena Division of the Sons of Temperance. A few months later temperance in Phillips County was "born at the polls," when the voters instructed the county's representatives in the state legislature "to obtain the passage of a special act, prohibiting the sale of vinous and spirituous liquors in less quantity than one quart."[16] A young officer in the local chapter of the Sons of Temperance was W. H. Kinsey, co-owner of a livery stable.[17] During the War between the States, General Cleburne was to cite Kinsey for valor and distinguished services on the field at the battles of Shiloh and Murfreesboro.

At this time Cleburne had not joined any church in Helena but had attended services occasionally at the Episcopal Church. The rector was strictly a high churchman, whereas Cleburne preferred the simpler service of a "low church." This congregation of twenty persons, including some of the most prominent people in the town, held services in a former store building. Cleburne frequently attended the Presbyterian Church, where his friend the Reverend Thomas R. Welch was pastor. Mr. Welch was also chaplain of the Masonic Lodge. Cleburne's early religious training and innate refinement were manifest — he disliked vulgarity and refused to listen to smut. Dr. Nash says, "I never heard him swear an oath."[18]

2

Early in 1854 Cleburne decided to leave the drug business

and become a lawyer. He began studying law in the office of Judge Thomas B. Hanly and Mark W. Alexander. Hanly, a former Circuit Court judge and a "powerful debater," was one of the ablest lawyers of Arkansas.[19] Mr. Alexander, from Virginia, was also a capable lawyer.

In April 1854 Cleburne and Dr. Nash sold the drug store, as the latter did not wish to operate it. Cleburne's profit from the sale was about $3,000. Drs. Grant and Nash moved their office to a building on Ohio Street.[20]

The Hanly & Alexander law office was in the "old Real Estate Bank," on Elm Street. For two years, Cleburne withdrew from social activities and studied law assiduously. A frequent visitor to the law office was Judge Hanly's son Sylvanus, a bright lad of thirteen.[21] Ten years later, Sylvanus, then Lieut. S. P. Hanly, was to serve on General Cleburne's staff.

After coming to Helena, Cleburne continued to advocate the Whig Party. However, he soon learned that the great majority of the leaders and influential people in the South were Democrats. He stayed by the Whig Party until 1856, by which time it had lost much of its following. Most of its local members were joining the recently formed American or Know Nothing Party. Cleburne came to believe, as local Democrats contended, that the Know Nothings in the North were against the constitutional rights of the South. Also, the Know Nothings were anti-foreign. They proposed that naturalized citizens should not hold governmental offices, and that the five years of residence required before becoming a citizen should be extended to twenty-one years. Facetiously explaining that he did not wish to be classed as a child, Cleburne left the Whigs and became a Democrat.[22] When the Know Nothing Party became active in Phillips County, political excitement ran high. A secret society, appealing to emotions and prejudices, some weak Democrats defected to it.

In June 1854, T. C. Hindman, a twenty-six-year-old lawyer, came to live in Helena. Hindman, a Tennessean, at age seventeen had enlisted in the army at the outbreak of the war with Mexico, and was a captain when the war closed. He later practiced law in Mississippi and served in the legislature of that state as a Democrat. Soon after coming to Helena, Hindman had a political altercation with another lawyer, an ardent Whig. Cleburne, learning that a duel was imminent between the two lawyers, sought the assistance of Gen. Gideon J. Pillow, who had known Hindman in Tennessee. Pillow, a wealthy Tennessee lawyer and planter and veteran of the Mexican war, spent much time on his Arkansas plantation, one of the largest in Phillips County. Pillow and Cleburne managed to have the duel called off without compromising the honor of either of the lawyers.[23]

For exercise and recreation, Cleburne frequently walked along the banks of the Mississippi River and hiked through the verdant forests to the hilltops of Crowley's Ridge.[24] Once, strolling through the hills, he met Miss Marion A. Yerby, a beautiful young lady called "Mitty." Her father, a native Virginian, then deceased, had been a planter in Phillips County.[25] Later, Cleburne was to pen the following lines in Mitty's autograph album:

9th July 1854

To Miss Y

Tell me, do your footsteps still
  Rone [*sic*] to yonder shady hill
Where the sweet May apple flowers
  Neath the pretty Dogwood bowers
Where the Mock birds varied song
  Echoes sweet tho [*sic*] woods among
First we met near yonder hill
  And fancy paints that meeting still

Oft I climb that solemn steep
  Where the silent spirits sleep
Oft in a pleasant waking dream
  I walk along the Cypress stream
And oft beneath the moon's pale ray
  Along the River's bank I stray
But one fair image haunts me still
  The one I met near yonder hill

Faithful then as I have been
  Unchanged through every changing scene
Will Mitty spare no thought to me
  One thought for weeks of constancy
Will she not send one fair bouquet
  To tell me she too minds that day

45

For let me wander where I will
Fond memory paints that meeting still

P R C.

We do not know how serious this romance was or why it terminated. Four years later Miss Yerby became Mrs. John D. Parrish.[26] But Cleburne's verse was preserved through the years, and a photostatic copy is on file at the Arkansas History Commission.

On February 16, 1855, by order of the state Circuit Court, Cleburne became "a naturalized citizen of the United States of America." About this time Hanly & Alexander moved their office to a temporary location on Ohio Street north of the courthouse. Three months later the firm moved again, this time to Porter Street, opposite the courthouse.[27]

Early in 1854 James T. Crary, a twenty-three-year-old lawyer, moved to Helena from Tennessee. A warm friendship developed between Cleburne and Crary, who was of "kind and courteous bearing" but impulsive and spirited.[28]

During the summer of 1855 Crary asked Cleburne to serve as his second in a street duel with Hoggatt Clopton, a planter's son. Despite his aversion to duels, Cleburne agreed to serve as a second for his friend. The duelists battled with both pistols and bowie knives until Crary fell to the ground, wounded. "Shoot him again," urged an onlooker. But Clopton refrained, saying, "I won't hurt him any more than I have to." Under Dr. Nash's care Crary recovered, and he and Clopton later became friends.[29]

Phillips County had become "the stronghold of Know-Nothingism" in Arkansas. In May 1855, the Phillips County Democratic Association organized "to marshal their forces" for the 1856 Presidential election, and to 'fight our secret skulking foe," Know Nothingism. At a large, enthusiastic meeting in the courthouse, Cleburne was one of eighty-four signers of the constitution for the Association. Other signers were Judge Hanly (who was elected president), James C. Tappan, Dr. Nash, and Hindman.[30] Tappan was to become a brigadier general in the Confederate Army. Hindman was to become a major general; and would command troops in several battles in which Cleburne, likewise, would be a commander.

In Paradise, a settlement in the northern part of the county, lived D. C. Govan, a planter and future general of the Confederacy. He was a native of North Carolina and a graduate of Columbia College, South Carolina. When the war came, he was to raise a company in his vicinity in Phillips County; and in 1863 and 1864 would be one of Cleburne's outstanding brigadier generals.

In August 1855, United States Senator William K. Sebastian of Arkansas, a resident of Helena, was elected president of the Phillips County Democratic Association; and Cleburne, secretary. In the ensuing weeks, the Association held political meetings in various townships of the county. Prominent Democrats addressed the dience "in opposition to the dangerous and anti-American doctrine of Know Nothingism." These meetings closed with a free barbecue for everyone.[31]

At such a meeting on Saturday, September 15, in Marianna, Cleburne was one of three speakers. A Democrat in attendance described the meeting in a Helena paper:

> The platform was erected under a delightful shade, made by interlaced vines, loaded with the lussious [sic] fruit of the Muscadine and the summer grape. The ladies were in attendance, and their bright eyes and winning smiles, lent additional attractions to the occasion .... Mr. Cleburne ... dwelt earnestly upon the monarchical and tyrannical tendencies of the new organization. ... We had a plentiful and substantial dinner, and universal good humor prevailed.[32]

Cleburne returned from Marianna to find Helena plagued with an epidemic of yellow fever. A boat from New Orleans had stopped, on September 5, bearing passengers suffering from the disease. For eleven days, Drs. Grant, Nash, and T. M. Jacks had fought frantically to save the lives of the victims. The streets of the town were "dreary and deserted," as most of the townspeople had fled to the country. The physicians sought volunteers to assist in the emergency. Three men responded — the young Methodist minister, the Reverend John H. Rice; T. C. Hindman; and P. R. Cleburne. Dr. Grant soon fell ill and almost died. The other two physicians and the three volunteers continued to battle this disease about which medical science knew so little at that time. Mr. Rice did his share of nursing and gave spiritual comfort. Cleburne and Hindman worked day and night, caring for the patients in every way, from preparing food to performing the most menial tasks; and even burying the dead. On October 3, after six victims had died, including the editor of the Helena *Democratic Star*, eighteen young men joined the volunteer workers. Among them were W. H. Kinsey and James T. Crary, the latter being elected chairman of a "Relief Committee." The band of workers labored until the disease subsided following several heavy frosts. By October 10 the residents who had fled from the town were returning and conditions were almost normal.[33]

During this disaster a friendship developed between Hindman and Cleburne.[34] Hindman, a forceful orator with an acrimonious disposition, had political ambitions; and soon became influential in the Democratic Party.

The middle of October, the Democratic Association resolved to hold a "Grand Mass Meeting" for two days in late November. Cleburne went to Memphis to procure a band for the occasion, and also to secure a "beautiful banner" for the ladies to present to the Association. The "thrilling and soul stirring" meeting was held under a large arbor erected at the foot of Crowley's Ridge, with some evening speeches in the courthouse. Gayety and enjoyment prevailed, featured by martial music, mounted processions, banners, artillery, fireworks, dinners, dancing, "a large collection of the beauty and chivalry of Helena," and "fair" and "charming" young ladies from adjacent counties and from Memphis. An overtone of the approaching war emerged in the following resolution which was unanimously adopted: "The repeal of the Kansas-Nebraska bill, or of the Fugitive slave law, or the refusal to admit Kansas as a slave State, would be grossly violative of the federal compact, and virtually a dissolution of the Union."

Noted orators — Jacob Thompson, ex-Governor Matthews of Mississippi, General Pillow, and Senator Sebastian — gave major addresses. J. R. McClanahan, chief editor of the Memphis *Appeal*, Hindman, Crary, Cleburne, and others, made shorter speeches. Cleburne spoke at the courthouse on the rostrum with ex-Governor Matthews.[35]

About this time Cleburne learned from his sister Anne that her husband James L. Sherlock, because of illness was no longer traveling on the steamboat. He was in his former position with Rogers & Sherlock, as receiving clerk at the Cincinnati dock.[36]

3

Late in December 1855, Judge Hanly was appointed a member of the state Supreme Court. About a month later, on January 22, 1856, on motion of James T. Crary, by order of the Circuit Court, "P. R. Cleburne" was enrolled as a member of the bar. Thereupon the law firm of Alexander & Cleburne was established, taking over the office of the former firm, Hanly & Alexander.[37]

Cleburne's first jury case attracted attention because of his popularity and the prominence of the parties to the suit. He represented a well-to-do widow who sought to eject a well-to-do tenant. In his summation to the jury, Cleburne ended an eloquent argument, pleading that a gentleman should have more respect for a lady than to compel her to come to court to protect her rights. At that point the spectators in the crowded court room thought that Cleburne had won his case. The opposing attorney, Charles W. Adams, a seasoned lawyer and former judge, quietly told the jury that the last thing in the world he would do would be to cause a lady unnecessary inconvenience; but that he could not change the law or the contract entered into by the parties. Reading a provision of the contract, he argued that the suit was patently without merit. Cleburne, seeing that the case stood to go against his client, angrily broke into the argument. "Mr. Cleburne," Adams replied smilingly and soothingly, "I have no feeling in the matter whatever, and disclaim any intention of wounding the feelings of anyone." The jury brought in a verdict for the defendant. Cleburne, disappointed and embarrassed, vowed that thereafter he would study the language of contracts more carefully and would make a conscious effort to control his temper.[38]

On a Saturday afternoon in late April of 1856, during a period of recreation, Cleburne had a sad experience. He was sailing on the Mississippi with Crary and Norman, a butcher, who was a skilled boatman. Norman was the owner of the bear in the dog and bear fight alluded to previously. As their skiff neared the eastern shore, two men and a boy asked to be taken to the Arkansas side. The boy, aged fifteen, was a pony express rider. With six aboard, Cleburne steered the skiff toward the western shore, combating a strong wind. He threw the skiff to the north to avoid a collision with a large steamboat, which was docking at a wharf boat 200 yards from the Helena shore. The skiff was turning toward Helena when the steamboat suddenly pulled away from the wharf. Instead of waiting for the steamboat to pass, Crary shouted, "No, dash on, we can pass her!" As they attempted to pass, the bow of the steamer intercepted the wind; and the skiff slowed down helplessly. The steamer crashed into the tiny boat, which capsized. Norman and one of the men from Mississippi reached the wrecked skiff and were saved.

The others, heading for shore in the rough waves, were soon widely separated. The other man from Mississippi, the boy, and Crary, were drowned. By his "matchless strength and strong will power," Cleburne succeeded in swimming ashore. A month later, the bodies of Crary and the boy were recovered 125 miles downstream. For long afterward, Cleburne could not speak of this tragedy "without the deepest emotion."[39]

The candidate for the state Senate on the Know Nothing ticket was W. D. (Dorsey) Rice, who had been serving in the Senate as a Democrat. The Democrats now dubbed the Know Nothing Party "the mulatto party." Early in May 1856, at the peak of the political campaign, Hindman published in a Helena paper, the *State Rights Democrat*, an unsigned article castigating Rice and calling him "the mulatto would-be Senator." Hindman and Rice quarreled through the medium of the local newspapers. Rice's brother-in-law, James T. Marriott, joined the quarrel. On May 24, 1856, Hindman heard that his enemies planned to attack him on the street as he went to dinner at the Commercial Hotel. Knowing that Cleburne was quick on the draw and a "crack shot," Hindman asked his friend to accompany him and see that he got fair play.

Cleburne left his law office armed with two Derringer pistols. A few minutes after one o'clock he and Hindman walked down Porter Street and turned left at Front Street. Lurking in an entrance of a dry goods store were Dorsey Rice and Marriott. As Hindman and Cleburne passed, Rice fired, striking Hindman in the right breast. Marriott shot but missed, and both assailants fled into the store.

Cleburne had just passed the entrance and turned around, his pistols still in their holsters, when he was shot in the back by Dorsey Rice's brother Jamison Rice, who was in a second entrance. Not seeing Jamison Rice, Cleburne thought that Marriott had shot him.

Hindman then darted around the corner, and through a side door fired at Marriott. Cleburne managed to walk to the corner, where he joined Hindman; and the two stood on the curb with their guns in their hands. According to the Helena newspaper, they "denounced W. D. Rice and Marriott as cowards and defied them to come out and fight like men." A third brother, F. H. Rice, and a friend advanced with drawn weapons and demanded that Cleburne not shoot. As written by the newspaper, Cleburne retorted that he had been wounded; "that he had a right to shoot — and would kill the scoundrel who had shot him." Marriott then appeared at the nearest door, pistol in hand. Cleburne calmly took aim and shot Marriott; then collapsed to the ground.[40]

Cleburne was shot just below the waist, near the spine, the bullet traveling upward at a forty-five degree angle. Spectators carried him to a room above a store while one of the bystanders ran for Dr. Nash. Becoming conscious of Dr. Nash's presence, Cleburne asked if he were going to die. "Cleburne, you are badly wounded," Dr. Nash replied, "the chances are all against you." After a while he asked, "Doctor, you are not going to leave me, are you?" Dr. Nash answered, "I will not leave your bedside, Cleburne, until you are out of all danger; nothing could induce me to leave you." Cleburne was taken to his room in Dr. Nash's house.[41]

Four days later, Marriott died from the wounds received during the affray. Cleburne hovered between life and death for about a week, but under the care of Drs. Nash and Grant, and with his stamina and determination to live, he survived.

For convalescence, Cleburne and Hindman went to the home of the latter's parents in north Mississippi. On July 10, Cleburne was able to return to Helena and resume his law practice. Only a few close friends were aware of the fact that for several years he continued to suffer ill effects from the wound and never completely recovered.[42]

Cleburne refused to prefer criminal charges against the Rice brothers and always regretted that the shooting had resulted in a death. Later, a friend quoted Cleburne as saying: "I had either to defend myself or run, and I was trained in a school where running formed no part of the accomplishments."[43]

A heart-warming adjunct of the affair involved Dr. Nash's dog Tom, who was devoted to Cleburne. He was accustomed to escorting the young lawyer back and forth from the house to the law office; and the day following the shooting, he refused to eat because he could not find his friend. The next day he followed a servant to Cleburne's room, licked his friend's hand and crawled under the bed, where he remained. As the story goes, he refused to eat until Cleburne recognized him. About two years later, Tom died and was buried in the Nash's yard. Cleburne had a coffin made for the faithful dog, provided a wooden grave marker with the date and place of his birth and death, and composed the following epitaph:

> Here lies Tom,
> My faithful friend;
> His life is spent,
> And he's come to his end.[44]

During the 1856 election campaigns in Phillips County, the bitter contest between the Democrats and the Know Nothings continued. In the August gubernatorial election, the Know Nothings carried Phillips and four other counties. But in the November Presidential race, to Cleburne's gratification, the Democrats carried Phillips County for Buchanan by some sixty votes. Cleburne was invaluable to his party in procuring the unanimous vote of the Irish workmen, by whom he was greatly admired.[45]

On December 5, 1856, Helena, now having a population of over 1,200, was chartered as a city. The population of the county was also increasing and land values were rising.[46]

With the city and county growth and prosperity, Cleburne prospered, too.

In addition to practicing law, Cleburne acted as a land purchasing agent. Dr. Nash having done some "speculating" in land, a company in North Carolina sought his services as agent for procuring large tracts of swamp land in eastern Arkansas. Unable to accept the offer, Nash referred it to Cleburne. Under an agreement that his remuneration would be in land, Cleburne became the agent. During the next two years, he spent much time inspecting and purchasing lands over a wide area, traveling by horseback and steamboat. He retained several thousand acres as his compensation.[47]

In 1853, Lafayette Lodge No. 16 had organized a joint stock company for the purchase of a lot and the erection of a Masonic Hall at Ohio and Porter Streets, diagonally across from the courthouse. The firm of Nash & Cleburne acquired a controlling interest in the hall by purchasing 100 shares, at $10 each, of the 433 shares issued. Subsequently Cleburne bought sixty additional shares; and, on the dissolution of his partnership with Dr. Nash, acquired the latter's stock. The modern two-story brick building was completed in 1854, and the lodge membership grew to over 150.[48] In 1856 Cleburne sold his stock; but remained an active Mason, being treasurer of the lodge until 1857, when he became secretary. On January 1, 1858, he reinvested in the Masonic stock company by purchasing 225 shares, which 4 weeks later he traded for a promissory note and a large tract of land in Poinsett County, Arkansas.[49]

In December 1856, Cleburne became a member of St. John's Episcopal Church. He was soon elected a vestryman, and served in that capacity until he left for the war. In 1860 he contributed generously to the construction of the church edifice, erected at Cherry and Rightor Streets.[50]

An illustration of Cleburne's interest in public and civic affairs is given in the Helena *State Rights Democrat* of July 16, 1857. The graduation exercises of "Miss Lindsay's *Female Institute*," held at the Presbyterian Church, reported the *Democrat*, "closed with a Musical Concert and an address from P. R. Cleburne, Esq . . . . The speech, like all that emanates from Mr. C., was worthy of the occasion and of himself."[51] Cleburne had time for some social life, as indicated by his occasionally hiring a horse and carriage on Sunday. He also found pleasure in fishing and now and then liked a cigar.[52]

In 1858 Dr. Nash retired and moved with his family to his Mississippi plantation. After the Nashs left, Cleburne took up residence at the Commercial Hotel, frequently visiting Dr. Nash on weekends.[53]

Thomas J. Key came to Helena in 1859 and became the editor of the Helena *Weekly Note-Book*. Key was to render distinguished service under Cleburne during the war as commander of Key's battery.

On May 23, 1859, Mark W. Alexander was elected Circuit Court Judge, necessitating the dissolution of his partnership with Cleburne. Using the same office, Cleburne became the senior member of the law firm Cleburne, Scaife & Mangum.[54] M. G. B. Scaife, aged twenty-three years, a South Carolinian, was of a planter family that had settled in Phillips County. L. H. Mangum, one year younger, a North Carolinian, had come to Helena in 1857, following his graduation from Princeton University. Cleburne and Mangum were to be closely associated in a way that neither anticipated, for in the war years that lay ahead, Mangum was to be an important member of Cleburne's staff.

During these busy years in Helena, Cleburne remained in contact with his family and participated in the plan for the rest of them to come to America. His stepmother, half sister Isabella, and half brothers Robert and Christopher, immigrated to the United States about 1856. They resided in Cincinnati, where Robert was employed as a machinist.[55] By 1860 the family group had settled in Newport, Kentucky. Christopher, eighteen years of age, was employed as a clerk with F. P. Corby & Co., Railroad Materials, at 4 Public Landing, Cincinnati. Isabella was a piano teacher in Newport. Anne's husband, James L. Sherlock, died in April 1860, and she and her children resided temporarily with her relatives in Newport. In 1857 a Ronayne cousin visited Cleburne in Helena.[56]

Cleburne and his partners had to compete with seasoned lawyers of Helena's outstanding bar. Through ability and hard work his firm fared well. In the 1860 United States Census, he placed a value of $20,000 on his real estate, and $2,000 on his personal estate.[57]

In 1859 and early in 1860, Cleburne made three major purchases of land — the first, solely on his own; the second, in combination with a wealthy land agent of Helena; and the third, with Dr. Grant. These ventures apparently absorbed all of Cleburne's available cash. For the balance of the purchase price of the lands, he executed several promissory notes (either individually or together with one of the other purchasers) totaling about $10,000. Only a portion of the notes was due when he went away to war, and small payments were made on two of them as late as 1863.[58] Manifestly he and his two associates — experienced investors — had a plan for the successful consummation of these ventures. Since most of the indebtedness was joint obligations, the amount that he would have been called upon to pay was much less than $10,000. It is safe to say that had there been no war, or had the Confederacy won, through appreciation in the value of his large land holdings Cleburne would have accumulated a sizable fortune.

Mangum, in after years, summarized Cleburne's ability and standing as a lawyer:

> While Cleburne was not a brilliant lawyer [not a Princeton graduate] he had all the elements of success and distinction in his profession. His reading was careful and extensive, his application constant, his judgment clear, and his earnestness always a marked characteristic of the man clothed him with real ability. He was scrupulously honest and upright, stood well among his brother lawyers, and commanded not only a good practice but a wide and deep respect among the people.[59]

Thus ended ten eventful years, during which Cleburne had become a highly esteemed citizen, and a part of, the thriving town in Arkansas which he had chosen as his home in America.

NOTES

CHAPTER III

1Nash, *Gen. Pat Cleburne*, 47; trust deed and deed recorded in Record Book "J," pp. 718, 732, Official Records of Phillips County, Ark. By the deed, dated Jan. 6, 1852, Dr. Hector M. Grant conveyed to Patrick R. Cleburne, "all his interest in and to the following described property being an equal undivided moiety of the same to wit: The drug store occupied by the firm of Grant & Nash built upon a lot leased from Henry L. Biscoe and John Preston, Jr., on Rightor Street in the Town of Helena in said County and State together with all the drugs, medicines, furniture and apparatus at this time contained in and in any way appertaining to said drug store."

2Helena (Ark.) *Southern Shield*, Jan. 10, 1852, p. 2; *ibid.*, Apr. 23, 1853, p. 1; p. 42, *Supra.*

3Helena (Ark.) *Democratic Star*, Mar. 15, 1854, p. 3; *ibid.*, March 22, 1855, p. 3.

4Nash, *Gen. Pat Cleburne*, 28-32, 35.

5Helena (Ark.) *Southern Shield*, Dec. 25, 1852, p. 3; "Temperance, Sons of," *New International Encyclopedia* (1925 ed.), XXII, 85.

6O'Hart, *Irish Pedigrees*, II, 118; Anne Sherlock Jordan to authors, Oct. 25, 1963.

7Albert J. Connelly, conversations with authors, July 17, July 18, 1962; Anne Sherlock Jordan to authors, Oct. 14, Oct. 25, 1963; George Mortimer Roe (ed.), *Cincinnati: The Queen City of the West* (Cincinnati, 1895), 370-71; Probate Court Marriage Record B3, 1852-53, p. 426, Official Records of Hamilton County, Ohio.

8Nash, *Gen. Pat Cleburne*, 29.

9*Ibid.*, 33; *cf.* Helena (Ark.) *Southern Shield*, June 28, 1851, p. 2.

10Nash, *Gen. Pat Cleburne*, 34.

11Helena (Ark.) *Southern Shield*, June 25, 1853, p. 3

12Nash, *Gen. Pat Cleburne*, 31; C. Eugene Smith, Secretary, Ancient and Accepted Scottish Rite of Freemasonry, Southern Jurisdiction of the United States, Valley of Little Rock, Ark., conversation with authors, Aug. 29, 1963.

13Johnson & Yerkes (print.), *Proceedings of the M: W: Grand Lodge of Free and Acccepted Masons of the State of Arkansas: Held at Little Rock, November 6th, 1854* (Little Rock, 1854), 27; Nash, *Gen. Pat Cleburne*, 29-30.

14Isabella C. Connelly to Hay, Apr. 12, 1918, in Hay Collection.

Manifestly, Cleburne's stepmother, half sister, and half brothers had surrendered the lease of Grange in Mar. 1850. Records show that by Aug. 20, 1851, they were no longer at Grange; in *Surveyors House Book*, dated July 22, 1848, p. 35, Map No. 11, as supplemented Aug. 20, 1851, Public Record Office of Ireland, Dublin, the name "Mrs. Cleburn" as "Occupier" of the property is stricken out. Their place of residence in Ireland after Mar. 1850 is unknown.

15Cleburne to his stepmother, Oct. 26, Oct. 27, 1853, in possession of Charles Cleburne Jordan.

16Helena (Ark.) *Southern Shield*, Nov. 12, 1853, p. 2; Helena (Ark.) *Democratic Star*, May 17, 1885, p. 1.

17Helena (Ark.) *Democratic Star*, Mar. 29, 1854, p. 2; CS, 1860, Phillips County, Ark., Sch. I, Vol. VI, p. 393R, RG 29, NA; File, Estate of Patrick R. Cleburne, Dec'd, Probate File No. C-2-104, Official Records of Phillips County, Ark., hereinafter cited as Est. of P. R. Cleburne, Dec'd.

18Nash, *Gen. Pat Cleburne*, 15, 35-38; Mangum, *Kennesaw Gazette*, II (June 15, 1887), 2.

19Mangum, *Kennesaw Gazette*, II (June 15, 1887), 2; Jesse N. Cypert, "Reminiscences of the Secession Convention," in John Hugh Reynolds (ed.), *Publications of The Arkansas Historical Association*, (Fayetteville, Ark., 1906), I, 321.

20Nash, *Gen. Pat Cleburne*, 80; Helena (Ark.) *Democratic Star*, April 19, 1854, p. 3; *ibid.*, Apr. 12, 1855, p. 3.

21Helena (Ark.) *Democratic Star*, Apr. 19, 1854, p. 3; Nash, *Gen. Pat Cleburne*, 80; CS, 1850, Phillips County, Ark., Sch. I, Vol. IV, p. 275, RG 29, NA.

22Nash, *Gen. Pat Cleburne*, 87-88: Helena (Ark.) *Democratic Star*, Mar. 1, 1855, pp. 2, 3.

23Nash, *Gen. Pat Cleburne*, 59-60.

24Mangum, *Kennesaw Gazette*, II (June 15, 1887), 2, 6.

25CS, 1850, Phillips County, Ark., Sch. I, Vol. IV, p. 237, RG 29, NA; *ibid.*, Sch. II, Vol. II, p. 275; Helena (Ark.) *Southern Shield*, May 31, 1851, p. 3.

26Marriage Transcript Record Book, Vol. I, p. 288, Official Records of Phillips County, Ark. In Census Schedule, 1850, note 25, *supra*, Miss Yerby's Christian name is listed as "Mary"; but her grave marker in the cemetery of Trenton Missionary Baptist Church, Trenton, Phillips County, reads "Marion N. Yerby wife of John D. Parrish."

27Circuit Court Record Book "12," p. 420, Official Records of Phillips County, Ark; Helena (Ark.) *Democratic Star*, Feb. 1, 1855, p. 3;

Helena (Ark.) *Southern Shield*, May 26, 1855, p. 1.

28Nash, *Gen. Pat Cleburne*, 39-40; Helena (Ark.) *Democratic Star*, Mar. 29, 1854, p. 3; obituary, James T. Crary, Helena (Ark.) *State Rights Democrat*, May 1, 1856, p. 2.

29Nash, *Gen. Pat Cleburne*, 40-44. Crary's law office was over the Licurgus Cage drug store, on Ohio Street, "opposite the Court House." — Helena (Ark.) *Democratic Star*, May 10, 1855, p. 1; Nash, *Gen. Pat Cleburne*, 42; advertisement of L. Gage drug store in Helena (Ark.) *Democratic Star*, Apr. 26, 1855, p. 3. More particularly, this property was "the north 21½ feet of the south 36 feet of Lot 89." — Deed to Licurgus Cage and John M. Rankin, dated July 8, 1859, recorded in Record Book "Q," p. 515, Official Records of Phillips County, Ark.

30Helena (Ark.) *State Rights Democrat*, Nov. 6, 1856, p. 2; Helena (Ark.) *Democratic Star*, May 17, 1855, p. 2; *ibid.*, May 24, 1855, p. 2.

31Helena (Ark.) *Democratic Star*, Aug. 30, 1855, p. 2; *ibid.*, Sept. 13, 1855, p. 3.

32*Ibid.*, Sept. 20, 1855, p. 2.

33*Ibid.*, Oct. 4, 1855, pp. 2, 3; *ibid.*, Oct. 11, 1855, pp. 2, 3; *ibid.*, Oct. 18, 1855, pp. 2. 3; Nash, *Gen. Pat Cleburne*, 52-56. Although the people did not realize that yellow fever was carried by mosquitoes, which the frost eliminated, they did associate the frosts with the subsiding of the disease. — Helena (Ark.) *Democratic Star*, Oct. 11, 1855, p. 3.

34Nash, *Gen. Pat Cleburne*, 56.

35Memphis *Daily Appeal,* Nov. 21, 1855, p. 2; Helena (Ark.) *Democratic Star*, Nov. 29, 1855, p. 2; *ibid.*, Dec. 6, 1855, p. 2, quoting Memphis *Appeal*.

36"Sherlock, James L.," *Cincinnati Directory*, 1851-52, p. 233; *ibid.*, 1856, p. 245.

37Circuit Court Record Book "13," p. 211, Official Records of Phillips County, Ark; Helena (Ark.) *Southern Shield*, Feb. 23, 1856, p. 1. The office of Hanly & Alexander, which in 1856 became that of Alexander & Cleburne, was located "north of the Court-House," "on Porter Street, two doors east of the post-office." — Helena (Ark.) *Democratic Star*, Mar. 1, 1855, p. 1; Helena (Ark.) *Southern Shield,* May 26, 1855, p. 1.

38Nash, *Gen. Pat Cleburne*, 80-82.

39Helena (Ark.) *State Rights Democrat*, May 1, 1856, p. 2; *ibid.*, May 8, 1856, p. 3, quoting *Memphis Appeal*; *ibid.*, May 29, 1856, p. 2;

Nash, *Gen. Pat Cleburne*, 44-46. The wharf-boat was a store moored in the water, for the sale of merchandise to passengers on boats. — Helena (Ark.) *Southern Shield*, July 20, 1850, p. 3.

40Helena (Ark.) *State Rights Democrat* May 1, 1856, p. 2; *ibid.*, May 15, 1856, p. 2, *ibid.*, May 29, 1856, p. 2; Nash, *Gen. Pat Cleburne*, 64-65, 70. The Myrtle & Moore dry goods store was on the northwest corner of Front and Porter Streets, extending to River Alley; more particularly, the south 60 feet of Lot 14. — Deed, James H. McKenzie to Myrtle & Fraser (William C. Myrtle, Robert H. and Jno. Fraser), dated Feb. 16, 1850, recorded in Record Book "J," p. 311, Official Records of Phillips County, Ark.; deed, Myrtle & Fraser to William F. Moore, dated Jan. 17, 1853, recorded in Record Book "N," p. 462, Official Records of Phillips County, Ark. The Commercial Hotel was on "Front Row, ... One door above Myrtle, Moore & Co." — Advertisement in Helena (Ark.) *Democratic Star*, Mar. 15, 1854, p. 3. There is no conveyance of record to the proprietor of the hotel, but the legal description of the property (Lot 15 and north 6 feet of Lot 14) appears in a deed, dated Feb. 25, 1861, to Mrs. Jane S. Whayne, recorded in Record Book "R," p. 731, Official Records of Phillips County, Ark. In 1861, Mrs. Whayne ran "Whayne's," a boarding house, the same structure which previously had been the Commercial Hotel.

41Nash, *Gen. Pat Cleburne*, 65-68; Mangum, *Kennesaw Gazette*, II (June 15, 1887), 2. Cleburne was first carried to a room over the Cage drug store, a little more than a block from where the shooting occurred. — Nash, *Gen. Pat Cleburne*, 66; note 29, *supra.*

42Helena (Ark.) *State Rights Democrat*, May 29, 1856, p. 2; *ibid.*, June 5, 1856, p. 2; *ibid.*, June 12, 1856, p. 3; *ibid.*, July 10, 1856, p. 2; Nash, *Gen. Pat Cleburne*, 69-70; Biscoe Hindman, "General Pat Cleburne," *Southern Historical Society Papers*, XXXI (1903), hereinafter cited as *S. H. S. P.*

43Mangum, *Kennesaw Gazette,* II (June 15, 1887), 2; Avery, "Patrick Ronayne Cleburne," 2.

44Nash, *Gen. Pat Cleburne*, 70-73.

45Helena (Ark.) *State Rights Democrat*, Nov. 6, 1856, p. 2; Nash, *Gen. Pat Cleburne*, 89.

46Helena (Ark.) *Democratic Star*, Oct. 18, 1855, p. 3; *ibid.*, Dec. 20, 1855, p. 2.

47Nash, *Gen. Pat Cleburne*, 85-86; File, Est. of P. R. Cleburne, Dec'd.

48Deed to president and directors of the "Masonic building now about to be erected," recorded in Record Book "L," p. 177, Official Records of Phillips County, Ark.; conveyance Nash to Cleburn, recorded in Record Book "M," p. 109; release, Nash to Cleburne, recorded in Record Book "O," p. 111, Official Records of Phillips County, Ark.; Nash, *Gen. Pat Cleburne*, 31-32; professional card of Underwood & Barrett, dated Nov. 9, 1854, Helena (Ark.) *Democratic Star*, Feb. 15, 1855, p. 1, which recites, "Office second room north of the Masonic Hall."

49Deed, Cleburne to Thomas H. Curry, recorded in Record Book "O," p. 110, Official Records of Phillips County, Ark.; Helena (Ark.) *Democratic Star*, Mar. 22, 1855, p. 3; Helena (Ark.) *State Rights Democrat*, June 4, 1857, p. 3; deed, Curry to Cleburne, recorded in Record Book "P," p. 122; deed, Cleburne to Daniel B. McKensie, recorded in Record Book "P," p. 120, Official Records of Phillips County, Ark.

50Records, St. John's Episcopal Church; Mangum, *Kennesaw Gazette,* II (June 15, 1887), 2. A deed dated Oct. 30, 1860 conveyed to the vestrymen of St. John's Church, of whom Cleburne was named as being one, the land upon which the church was built. Deed recorded in Record Book "R," p. 563, Official Records of Phillips County, Ark. ". . . to Gen. P. R. Cleburne, a liberal contributor, [and others named] all honor is due for their wisdom and generosity." — Clipping from Helena (Ark.) *World*, Feb. 1, 1899, in Records, St. John's Episcopal Church.

51Helena (Ark.) *State Rights Democrat*, July 16, 1857, p. 3.

52File, Est. of P. R. Cleburne, Dec'd; Biscoe Hindman, "General Pat. Cleburne," 164.

53Nash, *Gen. Pat Cleburne*, 85; CS, 1860, Phillips County, Ark., Sch. I Vol. VI, p. 393-R, RG 29, NA.

54Helena (Ark.) *State Rights Democrat*, May 22, 1860, p. 1. Only one legal pleading drafted by Cleburne is extant. Entitled on the cover, "Demurrer to Plea," and endorsed, "Filed December 8th 1859 Edw H Cowley Clerk," the pleading, in Cleburne's handwriting, is as follows:

S G Hanly)	In the Circuit Court of
vs)	Phillips County at the
A B Eclipse)	November Term 1859

"And the said Plaintiff saith that the said plea of the said Defendant and the matters therein contained in the manner and form as the same are above pleaded and set forth are not sufficient in law to quash the said Affidavit for Attachment the said Writ or the said Declaration and that the said Plaintiff is not bound by law to answer the same And this he is ready to verify Wherefore for want of a sufficient plea in this behalf the said Plaintiff prays Judgment and that said Defendant may answer further and the said Plaintiff according to the form of the statute in such case made and provided states and shows to the Court here the following causes of Dermurrer to the said plea that is to say

1st Said plea commences as a plea in Abatement and concludes as a plea to the Jurisdiction of the Court

2nd Said plea prays that the Writ Affidavit and Declaration may be quashed and also prays Judgment whether the Court can or will take cognizance of the action

3rd Said plea is not only of the nature of a plea in Abatement and a plea to the Jurisdiction but it also partakes of the nature of a Demurrer to the Court by by [sic] raising the question of law Whether the Declaration sets up a legal cause of action or not and also that said plea is in other respects informal uncertain and insufficient

P R Cleburne
Atty for Plf -

(MS in The Historical Society of Pennsylvania, Philadelphia, hereinafter cited as Hist. Soc. Pa.) Another legal document prepared by Cleburne reads:

NOTICE

Is hereby given, that after publication of this notice for six weeks, application will be made to the Commissioner of Pensions, for the issue of a duplicate of Land Warrant No. 23,003, act 28th Sept. 1850, issued to John Grist, (for 80 acres) private Capt. Gaffney's company, war 1812; the same having been lost or destroyed, and a caveat against its location having been entered in the General Land Office. Dated   , 1856.

P. R. Cleburne,
Atty for John Grist.

Sept. 25, '56 — 6w." — Helena (Ark.) *State Rights Democrat*, Dec. 11, 1856, p. 3.

The following year, the same newspaper carried this "Notice":

The firm of Curry & Dowty having been dissolved, and assets assigned to me, I will in pursuance of the deed of assignment so made, and as Trustee for the creditors of said late firm of Curry & Dowty, proceed to sell all the assets so assigned At Cost and Carriage for Cash. Said assets, to be sold as aforesaid, consist of Dry Goods, Clothing, Queensware, Hardware, Tinware, Tobacco, and a new general assortment of all articles usually found in a Dry Goods establishment.

July 30, '57.

P. R. Cleburne, Trustee. —
Helena (Ark.) *State Rights Democrat*, July 30, 1857, p. 2

The paper also had a news account: "Selling Off at Cost. — See advertisement of P. R. Cleburne, Esq., Trustee for the late firm of

Curry & Dowty, and call and make your purchases. The stock is large and new, and prices low.

"It is proper to say, that this sale is not because of the insolvency of the late firm, but solely for causes of a personal character, . . ." — *Ibid.*, p. 3.

55The 1857 *Cincinnati Directory*, p. 65, listed "Cleborne, Robt. . . . 66 12th," as a "finisher"; *i.e.*, machinist. In the 1860 Cincinnati Directory, p. 97, "Cleborne, *[sic]*" was listed as a "machinist."

56"Cleburne, Robt.," Newport, Ky. section of *Cincinnati Directory*, 1860, p. 370; CS, 1860, Campbell County, Ky., Sch. I, Vol. IV, p. 439-R, RG 29, NA; "Cleburne, Christopher,"*Cincinnati Directory*, 1860, p. 97; "Cleburne, Miss Isabella," Newport, Ky. section of *Cincinnati Directory*, 1869, p. 181; Albert J. Connelly, conversation with authors, Sept. 8, 1963; Records, Cemetery of Spring Grove, Cincinnati; "General P. R. Cleburne," *Kennesaw Gazette* V (Apr. 15, 1890), 1. In the 1860 U. S. Census, *supra*, the surname of General Cleburne's stepmother, brothers, and sister was recorded as "Clayburn."

57Mangum, *Kennesaw Gazette*, II (June 15, 1887), 2; CS, 1860, Phillips County, Ark., Sch. I, Vol. VI, p. 393-R, RG 29, NA.

58File, Est. of P. R. Cleburne, Dec'd.

59Mangum, *Arkansas Gazette*. Indicative of Dr. Grant's devotion to Cleburne, in October 1895 his infant son was named Cleburne. Unfortunately the little boy lived only eight months. — Marker, Grant family plot, Magnolia Cemetery, Helena.

CHAPTER IV

WAR CLOUDS

I am with the South in life or in death, in victory or defeat.
I never owned a Negro and care nothing for them,
but these people have been my friends and have stood
up to me on all occasions.

—From letter, Cleburne to his brother Robert, May 7, 1861.

In the spring of 1860, as war clouds gathered, the Helena *State-Rights Democrat* proclaimed, "Principle . . . is superior to the Union, especially when that principle is the safeguard of . . . independence and honor." The people of Phillips County were determined to resist what they believed to be encroachments upon their freedom.[1]

Few towns or counties of comparable population in the entire South were to produce the number of Confederate generals as "the remarkable group of general officers . . . of Helena, Arkansas, and its surrounding county of Phillips" — Major Generals Cleburne and Hindman and Brigadier Generals Lucius E. Polk, Govan, and Tappan.[2]

Generals Cleburne and Polk came from the Yell Rifles, an outstanding company. It was named in honor of Archibald Yell, former Governor of Arkansas and commander of an Arkansas cavalry regiment in the war with Mexico. Colonel Yell was killed in a counter-charge at the battle of Buena Vista. The Yell Rifles, assembled in the summer of 1860, was the first company organized in Phillips County, with Cleburne, Lucius Polk and Mangum among the first to enlist as privates.[3]

Lucius Polk, of the James K. Polk family, a North Carolinian by birth, was reared at Columbia, Tennessee, where his family had moved when he was a small child. Following graduation from the University of Virginia, he became a planter in Phillips County. Twenty-seven years of

63

age at the start of the war, Polk was to become a splendid brigadier general in Cleburne's division.

The Yell Rifles was "composed of the flower of the young men" in Helena and Phillips County.[4] The great majority were from the planter and large farmer class. Others were young professional and business men of Helena, three clerks, a miller, two master carpenters, and a mill laborer. Among the members were R. N. Yerby, brother of "Miss Mitty"; and James Clopton, younger brother of Hoggatt Clopton.[5]

The Yell Rifles elected Cleburne as their company commander. His experience in the British regiment proved valuable to the young Captain, who soon had a well trained company. He obtained the services of J. H. Calvert, a resident of Helena and a fellow Irishman, as drillmaster. Calvert, a former sergeant in the United States regular army,[6] later became an artillery officer in Cleburne's brigade.

A large percentage of other volunteer infantry companies in Phillips County was made up of small farm owners, thrifty tenant farmers, and herdsmen. This fact illustrates the contribution made by the "plain country folk" in the South's war effort. Thus, the L'Anguille Rebels (later Company A, 2nd Arkansas Infantry Regiment, Cleburne's division), came to Helena from as far away as fifty miles to enlist. The Helena *Southern Shield* described them: "Most of the company are hardy, industrious men, inured to toil and privation of frontier life, — the best material out of which to make the effective, reliable soldier, if properly armed, drilled and disciplined."[7]

The plain country folk gloried in expert markmanship with rifle and musket, derived from shooting matches and continual hunting. A typical shooting match attests to their skill. Some twenty "tall, stalwart, browned hunters; equipped in leather, with their broad knives by their sides, rifles in hand," would participate in the match. Each man would have a separate target — a piece of paper one inch square on a board against a tree forty yards distant for shooting off-hand, or sixty yards distant for shooting at rest from a prone position. In each contest of the match, eight rivals would take part with eleven shots each. A rifle would protrude over the top of a log, and upon its crack the bullet would likely split the paper. A half dollar would cover all eleven shots on a winner's target.[8]

Frank Lawrence Owsley, treating of small farm owners and herdsmen of the Old South, and of "those tenant farmers whose agricultural production . . . indicated thrift, energy, and *self*-respect," said that "their *self-description*" of " 'plain folks' " "connoted the sum of the solid virtues — integrity, independence, self-respect, courage, love of freedom, love of their fellow man, and love of God."[9] Men from all economic groups were to make up the gallant Army of Tennessee. But such small farmers and herdsmen as here described, from several states of the Confederacy, were to comprise the hard core of that army and Cleburne's division.

2

Cleburne was an earnest states'-rights man and a strict constitutionalist. He held the conviction that if war came, the struggle on the part of the Southern people would be for liberty — the right to manage their own affairs.[10] Cleburne scorned the idea that the fight would be for slavery. To be sure, slavery was an important part of the picture. But in his view, the abolitionists, in seeking to exterminate slavery, were interfering with the right of the South to govern its domestic affairs. The abolitionists had joined the newly formed and rising Republican Party. Although the party's candidate for President, Abraham Lincoln, believed that slavery in the states where it existed could not be interfered with, prominent members of his party, in many sections of the country, advocated its abolishment. A Helena paper of October 1860 high-lighted the threatening development, quoting extracts from the "Black Republican Bible":

> "We believe, that THIEVES, are as a general rule, less amenable to the moral laws than SLAVEHOLDERS."
> "SLAVEHOLDERS ARE MORE CRIMINAL THAN COMMON MURDERS *[sic]* ."
> ". . . we are wedded to one purpose, from which no earthly power can ever devorce *[sic]* us."
> "WE ARE DETERMINED TO ABOLISH SLAVERY AT ALL HAZARDS OF WHATEVER NATURE WHICH IT IS POSSIBLE FOR SLAVECRATS TO BRING AGAINST US. . . ."[11]

Cleburne abhored these misrepresentations. And he believed that this intermeddling was forbidden by the Tenth article of Amendment of the Constitution: "The powers not delegated to the United States by the Constitution, nor prohibited by it to the States, are reserved to the States respectively, or to the people."

Another grave issue was whether the Federal government should prohibit slavery in the territory acquired from Mexico. Cleburne believed that such action would be an encroachment beyond the constitutional power of the national government. His view accorded with a preamble adopted by the Tennessee Legislature (quoted in a Helena paper of September 1860), which asserted that territory ceded by Mexico "is the common property of all the people of the United States, and all have the right to move to it and take with them their property, ... Congress [cannot] say [slaves] shall cease to be property. To abolish slavery in the Territories . . . is an appropriation of the Territories to the people of one portion of our country to the exclusion of another whose blood and treasure flowed freely in the war which acquired it."[12] In April 1860, as a delegate from Phillips County to the Arkansas Democratic State Convention in Little Rock, Cleburne had voted for a less detailed resolution adopted at the convention that abolition of slavery in the territories would annul "the constitutional rights" of citizens.[13]

Cleburne was convinced that back of the agitation in the North over slavery in the territories was an effort of the industrial North to destroy the balance of power between it and the agricultural South, with their opposing social and economic systems; and thereby to exploit the South. The balance of power between the two sections had been recognized when the Constitution was adopted, and maintenance of the balance was safeguarded by the limitations upon the powers of the Federal government contained in the document. If slavery and the Southern system could be excluded from the territories — which would in due course become states — the North could upset the balance of power and maintain control of the Federal government. Then, through what Cleburne considered to be still further distortions of the Constitution, the North could achieve a more centralized government, and could accomplish such vital objectives as ship subsidies and internal improvements at national expense; a national bank; and, above all, an oppressive tariff — objectives that would strengthen the North and weaken the South. As Cleburne, in a considered statement, was to say in 1863 of the North's opposition to slavery, "It is merely the pretense to establish sectional superiority and a more centralized form of government, and to deprive us of our rights and liberties."[14]

With the election of "abolition candidates" for governor in Ohio, Indiana, and Pennsylvania, the Helena *Weekly Note-Book* of October 18, 1860, expressed the sentiments of the people of Phillips County:

"Hang out the banner of States Rights and political equality and let the watch be set.

"It is time to pray to God and keep our powder dry."

Cleburne was one of the judges and clerks, at Helena, in the presidential election of 1860. When the news reached Helena that Lincoln had been elected, with the backing of the extremists in the North who defied the Constitution, and on a platform hostile to the South which proclaimed that the party would bar the extension of slavery in the territories, Cleburne recognized that secession from the Union was near at hand.[15]

On December 20, South Carolina seceded; followed, in January 1861 by Mississippi, Florida, Alabama, Georgia, and Louisiana; the seceding states taking possession of Federal arsenals and forts within their borders.

3

Early in January 1861, Cleburne wrote to his brother Robert in Newport, Kentucky:

> The hopefulness and good humor with which you look the present gloomy state of Affairs in the face is really refreshing. Yours is the true philosophy — an honest heart and a strong arm should never succumb. Many will sink in the tempest that is now loosening every rivet of society but I hope and believe you will be one of those who will buffet it out. I never spent a

more gloomy Christmas. Our Court has been in Session for the last seven weeks and only adjourned three or four days ago. I was very busy all the time and most of the time I was working alone. My partners were participating in gaities I did not feel like sharing. I have been invited to twenty parties this Christmas and have not attended one.

I shook off books and business the day after the adjournment, got horse and gun and joined a party who were [out] for a wolf hunt in the hills back of town. I saw no wolves but shot a very large buck with antlers of the largest size. He was running before the hounds in full career and crossed me at forty or fifty yards distance. I let him have both barrels and with the last report he tumbled over. It will sound strange to you that in a country filled with game like this I have not had a shot gun in my hands for near two years until this hunt and I never fired at a deer before. When you remember the enthusiasm with which in other days I used to take the gun or whistle the dogs you will see I am greatly changed since then.

My health is better than it was in the summer but my lungs have never been well since I was wounded. I catch cold on the smallest provocation and an hour's excited debate in the Court House will sometimes fill my mouth with blood. When I first came here I thought nothing of wading all day through ponds and bayous after ducks. Now a broken boot will give me a bad cold. I never weighed over 148 lb. and at present I do not think I weigh over 135 lb. . . .

I hardly know what to say to you about politicks. This State has . . . ordered an election . . . for delegates to a convention. I cannot say what course they will adopt but the fever of revolution is very contagious and if blood is spilled and passion excited the reckless riflemen who inhabit our woods will inevitably take a hand. Even if the State should not secede it will be impossible to prevent armed volunteers from rushing to the scene of action. My own opinion is that the first blood shed on Southern soil in a collision between the Federal troops and the State authorities of any Southern state will be the signal for a civil war which must ultimately array the 15 Southern against the Northern States. I can now stand at my office window and see a foreign nation on the other side of the river. As to my own position I hope to see the Union preserved by granting to the South the full measure of her constitutional rights. If this cannot be done I hope to see all the Southern States united in a new confederation and that we can effect a peacable separation. If both of these are denied us I am with Arkansas in weal or in woe. I have been elected and hold the Commission of the State as captain of the volunteer Rifle Company of this place and I can say for my company that if the stars and stripes become the standard of a tiranical majority, the ensign of a violated league, it will no longer command our love or respect but will command our best efforts to drive it from the State.

I am not married and this is not a time for marrying or giving in marriage. If matters would get settled again and my lands had a value and I was certain that I would not be a permanent invalid I would wish to marry. As to being an invalid I sometimes think I will be; at other times I think my fears unnecessary. A few more years bent over law book will not help me.

The members of the bar of this circuit have recommended me to the Governor for the Office of Special Judge to try certain cases in which the regular Judge is disqualified. I expect he will appoint me.

The closing manifested Cleburne's continued love for the members of his family despite the distance and lapse of time that separated him from them:

Give my love to Mamma, Annie & her children, Issy and Christopher, and tell them I hope they have spent a less gloomy Christmas than I have. I do not certainly know your post office and cannot safely write. Please inform me in your next; also William's. Joey [Joseph] is well and at the old place, La Porte, Ind.

Your Brother
P R Cleburne

Enclosed find $10; buy some little Christmas present.[16]

On the front and back inside cover of his Book of Common Prayer, Cleburne glued two religious poems, clipped from newspapers. Each was a poem of sadness and suffering, and of trust and faith in God. Perhaps their special appeal to him lay in the tragedies of the drownings and the Marriott shooting, as well as the potentiality of his invalidism. One of these poems, which he placed in the prayer book scarcely six weeks after writing the letter to Robert, read:

I HOLD STILL.

From the German.

Pain's furnace heat within me quivers:
   God's breath upon the flame doth blow:
And all my heart in anguish quivers,

And trembles at the fiery glow;
And yet I whisper — As God will!
And in this hottest fire, hold still.

He comes and lays my heart, all heated,
On the hard anvil; minded so,
Into His own fair shape to beat it
With His great hammer, blow on blow;
And yet I whisper — As God will!
And at His hardest blows, hold still.

He takes my softened heart and beats it.
The sparks fly off at every blow;
He turns it o'er and o'er, and beats it,
And lets it cool, and makes it glow:
And yet I whisper — As God will!
And in His mighty hand, hold still.

Why should I murmur? For the sorrow
Thus only longer lived would be;
The end may come, and will, to-morrow,
When God has done His work in me.
So I say, trusting — As God will!
And trusting to the end, hold still.

He kindles for my profit merely
Affliction's fiery, glowing brand;
And all His heaviest blows are surely
Inflicted by a Master's hand.
So I say, praying — As God will!
And hope in Him, and suffer still.[17]

4

In January 1861, Cleburne equipped himself for war by purchasing a saddle horse and various significant articles: a comfort, a box of wads and two pounds of shot; a box of percussion caps; and, for his uniform, a pair of sleeve buttons.[18] On January 28, an exciting dispatch was sent from Little Rock to Memphis over a recently completed telegraph line; and relayed to Helena's new telegraph office. The wire reported a rumor that a steamboat, carrying a large body of Federal soldiers, was on its way to Little Rock to reinforce the United States arsenal there. The rumor was false. But unaware of the falsity of the report, citizens of Helena and Phillips County held a mass meeting and sent a wire to Gov. Henry M. Rector, offering their services in seizing the arsenal and expelling the United States troops. At the Governor's request, his adjutant-general sent a reply. His instructions to the adjutant-general are a matter of uncertainty; but the gist of the message dispatched by the adjutant-general has been recorded thusly:

"The governor has no authority to summon you to take possession of a Federal post, whether threatened to be reinforced or not. Should the people assemble in their defense, the governor will interpose his official position in their behalf."[19]

The Yell Rifles and another company which had been organized in the county, the Phillips Guards, prepared to depart for Little Rock.[20] With Captain Cleburne on horseback at the head of his command, the two companies marched along Ohio and Rightor Streets to the wharf. By steamboat they went down the Mississippi and then up the Arkansas River, arriving at Little Rock on February 5.

The enthusiastic patriots from Phillips County were greeted at the dock by one lone person, a private citizen. The companies formed on the hurricane deck of the boat, loaded their pieces, and marched to the Governor's mansion. The Governor professed surprise to see them and in a short address disavowed knowledge of the telegraphic message which had brought the volunteers to the aid of their state, and said that he was opposed to taking the arsenal unless the situation worsened. Disappointed and chagrined, the Yell Rifles and the Phillips Guards marched to the capitol grounds and set up camp for the night — resolved to seize the arsenal. During the night, they were joined by other volunteer companies from different parts of the state where a like telegram had been received.

The next day, at a mass meeting, residents of Little Rock resolved that if the Governor thought there was any danger of the volunteer troops taking the arsenal, or any necessity for such action, "we earnestly recommend him, as the only way to prevent the effusion of blood," to demand the surrender of the arsenal, and seize it by force if necessary. The City Council also requested the Governor to interpose his authority. Communications between the Governor and the commanding officer of the arsenal resulted, on February 8, in its voluntary surrender to state authorities.

Cleburne was pleased at the outcome, but shocked when following the surrender a group of Little Rock women who were Union sympathisers presented the Federal commander with a handsome sword. With the Governor's authorization, Cleburne procured a supply of minie balls for his company from the stockpile of ammunition at the arsenal.[21] He returned to Helena with the Yell Rifles, while the Phillips Guards remained to garrison the arsenal.

In Montgomery, Alabama, representatives of the seceded states were busily engaged in forming the government of the Confederate States of America. In early February the delegates elected Jefferson Davis provisional President and drafted a constitution.

On March 4 a state convention met in Little Rock to determine the course Arkansas should take in the crisis. Judge Hanly, an advocate of secession and soon to be serving in the Confederate Congress, was a delegate from Phillips County. Union sentiment was so strong that, after prolonged debate, the convention recessed without voting upon the question whether Arkansas should secede.

Captain Cleburne and the Yell Rifles continued to prepare for war. In a reorganization of the company, Polk was elected Second Lieutenant; and Mangum, Second Sergeant.[22] Diligently and effectively, Cleburne trained and disciplined his company.

In April 1861, after Confederate batteries had fired on Fort Sumter, President Lincoln called on Arkansas for 750 troops as part of an army of 75,000 to use in subduing the Confederate States. In his reply to the President, submitted on April 22, Governor Rector emphatically refused, knowing that Arkansas would not fight against the Confederacy. The Governor began preparing for secession, which was now inevitable. One step was to defend the Mississippi River by ordering several volunteer companies from eastern Arkansas, including the Yell Rifles, to "rendezvous" at Camp Frank Rector. This camp was located at Mound City, a village on the west bank of the river a few miles above Memphis.[23]

In Helena, the war fever rose so high that any man expressing sympathy for the North would have been killed by the local citizenry.[24] The city of Cincinnati had seized arms and munitions which were being shipped to Arkansas. In retaliation for this action, the City Council of Helena, about April 25, decided to seize all boats owned by Cincinnati interests. The Council directed Helena's mayor "to have all unmounted cannon mounted and to purchase two barrels of cannon powder for the defense of the city." On April 25, a Cincinnati steamboat, *Queen of the West*, came into sight, plying upstream. Amid a crowd of people assembled along the river bank, Captain Cleburne stood ready with Helena's biggest weapon, a little four-pounder cannon. He fired a ball in front of the bow of the steamboat and brought the vessel to shore.[25] Armed city officials and other armed citizens then demanded that the steamboat captain make known the ownership of the boat. The master replied that the owners were the Cincinnati firm Rogers & Sherlock, and the Helena officials promptly seized the boat.

The account, in Cleburne's own words in a letter to his brother Robert written a few days later, continues:

> Being assured that Th. [Thomas] Sherlock was part owner and knowing him to be a good Southern man, I beged [*sic*] our people as a favor to me to release the boat. On my assurances, they did release her, ... I thought of you all when I did this thing, that it might make you a friend in the crisis which is now upon us. I have scarcely shed a tear since Papa's death, but as I implored our armed men to release the boat, I cried on the public street like a woman. It came near involving one in a difficulty and criticism. My life perhaps, but life has always been a small matter with me when duty points the way. Capt. Scott, the captain of the boat, who lives in Covington, can give you the particulars, and if he has any gratitude in his soul, should befriend you for my sake. I wrote Sherlock a short note in regard to it. See whether he received it. I gave it to the clerk of the boat.[26]

On the morning of Sunday, April 27, a transport was waiting to take the Yell Rifles to Camp Rector. The company assembled on Ohio Street in front of the courthouse and marched to the Methodist Church, one block west, for services. The troops proudly bore the stars and bars of the

Confederate States, a flag which the young ladies of Helena had presented to Captain Cleburne on behalf of the company. The church was filled and hundreds of well-wishers stood on the outside. At the close of the service, Captain Cleburne was presented with a Bible for the company. Pale and touched with emotion, Cleburne responded in a scarcely audible voice. The minister then invoked on the company the blessing of the God of Battles; and the Rifles, after tender farewells, paraded to the steamboat landing. Gathered at the landing and along the river bank were hundreds of other people, with many waving the "Bonnie Blue Flag." Hindman, who had resigned from a second term in Congress to raise a brigade of Arkansas troops, made a talk. The Rifles then boarded the transport; and, amidst cheers and tears, departed to report for duty.[27]

The state convention reassembled at Little Rock on May 6; and the same day, the solemn and patriotic delegates adopted an ordinance of secession by a vote of sixty-nine to one. The spirit that prevailed in the state was described, thirty-seven years later, in a commentary by Judge T. J. Oliphint, a highly respected citizen of Little Rock and a Tennessean by birth. In the spring of 1861 Judge Oliphint had joined an Arkansas volunteer company, and had served throughout the war.[28] His commentary read: "I venture no state representing the Confederate cause responded to the call more freely than Arkansas, ... Well do I remember the excitement, the bonfires, the speeches stirring the young hearts to action, as well as the older."[29]

The day following Arkansas' secession, Cleburne wrote to his brother Robert from Camp Rector:

> I received your letter and one from Joseph. I find we are each on a different side, Joe with Lincoln, you for a neutrality that I believe can never be obtained.
>
> I am with the South in life or in death, in victory or defeat. I never owned a Negro and care nothing for them, but these people have been my friends and have stood up to me on all occasions. In addition to this, I believe the North is about to wage a brutal and unholy war on a people who have done them no wrong, in violation of the constitution and the fundamental principals of the government. They no longer acknowledge that all government derives its validity from the

consent of the governed. They are about to invade our peaceful homes, destroy our property, and inaugurate a servile insurrection, murder our men and dishonor our women. We propose no invasion of the North, no attack on them, and only ask to be let alone. They cannot conquer us but would turn the wolf from their own doors by letting this idle, brutal mob come here to be destroyed.

Joe speaks of joining the Northern army. He says the stars and stripes must be held up, that Davis or Lincoln must be president, that the laws must be enforced, the Government must be maintained, but there is not one argument, one reason in his letter. Let him ask himself why the free people of Arkansas should be robbed and murdered merely because they have determined to live under laws of their own making. Let him ask himself what the North will do with Arkansas. If she conquered it, will she keep a standing army of 30,000 men here to maintain her conquest? We are not striving to become tyrannical invaders. Our army is for protection, Lincoln's to subjugate and enslave the whole Southern people and divide their property among his vulgar unprincipled mob.

I am captain of a splendid company of Riflemen from Helena. The majority are the young planters of the county. We number 100 men and are armed with the latest improved army rifles. On tomorrow our election will take place for colonel of the 1st Arkansas Regiment of Volunteers stationed with other forces at this camp. All the companies appear determined to elect me colonel. This is a fearfully responsible position and I dread the honor but intend to turn my whole attention to it and do the best I can for the cause I am embarked in. I may die in this conflict and the South may suffer reverses, but mark me well (and I have seldom been a false prophet), the North will eventually retreat from this unholy war, shattered and disgraced.

Then followed the account above quoted about the seizure of the *Queen of the West*, and the letter continued:

Write to Joe and, if you can, keep him from joining our invaders. Send him a copy of this if necessary and tell him if he joins the North my honor forbids me from further correspondence with him during the war. . . . Write to William also and tell him about matters and things . . . . As for myself, I know nothing of the future, but I suppose I will have a conspicuous share in the events approaching.

Your brother
P R Cleburne

Give my love to Mamma, Issy & Chris and tell them I hope we shall one day meet again, if not on earth, in heaven.[30]

75

NOTES

CHAPTER IV

[1]Helena (Ark.) *State-Rights Democrat*, May 22, 1860, p. 2.
[2]Robert Selph Henry, "Foreword," in Ida Pace Purdue, *Papers Pertaining to the Confederacy* (Athens, Ga., 1961), p. ix.
[3]Mangum, *Arkansas Gazette*; Muster roll of Yell Rifles in clipping from unidentified Helena (Ark.) newspaper, 1903, in Scrapbk., U.D.C., Helena.
[4]Mangum, *Arkansas Gazette*.
[5](There were also four clerks who were sons of planters and a prominent merchant.) Two lists of Yell Rifles checked against CS, 1860, Phillips County, Ark., Sch. I, Vol. VI, and Sch. II, Vol. II, RG 29, NA. These lists were from muster roll of Yell Rifles cited note 3, *supra*, and Yell Rifles Mustered into Confederate Service (MS copied from Descriptive List of "Yell Rifles," Co. F,_____Ark., July 23, 1861, Confederate Voucher #3356), filed with 15th (Cleburne's — Polk's — Josey's) Arkansas Infantry, Muster and Pay Rolls, 1861-65, RG 109, NA.
[6]Mangum, *Arkansas Gazette*.
[7]Quoted in Little Rock *Arkansas State Gazette*, June 1, 1861, p. 2. About fifty-five percent of Capt. John Glendenning's Co. B, 23rd Regiment, Arkansas Volunteers, raised in Phillips County, were "plain country folk." Over forty percent of the company raised by D. C. Govan (which became Co. F, 2nd Arkansas Infantry, Cleburne's division) were "plain country folk." In the latter company nearly forty percent were of planter and large farmer families. — Muster rolls of these companies in newspaper clipping in Scrapbk., U.D.C., Helena, cited note 3, *supra*, checked against CS, 1860, Phillips County, Ark., Sch. I, Vol. VI, and Sch. II, Vol. II, RG 29, NA.
[8]Albert Pike, "A Shooting Match," in Octavius Coke (ed.), *The Scrapbook of Arkansas Literature* (Little Rock, 1939), 39.
[9]Owsley, *Plain Folk*, pp. vii, 8.
[10]Avery, "Patrick Ronayne Cleburne," 2; Benham, *Kennesaw Gazette*, IV (Jan. 15, 1889), 2; *ibid.*, (May 15, 1889), 6.
[11]Helena (Ark.) *Weekly Note-Book*, Oct. 4, 1860, p. 2.
[12]*Ibid.*, Sept. 27, 1860, p. 1.
[13]Little Rock *Arkansas True Democrat*, Apr. 7, 1860, p. 2.
[14]*The War of the Rebellion: A Compilation of the Official Records of the Union and Confederate Armies* (Washington, 1880-1901), Ser. I, Vol. LII, Pt. 2, p. 592, hereinafter cited as *O.R.; cf.* Frank Lawrence

Owsley, "The Irrepressible Conflict," in *I'll Take My Stand*, 72-91; Charles A. and Mary R. Beard, *The Rise of American Civilization* (New York, 1931), I, 714; *ibid.*, II, 3-6.

[15]County Court Record, Phillips County, Ark., Oct. Term 1861, Vol. "G," p. 161; Benham, *Kennesaw Gazette*, IV (Jan. 15, 1899), 2.

[16]Cleburne to his half brother Robert, undated, in possession of Charles Cleburne Jordan.

[17]Cleburne's Book of Common Prayer, on display in Helena Library. No copies of Helena newspapers during this period are extant. However, the same poem, in different type-face, appeared in the *Weekly* (Memphis) *Bulletin* of Feb. 28, 1861, p. 2. The justifiable inference is that Cleburne's clipping came from a Helena newspaper of about the same date. When leaving for the war, he gave the book to Miss "Sally" Alexander, sister of his former law partner. — Notation in Helena Library; Miss Lucy Alexander Sanders, daughter of Sally Alexander Sanders, conversation with authors, Aug. 31, 1965.

[18]File, Est. of P. R. Cleburne, Dec'd.

[19]John M. Harrell, "Arkansas," in Clement A. Evans (ed.), *Confederate Military History* (Atlanta, 1899), X, Pt. 2, pp. 6-8; Margaret Ross, "Chronicles of Arkansas," Little Rock *Arkansas Gazette*, Jan. 29, 1961, p. 3E.

[20]Cleburne purchased additional equipment consisting of a pair of saddle bags, $6.00; a pair of blankets, $3.00; a box of percussion caps; and two pounds of shot. — File, Est. of P. R. Cleburne, Dec'd.

[21]Benham, *Kennesaw Gazette*, IV (Jan. 15, 1899), 2; Little Rock *Arkansas State Gazette*, Feb. 9, 1861, p. 2; *ibid.*, Feb. 16, 1861, p. 2; Ross, "Chronicles of Arkansas," Little Rock *Arkansas Gazette*, Feb. 5, 1961, p. 4A.

[22]List of Yell Rifles, July 23, 1861. To his personal supplies, Cleburne added: "1 Box Cartridges, $1.50; 3/4 doz. Linen Handkerchief squares [likely for handkerchiefs and bandages], $6.35; . . . 1 Red Shirt, $1.75; 1 pr. Boots, $8.50; 1 Hat, $12.50; . . . 1 B. Gloves, $1.50; ½ ream letter paper, $2.55; comb, .10; 1 pr. Sleeve Buttons, .40." — File, Est. of P. R. Cleburne, Dec'd.

[23]T. J. Oliphint to C. E. Nash, Aug. 1898, in Nash, *Gen. Pat Cleburne*, 167-68; Cleburne to J. P. Benjamin, Jan. 18, 1862, C-212, Letters Received by the Confederate Adjutant and Inspector General, 1861-1865 (hereinafter cited as AIGO), 1862, M474/10, NA.

[24]*Cf.* killing of two men in other eastern Arkansas counties for being pro-Union. — "Bloody Affray in St. Francis," Little Rock *Arkansas State Gazette*, June 1, 1861, p. 1; "Abolitionist Hung," *ibid.*, June 15, 1861, p. 3. See also Oliphint to Nash, Aug. 1898, in Nash, *Gen. Pat Cleburne*, 165.

[25]Minutes of City Council of Helena, Ark., Apr. 25 (?), 1861, quoted in Centennial Ed., Helena *World*, Aug. 16, 1956, p. 3; Nash, *Gen. Pat Cleburne*, 178; "Appearance of the Mississippi," *Arkansas State Gazette*, May 11, 1861, p. 1; "River and Steamboat News," Cincinnati *Daily Commercial*, Apr. 26, Apr. 27, 1861.

[26]Cleburne to his half brother Robert, May 7, 1861, in possession of Charles Cleburne Jordan.

[27]M. T. Sanders, Address quoted in undated clipping from unidentified Helena, Ark., newspaper in scrapbook of Mrs. W. E. (Naomi Hays) Moore, in possession of Mrs. Moore Tappan, Helena, Ark.; "Cleburne," Memphis *Daily Avalanche*, Apr. 29, 1870, p. 3; *cf.* account in unidentified Helena, Ark., newspaper, 1861, concerning presentation of flag to Phillips Guards, quoted in clipping from unidentified Helena, Ark., newspaper, 1911, in Scrapbk., U.D.C., Helena.

[28]Hallum, *History of Arkansas*, I, 506-07.

[29]Oliphint to Nash, Aug. 1898, in Nash, *Gen. Pat Cleburne*, 165.

[30]Cleburne to his half brother Robert, May 7, 1861, in possession of Charles Cleburne Jordan. Neither William, Robert, nor Joseph served in the armed forces during the war. William was a surveyor with the Union Pacific Railroad; Robert continued as a machinist in Cincinnati. See *infra*, pp. 449-451. The occupation and where-abouts of Joseph during the war years are unknown, except for the inference that he lived in LaPorte, Ind. A thorough search of Union records at the National Archives failed to disclose a service record for Joseph Cleburne. Furthermore, the description of the Cleburne family in O'Hart, *Irish Pedigrees*, II, 117-18 (in the preparation of which William, and possibly some of his brothers and sisters, manifestly collaborated), set out that Patrick Ronayne and Christopher served in the Confederate Army; but made no mention of Joseph being in the Union Army.

In his sketch of Cleburne written in 1867, General Hardee said: "It was known that he had a brother in the Federal army, but he seldom mentioned his name, ..." — Hardee, "Major General Cleburne," 652. Manifestly, from the foregoing evidence, General Hardee was mistaken. Probably the brother to whom Hardee referred was William, construction of the Union Pacific being classified by the Federal government as a "military necessity." See *infra*, p. 449. Note in this connection letter to Editor, *Kennesaw Gazette*, from a Ronayne cousin of William and Patrick Ronayne: ". . . he [General Cleburne] never liked the somewhat doubtful position of his eldest brother toward the South, to which General Hardee alludes . . . ." — "General P. R. Cleburne," *Kennesaw Gazette*, V *(Apr. 15, 1890)*, 1.

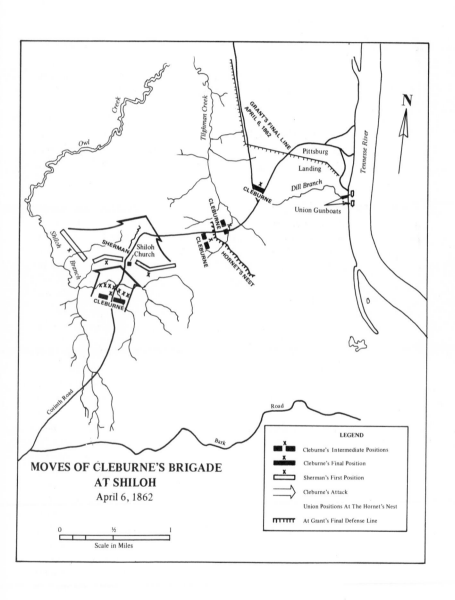

N

Owl

Creek

Tilghman Creek

GRANT'S FINAL LINE
APRIL 6, 1862

Pittsburg

Landing

Tennesse River

X
CLEBURNE

Dill Branch

Union Gunboats

Shiloh

CLEBURNE

X
CLEBURNE

SHERMAN

Shiloh
Church

X
CLEBURNE

X

HORNET'S NEST

Branch

X

X

XXX X X X X

CLEBURNE

Corinth Road

Road

Bark

**MOVES OF CLEBURNE'S BRIGADE
AT SHILOH**
April 6, 1862

LEGEND	
X	Cleburne's Intermediate Positions
X	Cleburne's Final Position
X	Sherman's First Position
	Cleburne's Attack
	Union Positions At The Hornet's Nest
	At Grant's Final Defense Line

0   ½   1

Scale in Miles

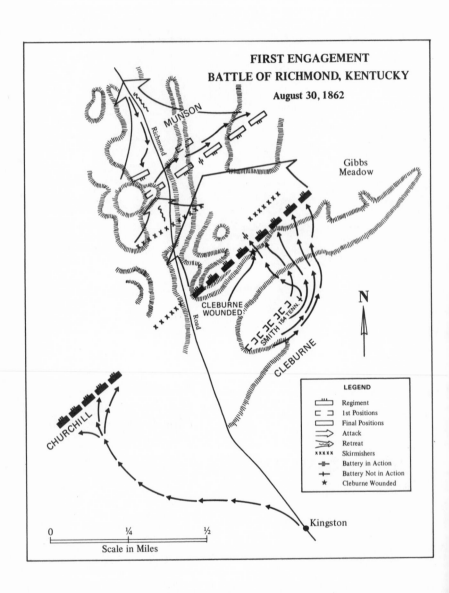

FIRST ENGAGEMENT
BATTLE OF RICHMOND, KENTUCKY
August 30, 1862

MUNSON

Richmond

Gibbs
Meadow

N

CLEBURNE
WOUNDED

SMITH 154 TENN.

CLEBURNE

Road

CHURCHILL

Kingston

LEGEND

⊏▥⊐	Regiment
⊏ ⊐	1st Positions
⊏ ⊐	Final Positions
⟹	Attack
⟫	Retreat
xxxxx	Skirmishers
⊣⊫	Battery in Action
+	Battery Not in Action
★	Cleburne Wounded

0   ¼   ½
Scale in Miles

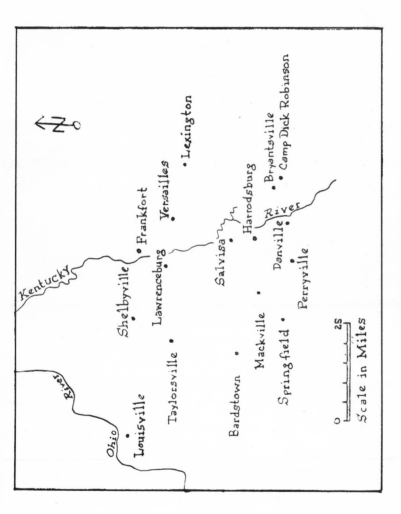

CENTRAL KENTUCKY

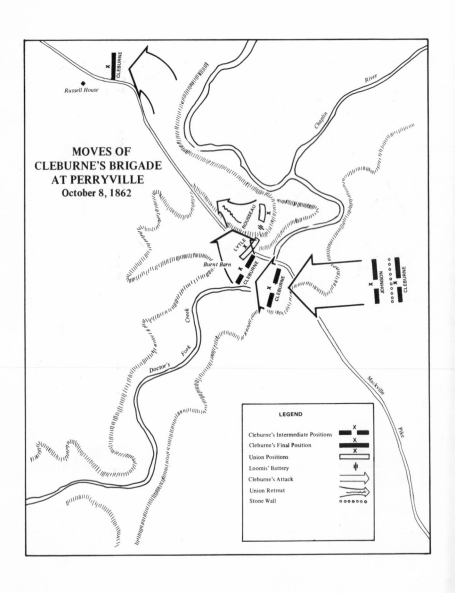

MOVES OF
CLEBURNE'S BRIGADE
AT PERRYVILLE
October 8, 1862

Russell House

CLEBURNE

ROUSSEAU

LYTLE

Burnt Barn

CLEBURNE

CLEBURNE

JOHNSON

CLEBURNE

River

Chaplin

Doctor's   Fork   Creek

Mackville   Pike

LEGEND

Cleburne's Intermediate Positions

Cleburne's Final Position

Union Positions

Loomis' Battery

Cleburne's Attack

Union Retreat

Stone Wall

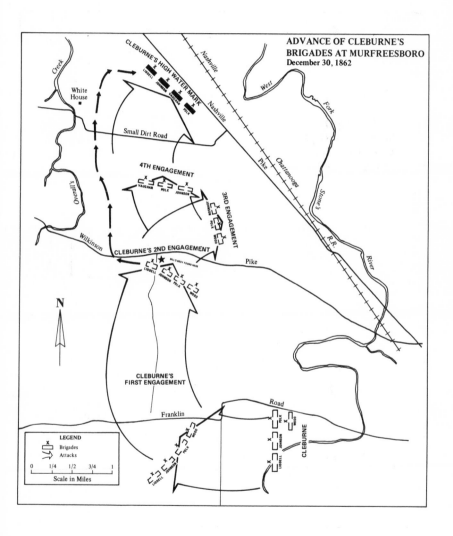

ADVANCE OF CLEBURNE'S
BRIGADES AT MURFREESBORO
December 30, 1862

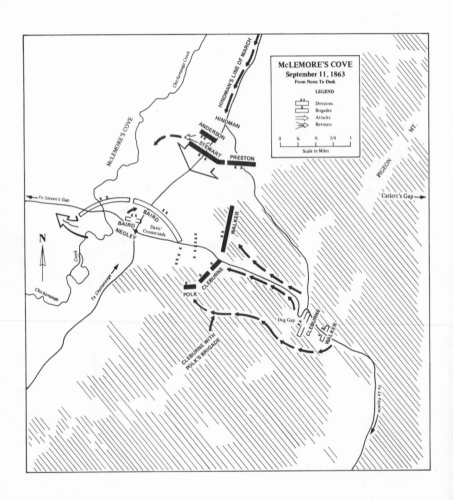

McLEMORE'S COVE
September 11, 1863
From Noon To Dusk

LEGEND

Divisions
Brigades
Attacks
Retreats

0   ¼   ½   ¾   1

Scale in Miles

HINDMAN'S LINE OF MARCH

Chickamauga Creek

McLEMORE'S COVE

HINDMAN

ANDERSON

STEWART

PRESTON

PIGEON MT.

To Steven's Gap

Catlett's Gap

BAIRD

BAIRD
NEGLEY

Davis'
Crossroads

WALKER

N

Creek

To Chattanooga

Chickamauga

POLK

CLEBURNE

Dug Gap

CLEBURNE
WALKER

CLEBURNE WITH
POLK'S BRIGADE

To La Fayette

CHAPTER V

FIRST YEAR OF THE WAR
(May 1861 — March 1862)

> He took great interest in everything connected with tactics,
> and personally taught it all, ...
> — *Cleburne as described by Gen. Basil W. Duke.*

The newly organized regiment mentioned in Cleburne's letter to his brother of May 7, 1861, was Arkansas' first regiment of infantry. Designated the First Infantry Regiment of Arkansas Volunteers, it consisted of nine companies from the eastern part of the state. Judge Oliphint, then a private in one of the companies, averred in his commentary: "I never before nor since saw as fine a body of men, or as well drilled, as was the Yell Rifles."[1] Cleburne's soft, pleasant voice with distinct enunciation had almost no Irish accent. But when irritated or giving commands, he often reverted to his native speech.[2]

The election of officers was deferred for a week awaiting authorization from the state convention. During this interval, Cleburne drilled his company and studied infantry tactics. As a man and soldier, he was held in high esteem by the troops of the regiment. When the election took place, on May 14, he was elected Colonel without opposition.[3] With much improved health, Cleburne thrived on army life.

On May 15, two attractive young ladies from Pine Bluff, Arkansas, arrived at Mound City to present two Confederate flags "of fine blue silk most elegantly wrought and decorated." One flag was for the Pine Bluff company, the Jefferson Guards of Cleburne's regiment, and the other for the regiment itself — "to fight under in the glorious struggle for Southern independence." A large crowd came from Memphis for the ceremonies on May 15 and 16. The Memphis *Evening Argus* reported that on May 16 the regiment marched "in all

'the pomp and circumstance of glorious war'" to the center
of the village for the presentation of the regimental flag.
"The bristling bayonets and the general paraphernalia
presented an imposing appearance. Each company was
composed of stalwart men — soldiers strong in bone and
muscle and nerve, and still stronger in hope and faith." "Our
hands have made it; your hearts must defend it," spoke the
young lady who presented the flag to the Captain of the
Jefferson Guards. The Captain in turn presented the flag to
Colonel Cleburne, who responded with "an able and eloquent
speech." The troops cheered loudly when Cleburne promised
that the flag would never be dishonored.[4]

In Little Rock the Arkansas state convention was still in
session, grappling with urgent problems. About May 15 the
convention appointed as Brigadier General of the eastern
district of Arkansas, one of its members, T. R. Bradley. A
wealthy planter of Crittenden County, Bradley had remained
"a Union man to the last moment."[5]

The Arkansas troops, consisting of Cleburne's regiment
and a few other companies, moved to Fort Randolph on the
east bank of the Mississippi, twenty miles north of
Memphis.[6] They had scarcely reached Fort Randolph when
Bradley arrived to assume command. Objecting to a "militia
general" as commander, the troops refused to serve under
Bradley and demanded Colonel Cleburne in his stead.
However, the Colonel recognized Bradley's authority and the
latter took command.

A few days later, Bradley became alarmed by a rumor
that Federal troops were moving from St. Louis to invade
Arkansas. He had his soldiers cross back over to Arkansas and
march twenty-five miles northward, to Bearfields Point on
the Mississippi River. While the troops encamped, Bradley
sent scouts — mostly from Cleburne's regiment — to locate
the enemy.[7]

On May 30, officials at Little Rock received three
telegrams from Memphis. Judge Hanly at the state convention received the first:

> Arkansas forces returned from Bearsfield Point · between
> two suns; a quantity of material abandoned; scouting party of
> picked men abandoned; no enemy nearer than Cairo; we are

the laughing stock of the Tennesseans; cause damaged in the north-east. Answer.

P. R. Cleburne.

The second message, to a military officer in Little Rock from the Captain of the Jefferson Guards, read: "We have deposed Bradley; appoint Col. Cleburne and satisfy regiment." Bradley sent the third message to Governor Rector, who was president of a military board created by the convention: "I have been suspended from my command; I am coming to Little Rock." The three telegrams were referred to the convention.

Circumstances prompting the messages were: After reaching Bearsfields Point, Bradley, becoming demoralized, precipitately ordered a retreat to Fort Randolph and left the scouts behind. Cleburne and his officers were incensed by Bradley's conduct and Cleburne suspected the "militia general" of treason. The day after the retreat to Fort Randolph, the abandoned scouts followed down the river in skiffs and reported that no enemy was near Bearsfields Point. Thereupon, Cleburne and some of his officers arrested the "militia general" for incompetence and cowardice, and placed guards on the boat where Bradley was quartered with instructions not to let him leave.[7] After awhile, the prisoner was released with the understanding that he would go to Little Rock.

Rid of Bradley, Cleburne's regiment, to which was attached a company of field artillery from Helena, moved to a high bluff on the east bank of the river thirty-eight miles north of Memphis. From this strategic point, selected by Cleburne, on the south side of a bend, the troops could fire on all boats coming down the river. Here Cleburne established the advance post in the region and began building fortifications. Until the end of June, he and his men labored, throwing up entrenchments and embrasures. The troops honored their Colonel by naming the works Fort Cleburne. However, in July the name was changed to Fort Pillow, for the general who was commanding the troops of the state of Tennessee.[8]

On June 18, to the indignation of the Arkansas troops,

the military board of Arkansas appointed a special court-martial to try Cleburne and five other officers of the regiment on charges of mutiny preferred by Bradley. A few days later, the court-martial convened at Mound City and took testimony. The trial did not proceed to conclusion, inasmuch as Bradley chose to leave the decision to Gen. Gideon J. Pillow, who promptly exonerated the defendants. Soon afterward, Bradley's appointment as Brigadier General was revoked and nothing more was heard of him.[9]

During the war years, Cleburne kept a diary in a series of pocket-sized notebooks. The first of these notebooks was extant in the late 1880's, in the possession of Maj. Calhoun Benham, assistant adjutant-general and chief of staff of Cleburne's division, then engaged in writing a sketch of the General's life. Research has failed to locate this notebook. Benham said that Cleburne's entries in the summer of 1861, in addition to covering incidents of garrison duty, revealed "much conscientious self examination."[10]

In his biography of Cleburne, Capt. Irving A. Buck stated that the General abstained from the use of liquor because "he felt responsible for the lives of his men, and feared the possible effect of intoxicants, for the proper discharge of his duties. He also said that a single glass of wine would disturb the steadiness of his hand in use of the pistol, and affect his calculations in playing chess, ..." Furthermore, he used no form of tobacco.[11]

At the end of June, Cleburne went to Memphis for several days. Here, no doubt he met Brig. Gen. William J. Hardee of the Confederate Army, recently appointed to an Arkansas command, who had arrived in Memphis by July 2.[12] The distinguished West Pointer immediately discerned military ability in the young Arkansas Colonel, and a lasting friendship was born.

Hardee selected Pittman's Ferry, Arkansas, as the site to assemble his command. Pittman's Ferry was located on the Current River 50 miles from the Mississippi and only 400 yards from the Missouri state line. Because of the terrain and the unusually wet season, travel to this base by water was more feasible than by land. The water route led down the Mississippi to the White River, up the White to the Black

River, up the Black to Pocahontas, a town near the mouth of the Current River; and up the Current to Pittman's Ferry.

The tenth company of the 1st Arkansas Regiment, the Crittenden Rangers, having just been organized had not joined the regiment, but its captain had come to Fort Pillow. On July 4, at Memphis, Cleburne wrote his first order of which there is a record. This order, to Capt. Josiah F. Earle of the Crittenden Rangers, read:

> You will encamp your company at Marian Crittenden Co Ark and prepare as quickly as possible to march to Pocahontas. You will receive from the Helena Artilery all their Mississippi Rifles and ammunition also enough sabres to equip your company. You will start for Pocahontas as quickly as possible. Making suitable arrangements for the subsistance of your men. The Commisery of the 1st Regiment will give you the necessary authority and detailed instructions.[13]

A few days thereafter, transports carrying Cleburne, his nine other infantry companies, and the Helena Artillery, steamed down the Mississippi. No doubt when the boats pulled in at Helena, the assembled citizens gave Cleburne and his command a rousing ovation.[14] Four days later, the transports were working their way up the narrow, meandering Black River toward the new base — Cleburne fully confident of Southern victory. The 1st Arkansas reached Pittman's Ferry about the middle of July and encamped. A regiment commanded by Hindman followed Cleburne and arrived at Pittman's Ferry on July 20.[15]

Hardee had traveled by stagecoach from Memphis to Little Rock. On July 15, he consummated an agreement with the military board for the transfer of the Arkansas forces then in service to the Confederate States of America. These forces consisted of seven infantry regiments plus a few cavalry regiments and artillery batteries. However, certain state leaders urged the Arkansas troops not to join Hardee's command. They argued that Arkansas soldiers were needed for the defense of their state and a contemplated campaign into Missouri, and should not go to eastern States to fight with the Confederate Army. Such was the situation when Hardee reached Pittman's Ferry on July 22.

Many of the companies at Pittman's Ferry and camps elsewhere in the state "went to pieces." Some of the men returned home and the rest joined other companies.[16] On July 23 Cleburne and eight of his companies transferred to the Confederate service. One of these companies was the Yell Rifles, seventy-one of whose members transferred, with Edward H. Cowley as captain.

The muster roll of the Yell Rifles for the period July 23 to August 31, 1861, is missing. But the muster rolls of the seven other companies for that interim show that "P R Cleburne Col Comg 1st Ark Vols," acting as Inspector and Mustering Officer, certified:

> Discipline: Only Tolerably Disciplined
> Instruction: Good
> Military Appearance: Good
> Arms: Armed with Minnie Rifles [One company was 'Armed with Sharps Rifles']
> Accoutrements: Very inferior.

Respecting "Clothing," the Colonel's comments were somber: "In a bad condition" (two companies); "In a bad condition having just a change of Shirts" (one company); "In a very bad condition many men without a single Shirt or Pr Pants" (four companies).[17]

Three days earlier, the Little Rock *Arkansas State Gazette* had noted, "Col. Cleburne's regiment has been in the field until their clothes are somewhat the worse of the wear," and suggested that "a complete new suit [be] made and forwarded to every soldier in that regiment."[18] Also about this time an epidemic of measles swept the camp.

The basic military unit of the Confederate Army was a company, which was authorized from 64 to 100 privates plus officers and noncommissioned officers. However, a large percentage of the companies had less than sixty-four when organized; and as the war progressed, sickness, casualties, transfers, and absenteeism drastically reduced the number of effectives. In turn, each regiment was authorized ten companies, although in practice many had less than this number — a few had more. Cleburne's regiment of eight companies mustered into the Confederate service aggregated

488 officers and men. The individual companies had from forty-eight to eighty-one officers and men.[19]

In the infantry organization of the Army of the Mississippi and the Army of Tennessee, there were usually four to six regiments in a brigade, commanded by a brigadier general. There were generally three or four brigades in a division, commanded by a major general; two or three divisions in a corps, commanded by a lieutenant general; and from two to four corps in an army. Artillery, usually, was attached to the brigades, divisions, or corps. The cavalry, except in the case of legion organizations, was comprised of units independent of the infantry.[20]

At every opportunity Cleburne studied Hardee's *Rifle and Light Infantry Tactics* — his commanding officer's revision and adaptation of a French tactics manual, for the American army. Hardee's manual was the standard work used by both the Union and Confederate armies.

The Federals' main force in Missouri had concentrated in the southwestern part of the state. They held eastern Missouri lightly, with some 4,000 "home guards" at St. Louis and other such regiments protecting the railroads emanating from that city. Eighty miles north of Pittman's Ferry at Ironton, the terminus of one of the railroads, were an estimated 3,000 Union soldiers. Other garrisons were at two points on the Mississippi River.

Acting under orders of Governor C. F. Jackson of Missouri, 2,000 Confederate troops of that state, commanded by Gen. Jeff Thompson, were at Bloomfield, Missouri. Confederate Maj. Gen. Leonidas Polk was in command at Memphis. At his direction Pillow, commanding 6,000 Tennesseans, crossed the Mississippi to New Madrid, Missouri. Polk's plan, concurred in by Hardee, was for Hardee, Thompson, and Pillow to join forces near Ironton; and after taking that garrison, to seize St. Louis. There, they would commandeer steamboats and proceed up the Missouri River raising troops, and drive the enemy from the state. By July 28, a third infantry regiment had arrived at Pittman's Ferry, bringing Hardee's force to 2,300, including cavalry and artillery. Hardee was eager to execute the plan and "free Missouri."[21]

On July 29, Hardee advanced into Missouri with 1,200

infantry and cavalry to drive back 1,000 Federal soldiers. This enemy force was moving upon Greenville, Missouri, thirty-five miles south of Ironton, "to plunder the secessionists." Cleburne's regiment was the vanguard in the forced march which was conducted over rough roads and through dense woods. With the enemy retreating to Ironton, Cleburne's regiment entered Greenville, followed by Hindman's regiment, and encamped. Hardee's third regiment remained at Pittman's Ferry to protect the hospital and supplies.

The Confederate commander's immediate plan was to cut communications between St. Louis and Ironton, an act which would prevent reinforcements from reaching the latter point. Then he would attack and take Ironton. The united forces of Hardee, Thompson, and Pillow would then seize St. Louis.

General Hardee met with difficulties. Pillow differed as to the first point to be attacked, and questioned the feasibility of the route from New Madrid to Ironton. A captain in the Missouri service who had promised to break the Ironton railroad did not carry out his mission. Hardee then secured Thompson's agreement to have 500 men destroy the railroad. But Pillow, bluffed by the Federals, thought that they were about to come down the Mississippi upon him in transports. Pillow prevailed upon Missouri's Governor to have Thompson march to his aid and not join in Hardee's undertaking. Hardee then ordered his own small cavalry force and some Missourians to destroy the railroad, but they failed to do so. Later, under misapprehension that the Federals were advancing down the Mississippi, Leonidas Polk detained Pillow at New Madrid; and when the facts were ascertained, Pillow delayed joining Hardee for other reasons.[22]

Cleburne's regiment remained at Greenville for nearly a month pending the joining of the Confederate forces, a plan which did not materialize. Basil W. Duke, temporarily an aide to Hindman and scout for Hardee (later a brigadier general in John H. Morgan's command), recalled seeing Cleburne at Greenville in his *Reminiscences*:

I cannot remember that I ever saw an officer who was so
industrious and persistent in his efforts properly to drill and
instruct the men under his command. He took great interest in
everything connected with tactics, and personally taught it all,
and was occupied from morning until night in superintending
squad, company, and battalion drill, guard mounting,
inspection and, indeed, everything mentioned in the books or
that he could conceive of. I have seen him during the hottest
hours of the hottest days of August instruct squad after squad
in the bayonet exercise until I wondered how any human
frame could endure the fatigue that his exertions must have
induced."[23]

Duke also observed that Cleburne was "an ardent botanist."

Cleburne made his headquarters in the village courthouse, where he used one room as his office and bedroom. A
lieutenant in the Missouri state guard with a small detail of
men came to Greenville, escorting some Federal prisoners
whom they had captured near Ironton. The group had
marched continuously for two or three days and nights, and
were exhausted when they reached Greenville. The prisoners
and the guard were quartered in the courthouse down the
hall from Cleburne's room. That night the Lieutenant, who
was a somnambulist, dreamed that the prisoners were
escaping. He sprang up screaming, and aroused everyone in
the building. There was much confusion in the dark. The
shouting sleepwalker rushed past the open door of Cleburne's
room. As he passed, Cleburne, thinking a prisoner was
escaping, fired and mortally wounded the man. For one
suddenly aroused from sleep to hit a target in a fraction of a
second was excellent marksmanship. The Lieutenant lived
only an hour, and in a dying statement exonerated Cleburne
of all blame. Cleburne was sorely grieved by the unfortunate
occurrence and regretted it the rest of his life.[24]

Cleburne, on August 17, hearing that Hardee's
cavalrymen on picket duty near Ironton expected a fight,
advanced his regiment to reinforce them. However, the fight
did not develop.[25]

By August 20 the Federal force at Ironton was greatly
strengthened, the railroad was heavily guarded, and sickness
in Hardee's force was widespread. Despite the Confederate
victory in southwest Missouri at Wilson's Creek, Hardee

concluded that he and Pillow could not march on St. Louis. The plan was abandoned, and Cleburne's and Hindman's regiments fell back to Pittman's Ferry the last of August. The troops were dispirited by this retreat from Missouri.[26]

By late summer Hardee's force had grown to an army of 5,000. On September 17 the General received an order to move his command from Pittman's Ferry on the Current River over to the Mississippi River, preparatory to joining Confederate forces in Kentucky. The shortest route, the Chalk Bluffs Plank Road, went around the north end of Crowley's Ridge in Missouri and across "the much dreaded and terrible 'Cache Bottoms'" to Point Pleasant on the Mississippi. Hardee feared that the condition of the road, which included six miles of trestle bridge, was so poor that wagons and artillery could not move over it. He sent Cleburne and his regiment as an advance force, entrusted with putting the road "in thorough repair" and other duties.[27] Cleburne's account of the mission is contained in his first report of military operations, dated September 27, 1861. From "Camp at east end Point Pleasant & Chalk Bluff Plank Road," he reported to "Major Genl Leonidas Polk Commanding C. S. forces on Mississippi River" as follows:

> By order of Br Genl Hardee the first [infantry] Regiment Arkansas Volunteers under my command left Pitmans [Pittman's] Ferry on the 19th inst for Point Pleasant. We have arrived at this point and will reach our destination early tomorrow. I am directed by Genl Hardee to report to you on my arrival and to take measures to have supplies sent us at Point Pleasant My command started with twelve days provisions and we will soon be out altogether. The whole command under Genl Hardee is already — or will in a day or two be — on the way. We will all need provisions for present use. Our supplies I understand will be shipped round by way of Napoleon [a port at the confluence of the Arkansas and Mississippi Rivers] and it will take some time to get them to Point Pleasant. I found the road across the Swamps of Black and the two Cache Rivers practicable for the march of an army. The plank road across the sunk Swamp lands was also in good condition. Genl Hardee's forces will therefore soon be at the Point.
>
> I have the Honor to be Sir
Your Obt Sevt

P R Cleburne Col Comdg
1st Regt Ark Volunteers
P. S. The matter of supplies is of so much importance to
us I have sent Lieut [Lucius] Polk of the 1st Regt to receive
your instructions and to give you the necessary information in
detail. One Company of Cavalry has arrived with us.
Respy
P R Cleburne Col[28]

Cleburne's regiment, eager for battle, remained for
several days at Point Pleasant awaiting the arrival of the rest
of the troops. Hardee's command, 4,000 effectives, then
marched to Columbus, Kentucky, arriving on October 6. Two
days later, one unit of the troops left for the command's
destination, Bowling Green, Kentucky, 150 miles to the east.
Their route by rail, 175 miles, was southeast, deep into
Tennessee; and then northeast to Bowling Green. Deficiency
of rolling stock compelled the command to move in units
several days apart; with Cleburne's regiment reaching Bowling
Green October 20 or 21. Fortunately, about this time the
Arkansas troops received a supply of clothing from their
home state, relieving the critical shortage.[29]

At Bowling Green the Confederates were assembling a
small army designated the Central Army of Kentucky.
Hardee was promoted to Major General in command of one
of the two divisions of the army. He immediately selected
Colonel Cleburne to command one of the three brigades. On
October 28, 1861, Cleburne, with headquarters in Bowling
Green, assumed command of the 1st Division's 2nd Brigade,
composed of the 1st and 5th Arkansas, the 6th Mississippi,
and the 5th Tennessee Regiments.[30]

Cleburne set about organizing the raw troops in his
command. A Confederate veteran wrote:

It was the writer's privilege to perform his first soldier's
duty under this exemplary officer whilst stationed at Bowling
Green, Ky. Well do I remember his bronzed features and what
I then thought his rigid rules .... He was plain unassuming
but resolute and determined. Everyone soon learned his orders
must be obeyed.[31]

The Commander of 2nd Brigade held frequent regimental inspections, reviews, and parades while at Bowling Green. Under Hardee's supervision, Cleburne learned the intricacies of brigade drill, including skill in maneuvers when in contact with the enemy. Cleburne's 1st Arkansas had been recognized as the best drilled regiment in the army. In a short time his 2nd Brigade became the best drilled brigade.

Cleburne employed his remarkable power of concentration in mastering infantry tactics, studying the science of war, and analyzing battle plans. Later, Hardee praised Cleburne's "unremitting study and labor" in perfecting himself as a commander, and said: "His mind was of a highly logical class. Before expressing an opinion upon a subject, or coming to a decision in any conjecture of circumstances, he wore an expression as if solving a mathematical problem."[32]

Gen. Albert Sidney Johnston, "one of the great soldiers and lofty souls of the Confederacy,"[33] was now commanding in the West with headquarters at Bowling Green. He had the task of defending more than a 300-mile front, from the southeastern border of Kentucky to the Mississippi, with a wholly inadequate force. Needing more than three times the number of troops in his command, Johnston's strategy was to thwart advances of the Federals by deceiving them as to his strength, ostensibly threatening attacks and keeping them on the defensive.

On November 9, Johnston received information that 500 of the enemy were in Jamestown and an additional enemy force was at Tompkinsville, respectively seventy-five miles east and forty-five miles southeast of Bowling Green. Johnston instructed Hardee to send 1,200 infantry and a half-section of artillery "under an intelligent officer" to Jamestown and Tomkinsville. This force was to be increased by a squadron of Terry's Texas Rangers (8th Texas Cavalry Regiment). The officer chosen was to be given these orders:

"... if the enemy are there, and not in too great force, attack and destroy them .... Inform him in advance that he moves through wooded country, ... If possible examine the roads leading to Gallatin, as it is reported that attempts will be made by the enemy to reach and cut the railway in that district. Report from time to time, and return to [Bowling Green] as soon as these orders are executed or it is apparent they cannot be. Create the impression in the country that this force is only an advance guard."³⁴

Hardee selected Colonel Cleburne for the mission. Cleburne's execution of the undertaking is reported in his communications to Hardee. The first was from "Camp at Jamestown, Ky., Monday Evening, [November] 11, 1861"; and read:

> We have just arrived safely at this point. I left in Scottsville one man hurt by falling from wagon and two sick. The people of Scottsville, as a general thing, appear to be with us. We had an enthusiastic reception. We took them by surprise. Not so here; they knew of our approach Saturday night, and seem bitterly hostile. Nearly every house has some member with friend in the Lincoln Army. We have forded some streams that in very rainy weather are impassable. One of our skirmishers of the advance guard saw 40 or 50 cavalry and infantry, doubtless of the enemy, within a mile of this camp. I have a party now on their track. We can get nothing from the inhabitants, except that the men are all absent and gone to some camp, but where the camp is I can't find out. I will start on my mission early in the morning.
> Since writing the above I have positive information that the enemy (probably in small force) are somewhere concealed in our neighborhood. You may rely on my taking every precaution. The country from here to Barren River is admirably adapted to a surprise. The ford over this river is from two to three feet deep. I will not have enough provision to last the expedition. I am just informed that there are 3,000 troops [at] Campbellsville, between 2,500 and 3,000 at Columbia, and an equal number at Lebanon. Some people advise me to go home by Glasgow.³⁵

Following his initial communication, Cleburne sent two additional dispatches to Hardee:

> Tompkinsville, Ky., November 13, 1861.
> [Salutation omitted.] We arrived at this place on yesterday evening about 5 o'clock. We did not find a friend along the whole road from Jamestown here; the houses were closed, the country apparently deserted. We saw a few women and children, but in almost every instance they were surprised and tried to run and conceal themselves at our approach; they have been told, and evidently believed, that we were burning,

killing, and destroying as we advanced. One old woman met us with an open Bible in her hand, said she was prepared and ready to die, and could not be convinced that we meant her no harm. As we entered this town, having sent a party in advance to prepare for our encampment, I ordered the advance guard to fall back, our bands to the front, our colors opened, bayonets fixed, and the march at attention resumed, for the purpose of making the strongest display we could. In this order we got nearly to the center of this town, when I was so astonished at the utter silence and desertion, not having seen a human being but two, who both fled, and not having heard from the party sent in advance, that I halted, under the belief the enemy must be at hand, sent our music away, loaded a strong advance guard, and sent out skirmishers, and advanced in this way until we met the party sent out under Major [John E.] Glenn to select a camp. I merely mention this as an illustration of the feeling existing among the people here. To-day most of the women and children have returned, but all the men (a dozen, perhaps, excepted) are absent in [Col. B. C.] Grider's camp at Columbia.

There is a rumor here that a detachment of [Gen. Lovell H.] Rousseau's force, 10,000 or 15,000 strong, is advancing, and but a few miles from here. This I regard as too false to base any calculation whatever upon it. I am satisfied of one thing, there is no force on any of the roads leading to Gallatin, Tenn., and no very immediate danger to the railroad in that quarter from any section of the country through which I have passed. The people here are under the impression that the Federals have possession of the railroad south of Bowling Green, and that we are only waiting a favorable opportunity to get away from there. This and the thousand other lies and influences brought to bear upon them have sent them by hundreds to Grider's camp at Columbia. This is the nearest camp to us. There are two regiments of Kentucky volunteers there, and hundreds have fled there in front of our advance. I am informed, however, they are dissatisfied with their officers, dispirited, badly armed, and many down with measles. I am reliably informed that there are few, if any, slave-owners among them, and the majority are fighting for the $13 a month and other pecuniary inducements. Did my instructions permit an advance on their camp, I would not hesitate to make it. I believe they would leave, and even if they fought, unless strongly re-enforced, I believe we could destroy them. The alacrity with which they fled from this strongly defensible country, leaving their wives, daughters, and children to the tender mercies of supposed ravishers, murderers, and barbarians, shows they are not yet very formidable as soldiers.

I made it my special business and used every effort to

convince the people we were friends to all but soldiers in arms against us and those giving them aid and information. I think on the whole we have succeded. No insult or injury to the person of any one has come to my notice. I am sorry to state that on yesterday, for the first time, the same respect was not paid to property. Our teamsters, rear guard, and guard with the teams, and individuals who fell back under the pretense of being sick, stole some poultry and other things along the road. I think this conduct was confined to a very few; but it was witnessed by officers, who never exercised their authority to put it down, and it only comes to my knowledge now when it is too late to repair it.

On reaching the residence of Colonel [John H.] Frame, a bitter enemy, in open arms against us, the chief circulator of all the slanders against us, a man who has ordered the plundering of all the southern-rights men he could find, I ordered his house, late headquarters of his camp at same place, to be searched for arms and ammunition. We found immense quantities of empty gun boxes, receipts for Lincoln guns sent through the country, and all other indications of a recruiting camp. I ordered one quartermaster to seize sheep enough on the place to do us for two or three days; also to take some tallow, sweet oil, and turpentine, which we were in great need of. I then ordered the house to be closed up and nothing else taken. Some unprincipled men took advantage of this circumstance to commence stealing on their own account.

In view of this state of affairs I immediately issued and caused to be read to the men the inclosed special order (marked A). [Not found.]

Friday, November 15, 1861.

I found it unsafe to send a dispatch back, unless with such a force as I could not spare. I am camped here, 7 miles west [east?] of Tompkinsville, and expect to be at Jamestown or beyond by night. On the 13th, 12 m., I advanced on the Columbia road, with the intention of taking the Burkesville and Glasgow road home. My guides represented it to me as the best road, and as my orders were silent as to route returning, I thought it best to take the easiest and that which would most advance the object in view, which, as I understood, was to make a strong impression (on the people of these hostile counties) as to our strength and readiness to exert it. I feared a return by same route might be construed into a retreat, especially as the enemy were reported on this road, within a few miles of our camp. For these and other good reasons, which I will give when I get back, I determined to take this route. We started at 12 m., intending to make McRea's Cross-Roads (9 miles distant, as I was informed by everybody at Tompkinsville, but which I found utterly untrue). I managed it so as to make the

93

impression on everybody I would take a different road, and then suddenly turned off on this road. Two miles from town, my advanced guard jumped the enemy's pickets. The Texas Rangers, 10 in front, gave chase, followed 4 miles, when they suddenly found themselves in presence of 40 U. S. cavalry. Our men fell back and sent for re-enforcements. I sent on 20 more cavalry to join them, and ordered 60 more to keep well in advance of our infantry and to keep up communication with the party in chase. By the time we had advanced 7 miles night was coming on, I found the Cross-Roads were 16 instead of 9 miles distant, and the enemy's scouts were seen on our flanks and even in our rear.

In this state of affairs I halted the main body, taking up a strong position on Skaggs' Creek. I could not tell whether we were approaching an army or a mere scouting party; I was completely in the dark. I knew nothing of the general movements of the enemy, not having heard from Bowling Green since I left. I knew, however, they were in great force in front and might get in our rear. In this emergency I determined to have our train loaded for any movement. A hotly pressed retreat through 50 miles of hostile country would, I feared, prove very disastrous, and I determined not to be caught in such a trap. I had false camp fires lighted on every surrounding hill, and a wide line of outlying pickets. In the mean time our cavalry pressed the enemy in the direction of the Cross-Roads so closely that they got confused and dispersed in the woods at McRea's Cross-Roads. Our cavalry fell on the main body of the enemy's cavalry, about 100 strong, and after a little skirmish, in which the enemy broke and left and got 2 of their men killed, other men and horses wounded, without damage to us, our cavalry fell back 5 miles to camp for the night.

During the evening and night we captured a number of U. S. dragoon horses, fully accoutered, a number of muskets, pistols, and sabers. A great deal of credit is due Major [Thomas] Harrison, of the Rangers, also Captain [B. F.] Phillips, volunteer, for the way they managed to disorganize and disperse this large body of the enemy's cavalry in an unknown country in the night, and without one friend among the country people. My infantry pickets captured several U. S. horses, fully accoutered in the most approved style, within our lines. The truth is, the rush of the Rangers so dispersed and confused the enemy that they got lost and were wandering about in every direction, and this accounts for their appearance on our flanks and rear.

I sent Lieutenant [John W.] Cage, of my regiment, with a dispatch to Major Harrison at midnight, ordering him to fall back on me. Cage and his escort lost their way, got almost into the enemy's lines, and in returning were fired on by our cavalry picket, and returned the fire before the sad mistake was found out. Cage was shot in the leg, his horse was twice shot, and Bankhead, of the Rangers, was shot badly in the leg and arm.

Yesterday morning, finding the road clear beyond the Cross-Roads, the enemy all fled, and thinking [it] imprudent to advance, blindfold as I was, I commenced returning by the same route I came, and am here this morning. The Rangers advanced to and beyond the Cross-Roads and up the Glasgow road; they heard artillery in the direction of Columbia, and believe a force is advancing along that road. They left Cross-Roads at 1 o'clock yesterday and reached here, a distance of 23 miles, last night.

I doubt whether any force is advancing, and do not think the enemy's cavalry will visit this section soon again. If energetic, the enemy may advance along the Columbia and Jamestown road and attempt to cut us off. I have sent a strong cavalry force ahead to guard against this. The road mentioned is a good one, and Jamestown is as close to Columbia as Tompkinsville. Our advance has been fired at twice from the woods. No damage done. My seven days' provisions are almost out. I think some ought to be sent me.[36]

Cleburne's last report to Hardee on this expedition was from "New York, Ky., November 16, 1861," and read:

We crossed Barren River at this point yesterday evening all safe. There is a small body of mounted Union men somewhere in this neighborhood, but we could not find them. I arrested a man to-day who says he has just escaped from the North. I believe him to be a Northern spy. I took some Cincinnati papers from him. He says the enemy were falling back from Columbia to Camilsville [Campbellsville]; that they were in consternation; that he met a party carrying some wounded to Columbia; that they seemed frightened, and did not stop to question him. One of the men killed at Cross-Roads was Lieutenant Clark, a renegade Tennessean, of Captain Dickenson's company, U. S. Cavalry (he was shot in the stomach, and died in six hours); the other was shot below the left shoulder. Others were wounded.

I have examined into the circumstances of the pickets firing on each other. The picket stationed was not to blame. Mr. Cage and his escort got north of the picket and came galloping back from the direction of the enemy, riding captured horses with their gaudy trappings, and were mistaken for the enemy; and when the firing commenced, instead of

95

calling out the name of one of the Rangers whom the picket
would have known, they called, "It's Cage! It's Cage!" This
confirmed the picket, and they kept up the fire. I have paid
out of my own pocket for the articles stolen by our men.
Confidence is restored, all the houses open, and families
returned. Trunks and other articles found by our flankers in
the woods I had carried to the house and labeled "Returned by
Southern soldiers." The people all acknowledge they have been
grossly lied to. Colonel Frame has another farm here at the
river. I supplied our men with meat from it last night, and left
word for the colonel that I would settle with him if he would
come and see us at Bowling Green.[37]

In paying for the stolen articles Cleburne trustingly
accepted loose statements of loss and value. But he disal-
lowed one claim, refusing to believe a woman who said
troops had stolen her Bible.[38]

Cleburne's expedition accomplished Johnston's fullest
hope. Thinking that the Confederates might be moving in
force toward Lexington, Federal Gen. W. T. Sherman, at
Union headquarters in Louisville, ordered Gen. George H.
Thomas to withdraw his 9,000 troops from eastern Kentucky. The vanguard of Thomas' force, 5,000 troops commanded by Gen. Albin Schoepf, was then moving against
Confederate Gen. F. K. Zollicoffer in southeast Kentucky.
Schoepf feared that the Confederates were advancing on his
flank; a wild stampede of his men ensued; and the expedition
against Zollicoffer was abandoned.

On November 23 Cleburne left for Nashville, Tennessee,
on a forty-eight hour leave of absence "to purchase some
military clothing." News of his successful expedition in
Kentucky preceded him, and at the end of the four-hour ride
in the cars he was warmly welcomed at the railroad station.
He wrote in his diary that he felt he had made a new friend in
Gov. Isham G. Harris and was embarrassed by the Governor's
extreme kindness. He found the Governor most "active
minded . . . fully alive to the exigencies of the hour and
bending every energy . . . for the advancement of the
cause."[39] After returning to camp from Nashville, whenever
the weather permitted Cleburne continued to drill his men,
now "splendidly armed . . . with the Enfield Rifle." Too, he
and his command took part in building forts on the hills

surrounding Bowling Green.[40]

Near the end of December, Mrs. Frank (Ella H.) Newsom, a nurse, later known as "The Florence Nightingale of the Confederate Army," came to Bowling Green to care for the soldiers in the hospitals. Mrs. Newsom, a young widow from Phillips County, Arkansas, had taken a training course at a Memphis hospital. She arrived in Bowling Green with five servants and a carload of hospital supplies purchased and transported at her own expense. In addition to long hours of nursing, Mrs. Newsom organized and supervised the work at the hospitals. She was encouraged in her work by the cooperation of Cleburne and other officers.[41]

Despite his recent military successes, Cleburne expressed his humility by an entry in his diary on January 1, 1862: "Oh! my God! whom I believe in and adore, make thy laws plainer to my erring judgment, that I may more faithfully observe them, and not dread to look into my past."[42]

That same month, the 1st Arkansas Infantry Regiment was redesignated as the 15th Arkansas Infantry by the Secretary of War at Richmond. At the urgent solicitation of the men in the regiment, on January 18, 1862, Cleburne wrote the Secretary pointing out that the 1st Arkansas Infantry Regiment was the first organized in the state "for the defence of the South," and requesting "a designation more suitable to our early exertions in favour of the Southern Confederacy."[43] The request was not granted. Cleburne's command was now composed of the 15th Arkansas, the 6th Mississippi, and the 5th, 23rd, and 24th Tennessee Regiments.

On January 19, 1862, Confederate Generals Zollicoffer and G. B. Crittenden were defeated by Thomas at Logan's Crossroads in eastern Kentucky. Zollicoffer was killed; and the right flank of Johnston's defense line, turned. Compelled to abandon his artillery, and most of his ammunition, small-arms, wagons, horses, mules, and stores, Crittenden retreated to Chestnut Mound, fifty-five miles east of Nashville. Johnston dispatched Cleburne to Chestnut Mound to ascertain "all the wants" of Crittenden's command.[44]

3

On February 6, immediately after Cleburne's return to

Bowling Green, disaster struck. Union gunboats captured Fort Henry on the Tennessee River at the Tennessee-Kentucky line. With General Johnston's line of defense severed, Union boats now could pass up the wide river, through the state of Tennessee, and into Alabama. Also, having lost Fort Henry, there was danger that Fort Donelson, several miles to the east on the Cumberland River, would fall. In that event, with Federal gunboats commanding the Cumberland, the Confederate Central Army of Kentucky would be outflanked and destroyed. Hence, the evacuation of Bowling Green by the Confederates became imperative.

On February 7 Hardee and Cleburne began supervising the quiet removal of artillery and supplies. On February 11 the Confederate column started its retreat. Except for a brigade covering the rear, Cleburne's was the last brigade to leave Bowling Green. As they marched from the city, his troops were fired upon by artillery from a hill across the Barren River, the advance guard of the Federal army under Gen. Don Carlos Buell.[45]

Several company commanders of the 15th Arkansas recorded the withdrawal to Nashville. The commander of Company D wrote: "This Co. marched with Gen Cleburne's Brigade from Bowling Green, Ky. on Feb 13th 1862 to Nashville, a distance of 79 miles, reaching Nashville on Feb 17th/62. Our line of march was on the Louisville & Nashville pike road." Reports of other captains give further details. Company B: "Marched but a few miles out [from Bowling Green] encamped having Snow during the night. Continued the March the next morning over Turnpike Road quite slopy and disagreeable. . . . Saturday 15 remained half day at Camp. Sunday 16 Marched to Nashville Tenn. distance 33 miles. 'Troops' well worn out hunger & tired." Company E: "[Arrived at Nashville] after a fatiguing and disagreeable march having encountered no [nothing] but snowstorms with much rain."

At Nashville the army received news of a greater disaster: On February 16, Fort Donelson was captured by Gen. U. S. Grant. The fall of this fort meant losing the state of Kentucky, the key city of Nashville, and half of Tennessee to the Union forces.

"Camped in Nashville Court & Market House until the 18th, when we move 4 miles South Nashville," recorded the Captain of Company D, 15th Arkansas. The Captain of Company F saw a brighter side: ". . . had a nice time in 'N' wading through mud knee deep and getting good Confederate clothes by whole sale and 'Nary Red' to pay."[46]

Under Johnston's order to go to Murfreesboro, thirty miles southeast of Nashville, Cleburne's brigade resumed marching on February 18 and 19. "After three days ploughing through the mud," it arrived at Murfreesboro on the 21st. General Johnston recorded that the people of Nashville were "terrified" by the approach of the Federals and some of the Confederate troops, were "disheartened," with "discouragement . . . spreading."[47]

General Johnston, in concert with Gen. T. G. Beauregard, who had evacuated the base at Columbus, Kentucky, decided upon a plan to offset the disaster at Donelson. Their forces would unite with other Confederate forces at Corinth, Mississippi, a strategic railroad center, and drive back the enemy.

On February 28, Johnston's army began a march to Decatur, Alabama, via Shelbyville and Fayetteville, Tennessee. For a few days, beginning March 4, Hardee, Cleburne, and most of his brigade remained at Shelbyville. The 15th Arkansas was detached to guard the railroad bridge across the Tennessee at Decatur. Hardee and Cleburne arranged shipment of four million pounds of government meat to Grenada, Mississippi, while the latter's troops with cavalry acted as the rear guard.[48]

During this interval, in recognition of his ability as an organizer and commander, Cleburne was appointed Brigadier General, to rank from March 4, 1862. The appointment had been requested by his field grade officers and highly recommended by Hardee.[49] When Hardee and Cleburne left Shelbyville for Huntsville, Alabama, Cleburne's troops marched to Fayetteville and Decatur to join the main body. Huntsville was a key point on the Memphis & Charleston Railroad, which ran through Corinth. At Huntsville the two generals spent several days forwarding commissary supplies and arranging for the overburdened railroad to supply all possible transportation for Johnston's troops. Cleburne stayed in the residence of Addison White, a planter who lived on the outskirts of the city. General Cleburne wrote to Mrs. Newsom, who was then at the Empire House Hospital in Atlanta, and asked that she procure hospital supplies and clothing from aid societies in Atlanta and go immediately to Corinth to set up hospitals there.[50]

Cleburne left Huntsville about March 18 and rejoined his troops on their westward march. The first units of the command, proceeding by foot and rail, reached Corinth on March 27. By the end of the month all of the brigade had arrived at Camp Hill, two and a half miles south of the town.[51]

Benham, in his sketch of Cleburne, told of the General's deep concern in the South's losing Forts Henry and Donelson, and said that Cleburne, in his diary, had described the retreat from Bowling Green to Corinth. This is the missing diary previously mentioned.[52]

The forces of Generals Beauregard from Columbus, Braxton Bragg from Pensacola, Mobile, and New Orleans; and Johnston, were now concentrated in the vicinity of Corinth. With General Johnston in command, the combined force, numbering about 38,000 men, was designated the Army of the Mississippi.

NOTES

CHAPTER V

[1] Oliphint to Nash, Aug. 1898, in Nash, *Gen. Pat Cleburne,* 168.

[2] Basil W. Duke, *Reminiscences of General Basil W. Duke, C.S.A.* (New York, 1911), 69; Avery, "Patrick Ronayne Cleburne," 3; Buck, *Cleburne,* 117.

[3] Benham, *Kennesaw Gazette,* IV (Jan. 15, 1889), 2. "I have been elected Colonel 1st Regiment today." — Cleburne to his half brother Robert, undated letter in possession of Charles Cleburne Jordan. Benham said the election took place on May 14, 1861.

[4] Little Rock *Arkansas State Gazette,* June 1, 1861, p. 2, referring to accounts in Memphis *Evening Argus* and Memphis *Avalanche.*

[5] Susan Fletcher to her sister Fannie, June 18, 1861, in J. H. Atkinson (ed.), *The Civil War Letters of Captain Elliot H. Fletcher of Mill Bayou, Mississippi County, Arkansas: July to December 1861* (Little Rock, 1963), 36; "Proceedings of the State Convention," Little Rock *Arkansas State Gazette,* May 18, 1861, p. 2.

[6] Oliphint to Editor, *Arkansas Gazette,* Oct. 1899, quoted in Little Rock *Arkansas Gazette,* Oct. 11, 1899, p. 8; J. R. Thomas to Editor, *Arkansas Gazette,* Sept. 16, 1899, quoted in Little Rock *Arkansas Gazette,* Sept. 28, 1899, p. 8; Sam W. Williams to Editor, *Arkansas Gazette,* Sept. 21, 1899, quoted in Little Rock *Arkansas Gazette,* Sept. 22, 1899, p. 8.

[7] Johnson & Yerkes (print.), *Journal of Both Sessions of the Convention of the State of Arkansas, Which Were Begun and Held in the Capitol, in the City of Little Rock* (Little Rock, 1861), 417, 423-24; Thomas to Editor, *Arkansas Gazette,* Sept. 16, 1899; Avery, "Patrick Ronayne Cleburne," 3.

[8] Cleburne to Benjamin, Jan. 18, 1862, C-212, 1862 (AIGO) M474/10, NA; Thomas to Editor, *Arkansas Gazette,* Sept. 16, 1889; List of Organization, July 3, 1861, from record, Co. E, 15th (Cleburne's — Polk's — Josey's) Arkansas Infantry, M317/139, NA; *cf.* Benham, *Kennesaw Gazette,* IV (Jan. 15, 1899), 2.

[9] Williams to Editor, *Arkansas Gazette,* Sept. 21, 1899; Ora, "Our Army Correspondence," Mobile *Advertiser and Register,* Jan. 1, 1863, p. 1.

[10] Benham, *Kennesaw Gazette,* IV (Jan. 15, 1899), 2.

[11] Buck, *Cleburne,* 80.

[12] W. J. Hardee to Mrs. Felicia Lee Shover, July 2, 1861, in William J. Hardee Correspondence: 1861-1862, Library of Congress. At "Memphis, Tenn. July 1st 1861," P. R. Cleburne and one G. W. Hurley executed a promissory note in the sum of $1,067, payable to

P. B. Hendrix & Co. in thirty days "at Branch, Union Bank at Memphis." On July 23, 1861, $960.30 was paid on this note. — File, Est. of P. R. Cleburne, Dec'd.

[13]Cleburne to Captain Earle, Crittenden Rangers, July 4, 1861, in files, Ark. Hist. Com.

[14]No Helena newspaper of 1861 is extant. However, Hindman's regiment left Memphis a few days later, traveling the same route. A captain in Hindman's regiment said the transports carrying that regiment stopped at Helena; and, "We were complimented by quite an interesting ovation." — E. H. Fletcher, Jr. to his father, July 19, 1861, in Atkinson (ed.), *Fletcher Letters*, 3.

[15]Mangum, *Arkansas Gazette*; Fletcher, Jr., to his father, July 20, 1861, in Atkinson (ed.), *Fletcher Letters*, 4.

[16]Oliphint to Nash, Aug. 1898, in Nash, *Gen. Pat Cleburne*, 169; Nathaniel Cheairs Hughes, Jr., *General William J. Hardee: Old Reliable* (Baton Rouge, 1965), 75-76.

[17]List of Yell Rifles, July 23, 1861, and Muster Rolls of Cos. A, C, D, E, F, G, and H, 1st Regiment, Arkansas Volunteers, for July 23 to Aug. 31, 1861, filed with 15th (Cleburne's — Polk's — Josey's) Arkansas Infantry, Muster and Pay Rolls, 1861-65, RG 109, NA. "Minie. — A kind of rifle invented by Captain Minie, of France, which carries a conical ball, hollow at the base." — J. B. Lippincott & Co. (pub.), *United States Infantry Tactics, for the Instruction, Exercise, and Manoeuvres of the United States Infantry* (Philadelphia, 1862), 530.

[18]Little Rock *Arkansas State Gazette,* July 20, 1861, p. 2.

[19]D.C. Govan to his wife, July 28, 1861, in Daniel C. Govan Papers, Southern Historical Collection, The University of North Carolina Library, hereinafter cited as Uni. N.C.; Fletcher, Jr. to his father, Aug. 2, 1861, in Atkinson (ed.), *Fletcher Letters*, 6-7; List and muster rolls cited note 17, *supra.*

[20]At Shiloh, Hardee's "corps" had only one division and a brigade; and Breckinridge's "corps," only one division. In Gen. Braxton Bragg's organization, each corps also had a small brigade of cavalry.

[21]*O.R.,* III, p. 629.

[22]Hardee to Mrs. Shover, Aug. 19, 1961, in Hardee Correspondence, Library of Congress; Fletcher, Jr. to his father, Aug. 2, 1861, in Atkinson (ed.), *Fletcher Letters*, 6, 35; Duke, *Reminiscences*, 60.

[23]Duke, *Reminiscences*, 68-69.

[24]*Ibid.,* 69-70.

[25]Govan to his wife, Aug. 17, 1861, in Govan Papers.

[26]Hardee to Mrs. Shover, Aug. 19, Sept. 4, 1861, in Hardee Correspondence, Library of Congress; Stations of Cos. A, C, and H, 15th (Cleburne's — Polk's — Josey's) Arkansas Infantry, on Aug. 31,

1861, from Muster Rolls of said companies for July 23 to Aug. 31, 1861, M317/139, NA; Elliot H. Fletcher to his daughter Fannie, Sept. 12, 1861, in Atkinson (ed.), *Fletcher Letters*, 35.

[27]*O.R.*, III, pp. 703, 706; Fletcher, Jr. to his father, Sept. 26, 1861, in Atkinson (ed.), *Fletcher Letters*, 12.

[28]Cleburne, Report of Military Operations, Sept. 27, 1861 (MS in War Department Collection of Confederate Records, Miscellaneous Papers of Officers, 1862-1864, RG 109, NA).

[29]Hardee to Mrs. Shover, Oct. 11, 1862, in Hardee Correspondence, Library of Congress; *O.R.*, IV, p. 445; Hughes, *General Hardee*, 82; Fletcher, Jr. to his father, Oct. 20, 1861, in Atkinson (ed.), *Fletcher Letters*, 16.

[30]*O.R.*, IV, p. 484; Cleburne to J. J. Thornton, Nov. 3, Nov. 22, 1861, in J. J. Thornton Scrapbook, 351, 356, Mississippi Department of Archives and History, Jackson. The 6th Mississippi was also called the 7th Mississippi. — See list of officers, 6th Mississippi Infantry, M269/155, NA. The end of Oct., Cleburne with his brigade, apparently on reconnaissance, advanced and encamped five miles from Bowling Green in the direction of the enemy. — *O.R.*, LII, Pt. 2, p. 190.

[31]S. P. Emerson to Cleburne Shaft Committee, Dec. 1890, quoted in unidentified Helena (Ark.) newspaper, Jan. 26, 1891, in Scrapbk., U.D.C., Helena.

[32]Cleburne to Thornton, Nov. 3, 1861, Jan. 24, 1862, in Thornton Scrapbook, 351, 391; Avery,"Patrick Ronayne Cleburne," 3; Hardee, "Major General Cleburne," 643, 651; Hughes, *General Hardee*, 85; Sanders, Address.

[33]Robert Selph Henry, *The Story of the Confederacy* (New York, 1936), 73.

[34]*O.R.*, IV, p. 531.

[35]*Ibid.*, pp. 537-38.

[36]*Ibid.*, pp. 545-48.

[37]*Ibid.*, pp. 558-59.

[38]Benham, *Kennesaw Gazette*, IV (Jan. 15, 1889), 2.

[39]Cleburne to D. G. White, Nov. 22, 1861, in CSR (Gen. Officer) of P. R. Cleburne, M331/57, NA; Benham, *Kennesaw Gazette*, IV (Jan. 15, 1889), 2.

[40]Fletcher, Jr. to his father, Nov. 30, 1861, in Atkinson (ed.), *Fletcher Letters*, 27; Govan to his brother, Dec. 3, 1861, in Govan Papers; Questionnaire of W. T. Jones, veteran of 24th Tennessee Infantry, received Dec. 18, 1922 (Tennessee State Library and Archives, Nashville, hereinafter cited as Tenn. Lib. and Arch.), 1. The Enfield rifled musket, manufactured in England, was the type shoulder arm most generally imported by the Confederates.

[41]J. Fraise Richard, *The Florence Nightingale of the Southern Army* (New York, 1914), 26, 31, 39, 57-58, 72-73.

[42]Benham, *Kennesaw Gazette,* IV (Jan. 1, 1889), 2.

[43]Cleburne to Benjamin, Jan. 18, 1862, C-212 (AIGO) 1862, M474/10 NA. On Jan. 14, 1862, Cleburne's headquarters were at Camp White, near Bowling Green. — Cleburne to Thornton, Jan. 14, 1862, in Thornton Scrapbook, 391. By Jan. 18, he again had headquarters at Bowling Green. — Cleburne to Benjamin, *supra.*

[44]William Preston Johnston, *The Life of Gen. Albert Sidney Johnston* (New York, 1878), 406.

[45]Benham, *Kennesaw Gazette,* IV (Jan. 15, 1889), 2; James A. Jones, "About the Battle of Shiloh," *Confederate Veteran,* VII (1899), 556.

[46]Record of Events from Muster Rolls of Cos. B, D, and E, 15th (Cleburne's — Polk's — Josey's) Arkansas Infantry, Jan. and Feb. 1862, M317/139, NA. (All company Records of Events cited hereinafter are from the bimonthly muster rolls. In NA, all Records of Events from muster rolls of companies in the same regiment have the same microfilm publication and roll number. Herein, subsequent citations of Records of Events from the muster rolls of companies in the same regiment will omit microfilm publication and roll numbers, irrespective of the months involved.)

[47]*O.R.,* VII, p. 259.

[48]Hardee to T. U. Cole, Mar. 9, 1863, in William Joseph Hardee Papers, Alabama Department of Archives and History, Montgomery, hereinafter cited as Ala. Arch. and Hist.; *O.R.,* X, Pt. 2, pp. 297, 302; Record of Events, Cos. A, E, and F, 15th (Cleburne's — Polk's — Josey's) Arkansas Infantry, Jan. and Feb. 1862. "Started from Murfreesboro [for Decatur, Ala.] on the 21st [of Feb.] but with a change in our mode of traveling — this time being jammed into cars having just enough room to turn round provided five men went on the platform." — Record of Co. E, 15th Arkansas, *supra.*

[49]The Military Secretary's Office, U.S. War Department, *Memorandum Relative to The General Officers Appointed by the President in the Armies of the Confederate States, 1861-1865: Compiled from Official Records* (Washington, 1905), 19; Hardee, "Major General Cleburne," 643; Benham, *Kennesaw Gazette,* IV (Jan. 15, 1889), 2. There is a reference to a letter of Jan. 4, 1862, wherein Cleburne's appointment as Brigadier General was requested by "Col. B. J. Hill & others." — C-79 (AIGO) 1862, M474/10, NA. Colonel Hill was commander of the 5th Tennessee Infantry in the brigade commanded by Cleburne.

[50]*O.R.,* X, Pt. 2, pp. 334, 338; Hardee to Mrs. Shover, Mar. 22, 1862, in Hardee Correspondence, Library of Congress; Miss Edith Coulson, Huntsville resident for nearly thirty years beginning about 1890,

conversation with authors, Dec. 27, 1962; Richard, *Florence Nightingale of Southern Army,* 41; Cordella Powell Odenheimer, "From the President General," *Confederate Veteran,* XXIV (1916), 468.

[51]Cleburne to W. D. Pickett, Mar. 24, 1862, in CSR (Gen. Officer), Cleburne; Record of Events, Co. A, 24th Tennessee Infantry, Dec. 31, 1861 to Apr. 30, 1862, M268/215, NA; Record of Events, Co. A, 15th (Cleburne's — Polk's — Josey's) Arkansas Infantry, Feb. 28 to June 30, 1862; George J. Blakemore Diary (MS in Tenn. Lib. and Arch.), Apr. 29 and 30, 1862.

[52]Benham, *Kennesaw Gazette,* IV (Jan. 15, 1889), 2.

CHAPTER VI

SHILOH AND AFTERMATH
(April – July 1862)

And he won his stars on that field of Mars
Where the glorious Johnston bled!
— *"Cleburne," in Dublin (Ireland) Nation.*

Shiloh Church, located in southwest Tennessee, was twenty miles northeast of Corinth, Mississippi. The little log church, built by a Methodist minister, was the place of worship for farm people in the vicinity. It stood in the center of a wooded plain, cut by scattered hollows and ravines as deep as fifty feet. Except for a few clearings, the area was covered with dense undergrowth. At the foot of a high bluff, two and a quarter miles northeast of the church, was Pittsburg Landing on the Tennessee River. West of the church ran Owl Creek; and to the east, Lick Creek. The two creeks, three to five miles apart, flowed northeast toward the Tennessee. Shiloh Branch, feeding into Owl Creek, was four hundred yards south of the church.[1]

On March 18, 1862, Union troops began disembarking in large numbers at Pittsburg Landing. Within a week, an army of 5 Federal divisions, some 37,000 men commanded by Grant, now a major general, encamped on the plain. The troops pitched tents in the area bounded by Owl and Lick Creeks and Shiloh Branch. On a steep ridge parallel to Shiloh Branch, Sherman, unofficially second in command, aligned the tents of his division over a stretch of a mile, ending near Owl Creek.

In this camp site of about nine square miles, the Union troops lay inactive awaiting the arrival of Buell's army of 25,000, marching from Nashville. The two forces, once united, were to move against Corinth. Johnston, with the aim of recovering Tennessee and Kentucky, planned to attack and

106

defeat Grant's army where it lay encamped before Buell could join the main Federal force.

Capt. I. W. Avery, who later became a warm friend of Cleburne, commanded a company of independent Georgia cavalry stationed near Corinth. On daily trips to the town, he observed a particular brigade being skillfully and vigorously drilled. He later recorded: "The leader was a plain-looking officer, dressed in faded gray, topped with a weather-beaten slouched gray hat, riding an ungainly gray steed of peculiar power, the rider and horse being singularly matched, and giving an idea of rugged strength. That uncouth and indefatigable driller was Cleburne."[2]

Information reached the Confederates that Buell was advancing from Nashville via Columbia. Probably on the evening of April 1, most of the generals of the Army of the Mississippi (no doubt including Cleburne) met in Corinth at the residence of Dr. Joseph Stout for a council concerning the imminent battle.[3] About midnight on April 2, Johnston decided to march the Confederate army forthwith toward Shiloh.

Orders were for the army to concentrate in the vicinity of the Michie house,[4] five and a half miles southwest of Shiloh Church, and to be in position and prepared to attack Grant's army early Saturday morning, April 5. From Corinth two roads led toward Michie's. One, the Ridge Road, for four miles went due north and then swung northeast for ten miles, to Michie's. The second, the Monterey Road, ran east, then north, for ten miles to Monterey, three miles south of Michie's. From Monterey running north was the Savannah Road, which crossed the Ridge Road at Michie's. Also from Monterey, running northwest, was the Purdy Road, which crossed the Ridge Road three miles southwest of Michie's.[5]

Leaving Corinth about noon, Thursday, April 3,[6] via the Ridge Road, Cleburne's 2nd Brigade led the main body of the army, composed of Hardee's division (referred to as a "corps") and Leonidas Polk's corps. A corps commanded by Bragg used the Monterey, Savannah, and Purdy Roads.

Cleburne's brigade marched along winding narrow Ridge Road in pelting rain, bivouacking at dark. A member of the 23rd Tennessee Infantry, a regiment of Cleburne's brigade, later recounted:

> Gen. Cleburne addressed our regiment, telling us that we
> were soon to be engaged in a great battle, and that if we did
> our duty as good soldiers he was satisfied we should gain a
> great victory, and that we should regain Tennessee and be in a
> measure restored to our families and homes. He said that we,
> as Tennesseans, had more to fight for than he or his own
> Arkansans, as we were to make the "fight for our homes and
> firesides."[7]

The General likely made similar talks to other regiments that night.

Cleburne's brigade and the other brigades of Hardee's corps reached Michie's the next morning, April 4.[8] Bragg's corps reached Monterey about the same time, and one of his divisions advanced to join with Hardee at Michie's.

From Michie's, running eastward was Bark Road, which after three miles intersected the Corinth and Pittsburg Road, called the Corinth Road. From this intersection, the Corinth Road ran northeastward two and a half miles to Shiloh Church, then swung almost due east and continued to Pittsburg Landing.

The afternoon of April 4, Cleburne's brigade, followed by the rest of Hardee's corps, advanced from Michie's via Bark Road. Marching in a heavy rain, by four o'clock they were approaching Corinth Road. In a hollow on their left, a detachment of Federal cavalry was sighted moving in the opposite direction. Immediately facing left, Cleburne's men parallel to the Federals, "opened a tremendous volley at them." A Confederate artillerist recalled: "Our infantry fire was tremendous to me, and the most intensely exciting thing I had ever heard, being the first musketry fire at a real enemy that I and most of the army had ever heard, and the yell that went down the line of infantry following showed their readiness for the fray."[9] About a dozen of the Federal reconnaissance cavalry were killed, wounded, or captured. Incongrously, despite this episode the Union army remained unaware of its peril.

Cleburne's brigade, still leading the rest of Hardee's corps, turned onto Corinth Road toward Shiloh Church and bivouacked, expecting to attack early the next morning,

April 5. That night, Hindman, who led a brigade in Hardee's command, ordered Captain Avery to locate a guide for him — Captain Phillips of Cleburne's staff. As Avery approached Cleburne's tent a gruff voice inquired about his mission. After Avery explained the circumstances the same voice replied that Phillips had work to do the next day and needed sleep; that Hindman should get his own guide. However, Phillips, having been awakened, offered to assist Hindman. Cleburne then invited Avery in out of the storm while Phillips was dressing. Thus Avery and Cleburne met.[10]

To move forward at 3 A.M. as planned was impraticable because of swollen streams and flooded ravines. About three hours later Hardee's command, now augmented by a brigade from Bragg's corps, advanced to within a mile and a half of Shiloh Church and deployed into line of battle across Corinth Road.[11] Cleburne's brigade formed the extreme left of the line, which terminated nearly a mile from Owl Creek. Over 300 men of the 2nd Tennessee Regiment, who had just arrived, were placed under Cleburne and assumed position on the far left of the line. These men had been on furlough from service in Virginia and had voluntarily assembled at Corinth to fight in the battle.[12]

All day Hardee's troops waited for the order to attack. Bragg's second division and Leonidas Polk's corps had become intermingled as they approached the battle area. Large bodies of troops were blocked at forks in a labyrinth of small roads. Marching from an outpost, a reserve division under Gen. John C. Breckinridge arrived late in the afternoon. The confusion and delay are attributed to inexperienced officers and troops, the weather, soggy roads, and to the misunderstanding of orders or the failure to observe them. Because of the delay and confusion the attack was postponed until Sunday morning the 6th — twenty-four hours later than planned.

Before dusk, the army was deployed into three lines with Hardee's command forming in the front. Eight hundred yards to his rear was the second line, Bragg's corps. In Bragg's rear were Polk's corps and Breckinridge's division. This disposition of the army was faulty. Hardee's, Bragg's, and Polk's corps should have deployed on a solid front with each general assigned a definite sector of the line.

Johnston's plan of battle was to turn the Federal left flank, thus cutting Grant off from the Tennessee River, and then drive him into the swamps along Snake and Owl Creeks, where he would be isolated and could be destroyed.

At dawn, Sunday, April 6, Hardee's skirmishers became engaged with a Federal reconnoitering party. At the sound of the firing the Confederate army was ordered forward. Cleburne's account of this initial action is given in his report to Hardee's assistant adjutant-general:

> On the morning of the 6th my brigade was formed in line of battle on the left of your division. It consisted of the following regiments, viz: The Twenty-third Tennessee, Lieut. Col. James F. Neill commanding; Sixth Mississippi, Col. J. J. Thornton; Fifth Tennessee, Col. Ben. J. Hill; Twenty-fourth Tennessee, Lieut. Col. Thomas H. Peebles commanding; Fifteenth Arkansas, Lieut. Col. A. K. Patton commanding, and the Second Tennessee, Col. W. B. Bate. The regiments were placed in the following order: Twenty-third Tennessee on the right, Sixth Mississippi next, Fifth Tennessee next, Twenty-fourth Tennessee on the left, Fifteenth Arkansas deployed as skirmishers in front of the line, with their reserve near the left, and the Second Tennessee en echelon[13] 500 yards in rear of my left flank, with a strong line of skirmishers covering the interval between its left and that of the Twenty-fourth Tennessee.
>
> In this formation, soon after daylight, I advanced with the division against the enemy, keeping the proper distance from and regulating my movements by those of General [S. A. M.] Wood's brigade, which was on my right. I remained myself near the right of my brigade so as to preserve, as far as possible, my connection with the division. Trigg's battery[14] followed near the right of my brigade, but was under the control of the chief of artillery, and left me after the first encounter. I advanced some distance through the woods without opposition.[15]

Sherman's division was in line of battle on high ground 200 yards north of the deep, marshy ravine through which flowed Shiloh Branch. A Federal battery was stationed in front of Shiloh Church, and another had its guns on a ridge 200 yards east of Corinth Road and 150 yards north of the ravine.

In advancing, Hardee's line had veered somewhat to the right, so that the middle of Cleburne's brigade was now on the Corinth Road. Thus, about 8:00 A.M., Cleburne's brigade approached the most formidable, and an almost impenetrable part of the Federal line of defense. Continuing with Cleburne's report:

The enemy first showed himself about 400 yards off towards my left flank. I ordered Captain [John T.] Trigg to send a howitzer in this direction and wake him up with a few shells. Continuing to move forward, the Fifteenth Arkansas engaged the enemy's skirmishers and drove them in on their first line of battle.16 My skirmishers then fell back on their reserve.

I was soon in sight of the enemy's encampments, behind the first of which he had formed his line of battle. He was very advantageously posted and overlapped my left flank by at least half a brigade. His line was lying down behind the rising ground on which his tents were pitched, and opposite my right he had made a breastwork of logs and bales of hay. Everywhere his musketry and artillery at short range swept the open spaces between the tents in his front with an iron storm that threatened certain destruction to every living thing that would dare to cross them. An almost impassable morass, jutting out from the foot of the height on which the enemy's tents stood impeded the advance of my center, and finally caused a wide opening in my line. The Fifth Tennessee and the regiments on its left kept to the left of this swamp, and the Sixth Mississippi and Twenty-third Tennessee advanced on its right. My own horse bogged down in it and threw me, and it was with great difficulty I got out. My brigade was soon on the verge of the encampments and the battle began in earnest. Trigg's battery, posted on some high ground in the woods in my rear, opened over the heads of my men, but so thick were the leaves, he could only see in one direction, while the enemy were playing on him from several. The result was he was unable to accomplish much, and was ordered to a new position. I had no artillery under my command from this time forward.

The Sixth Mississippi and Twenty-third Tennessee charged through the encampments on the enemy. The line was necessarily broken by the standing tents. Under the terrible fire much confusion followed, and a quick and bloody repulse was the consequence.17

A veteran of the 23rd Tennessee Regiment recalled

111

General Cleburne riding up to the regiment and saying, " 'Boys, don't be discouraged; that is not the first charge that was ever repulsed; fix bayonets and give them steel.' Then he ordered, 'Forward! Charge!' "[18]

Continuing with Cleburne's account of the battle:

> The Twenty-third Tennessee was with difficulty rallied about 100 yards in the rear; again and again the Sixth Mississippi, unaided, charged the enemy's line, and it was only when the regiment had lost 300 officers and men killed and wounded, out of an aggregate of 425, that it yielded and retreated in disorder over its own dead and dying. Colonel Thornton and Major [Robert] Lowry, the field officers,[19] were both wounded. It would be useless to enlarge on the courage and devotion of the Sixth Mississippi. The facts as recorded speak louder than any words of mine.[20]

A lieutenant in the 6th Mississippi later said of this tribute, "Praise from the intrepid Cleburne is praise indeed."[21] Cleburne continued:

> Col. Mat. Martin, former commander of the Twenty-third Tennessee, arrived on the field just as his old regiment broke; though not then on duty, he voluntarily assisted me in rallying and inspiring the men with renewed determination, and remained with it until severely wounded at a subsequent period of the day.
>
> While my right was reforming I galloped around the morass to my left, which, after a desperate fight and heavy loss, caused chiefly by the fact that the enemy flanked me on the left, had driven him back at all points, and was now in possession of his first line of encampments.
>
> Here the Second Tennessee, coming up on the left, charged through a murderous cross-fire. The gallant major, William R. Doak, fell mortally wounded, and the colonel, W. B. Bate, had his leg broken by a Minie ball. Tennessee can never mourn for a nobler band than fell this day in her Second Regiment.
>
> Here the Twenty-fourth Tennessee won a character for steady valor, and its commander, Lieutenant-Colonel Peebles, showed that he possessed all the qualifications of a commander in the field.
>
> Here the Fifteenth Arkansas inflicted heavy loss upon the enemy, and lost many good men, and its major, J. T. Harris. He scorned to pay any regard to his personal safety; he moved up within pistol range of the enemy, and was shot dead while

firing on them with his revolver.[22]

When taking Sherman's encampment, Cleburne's men were supported by units of the second and third Confederate lines. Cleburne's report continued: "Finding my advance on the left wing for the present unemployed, I galloped back to my right. About half of the Twenty-third Tennessee and 60 men of the Sixth Mississippi had reformed. With these I advanced directly to my front, through the enemy's encampment, the enemy having retreated as soon as my left had broken their right."[23]

About 10 A.M. Cleburne, along with troops from the other Confederate lines, advanced past Shiloh Church. Whole regiments of Sherman's terrified men fled. Thousands sought shelter at the foot of the bluff on the river bank and the protection of the gunboats. As Cleburne continued forward he engaged Maj. Gen. John A. McClernand's Federal division, which was in support of Sherman.

Cleburne's advance followed the Corinth Road toward Pittsburg Landing. Because of the unorthodox Confederate formation, the terrain, and the concealed character of the country, troops from different commands fought in small units of brigade size and less. Cleburne said "Colonel [William K.] Patterson of the Eighth Arkansas [Wood's brigade], connected his regiment with my remnants of two regiments, and remained fighting with me until about 12 or 1 o'clock." [24]

Meanwhile, the center and right wing of the Confederate Army forged ahead, bending back Grant's left flank. The Federal commander sent a hurriedly penciled note, addressed to Buell at Savannah, seven miles downstream, "If you will get upon the field, . . . it will . . . possibly save the day to us."[25]

The Southerners almost had victory in their grasp, when about 10:30 A.M., B. M. Prentiss' and W. H. S. Wallace's Federal divisions moved into a natural fortress on a sunken road. This site, later known as the "Hornet's Nest," began a half mile northeast of Shiloh Church and extended eastward for three quarters of a mile. To assail it, the Confederates had to cross an open field enfiladed by Federal artillery fire. For hours the two Union divisions valiantly resisted Confederate assaults. Returning to Cleburne's account:

> At [about 12 or 1 P.M.] Captain [W. A.] Harper, commanding the remnant of the Sixth Mississippi, marched it to the rear. Its terrible loss in the morning, the want of all its field and most of its company officers, had completely disorganized it and unfitted it for further service. I saw it no more during the battle, ...
>
> Soon after this I ordered the Twenty-third Tennessee to the rear, with directions to reunite with other portions of the regiment which had got separated from it in the repulse of the morning. I was now left without a command on this part of the field, and was proceeding along the rear of our line to join my left wing, when I met General Hardee. I reported my situation to him. He ordered me to collect and bring into the fight a large body of stragglers who were thronging the encampments in our rear. This, after great exertion, I partially succeeded in doing, but finding this kind of a force would not stand anything like a heavy fire, I determined to rejoin my command on the left, which I did about 2 P.M.
>
> I found the Fifth and Twenty-fourth Tennessee and Fifteenth Arkansas halted under the brow of an abrupt hill. The Second Tennessee had suffered so severly in its charge of the morning it had to be moved back to reform. Moving forward immediately after I lost sight of it, and it did not connect itself with my brigade any more during the fight . . . .
>
> On reaching the ground I ordered an immediate advance. It was delayed, however, by one of our own batteries firing across the line of my intended advance. As soon as I succeeded in stopping this fire I sent out skirmishers and pushed directly forward. The Twenty-third Tennessee Regiment, under the command of Lieutenant-Colonel Neil, came up at this juncture and advanced with me.
>
> After moving forward about half a mile I was fired on by the enemy again, my skirmishers driven in, and soon my main body (the Fifteenth Arkansas excepted) was heavily engaged. This engagement lasted half an hour, when the enemy gave way.[26]

This attack was made east of Tilghman Creek, upon McClernand's sixth line. One of Cleburne's regimental commanders a few days later wrote that the Federals "left the woods strewn with their dead and dying."[27] Following this engagement, Cleburne called for volunteer sharpshooters and placed them on a ridge in his front to pick off Federal artillerymen supporting Prentiss.[28] Cleburne's report continued: "My men were out of ammunition. Owing to the nature of the ground my ammunition wagons could not follow, so I had to send a strong fatigue party back, and the men carried boxes of ammunition on their shoulders up and down the steep hills for more than a mile. As soon as supplied with ammunition I again advanced, ..."[29]

Finally, with fire from sixty-two guns assembled by Gen. Daniel Ruggles — the greatest concentration of artillery up to that time assembled in North America — the Confederates forced out of action the batteries supporting Prentiss and Wallace. Several Confederate brigades, including Cleburne's, made a simultaneous attack on the Hornet's Nest.[30] Prentiss' surrender at 5:30 was "the high-water mark of Southern success during the battle."[31] About the same time, Cleburne's brigade received word of the death of General Albert Sidney Johnston, which had occurred three hours earlier.

Cleburne said, "[I] continued to move forward until checked by a heavy fire of artillery from the enemy's field artillery and gunboats. When this firing ceased I again advanced until halted by an aid of General Beauregard [Johnston's successor], who informed me we were not to approach nearer to the river."[32] When halted, Cleburne was within 400 yards of Pittsburg Landing.[33]

By now only about 7,000 effective fighters were left in Grant's army, crowded in a semicircle adjacent to Pittsburg Landing. Federal artillery was located on a ridge a quarter of a mile from the landing. Taking the landing and severing the Union supply line would have brought about the capitulation of the Federals. However, with the Confederates disorganized and, in Beauregard's judgment, the battle out of hand, he ordered the troops to withdraw from action until the next morning.

"It was now dark," Cleburne said in his report, "so I returned, and encamped in one of the enemy's encampments near the [Corinth] road."[34] Cleburne's report continued:

> It rained heavily during the night. Every fifteen minutes
> the enemy threw two shells from his gunboats, some of which

115

burst close around my men, banishing sleep from the eyes of a few, but falling chiefly among their own wounded, who were strewn thickly between my camp and the river. History records few instances of more reckless inhumanity than this.

Soon after daylight on Monday morning I received notice that the enemy were pushing forward and driving in our cavalry pickets. It now became plain Buell had arrived and we had a fresh army to fight. In a few moments I received orders from General Hardee to advance on the [Corinth] road. I reformed my brigade and fired off my wet guns.

My brigade was sadly reduced. From near 2,700 I now numbered about 800. Two regiments, the Second Tennessee and Sixth Mississippi, were absent altogether. Hundreds of my best men were dead or in the hospitals, and, I blush to add, hundreds of others had run off early in the fight of the day before — some through cowardice and some loaded with plunder from the Yankee encampments.

With the gallant few still with me I advanced about a mile to a place where I found a line of battle. It was halted, and, I was informed, was a part of General Breckinridge's command. I formed on the left of this line [immediately south of Corinth Road, a mile and a half southwest of Pittsburg Landing], halted, and ordered my men to lie down. I could plainly see the enemy's line in my front and that it stretched beyond my left as far as the eye could see.

At this time a battery of six guns came up in my rear and offered its assistance. I think it was the Washington Battery.[35]

About half a mile to my left, in a neck of woods, I could see troops moving from the direction of the enemy and passing far in rear of my line. Soon a heavy fight commenced in this direction. I endeavored to discover the character of these troops, but could not. Finally Colonel [J. H.] Kelly, of your [Hardee's] division, rode up, and informed me they were enemies. The battery immediately opened on their flanks and soon cleared them out of the woods.

An officer now bore me an order from General Breckinridge to move forward with his line and attack the force in our front. I sent back word that I was completely without support and outflanked on the left and would be destroyed if I advanced. I received for answer that the order was from General Bragg, that it was positive, and I must immediately advance. I did so, but had not gotten far before a battery on the left of General Breckinridge's line commenced firing across my front, obliging me to halt.

The enemy soon replied with rifled guns. This duel was carried on diagonally across the line of my proposed advance. I moved my line forward [a quarter of a mile north of Corinth

Road] into a valley that separated me from the enemy so as to permit the Washington Battery to take part in the fight by firing over my line. The enemy brought up another battery, and for half an hour an artillery fight was carried on over my line the fiercest I saw during the day. The whole line of infantry on my right had halted and were merely spectators of the fight.

Here I had some men killed by limbs cut from the trees by our own artillery. It soon became apparent that our artillery was overmatched. It ceased firing, and the whole line of infantry charged the enemy. There was a very thick undergrowth here of young trees, which prevented my men from seeing any distance, yet offered them no protection from the storm of bullets and grape shot that swept through it. I could not see what was going on to my right or left, but my men were dropping all around before the fire of an unseen foe.

Here Captain Cowley, acting major of the Fifteenth Arkansas, a true and tried officer, was shot in the head, and Lieutenant-Colonel Neil, of the Twenty-third Tennessee, was shot through the body.

My brigade was repulsed and almost completely routed in this unfortunate attack. As far as I know the Fifteenth Arkansas was the only regiment rallied anywhere near the scene of disaster. In the face of a deadly fire and an exultant foe the regiment reformed near two abandoned cannons and fell back in order behind a ridge. From this point, seeing some re-enforcements coming up, I led them in a charge on the advancing foe. The enemy fled back faster than they came.

In this charge Lieutenant-Colonel Patton, the sole remaining field officer of the Fifteenth Arkansas, was shot dead. He did his duty nobly in this battle and secured the love and confidence of every man in his regiment. The Fifteenth Arkansas continued to pursue the enemy until out of ammunition, when 58 men, all that were still together, fell back to replenish.

My brigade was now completely scattered and disorganized. Many of my officers and men continued fighting in the ranks of other commands or on their own responsibility, but not again in any organization which I could control.

For myself, I endeavored to rally stragglers, form them in lines, and do what else I could to secure the retreat. Fortunately the enemy had suffered too severely to pursue, and drew out of the fight while yet we were in possession of one-third of their encampment.

I remained on the field destroying property which could not be carried off and trying to succor the wounded until after sunset, when by General Hardee's orders I left for Corinth.

My brigade, including Trigg's and [J. H.] Calvert's

batteries, numbered on the morning of the 6th 2,750 men; out of this number 1,000 were killed and wounded and 32 missing.

This was the first battle my men were ever engaged in. They led the advance of our army on Shiloh and engaged and repulsed the enemy's cavalry the Friday before the battle. They fought in the foremost line both days and were never rested or relieved for a moment. They captured many stands of colors and assisted in the capture of General Prentiss' Federal brigade on the left.

I would like to do justice to the many acts of individual valor witnessed during the fight, but they were too numerous to mention. Privates William Dixon, William Pierce, W. H. Kinsey, H. A. Sale [misspelled Sales] Sergt. T. H. Osborne, and Lieutenant [John E.] Josey, of the Fifteenth Arkansas; Col. Ben. Hill, of the Fifth Tennessee; Lieutenant-Colonel Peebles, of the Twenty-fourth Tennessee; Lieut. R. H. Keeble, Captain [J. A.] Ridley, and Lieutenant-Colonel Neil, of the Twenty-third Tennessee, were among the number.[36]

The loss sustained by Cleburne's brigade (revised figures are 1,013 out of 2,700) was the heaviest of any brigade in the army. "In an assault," William Preston Johnston observed, this percentage of loss, "is one of the surest signs of honest, hard fighting."[37] Company C (formerly Yell Rifles), 15th Arkansas, went into the battle with fifty men (including Cowley). Five were killed or mortally wounded; and four, seriously wounded.[38]

Hardee said in his report: "During the action Brigadier-General Cleburne conducted his command with persevering valor. No repulse discouraged him; but after many bloody struggles he assembled the remnant of his brigade and was conspicuous for his gallantry to the end of the battle."[39]

In his sketch of Cleburne, Avery wrote of meeting the General near the end of the battle. Avery was pushing skulkers to the front when he was hailed by Cleburne, who was alone without even a staff officer. The two joined in rounding up stragglers. Although Cleburne with pistol in hand ordered the shirkers back to duty, Avery described his tenderness in voice and manner when they came upon a dying Confederate soldier. Avery reported the exhausting ride back to Corinth as follows:

As we passed through a camp we saw some immense hard-tacks, a bucket of butter and a half sack of corn. The writer lifted the corn to the front of Cleburne's saddle, by his direction. I then buttered for each of us one of the huge areas of biscuit, and, swinging the bucket on my own arm for further use, on we rode, eagerly munching the tough provender. I often afterward joked the general upon his comical appearance holding with one hand the bulky sack of grain on his saddle pommel, and with the other grasping a sheet of cracker as broad as the map of the United States, and cramming it in heavy relays down his throat. The rain began to fall, adding to the gloom of the disaster. It became heavier until it grew to a steady pour, and the road was converted into a deep slop and the way impenetrably dark, and we could go only by the occasional flash athwart the cimmerian darkness. We fed our horses about nine o'clock, and then resumed our weary ride to Corinth. Men and animals were worn out. We rode sleeping, and would be awaked by jostling against some one, or a deep oath from some startled tramper. The horses would stop to drink in crossing branches and fall asleep. Frequently I would awake and find my horse stark still, and a blinding flash of lightning would reveal the general's gray hugging closely to my mare, the general snoozing away as if he had made a special contract to sleep.

At length, far in the night, we arrived at a broad creek, and let our stock drink, and, of course the writer went to sleep. I was awakened by a deafening clap of thunder. I called for my companion but he was gone, and I saw him no more for several days. Cleburne told me afterward that he awoke and found me missing, and shouted lustily for me, and then rode on and brought up finally at a farm house. The road forked beyond the creek, and we took different routes.[40]

2

Months later, speaking of Shiloh, Cleburne is reported to have said, "It was a battle gallantly won and as stupidly lost." He was manifestly referring to General Beauregard's order which stopped the fighting on the 6th.[41] Cleburne's statement was in accord with the consensus of the Confederate officers and soldiers who were in the battle. However, from an historical perspective, Beauregard's order probably did not lose the battle. When the order was received, Buell's army was crossing the river to reinforce Grant. The Confederates only had a few minutes within which to break through the beleagured Union troops adjacent to Pittsburg Landing and capture the landing. Certainly, however, Beauregard should have ordered the attack. No one knows what the outcome would have been. "Grant's front may have been a brittle shell."[42]

Had Shiloh been fought a day earlier as planned, defeat of the Union army would have been almost a certainty, and a Confederate victory there would have certainly increased the South's chances of winning the war.[43]

3

From the battlefield of Shiloh, Cleburne returned to his headquarters at Camp Hill, south of Corinth. He set about rebuilding the brigade and replenishing supplies. Each day an ordnance officer was sent to town to try to get Enfield and Minié rifle cartridges. Finally, on April 24 Cleburne wrote to Hardee's adjutant-general about the "very limited" supply of rifle cartridges in the brigade and on none being available.[44]

On April 23, Cleburne selected Pvts. Isaac S. Ray of the 5th Tennessee and W. R. Empie of the 15th Arkansas to take trophies of the battle of Shiloh to Richmond. Both men had displayed gallantry in the battle.[45]

At Camp Hill, Cleburne inaugurated an unique method of military instruction. A group composed of one line officer from each regiment, selected by his colonel for intelligence and aptitude, received instruction at headquarters. Under Cleburne's supervision, members of his staff instructed the group in special phases of infantry tactics. The line officers then instructed the other officers in their regiments, who in turn instructed the men.[46]

On April 29, Lieut. George J. Blakemore of the 23rd Tennessee entered in his diary: "Gen Cleburne in person was in our camp this morning he ordered after talking to his many lovers all around him for some time a detail of the best bravest & colles [coolest] men (the no. of 5) from each company to form a co of sharp shooters, ..." Blakemore (later mortally wounded at Chickamauga) told in his diary of being chosen company commander: "it has fallen upon me I am aware tis a dangerous & perilous Position in all engagements still I'll not chide because I was appointed by the Col. but will accept for I am willing to do any thing for my country."[47] Thus Cleburne organized the first units of sharpshooters, who were to become highly valuable in his brigade and division.

In ‚April and early May, Cleburne reorganized his companies and regiments. Lieut. Lucius Polk having demonstrated qualities of leadership at Shiloh, was elected Colonel of the 15th Arkansas; and Pvt. W. H. Kinsey, Captain of its Company C (formerly Yell Rifles).[48]

Meanwhile, back at Shiloh, under slow-moving Gen. Henry Wager Halleck, the Federals had assembled an army of more than a hundred thousand men. Beauregard's army at Corinth had increased also. With the augmentation of 16,000 men from Arkansas and Missouri under Gens. Earl Van Dorn and Sterling Price, his total strength numbered some 80,000. However, sickness was so rampant that effectives numbered only 53,000.

Finally, on April 29, Halleck started moving his army toward Corinth, with Gen. John Pope in command of the left wing. This wing was comprised of three infantry divisions, commanded by Gens. E. A. Paine, D. S. Stanley, and Schuyler Hamilton, plus a cavalry division. Confederate engineers were busy constructing a line of works encircling most of the town about a mile and a half out. Hardee, defending the Confederate right, placed Cleburne's brigade in the works, east of Corinth.[49]

About noon on May 3, Hardee, after receiving information that a strong Federal force of undetermined size was approaching Corinth from the northeast, on the Hamburg Road, ordered Cleburne's brigade to engage "the advance of the enemy." Later, in a letter to a friend Hardee explained that, "The object was not to bring on a fight but to feel the enemy & to fall back."[50] Early in the afternoon, Cleburne moved forward on the Hamburg Road and through the small town of Farmington. Three quarters of a mile beyond the town, he posted his brigade east of Seven Mile Creek. The enemy soon appeared; and after a brief exchange of fire, Cleburne fell back to a new position, destroying the bridge across the creek and obstructing the road with felled timber. Thus he delayed the enemy's advance for two hours. Finally, when the Federals were opposite Cleburne's new position, an hour of spirited artillery and infantry firing ensued. In the late afternoon Cleburne withdrew to the

Confederate line of works.[51]

With no further enemy attack, on May 5 Cleburne's brigade was relieved in the line but remained within supporting distance.[52] Returning to the works the next day, Cleburne sent the following message to Hardee from "Farmington Road":

> If the earth works here are of any importance, I must say I think they are being neglected. No Engineer to be found, my men were ordered in advance to protect workmen but there are no workmen to protect, everything seems out of joint, I think Some of the Genls ought to come out and see how these works are being done, had we been attacked up to this time I think the work done of no value.
>
> My Aid and escort occupied (at daylight this morning) the Houses occupied by the enemies pickets at sunset yesterday the enemy seem to have their out post at Farmington and to be encamped ¼ mile back of that place. I sent Phillips out with Telescope to get fuller intelligence A Negro near their lines told us that they were as thick as bees behind Farmington We can hear their Drums very plain.[53]

The next day Cleburne moved Camp Hill nearer the line of works and set up headquarters in Corinth, at the residence of Mr. S. Hay, located at 915 Waldron Street.[54] The Federal force Cleburne had met on May 3 proved to be a reconnaissance of one division, which remained in the vicinity of Farmington.

In an "historic crawl,"[55] by May 2 Halleck had advanced ten miles in four days. During the next twenty-two days he averaged only a third of a mile a day. Twice in this period, units of the Confederate army, including Cleburne's brigade, made a sortie toward Federal advance forces at Farmington. The first, on the 9th, developed into a skirmish, but Cleburne did not become engaged. The second sortie, on May 22, was a long detour to attack, but obstacles rendered the advance impracticable.[56] On May 24 Halleck began to build a fortified line near Corinth and to mount heavy siege guns.

On May 25, in order to save his army, Beauregard decided to evacuate Corinth secretly. The next day, while supplies were being loaded for the evacuation, enemy pickets came so near on the east side of the town that one of Cleburne's companies, on picket duty, had a skirmish with them.[57]

May 28, Cleburne met the enemy at the Shelton house, located on a hill north of "the lower Farmington road." This site, southwest of Farmington and two and a half miles east of Corinth, was a half mile north of the Memphis & Charleston Railroad.[58] A small creek, a branch of Clear Creek, running south crossed the road a hundred yards west of the house.

Giving no details, Avery said that Cleburne "distinguished himself in the brilliant affair of 'Shelton House.' "[59] On the monument at Cleburne's grave in Helena, Shelton House is listed with five important battles. Several other important battles in which Cleburne had a prominent part are not listed. When planning the inscription, men familiar with Cleburne's career must have had knowledge of some distinguished service performed by the General in the little known affair at Shelton House. In his report of the operations, Cleburne's modesty forbade expanding on his role. Research has failed to reveal the distinguished service, unless it be his leadership and determination in a difficult situation.

Cleburne's detailed report to Hardee concerning the Shelton House affair is given below in its entirety for little else can be found on this engagement:

> On the morning of the 28th of May, 1862, I received an order from your headquarters informing me that our pickets had been driven in on the lower Farmington road, and directing me to take my brigade and replace them, also that Colonel [Sidney S.] Stanton was already there with two regiments and would be under my command. About 11 a.m. I marched with four regiments of my brigade to carry out the order, viz, the Fifth, Forty-eighth, Twenty-fourth, and Second Tennessee Volunteers. The Fifteenth Arkansas and Calvert's battery had left previously for Tuscumbia Creek and were not with me on this occasion. Marching past your headquarters, I reported to you in person, and was directed by you to reconnoiter the enemy before attacking. Before passing outside of the lines I sent Lieutenant [James] Mayo, Fifteenth Arkansas, to see Colonel Stanton, to inform him that I was coming up with my brigade, to ascertain from him the position of his force, and what he knew of the enemy. Lieutenant Mayo soon returned, informed me that he had delivered my message; that Colonel Stanton's force was on the right of the lower

Farmington road; that Colonel Stanton informed him that the enemy were in position in his front and to his left; that he believed they occupied the Shelton house, but did not think there were any on this side of the creek; that he needed support on his left, and wished me to hurry up as fast as I could. On reaching the first open ground outside the line of earth-works, at a place where an old cotton gin stands, I formed my brigade in line. While engaged in forming my line I was approached by Captain Steadman with some message from Colonel Stanton. (I do not recollect sending any message by Captain Steadman to Colonel Stanton.) I, however, requested Captain Steadman to go as quickly as possible to a point on the Memphis and Charleston road, where General Van Dorn had erected an earth-work on a hill commanding a view of the enemy's position at the Shelton house, and get all the information he could from the commander of the earth-work. I believed this the only point from which we could reconnoiter the enemy.

I had scarcely formed my line before the enemy's skirmishers commenced firing from the opposite side of the open ground and drove in some cavalry pickets from the left of it. I sent Lieutenant Jetton with six sharpshooters to reconnoiter in this direction. I threw out skirmishers in front of my whole line, ordering them to keep about 100 yards in front of the main body and regulate their movements by those of the main body. About this time Captain Steadman returned with the information that General Van Dorn had shelled the enemy out of the Shelton house, and they were nowhere to be seen; that I could now advance and take possession of the house.[60] I now ordered my brigade forward, ordered each regiment to preserve brigade distance from, and keep dressed by, the regiment on its right; at the same time sent Colonel Stanton word that I was on his left, advancing; that he must immediately advance on the right. Lieutenant Hanly, Fifteenth Arkansas, attached to my staff, informed me that he delivered the message to Colonel Stanton; that he found Colonel Stanton's men lying down on the ground to the right of the road; that on receiving the order Colonel Stanton called his men to attention and moved them forward by a flank along the Farmington road. I advanced to the edge of the woods on the far side of the open ground before mentioned, driving the enemy's skirmishers on my left. At this time I received an urgent message from Colonel Stanton, desiring me to connect with his left. I galloped forward, examined the ground, and did not consider it advisable, but moved as far as the ground would well permit by the right flank.

Finding at the same time that Colonel Stanton, instead of obeying my orders to advance, was waiting to make connections with my line, I dispatched Lieutenant McClelland, late of the Fifth Tennessee Volunteers, on my staff, to again inform Colonel Stanton that I was advancing with my brigade on the left, and to direct him to advance on the right. On returning, Lieutenant McClelland informed me he had delivered the order to Colonel Stanton; that Colonel Stanton stated he would comply with it; that he found Colonel Stanton's men advanced to within twenty paces of the branch of the creek nearest to Corinth. I halted for three or four minutes, to give the message time to reach Colonel Stanton. These dispositions having been made, I took up my position on the right, with Colonel Hill's regiment. I sent my aide, Captain Phillips, down my line to the left with orders to instruct the regiments to keep the proper distance, and, as the undergrowth was so thick I could not see twenty paces, that each regiment must direct its movements by the regiment on its right. I also ordered Captain Phillips to collect some cavalry and place them so as to watch our left flank; also to remain himself on the left of the line and keep me posted as to the state of affairs on that flank. In the meantime Colonel Hill, of the Fifth Tennessee, had gone forward with a few resolute men to reconnoiter. Returning at this time, he informed me he had been within a few yards of the Shelton house; that all was quiet there, and there was no appearance of the enemy. I now determined to take possession of the Shelton house, but before doing so I ordered Lieutenant [James F.] Sanford, Fifteenth Arkansas, attached with my staff, to go with all speed to Colonel Stanton and tell him to be careful and not to fire on any of my men in mistake for the enemy. I thought this precaution necessary, as I might possibly reach the Shelton house first. Lieutenant Sanford informs me he found Colonel Stanton with his regiment on the Farmington road. The head of his column was halted, the rear closing up as though he was about to make a forward movement.

About this time firing was heard in the direction of the Shelton house. Lieutenant Sanford states that he hallooed to the men in a very loud voice, which he is confident Colonel Stanton could have heard, "For God's sake, men, move forward; your friends are fighting on the left." In the meantime I had ordered the brigade forward in loud and distinct tones. In a few minutes our skirmishers, advancing out of the hollow to the high land around the Shelton house, were fired on by the enemy, who had been attempting to erect a redoubt at the Shelton house, and were concealed all about it and in the wooded ravines on its right. The main body of the Fifth Tennessee now rushed forward with a loud cheer to storm the place. They were met by a heavy fire of musketry and artillery. The musketry was chiefly from the wooded hollow

on our right flank. Knowing Colonel Stanton's command
flanked this position of the enemy, I waited with painful
anxiety to hear his musketry open to my right. I was doomed
to disappointment. Colonel Stanton, for some strange reason,
never advanced. Unsupported, the Fifth Tennessee had
followed their gallant leader forward, driving the enemy before
them. They soon disabled one of the enemy's batteries, killing
most of the horses and driving the artillerymen in flight from
their guns. They advanced some distance beyond the buildings,
when a fresh battery opened on them from a new direction,
while the fire continued on their flank and increased on their
front. At this time Colonel Hill fell, stunned by a shell. His
men were forced to abandon their first successes, and fell back
to the cover of the woods.

My attention was directed to the fight progressing in my
front, and some ten or fifteen minutes elapsed before I
discovered that the left of my brigade had failed to advance. I
immediately galloped to the front of the position where the
Twenty-fourth, Colonel [R. D.] Allison, ought to have been,
but could see nothing of them. I then rode back into the
wooded bottom to look for them. I advanced on their
sharpshooters from the direction of the enemy and found
them lying down in the rear of the creek. I upbraided Colonel
Allison with his shameful dilatoriness, and again ordered him
forward. He made some difficulty about crossing the creek —
said he had been stopped by some very thick undergrowth. I
found him dismounted and with his uniform off. At length I
got him to move forward. His regiment arrived on the ground
just as the Fifth Tennessee were falling back. The regiment
fired one ineffectual volley, and then most of the men,
especially on the right, ran away. Those who did not run off I
ordered to fall back and reform. I am happy to bear testimony
that the present commander of the regiment, Major [Hugh L.
W.] Bratton was conspicuous among those who remained and
did their duty. I am also informed that some of the companies
on the left stood their ground. This regiment, under different
auspices, fought well at Shiloh. It is painful to be forced to
record this instance of its failure to do so. Colonel Allison not
only disobeyed my order to advance, but through the whole
affair he showed none of the qualities of an officer. I was
forming the Forty-eighth and Second Tennessee for another
attempt, when I received an order from you to draw out of the
fight and keep my pickets along the western border of the
creek. I fell back some fifty or seventy-five yards, and put out
my pickets. Colonel Allison, by failing to move forward,
delayed the movement of the Forty-eighth and Second
Tennessee. They but conformed to my orders in directing their
movements by his. I saw no disposition to falter in these

regiments, though exposed for some time to a galling fire of artillery. Colonel Stanton failed to obey my reiterated order to advance. On being questioned by me as to his failure, he stated he had received no communication from me but one through Captain Steadman, ignoring him. Four of my officers stated positively they bore communications from me to him. My loss in killed and wounded and missing was between eighty and ninety. The Fifth Tennessee were the principal sufferers, though Lieutenant_____, of the Forty-eighth, one of the most promising young officers in the brigade, was killed by a shell on the field. A number of the enemy lay dead on the field. The Fifth Tennessee took one officer and one private of the enemy's sappers and miners prisoners.[61]

Thirty-four years later in an address commemorating Cleburne, Capt. O. T. Plummer of the 48th Tennessee recalled the encounter at Shelton House. He told of General Hardee rushing to the front, ordering a halt, and saying that he had not ordered Cleburne to bring on a general engagement. Captain Plummer quoted Cleburne as replying, "Did you expect me to send General Pope a flag of truce requesting him to fall back and allow me to extend our picket line to its former position, or to drive him back?" This, the Captain said, shows Cleburne's mettle and his manner of dealing with the enemy.[62]

During the night of May 29, without detection by the enemy, Beauregard cleverly withdrew his army to a point seven miles south of Corinth, across Tuscumbia Creek. Cleburne's 15th Arkansas, Calvert's battery, and four cavalry companies, who for several days had been holding the turnpike bridge over the creek, stood guard while Beauregard's army crossed. Then the men of the 15th burned the bridge. The railroad bridge over the creek was guarded by Cleburne's 23rd Tennessee and a section of artillery. After all the cars were across, this bridge was also burned. Early the next morning, with "weather very warm," the main Confederate forces began marching to Baldwyn, twenty-six miles farther south.

Halleck, becoming aware of the Confederate evacuation at daylight on the 30th, sent troops in pursuit. For two days the 15th Arkansas and a section of artillery held weak Federal infantry attacks in check at the creek. Then the 15th

Arkansas and the 23rd Tennessee marched throughout the night of May 31 and all the next day to Baldwyn.[63]

Halleck discontinued pursuit of Beauregard's army, redirected his forces, and started Buell with an army toward East Tennessee. On June 7, the Confederate army left Baldwyn for Tupelo, Mississippi, nineteen miles farther south. Camping on high land and with pure water available, the troops were soon in better health and occupied a sound defensive position.

Beauregard, unwell and compelled to take sick leave, left Braxton Bragg in command. A few days later, on June 27, Jefferson Davis grasped this opportunity to appoint Bragg, a favorite of his, permanent commander of the Army of the Mississippi. The army remained near Tupelo until the last week of July. Cleburne used these weeks for drilling, training, and instructing his command.[64]

The General had been saddened by the loss of the many men of his command who perished at Shiloh and the failure to achieve the victory so nearly attained. But he faced the future with high resolve and confidence in the ultimate success of the South.

NOTES

CHAPTER VI

[1] The Tennessee at this point flows north. Lick Creek empties into the Tennessee; and Owl Creek, into Snake Creek. The latter empties into the river a mile below Pittsburg Landing.

[2] Avery, "Patrick Ronayne Cleburne," 3.

[3] W. R. Stout, son of Dr. Joseph Stout, to Mrs. R. E. Price, Dec. 12, 1931, in possession of Mrs. R. E. Price, Corinth.

[4] Orders of officers engaged in the battle, battle reports, and contemporary maps, spelled the name "Mickey," as it was pronounced. However, the correct spelling is "Michie." — Monroe F. Cockrell to authors, Aug. 28, 1967; James W. Holland, Superintendent, Shiloh National Military Park, memorandum for the Director, Sept. 15, 1945, photostat in papers of Monroe F. Cockrell, Evanston, Ill.

[5] See Atwell Thompson "Map of the territory between Corinth, Miss. and Pittsburg Landing, Tenn. showing positions and route of the Confederate Army in its advance on Shiloh," in D. W. Reed (comp.), *The Battle of Shiloh and the Organizations Engaged* (Washington, 1909), opp. p. 66.

[6] *O. R.*, X, Pt. 1, p. 400.

[7] Jones, "Battle of Shiloh," 556.

[8] T. Harry Williams, in *P. G. T. Beauregard: Napoleon in Gray* (Baton Rouge, 1955), 126-27, 129, expressed the view, based on Special Orders No. 8 authorized by Johnston the night of Apr. 2 (*O. R.*, X, Pt. 1, pp. 392-95), that the initial intention of Johnston and Beauregard was to concentrate the army around Michie's the night of Apr. 3 and attack the morning of Apr. 4. Such intention presupposed the army being put in motion in the early forenoon of Apr. 3. Various delays necessitated a new time schedule whereby Michie's would be reached on Apr. 4, and the attack would begin on the 5th. Cleburne's movements conformed to the new schedule.

[9] J. R. M'Daniel, "A Story of Shiloh," Nashville *American*, Apr. 6, 1908, p. 4.

[10] Avery, "Patrick Ronayne Cleburne," 3.

[11] A line of battle normally consisted of troops in two ranks.

[12] S. F. Wilson, Address 1905 at unveiling of monument honoring 2nd Tennessee Regiment, in "The Confederate Monument at Shiloh," *Confederate Veteran*, XIII (1905), 439.

[13] "Echelon (A French word, meaning ladder). — A formation of troops, where battalions or brigades follow each other on separate

lines like the steps of a ladder." — Lippincott (pub.), *U. S. Infantry Tactics*, 419.

[14]A field battery usually consisted of six or four pieces of artillery, with its compliment of artillerymen, horsemen, caissons, and horses. A battery section was composed of two pieces of artillery, men, horses, and necessary equipment.

[15]*O. R.,* X, Pt. 1, p. 580.

[16]Cleburne's infantry moved to the attack "in fine order, with loud and inspiring cheers." — *Ibid.,* p. 403.

[17]*O. R.,* X, Pt. 1, pp. 580-81.

[18]J. A. Wheeler, "Cleburne's Brigade at Shiloh," *Confederate Veteran,* II (1894), 13.

[19]"Field Officers. — The colonel, lieutenant colonel, and major of a regiment are called field officers." — Lippincott (pub.), *U. S. Infantry Tactics*, 420.

[20]*O. R.,* X, Pt. 1, p. 581.

[21]Pat Henry, "Regimental Losses," *Confederate Veteran,* XXIII (1915), 521.

[22]*O. R.,* X, Pt. 1, p. 581.

[23]*Ibid.,* pp. 581-82.

[24]*Ibid.,* p. 582.

[25]*Ibid.,* Pt. 2, p. 95.

[26]*Ibid.,* Pt. 1, p. 582.

[27]T. H. Peebles to his wife, Apr. 19, 1862, in "From Participant in Battle of Shiloh," *Confederate Veteran,* XVI (1908), 281.

[28]Reed (comp.), *Battle of Shiloh,* 71; Jones, "Battle of Shiloh," 556.

[29]*O. R.,* X, Pt. 1, p. 582.

[30]Reed (comp.), *Battle of Shiloh,* 48, 49; J. A. Wheeler, "Letters from Veterans," *Confederate Veteran,* II (1894), 340; John W. Woodward, "Contributors Should be Accurate," *Ibid.,* XIX (1911), 216.

[31]Otto Eisenschiml, *The Story of Shiloh* (Chicago, 1946), 80.

[32]*O. R.,* X, Pt. 1, p. 582.

[33]Hardee, "Major General Cleburne," 643.

[34]*O. R.,* X, Pt. 1, p. 582. Corinth Road, mistakenly referred to as Bark Road in Cleburne's report, was erroneously so designated on the map used by the Confederate generals.

[35]This battery had a company of 156 members and was a part of the noted Washington Artillery of New Orleans. Throughout the war, a battalion of this artillery served in the Army of Northern Virginia; and the battery Cleburne mentioned was with the Army of the Mississippi and Army of Tennessee.

[36]*O. R.,* X, Pt. 1, pp. 582-84.

[37]W. P. Johnston, *Albert Sidney Johnston,* 607.

[38]Muster Roll of Co. C, Feb. 28 to June 30, 1862, 15th (Cleburne's —
Polk's — Josey's) Arkansas Infantry, Muster and Pay Rolls, 1861-65,
RG 109, NA; Muster roll of Yell Rifles in clipping, "Confederate
Soldiers," from unidentified Helena (Ark.) newspaper, 1903, in
Scrapbk., U. D. C., Helena.

[39]*O. R.*, X, Pt. 1, p. 570.

[40]Avery, "Patrick Ronayne Cleburnne," 3.

[41]H. J. Cheney, "Reminiscences of War Incidents," *Confederate
Veteran*, XVIII (1910), 518.

[42]Eisenschiml, *Story of Shiloh*, 46-47.

[43]For the military results which probably would have resulted from a
Confederate victory at Shiloh, see, *e. g.*, Basil W. Duke, *A History of
Morgan's Cavalry* (Reprint; Bloomington, Ind., 1960), 154-55; and
W. P. Johnston, *Albert Sidney Johnston*, 638. Furthermore, the
Union army's defeat probably would have been the end of U.S.
Grant.

[44]Cleburne to T. B. Roy, Apr. 24, 1862, in CSR (Gen. Officer),
Cleburne.

[45]Cleburne to Thomas Jordan, Apr. 23, 1862, and Ben J. Hill to
Jordan, Apr. 23, 1862, in CSR (Gen. Officer), Cleburne.

[46]Drake, "General Cleburne," 244.

[47]Blakemore Diary, Apr. 29, 1862.

[48]Cleburne to G. W. Randolph, Oct. 30, 1862, C-2327, 1862 (AIGO),
M474/14, NA; Muster Roll of Co. C, Feb. 28 to June 20, 1862, 15th
(Cleburne's — Polk's — Josey's) Arkansas Infantry, Muster and Pay
Rolls, 1861-65, RG 109, NA; Cleburne to Hardee, May 3, 1862, in
CSR (Gen. Officer), Cleburne.

[49]*O. R.*, LII, Pt. 2, pp. 309-10.

[50]Hardee to Mrs. Shover, May 7, 1862, in Hardee Correspondence,
Library of Congress.

[51]*O. R.*, X, Pt. 1, pp. 714-15; "News of Bygone Days," (Memphis)
Commercial Appeal, May 4, 1937, p. 6.

[52]*O. R.*, X, Pt. 2, p. 488; Blakemore Diary, May 6, 1862.

[53]Cleburne to Hardee, May 6, 1862, in CSR (Gen. Officer), Cleburne.

[54]*O. R.*, X, Pt. 2, pp. 488, 497; "Headquarters of Confederate Generals
Stationed in Corinth during 1862," compiled about 1920 by Corinth
Chapter, United Daughters of the Confederacy, with assistance of
veterans in the vicinity (MS in possession of Mrs. Fred E. Rogers,
Corinth, former chapter president).

[55]Monroe F. Cockrell, "Outline of Address at Lake Forest Academy,
Mar. 8, 1946," 1, in *Notes and Articles by by Monroe F. Cockrell for
His Maps of the War between the States*, (Evanston, 1950), (MSS in
Library of Congress).

[56]Blakemore Diary, May 9, May 12, 1862; Hardee to Mrs. Shover, May

26, 1862, in Hardee Correspondence, Library of Congress.

[57] Record of Events, Co. D, 35th (formerly 5th) Tennessee Infantry, May and June 1862, M268/261, NA.

[58] See Atwell Thompson "Map of Territory between Corinth and Pittsburg Landing."

[59] Avery, "Patrick Ronayne Cleburne," 3.

[60] An entire division of the enemy occupied the area adjacent to the Shelton House. — *O. R.*, X, Pt. 1, pp. 722-23.

[61] *Ibid.*, LII, Pt. 1, pp. 33-36. On May 29, General Beauregard issued a general order, which was read at dress parade, commending "the distinguished conduct of Col. B. J. Hill and his regiment, the Fifth Tennessee Volunteers, in an affair with the enemy yesterday." — B. L. Ridley, "The Fifth and Sixteenth Tennessee," *Confederate Veteran*, VIII (1900), 101-02.

[62] O. T. Plummer, Address, Cleburne, Tex., about 1896, at memorial service honoring General Cleburne, quoted in undated and unidentified newspaper clipping in "Scrap Book" in Cleburne Public Library.

[63] Cleburne to Randolph, Oct. 30, 1862, C-2327 (AIGO) 1862, M474/14, NA; Record of Events, Cos. C and E, 23rd Tennessee Infantry, May and June 1862, M268/209, NA; Record of Events, Co. A, 35th (formerly 5th) Tennessee Infantry, Feb. 28 to June 30, 1862; Record of Events, Co. A, 15th (Cleburne's — Polk's — Josey's) Arkansas Infantry, Feb. 28 to June 30, 1862; *O. R.*, X, Pt. 2, pp. 558, 563-64; Hardee to Mrs. Shover, June 1, 1862, in Hardee Correspondence, Library of Congress.

[64] Drake, "General Cleburne," 244.

CHAPTER VII

KENTUCKY CAMPAIGN
(August — November 1862)

And treasured tales of victory,
 'Midst loud triumphant cheers,
Bring Richmond's name and Cleburne's fame
 Re-echoing down the years.
 ••••
Ye who'd recount of heroes dead
 Tales that inspire and thrill,
Tell of the charge Pat Cleburne led
 That day at Perryville.
 — *William Hogan, Cobh, Ireland (1965).*

Toward the end of July 1862, Braxton Bragg decided to move the major part of his army to Chattanooga, leaving Van Dorn and Price in Mississippi. Hamstrung by orders from Washington, Buell's immobile army stretched from Nashville to within thirty miles of Chattanooga. Buell was further impeded by the Confederate cavalry of Gen. Nathan B. Forrest and Col. John Morgan. Bragg planned to gain the rear of Buell and cut off his supplies. Then by joining forces with Gen. E. Kirby Smith's small army in East Tennessee, Bragg would take the offensive.

The Confederate infantry went by rail, via Mobile and Atlanta; the artillery and wagons traveled across country. Cleburne's brigade left Tupelo on July 26, and arrived in Chattanooga about August 1.[1] Bragg and Kirby Smith agreed upon a plan of cooperation. Smith's army, at Knoxville, would move against Federal Gen. George W. Morgan's force of 9,000, in Cumberland Gap, about 80 miles distant by the tortuous mountain route. For this expedition, Bragg temporarily assigned Kirby Smith a division commanded by Cleburne. The division consisted of Cleburne's brigade commanded by Col. Benjamin J. Hill and Col. Preston Smith's brigade.[2] When his wagon trains arrived, Bragg would move to Middle Tennessee to cut off Buell; and be joined by Kirby Smith if he had been successful at Cumberland Gap. By August 10 the Confederate generals contemplated the likelihood of a campaign into Kentucky rather than Middle Tennessee, and considered the advisability of Kirby Smith bypassing the Federals at Cumberland Gap and moving to Lexington.

Cleburne's division took the cars to Knoxville about August 6. This division increased Kirby Smith's army to about 20,000. At sunrise on August 14, the divisions of Cleburne and Gen. T. J. Churchill began marching to the vicinity of Cumberland Gap, with Cleburne's the vanguard. To flank Morgan and gain his rear, the troops traversed the wild, rugged Cumberland Plateau as fast as possible, by day and into night over hardly passable roads. They sometimes pulled wagons and artillery by hand over rocks and precipices. Gen. Henry Heth's division, of Kirby Smith's command, went by another route. Gen. C. L. Stevenson with 9,000 men, already a short distance south of the gap, moved to its entrance and was left by Kirby Smith to invest the Federals there. Kirby Smith with Cleburne's and Churchill's divisions reached Barboursville, Kentucky, about thirty miles north of the gap, on August 18.[3]

Capt. W. H. Kinsey, in the "Record of Events" of Co. C, 15th Arkansas, told of the march to Kentucky: "... marched by land via Big Creek Gap in Cumberland Mts, crossed the mountains at Wilsons Pass Cut off Federal communication with Cumberland Gap at Barboursville Ky Subsisted for seven days on Green Corn and Beef without any Bread."[4]

On August 21, having decided to advance into central Kentucky, Kirby Smith instructed Col. John S. Scott, commanding a cavalry force of 900, to cover the movement toward Richmond, Kentucky. Six days later, Smith with Cleburne's and Churchill's divisions (Cleburne's division leading) began forced marches along ridges and through narrow gaps in the wild mountain region.[5] Smith's army was now designated the Army of Kentucky; Cleburne's, the 4th Division.

The morning of August 29, Cleburne's men descended

the steep slope of Bighill Mountain into the blue-grass region.[6] Eight miles from the foot of the mountain, the turnpike running north by northwest led through the village of Kingston; and eight miles farther, entered Richmond. Cleburne detailed his activities during the early part of this campaign in two reports to Kirby Smith commencing with his operations on August 29:

> On the morning of the 29th ultimo I was ordered by you to advance on the Richmond road to a point where the road emerged from a gap in the hills about 5 miles from the foot of Big Hill, and to act as advance guard of the army.
> About 5 P. M. I heard cannonading in my front, and learned that Colonel Scott's cavalry were being driven in and they had already lost one of the mountain howitzers. Subsequently the cannonading ceased, and Colonel Scott, coming into camp, informed me he was encamped in the road in my front; that our whole front was well picketed; that the enemy were not advancing. Still feeling uneasy about our situation, with an unknown force of the enemy in our front, I determined, as a matter of precaution, to form line of battle facing the supposed direction of the enemy. This was not accomplished until some time after dark. I then warned commanders of regiments at the first alarm to bring their regiments to their prescribed positions on this line, and then dismissed them, retaining, however, my battery and company of sharpshooters on the line. I had scarcely dismissed them, however, before firing and yelling was heard in our front, and almost simultaneously a multitude of stragglers, consisting of part of Colonel Scott's cavalry brigade, sick men, baggage wagons, servants leading horses, came flying in in the utmost consternation, closely pursued by the whole of Colonel [Leonidas] Metcalfe's command of United States cavalry, who were firing on them and yelling as though they were all excited with liquor. I reformed my line rapidly, leaving the road clear. When within 25 steps two companies of the Forty-eighth Tennessee fired on the enemy's advance and checked it. The enemy then dismounted one regiment of cavalry and again advanced. It was very dark and they could not see my line of battle, but they kept up a continuous fire on our camp-fires, which were blazing brightly 300 yards in our rear. A few sharpshooters were now pushed forward, the enemy showing great reluctance to advance, and in spite of curses and threats, which we could plainly hear, the whole force of the enemy precipitately retreated.
> In this affair we had but one man wounded. The enemy

had several dangerously wounded. We captured 30 prisoners, 100 stand of arms, and several horses. The enemy retreated in such haste they cut the reins of their horses, which, as before stated, they had hitched for the purpose of advancing on foot, fearing it would take too much time to unhitch them. My men slept in line of battle without any supper, and at daylight [August 30] again advanced in search of the enemy.[7]

The battle of Richmond took place on August 30, 1862. Cleburne's second report to Kirby Smith set out the initial phase of the battle:

> On the night of the 29th ultimo I was informed by Colonel [W. R.] Boggs, of your staff, that you desired me to move forward with my division and the two batteries attached at daylight and attack the enemy, supposed to be immediately in my front. At daylight I commenced the movement. The Second Brigade and the battery of Captain [James P.] Douglas (commanded by Col. B. J. Hill) was in front. The First Brigade, under Acting Brig. Gen. Preston Smith, with the battery of Captain [J. M.] Martin, followed at the distance of a quarter of a mile. I sent the Buckner Guards (a company of Scott's cavalry) in front to find the enemy. Half a mile north of the village of Kingston the cavalry encountered the advance guard of the enemy and soon after discovered their line of battle about 500 or 600 yards in rear of their advance guard.[8] Going forward to reconnoiter I could distinctly see their first line facing us at right angles to the Richmond road, with one regiment to the right of the road, the others in the timber to the left. They had a battery masked near the Richmond road. I immediately placed Colonel Hill's brigade in line behind the crest of a low hill which ran parallel to and about 500 yards from the enemy's line. I placed Douglas' battery on the crest near my center. I ordered Smith's brigade to be formed in line within supporting distance; he accordingly formed his brigade in line behind the crest of a second hill in my rear. While making these dispositions the enemy, showing only one regiment, kept up a ridiculous fire on us from a little mountain howitzer which they had captured the day before from Colonel Scott.

The battle lines of the opposing forces, each about a quarter of a mile long, were in Gibbs Meadow.[9] Continuing with Cleburne's report of the battle of August 30:

> I now ordered the battery of Captain Douglas to open on what appeared to be a squad of cavalry on the Richmond road.

In a moment this squad disappeared, unmasking a battery, which opened a rapid fire. I sent out skirmishers along our front and toward our right flank, and extended my line to the left across the Richmond turnpike with a strong company of skirmishers. This company held the regiment of the enemy's infantry on the same side of the road in check during the whole of the first fight and effectually protected my left flank. Finding a good position for a second battery I sent orders to acting Brig. Gen. Preston Smith to send Martin's battery to the front. I placed it on the hill near the right of my brigade and opened on the enemy. At this juncture I received an order from you [Kirby Smith], directing me to avoid a general battle until General Churchill's division could get up. I now directed the artillery to fire very slowly and not waste a round. The battle continued a mere fight of artillery and skirmishers for over two hours, when the enemy commenced moving toward my right flank, driving back my skirmishers on that flank. I ordered a regiment of Smith's brigade (the One hundred and fifty-fourth Tennessee) to be sent forward, and placed it in line on the right of my brigade. A close fire soon commenced on the right, and became so heavy I found it necessary to sustain the right with a further re-enforcement. I detached Col. [L. E.] Polk, commanding the Thirteenth and Fifteenth Arkansas Regiments, to the support of the One hundred and fifty-fourth Tennessee. A very heavy musketry fight ensued, and learning that the enemy were still concentrating against my right, and believing that General Churchill must now be within supporting distance, I ordered Acting Brig. Gen. Preston Smith to immediately move forward the remaining three regiments of his brigade, to place them on the right of the line already engaged, and if his line overlapped that of the enemy to lap around their left flank. At this time it was evident that the enemy had staked everything on driving back or turning our right flank and that they had weakened their center to effect this object. I therefore determined the moment I could hear Smith's musketry on the enemy's left flank to move Hill's brigade rapidly on the center. With this view I galloped to the right to satisfy myself that Smith's brigade was getting into position. I found them moving into the position rapidly and in admirable order. I then moved back to give my personal attention to the advance of Hill's brigade, including the two batteries. Before I got far, however, I was adressed by Colonel Polk, who was being carried wounded to the rear. I stopped an instant to reply and while doing so received a very painful wound in the mouth, which in a few minutes deprived me of the powers of speech and rendered my further presence on the field worse than useless. I sent aides to

inform General Preston Smith of my mishap and to direct him
to take command of the division; also to inform Colonel Hill
and yourself of the situation of affairs.

"Including the batteries, I had less than 3,000 men in my
division."[10]

A Union general in the battle reported: "It was . . .
impossible, with the troops composing our lines, to stand
against the impetuosity of [the enemy's] charge." The
Federal center and right flank gave way, most of the Union
regiments fleeing through the fields to the rear. Thus, in
Cleburne's first handling of an independent command, his
tactics broke the enemy line and won the victory.[11]

Most of the Federals were farm boys from Indiana.
Although green, there was no better raw material in the
Union Army. Rested, well fed, and well armed, they fought
well until their lines gave way.

Between Gibbs Meadow and Richmond, part of the
Northern army was reinforced and made an unsuccessful
stand against the pursuing Confederates. They also made a
brief, futile stand behind fences and tombstones in a
cemetery located on a ridge near the edge of the city.

The Confederate victory was complete. Of the 7,000
Union troops engaged (including cavalry), 206 were killed,
844 were wounded, and 4,303 were captured or missing
excluding many who escaped. Also captured were 9 pieces of
artillery, 10,000 stands of small arms, and large quantities of
stores. The Confederate loss was 78 killed, 373 wounded, and
1 missing. With headquarters in Louisville, Gen. William
Nelson, commander of all Federal forces in Kentucky, rode
from Lexington to Richmond. He arrived in time to take
command of the Union forces in the final stand, replacing
Gen. Mahlon D. Manson. During the action on the 20th,
Nelson was wounded and Manson was captured.

Bellicose William Nelson, six feet two inches tall and
weighing 300 pounds, was called "Bull" by his troops. Soon
thereafter, speaking of the battle, Cleburne said, "His army
was broken up, and 'Bull' Nelson sent howling back to
Louisville with a bullet through his leg."[12]

Although Confederate sympathizers, the people in the
area opened their homes to the wounded of both armies.

Cleburne was taken from the battlefield to a farmer's home near Gibbs Meadow. Research has failed to reveal the name of the farmer who cared for the General. A bullet had entered Cleburne's left jaw, destroying two lower teeth and lodging in his mouth.[13] Despite his injury, two days later he wrote the two battle reports quoted above.

The arrival of Heth's division and a brigade from Stevenson's division between the 2nd and 6th of September increased the Confederate infantry to 11,000. John Morgan's cavalry, 1,100 strong, then assigned to the Army of Kentucky, on September 3 entered Lexington, and thus rounded out the substantial force of the Southerners in this area.

Part of the army fanned out from Lexington, recruiting troops and collecting supplies. Advance forces under Heth marched to the vicinity of Covington, and threatened Cincinnati. During the absence of its commander, Cleburne's division was divided, with part of it occupying Frankfort, the state capital, about twenty miles northwest of Lexington. Other units of his division, commanded by Heth, marched north of Lexington to Georgetown, Paris, Cynthiana, Williamstown, and Crittenden — thirty miles from Cincinnati.[14]

The 15th Arkansas and the 2nd Tennessee Regiments of Cleburne's division marched directly from Lexington to Covington. The Arkansans reached this town on the Ohio River on September 11; and the Tennesseans, the next day. Three companies from these two regiments assisted in "driving the enemy into his fortifications." Covington was the nearest the Confederates came to Cincinnati, although their cavalry entered Augusta, Kentucky, on the Ohio forty miles southeast of Covington.

Kirby Smith, who remained at Lexington, had given orders to the Confederate advance forces not to take Covington until joined by Preston Smith's brigade and the command of Gen. Humphrey Marshall. The latter was en route from West Virginia with 6,000 troops. When part of Preston Smith's brigade was within thirty miles of Covington, Kirby Smith decided that a Confederate attack was inadvisable because the Union force at Cincinnati had been increased. He instructed Heth to withdraw slowly to about twenty miles north of Lexington.

On the night of the 12th, the 15th Arkansas and the 2nd Tennessee were withdrawn. The next day, a Cincinnati newspaper reported the capture of four prisoners from the 15th Arkansas and one from the 2nd Tennessee, who "were sick, and had, in consequence, been left behind by the retreating army."[15]

2

When, on September 18, Cleburne's command of nearly 3,000 men was in the process of reuniting, Kirby Smith temporarily assigned it to Bragg's Army of the Mississippi, and gave orders for the division to march to Shelbyville, Kentucky, twenty-eight miles east of Louisville.[16] With Kirby Smith's support, Bragg planned to attack Louisville, the supply base for Buell's army, which was strategically a far greater prize and a great deal more important than was Cincinnati. Thousands of Federal recruits were pouring into Louisville, augmenting the small force occupying it. But they were hastily assembled raw levies with few experienced officers and scant artillery.

Just prior to September 25, Cleburne had recovered from his painful face wound and had rejoined his command at Frankfort.[17] A short beard concealed the scar on his cheek. He was delayed in starting to Shelbyville because of an order, later revoked, for him to go to Bloomfield. From "Hqrs Division Army of Ky, Shelbyville, Ky, 26th Sept. 1862," Cleburne reported to "General Braxton Bragg, Comg. C S forces in Ky" as follows: "I arrived here early yesterday morning with my command. Col. Scotts cavalry are several miles in my front. there is no appearance of the enemy in this neighborhood. A small train of waggons loaded with flour started from this place to Bardstown this morning."[18]

Turning from Kirby Smith's activities in Kentucky to the operations of the Army of the Mississippi: Late in August of 1862, Bragg left Chattanooga, marching north and slightly westward. Not knowing whether Bragg's destination was Nashville or Kentucky, Buell concentrated his army at Murfreesboro, and later at Nashville. Upon discerning that Bragg was headed for Kentucky, Buell started marching his troops there by the turnpike and railroad right of way from Nashville because the railroad was out of commission as far as Bowling Green.

As the race north developed, Bragg had a head start. His army of 27,000 men reached Glasgow, Kentucky, on September 13. Buell, with 35,000 troops, reached Bowling Green two days later. Bragg planned to march from Glasgow to Louisville via Bardstown. On September 15, he ordered Kirby Smith to be ready to attack Louisville on the 23rd. Hence Kirby Smith immediately ordered Cleburne's division to Shelbyville.

Later the same day Bragg learned that on September 14 a Confederate cavalry brigade, acting without orders, had been defeated when attacking a Federal garrison at Munfordville, Kentucky. The Federal force was assigned to guard the crucial position where the railroad to Louisville crossed the Green River. Deciding to avenge the defeat, Bragg diverted his army to Munfordville; and at midnight on September 16 forced the Federal garrison to surrender without a fight.

The next morning, Bragg planned to await an attack from Buell, who was some twelve miles south of Munfordville. The Confederate commander stationed his army behind a crest south of the Green River in "a position of unusual strength," thus placing his army between Buell and Louisville. Bragg's generals were jubilant because of their "good luck in getting Buell where he would be compelled to fight [them] to such a disadvantage." Further, Kirby Smith, only a hundred miles away, would be in a position to detach some 10,000 men to reinforce Bragg.[19]

Braxton Bragg's determination and confidence soon changed to vacillation and apprehension. By the night of the 17th, he made the lamentable decision to abandon his strategic position and join Kirby Smith. The troops were to march on September 19; but on the 18th, fearing an attack by Buell's army, Bragg countermanded the marching order. The night of the 18th, he became highly agitated from fear of an attack on his lines or a flank movement. No direct assault or flank move having taken place, he calmed down somewhat the next day. Early on the morning of the 20th, Bragg made the irreparable mistake of vacating his position and turning his force northeast. Marching his army to Bardstown, the Confederate commander allowed Buell to pass on to Louisville unopposed.[20]

Bragg's mishandling of this situation is explained by his basic instability. He was of superior intelligence, fifth in his class at West Point, a brave soldier in the Mexican War, a highly patriotic Confederate, and an excellent military organizer. However, "ill in body and mind," when the time came he could not face fighting a crucial battle.[21] He would avoid the engagement and escape reality until battle was forced upon him. Then he was likely to make unwise decisions to which he would stubbornly cling. In military operations, he seemed incapable of carrying through to victory.

The head of the Confederate column reached Bardstown on September 22. Five days later, continuing his puzzling behavior, Bragg left his army in Bardstown with Gen. Leonidas Polk in command and started on a "tour of inspection." The tour, via Springfield, Perryville, and Danville, brought him to Lexington on October 1.[22] There, he dramatically arranged for the installation of Richard Hawes as Confederate Provisional Governor. The ceremonies were to take place three days later at Frankfort.

Buell's army reached Louisville between September 25 and 29, Buell himself arriving the 25th. With speed and diligence, he reorganized his army by judiciously mixing raw troops with veterans and by the end of the month was ready to assume the offensive with 61,000 men.

Meanwhile, at Shelbyville, Cleburne was operating under orders from General Bragg and reporting on the situation in his front. Two of his reports were addressed to Col. George G. Garner, assistant adjutant-general, Army of the Mississippi. From "Hd Qrs Division Army of Ky.," on September 28, Cleburne wrote: "I know of no enemy beyond a few pickets between here and Louisville. Scott met three pickets between Middletown & Louisville last night. He sent a party to LaGrange & another town on the R Road 10 miles from Louisville and got two Telegraph instruments."[23] Two days later, on September 30, Cleburne wrote,

On night before last the enemy pushed forward a strong body of cavalry in this direction driving back our pickets. Col Scott advanced on them yesterday with his Brigade and after a slight skirmish in which no body was hurt he caused them to fall back following them beyond Middletown and replacing our pickets.

My chief danger here is from an approach by way of the Louisville & Lexington Rail Road. They are running cars a short distance on this road. Our pickets heard their cars during all of night before last. We have a small camp of fresh Kentucky cavalry at Christiansburg on this road. They have promised to give me early information of an approach. In addition Scotts Cavalry have taken proper precautions to protect our flanks. Should Scotts whole force be withdrawn I will be without any cavalry & will feel very uneasy here as there are several roads leading from Louisville to our rear.

Genl Smith appointed a military commission consisting of three Officers to try plunderers in this division, one of these Officers Lt Col [John A.] Butler was killed at the Battle near Richmond. I would ask that Major [R. A.] Duncan of the 13th Arkansas be ordered to fill the vacancy.

Before leaving Tupelo Genl Hardee was, endeavouring to procure a consolidation of the 13th Ark with the 15th Ark. Will you inform me if the order for this consolidation has been procured. Both together will not make over ½ a Regiment.

Is there any way by which I could get some pay for my men most of them have not been paid in nine months. Has an order been issued by the Commanding General making our money a legal tender every where within our lines?[24]

At 10 P.M., October 1, Cleburne sent the following report to "Major General L. Polk, Com'g Army Mississippi":

I have undoubted evidence that the enemy are advancing on me in very strong force [of] Infantry Cavalry & Artilery. They are advancing on the Louisville & Frankfort Pike also on two roads one north the [other] south of and both paralel to the Pike Scotts cavalry has skirmished with them all day but is forced to fall back before their rifled Artilery. they are within 5 or 6 miles of here *now* Roanscanx [Rosecrans] is said to command one of the divisions. I will be forced to leave and will carry out the instructions recd from Genl Bragg, they are to fall back on Frankfort and hold that position. This is evidently a move in force I would like to have further instructions in case of my being attacked by overwhelming numbers at Frankfort. Also what I should do with the Frankfort Artilery. Of course if the necessity is upon me before I can have further orders I will act on my own Judgement.[25]

At midnight Cleburne began to fall back to Frankfort.[26] A Cincinnati newspaper carried the following account from the Louisville *Journal* of October 4:

> It is reported says the Journal that when the rebel forces under General Claiborne, at Shelbyville, retreated in such haste from that place on Wednesday night, they gave assurances to rebel sympahizers there that they would fall back to a point fourteen miles beyond Shelbyville, and make a stand against the Federal force that was advancing upon them. Without re-enforcement General Caliborne's army of four thousand would be powerless against the army under General [J. W.] Sill which threatens him, and, from our knowledge of the situation of the rebel forces in the interior, we think it very improbable that Claiborne could hope to strengthen his command this side of the Kentucky river.[27]

Cleburne's relatives in Newport no doubt read this account with avid interest.

On October 2, Leonidas Polk learned that in addition to the Union column moving toward Frankfort, the Federals were marching from Louisville in the direction of Bardstown in strong force on all roads. From Frankfort, Bragg sent Polk an order to attack the column moving toward the capital city. Polk chose not to comply with the order as it indicated that Bragg was unaware of the military situation. Instead, Polk availed himself of a measure of discretion previously given by Bragg and fell back toward Harrodsburg, thirty-two miles south of Frankfort, in the direction of Bryantsville and Camp Dick Robinson, the Confederate supply bases.

Bragg was recognized by Kirby Smith as also being in over-all command of his army, composed of Heth's and Churchill's divisions and newly-arrived Stephenson's division. On October 3, at Bragg's direction, Kirby Smith's army was concentrated at Frankfort for the gubernatorial inaugural ceremonies. On the 4th, Federal guns near Frankfort cut short the ceremonies and forced Kirby Smith to retire toward Harrodsburg.

Bragg now planned to concentrate all the Confederate

forces in Kentucky at Harrodsburg and then strike the enemy. Cleburne was ordered to move from Frankfort toward Harrodsburg in support of General Heth. Going by way of Lawrenceburg and Salvisa, he reached Harrodsburg on October 5.[28] There, the temporary division commanded by Cleburne was divided, with Preston Smith's brigade going back to B. F. Cheatham's division of the Army of the Mississippi and Cleburne resuming direct command of his old brigade. The Confederate generals were uncertain as to where Buell was directing his main attack. The Union force which had opened fire on Kirby Smith's troops during the inaugural ceremony had not pushed their attack on Frankfort. On October 5 the Confederates learned that this force was a single division of Maj. Gen. A. McDowell McCook's corps. By October 5, part of Kirby Smith's command was twelve miles southeast of Frankfort, at Versailles, and the rest, between there and Harrodsburg. Smith believed that Frankfort and also Lexington were threatened by the rest of McCook's corps, which was then in the vicinity of Taylorsville under McCook's personal command. Therefore, on October 6 he sent urgent pleas to Bragg for reinforcements, at the same time informing the Confederate commander that a heavy Federal force had shelled Frankfort.

Bragg was now firmly convinced that Buell's objectives were Frankfort and Lexington with the main attack directed against Smith's army. On October 7, the right wing of the Army of the Mississippi, directly commanded by Polk, had reached Harrodsburg; and the left wing, commanded by Hardee, was nine miles south, at Perryville. Early that morning, Bragg at Harrodsburg issued a circular outlining his revised plan — to concentrate the armies for battle at Versailles. Cheatham's division would move that night to join J. M. Withers' division of Polk's command, between Harrodsburg and Lawrenceburg; and both divisions would move on to Versailles. Hardee would follow as circumstances allowed and Kirby Smith would assemble all his forces at Versailles, including Marshall's command, which was at Lexington. News on October 7 seemed to support Bragg's conviction when a cavalry colonel reported two Union divisions, under George H. Thomas and O. M. Mitchel, were moving from Bardstown toward Lexington and a Federal column under T. L. Crittenden was moving on Frankfort. Also, Colonel Scott of the cavalry reported that the enemy had crossed the river at Frankfort with an estimated force of 20,000.[29]

However, in the forenoon and afternoon of October 7, Bragg received tow ominous dispatches from Perryville. The first was a message from Joseph Wheeler, Confederate cavalry commander, to Hardee transmitted by Hardee to Leonidas Polk, and by Polk on to Bragg. The second message, written by Hardee at 3:20 P.M., was sent directly to Bragg. Both reports were to the plain effect that "a strong force" of the enemy was moving on Hardee's position. Hardee requested Bragg "unless pressed in another directon to send forward all the reinforcements necessary, take command in person and wipe [the enemy] out."[30]

Bragg remained convinced, however, that the main advance of the Federals was toward Frankfort and Lexington and assumed that the enemy infantry near Perryville was a small portion of Buell's army which could be handled easily. Late in the afternoon of October 7, Bragg countermanded the order for Cheatham to march north and directed Polk to proceed with Cheatham's division to Hardee's support; to "give the enemy battle immediately. Rout him, and then move to our support at Versailles." Cleburne, ordered that afternoon to move to Perryville, reached there the night of October 7.[31]

The same night Bragg received a report from Kirby Smith announcing, "The enemy has made no move from Frankfort nor do I think they have crossed the river in very large force"; and that he had requested Withers and Cheatham to halt at Lawrenceburg until "the enemy's plans develop themselves." Furthermore, Bragg received word that Federal Gen. A. McDowell McCook was at Mackville, twelve miles northwest of Perryville. About midnight came another dispatch from Hardee advising Bragg not to scatter his forces, but to use his whole force in striking the enemy at Versailles or "the Army in front of me." Despite these significant messages the night of the 7th, Bragg inflexibly held to his conviction that only a fraction of Buell's army was near

Perryville, and that "the great battle of Kentucky" would be in the Varsailles area.[32]

The next day, October 8, the battle of Perryville took place, with the main fighting occurring northwest of the village. When Bragg reached the battlefield about 9:30 A.M., Polk had not made the attack ordered and explained that he had assumed the "defensive-offensive" because of the enemy's numerical superiority. By 11 A.M., 16,000 Confederates opposed a Federal force of about 27,000. But Bragg refused to accept the fact that the Confederates were confronting an army and held to his tactics planned for opposing a modest force. After adjusting the line of battle, he ordered Polk to attack; and when Polk delayed, Bragg personally put the troops in motion about 1 P.M.

General Cleburne's 2nd Brigade was in Hardee's left wing of the army, in the division of Maj. Gen. S. B. Buckner, and now consisted of the 15th and 13th Arkansas (consolidated), 5th and 2nd Tennessee, and the 5th Confederate, all, of course, infantry regiments. Cleburne was riding Dixie, a mount noted for "bravery and sagacity" on the battlefield.[33] Cleburne's official report of the battle stated: "About midday on the 8th of October, instant, my brigade was ordered to be formed in line of battle east of the Harrodsburg and Perryville road, supported by the brigade of General [St. John] Liddell. From this position we were ordered to advance [westward] across Chaplin [River] and support the brigade of Brigadier-General [Bushrod] Johnson."[34]

Northwest of Perryville is Doctor's Fork Creek, which generally flows northeasterly and into Chaplin River. But about a mile from the village, it bends and flows directly north for a half mile. For this half mile, the east bank is a gentle slope and the west bank is a rock cliff rising eighty to ninety feet above the creek bed. About the center of this half-mile stretch, through a gap in the west bank, the Mackville Pike crossed the creek. The creek was dry except for scattered pools.[35]

By 11 o'clock the morning of October 8, Union forces were posted in strength on the heights along Doctor's Fork and Chaplin River. The key of the enemy position was where the Mackville Pike crossed the creek. Along the creek's west bank, and then northwest, the enemy's lines formed an obtuse angle. South of the road was a large barn, later termed the "burnt barn." Over three-quarters of a mile west of the creek and south of the road, was the Russell house, or the "white house."

Pursuant to Bragg's order, Cheatham's division attacked the left of the Federal line. Then, on Cheatham's left Buckner threw forward his first line, Johnson's brigade. Cleburne reported, "We continued to advance, keeping within supporting distance of General Johnson's brigade until he became hotly engaged with the enemy at the point where the Mackville road [Pike] crosses [Doctor's Fork]." Sheltered by a stone fence, Cleburne's brigade awaited the order to attack. The middle of his brigade was about opposite the obtuse angle of the enemy's line.[36]

Continuing with Cleburne's report: "The enemy lined the ridges west and south of the creek. They were strongly posted behind stone walls and were keeping up a rapid fire on the brigade of General Johnson, which was trying to ascend the ridges in the face of this galling fire. We now received the order to advance quickly to his support."[37]

Cleburne led his brigade in the charge. Crossing the stone fence, his soldiers changed front to the left about twenty degrees in order to assail the south side of the Federal's key position. A captain, who participated in the charge, afterward related: "It seemed to me that there were cannons on our right, cannons on our left and cannons on our front, bearing upon that plateau as we passed over it."[38]

Another of Cleburne's captains described the charge: "Picture it in your mind, half a mile of open field, fronted by an entrenched enemy behind a breast-high rock wall, supported by a double infantry line, and numerous batteries, their beautiful new flags flying, their bands in full view playing their level loudest. . . . it was beautiful. It was only such a man as Cleburne who could inspire men to go up against such odds, and win — and he did."[39]

Crossing the Mackville Pike, the brigade moved rapidly to the bed of Doctor's Fork. In Cleburne's words: "We advanced down the open ground into the creek bottom exposed to a heavy fire of artillery and small arms. I ordered the brigade to advance in double time and we were soon in the rocky bed of the creek so immediately under the enemy that their fire passed harmlessly over us. General Johnson's brigade was still on the side of the acclivity in our front, exchanging a rapid fire with the enemy."[40] During the charge, Cleburne was painfully wounded near the ankle but remained in the battle. His prized mount, Dixie, was killed. In the rocky bed of the creek, Cleburne ordered, "On the center dress!" Officers repeated the command; and the troops with eyes on the colors, "dressed on the center" — a dress parade under fire on the battlefield.[41]

Cleburne's report continued:

> By moving the Fifteenth Arkansas Regiment a short distance farther to the right of my line, and then changing front forward on the left company, I placed this regiment against a stone wall lining the Mackville road. This movement placed the Fifteenth Arkansas on the hill side with its line at right angles to that of General Johnson and the enemy, and so situated as to give me a flank fire on the enemy's left without being myself exposed at the same time. General Buckner got a battery into such a position to the left of General Johnson's line of battle as to enfilade the stone wall from behind which the enemy were firing. About this time General Johnson's brigade had exhausted their ammunition and fell back into the bed of the creek; at the same time I moved forward and occupied the position previously occupied by his brigade. On examination I found the enemy had been driven back from the stone wall near the crest of the ridge and were now sheltering themselves behind the crest. I ordered the Fifteenth Arkansas back to their position on the right of my line and sent forward skirmishers to reconnoiter the enemy's line preparatory to an advance.
>
> In this I received great assistance from Captain [George] Dixon, of the Fifteenth Arkansas. He advanced alone to within thirty steps of the enemy's line, and gave me much information and made some useful suggestions which were afterward turned to good account. (Whether as private or captain I have found this soldier on every battle-field I have engaged in since the war began, skillfully leading the van. I recommend him to the special notice of the general commanding.) I now advanced in line of battle, my skirmishers ten paces in front of the line and carrying the battle-flags of the regiments. As we ascended the hill we were fired into by our own artillery in the rear. Several of our men were killed and wounded, and we had to

fall back. I sent an aide to stop this battery. I can only account for this blunder from the fact that most of our men had on blue Federal pants. We again advanced in the same order. The moment our flags, carried by the line of skirmishers, appeared above the crest of the hill, the enemy, supposing our line of battle was in view, emptied their guns at the line of skirmishers. Before they could reload our true line of battle was upon them; they instantly broke and fled, exposed to a deadly fire. Their brigade commander, Colonel [William H.] Lytle, rallied about 100, but they were routed in a moment with heavy loss.[42]

During Johnson's attack the large barn, filled with hay, had caught fire and burned. General Liddell, whose brigade was held in reserve, recorded: "From my stand point on the ridge, I saw Genl Cleburne's Brigade assault and carry the 'burnt barn,' and then hold the place against the repeated attacks of fresh troops thrown against them." At the burnt barn, Cleburne was wounded in the body and again dismounted; but continued in command until the close of the battle. After crossing back over the Mackville Pike, Cleburne's men fell upon the rear of Lytle's lines and occupied the north sector of the key position; from here they drove the Federals from the heights.[43]

Cleburne stated that his brigade, then moving westward, "continued to advance through a corn-field, [but] became so scattered in the pursuit" that he found it necessary to halt the brigade and reform the line of battle. "This I did," he reported, "my left resting on the Mackville road, my line at right angles to this road [and] I again advanced until within seventy-five yards of the position known as the white house, where a fresh line of the enemy were strongly posted, flanked by artillery."[44]

This advance by Cleburne's brigade, as viewed by the commander of the opposing Federal division, Gen. Lovell H. Rousseau, was thus described:

> . . . I saw a heavy force of the enemy advancing upon our right, the same that had turned Lytle's right flank. It was moving steadily up, in full view of where [Federal] General [C. C.] Gilbert's army corps had been during the day, the left flank of which was not more than 400 yards from it. . . .
> I then rode up to [Cyrus O.] Loomis' battery and directed

him to open upon the enemy. .... He at once opened fire with alacrity and with fearful effect upon the ranks of the enemy. It was admirably done; but the enemy moved straight ahead, his ranks now raked by the battery and terribly thinned by the musketry of the Seventeenth [Lytle's] Brigade, but he scarcely faltered; and finally hearing that re-enforcements were approaching, the brigade was ordered to retire and give place to them, ...45

Returning to Cleburne's account of the action at Perryville:

At this juncture I had no artillery and no supporting force upon my left. I sent Captain [Charles H.] Carlton, commanding a few sharpshooters, to watch my left. A large regiment posted in the valley to my right gave way, and most of them, in spite of my entreaties, fled to the rear, leaving my small brigade of not over 800 men in the center of the battle, unsupported on either flank. A furious cannonade between our own artillery, posted on the hill we first carried on the right of the Mackville road, and the enemy's artillery, posted on the right of the white house before mentioned, was carried on [over] our own line. This, together with the fact that [we] were almost out of ammunition, prevented us from advancing farther. We held the position we had taken until night closed in, when the enemy, flanked and surprised by Brigadier-General Liddell's brigade, retired altogether from this part of the field.46

So pleased was Cleburne with the manful defense made by his sharpshooters on the exposed left flank that in approbation he addressed them as "boys," much to their gratification.47 On Buckner's right, Cheatham's division and other troops nearer had driven the enemy back nearly a mile. On Buckner's left, the Confederates had contained the Federals.

Those Confederates who had advanced lit bivouac fires on the ground they had won, confidently expecting to resume the battle the next morning. To their amazement and bitter disappointment, however, between 9 P.M. and midnight, all Confederate brigades received orders to retire from the field. Cleburne's report concluded:

I then collected my wounded and 375 stand of small-arms, and with the permission of Major-General Polk returned to my camp on the Harrodsburg road. Colonel Polk, of the Fifteenth Arkansas Regiment, displayed his usual judgment and gallantry on this occasion. The conduct of both these officers deserves special mention. Lieutenant Seay, of my staff, was shot dead at my side. In him the country has lost one of her most gallant and useful officers.[48] Captain Carlton, commanding the brigade sharpshooters, distingished himself for coolness and bravery.[49]

About 6 P.M., a force of the enemy had been discovered passing to the left rear of Bragg's lines, which was determined to be an entire Federal corps that had not been engaged in the battle. Now it was apparent that the Federal objective had not been Frankfort and Lexington; that the Union troops near Frankfort were only a small part of the Federal army, employed as a feint; and that Buell's main army was at Perryville. If Bragg's small army remained at Perryville, it would be surrounded the next morning.

Informed at headquarters of the situation, Bragg at first could not believe it was true. When realization came, he paced the floor in anguish, wringing his hands; and finally, on the advice of Leonidas Polk and Hardee, issued orders for the withdrawal of the army to Harrodsburg. He sent instructions to Kirby Smith to form a junction with him at that town and had his army moved there the next morning.[50] Cleburne, suffering from his wounds, no doubt rode in an ambulance during the withdrawal.

Kirby Smith reached Harrodsburg on October 10. Thus, the armies of Smith and Bragg were united for the first time, except for some of the latter's troops who had marched to the Confederate supply base Camp Dick Robinson, twelve miles to the southeast.

Buell's army was reported to be advancing from Perryville. Intending to engage the Federals, Bragg and Smith placed their forces in an advantageous position two miles south of Harrodsburg and awaited the Federal assault. The Confederate troops exulted at the prospect of a decisive battle. At first Bragg appeared confident and determined; but later in the day and that night exhibited vacillations which to

Leonidas Polk, Hardee, and Kirby Smith, were "appalling."[51] At dawn Bragg withdrew toward Camp Dick Robinson.

On October 11, the entire Confederate force was concentrated in Camp Dick Robinson, at the junction of the Kentucky and Dicks Rivers, a position difficult to assail. With the additional troops under Stevenson and Marshall, Bragg had about 45,000 effectives — a fine army of combat veterans. On the 12th Bragg called a council of some of his generals (Cleburne not included), to present the question whether the army should fight or evacuate Kentucky. Bragg advocated evacuation, assigning as reasons: the Confederates were outnumbered and far removed from their base; the enemy was near his base and drawing ample supplies of men and subsistence; Kentucky having furnished only a few recruits, the prime object of the campaign had failed; the fate of the Confederacy should not be risked upon an unequal engagement with the enemy, or by the dangers of delay; to wait until the enemy could get in rear of the army, or until the autumn rains made the roads impassable, would be disastrous; reports were that Van Dorn and Price, to whom the Confederates were looking for the defense of Mississippi and Tennessee, had been defeated at Corinth. All but Kirby Smith and Marshall approved of a retreat. Col. Thomas Claiborne, aide to General Buckner, quoted Buckner as saying, immediately after the conference, and Hardee concurring, "The army [*i.e.*, the generals] had lost confidence in Gen'l. Bragg and there was left no other course to pursue [except retreat]."[52]

3

On October 13, the Confederates began moving toward East Tennessee, Bragg's army via the village of Crab Orchard; and Kirby Smith's, via Bighill Mountain. Cleburne's division was with Bragg. Two captains in the 15th Arkansas recorded in their company records, that they had "started on that inglorious retreat."[53]

Kirby Smith's army on October 15, pressed in the rear by pursuing Federals, approached Bighill Mountain, towering 625 feet. For about a mile a dirt road ran straight up the side of the mountain to the top. Thick sandstone ledges made the steep road almost impassable. The Confederate infantry was obstructed by seven miles of wagons and was unable to pass over the mountain. The wagons were the trains of both Kirby Smith's and Bragg's army, the latter having mistaken their way. Twenty thousand rifles which the Confederates had taken to Kentucky to arm volunteers they had hoped to recruit were being carried back. Other wagons contained 17,000 rifles and some two million cartridges which had been captured at Richmond and Perryville. There were also provisions and supplies which had been procured in Kentucky, as well as several hundred wagons and numerous teams that had been captured from the Federals.

Faced with the necessity of saving his troops, General Smith had almost despaired of saving any of the trains. "Park the wagons off of the road," he ordered, "ready for burning, then move forward those which contain commissary and quartermasters' stores, but keep the road open for my troops." From Heth's division, 1,500 men were detailed to try to move the wagons.

Cleburne appeared, still off duty because of his wounds, and urged that the trains not be burned. Volunteering to take charge of moving them, he requested and was granted unlimited authority. He organized the 1,500 troops into fatigue parties, infusing into them some of "his wonderful energy." He stationed guards along the road to arrest the many stragglers and press them into service. Other officers and soldiers passing by were also put to work. Serg. B. J. Semmes of the 154th Tennessee came along on horseback. Unable to use both stirrups because of a wounded leg, he was riding "lady-fashion." Cleburne ordered Semmes to dismount and go to work. Semmes replied if the General would help him down from the saddle he would try. Grasping the situation, Cleburne laughingly said, "Madame, ride on."

From the base of the mountain to the summit, soldiers lined the road on both sides. The multi-teams struggled up the steep road, with the troops lifting and pushing the wagons over the roughest spots. "All day, and throughout the night and until noon the next day, the trains, in an unbroken stream," poured over the mountain. The small arms, saved by Cleburne, were of utmost value to the Confederacy; and without the provisions the armies could not have made the long march through the rugged, sterile country.[54]

At London, Kentucky, the Union pursuit ceased. Bragg's and Kirby Smith's armies reuniting at that point, struggled on to Knoxville, via Cumberland Gap. "After a hard and wearisome march," Cleburne's brigade reached Knoxville, in scattered units, between the 20th and 26th of October and encamped. At Knoxville the General, now recovered from his wounds, resumed command of his unit.[55]

While at Knoxville, Cleburne wrote a letter to Secretary of War Randolph recommending the promotion of Lucius Polk, colonel of the 15th Arkansas, to the rank of Brigadier General. The letter described qualities possessed by Polk which Cleburne considered of primary importance in a general officer. After outlining Polk's skill, bravery, and leadership demonstrated in the field, Cleburne concluded: "I believe him to possess the requisite judgement, knowledge of the military art, and knowledge of human nature, to prepare a Brigade for action and command it in battle."[56]

About this time young Christopher Cleburne came to Tennessee to join his brother in fighting for the Confederacy. The General explained to Chris that he could give him a position on his staff, but suggested that he enlist as a private and win promotion on his own. He advised his young brother to join Morgan's cavalry and bought him a fine horse. Morgan was near Gallatin, Tennessee, having traversed Kentucky and made daring raids on the Federal rear. On November 15, at Alexandria, Tennessee, Chris Cleburne joined Morgan's 2nd Kentucky Cavalry, as a private in Co. I.[57]

Beginning about November 1, Cleburne's brigade traveled by train from Knoxville to Estill Springs, Tennessee, a settlement on the Elk River fifty miles northwest of Chattanooga. Company records of the 15th Arkansas show that it entrained on November 4, and after stopping one night at Chattanooga and two days at Bridgeport, Alabama, arrived at Estill Springs on November 8. The other regiments under Cleburne, using the same route, reached the destination within a few days of such time. Cleburne's entire brigade camped at Estill Springs.[58]

Cleburne was dissillusioned by the Kentucky campaign.

He was keenly disappointed that the Confederate command had not capitalized on the victory at Richmond; that the achievements of the Confederates at Perryville had been dissipated; and that instead of destroying Buell's army at Harrodsburg they had evacuated Kentucky. He felt that Bragg's want of generalship was responsible for the failure to achieve the momentous results which the auspicious start of the campaign presaged.

Sixteen months later a resolution was adopted by the Confederate Congress tendering thanks to Gens. Kirby Smith, Cleburne, and Churchill and Col. Preston Smith for the victory in the battle of Richmond; and for "planting the Confederate flag upon the capitol of Kentucky, and upon the shores of the Ohio River, in front of the great city of Cincinnati."[59]

NOTES

CHAPTER VII

[1] Record of Events, Co. C, 15th (Cleburne's — Polk's — Josey's) Arkansas Infantry, July and Aug. 1862. From Mobile to Montgomery, Ala., the troops moved by both rail and river.

[2] *O.R.*, XVI, Pt. 2, pp. 744-45, 753-54.

[3] Kirby Smith to his wife, Aug. 19, Aug. 20, Aug. 21, and Aug. 23, 1862, in Edmund Kirby Smith Papers, Uni. N.C.

[4] Record of Events, Co. C, 15th (Cleburne's — Polk's — Josey's) Arkansas Infantry, July and Aug. 1862.

[5] Kirby Smith, "Kentucky Campaign" (Typescript in Edmund Kirby Smith Papers), 6-7.

[6] *O.R.*, XVI, Pt. 1, p. 933.

[7] *Ibid.*, p. 944.

[8] Reconstructing the location of the Federal line of battle from examination of the terrain in light of Cleburne's report, this line appears to have been about one and two-fifths miles from the center of Kingston.

[9] Miss Emma Watts, Richmond, Ky., conversation with authors, Nov. 16, 1967.

[10] *O. R.*, XVI, Pt. 1, pp. 945-46.

[11] *Ibid.*, p. 920. See also: *O.R.*, XVI, Pt. 1, p. 932; Hardee, "Major General Cleburne," 643.

[12] Buck, *Cleburne,* 108.

[13] Miss Watts, conversation with authors, Nov. 16, 1967; Buck, *Cleburne*, 107, 110; Nash, *Gen. Pat Cleburne*, 202; Harrell, Arkansas," 338. A Confederate veteran told that upon receiving the wound, Cleburne "jest spit the bullet out an' kept a-fighting." — George M. Moreland, "Pat Cleburne," Memphis *Commercial Appeal*, Feb. 6, 1927, Sec. V, p. 12.

[14] Record of Events, Co. E, 47th Tennessee Infantry, Sept. and Oct. 1862, M268/308, NA; Record of Events, Co. A, 13th Tennessee Infantry, May 8, 1863, M268-169, NA; Record of Events, Co. A, 2nd (Robison's) Tennessee Infantry, Sept. and Oct. 1862, M268/114, NA.

[15] Record of Events, Cos. C and H, 15th (Cleburne's — Polk's — Josey's) Arkansas Infantry, Sept. and Oct. 1862; Record of Events, Co. A, 2nd (Robinson's) Tennessee Infantry, Sept. and Oct. 1862; Cincinnati *Daily Commercial*, Sept. 13, 1862, p. 3. The newspaper listed the prisoners as Privs. F. E. Bridges and Crawford Montgomery, Co. A, and Privs. John Haney and G. W. Seaburn, Co. F, 15th

Arkansas; and Priv. Curry Hoover, Co. A, 2nd Tennessee.

[16]*O.R.*, XVI, Pt. 2, pp. 844, 866.

[17]*Ibid.*, pp. 874-75.

[18]Cleburne, Report of Military Operations, Sept. 26, 1862 (MS in William P. Palmer Collection, The Western Reserve Historical Society, Cleveland, hereinafter cited as West. Res. Hist. Soc.). An advance regiment had arrived at Shelbyville on Sept. 22. — Record of Events, Co. A, 2nd (Robison's) Tennessee Infantry, Sept. and Oct. 1862.

[19]*O.R.*, XVI, Pt. 1, p.1090; J. Stoddard Johnston, "Bragg's Kentucky Campaign" (Typescript, Jan. 1863, in Josiah Stoddard Johnston Papers, The Filson Club, Inc., Louisville), 4; Don Carlos Buell, "East Tennessee and the Campaign of Perryville," in Robert U. Johnson and Clarence O. Buel (eds.), *Battles and Leaders of the Civil War* (New York, 1887), III, 42; Henry, *Confederacy*, 195, 196; Duke, *Reminiscences*, 307-09; Joseph Wheeler, "Bragg's Invasion of Kentucky," in *Battles and Leaders*, III, 10.

[20]Don C. Seitz, *Braxton Bragg: General of the Confederacy* (Columbia, S. C., 1924), 178; *O.R.*, XVI, Pt. 2, pp. 848-49; L. Polk to N. B. Forrest, Sept. 19 (1:30 A.M.), 1862, Ch. II, Vol. 13, RG 109, NA; *Diary of Brigadier-General Marcus J. Wright, C.S.A., April 23, 1861 – February 26, 1863* (n.p., n.d.), 6, entries Sept. 17, Sept. 18, Sept. 19, 1862.

Buell had determined to attack Bragg's position upon the arrival of a division from Nashville, which reached him on the 20th. In his report, Bragg said that he withdrew because (1) he was reduced to three days' rations; and (2) Buell, by-passing him on the west, could take a circuitous route to Louisville. — *O.R.*, XVI, Pt. 1, p. 1090. Neither reason is valid. As to the first, the region in the immediate vicinity of Bragg's army could have provided at least a few days' subsistence. — Duke, *Reminiscences*, 315-16. Furthermore, Bragg had ordered Kirby Smith to send him fifty wagons of supplies from Danville. — *O.R.*, XVI, Pt. 2, p. 850. As to Bragg's second reason, had Buell taken the circuitous route, Bragg could easily have beaten him to Louisville, or could have assailed him while in motion.

[21]Clifford Dowdey, *The Land They Fought For* (Garden City, N.Y., 1955), 227-28; Mary Johnston, *Cease Firing* (Boston, 1912), 225; Arndt M. Stickles, *Simon Bolivar Buckner: Borderland Knight* (Chapel Hill, 1940), 236; James L. Morrison, Jr. (ed.), "The Memoirs of Henry Heth," *Civil War History*, VIII (1962), 23-24; D. W. Yandell to William Preston Johnston, Nov. 8, 1862, in Mrs. Mason Barret Collection of Albert Sidney and William Preston Johnston Papers, Tulane University Library.

[22]*O.R.*, XVI, Pt. 1, p. 1087; Duke, *Reminiscences*, 319.

[23]Cleburne, Report of Military Operations, Sept. 28, 1862 (MS in Hist. Soc. Pa.).

[24]Cleburne, Report of Military Operations, Sept. 30, 1862 (MS in Miscellaneous Papers of Officers, RG 109, NA).

[25]Cleburne, Report of Military Operations, Oct. 1, 1862 (MS in Braxton Bragg Papers, West. Res. Hist. Soc.).

[26]*O.R.*, XVI, Pt. 2, pp. 898, 901; Record of Events, Co. E, 15th (Cleburne's — Polk's — Josey's) Arkansas Infantry, Sept. and Oct. 1862.

[27]Cincinnati *Daily Gazette*, Oct. 6, 1862, p. 2.

[28]*O.R.*, XVI, Pt. 2, p. 917; Record of Events, Co. E, 47th Tennessee Infantry, Sept. and Oct. 1862; Record of Events, Co. C, 15th (Cleburne's — Polk's — Josey's) Arkansas Infantry, Sept. and Oct. 1862.

[29]Thomas Lawrence Connelly, *Army of the Heartland: The Army of Tennessee, 1861-1862* (Baton Rouge, 1967), 254-58.

[30]Joseph Wheeler to Roy (MS in Bragg Papers, West. Res. Hist. Soc.), Oct. 7, 1862, 8 A.M., with endorsement, Hardee to Polk, 9:30 A.M.; Hardee to Braxton Bragg (MS, *ibid.*), Oct. 7, 1862, 3:20 P.M.; George William Brent Diary, Oct. 1, 1862 — Dec. 2, 1863 (MS, *ibid.*), Oct. 7, 1862. Colonel Brent was assistant adjutant-general to Bragg, and at intervals acting chief of staff.

[31]*O.R.*, XVI, Pt. 1, p. 1096; Record of Events, Co. A, 2nd (Robison's) Tennessee Infantry, Sept. and Oct. 1862.

[32]*O.R.*, XVI, Pt. 2, p. 920; Connelly, *Army of the Heartland*, 259; Hardee to Bragg (MS in Bragg Papers, West. Res. Hist. Soc.), Oct. 7, 1862, 7:30 P.M.; W. K. Beard to Bragg, Apr. 24, 1863, *ibid.*; J. Stoddard Johnston, "Memoranda of Facts Relating to General Bragg's Kentucky Campaign" (Typescript, Jan. 8, 1863, in Josiah Stoddard Johnston Papers), 4. Lieutenant Colonel Johnston was a volunteer aide-de-camp on Bragg's staff. Lieutenant Colonel Beard's letter inferred that after receipt of Hardee's letter the night of Oct. 7, 1862, Bragg believed that the major battle would be at Perryville. This inference is contradicted by (1) Johnston's "Memoranda of Facts," *supra*; (2) Bragg's failure to order any of the forces under Kirby Smith to Perryville after receipt of the letter; and (3) Bragg's deliberately attacking the enemy the next day at Perryville with a fraction of his army.

[33]Francis Trevelyn Miller, (ed.), *The Photographic History of the Civil War* (New York, 1912), IV, 318; A. H. Brown, "Reminscences of a Private Soldier," *Confederate Veteran*, XVII (1909), 449. The 5th Confederate Regiment was more particularly designated as the 5th Confederate Infantry or the 5th Confederate Regiment, Tennessee Infantry. — Records, RG 109, NA.

[34]*O.R.*, LII, Pt. 1, p. 51.

[35]*Ibid.*, XVI, Pt. 1, p. 1120; S. B. Buckner, "Report of the Battle of Perryville," dated Nov. 6, 1862 (MS in Henry E. Huntington Library and Art Gallery, hereinafter cited as Huntington Library), 5.

[36]*O.R.*, LII, Pt. 1, p. 51; Plummer, Address; Buckner, "Perryville," 5.

[37]*O. R.*, LII, Pt. 1, p. 51.

[38]Hardee, "Major General Cleburne," 644; Plummer, Address; *cf.* Buckner, "Perryville," 5.

[39]W. E. Yeatman, Address by, given at dinner for Confederate veterans sponsored by Knoxville Chapter, United Daughters of the Confederacy, Knoxville (Tenn.) *Sentinel*, date not shown, quoted in undated clipping from Helena (Ark.) *World*, in Scrapbk., U.D.C., Helena.

[40]*O.R.*, LII, Pt. 1, p. 51.

[41]Buckner, "Perryville," 10; Avery, "Patrick Ronayne Cleburne," 3; Irving Buck to his sister Lucie, Feb. 8, 1863 (Microfilm copy in Irving A. Buck Papers, Uni. N.C.); Buck, *Cleburne*, 114; Miller (ed.), *Photographic History*, IV, 318; Plummer, Address.

[42]*O.R.*, LII, Pt. 1, pp. 51-52.

[43]St. John Richardson Liddell, "Record of the Civil War" (MS in Govan Papers), 78, 85; Buckner, "Perryville," 10; Irving Buck to his sister Lucie, Feb. 8, 1863, microfilm copy in Buck Papers; *O.R.*, XVI, Pt. 1, p. 1047.

[44]*O.R.*, LII, Pt. 1, p. 52.

[45]*Ibid.*, XVI, Pt. 1, p. 1047.

[46]*Ibid.*, LII, Pt. 1, p. 52.

[47]Drake, "General Cleburne," 242.

[48]Research to ascertain the full name of Lieutenant Seay was unsuccessful. The research included a thorough examination of the records in National Archives Record Group 109, the Arkansas History Commission, and "Notes and Memoranda on Kentucky Campaign of 1862" in the Edmund Kirby Smith Papers, Uni. N.C.

[49]*O.R.*, LII, Pt. 1, p. 52-53. "My men seemed deeply concerned and shed tears at leaving the field, as it was generally believed by them that Bragg surely would not lose the chance of pushing the advantage gained and bring up all his force." — Liddell, "Record," 85.

[50]Thomas Claiborne, "The Campaign of 1862 into Kentucky of Gen'l Braxton Bragg" (MS in Thomas Claiborne Letters and Reminiscences, 1849-1929, Uni. N.C.), 18; William M. Polk, *Leonidas Polk: Bishop and General* (New York, 1915), II, 158-59; *O.R.*, XVI, Pt. 1, p. 1093; Brent Diary, Oct. 9, 1862.

[51]*O.R.*, XVI, Pt. 1, p. 1093; J. Stoddard Johnston, "Memoranda of Facts," 4-5; Polk, *Leonidas Polk*, II, 163; Paul F. Hammond, "Campaign of General E. Kirby Smith in Kentucky in 1862,"

S.H.S.P., X (1882), 71-73; Joseph Howard Parks, *General Edmund Kirby Smith, C.S.A.* (Baton Rouge, 1962), 237-38.

[52]Brent Diary, Oct. 11, Oct. 12, 1862; J. Stoddard Johnston, "Memoranda of Facts," 4-5; Claiborne, "Campaign of 1862," 19.

[53]Record of Events, Co. B, 15th (Cleburne's — Polk's — Josey's) Arkansas Infantry, Aug. 31 to Oct. 31, 1862; Cos. D and H, *ibid.*, Sept. and Oct. 1862.

[54]Hammond, Kirby Smith's Campaign," 75; Hardee, "Major General Cleburne," 644; Buck, *Cleburne,* 116-17; B. J. Semmes to Mrs. W. E. Moore, Apr. 30, 1891, undated clipping from unidentified Helena (Ark.) newspaper, in scrapbook made by Mrs. Naomi Moore (in Helena Library); *O.R.*, XVI, Pt. 2, pp. 943, 949.

[55]Record of Events, Cos. B and G, 15th (Cleburne's — Polk's — Josey's) Arkansas Infantry, Aug. 31 to Oct. 31, 1862; Cos. D, E, and F, *ibid.*, Sept. and Oct. 1862; Co. H, *ibid.*, Nov. and Dec. 1862; Record of Events, Cos. E and F, 2nd (Robison's) Tennessee Infantry, Sept. and Oct. 1862; *cf.*, Liddell, "Record," 85.

[56]Cleburne to Randolph, Oct. 30, 1862, C-2327 (AIGO) 1862, M474/14, NA.

[57]CSR of Christopher Cleburne, M319/10. The first entry is spelled "Claiborne."

[58]Record of Events, 47th Tennessee Infantry, Sept. and Oct. 1862; Record of Events, Cos. F and H (Cleburne's — Polk's — Josey's) Arkansas Infantry, Nov. and Dec. 1862.

[59]*O.R.*, XVI, Pt. 1, pp. 1161-62.

CHAPTER VIII

MURFREESBORO – TULLAHOMA CAMPAIGN
(December 1862 – June 1863)

As the whirlwind's path
Shows its fiercest wrath
Through the lordliest forest pines,
So the deepest wave
Of the fallen brave
Told where Cleburne crossed their lines.
— *From "Cleburne," Dublin (Ireland) Nation.*

On November 16, 1862, Cleburne's brigade began leaving Estill Springs. The men marched northwest for two days to Shelbyville, Tennessee, where they remained until December 6.[1]

The Federal army in Kentucky, marching via Bowling Green and Glasgow, returned to Middle Tennessee. It had a new commander now, Maj. Gen. W. S. Rosecrans having succeeded Buell. Rosecrans occupied Nashville, his right extending southward toward Franklin.

Bragg's army was now designated the Army of Tennessee. Kirby Smith was with Bragg only a few days in December; and of his army, only C. L. Stevenson's and J. P. McCown's divisions remained with Bragg. This loss was partially offset by the addition of a division under Gen. John C. Breckinridge.

Facing Nashville, the Army of Tennessee formed a wide arc with Murfreesboro at its center. To form part of the left wing commanded by Hardee, Cleburne's brigade marched to College Grove, twenty miles southwest of Murfreesboro. Arriving on December 7, the brigade remained in this village for three weeks. On December 12 the brigade interrupted its drilling to march twelve miles along the road to Franklin in a demonstration, and returned the next day.[2]

162

From December 12 to 14, President Davis visited the Army of Tennessee. Buckner's transfer to other duties had created a vacancy in the command of his former division. Davis now commissioned Cleburne as Major General and appointed him to fill the vacancy. Cleburne was proud of this recognition, which had been accorded him in preference to two senior brigadier generals, S. A. M. Wood and Bushrod Johnson, the latter a West Pointer. Cleburne had earned the promotion by his aggressive leadership in battle as well as by demonstrating a high order of military judgment. General Bragg had given him a strong endorsement: "Cleburne is young, ardent, exceedingly gallant, but sufficiently prudent; a fine drill officer, and has the admiration of his command as a soldier and a gentleman." Buckner also had recommended Cleburne's promotion. Hardee's recommendation, however, seems to have carried the greatest weight with the President. Hardee wrote:

> Gen Cleburne has been a Brigadier under my command for about a year, & has given unmistakable proofs of military talent of a high order. He unites the rare qualities of a strict disciplinarian, a brave and skillful leader and a popular commander.
>
> General Cleburne has distinguished himself in every engagement of the campaign. At Shiloh, his Brigade was among the first to go into action, the last to come out, and suffered more severely than any other Brigade in the Army of the Mississippi.
>
> When the army reached Chattanooga, Cleburne's & Preston Smith's Brigades were detached for duty with Maj Gen Kirby Smith; and as shown in the official report of that officer to Gen. Bragg, these two brigades, under command of Gen Cleburne, completely routed the enemy in the first action at Richmond, before the remainder of the column could be deployed into line. Gen Cleburne was wounded in this engagement. At Perryville, his Brigade pierced the Center of the Federal forces, and was the first to break their lines. Here he was again wounded.
>
> [I feel] assured that the services of this gallant officer will meet with the recognition they merit, and [am] convinced that the interest of the service would be advanced by his promotion,. . . . [3]

General Liddell related that Davis, while at Murfreesboro,

said that he had "yielded finally" to Hardee's request for Cleburne's promotion and that it reminded him of an incident at West Point. The story ran: When Davis was a cadet at West Point, "there was a famous bugler leading the band, named Willis, who in time had a pupil (Barnes or some such name), nearly *equal to himself.* Mr. Davis perceiving it, sought to compliment Willis upon the skill of his pupil. 'Yes,' said Willis deliberately, 'Yes, *Barnes* is a good bugler; Barnes *can't* be beat: — Barnes is the *best* bugler in the U.S.; *I* made Barnes.' The application was apparent and the subject of amusement. Mr. D. desired to compliment Hardee with making Cleburne, and when Hardee told the story to me, he said with a laugh, 'Yes, *I* made Cleburne.' "4

Cleburne's division consisted of his old brigade, now commanded by newly appointed Brig. Gen. Lucius E. Polk, Liddell's Arkansas brigade, Bushrod Johnson's Tennessee brigade, and S. A. M. Wood's Alabama and Mississippi brigade. Attached to the division were Calvert's Arkansas battery (commanded by Lieut. Thomas J. Key), Charles Swett's Mississippi battery (Warren Light Artillery), Putnam Darden's Mississippi battery, and Henry C. Semple's Alabama battery. Shortly after becoming Major General, Cleburne enlarged his staff. New members included Maj. Calhoun Benham and Capt. Irving A. Buck. Benham, aged thirty-nine, born in Cincinnati, had practiced law in San Francisco. He served as a volunteer aide on the staff of Albert Sidney Johnston; after the latter's death, he acted in the same capacity on Beauregard's staff; and in October 1862, was assigned to Breckinridge's staff. Buck, aged twenty-two, a native of Front Royal, Virginia, enlisted as a private in the 17th Virginia Regiment on July 25, 1861, immediately after the battle of First Manassas. He was promptly placed on detached service as a clerk at Beauregard's headquarters. In February 1862, Buck accompanied Beauregard to the western theater; and continued to serve as a clerk at headquarters during and after the battle of Shiloh. In early September, in the same capacity he went with Beauregard to Charleston, where the latter commanded the Department of South Carolina and Georgia. In late December, Buck was ordered to report for duty to Cleburne as an assistant adjutant-general.

On December 26, Rosecrans began advancing upon Bragg with an army of about 54,000 men. Bragg had about 37,000 men, his army having been weakened some days earlier when Davis instructed that Stevenson's division be sent to Vicksburg. While Confederate cavalry and infantry outposts impeded the Federal advance, Bragg formed his army for battle near Stone's River. This stream flowing to the north, was about a mile and a half west of Murfreesboro.

It is to the point to quote from Cleburne's report respecting Murfreesboro, written on January 31, 1863:

> On December 26, 1862, three brigades of my division were stationed at College Grove, near Eagleville, about 20 miles west of Murfreesborough. The Fourth Brigade, under command of Brig. Gen. S. A. M. Wood, was stationed at Triune, 4 miles north of College Grove, on the Nashville and Shelbyville turnpike.
>
> On the evening of the same day I had information that the enemy had driven back the cavalry and occupied Nolensville, in my front.
>
> During the night I received orders from General Hardee, who had gone in person to the front, to have everything in readiness for a movement and to be prepared for any emergency. I also received instructions as to the roads to be taken by my train and fighting force, respectively, in case of a retreat on Murfreesborough.
>
> Early on the morning of the 27th, I received orders from the same source to take up a position on the turnpike about 1 mile north of my encampment. While making this disposition, I received orders from General Hardee to move the three brigades with me to Murfreesborough by the routes previously decided upon; also that Wood's brigade would remain at Triune and assist General Wharton's cavalry to retard the farther advance of the enemy.
>
> . . . .
>
> I immediately moved as directed; marched all day, part of it over a miserable road and through a cold, drenching rain, and encamped after nightfall on the Salem turnpike, within 1 mile of Stone's River.[5]

A quarter of a mile from the Salem Turnpike was a large brick plantation house with a small square office about twenty-five feet to its rear. Desirous of quarters for his cold, wet, and weary General, one of Cleburne's aides approached the house. The occupant, one Dave Spence, a Yankee sympathizer, had gone North and left his wife in charge. The indignant Mrs. Spence refused to allow the General to occupy the little office building, saying that no Confederate could sleep on her premises. Hearing of the incident, Cleburne's soldiers were soon warming their feet by campfires fed by a mile of the woman's cedar-rail fence along the pike. For once Cleburne'e men were allowed to destroy private property.[6]

Cleburne's report continued:

> On the morning of the 28th, General Hardee ordered me to form line of battle north of Murfreesborough and east of Stone's River, my line to face north, its left resting on the river, its right near the Lebanon turnpike, 800 or 1,000 yards in rear of a line already occupied by Breckinridge's division.
>
> Wood's brigade, falling back slowly before General Mc-Cook's army corps, impeding his advance wherever opportunity offered, finally reached Stone's River and rejoined the division on the morning of the 29th.[7]

The fighting on the first day of "the great battle of Murfreesboro," December 31, took place west and northwest of the town. The south end of the battlefield was about a mile below the Franklin Road, which ran west. One and a half miles north of and parallel to this road, was the Wilkinson Turnpike. A mile farther north and also parallel, was a "small dirt road." The battlefield, about three miles wide, was bounded on the east by Stone's River and on the west by Overall's Creek. A short distance apart and directly northwest from Murfreesboro, ran the turnpike and railroad to Nashville.

On the 30th, the Confederate divisions of Generals McCown, J. M. Withers, and Cheatham lay in line of battle near the eastern edge of the area which would soon become the battlefield. McCown's division formed a line south of the Franklin road. Beginning at that road Withers' division extended to a point immediately north of the Nashville Turnpike and railroad, with Cheatham's division in a line behind Withers. Breckinridge's and Cleburne's divisions, north of Murfreesboro, were separated from Withers and Cheatham by Stone's River. Rosecrans concentrated his army facing the Confederate divisions, both on the west and north.

At some points the two armies were less than six hundred yards apart.

Cleburne further reported:

> I lay, inactive, in line of battle until the evening of the 30th, when I received orders to move from the right to the left of the army. Arriving at the fording place on Stone's River, I received orders to remain there until General Hardee had examined the ground and determined my position. It was dark when staff officers were sent to order me forward and show me my position. The passage of the river in the night was attended with many difficulties, and my whole division was not in position before midnight. As well as I could judge from the camp-fires, my line was a prolongation to the left of Cheatham's line, and was 400 or 500 yards in rear of McCown's division.[8]

Cleburne set up headquarters in an abandoned farmhouse and summoned his brigade commanders to a council. During the meeting the generals were briefed on the locations of the brigades in the divisions of McCown and Cheatham, which were also in Hardee's corps.

Cleburne's report continued:

> Soon after midnight I received an order from General Hardee, on which I based and issued the following circular, viz:
>
> "Generals of brigades will have their respective commands in readiness to move upon the enemy at 4:30 o'clock this morning. The several commands will fall into line without signal of bugle or drum."
>
> Before daylight I formed line, placing Polk's brigade, with Calvert's battery on the right; Johnson's brigade, with Darden's battery, in the center, and Liddell's brigade, with the Warren Light Artillery, commanded by Lieutenant [H.] Shannon, on the left. Wood's brigade I placed a short distance in rear of Polk's. This brigade had no battery in the fight, its battery (Semple's, of six Napoleon guns) having been detached the day before to support [R. W.] Hanson's brigade, of Breckinridge's division, and having remained with that brigade on the right of the army. [The line thus formed, facing west, perpendicular to the Franklin Road, extended about three-quarters of a mile south of the road.]
>
> On account of the absence on duty of my chief of artillery, I ordered my chief of ordnance (Captain [T. R.] Hotchkiss) to act as chief of artillery, and Robert [D.] Smith,

ordnance officer of Polk's brigade, to act as division ordnance officer.[9]

Both Bragg and Rosecrans had formed the same plan, to be executed the same morning — to attack with the left and drive back the enemy's right wing. The Confederates, however, advanced earlier in the cold, frosty morning. Cleburne's report continued:

It was not yet clear day when I received orders from General Hardee to advance. Swinging to the right as I moved forward, I rapidly communicated these instructions to brigade commanders, caused my division to load, and moved forward, stepping short upon the right and full upon the left, so as to swing round my left as directed. General Cheatham's left did not move forward at the same moment as my right, and my division, inclining to the left as it advanced, a gap was soon left between us, which General Hardee directed General Wood's brigade to fill. My whole division (Semple's battery excepted) was now advancing in line of battle, gradually wheeling to the right as it advanced. My left had not moved half a mile when heavy firing commenced near its front, supposed to be McCown's division engaging the enemy. A few moments more, and the enemy's skirmishers opened fire along the right and left center of my division, indicating that instead of being a second line supporting McCown's division, I was, in reality, the foremost line on this part of the field, and that McCown's line had unaccountably disappeared from my front. Skirmishers were immediately thrown forward, and I pressed on, continuing the difficult wheel under fire, through a country cut up with numerous fences and thickets. There was a great deal of crowding and improper opening out in the center of my line. Polk's and Johnson's brigades had to be moved by the flank more than once to regain their true positions. [By this time, the line faced northeastwardly.] Driving back the enemy's skirmishers in the face of a heavy fire of shot and shell, I encountered his first solid line of battle at an average distance of three-fourths of a mile from the scene of my bivouac of last night. The left of his line (opposite Wood's and Polk's brigades) stretched through a large cedar brake; the right (opposite Liddell's and Johnson's) through open ground. In many parts of the brake the enemy found natural breastworks of limestone rock. In the open ground he covered most of his line behind a string of fence. Opposite my left, where the ground was open, a second line of the enemy, supported by artillery, could be seen a short distance in rear of his first. Here was my first important fight of the day. It extended along my whole line, and was participated in by [Evander] McNair's brigade, of McCown's division, which had been placed on my left, and which a few moments before had surprised and driven the enemy from the ground over which my left had passed. The fight was short and bloody, lasting about twenty-five minutes, when the enemy gave way, both in the cedars and open ground, and fled back on his second line, which was immediately encountered in the woods, pastures, and open ground in rear of his former position. His second line soon gave way, and both went off together. My first fight may be said to have ended here. Its results were important.

The Eighth Arkansas, of Liddell's brigade, captured two stand of colors. They were handed to Colonel [John H.] Kelly on the field by Private James Riddle, of Company C, and Corpl. N. A. Horn, of Company E. In the rapid pursuit which followed, Colonel Kelly could not carry them; they were left on the field, and, I fear, appropriated by some person who had no title to them.

The Second Arkansas [Infantry], of Liddell's brigade, again encountered and defeated the Twenty-second Indiana (the same regiment it had so severely handled at the battle of Perryville), wounding and capturing its lieutenant-colonel. This brigade also captured two rifled cannon, with suitable ammunition; these Lieutenant Shannon added to his battery, and used on the enemy at subsequent periods of the battle. In Johnson's brigade, the Seventeenth Tennessee charged and captured a battery of four guns. In Wood's brigade, the Sixteenth Alabama wounded and captured the colonel and killed the lieutenant-colonel and major of the One hundred and first Ohio. My losses were very severe, especially on my left wing, where Johnson's and Liddell's brigades suffered more than in all the subsequent fighting of the day. In Johnson's brigade, Colonel [A. S.] Marks, of the Seventeenth Tennessee (one of the best officers in the division), was severely wounded. Major [H. C.] Ewin, Forty-Fourth Tennessee, was mortally wounded. Colonel [Moses] White and Lieutenant-Colonel [R. D.] Frayser, Thirty-seventh Tennessee, were wounded. Colonel [J. M.] Hughs, Twenty-fifth Tennessee, was wounded. In Polk's brigade, Majors [C. H.] Carlton and [R. A.] Duncan, Fifteenth and Thirteenth Arkansas, were wounded. In Wood's brigade, Lieutenant-Colonel [A. H.] Helvenston and Major [J. H.] McGaughy, Sixteenth Alabama, were wounded. In all, nine field officers, and a proportionate number of company officers, non-commissioned officers, and privates were killed or wounded in this fight.[10]

In single line of battle, Cleburne in his "first fight"

assaulted the corps of General McCook, the right wing of the Federal army. The Federal commander, General Rosecrans, in his official report said, ". . .fugitives and stragglers from McCook's corps began to make their appearance through the cedar-brakes in such numbers that I became satisfied that McCook's corps was routed." Lieut. Col. G. C. Kniffin, on the staff of Maj. Gen. T. L. Crittenden commanding the Federal left wing, was more descriptive: "The rear of a line of battle always presents the pitiable spectacle of a horde of skulkers, ... But the spectacle of whole regiments of soldiers flying in panic to the rear was a sight never seen by the Army of the Cumberland except on that occasion." Kniffin stated that strong reinforcements from the Federal center and right formed a new front, a half mile long. He then said, "It was a trying position to these men to stand in line while the panic-stricken soldiers of McCook's beaten regiments, flying in terror through the woods, rushed past them."[11]

Cleburne's report continued:

> My division was now engaged in a rapid, but not very orderly, pursuit of the enemy, which was continued until a fresh line of his infantry and artillery came in view. This line was drawn up on the south side of, and parallel to, the Wilkinson turnpike, its right resting in open woods, its left in open fields. It checked or pushed back portions of my command, which, in the ardor of pursuit, had advanced beyond the general line. My whole division (the right of Johnson's brigade, which had delayed to replenish its ammunition, excepted) again engaged the enemy. Advancing steadily in the face of a heavy fire of infantry and artillery, Liddell's brigade, and the Seventeenth Tennessee, of Johnson's brigade, drove back the enemy's right. Wood's and Polk's brigades encountered a more obstinate and protracted resistance to the open fields where they fought; but here, too, success again rewarded the bravery of my men. The enemy were driven across the Wilkinson pike, and took refuge in the woods and heavy cedar brake on the north side. In this fight I captured 2 hospitals, nearly 1,000 prisoners, a train of ammunition wagons, 1 piece of artillery, 3 or 4 caissons, and 2 wagons loaded with medical stores. The Federal General [J. W.] Sill was killed near one of the hospitals. The Seventeenth Tennessee, of Johnson's brigade, and the Second Arkansas, of Liddell's brigade, contend for the honor of having first

captured the hospital and killed General Sill.

My line was now far advanced beyond that of Withers and Cheatham. I began to discover from the firing that I was getting in rear of the right flank of the enemy's center. My right wing and left center were exposed to a heavy enfilading fire as they crossed the open ground near the turnpike from a powerful battery planted near the north side of the pike. Captain Hotchkiss, acting chief of artillery, placed Darden's and [J. H.] Calvert's batteries in position, and boldly attacked the Parrott and rifled artillery of the enemy. Wood's brigade having moved back to get a fresh supply of ammunition, Brigadier-General Polk moved forward, but was forced by the enfilading fire to change front forward on his first battalion, so as to place his line at right angles to the pike and facing eastwardly. This done, he advanced and attacked the supports of the battery, while Hotchkiss, though greatly overmatched in number and caliber of guns, continued to fire on them. The enemy abandoned the position, leaving several pieces of artillery. The Fifth Confederate and First Arkansas passed through and beyond these guns, and fairly deserve the honor of having captured them. Colonel [P. B.] Hawkins, of the Eleventh Kentucky, commanding a Federal brigade, was killed by the First Arkansas [Infantry] during this fight. Relieved of the enfilading fire, Brigadier-General Polk again changed front and resumed his original line of advance.

In the mean time Wood's brigade had come up and been ordered by me to the left of Polk's brigade. Johnson's brigade had also come up, and, like Polk's, had been forced by the enfilading fire to change front. I had ordered Brigadier-General Johnson to throw forward a strong company of sharpshooters and advance on the battery to Polk's assistance; but just at this time the firing ceased, and I discovered the enemy had been driven back, as before stated. I then changed the direction of Johnson's advance to correspond with Polk's, and moved his brigade on the right of Polk's, whose guns were again heard in conflict with the enemy. On examination, I found the enemy had made another stand in a heavy cedar brake north of the Wilkinson pike, and in front of where my right crossed it. He had again found natural breastworks of limestone rock, and covered most of his line behind them. He made an obstinate and destructive resistance, during which Polk's brigade suffered a severe repulse; but he was finally dislodged and driven from the cedars. Toward the close of this fight, [Preston] Smith's brigade, of Cheatham's division, under command of Colonel [A. J.] Vaughan, [Jr.,] came up on my left and rendered us material assistance.

In this fight Sergeant [John F.] Lovin, of the Third Confederate Regiment, of Wood's brigade, captured a stand of colors, which I herewith transmit. Lieut. Col. Don McGregor, of the First Arkansas, fell mortally wounded, and Major [J. T.] McReynolds, the last field officer of the Thirty-seventh Tennessee, was mortally wounded.

The commanding officers of Brigadier-General Wood's regiments again reported their ammunition expended; he moved the brigade in rear of the Wilkinson pike to procure a supply. While there information reached General Hardee that the enemy was threatening our left flank, and he ordered Wood's brigade to remain in the rear and protect the trains. This was the smallest brigade I had, numbering on the morning of the fight not over 1,100 officers and men. It was without a battery, as before explained; was on the extreme right of my line (the most exposed position) up to the time of crossing the pike, and at this time did not number 500.

The enemy was now driven out of the cedars in our front, but to the right of my division he still remained undisturbed, and as I again attempted to advance I found myself flanked on the right and again exposed to an enfilading fire. I therefore determined to advance on a line farther to the left, and where my right flank would not be so fearfully exposed. With this view, I ordered General Johnson to move his brigade to the left, where Liddell's brigade would again connect with him.

But here it would be proper to give a statement of the doings of Liddell's brigade since last mentioned as having driven back a line of the enemy on the south side of the Wilkinson pike. While my other brigades inclined to the right, as stated, Brigadier-General Liddell moved diagonally to the left for a considerable distance through open woods. He met the enemy on the far edge of these woods and drove him over the crest of the high ground beyond. Throwing forward skirmishers, it was found he had made another stand in the valley of Overall's Creek, 400 or 500 yards beyond the crest. Liddell moved his battery to the crest and drove him back until he disappeared from view behind the embankment of the Nashville railroad. From the high point where his battery now was, Liddell was in full view of the Nashville turnpike and the enemy's trains. He opened with his artillery on one portion of the train, while General [John A.] Wharton, with the cavalry, charged another. The trains disappeared in haste and confusion. At this time Liddell's brigade was the extreme left of the infantry of the army, and there was a gap of three-quarters of a mile between his right and the left of the other portion of the division. I determined to unite the division opposite this gap and advance. I ordered Johnson to move on the left of Polk's brigade, and at the same time sent orders to Brigadier-General Liddell to move his brigade by the right flank[12] until he had reconnected with Johnson's brigade.

172

While these commands were being executed, I met a brigade of McCown's division retreating in great disorder. I think this brigade must have attempted to advance through the gap in my division and been repulsed.

By moving inward and uniting in the gap mentioned, my division again advanced on a line midway between the diverging lines which the two portions had before pursued. I advanced with four brigades, disposed as follows: Polk's brigade on the right, Liddell's on the left, Smith's brigade, of Cheatham's division, the right center, Johnson's the left center. I had not moved 100 yards when Liddell's brigade became hotly engaged with a line of the enemy drawn up across a neck of woods and prolonged into the fields on each side. This, I think, was a continuation to the left of the same line which my other brigades had defeated farther to the right, or it may have been the line which had caused the repulse of McCown's division (just mentioned) and which was pursuing. However this be, Liddell met the enemy here in force and engaged in the most obstinately contested and (to the enemy) most destructive fight which had yet occurred. Not until Liddell had closed within 25 paces of him would the portion of his line in the woods give way.

Colonel Kelly, of the Eighth Arkansas, and Colonel [S. G.] Smith, of the Sixth and Seventh Arkansas, were wounded here.

Lieutenant-Colonel [John E.] Murray, of the Fifth Arkansas, bore the colors of his regiment through the hottest of the fight, and by his own bright example encouraged his men to despise danger.

J. K. Leslie, a brave and intelligent private of Company C, of this regiment, captured a beautiful stand of colors belonging to one of the enemy's regiments of regulars. This flag I also herewith transmit.

The enemy gave way and fled, leaving a large number of dead behind him. Johnson's, Smith's, and Polk's brigades moved rapidly in pursuit, obliquing to the left as they advanced. Liddell rapidly reformed his line and followed, en echelon, about 100 yards in rear of Johnson. My orders, frequently received from General Hardee during the day, being to push the enemy, and, if possible, give him no time to rally or select positions, I did not halt the division or lose any time in rectifying distances or alignments. The line had not advanced a quarter of a mile when a fresh line of the enemy was discovered in open fields. He was supported by numerous and well-served batteries. At this time I had but one battery (Liddell's). Polk's could not follow through the heavy woods and Johnson's had been ordered by General Hardee to remain in reserve near the Wilkinson pike. My line advanced steadily, pouring in a deadly fire, and drove the enemy across a small dirt road. That portion of his line opposite Johnson rallied behind a fence on the far side of the dirt road, but was driven from there also, when his whole line disappeared in the cedar woods, which here border the Nashville pike, and were close behind him. Still another line of the enemy showed itself on the edge of these cedars. A heavy fire of small-arms was immediately directed upon him. He fled back in the woods, leaving the ground in front of Johnson's brigade thickly covered with dead and wounded. Following up their success, our men gained the edge of the cedars — Johnson's brigade capturing a battery of Parrott guns — and were almost on the Nashville turnpike, in rear of the original center of Rosecrans' army, sweeping with their fire his only line of communication with Nashville; but it was now after 3 o'clock; my men had had little or no rest the night before; they had been fighting since dawn, without relief, food, or water; they were comparatively without the support of artillery, for the advance had been too rapid to enable my single battery to get in position and answer the enemy; their ammunition was again nearly exhausted, and our ordnance trains could not follow.

At this critical moment the enemy met my thinned ranks with another fresh line of battle, supported by a heavier and closer artillery fire than I had yet encountered. A report also spread, which I believe was true, that we were flanked on the right. This was more than our men could stand. Smith's brigade was driven back in great confusion. Polk's and Johnson's followed. As our broken ranks went back over the fields before the fire of this fresh line, the enemy opened fire on our right flank from several batteries which they had concentrated on an eminence near the railroad, inflicting a heavier loss on Polk's brigade than it had suffered in all the previous fighting of the day. The division was rallied on the edge of the opposite woods, about 400 yards in rear of the scene of disaster, though some of the men could not be stopped until they reached the Wilkinson pike. Liddell's brigade, en echelon on my extreme left, was not engaged in this last fight and was moved back in good order to the line where the other brigades rallied. Here I reformed my division as rapidly as possible, Polk's brigade on the right, Johnson's in the center, and Liddell's on the left. A fresh supply of ammunition was served out, and I waited in momentary expectation for an advance of the enemy in overwhelming force. He never advanced a foot, and the question presented itself, Ought I to again advance? I was now in possession of 3 miles of ground conquered from the enemy, large numbers of prisoners, cannon, and small-arms. Another repulse, and I might lose all these and cause the demoralization and destruction of my division. I immediately reported the situation to General Hardee, and was ordered by him to hold the ground I had won, rest, and reorganize my division and await further orders. Pushing my pickets well forward, I bivouacked in line of battle on the same line which the division rallied on after the repulse.[13]

Cleburne, in his report, summarized the accomplishments of his division, and the brigades of McNair and A. J. Vaughn:

> To the courage and patriotism of the officers and men, the good discipline which existed among them, and the unexpected suddenness of the attack, are alone due the success which attended my advance upon the enemy's right. With the exception of the wheel of my division, directed by General Hardee, on the morning of the great battle, there was no strategic movement attempted. It was one determined charge, sometimes checked, and even repulsed, by the enemy; sometimes delayed to procure a fresh supply of ammunition, but ever renewed and successful, until McCook's Federal corps of 18,000 men, composing the right wing of Rosecrans' army, had been swept away, and two or three lines of his successors had shared the same fate.[14]

Liddell said that in his heaviest engagement, the enemy left "a long line of dead and wounded, on the ground, they were standing when struck."[15] From the three-mile stretch of battlefield over which Cleburne's division passed, "The Enemy was driven with most prodigious loss, the ground being filled with Yankee corpses," said a young man who witnessed the battle. "Gen'l. Cleburne . . . fought, as usual, like a lion."[16]

Hardee gives these reasons, in his report, why Cleburne's success was not decisive of the battle:

> If, at the moment when the enemy were driven from the thick woods north of the Wilkinson turnpike, a fresh division could have replaced Cleburne's exhausted troops and followed up the victory, the rout of Rosecrans' army would have been complete. The interval required to collect and reform our lines, now shattered by four successive conflicts, was occupied by the enemy in planting heavy batteries and massing fresh columns of infantry to oppose our further advance. I sent for

re-enforcements. The commanding general replied he had none to give me.[17]

During the forenoon Bragg called on Breckinridge for two brigades to reinforce Hardee, but countermanded the order when Breckinridge, under misapprehension, represented that a heavy force of the enemy was advancing on him.

In Cleburne's front the Federal right wing was doubled back upon the center of the Union army. In front of Withers' and Cheatham's divisions, commanded by Leonidas Polk, the Federal right wing and part of the Union center finally were driven back; but at the salient where the Union center joined the left wing, the Federal lines remained intact.

The next morning, January 1, 1863, soon after daybreak, Cleburne rode along his lines. Then he rode beyond the Confederate pickets and within easy range of the enemy sharpshooters in order to fetch a particular type of Yankee gun. He was accompanied by his aide Captain Buck, who later said in a letter: ". . . he seemed to be perfectly cool — although the bullets were flying within a few inches of us, & did not leave until he secured the gun — as for myself I felt very uncomfortable but as a matter of course, did not leave until he did."[18]

Cleburne's own report continued:

> On the morning of January 1, there were rumors that the enemy was retreating. I was ordered by General Hardee to push forward, feel the enemy, and ascertain the true state of affairs in our front. Liddell's brigade was moved forward and to the left, and drove the enemy's skirmishers back at least a quarter of a mile, and beyond a white house used as a Federal hospital, and situated on the small dirt road near which our last fight of the day before occurred.[19]
>
> During this fight Lieutenant-Colonel [F. J.] Cameron, Sixth and Seventh Arkansas Regiment, was wounded.
>
> Liddell again swept the Nashville turnpike with his artillery, and greatly disturbed the enemy's trains, which could be seen on and near it. Receiving another message from General Hardee to the effect that he had ordered me to feel the enemy, and could not hear my guns, and at the same time receiving information from General Liddell that he was in line of battle near the hospital just mentioned, and needed immediate support on his right, I ordered General Wood to

move his brigade forward cautiously, and support Liddell on
the right, but I also informed him that the object was merely
to ascertain whether the enemy was still in force in our front,
not to bring on a general battle. Wood's brigade moved
forward, and I moved Johnson's skirmishers forward en
echelon on Wood's right flank, so as to protect him as much as
possible. Wood's brigade formed line close to the dirt road last
mentioned, and immediately became hotly engaged with a
very large force of the enemy, which advanced on him out of
the cedars where our repulse of the day before occurred. He
found that Liddell was not on his left, as expected, having
previously fallen back; he also discovered that the enemy were
flanking him on the left with another heavy force. At this time
he received an order direct from General Hardee not to bring
on a general battle. He ceased firing and fell back, leaving
several killed and wounded on the ground. Some of the men of
the Forty-fifth Mississippi Regiment had gone so far ahead
that retreat was impossible; they remained where they were,
and fell into the hands of the enemy. Wood must have lost
nearly 100 in killed, wounded, and prisoners in this fight. It
was now clear the enemy was still in force in my front, and I
so reported it.[20]

In the fight on the 31st Rosecrans was so badly whipped
that he was on the verge of retreating but finally decided to
hold on. The night of the 31st the Federals withdrew from
the salient to consolidate their lines and Leonidas Polk
occupied it the next morning. Bragg had expected Rosecrans
to retreat, and when he did not do so, Bragg was perplexed.
He was at a loss as to how to force the enemy to evacuate the
battlefield.[21]

Cleburne himself reported:

On Friday morning, January 2, I was satisfied that the
enemy was fortifying his position. On consultation with my
brigade commanders, I addressed a note to General Hardee,
which I requested him to forward to General Bragg, stating
this important fact, and that I feared, if my single, and now
reduced, line was pushed on the enemy in his fortified
position, the result would prove very disastrous, but that I
believed I could hold a defensible position against any assault
of the enemy.[22]

About noon on Friday the 2nd, Bragg concluded that to
protect Leonidas Polk from being enfiladed, an enemy force

must be dislodged from a low ridge a half mile east of the river. Accordingly he ordered Breckinridge to take the position by a vigorous attack. Breckinridge protested, pointing out that his troops would be raked by enemy fire from high ground on the west side of the river. Polk also advised Bragg against the attack, explaining that Confederate control of the hill was unessential to his protection. Hardee had no knowledge that the attack was to be made. Despite the advice of Breckinridge and Polk, Bragg failed to foresee the peril and could not be shaken from his plan. In this connection, the Cleburne report said:

> Semple's battery rejoined me on the 1st. On the 2d, Friday evening, I was ordered to send four of his guns to support an attack about to be made by Major-General Breckinridge's division. My acting chief of artillery, Captain Hotchkiss, having been twice wounded while gallantly discharging his duty, I ordered him to quit the field (which he reluctantly did) and directed Captain Semple to act as chief of artillery. Captain Semple sent four of his 12-pounders, under Lieutenant [E. J.] Fitzpatrick, to General Breckinridge's division.[23]

That afternoon at 4 o'clock Cleburne and his division heard firing from Breckinridge's attack, more than two miles away.[24] Finally, shouts of victory came from the Federals. Breckinridge's men had gained the ridge but then had been mowed down by the fire from fifty-eight pieces of Federal artillery massed on a bluff just west of the river. Eighteen hundred Confederate soldiers lay killed or wounded by the artillery barrage.

Cleburne's report concluded:

> In the desperate conflict which took place on the right that evening, [Semple's] battery bore a conspicuous part. Out of 45 men and officers, 20 were killed and wounded; among them Lieut. Joseph Pollard, who is represented as having fought most bravely, and only yielded when his leg and arm were both broken; 14 horses were killed and wounded, and one piece of artillery was lost. . . .
> About 11 o'clock that night the enemy made a reconnaissance in force in front of my division; he was driven back by my skirmishers. Immediately afterward I received orders to withdraw my pickets and resume the position held by me on

the morning of December 30, on the right of the army, in rear of Breckinridge's division. Here I remained, enduring the incessant cold rain of that night and the next day, until 11 p.m. of the 3d, when I commenced retreating on Manchester.

After the battles of Wednesday, I collected a large number of guns and sent them to General Bragg's chief of ordnance. I also got several artillery horses, with which I replaced most of the disabled horses in my batteries; also a large quantity of artillery ammunition, harness, and other articles necessary in batteries. . . .

To Brigadier-Generals Johnson, Wood, and Polk, and Colonel Vaughan, commanding Smith's brigade, of Cheatham's division, the country is indebted for their great exertions on this occasion. Brigadier-General Liddell led his brigade with a skill, courage, and devotion which, I believe, saved my left flank from being turned by the enemy.

I found the following officers of my staff very efficient in this battle; they were at their posts all the time, and discharged their difficult duties with a courage, promptness, and intelligence not often equaled, viz: Col. W. W. Kirkland, chief of staff; Maj. Calhoun Benham, assistant-inspector-general; Capt. Irving A. Buck, assistant adjutant-general; Lieuts. J. W. Jetton and J. K. Dixon (the latter was wounded); Capt. T. R. Hotchkiss (wounded); John M. Johnson, chief surgeon; Surg. J. H. Erskine, chief inspector. Dr. Johnson showed the same zeal, courage, and energy in this battle which has distinguished him on every other occasion, and made me feel that my division was very fortunate in having secured his services.

In addition to the officers and men already mentioned in my report, the following officers and men have been brought to my notice for distinguished services on the field. I hope it will be considered no disparagement of the services of other brave men of my division, some of whom laid down their lives or lost limbs on this field, if their gallant deeds have been overlooked in this report.

In Wood's brigade I must specially mention the following officers and men of the Sixteenth Alabama, viz: Col. W. B. Wood and Adjt. B. A. Wilson (wounded); Captain [William] Hodges, Company F; Lieutenant [C.] Davis, Company B; Lieutenant [G. W. W.] Jones, Company G; Lieutenant [G.] Pride, Company A; Lieutenant [C. F.] Carson, Company C, who remained fighting after he was wounded; Lieutenant [D. O.] Warren, Company F; Lieutenant [Thomas J.] Salter, Company D, who was wounded, but returned to the field the moment his wound was dressed; Sergt. Maj. Robert H. Cherry and Private Harvey G. Sargent, of Company H; Privates William Boyce and James Peeden, of Company C; Sergeant [W. D.] Bowen, Company H; Sergt. H. W. Rutland, Company A;

Privates Peter White, Company F; Robert Williams, Company
B, and H. D. Smith, Company A; the latter, wounded in both
legs, deserves promotion. In the Forty-fifth Mississippi: Lieu-
tenant-Colonel [R.] Charlton, Major [E. F.] Nunn, Adjt.
Frank Foster, jr., Sergeants [S. L.] Asberry, [W. E.] Doolittle,
[J. C. F.] Morrison, [A. J.] Vaughan, [John A.] Stewart,
Lieut. G. W. Williams, Sergeant-Major [J. M.] Kern, Corporals
[J. H.] Mallett, [J. P.] Hackler, and [Joseph D.] Read, and
Private McChadin. Corporal Read volunteered to carry the
colors after the color-bearer had been shot down. He is well
qualified as an officer, and ought to be promoted. In the
Thirty-third Alabama: Colonel [Samuel] Adams, Captains [W.
E.] Dodson and Thomas Seay (severely wounded, in advance),
Sergeant-Major [N.] Mizell (mortally wounded), Corpl. Isaac
R. Smith, Company C; Sergeant Stewart, Company H; Privates
Byrd, Company I,[25] [J. D. or John J.] Foster, Company E,
and [W. C.] Riley, Company D. In the Third Confederate:
Major [J. F.] Cameron. Wood's Sharpshooters: Captain [A.
T.] Hawkins.

Polk's Brigade. — In Fifth Confederate: Col. J. A. Smith
and Adjt. F. T. Smith. In First Arkansas: Colonel [John W.]
Colquitt, Lieut. Col. Don McGregor, Adjt. S. N. Greenwood.
Captain [William A.] Alexander, Company B (wounded);
Captain [W. H.] Scales, Company C (wounded); Captain [O.
F.] Parrish, Company D (wounded); Lieut. John E. Letson
(wounded); Corpls. Green M. McKenzie, Company A (killed);
John S. T. Hemphill, Company B (wounded); Privates G. W.
Sallee, Company C; J. C. Bogy, Company D; W. W. Chaney,
Company E; Hardee J. Bullion, Company F, and A. P. Green,
Company G (killed); James Beeson, Company H; John H.
Curd, Company I (killed); Ocean C. Choat, Company K
(killed). In Thirteenth and Fifteenth Arkansas: Capt. Thomas
H. Osborne, Companies B and H, Fifteenth Arkansas; Lieut.
John Dolan, Company A, Thirteenth Arkansas, ought to be
promoted; Color-bearer Felix E. Lipe, Thirteenth Arkansas
(wounded); First Sergt. J. M. Harkleroad, Company F,
Fifteenth Arkansas; Private William Sandford, Company E,
Thirteenth Arkansas (wounded), ought to be promoted; Lieut
William [H.] Pearce and Captain [W. H.] Kinsey, Fifteenth
Arkansas. In Fifth Tennessee: Col. B. J. Hill, well worthy of
promotion. Calvert's Battery: Joseph Lemon, color-bearer,
deserves promotion.

Liddell's Brigade. — In Second Arkansas: Lieutenants [H.
C.] Collier and [B. L.] Clegg, I fear killed; Lieutenant Colonel
[Reuben F.] Harvey; Captain [J. K.] Phillips, Company F,
ought to be promoted; Lieutenants [C. S.] Emerson, Com-
pany A; [M. D.] Brown, Company K, and [R. E.] Smith,
Company G. In Eighth Arkansas: Adjutant [H. J.] McCurdy, a

180

brave young soldier (killed); Lieutenant [S. B.] Cole, Company I; Lieut. Calvin East, Company H; Lieut. T. H. Beard, Company F (killed); Lieutenant [W. M.] Bass, Company E; Captain [W. H.] Lankford, Company A; Lieutenant [B. A.] Terrett, Company E. In Fifth Arkansas: Captain [A. B.] Washington, Company K; Privates John Atkinson, Company C; B. W. Maret, Company I, and C. Mattix, Company F. This soldier was too badly wounded to carry his gun. He asked to be allowed to carry the colors, and did so through the rest of the day. Three color-bearers had been shot down previously. In Sixth and Seventh Arkansas: Captain [J. W.] Martin, Lieutenant [J. A.] Reeves, and Captain [S. C.] Brown, ever foremost in leading their men; Captains [J. G.] Fletcher, [W. E.] Wilkerson, and [M. M.] Duffie (wounded); Sergeant-Major [W. P.] Eddins, Sergeant [A. W.] Bratton, Company H; Private [J. V.] Hulse, Company K; the color-bearer, whose name has not been furnished to me.

Johnson's Brigade. — In Twenty-fifth Tennessee: Capt. A. Green, Company G; Capt. G. H. Swope, Company H; First Lieut D. S. Walker, Company D. In Forty-fourth Tennessee: Maj. H. C. Ewin and Capt. Samuel Stiles, Company A; Adjt. R. G. Cross, Lieutenants [F. M.] Kelso, Company B; [J. W.] Dickins, Company C; [W. H.] Gibbs, Company F; A. P. Forester, Company K (wounded); Color-Sergt. M. J. Turner and Corpl. I. S. Berry, Company I (wounded); Corpl. John W. Gill, Company F (killed); Privates J. D. Stone, Company B; S. G. Heflin, Company C (killed); B. P. Hargroves, Company E (wounded); James D. Crenshaw, Company H (wounded), and J. M. Sellers, Company K. In Twenty-third Tennessee: Capt. N. R. Allen, Company E; Capt. W. H. Harder, Company G; Privates Henry C. Haynes, Company E, and Stephen M. Foster, Company C. In Seventeenth Tennessee: Adjt. James [B.] Fitzpatrick.

I wish to call particular attention to the gallant conduct of Sergt. William N. Cameron, color-bearer of Twenty-fifth Tennessee Regiment. In the last fight he advanced in front of his regiment so far that when it fell back he was unable to follow, and was captured. He tore the colors from the staff, concealed them upon his person, and made his escape from Bowling Green, bringing with him the flag of the Twenty-fifth Tennessee Regiment.

In conclusion, I would state that I carried into the fight 6,045 men, out of which I lost 2,081 killed, wounded and missing.26

From Murfreesboro, via Manchester, with rain falling "in torrents upon [them]" from midnight until morning, Cle-

burne's division marched "in fine order" back to Estill
Springs. At the end of the forty-eight mile march, they
pitched tents on January 6. Two days later the division
marched north to Tullahoma, south of Duck River and
thirty-five miles south of Murfreesboro.[27] Hardee's corps was
stationed at Tullahoma; and Polk's corps, at Shelbyville.
Rosecrans' army remained at Murfreesboro.

2

The proposal to retreat from Murfreesboro was advanced
first by Withers and Cheatham, the night of January 2, 1863,
in a joint letter to Bragg, sent through Leonidas Polk.
Withers' and Cheatham's assigned reason was that much of
the army was exhausted; but another, unstated, reason for
their proposal seems to have been that they had lost
confidence in the commanding General's ability to meet the
situation.[28] Bragg at first rejected the idea of retreat; but
upon reconsidering and thinking the enemy was receiving
large reinforcements, he decided to withdraw. Hardee and
Polk concurred.

Following the retreat from Murfreesboro, Southern newspapers renewed their attack on Bragg. Seeking the support
of his corps and division commanders, the commanding
General sent them a circular letter, dated January 11, saying:

> It has come to my knowledge that many of [the]
> accusations and insinuations are from staff officers of my
> generals, who persistently assert that the movement was made
> against the opinion and advice of their chiefs, . . . Unanimous
> as you were in council in verbally advising a retrograde
> movement, I cannot doubt that you will cheerfully attest the
> same in writing. I desire that you will consult your subordinate
> commanders and be candid with me, ...[29]

Cleburne replied to Bragg's request with a letter from
"Tullahoma, January 13th, 1863." It read as follows:

> General,
>   I have received your communication of the 11th inst. with
> enclosures, and will answer candidly as you desire.
>   I understand the retrograde movement to have been
> decided upon, and partially executed before we met in council
> on Saturday night (the 3 inst.) and the only question

presented to me, and the only question before us there, to be whether the movement should be suspended as far as practicable, for twenty four hours. To this I replied, that in my opinion it could be suspended, I offered advice on no other point.

Subsequently on learning fully the condition of Genl Polks Corps and Genl Breckinridge's Division, I felt it my duty to say to you, that in answering as I had just done, I had looked only to the condition of my own Division, that *it* had been successful in the fight, and notwithstanding its losses and weariness, was still capable of making a firm resistance, that I was also influenced by the fact that my men had had no sleep the previous night, having suffered and repelled a night attack of the enemy and immediately thereafter been moved from the extreme left to the right of the Army, which led me to fear that in case of a retreat, involving as it must the loss of another nights rest, large numbers of my men would fall out by the way, and I might in this manner lose as many as in an attack by the enemy in our then position. I further stated that in case the enemy attacked us, I believed the chances were in favor of our repulsing him, but that it might turn out otherwise, and that it was for you to decide whether our cause should be risked on a cast, the issue of which was doubtful; that I believed the final success of our cause depended in a great measure upon the safety of this Army.

I have consulted with all my Brigade Commanders at this place as you request — showing them your letter and enclosures, and they write with me in personal regard for yourself, in a high appreciation of your patriotism and gallantry and in a conviction of your great capacity for organization, but at the same time they see, with regret, and it has also met my observation, that you do not possess the confidence of the Army, in other respects, in that degree necessary to secure success.[30]

Hardee's response to Bragg's circular letter went even further, pointedly stating he had conferred with Cleburne and Breckinridge and that all three had agreed a change in the command of the army was necessary.[31] President Davis instructed Gen. Joseph E. Johnston to proceed to Bragg's headquarters in Tullahoma and decide what the best interests of the service required. After an investigation Johnston recommended that Bragg be left in command.

3

At Tullahoma, Cleburne had his men construct earthworks and fortifications, part of a system of field works around the town. He established his headquarters in a wooden structure erected by his men immediately behind the earthworks. The crude little building stood a mile north of the center of town and about fifty yards west of the railroad. During the winter lull of battle, Cleburne attended to the defense and safety of his division; insisted upon cleanliness in the camp and obedience to orders; and saw to it that the men's needs for food and medical care were met in every way possible.[32]

Because of his "conspicuous part in the battle of Murfreesboro," Cleburne was made the subject of a sketch in a Mobile paper. The sketch, written January 14, 1863, by a special army correspondent, gave this description of the General: "He is about five feet ten inches in height, well made, light complexion, a fine piercing gray eye, with a large pupil, wears a moustache and goatee, is quite prepossessing, and is remarkably quiet and modest."[33]

Cleburne's division drilled regularly, weather permitting. When snow fell the Alabama soldiers enjoyed snowball fights. At first companies of the 33rd Alabama fought each other. Then the whole regiment, with Col. Samuel Adams in command, charged other Alabama regiments.[34]

Cleburne now had some spare time for reading a favorite book of poetry and a two-volume set which he carried with him — William and Robert Chambers (eds.), *Chambers's Information for the People.* The publication contained articles on "the most important branches of science," which he enjoyed reading and discussing. In artillery and rifle fire he utilized "laws of projectiles" set out in the article on "natural philosophy." There was also a little time for recreation, as Buck spoke of the General enjoying some social life in Shelbyville, twenty-four miles northwest of Tullahoma.[35]

During the winter and spring, there were "splendid" reviews of the entire corps, in which the band of Cleburne's division no doubt participated. In the files of National Archives is a voucher, dated March 26, 1863, Tullahoma, Tennessee, in the amount of $3.75, signed by a local merchant, reading: "One and a half yards fine Domestic at $2.50 per yard. This article was purchased to repair the battle flags of Cleburnes Division." On one occasion Buck recorded, "Genl C sent me to S[helbyville] after a load of ladies . . . . I called upon several and brought them down yesterday morning, gave them a fine review, horse race and tournament, and a good dinner in the evening."[36]

Late in March, Cleburne and six other generals of the Army of Tennessee were appointed as a general court-martial to try Major General McCown on charges preferred by Bragg of, "Conduct to the prejudice of good order and military discipline." The court-martial convened at Shelbyville on March 25, found McCown guilty, and sentenced him to be suspended from rank for six months.[37]

On April 23, Hardee's corps advanced across Duck River to form the right wing of the Army of Tennessee, in the vicinity of Wartrace, twenty miles south of Murfreesboro. As usual, Cleburne's division formed the vanguard in the advance.[38] He stationed three of his brigades at Wartrace; and ordered the fourth, Liddell's, to Bell Buckle, a village five miles north of Wartrace. Through a chain of hills between Wartrace and Murfreesboro were three defiles: Liberty Gap and Bell Buckle (or Railroad) Gap, a few miles north and northwest of Bell Buckle; and Hoover's Gap, five miles east of Liberty Gap.

Cleburne made his headquarters in the home of Rice Coffee, a prominent citizen of Wartrace. This "very comfortable," spacious, two-story frame house still stands on the northwest edge of the town. General Cleburne made a lasting impression on Mr. Coffee's small son, Ison, who years later named his son Patrick Cleburne Coffee.[39]

During the two months at Wartrace, in close proximity to the enemy, Cleburne exercised "his high soldierly qualities of vigilance and activity," as described by Hardee. Benham also spoke of Cleburne's "sleepless vigilance." Cleburne labored incessantly in training his division. It was trained daily in three categories: drill, weapon maintenance, and rifle shooting. Company and regimental drills were held daily except in stormy weather and on Sundays. Morning drill began at 8 or 9 o'clock; afternoon drill, at 2 o'clock; dress parade, at sunset. There were occasional brigade drills.[40]

Once, during drill a regiment was halted at a front face. At that moment, Cleburne, who was observing, rode forward and called, "Attention, battalion! By the right of companies —" When he hesitated an instant, a company captain sprang to the front and commanded, "Company, right face!" Cleburne called out, "Hold on there, Captain, you don't know but that I was going to say by the right of companies into the moon." Amid the laughter of the troops, the General finished the order by adding, "To the rear into column!"[41]

Cleburne was more exacting of officers than of the rank and file. He generally held a company captain responsible for any mistake which marred the precision of a movement. Through respect and admiration for their General, officers and men strove to measure up to his high standards. Cleburne's division probably became the best drilled in the Army of Tennessee. The General stressed the cleaning and care of the rifle and the bayonet. The man having the cleanest gun among the detail for daily guard duty was excused from a round of duty. Likewise, at regimental guard mount the same test applied and five men would be excused.[42]

On one occasion Cleburne went to Bell Buckle for the inspection of one of Liddell's regiments. All was well as he went slowly down the line until he reached Pvt. Ben Stewart, who seldom cleaned his gun. The General took the gun, examined it closely, and handed it back. Looking the soldier in the face with reproach, he said, "I hope I do you no injustice, my man, but I don't think you have washed your face for several days." After that, Private Stewart's gun and face were always ready for inspection.[43]

The Arkansan placed great stress on instruction in rifle shooting. He secured a book on the subject used by the English Army — doubtless *Regulations for Conducting Musketry Instruction in the Army*, compiled by the School of Musketry, Hythe (London, bet. 1855 and 1860). After he mastered the text, he had Benham study it. The General then employed a method of instruction similar to that which he had used at Corinth. Under his supervision, Major Benham taught a group of line officers — one from each regiment — selected on the basis of their intelligence and skill with the rifle. When they had completed the course, they instructed the other regimental officers, who in turn instructed the men in each of the companies. In the forenoon the selected group of officers studied the parts and function of the rifle and the laws of projectiles. During part of the afternoon they were trained in estimating distances, "with human flesh and blood for markers." The rest of the day. was spent in rifle practice.[44]

Cleburne was among the first to appreciate the Whitworth rifle and made extensive use of it. Equipped with telescopic sights, it was the best long-range rifle manufactured. Made in England, each rifle, with one thousand rounds of cartridges, cost the Confederate government $1,000. When at Wartrace, Cleburne had five Whitworth rifles. In a contest among the best riflemen from the regiments in his division, the five who scored highest were chosen to use the prized weapons. The selected soldiers were detached from their regiments and organized into a special squad of Whitworth sharpshooters. One of their number was appointed Lieutenant to command. This squad was the first detachment of Whitworth sharpshooters in the Army of Tennessee.[45]

The General believed that self-respect was an essential of a good soldier. He refrained from inflicting punishment for breach of military rule which would humiliate a man, such as bucking and gagging, having to wear a barrel shirt, or carrying a fence rail or wooden pole while marching. His punishment, however, was swift and sure; and usually consisted of confinement at guard quarters while doing extra police duty, or withdrawal of privileges for a given period. In case of a serious charge, the accused was court-martialed.[46]

The spirit of Cleburne's troops was reflected in company reports. While at Tullahoma, 2nd Lieut. E. D. Lee, commanding Company K, 33rd Alabama, recorded, "We are ready to be again introduced to the friends of Southern misery who are said to be 'just over the way.' " Capt. P. C. Ewan, Company F, 15th Arkansas, reported at Wartrace, ". . .we now remain in good spirits, patiently waiting for peace or another fight & it matters but little to us which comes first — so that we are victorious." Lieut. Elias Wellborn, Company C, 15th Arkansas, wrote while at Wartrace: ". . .we are now preparing to give the Yanks another twist."[47]

Cleburne's men frequently referred to their leader as "Old Pat." The term was one of respect and affection, as in the Army of Northern Virginia, Longstreet was called "Old Pete," and Jackson was "Old Jack."[48] Some months earlier, the members of Cleburne's former regiment, the 15th Arkansas, had decided to present the General with a handsome sword as an expression of their admiration and devotion. The sword, coming through the blockade from Bermuda, arrived while Cleburne's division was in Wartrace. The fine Damascus blade was in a polished steel scabbard and a shamrock was engraved on the hilt. The belt rings and scabbard bands were of solid gold, as was the presentation plate of the scabbard. Cleburne cherished the gift and never wore it in battle, always leaving it safely in the rear.[49]

A special affinity existed between Cleburne and the 5th Confederate Regiment of his division. This regiment, except for two companies, was composed almost entirely of Irishmen from Memphis. Said Capt. C. W. Frazer, one of its officers: "The hero-worship (amounting almost to idolatry) on the one hand, and the sympathy and admiration on the other, that existed between this regiment and Cleburne was remarkable, and can only be partially accounted for by their common birthplace, their thorough devotion to the Southern cross, and the ties that bind men who have often met a common foe in the death-grapple."[50]

Cleburne's division had a distinctive battle flag which Hardee had adopted before the battle of Shiloh. Nearly all of the regiments commanded by Hardee at Shiloh were now in the Arkansan's division. Cleburne retained this flag — a blue field with a white border and a large white circle or ellipse near the center. In the circle was "the significant device of the 'crossed cannon inverted.' " On May 1, 1863, the Congress at Richmond adopted the Confederate States "National Flag"; and orders were issued at Wartrace for that flag to replace all other battle flags. When the members of Cleburne's division learned that their blue flag, carried by each regiment, was to be displaced, they strongly protested; and urgently requested that they be permitted to retain their distinctive battle flag. Their request was granted, and each regiment in the division was given a new "blue flag." Inscribed on each flag were the names of the battles in which the regiment had fought. Cleburne's was the only division in the Army of Tennessee allowed to carry into action a flag other than the national colors. "Friends and foes," said Hardee, "soon learned to watch the course of the blue flag that marked where Cleburne was in the battle."[51] Arthur Louis Peticobas, in his poem "Patrick Ronayne Cleburne," wrote:

> He led a division that proudly adored him;
> In the forefront of battle their blue flags were
> known, ...

Cleburne's friend Avery (who had risen to colonel in the cavalry) spent a day with the General at Wartrace. His description of Pat Cleburne on that occasion follows:

> He had donned better toggery than he used to wear, and I thought that in his laced uniform he looked actually handsome. The gray with its Hungarian tracery of braid on the arm became him well. Smoothly shaven, with his lithe and rather slender form, his blue eye, soft in his social moments, but flashing in fight, and the mouth so stern in battle, wreathed in friendly smiles, he was quite an attractive warrior.[52]

It was at Wartrace that Cleburne entertained the British army officer, Lt. Col. James Arthur Lyon Fremantle. On June 1, Fremantle, Cleburne, and Hardee rode to Bell Buckle for a review of Liddell's Arkansas brigade. With them were three carriages of ladies. Fremantle noted the numbers in Liddell's brigade — to which the 15th Arkansas now belonged — were much diminished through attrition. His description of the Arkansas troops ran:

> The men were good-sized, healthy, and well clothed, though without any attempt at uniformity in color or cut, but nearly all were dressed either in gray or brown coats and felt hats.
> I was told that even if a regiment was clothed in proper uniform by the government, it would become parti-colored again in a week, as the soldiers preferred wearing the coarse homespun jackets and trousers made by their mothers and

sisters at home. The generals very wisely allow them to please themselves in this respect, and insist only upon their arms and accoutrements being kept in proper order.

During Fremantle's stay at Wartrace, the Right Reverend Stephen Elliott, Episcopal Bishop of Georgia, held an "open-air preaching" in Brigadier Wood's camp. Attending the service were "Generals Bragg, Polk, Hardee, Withers, Cleburne," "endless brigadiers," and "nearly 3000 soldiers," reported the British officer.[53]

Near the first of June 1863, Federal activities indicated that Rosecrans might be preparing to advance south in Tennessee or to send a portion of his forces to Grant in Mississippi. On June 3, Bragg ordered a heavy reconnaissance by Hardee's corps in an effort to determine the enemy's intent. Cleburne, in charge of one of two columns, moved over a narrow road through the three-mile length of Hoover's Gap, and beyond to within four miles of Murfreesboro. He drove in Federal pickets; had light skirmishes with the enemy; in Buck's words, "gave them a terrible scare"; and returned to Wartrace the next day.[54]

A few days earlier, the Confederate high command had sent McCown's division and most of Breckinridge's division to Mississippi to reenforce Joseph E. Johnston, opposing Grant. To replace the latter force, a small division was organized for Hardee's corps. On June 6, A. P. Stewart was promoted to Major General and assigned to command the new division. In the reorganization, Bushrod Johnson's excellent Tennessee brigade was transferred from Cleburne to Stewart; and Cleburne acquired an excellent Texas brigade commanded by Brig. Gen. Thomas J. Churchill, including Capt. James P. Douglas' Texas battery.

4

When military operations known as the Tullahoma campaign began, Rosecrans had an army of about 60,000 men; Bragg, about 47,000, of whom nearly 14,000 were cavalry. A report by Cleburne written on August 3, 1863, commenced:

On June 24 last, I was stationed at Wartrace, Tenn., with two brigades of my division. Polk's brigade was at Tullahoma, fifteen miles south of Wartrace, and Liddell's brigade was at Bellbuckle [Bell Buckle], a village 5 miles north of Wartrace. A range of hills dividing the headwaters of Duck River from the headwaters of Stone's River separated our positions from those of the enemy. There were several gaps or good roads through these hills, two of which led directly on Liddell's position at Bellbuckle, viz, Railroad Gap, via New Fosterville,[55] and Liberty Gap. Both of these gaps Liddell was ordered to picket. The former was 4, the latter 3 miles from Bellbuckle. Two other gaps (Dismal Hollow and Hoover's) gave ingress to the country immediately on the right of Liddell's position; these were held by some cavalry of Wheeler's division.[56]

To the east, the range of hills terminates a little beyond Hoover's Gap. The narrow road through Hoover's Gap continued narrow and winding to Manchester, twenty miles southeast. West of Bell Buckle, the chain of hills begins to level off north of Shelbyville and terminates a short distance northwest of the town.

In view of the favorable terrain and wide turnpikes between Murfreesboro and Shelbyville, Bragg had expected Rosecrans' army to advance toward Shelbyville, or at least could be "drawn" near Shelbyville. Dispositions of Confederate troops had been made accordingly. The larger part of the army, the three divisions of Leonidas Polk's corps, remained at Shelbyville and constructed extensive fortifications. In Hardee's corps, Cleburne's division held Wartrace, on the railroad, and Bell Buckle and Liberty Gaps. Stewart's troops were placed at intervals over a stretch of several miles from the south end of Hoover's Gap past Fairfield, a village five miles northeast of Wartrace. Should Rosecrans' army advance to Liberty Gap, Bragg hoped to move Polk's troops from Shelbyville and strike the Federals on the flank. Should the bluecoats advance through Hoover's Gap, it is uncertain whether Bragg hoped that Polk could assail them in flank, or hoped to stop the enemy by some other means.[57]

Cleburne reported:

On the evening of June 24, I had information from the corps commander that the enemy had suddenly advanced in force simultaneously on Liberty and Hoover's Gaps and had carried both positions.

On the morning of the 25th, in pursuance of orders, I advanced Wood's brigade to Bellbuckle. I found Liddell still guarding the approaches via Liberty Gap and New Fosterville. He was holding two wooded hills a mile south of Liberty Gap. On the evening of the 25th, Liddell, supposing the enemy retiring, advanced on the gap; but after some heavy fighting, in which he inflicted a considerable loss on the enemy and suffered little himself, he fell back to his former position. I was now satisfied the enemy was still in force at Liberty Gap; that he had at least a division of infantry, besides cavalry and artillery, so I ordered up three regiments of Wood's brigade and a section of Semple's battery to Liddell's support. One regiment of Wood's and one of Liddell's brigade, with the other section of Semple's battery, were guarding the approaches via New Fosterville.

On the morning of the 26th, this section of artillery and the two regiments rejoined their brigades in front of Liberty Gap, and were replaced by a regiment of Churchill's brigade, of my division, which arrived at Bellbuckle on the morning of the 26th. The remaining two regiments of Churchill's brigade I moved up as a reserve to the force in front of Liberty Gap. The enemy kept up a constant firing all day, the 26th, and advanced twice with double lines of skirmishers. They were driven back, and at night both parties held their former positions. I had no ammunition to spare, and did not reply to the continual fire of the enemy except with five Whitworth rifles, which appeared to do good service. Mounted men were struck at distances ranging from 700 to 1,300 yards. During the day the enemy, advancing in overwhelming force through Hoover's Gap, forced back Stewart's division almost to Fairfield, thus threatening to cut me off from Wartrace.

At night I received orders to retreat on Tullahoma, via Schoefner's Bridge,[58] at daylight on the 27th, which I did without any loss, although my men were much wearied by the watching and fighting in front of the gaps, for it rained incessantly during most of the time. The men had no changes of clothing, no tents, and could not even light fires to dry themselves. Many had no shoes, and others left their shoes buried in the deep mire of the roads.

My entire loss in the several fights amounted to 121.[59]

In the fight on June 24, 1863, a Federal division of three brigades opposed Liddell's Arkansas brigade, the only part of Cleburne's division engaged. In the fight against this brigade on the afternoon of the 25th, the Federal division was reenforced by two more brigades. One of the Union generals thought they were fighting "the whole of Cleburne's division," and a Union colonel thought that the Federals were "stubbornly opposed by a much larger force than ours." Another Union colonel said, "When we were within one-half or three-fourths of a mile of the enemy, the effect of their sharpshooters was terrible." The commander of the Union division reported, "The affair at Liberty Gap will always be considered a skirmish, but few skirmishes ever equaled it in severity."[60] The Federal casualties were 267.

The fighting of the Federals at Liberty Gap was a small part of an offensive campaign Rosecrans had started on June 23. The Union General's strategy was excellent; and its execution, masterful. His forces were to advance simultaneously toward Shelbyville, Liberty Gap, and Hoover's Gap. The advance on Shelbyville was to be a feint, and Liberty Gap was merely to be seized and held. The main body of the Federal army would move through Hoover's Gap, with one corps going around the eastern end of the range of hills. From Hoover's Gap they would push on to Manchester, where all of Rosecrans' forces would be consolidated.

Bragg's belief that the battle between the two armies would be fought at Shelbyville seemed to be confirmed on the 24th. A Federal cavalry division attacked Confederate cavalry in force near Bragg's partially open flank northwest of the town. That night to the rear of their cavalry the Federals spread the countryside with campfires, convincing Bragg that heavy infantry forces were advancing on Shelbyville. By the 25th, the pressure against Shelbyville had diminished; and on the 26th Bragg thought the main attack would be through Liberty Gap. But before Polk's corps began to move to the gap for a flank attack, Bragg learned early the evening of the 26th that Rosecrans' main forces had passed through Hoover's Gap and had reached Fairfield. Realizing that his right was turned and that he must evacuate Shelbyville, Bragg ordered Polk's corps early on the 27th to begin a retreat to Tullahoma.

At Duck River, Cleburne, with one of his brigades, fell in line behind Cheatham's division as the rearguard in the retreat. Also covering the rear was Colonel Avery with his cavalry regiment and a Texas cavalry regiment. The cavalry had dismounted and were fighting "infantry fashion." Retiring slowly, Cleburne's skirmish line and Avery's troops engaged the Federals in occasional skirmishes. An order came for the cavalry to mount and ride to the flank. Avery related:

> Drawing back under hot fire, we slowly and sullenly retrograded through the infantry skirmishes [skirmishers?], with Cleburne in person commanding. A quick grasp of the hand, a hasty, but cordial, salutation, a hurried inquiry from him as to the troops in front, and a swiftly-spoken good-bye and we parted, the gallant Irishman pushing his deployed line rapidly to the front amid the whizzing bullets and occasional shell.[61]

On the 29th and 30th, Bragg's army, including Cleburne's division, remained in line of battle in entrenchments at Tullahoma. Part of Rosecrans' army took battle formation and advanced toward the Confederates — a feint to mask a flank movement through the woods in the rear of Bragg's position. Hence, the night of the 30th, Bragg was compelled to evacuate Tullahoma, Cleburne's division covering the retreat of the army.[62]

The next day, the army withdrew to the east side of the Elk River, Cleburne's division crossing at Bethpage Bridge, two miles above the railroad bridge. From the high ground his men commanded the bridge with artillery placed behind hastily constructed embrasures. Late in the afternoon, the Texas Brigade of Cleburne's division recrossed the Elk, as described in the diary of Benjamin M. Seaton, private in Company G, 10th Texas:

> we crost back again and went some 2 miles back to meet the enmy. We were drawn up in battle line some 2 or 300 yds from the Feds — the pickets soon commenced firing on them and repulsed them 3 times and drove them back. I thought we were into it then when ther balls fell close around us but they did not come and shortley after dark we fell back across the river again and cut the bridge down — we remained thar all night.[63]

Bragg, on July 10, after hours of much wavering and

indecision as to his next move and whether to fight or retreat across the Cumberland Mountains to Chattanooga, decided to retreat. During these critical hours he seemed confused and dazed.[64]

"On the morning of the 3rd," recorded the Captain of one of Cleburne's Arkansas companies, "we ascended the mountains that lay in the rout to Chattanooga, Tenn. — traveled on the top of those mountains several days." By this time the enemy was far behind and Cleburne's division was no longer serving as rearguard. After the army had camped overnight near the University of the South, at Sewanee, the march order of the day was: Hardee's corps in front with Cleburne's division leading. Positive orders were for no troops to precede that division. Early in the morning, as Cleburne marched his division into the road, he found a brigade marching in front of his lead regiment. He located the commander, whom he knew only slightly — Brig. Gen. John C. Brown of Stewart's division. In a peremptory manner permitting no reply, Cleburne ordered Brown to halt the brigade until his troops had passed. When returning to the head of his division, Cleburne met Hardee and learned that a change had been made in the original order, placing Brown's brigade in front. Without comment, Cleburne immediately galloped back to Brown; and in the presence and hearing of those who had witnessed the previous meeting, he graciously apologized. Thus began a strong friendship between the two generals.[65]

Hardee, on July 6, after his corps had marched through Jasper, departed for Chattanooga, placing Cleburne temporarily in command of his two divisions. The corps crossed the Tennessee River, on pontoon bridges, at Kelly's Ford in Lookout Valley on July 6 and 7. This ford was about nine miles west of Chattanooga as the bird flies but about twelve miles by the railroad and dirt road. The 15th Arkansas was dispatched by train to Chickamauga Station, eight miles southeast of Chattanooga.[66] Its orders probably were to guard the depot on the Western & Atlantic Railroad leading to Atlanta, and two nearby railroad bridges. By July 10, on foot and by rail Cleburne moved the rest of Hardee's corps to Tyner's Station.[67] This hamlet, nine miles east of

Chattanooga, was on the railroad to Knoxville. Cleburne's division encamped in and about the village, with Stewart's division nearby, and Polk's corps, in and below Chattanooga.

NOTES

CHAPTER VIII

[1]Record of Events, Cos. A and C, 15th (Cleburne's — Polk's — Josey's) Arkansas Infantry, Nov. and Dec. 1862. During the stay in Shelbyville, several parties were given honoring the generals. Mrs. W. M. Gentry, a noted "beauty" of a prominent family, years later reminisced about dancing with Generals Hardee, Buckner, Cleburne, James E. Rains, and Bushrod Johnson. — "Surgeons of the Confederacy: Dr. W. M. Gentry of Tennessee," *Confederate Veteran*, XL (1932), 336-37.

[2]Record of Events, Cos. B and H, 15th (Cleburne's — Polk's — Josey's) Arkansas Infantry, Nov. and Dec. 1862; C. W. Frazer, "Fifth Confederate," in John Berrien Lindsley (ed.), *The Military Annals of Tennessee (Confederate)* (Nashville, 1886), 148.

[3]*O.R.*, XX, Pt. 2, p. 509; *cf.* Nash, *Gen. Pat Cleburne*, 202. "I feel it due to Brig. General Patrick R. Cleburne, to call your attention to his able and gallant services during the recent action at Perryville, Ky. His conduct was in every particular entitled to the highest praise and is deserving of promotion." — Buckner to Hardee, Oct. 28, 1862 (AIGO), M474/25, NA. Hardee to S. Cooper, Oct. 28, 1862, *ibid.* Hardee enclosed the Buckner letter, and the recommendations were approved and forwarded by 'L Polk, Maj. Genl. Comd." — *Ibid.* The date of appointment as Major General was Dec. 20, 1862, to rank from Dec. 13. — Military Secretary's Office, *Memorandum Relative to General Officers*, 9.

[4]Liddell, "Record," 91-92.

[5]*O.R.*, XX, Pt. 1, p. 843.

[6]Frazer, "Fifth Confederate," 149; Mary B. Hughes, *Hearthstones: The Story of Historic Rutherford County Homes* (Murfreesboro, Tenn., 1942), 29. For generations, the house had been the home of the Ledbetter family. After Capt. William Ledbetter had joined the Confederate Army, Spence through legal manipulation dispossessed the Ledbetter family. Hughes, *Hearthstones*, incorrectly states that Spence acquired the property after the close of the war. The exact date the Ledbetter family lost the home is not known, because some courthouse records were burned by the Federals following the battle of Murfreesboro. However, when Captain Ledbetter came home from the war, Spence was in possession of the house; and manifestly was in possession when Cleburne's division encamped on the turnpike. — William Ledbetter, Jr., great-grandson of Captain Ledbetter, conversation with authors, Feb. 23, 1970.

[7]*O.R.*, XX, Pt. 1, p. 843.

[8]*Ibid.*, p. 844.

[9]Liddell, "Record," 94; *O.R.*, XX, Pt. 1, p. 844.

[10]*Ibid.*, pp. 844-45.

[11]*Ibid.*, p. 193; G. C. Kniffin, "The Battle of Stone's River," in *Battles and Leaders*, III, 623.

[12]Moving by the right flank. — A maneuver in which troops in line of battle faced right and marched in a column, four abreast, parallel to the original line.

[13]*O.R.*, XX, Pt. 1, pp. 845-49.

[14]*Ibid.*, p. 850.

[15]Liddell, "Record," 99.

[16]Alvin Buck to his sister Lucie, Jan. 15, 1863, microfilm typescript in Buck Papers.

[17]*O.R.*, XX, Pt. 1, p. 777.

[18]Irving Buck to his sister Lucie, Feb. 8, 1863, microfilm copy in Buck Papers.

[19]This house still stands, in good condition.

[20]*O.R.*, XX, Pt. 1, p. 849.

[21]Stanley F. Horn, *The Army of Tennessee* (Norman, Okla., 1959), 205-06.

[22]*O.R.*, XX, Pt. 1, p. 849.

[23]*Ibid.*, pp. 849-50.

[24]*Cf.* Liddell, "Record," 100.

[25]Unable to identify because there were ten Byrds in Co. I, five of whom were privates in the battle of Murfreesboro.

[26]*O.R.*, XX, Pt. 1, pp. 850-52. By a general order of the Adjutant and Inspector General's office, issued Oct. 3, 1863, the names of officers, noncommissioned officers, and privates of the Confederate armies, conspicuous for "courage and devotion on the field of battle," were to be inscribed on a Roll of Honor to be preserved in that office "for reference in all future time." This Roll of Honor was initiated because of difficulty in procuring medals and badges authorized by an earlier Act of Congress. The following names of members of Cleburne's division were inscribed on the Roll of Honor for their part in the battle of Murfreesboro: *Arkansas. — 1st Regiment of Infantry:* Lieut. Col. D. McGregor, *k*, Adjt. S. N. Greenwood, Capt. O. F. Parrish, Co. D; Lieut. J. E. Letson, Co. D; Capt. W. H. Scales, Co. C; Corpl. G. M. McKenzie, *k* Co. A; Priv. J. S. T. Hemphill, Co. B; Priv. G. W. Sallee, *k* Co. C; Priv. G. Bogy, Co. D; Priv. W. W. Chaney, Co. E; Priv. H. J. Bullion, Co. F; Priv. A. P. Green, *k* Co. G; Priv. J. Beeson, Co. H; Priv. J. H. Curd, *k* Co. I; Priv. O. C. Choat, *k* Co. K. *Mississippi. — Darden's battery:* Capt. P. Darden; Maj. R. B.

Snowden, assistant adjutant-general. *Tennessee. – 2nd Regiment of Infantry:* Color-Sergt. John C. Ferris. *5th Regiment of Infantry:* Sergt. J. P. Hardcastle, Co. A; 2nd Lieut. Z. B. Hamrick, Co. B; Color-Sergt. W. Davis, Co. C; 1st Lieut. W. T. Grisson, Co. C; Capt. R. B. Roberts, Co. D; 2nd Lieut. W. W. Masey, Co. E; 1st Lieut. J. B. Blair, Co. G; Sergt. J. Swan, Co. G; 2nd Lieut. S. R. Richards, Co. H; 2nd Lieut W. H. Ballard, Co. L; Corpl. W. F. Diggs, Co. A; 2nd Sergt. J. A. Aguilar, Co. B; Sergt. L. D. Holland, Co. C; Priv. W. T. Ballard, Co. D; Corpl. W. A. Thompson, Co. E; Priv. J. J. Hagler, Co. F; Priv. D. C. Baucum, Co. G; Priv. W. C. Malin, *k* Co. H; Priv. G. W. Costen, *k* Co. I; Corpl. J. B. Johnson, Co. K. *17th Regiment of Infantry:* Col. A. S. Marks; Lieut Col. W. W. Floyd; Adjt. James B. Fitzpatrick; Capt. F. B. Terry, Co. A; 1st Lieut. G. W. Corn, Co. D; 1st Lieut. H. M. Kinsey, Co. B; 2nd Lieut. M. W. Black, Co. E; Corpl. John N. Lowry, *k* Co. A; Sergt. P. L. Shaffner, Co. B; Sergt. W. T. Jones, Co. C; Sergt. Robert Rollins, Co. D; Priv. J. D. Martin, Co. E; Priv. John L. Conley, Co. F; Priv. J. H. Gober, Co. G; Priv. M G. Liggett, *k* Co. H; Priv. T. C. Mitchell, Co. K; Co. I declined making selection. *23rd Regiment of Infantry:* Lieut Col. R. H. Keeble; Capt. W. H. Harder, Co. G; Capt. N. R. Allen, Co. E; Pri. W. M. Haynie, Co. A; Priv. W. J. Pennington, Co. B; 1st Sergt. J. N. Holt, Co. D; Priv. H. C. Haynes, *k* Co. E; Priv. S. M. Foster, Co. C; Priv. Jasper M. Harris, *k* Co. F; 1st Sergt. William K. Kelly, Co. G; Corpl. L. W. Jernigham, Co. H. *25th Regiment of Infantry:* This regiment declined making any selections. *37th Regiment of Infantry:* Maj. J. T. McReynolds. *44th Regiment of Infantry:* Col. John S. Fulton; Lieut. Col. J. L. McEwen, Jr.; Maj. H. C. Ewin; Capt. Samuel Jackson, Co. I; Priv. James D. Stone, Co. B; Priv. S. G. Heflin, *k* Co. C; Corpl. John W. Gill, *k* Co. F; Corpl. J. D. Crenshaw, Co. H; Corpl. Isaac S. Berry, Co. I; Priv. J. M. Sellers, Co. K — *Ibid.*, pp. 972-74, 976-78. *k* Killed in action.

[27] Record of Events, Field and Staff and Co. G, 15th (Cleburne's — Polk's — Josey's) Arkansas Infantry, Dec. 31, 1862 to Feb. 28, 1863; *ibid.*, Co. H, Jan. and Feb. 1863; Buck, *Cleburne*, 125.

[28] Polk, *Leonidas Polk*, II, 194-95.

[29] *O.R.*, XX, Pt. 1, p. 699.

[30] Cleburne to Bragg, Jan. 13, 1863 (MS in Bragg Papers, West Res. Hist. Soc).

[31] *O.R.*, XX, Pt. 1, p. 683.

[32] W. E. Preston, "Memoirs of the War" (Undated MS in Compiled Data, 33rd Alabama Infantry Regiment, Ala. Dept. Arch. and Hist.), 16; General Orders dated Jan. 11, 1863, Headquarters Cleburne's Division, Army of Tennessee, RG 109, NA; Paul W. Pyle, Tullahoma, conversation with authors, Feb. 27, 1970; map, dated Mar. 22, 1863, showing the Confederate camp at Tullahoma The map is a

reproduction of a freehand drawing made by Pvt. William Austin Smith, 2nd Tennessee Regiment, Cleburne's division, in a diary in possession of Stanley F. Horn, Nashville. Distances, estimated by Pyle, are based on landmarks.

33"Ora," Mobile *Advertiser and Register.*

34Record of Events, Co. K, 33rd Alabama Infantry, Jan. and Feb. 1863, M311/350, NA; Preston, "Memoirs," 17.

35Benham, *Kennesaw Gazette*, IV (Jan. 1, 1889), 2; William and Robert Chambers (eds.) *Chambers's Information for the People* (Philadelphia, 1857), I, Preface and p. 157; Avery, "Patrick Ronayne Cleburne," 4; Irving Buck to his sister Lucie, Apr. 11, June 12, 1863, microfilm copies in Buck Papers.

36"W. T. Barnes," *Confederate Veteran*, XXVI (1918), 122; Voucher, Duffer, Joseph F. (MS in Citizens' File, RG 109, NA); Irving Buck to his sister Lucie, Feb. 8, Mar. 22, Apr. 11, 1863, microfilm copies in Buck Papers.

37*O.R.*, XXIII, Pt. 2, pp. 653, 722; General Orders No. 83, Richmond, June 13, 1863, RG 109, NA.

38Hardee, "Major General Cleburne," 645.

39Irving Buck to his sister Lucie, Apr. 26, 1863, microfilm copy in Buck Papers; Jerry Cleveland Sims, Wartrace, conversation with authors, Aug. 18, 1968. Hardee, Cleburne, and other generals were entertained with parties at Beechwood, the home of Mrs. Andrew Erwin, at Beech Grove, near Wartrace. — Miss R. C. Webster, "Some Reminiscences," *Confederate Veteran*, VII (1899), 324.

40Hardee, "Major General Cleburne," 645; Benham, *Kennesaw Gazette*, IV (Jan. 1, 1889), 2; Preston, "Memoirs," 18, 19.

41J. M. Berry, "The Quiet Humor of Gen. Pat Cleburne," *Confederate Veteran*, XII (1904), 176.

42Drake, "General Cleburne," 242, 243; D. H. Hill, "A Sketch of Maj. Gen. P. R. Cleburne," in Hill (ed.), *The Land We Love*, II (1867), 462; Preston, "Memoirs," 18.

43Berry, "Quiet Humor of Cleburne," 176.

44Drake, "General Cleburne," 244-46; Buck, *Cleburne*, 128.

45"Attention, Whitworth Sharpshooters," *Confederate Veteran*, I (1893), 117; Benham, *Kennesaw Gazette*, IV (Sept. 15, 1899), 4; Frank H. Smith, Interview with Capt. A. Buck Schell, Jan. 16, 1907, in Maury County Historical Society (comp.), *Frank H. Smith's History of Maury County, Tennessee* (Columbia, Tenn., 1969), 219; Buck, *Cleburne*, 128; *O.R.*, XXIII, Pt. 1, p. 587.

46Preston, "Memoirs," 19; Buck, *Cleburne*, 128.

47Record of Events, Co. K, 33rd Alabama Infantry, Jan. and Feb. 1863; Record of Events, Cos. C and F, 15th (Cleburne's — Polk's — Josey's) Arkansas Infantry, Jan. and Feb. 1863.

[48]See, *e.g.*, Irving Buck to his sister Lucie, Aug. 8, 1863, microfilm copy in Buck Papers; War Correspondent "290," "The Battle of Ringgold," Atlanta *Daily Intelligencer*, Dec. 25, 1863, quoted in *Kennesaw Gazette*, I (Mar. 1886), 1.

[49]Buck, *Cleburne*, 129.

[50]Frazer, "Fifth Confederate," 146, 152.

[51]Hardee, "Major General Cleburne," 650; Buck, *Cleburne*, 130; "Facts about 'the Cleburne Flag,' " *Confederate Veteran*, XVII (1909), 348; Lord (ed.), *Fremantle Diary*, 125; By Authority of the United Confederate Veterans, *The Flags of the Confederate States of America* (Baltimore, 1907), 2.

[52]Avery, "Patrick Ronayne Cleburne," 4.

[53]Lord (ed.), *Fremantle Diary*, 123-24; Buck, *Cleburne*, 127.

[54]Bragg to W. W. Mackall, June 2, 1863; Bragg to Buckner, June 2, 1863; Hardee to Bragg, June 3, 1863; Hardee to Bragg, June 3, 1863; 4:30 P.M.; Hardee to Bragg, June 3, 1863, 8 P.M.; Hardee to Bragg, June 4, 1863 (MSS in Bragg Papers, West. Res. Hist. Soc.); Irving Buck to his sister Lucie, June 12, 1863 (microfilm copy in Buck Papers).

[55]Now Fosterville.

[56]*O.R.*, XXIII, Pt. 1, p. 586.

[57]Bragg to Hardee, June 6, 1863 (MS in Bragg Papers, West. Res. Hist. Soc.); Thomas Lawrence Connelly, *Autumn of Glory: The Army of Tennessee, 1862-1865* (Baton Rouge, 1971), 117-19.

[58]This bridge over the Duck River was about five miles from Wartrace in the direction of Shelbyville.

[59]*O.R.*, XXIII, Pt. 1, pp. 586-87. Regarding the fight on June 25, Liddell reported, "Our soldiers were exceedingly eager and excited, and gallantly maintained the contest . . . ." And further, "The defiant shouts of our soldiery in the face of the enemy during these different engagements indicates an obstinate resolution in the cause of their country. . . ." — *Ibid.*, pp. 590, 591.

[60]*Ibid.*, pp. 485, 489, 490, 505.

[61]*Ibid.*, p. 591; *ibid.*, Pt. 2, p. 888; Avery, "Patrick Ronayne Cleburne," 4. ". . .he [Cleburne] often went with the skirmish line." — Frazer, "Fifth Confederate," 151.

[62]Harold B. Simpson (ed.), *The Bugle Softly Blows* (Waco, 1965), 35; Hardee, "Major General Cleburne," 645. The night of June 29, the 15th Arkansas Regiment went by rail from Tullahoma to the village of Allisonia to guard the railroad bridge across the Elk River; and stayed there until July 1. — Record of Events, Field and Staff and Cos. C and F, 15th (Cleburne's — Polk's — Josey's) Arkansas Infantry, May and June 1863; *ibid.*, Co. A, July and Aug. 1863.

[63]*O.R.*, XXIII, Pt. 1, p. 408; Simpson (ed.), *Bugle Softly Blows*, 35.

The captain of another Texas company recorded: "On the 1st July deployed as skirmishers west of Elk ı.ver engaged the enemy's skirmishers & Sharpshooters for near two hours & until the latter retreated." — Record of Events, Co. A, 10th Texas Infantry, July and Aug. 1863, M323/337, NA.

[64]Connelly, *Autumn of Glory*, 132-33.

[65]Record of Events, Co. F, 15th (Cleburne's — Polk's — Josey's) Arkansas Infantry, July and Aug. 1863; Record of Events, Cos. B and D, 33rd Alabama Infantry, July and Aug. 1863; Mangum, *Kennesaw Gazette*, II (June 15, 1887), 2; Benham, *Kennesaw Gazette*, IV (Jan. 1, 1889), 2.

[66]*O.R.*, XXIII, Pt. 2, p. 901; Record of Events, Cos. A and C, 15th (Cleburne's — Polk's — Josey's) Arkansas Infantry, July and Aug. 1863.

[67]Buck, *Cleburne*, 134; Record of Events, Cos. C and F, 35th (formerly 5th) Tennessee Infantry, July and Aug. 1863.

Ambrotype of P.R. Cleburne, Aged 21

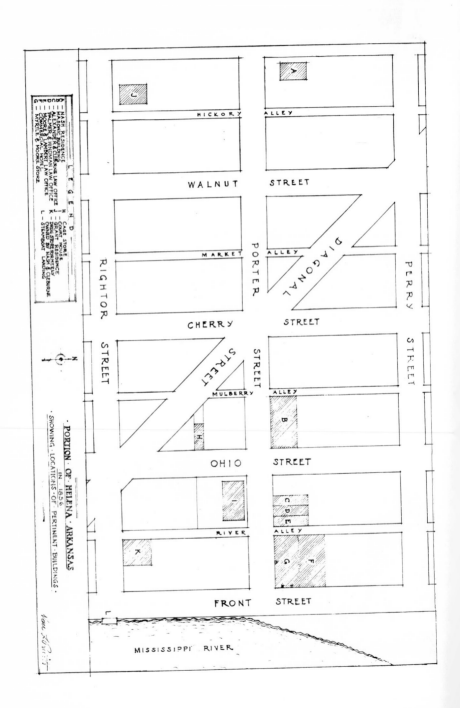

· PORTION · OF · HELENA · ARKANSAS ·
· IN · 1856 ·
· SHOWING · LOCATIONS · OF · PERTINENT · BUILDINGS ·

LEGEND

A — NASH RESIDENCE
B — ALEXANDER & CLIBURNE LAW OFFICE
C — PALMER & HINDMAN LAW OFFICE
D — MOORE & JAMES LAW OFFICE
E — COOPER LAW OFFICE
F — COMMERCIAL HOTEL
G — MYRTLE E. MOORE STORE

H — CAGE STORE
J — COURT HOUSE
K — GRANT RESIDENCE
L — DWELLING OCCUPIED BY NASH & CLIBURNE
L — STEAMBOAT LANDING

N

HICKORY ALLEY

WALNUT STREET

RIGHTOR STREET

PORTER STREET

PERRY STREET

MARKET ALLEY

DIAGONAL

CHERRY STREET

MARKET STREET

MULBERRY ALLEY

B

OHIO STREET

H

C
D
E

RIVER ALLEY

K
I

F
G

FRONT STREET

MISSISSIPPI RIVER

Battle Flag of 1st. Arkansas Infantry, Cleburne's Division
Now in Old State House, Little Rock

KEY'S BATTERY MOVING OUT PEACHTREE ROAD — BATTLE OF PEACHTREE CREEK - JULY 20. 1864

Drawing by Wilbur G. Kurtz 1939

Gen. Joseph E. Johnston's Headquarters, Dalton, Ga., January 1864,
where Gen. Cleburne advanced his proposal for enlisting
and freeing slaves.
Photograph Taken in 1972

Gen. James Deshler Killed at Chickamauga, Sept. 20, 1863

Brig. Gen. Lucius E. Polk   Brig. Gen. M.P. Lowrey

Brig. Gen. D.C. Govan   Brig. Gen. H.B. Granbury

"Four Better Officers Are Not in the Service of the Confederacy."

—*P.R. Cleburne, December 9, 1863*

CLEBURNE'S REPULSE OF SHERMAN AT MISSIONARY RIDGE.
Opposite Boyce Station, on the Western & Atlantic Railroad.
November 25, 1863.

GEN. BRAXTON BRAGG,
Commanding Confederate States Army.

GEN. U. S. GRANT,
Commanding United States Army.

BATTLE OF RINGGOLD, GA.
On the line of the Western & Atlantic Railroad.
November 27, 1863.

GEN. PATRICK R. CLEBURNE,
Commanding Confederate States Forces.

GEN. JOSEPH HOOKER,
Commanding United States Forces.

BATTLE OF PICKETT'S MILL—FIRST VOLLEY FROM THE CONFEDERATES.
Near New Hope Church, west of the Western & Atlantic Railroad.
May 27, 1864.

GEN. PATRICK R. CLEBURNE,
Commanding Confederate States Forces.

GEN. O. O. HOWARD,
Commanding United States Forces.

THE TRUCE IN THE MIDST OF THE BATTLE OF KENNESAW MOUNTAIN.
On the line of the Western & Atlantic Railroad, near Marietta, Ga.
June 27, 1864.
The Confederates and Federals rescuing the Federal wounded from the burning timber.

GEN. JOSEPH E. JOHNSTON,
Commanding Confederate States Army.

GEN. WM. T. SHERMAN,
Commanding United States Army.

Portrait of Miss Susan Tarleton

CHAPTER IX

McLEMORE'S COVE — CHICKAMAUGA
(September 1863)

Folded now is Cleburne's banner,
But one day it gleamed along
When the war-drum's stern hosanna
Echoed in a nation's song!
Shiloh saw it sweep from under
Like a tempest in its wrath;
Chickamauga heard its thunder,
Felt the lightning of its path.
— *John Trotwood Moore, "Cleburne's Banner."*

At Tyner's Station Cleburne presumedly made his head-quarters in the residence of J. S. Tyner, captain in the Confederate Army, for whose family the community was named. This two-story frame farmhouse was located north of the railroad station.[1] Upon reaching the village, Cleburne learned that some "homemade Yankees" from East Tennessee had destroyed two trestles near Tyner's Station. Hence he ordered Stewart to have a brigade guard the railroad bridges for a distance of seventy miles eastward.[2]

The Confederates, for two reasons, assumed the Union army would attempt to cross the Tennessee above Chattanooga. First, the terrain below Chattanooga was difficult. Second, Federal Gen. Ambrose E. Burnside would advance from the direction of Knoxville and join forces with Rosecrans. To defend the railroads and the approach to Chattanooga, Cleburne immediately began constructing four large, round forts in and near Tyner's Station. Twelve feet high and 200 to 300 feet in diameter, with embrasures for cannon and openings for rifles, the forts were surrounded by rifle pits.[3] Traces of three of these fortifications are still discernible.

On July 12, 1863, Cleburne sent most of Wood's brigade

to the town of Harrison, on the Tennessee River eleven miles northeast of Chattanooga, to guard river crossings.[4] Harrison, with about 400 inhabitants, was the county seat of Hamilton County. (Chickamauga Lake, created by the Tennessee Valley Authority, now covers the site of the town.)

Hardee had scarcely resumed command of his corps when, on July 14, because of the fall of Vicksburg, he was ordered to join Gen. Joseph E. Johnston's army at Jackson, Mississippi. Hardee again placed Cleburne in charge of the corps pending arrival of the new commander, Lieut. Gen. D. H. Hill. Daniel Harvey Hill, traveling from Richmond, reached Chattanooga on July 19. The distinguished veteran of the Army of Northern Virginia and Cleburne, distinguished veteran of the Army of Tennessee, immediately established mutual respect for one another.

During his stay at Tyner's Station, Hill was impressed with Cleburne's method of drill and instruction, and noted his Irish accent:

> . . . when giving emphatic orders on the field, the harsh rolling of his Rs was sometimes startling. Not one of his soldiers but can recall the peculiar intonation given to his command "For-ward MAR-R-R-C-H!" the first word, being syllabled with remarkable distinctness, while the latter was given with the broadest brogue imaginable. Nor can we forget his truly Irish rendering (bar-r-r-'l) of the word "barrel" when lecturing his class of officers on the rifle, its parts, uses &c.

Hill further said of Cleburne: "Habitually thoughtful and grave, he was considered cold and repellant in manner by those who only met him in his official capacity; but to his intimate friends, he was genial and pleasant in conversation; with, at times, a real sparkling of Irish wit and humor that would bring the hearty laugh from auditors responsive to his rather grim smile."[5]

Cleburne continued to command Hardee's old corps at intervals after Hill's arrival when the latter was elsewhere.[6] During the relatively quiet weeks at Tyner's Station, Cleburne attended meetings of Masonic Lodge No. 199 in Chattanooga.[7]

On August 2 Cleburne learned that bluecoats had appeared on the right bank of the Tennessee at Bridgeport, twenty-four miles west and south of Chattanooga. He at once dispatched the 32nd Mississippi Regiment to guard the crossing at Blythe's Ferry, thirty-one miles northeast of Chattanooga, where the Hiwassee River enters the Tennessee. On August 8, Captain Buck wrote his sister: "It was reported, about the time of the Liberty Gap fight, that General Cleburne was killed, the Yankees are determined if they cannot kill him in reality they will in imagination, on paper, but he is alive and will worry them yet before he 'goes up.' His men are very fond & proud of him, ..."[8]

While at Tyner's Station, Cleburne conceived the idea of "Comrades of the Southern Cross," a secret order of Southern soldiers. This military brotherhood would foster patriotic sentiment and strengthen bonds of fellowship. Cleburne believed such an organization could be a strong factor in winning the war by effecting a unity of purpose and "exalted oneness of action" among the oath-bound members. The General met with several officers one evening at Tyner's Station to study the subject. Gen. Leonidas Polk, unable to attend, sent as his representative, Chaplain (later Bishop) Charles Todd Quintard. The six or eight men present agreed upon the purposes of the order; and appointed as a committee to draft a constitution, Generals Cleburne, Liddell, and Brown, and Chaplain Quintard. The committee met daily for over a week in writing the document. On August 28 the organizers and several other officers met to adopt the constitution and plan expansion of the order throughout the army. The meeting was held at Gray's Mill, an old water mill a half mile southwest of Graysville, Georgia, a town twelve miles below Chattanooga on the railroad to Atlanta. The men, sitting on grain sacks, listened as Chaplain Quintard read the constitution; it was adopted unanimously.

The battle of Chickamauga, taking place soon after the ritual was perfected, and the investment of Chattanooga, which followed, prevented the dissemination of the Order in the Army of Tennessee as planned. However, in the spring of 1864 several chapters were formed. The exigencies of the campaigns which began in May 1864 left no opportunity for enlarging the organization. The United Confederate Veterans subsequently embodied some of the features of the Comrades of the Southern Cross.[9]

2

On August 21 Union troops, in some numbers, appeared on the river bank opposite Chattanooga and threw shells into the city. At 1 P. M. on the same day, other Federal troops appeared on the north bank of the river at Blythe's Ferry. That same day, Cleburne was ordered to advance from Tyner's Station to Harrison with his troops. After a personal reconnaissance up the river on horseback, he sent Polk's brigade to Thatcher's Ferry, about midway between Harrison and Blythe's Ferry; and to Gardenshire's Ferry, twelve miles above Harrison. Rifle pits were dug and artillery was placed at those points. A few companies were sent to other ferries and landings along the river, from the mouth of Chickamauga Creek, two miles above Chattanooga, to the Hiwassee.[10] Cleburne had Captain Phillips make a thorough examination of the river between Harrison and Chickamauga Creek. At intervals along the river Cleburne had troops picketing, and also sent scouts across the river.[11]

Units of a large Federal force, which the Confederates thought was a corps, reconnoitered on the north side of the Tennessee; and on August 22, one of the units shelled Harrison. On the 24th, Cleburne left Harrison for a two-day reconnaissance to Blythe's Ferry and beyond. A Confederate company commander at Gardenhire's Ferry recorded that on August 26, his company "was shelled in [their] Camps from the enemy's guns, on the opposite side of the river." At Thatcher's Ferry, two company captains recorded for that date: "Slight skirmish with the enemy," and "engaged in two picket skirmishes."[12]

Buck wrote his sister from "Harrison Landing," on August 29:

> . . . a battle was considered as imminent — it has not transpired although the enemy is still in our front & shells our position every day or two — but so far has succeeded in killing only one man, a sharpshooter attached to these Hdqrs, ... Genl Cleburne was watching the fight with one of their batteries yesterday, when they threw a shell which fell about three feet in front of him but fortunately did not explode . . . . Am afraid his intrepidity will cause his death yet. A battle may be fought very soon.

At Chickamauga Station, Captain Kinsey, in the Record of Events of Company C, 15th Arkansas, for July and August, 1863, penciled: "We are expecting a fight here soon. Rosey [Rosecrans] is pegging away at Chattanooga from the opposite bank of the river & I can hear the booming of his cannon while I write."[13]

Near the end of August Bragg made a change in Hill's command. Breckinridge's division, coming up from Mississippi, was assigned to Hill's corps; and Stewart's division was ordered to Buckner's corps, which had evacuated Knoxville and was falling back toward the Hiwassee.

On the night of August 31 came the surprising report that the main force of Rosecrans' army had crossed the Tennessee at points twenty-two and thirty-two miles southwest of Chattanooga. By September 4, large forces of the enemy were known to be in Wills Valley, west of Lookout Mountain. This mountain, high and rugged, rising at the edge of a horseshoe bend in the Tennessee River, two miles southwest of Chattanooga, extends southwestward for more than eighty miles. Part of the Federal army was reported to be moving south in the valley, and perhaps would cross the mountain at Winston's Gap, forty-two miles from Chattanooga, in an effort to sever the Confederate supply line from Atlanta. Bragg sent cavalry to observe this movement of the enemy and to protect his communications.

The Southern commander considered attacking the isolated Union force across the Tennessee from Cleburne and Hill. In a private letter to Hill, dated September 4, outlining the proposal, Bragg said: "Consult Cleburne. He is cool, full of resources, and ever alive to a success. Then give me your views, or call with Cleburne and see what our resources are." At 10 P. M. the next day, Cleburne having just received a copy of Bragg's letter, wrote Hill: "I am of the opinion that we should crush the corps opposite us if we can. I do not know, however, what force you have. I have a fraction over 5,000 men. I do not know how we could cross our artillery. This is a necessary calculation, as the enemy have had time to fortify, and doubtless have done so at the foot of the mountain."[14] Bragg promptly abandoned the idea.

Starting early on September 6 from Harrison and other

points along the river, Cleburne's troops marched via Tyner's Station to Chattanooga, arriving there during the evening and night.[15] The movements of the Union forces in Wills Valley were concealed by Lookout Mountain. Bragg concluded that they were likely going to Rome, Georgia, to sever the railroad communications with Atlanta and the South. The Confederate commander decided to evacuate Chattanooga and march toward Rome, so as to interpose his army between the Federals and the railroad. The dirt road to Rome, known as the "Chattanooga-LaFayette Road" or the "LaFayette Road," led through LaFayette, Georgia, a town of about 200 inhabitants, 26 miles south and slightly east of Chattanooga.

At dusk on the 7th, the Army of Tennessee, with Cleburne's division leading the first column, set out on the LaFayette Road.[16] As the troops marched southeast, steep Missionary Ridge, rising 200 to 400 feet, loomed ahead. The ridge, beginning four miles northeast of Chattanooga, a mile south of the Tennessee River, extends about twelve miles southwesterly, practically parallel to Lookout Mountain, and then tapers.

Five miles from Chattanooga, the column passed through the hamlet of Rossville, at the foot of Missionary Ridge; and thence through Rossville Gap. A short distance farther on, the LaFayette Road swerved southward through wooded country, with tangled undergrowth and cedar thickets. About two miles to the left, roughly paralleling the road, flowed West Chickamauga Creek, called "the Chickamauga" by the soldiers. The large creek with steep banks meandered northward. The Confederate column was now marching on the site which, twelve and thirteen days hence, would be the battlefield of Chickamauga, "the great battle of the West, and the bloodiest two days of the war."[17] The second column of Bragg's army moved along a parallel road on the east side of Chickamauga Creek.

Seven and a half miles past Rossville Gap, the LaFayette Road turning east, immediately crossed Chickamauga Creek, which winds northeastward. Here, on the west side of the creek, was located "Lee & Gordon's Mills." The column led by Cleburne's division halted, and the division bivouacked by the mill for the rest of the night.[18] The next day, September

8, Hill's corps, Cleburne's division still in the van, continued marching slightly east and then south, fourteen miles to Lafayette.[19] Pursuant to Bragg's orders, Hill's corps concentrated at LaFayette, and the rest of the army took position near Lee & Gordon's Mills and southward toward LaFayette.

Thirty-two miles south of Chattanooga, a spur from Lookout Mountain projects northeasterly, then veers north. Known as Pigeon Mountain, the spur continues for nearly twenty miles, paralleling Lookout Mountain. McLemore's Cove, the valley between steep Lookout and Pigeon Mountains, is a cul-de-sac about five miles wide. The only outlets are a few gaps in Pigeon Mountain and a few shallow "gaps" on Lookout Mountain. Chickamauga Creek, starting at the south end of McLemore's Cove, flows northerly through the valley. Four miles in a direct line northwest of LaFayette, Dug Gap crosses Pigeon Mountain. However, between the town and the gap is a steep, high ridge paralleling the mountain; and by the circuitous road the distance was more than five miles. Two miles northwest of Dug Gap lies Davis' Crossroads in McLemore's Cove. On the other side of the cove, northwest of Davis' Crossroads, Steven's Gap and Cooper's Gap, two miles apart, ascend Lookout Mountain.

The afternoon of September 9, "Yankees began to pour down" into McLemore's Cove from Steven's and Cooper's Gaps. From LaFayette, Cleburne sent Wood's brigade to the top of Pigeon Mountain to hold Dug Gap, Catlett's Gap (two miles north of Dug Cap), and Bluebird Gap (one and a half miles south of Dug Gap). The three gaps already had been obstructed with felled timber. Cleburne's other two brigades remained stationed at LaFayette. That night Cleburne established headquarters in a bivouac by the road leading to Dug Gap.[20]

After daylight, September 10, Hill at LaFayette received an order, through Bragg's chief of staff, dated September 9, 11:45 P. M., Lee & Gordon's Mills:

> I inclose orders given General Hindman [commanding a division]. General Bragg directs that you send . . . Cleburne's division to reunite with Hindman at Davis' Cross-Roads to-morrow morning. Hindman starts at 12 o'clock to-night, and has 13 miles to make. The commander of the columns

> thus united will move upon the enemy at the foot of Stevens'
> Gap, said to be 4,000 or 5,000. If unforeseen circumstances
> should prevent your movement, notify Hindman . . . . Open
> communication with Hindman by your cavalry in advance of
> the junction. He marches on the road from Dr. Anderson's to
> Davis' Cross-Roads.[21]

Dr. Anderson's house was on the LaFayette Road four miles
southeast of Lee & Gordon's Mills.

Hill replied that Cleburne had been sick in bed all day;
that two of Cleburne's regiments had not arrived from picket
duty at Harrison; that one of Cleburne's brigades had to be
relieved from picketing the gaps; that hours would be
required to remove the obstructions from the gaps; that since
Cleburne would have nearly as long a march as Hindman, the
intended junction would be impossible, and no surprise could
be effected. Hill did not order the movement and took no
step toward effecting the junction.

A month later, October 15, 1863, when his friend Hill
was being censured for failing to execute Bragg's order,
Cleburne wrote a letter in Hill's defense. In the letter,
addressed to Hill, Cleburne explained that to unite his
(Cleburne's) division would have required "several hours";
"Dug Gap was heavily obstructed with fallen timber which it
would take a considerable time to remove"; Davis' Crossroads
was "between nine and thirteen miles from LaFayette, [by]
the only practicable road then known to us"; the order for
the movement, received by Hill at 4:30 A. M. on September
10, specified that the junction with Hindman at the
Crossroads was to be that same morning. "With these facts
before me I am convinced that General Bragg's order could
not have been carried out and that the contingency existed
which (under the terms of the order itself) made it your duty
to postpone the movement."[22]

Cleburne was only able to conclude that the circumstances justified "postponing" the movement. Granted it was
impossible for Hill to make the junction that forenoon as
ordered, why did Hill do nothing toward uniting with
Hindman early in the afternoon? Why did not the aggressive
Hill notify Bragg that circumstances prevented execution of
the order in the forenoon; that he forthwith would prepare

for the movement, and requested instructions whether to
effect the junction early in the afternoon or cancel the
movement? The troops who had felled the trees across the
road through Dug Gap were under Brig. Gen. Will T. Martin.
Commanding a Confederate cavalry division in McLemore's
Cove, Martin had his headquarters in LaFayette. Before
replying to Bragg, why did Hill not learn from Martin how
quickly the obstructions could be removed? Martin's reply
would have been that with a proper detail he could remove
the obstructions in two hours.[23] Hill could have ordered
Cleburne to have a detail from Wood's 500 men at Dug Gap
clear away the timber while the other two brigades were
marching from LaFayette to Dug Gap.

The other reasons Hill gave for not uniting with Hindman
are worthless. Illness of a division commander is no justifica-
tion for a corps commander not making an attack. In fact,
Cleburne was not sick;[24] Hill must have been misinformed.
The absence of two of Cleburne's regiments is irrelevant.

The real reason for not executing Bragg's order probably
is gleaned from a post-war article written by Hill in which he
said that Bragg, more than once, issued "'impossible' orders,
and therefore those entrusted with their execution got in the
way of disregarding them." Hill believed that "the mass of
the Yankee Army" was behind Lookout Mountain.[25] He did
not know what they would meet should he and Hindman
move upon the Federals at Steven's Gap — 5,000 Union
troops or an additional force of overwhelming strength. Had
Hill thought there would be a force of only 5,000, nothing
could have prevented his and Hindman attacking.

On the morning of September 10, a Union force
advanced from Steven's Gap toward Davis' Crossroads, and
Cleburne's skirmishers of Wood's brigade engaged those of
the Federals. Just before 11 o'clock, advancing to Chickamauga Creek, a half mile west of Davis' Crossroads, Union
infantry and artillery drove back Confederate cavalry and
continued an advance to within three-quarters of a mile of
Dug Gap before withdrawing.

Hindman, who had marched his division to a point four
miles north of Davis' Crossroads, was informed of the Union
movements; and received reports that a Union division had

211

reached the crossroads and that another division was at Steven's Gap. In the afternoon, a contingent of Federals from Davis' Crossroads demonstrated against Hindman's cavalry. Hence, Hindman became apprehensive as to the strength of the Federals in the cove. Because of Hill's refusing to cooperate, Hindman remained north of Davis' Crossroads the rest of the day without attacking. Per Bragg's orders, Bucker's corps marched from Dr. Anderson's, joining Hindman late in the afternoon.[26] Command of the joint forces was given to Hindman, who turned over command of his division to one of his brigadiers, Patton Anderson.

The intelligence Bragg had received regarding the isolated fragment of Rosecran's army at the foot of Steven's Gap had come from Martin. At Cleburne's headquarters near Dug Gap, on the 10th, Cleburne and Martin discussed the movement which they anticipated making in conjunction with Hindman.[27] The same day, the reserve corps of Maj. Gen. W. H. T. Walker, recently arrived from Mississippi and stationed near LaFayette, marched to LaFayette. Liddell's brigade was temporarily transferred from Cleburne's division to Walker's corps.

Between midnight and daylight on the 11th, the rest of Cleburne's troops — Lucius Polk's brigade and the Texas Brigade (now commanded by Brig. Gen. James Deshler) — marched from LaFayette to Dug Gap, followed by Walker's corps. At Bragg's direction, before daylight Cleburne had troops of Wood's brigade remove the obstructions from the gap. The removal took three hours.[28]

At 4:20 A. M. on September 11, Hindman received a dispatch from Bragg's assistant adjutant-general sent from LaFayette at midnight:

> Headquarters are here and the following is the information: Crittenden's corps is advancing on us from Chattanooga. A large force from the south has advanced within 7 miles of this. Polk is left at Anderson's to cover your rear. General Bragg orders you to attack and force your way through the enemy to this point at the earliest hour that you can see him in the morning. Cleburne will attack in front the moment your guns are heard.[29]

At daylight, Cleburne, with two of his brigades deployed at the edge of the cove, awaited the opening of Hindman's guns to move on the Union flank and rear. There was no sound of an attack by Hindman. Cleburne dispatched an officer and couriers along the top of Pigeon Mountain to Catlett's Gap, to detect any firing of artillery or small-arms. From a nearby elevation on Pigeon Mountain, the Federal troops, mostly deployed in woods, were discernable, facing north with their battle line in an arc pretty much centered on Davis' Crossroads. Bragg, as time passed and there came no sound or word of Hindman's guns, paced back and forth on this elevation, digging his spurs in the ground. Maj. J. K. Dixon made a daring reconnaissance under fire, which enabled Cleburne to improve the disposition of his command for striking the Federals. He formed his third brigade into a line behind the right of the Union rear, joining this brigade with the left of his two other brigades. About noon, when no signal had come from Hindman, Bragg ordered Cleburne and Walker to attack. Sharpshooters of Wood's brigade, advancing in handsome style, drove back the Union pickets and skirmishers. Cleburne's entire force was advancing in line of battle when suddenly it was halted at Bragg's order.

Hindman, a little before sundown, finally attacked, after learning the Federals were retiring toward Steven's Gap. He attempted to intercept the retreating Federal column. At Hill's direction, 150 Confederate cavalrymen charged the enemy's rear; and Semple's battery silenced the Federal rearguard, making a stand on the west side of Chickamauga Creek. Cleburne's line united with Hindman's line at Davis' Crossroads about dark, but by this time nearly all of the enemy force was behind low ridges in front of Steven's Gap. Declaring, "We can't stay here," Bragg ordered that most of his command march to LaFayette.[30]

Thus the golden opportunity was lost to annihilate or compel the surrender of 12,000 Federals in McLemore's Cove. Masters of the situation, the Confederates could have destroyed piecemeal the rest of Rosecran's divided army. Cleburne's and Walker's men were heartbroken that the opportunity for a decisive victory had been dissipated.[31]

Who was responsible for the fiasco on September 11 at

McLemore's Cove? Hindman, Bragg, and to a lesser degree the generals under Hindman, were culpable. At 8 P. M. on the 10th, Hindman had first received word from Bragg that Crittenden's corps was marching southward from Chattanooga; and Hindman was urged to hasten the attack on the Union troops in Steven's Gap. An hour and a half later Hindman had received another message from army headquarters: "The enemy is now divided. Our force at or near LaFayette is superior to the enemy. It is important now to move vigorously and crush him."[32]

Concerned about the strength of the Union force in the gap, and alarmed by Crittenden's approach, Hindman, Buckner, and Anderson had unanimously agreed that the best course was to turn on Crittenden. Hindman had sent a communication to this effect to army headquarters by an aide, Maj. James Nocquet.

Nocquet had reached Bragg's headquarters, at LaFayette, shortly before midnight on the 10th. Hindman's and Bragg's reports are in conflict as to Bragg's response to Nocquet. According to Hindman, when Nocquet returned at 6:30 A. M. on the 11th, he reported that Bragg had said that Hindman could carry out his own plans and Bragg would sustain him. But according to Bragg, "I verbally directed the major to return to General Hindman and say that my plans could not be changed, and that he would carry out my orders." At the same time, Bragg by courier also dispatched to Hindman the written order to attack which the latter received at 4:20 A. M., before Nocquet's return. The weight of the evidence sustains Bragg. Martin and Liéut. Col. David Urquhart, assistant adjutant-general, were present during Bragg's conversation with Nocquet and their subsequent statements fully corroborate the commanding General.

On the 11th, why did not Hindman forthwith obey the order to attack? Apparently he and the general officers in his command had the same lack of confidence in Bragg entertained by Hill. Hindman, Buckner, and Anderson, all distrusted Bragg's orders. Not only were they apprehensive that the bluecoats in their front would be too numerous but they also feared that Federals in great strength lurked on Lookout Mountain and at the base of Steven's Gap. They also thought that Hindman's column marching toward Davis' Crossroads would be seen by the enemy atop Lookout Mountain in time for support to be rushed to the Federals in the cove. Further, Crittenden, approaching from behind, might by-pass the Confederate force protecting thier rear. The three Confederate Generals feared that they were about to be enveloped while in the cove.

Hindman, Buckner, and Anderson made the fateful error of deferring the attack until they could get more definite information. They procrastinated for hours, advancing cautiously and timidly, with scouting and frequent reconnaissances. Finally, about noon, they deployed to attack, their foremost division being almost a mile from the Federal line. Hindman was about to order an immediate advance when receipt of the written message from Bragg referred to below caused him to delay the movement until further information of the strength of the enemy could be obtained. Hindman finally concluded to abandon the undertaking, and was preparing to withdraw his force to Catlett's Gap when scouts reported that the Federals were retreating. Hindman then started his ineffectual pursuit.[33]

Bragg, also, was grievously at fault. In the late forenoon and early afternoon of the 11th, he showed the same vacillation and lack of confidence he had displayed in the Kentucky campaign; and seems to have panicked. He estimated the Federals in the cove, which he knew to be part of George H. Thomas' corps, at 12- to 15,000. At 11 A. M., when "5 Miles on the Road from LaFayette to Steven's Gap," through his chief of staff, he dispatched an order to Hindman: "If you find the enemy in such force as to make an attack imprudent, fall back at once on Lafayette by Catlett's Gap, ..."[34] Bragg followed up this order by sending a staff officer to learn if Hindman felt certain of making his way out through Catlett's Gap.[35] The commanding General gave these instructions despite the fact that he had on hand, in Hindman's, Cleburne's, Walker's, and Martin's commands, about 27,000 seasoned soldiers, who could have converged on the enemy from three directions. Furthermore, as already noted, Bragg started an attack by Cleburne and Walker; but stopped it as soon as it was under way.

Following the fiasco in McLemore's Cove, Cleburne's division stayed at Pigeon Mountain to guard the gaps. Remaining at this location was important because the enemy was still on the opposite side of the cove. Bragg, arriving at LaFayette about 9:30 P. M. on the 11th, learned, contrary to his fear, that Crittenden's corps had not been marching to McLemore's Cove. Instead, two of Crittenden's divisions were reported being at Ringgold, Georgia, a town on the railroad to Atlanta fifteen miles southeast of Chattanooga; and his third division, at Lee & Gordon's Mills. Also, Bragg must have learned that the enemy force which he had believed threatened him from the south was only a cavalry reconnaissance.

On September 12 and the morning of the 13th, Bragg issued orders to have Leonidas Polk's corps strike Crittenden near Rock Spring Church, located between LaFayette and Lee & Gordon's. The operation was unsuccessful because of misinformation as to the movements of Crittenden's divisions from Ringgold and Polk's belief that the Federal General was supported by reserve forces from other corps. Crittenden concentrated his corps at Lee & Gordon's without being attacked. Bragg then ordered Polk not to attack and to return to LaFayette, which the commanding General believed was threatened from the south by McCook's corps.

Cleburne's division now guarded the gaps on Pigeon Mountain against Major General Thomas' entire corps on the other side of McLemore's Cove, in front of Steven's and Cooper's Gaps. The report of McCook's advancing upon LaFayette proved to be false. However, the report had been sufficiently plausible for Hill, on the 12th, to summon Lucius Polk's brigade from Cleburne's division and prepare for battle. This brigade returned to Pigeon Mountain on the 13th.[36] On September 14, Deshler's Texas Brigade, Cleburne's division, in a formation which included a strong line of skirmishers, was drawn up at the mouth of Catlett's Gap. Deshler's brigade opposed a brigade of Thomas' corps on reconnaissance, and its presence forced the Federals to withdraw. Two days later the Texans at this gap "strongly posted" with two pieces of artillery and "in force" according to Thomas, twice prevented the same Federal brigade from advancing. The spirit of the Texans in Cleburne's command is exemplified by the self-styled motto of Co. F, 10th Texas Infantry, "All for Duty."[37]

Rosecrans, having thought for a week that the Confederates were in full flight, had seriously erred in separating his three major corps. Thomas was more than a day's march from Crittenden. McCook, at Alpine, forty-two miles below Chattanooga and just east of Lookout Mountain, was a three-day march from Thomas. The only practicable route was back across Lookout Mountain, north through Wills Valley, and east across Lookout to McLemore's Cove. On September 12, Rosecrans, realizing that the enemy had turned on him and his divided forces were in peril, hastened to concentrate the three corps. On the 16th, the advance of McCook's corps joined Thomas in McLemore's Cove. Meanwhile, Bragg had discarded the strategy of attack on the scattered fractions of the Union army; and planned, by moving toward Chattanooga, to force Rosecrans either to fight or cross back over the river. To meet the heavy Union concentration in front of Catlett's Gap, Deshler was reenforced by Breckinridge's division.[38] However, no conflict ensued; Thomas and McCook were bent on consolidating with Crittenden.

On September 17, Thomas and McCook, west of Pigeon Mountain, and the Confederates, east of the mountain, both marched northward toward Lee & Gordon's Mills. Bragg's immediate purpose now was to throw his forces along the east side of the Chickamauga, with his right at Reed's Bridge, four and a quarter miles northeast of Lee & Gordon's. Starting at daylight on the 18th, Cleburne's division marched to Dr. Anderson's (four miles southeast of Lee & Gordon's) and formed line of battle as the left flank of the Confederate army.[39]

3

Early on September 18, the Federal left flank rested at Lee & Gordon's Mills. That afternoon, while fighting Union cavalry and mounted infantry, the Confederates were able to cross the Chickamauga at Reed's Bridge and at a ford a short distance to the south. These crossings, by Bushrod Johnson's division and Walker's corps of two divisions, were pursuant to

Bragg's plan to strike the exposed left of the Union army and interpose his force between Rosecrans and Chattanooga.

Early on the 19th, Walker's corps, comprising the right of the Confederate army, was engaged by Thomas, who had marched all night from McLemore's Cove to take position on extreme Union left. Fighting grew in volume as additional divisions of the Confederate army, from right to left, crossed over the stream and as fresh Federal divisions reached the field of battle. Desperate and inconclusive fighting continued along the entire front during the 19th.

Cleburne's original handwritten report of the battle of Chickamauga, dated October 18, 1863, bearing his signature, began: ". . . During the afternoon of Saturday, the 19th ultimo, I moved my Division in a westerly direction across the Chickamauga River, at [Thedford's] Ford, and having received orders to report to Lieut. Genl. Polk, commanding the right wing of the army, I did so, ..."[40] Thedford's Ford was about three miles northwest of Dr. Anderson's; and two and a half, northeast of Lee & Gordon's. Moving at quick step on a road cluttered with artillery and wagons, Cleburne's troops approached the ford. "Boys, go through the river," Cleburne said, "We can't wait." Amid the roar of cannon, the soldiers removed all clothing below their waists and waded through Chickamauga Creek. Redonning their clothes, they hurried northward on a lane paralleling the creek.[41]

Some distance in the woods and to the left of Cleburne's column, the Confederate line paralleled this lane. A Georgia regiment had fallen back and taken position behind a small hill near the lane. Later, a veteran of the regiment wrote, "While the Command was behind this hill, and about twilight, the steady tramp of Gen. Pat Cleburne's men was heard advancing, and as these heroes passed us we gave them a shout."[42] Farther along the lane, during a lull in the battle, Confederate cavalry General Nathan Bedford Forrest was asked by an artillery corporal, "General, is the fighting over for today?" Pointing up the lane, Forrest replied, "Do you see that large body of infantry marching this way in columns of fours? That is General Pat Cleburne's division; hell will break loose in Georgia in about fifteen minutes."[43]

Continuing with Cleburne's report:

... [I] was directed [on September 19] by [General Polk] to form a second line in rear of the right of the line already in position. Accordingly, soon after sun-set, my Division was formed partially in echelon, about three hundred yards in rear of the right of the first line. My right rested in front of a steam saw-mill [two and a half miles from Thedford's Ford], known as Jay's Mill, situated on a small stream, running between the Chickamauga and the road leading from Chattanooga to LaFayette [Chattanooga-LaFayette Road]. My line extended from the Saw Mill almost due South for nearly a mile, fronting to the west.

[Lucius] Polk's Brigade, with Calvert's Battery (commanded by Lieut. Thomas J. Key), composed my right wing; Wood's Brigade, with Semple's Battery, my center; and Deshler's Brigade, with Douglas' Battery, my left wing.

I now received orders from Lieut. Genl. Hill to advance — passing over the line, which had been repulsed — and drive back the enemy's left wing.

The men in the line, Walker's corps, lay prone on the ground. They recognized the blue and white battle flag of Cleburne's division and cheered as the troops passed by them.[44]

Cleburne's report of Chickamauga continued:

In my front were open woods — with the exception of a clearing (fenced in) in front of my centre, the ground sloping upwards as we advanced. Ordering the Brigades to direct themselves by Wood's (the centre) Brigade, and preserve Brigade-distance, I moved forward — passing over the first line — and was in a few moments heavily engaged along my right and centre. The enemy, posted behind hastily-constructed breastworks opened a heavy fire of both small arms and artillery."[45]

Cleburne's part in the battle was graphically described by Benham:

Cleburne was magnificent in the battle of this evening [September 19]. The enemy opened, from the first step the line took in advance, with every conceivable projectile — shot and shell and cannister and the deadly minnie. Fortunately it was too dark for much execution, but the roar was tremendous, and the crashing of the forest and the thick rattling of the smaller missles against the trees added to the fury of the storm.

Fiends and malignant demons seemed at work. But that

line, with that commander was superior to terror. It might feel it but it never blanched. It kept its course. Cleburne was determined that it should. Moving along it, near behind the file closers, he cheered to the men above the noise of battle.

He rode like a fury from brigade to brigade — horse and rider seemed frenzied alike. The men responded to him. They knew him. They were intoxicated by his appeals and example. The enemy could not stand before the charge. A charge made with such an elan as that nobody stands before.

I never saw Cleburne before or afterward so demonstrative. I suppose, knowing it was indispensible the charge should be successful, and reflecting that his men — called to take the place of a line which had been repulsed, had not seen a regular battle for nine months, he deemed it necessary to encourage them as much as possible.[46]

Returning to Cleburne's report concerning the action of the 19th:

> For half an hour the firing was the heaviest I had ever heard; it was dark, however, and accurate shooting was impossible. Each party was aiming at the flashes of the other's guns, and few of the shot from either side took effect. Maj Hotchkiss (my Chief of Artillery), placed Polk's and Wood's Artillery in position in the cleared field in front of my centre. Availing themselves of the noise and the darkness, Capt Semple and Lieut Key ran their batteries forward within sixty yards of the enemy's line, and opened a rapid fire. Polk pressed forward at the same moment on the right, when the enemy ceased firing, and quickly disappeared from my front.
>
> There was some confusion at the time, necessarily inseparable, however, from a night attack. This, and the difficulty of moving my Artillery through the woods in the dark, rendered a further advance inexpedient for the night.
>
> I consequently halted, and after readjusting my lines, threw out skirmishers a quarter-of-a-mile in advance, and bivouacked.
>
> In this conflict the enemy was driven back about a mile-and-a-half. He left in my hands two or three pieces of Artillery, several Caissons, two or three hundred prisoners, and the Colors of the Seventy-seventh Indiana and those of the Seventy-ninth Pennsylvania.[47]

Gen. D. H. Hill, veteran of several major battles of the Army of Northern Virginia, reporting on the attack of

Cleburne's men said: "I have never seen troops behave more gallantly than did this noble division, and certainly I never saw so little straggling from the field." In a later account, Hill said that he saw "not one deserter" from Cleburne's division.[48]

During the night, as Cleburne's men slept in line of battle,[49] Lieut. Gen. James Longstreet with two brigades arrived from the Army of Northern Virginia, three of his brigades having preceded him. The same night, Bragg reorganized his army into two wings — the left, under Longstreet and the right, under Leonidas Polk — a hazardous change during the battle. Because of the deficient reorganization, darkness, and confusion, an attack at daylight on the 20th ordered by Bragg did not take place. Orders went astray and commanders could not be located in the woods.

Toward morning, Cleburne received an order directly from Polk, explaining that he had sought in vain to locate Hill and directed Cleburne to attack the enemy as soon as he could get in position. Polk sent an identical order to Breckinridge, now in position on Cleburne's right. About 7 A. M., Hill received a copy of these orders. He immediately sent a message to Polk, explaining that he had been trying to locate the corps commander for orders and that it would be an hour before his divisions could move. Hill's message continued, significantly:

"General Cleburne reports that the Yankees were felling trees all night, and consequently now occupy a position too strong to be taken by assault. What shall be done when this point is reached?"[50] Bragg, however, when in position near the right wing of the army at about 8 A. M., ordered Hill to attack as quickly as possible.

Meanwhile, in Cleburne's words, "I rode up and down my line more than once," observing the enemy position.[51] On receipt of the order to proceed with the attack, he responded just as he had on the second day at Shiloh, when in his view an attack was unwise had been overruled — he obeyed and did his utmost to succeed.

Again referring to Cleburne's official report of Chickamauga:

221

At about ten o'clock next morning [the 20th] I received orders from Lieut Gen. Hill to advance, and dress on the line of Gen. Breckinridge, who had been placed on my right. Accordingly, directing each Brigade to dress upon the right, and preserve its distance, I moved forward. Breckinridge was already in motion. The effort to overtake, and dress upon him, caused hurry and some confusion in my line, which was necessarily a long one.

Before the effects of this could be rectified, [Lucius] Polk's Brigade, and the right of Wood's encountered the heaviest Artillery-fire I have ever experienced. I was now within short canister range of a line of log breast-works, and a hurricane of shot and shell swept the woods, from the unseen enemy in my front.

This deadly fire was direct, and came from that part of the enemy's breast-works, opposite to my right and right centre; the rest of my line — stretching off to the left — received an oblique fire from the line of breast-works, which at a point opposite my centre formed a retiring angle, running off towards the Chattanooga-LaFayette road behind.

The accompanying map, showing the shape of the enemy's line of works opposite my line, will explain our relative positions.

Upon reference to it, it will be seen that opposite to my right and right-centre, the enemy's works ran about a half-a-mile north and south, and nearly parallel to the Chattanooga-LaFayette road, which was about three hundred yards behind; that at a point opposite my centre his works formed, as before stated, a retiring angle, running in a westerly, and somewhat oblique direction, to the Chattanooga-LaFayette road, and that at a point nearly opposite my right his works formed another retiring angle running back also to the road.

My right and right-centre, consisting of Polk's Brigade, and [M. P.] Lowrey's Regiment of Wood's Brigade, were checked within one hundred and seventy-five yards of the advance part of this portion of the enemy's works, and the rest of the line was halted in compliance with the order previously given to dress upon the right.

Passing toward the left at this time, I found that the line of advance of my Division, which was the left of the Right Wing of the Army, converged with the line of advance of the Left Wing of the Army; the flanks of the two wings had already come into collision — part of Wood's Brigade had passed over [William B.] Bate's Brigade of Stewart's Division, which was the right of the Left Wing; and Deshler's [Texas] Brigade, which formed my left, had been thrown out entirely, and was in rear of the Left Wing of the Army. I ordered Wood to move forward the remainder of his Brigade; opening at the same time in the direction of the enemy's fire with Semple's Battery.

That part of Wood's Brigade to the left of Lowrey's Regiment, and to the left of the Southern angle of the breast-works, in its advance at this time, entered an old field bordering the road (Chattanooga-LaFayette), and attempted to cross it in the face of a heavy fire from works in its front; it had almost reached the road, its left being at Poe's house (known as the Burning House), when it was driven back by a heavy oblique fire of small arms and Artillery which was opened upon both its flanks. The fire from the right coming from the South face of the breast-works, which was hid from view by the thick growth of scrub-oak bordering the field. Five hundred men were killed and wounded by this fire in a few minutes. Upon this repulse Lowrey's Regiment having also in the meantime been forced to retire, I ordered the Brigade still further back to reform. Semple's Battery, which had no position, I also ordered back.

I now moved Deshler's Brigade by the right flank, with the intention of connecting it with Polk's left, so filling the gap left in my centre by the withdrawal of Wood. This connection, however, I could not establish, as Polk's left had in its turn been also driven back. Finding it a useless sacrifice of life for Polk to retain his position, I ordered him to fall back with the rest of his line, and with his and Wood's Brigades I took up a strong defensive position, some three or four hundred yards in rear of the point from which they had been repulsed. Deshler's Brigade had moved forward towards the right of the enemy's advanced works, but could not go beyond the crest of a low ridge, from which Lowrey had been repulsed. I therefore ordered him to cover himself behind the ridge, and hold his position as long as possible. His Brigade was now en echelon about four hundred yards in front of the left of the rest of the Division, which here rested for some hours.

In effecting this last disposition of his command, Genl. Deshler fell — a shell passing fair through his chest. It was the first battle in which this gentleman had the honor of Commanding as a General Officer. He was a brave and efficient one. He brought always to the discharge of his duty a warm zeal, and a high conscientiousness. The Army and the Country will long remember him.[52]

Referring to the attack that morning by his two division commanders, Cleburne and Breckinridge, Hill wrote: "The faultiness of our plan of attack was now but too apparent. Perhaps never before in the history of war had an attack been made in a single line without reserves or supporting force. It was still more unfortunate that our attack was directly in front, against breastworks."[53]

Nevertheless, the attack made by Cleburne's and Breckinridge's divisions affected the outcome of the battle. Their assaults were so forceful that Thomas, commanding the Union left, repeatedly called for assistance. Rosecrans, convinced that the Confederate army planned to turn his left, hurried heavy reenforcements to Thomas from the Federal right. At about the same time that Rosecrans weakened his right, Confederate Generals Longstreet and John B. Hood launched an attack from the Confederate left, Hood being seriously wounded at the height of the assault. About 11 A.M., because of the shifting of Federal forces from the right to the left, a wide gap was created in the weakened Federal right-center.

The Confederates commanded by Longstreet surged through the opening.[54] Disregarding the order of the day to bear to the left, Longstreet with soldierly acumen wheeled his troops to the right and struck the exposed Federal right flank. The Union right and center were routed and fled the field. The bulk of the demoralized Federals fled to Chattanooga, as did Generals Rosecrans, Crittenden, and McCook, and Assistant Secretary of War Charles A. Dana. The latter was present at the battle as a special observer for Secretary Edwin M. Stanton. Dana wrote that he made his way into the city, "through a panic-stricken rabble."[55] Federal Gen. Philip H. Sheridan and part of his division ceased fleeing upon reaching a gap in Missionary Ridge but did not return to the battlefield.

Thomas formed a new line to his rear, on Snodgrass (or Horseshoe) Hill, at right angles to the Union left; and made a stubborn stand which arrested Longstreet's onslaught. Reenforced by a reserve corps under Gordon Granger which marched from Rossville to his battle line, Thomas resisted Longstreet's vigorous assaults throughout the long afternoon and until dusk when the "Rock of Chickamauga" retreated toward Chattanooga.

During the afternoon of the 20th, Cleburne and Breckinridge regrouped their troops for another general assault.

Breckinridge's command, in reforming, closed in on Cleburne's right, leaving a wide gap in the Confederate line almost opposite the angle formed by the left of the Union works. Two brigades of Cheatham were ordered to fill part of the gap, connecting with Breckinridge's left. Cleburne received an order from Leonidas Polk to move part of his division forward and to the right so as to fill the rest of the opening. Cleburne, as usual wished to examine the ground to be occupied. He had Polk's staff officer, Maj. W. W. Carnes, who had delivered the order, go with him and point out how far his line was to extend. As they were returning, Carnes "ventured to suggest" that the General was within shot-range of the Union guns, but Cleburne ignored the warning and did not change his horse's course or gait. When Federal infantry fire opened suddenly and minié balls whizzed by, the General turned his horse to the left and dashed quickly out of range into the timber.[56]

Again taking up Cleburne's report:

At about half-past-three o'clock P.M. I received orders from Lieut. Polk to move forward on a line with my left (Deshler), connecting my right with [John K.] Jackson's Brigade [of Cheatham's division], and when I had formed my line, to remain, and hold the position. I, accordingly, advanced with my centre and right-wing, drove in the enemy's skirmishers, and found his line behind the works from which he had repulsed us in the morning.

The Left Wing of the Army had been driving the enemy; the Right Wing now attacked, Lieut. Gen. Polk ordering me to advance my heavy Batteries, and open on the enemy. Capt Semple, my Acting Chief of Artillery (Maj. Hotchkiss, my Chief of Artillery, being disabled by a wound received the day before) selected positions in front of the line, and placed his own and Douglas' Batteries within two hundred yards of the enemy's breast-works, and opened a rapid and most effective fire, silencing immediately a Battery, which had been playing upon my lines. About the same time Brigadier-Genl. Polk charged, and soon carried the north-western angle of the enemy's works, taking in succession three lines of breastworks. In this brilliant operation he was materially aided by Key's Battery, and towards its close by Douglas' Battery, which had again been moved by my orders to my extreme right, where it was run into position by hand.

A large number of Prisoners (Regulars) was here captured;

the enemy abandoned his works, and retired precipitately. Brigadier Genl. Polk pursued to the Chattanooga-Lafayette road, where he captured another piece of artillery.

I here received directions from Lieut. Genl. Hill to halt my command until further orders.

I cannot close this report without an acknowledgement of distinguished services rendered by various Officers and men, which would, otherwise, pass unnoticed.

I have already incidentally called attention to the gallant conduct of Brig. Gen. Polk, but it is due to him and to the Country, which wishes to appreciate its faithful servants, to say that to the intrepidity and stern determination of purpose of himself and men, I was principally indebted for the success of the Charge on Sunday evening [September 20], which drove the enemy from his breast-works, and gave us the battle.

Col. [Roger Q.] Mills, also, is entitled to be remembered. Leading his regiment through the battle until the fall of his Brigadier, the lamented Deshler, he was then called by Seniority to Command the Brigade, which he did with gallantry and intelligence.[57]

Cleburne then expressed indebtedness to his staff "for the faithful and indefatigable manner, in which they performed their vital though perhaps not showy duties, throughout the operations." He again cited Benham, "who received a contusion on the right sholder"; Buck, "whose horse was shot under him"; Hotchkiss, "who received a wound from a Minie ball in the foot on Saturday, which deprived me of his valuable services afterwards"; Erskine; and J. K. Dixon. Other staff members cited were: Capt. B. F. Phillips, Assistant Inspector General; Capt. Henry C. Semple, who replaced Hotchkiss as Chief of Artillery; Capt. C. F. Vanderford, Chief of Ordnance; Lieut. L. H. Mangum; and Lieut. S. P. Hanly, who received a contusion from a grape-shot.[58]

The report continued;

Maj. T. R. Hotchkiss, Chief of Artillery, Capt. Semple with his Battery, and Lieut. Thomas J. Key, commanding Calvert's Battery, rendered invaluable service, and exhibited the highest gallantry, on Saturday night, in running their pieces up, as they did, within sixty yards of the enemy. In this they were ably sustained by Lieut. Richard Goldthwaite of Semple's Battery. Here Maj. Hotchkiss received his wound.

Capt. Semple also displayed skill and judgment, as acting

Chief of Artillery; particularly in the selection of a position for his own and Douglas's Batteries on Sunday evening, which gave an oblique fire upon the enemy in his works, contributing to the success of the final charge of Polk's Brigade.

Capt. O. S. Palmer, A.A. Gen of Wood's Brigade, was conspicuous for his coolness and attention to duty on the field, and has my thanks.

I am much indebted also to Dr. D. A. Linthicum, Chief Surgeon of my Division. The completeness of his arrangements, his careful supervision of subordinates, both on the field — under fire and elsewhere, and in the Hospitals, secured our gallant wounded prompt attention, and all the Comfort, and alleviation of pain, attainable in the exigencies of battle.

... Assistant Surgeon Alfred B. DeLoach particularly distinguished himself by his unselfish devotion — going repeatedly far forward under fire, and amongst the skirmishers, to attend the wounded.

James P. Brady, and Melvin L. Overstreet, privates in the Buckner Guards (my escort), specially detailed to attend me through the battle, went with me whereever [sic] my duty called me. Brady was wounded in the hand — Overstreet had his horse shot.

To Capt C. F. Vanderford, my Chief of ordnance, my thanks are specially due. His trains were always in the best order, and in the most accessible position, and to his care in this respect, I am indebted for a prompt supply of ammunition in every critical emergency which arose.

I carried into action on Saturday (the 19th) five thousand one hundred & fifteen (5,115) officers and men — four thousand eight hundred and seventy five (4,875) bayonets. On Sunday (the 20th) I carried in four thousand six hundred and seventy one (4,671) Officers and men — four thousand and four hundred and thirty seven (4,437) bayonets. In the two days my casualties were two hundred and four (204) killed, fifteen hundred and thirty nine (1,539) wounded, six (6) missing, making in all one thousand seven hundred and forty nine (1,749).[59]

Capt. H. W. Kinsey, Company C (formerly Yell Rifles), 15th Arkansas, Cleburne's friend of Helena days, serving in Liddell's brigade, Walker's corps, was fatally wounded.

Cleburne was unaware that the Union troops in the position attacked by Lucius Polk were preparing to withdraw, Thomas having ordered a general retirement from the field. Under the cover of night Thomas retreated to Rossville, and the triumphant Confederates were in possession of the entire battlefield. Thomas posted troops at Rossville Gap in a position which he said was "untenable," and so on the next night, September 21, fell back to Chattanooga.[60]

The evidence is convincing that Bragg did not realize on the afternoon and evening of the 20th that the Confederate army had won a great victory. He refused to accept the fact that the victory was achieved without following his battle plan.[61] On the morning of the 21st, Bragg's generals awaited orders to pursue and destroy Rosecrans while the Federals were defeated and demoralized, and, as yet, had not entrenched at Chattanooga. Even later in the day, when Bragg came to realize that there had been a complete Confederate victory, he failed to press forward rapidly and reap the benefits. By vacillation and indecision he had wasted the great opportunity purchased at a tremendous price in killed and wounded.

NOTES

CHAPTER IX

[1]John E. Conner, Chattanooga, conversation with authors, Feb. 22, 1970. Mr. Conner was born (1898) and reared two miles from Tyner's Station. Living in the area were veterans of Cleburne's division, and children and grandchildren of Cleburne's veterans. It was an accepted fact that the "much loved" General Cleburne had his headquarters in the Tyner house.

[2]*O.R.* XXIII, Pt. 2, p. 904-05.

[3]Conner, conversation with authors, Feb. 22, 1970.

[4]Buck, *Cleburne*, 134; Record of Events, Co. H, 33rd Alabama Infantry, July and Aug. 1863. At least one regiment of Wood's brigade, the 32nd Mississippi, remained at Tyner's Station. — Record of Events, Cos. A, C, D, E, and G, 32nd Mississippi Infantry, May and June 1863 (dated July 20, 1863), M269/347, NA; and Cos. B, F, H, I, and K, July and Aug. 1863.

[5]Hill, "Maj. Gen. Cleburne," 460.

[6]Circular dated July 21, 1863, Headquarters Hill's Corps, Army of Tennessee, By command of Cleburne, to A. P. Stewart, RG 109, NA; *O.R.*, XXX, Pt. 4, pp. 544-45.

[7]Conner, Conversation with authors, Feb. 22, 1970.

[8]Record of Events, Co. A, 32nd Mississippi Infantry, July and Aug. 1863; Irving Buck to his sister Lucie, Aug. 8, 1863, microfilm copy in Buck Papers.

[9]Arthur Howard Noll (ed.,), *Doctor Quintard, Chaplain C.S.A. and Second Bishop of Tennessee* (Sewanee, Tenn., 1905), 92-94; Hill, "Maj. Gen. Cleburne," 462; R. Q. Mills to J. P. Douglas, Jan. 10, 1901, in "Concerning Re-Enlistment at Dalton," *Confederate Veteran*, IX (1901), 13; handwritten notations, undated, on Burke Boykin & Company (print.), *Constitution of the Comrades of the Southern Cross: Adopted August 28th, 1863* (Macon, Ga., 1863), Uni. N.C. The pocket-sized printed pamphlet contains the constitution of twelve pages, and ten pages of specially composed prayers and hymns. To qualify for membership, one had to be "a commissioned officer or enlisted soldier in the Confederate States service, a free white male over eighteen years of age, intelligent in his military duties and of known patriotism and integrity, ..." The initiation fees were: general officers, $25.00; field officers, $15.00; captains, $10.00; lieutenants, $5.00; and privates, $2.00. Also there were monthly dues. The constitution provided for an insurance or "Charity Fund," to which members were required to contribute half

of one month's pay annually for two years. This fund would be for
the relief of wounded and disabled members, and indigent widows
and orphans of members who lost their lives in "the military service
of the Confederate States." Each meeting of an "Encampment" was
to begin by the reading of a Scripture lesson, followed by a hymn
and one of the prayers. An illustrative portion of a prayer was: ". . .
save and deliver us, we humbly beseech Thee, from the hands of our
enemies — abate their pride, assuage their malice, and confound their
devices; that we being armed with Thy defence, may be preserved
evermore from all perils, to glorify Thee who art the only giver of all
victory; . . . ." A typical stanza read:

> Now, in our deep distress,
> Oh! deign our cause to bless,
>   And hear our prayer;
> Now, while the din of war,
> And the loud cannon's roar,
> Resound from shore to shore,
>   Be ever near. — *Constitution, supra.*

It is a fair inference that Chaplain Quintard composed the prayers;
and Cleburne, the words of some of the hymns.

[10]Buck, *Cleburne*, 134; *O.R.*, XXX, Pt. 2, P. 137; *ibid.*, Pt. 4, pp.
532-33, 545; Record of Events, Cos. B and C, 35th (formerly 5th)
Tennessee Infantry, July and Aug. 1863; Record of Events, Co. B,
1st (Colquitt's) Arkansas Infantry, June 30 to Aug. 31, 1863,
M317/46, NA; Co. C, *ibid.*, July 1 to Aug. 31, 1863; Co. H, *ibid.*,
June 30 to Aug. 31, 1863; Record of Events, Cos. F, H, and I, 48th
(Nixon's) Tennessee Infantry, July and Aug. 1863, M268/312, NA;
Cos. G and I, *ibid.*, Sept. and Oct. 1863.

[11]*O.R.*, XXX, Pt. 4, p. 545; Record of Events, Co. E, 10th Texas
Infantry, Sept. and Oct. 1863; Record of Events, Co. D, 33rd
Alabama Infantry, July and Aug. 1863.

[12]*O.R.*, XXX, Pt. 4, pp. 532, 545, 553; Record of Events, Co. I, 48th
(Nixon's) Tennessee Infantry, July and Aug. 1863; Record of Events,
Co. A, 1st (Colquitt's) Arkansas Infantry, June 30 to Aug. 31, 1863;
Co. K, *ibid.*, July 1 to Aug. 31, 1863.

[13]Irving Buck to his sister Lucie, Aug. 29, 1863, microfilm copy in
Buck Papers; Record of Events, Co. C, 15th (Cleburne's — Polk's —
Josey's) Arkansas Infantry, July and Aug. 1863.

[14]*O.R.*, XXX, Pt. 4, pp. 594, 601.

[15]*Ibid.* p. 601; Record of Events, Co. H, 32nd Mississippi Infantry,
Sept. and Oct. 1863; Record of Events, Cos. B and E, 33rd Alabama
Infantry, Sept. and Oct. 1863.

[16]*O.R.*, XXX, Pt. 4, p. 622.

[17]Henry, *Confederacy,* 309.

[18]Record of Events, Co. B, 33rd Alabama Infantry, Sept. and Oct. 1863.

[19]*O.R.*, XXX, Pt. 4, p. 627; Record of Events, Co. D, 1st (Colquitt's) Arkansas Infantry, Sept. 1 to Oct. 31, 1863; Record of Events, Co. D, 32nd Mississippi Infantry, Sept. and Oct. 1863; Record of Events, Co. B, 33rd Alabama Infantry, Sept. and Oct. 1863.

[20]*O.R.*, XXX, Pt. 2, pp. 137, 299-300; Cleburne to D. H. Hill, Oct. 15, 1863, in D. H. Hill Papers, Virginia State Library, Richmond; Daniel H. Hill, "Chickamauga — The Great Battle of the West," in *Battles and Leaders,* III, 641; Buck, *Cleburne,* 136.

[21]*O.R.*, XXX, Pt. 2, pp. 137-38.

[22]Cleburne to Hill, Oct. 15, 1863, in Hill Papers, Virginia State Library.

[23]Will T. Martin to Bragg, undated but written in fall of 1867, University of Texas Library.

[24]Martin to Bragg, undated, cited note 23, *supra*; Bragg to E. T. Sykes, Feb. 8, 1873, in Polk, *Leonidas Polk,* II, 309.

[25]Hill, "Chickamauga," 646; *O.R.*, XXX, Pt. 2, p. 137.

[26]*O.R.*, XXX, Pt. 1, p. 326; *ibid.*, Pt. 2, pp. 138, 293, 299-300; *ibid.*, Pt. 4, p. 633; Record of Events, Cos. C and D, 32nd Mississippi Infantry, Sept. and Oct. 1863.

[27]Martin to Bragg, undated, cited note 23, *supra.*

[28]*O.R.*, XXX, Pt. 2, pp. 29, 138; Benham, *Kennesaw Gazette,* IV (Mar. 15, 1889), 2.

[29]*O.R.*, XXX, Pt. 2, pp. 294-95.

[30]*Ibid.*, p. 297.

[31]*Ibid.*, Pt. 1, pp. 247, 271-72, 327; *ibid.*, Pt. 2, pp. 29, 138-39, 296-97, 316; Benham, *Kennesaw Gazette,* IV (Mar. 15, 1889), 2; Buck, *Cleburne,* 139 (n) ; Martin to Bragg, undated, cited note 23, *supra*; Record of Events, Co. F, 35th (formerly 5th) Tennessee Infantry, Sept. and Oct. 1863; Record of Events, Cos. D and H, 32nd Mississippi Infantry, Sept. and Oct. 1863; Record of Events, Cos. B, D, E, F, and H, 33rd Alabama Infantry, Sept. and Oct. 1863. The Federal force in McLemore's Cove consisted of parts of Thomas' corps, *viz.:* James S. Negley's division, which entered the cove late on Sept. 9; two brigades of A. Baird's division, which joined Negley's division at Davis' Crossroads at 8 A.M. on Sept. 11; and one brigade of Joseph J. Reynold's division, which reached Negley two hours later. — *O.R.*, XXX, Pt. 1, pp. 247, 270.

[32]*O.R.*, XXX, Pt. 2, p. 301.

[33]*Ibid.*, pp. 29, 294-96, 301, 308, 311, 315-16; *ibid.*, Pt. 4, p. 636; Martin to Bragg, undated, cited note 23, *supra.*

[34]*O.R.*, XXX, Pt. 2, p. 296. The original communication is in T. C.

Hindman Papers, RG 109, NA. These papers also contain all the other communications quoted by Hindman in his "Report of Operations in McLemore's Cove on September 10 and 11, 1963," and accompanying exhibits, *O.R.*, XXX, Pt. 2, pp. 292-302, several of which are cited notes 20, 26, 29, 31, 32, and 33, *supra*.

[35] Bragg said in his report that he repeatedly sent couriers and staff officers to Hindman during the day, "urging him to move with promptness and vigor." — *O.R.*, XXX, Pt. 2, p. 29. However, there is a record of only one such message, sent at 3 P.M.: "Time is precious. The enemy presses from the north. We must unite or both must retire. . . . we only wait for your attack." — *Ibid.*, Pt. 4, p. 634.

[36] *Ibid.*, Pt. 2, p. 139; Record of Events, Co. F, 35th (formerly 5th) Tennessee Infantry, Sept. and Oct. 1863.

[37] *O.R.*, XXX, Pt. 1, p. 248; Record of Events, Co. F, 10th Texas Infantry, Sept. and Oct. 1863; Nov. and Dec. 1863.

[38] *O.R.*, XXX, Pt. 2, p. 139.

[39] *Ibid.* pp. 31, 139-40.

[40] Cleburne, "Report of Battle of Chickamauga" (MS in Benjamin Franklin Cheatham Papers, Tenn. Lib. and Arch.), 1. The same report, with differences in paragraphing and other slight editing, appears in *O.R.*, XXX, Pt. 2, pp. 155-58.

[41] "To the Memory of John A. Cathey and John R. Loftin," *Confederate Veteran*, XXVIII (1920), 70; Preston, "Memoirs," 20; Hill, "Chickamauga," 651.

[42] W. K. Pilsbury, "The Fifth Georgia at Chickamauga," *Confederate Veteran*, III (1895), 330.

[43] "James H. Wilkes," Columbia (Tenn.) *Daily Herald*, Mar. 13, 1907, p. 2.

[44] Cleburne, "Battle of Chickamauga," 1; Buck, *Cleburne*, 144; Preston, "Memoirs," 20.

[45] Cleburne, "Battle of Chickamauga," 1-2.

[46] Benham, *Kennesaw Gazette*, IV (Apr. 1, 1889), 2.

[47] Cleburne, "Battle of Chickamauga," 2-3. Years later, a Federal soldier wrote of the kindness of a squad from Cleburne's division as he lay wounded: ". . . just at dusk . . ., my leg was broken by a musket ball sent out by the Johnnies in our front. This occurred in the woods about a half mile to the west of Jay's Mill, and we were falling back at the time. Soon after our lines had fallen back the Confederates established their pickets for the night. A squad (five, if I remember correctly) were passing to the front about fifty yards from where I had fallen. I called to them. They halted, and asked who I was and what I wanted. I replied that I was a wounded Federal soldier, and wanted to be helped into an easier position, as I was

suffering from a broken leg. They came to me promptly and assisted me as gently as if I had been one of their own men or a brother to a large tree where I would be protected from the fire of our own men, first taking off my woolen blanket and spreading it down for me to lie on, placing my cartridge box under my head for a pillow and spreading an oilcloth over me.

"The tenderness with which they had lifted me touched me, and I said: 'Boys, an hour or two ago we were engaged in shooting each other, and now you are treating me with the greatest kindness. I hardly know how to thank you for it in return.' They only replied, 'Well, old fellow, we are doing to you only as we should like to be done by. It may come our turn next, and they passed on to the front picket line for the night. . . . the next morning, when I awoke from a half-feverish, dreamy sleep, I found that one of them had spread half of a homemade calico quilt over me, saying nothing about it, and doubtless keeping the other half to shelter him in his nightlong watch on picket post.

". . . The Confederates near our part of the line were of Cleburne's Division, ..." — W. C. Brown, veteran of 93rd Ohio Volunteer, "How Confederates Treated a Federal," *Confederate Veteran*, XIII (1905) 228.

[48]*O.R.*, XXX, Pt. 2, p. 140; Hill, "Chickamauga," 652.

[49]Preston, "Memoirs," 20; Record of Events, Co. F, 48th (Nixon's) Tennessee Infantry, Sept. and Oct. 1863; Record of Events, Cos. E and H, 33rd Alabama Infantry, Sept. and Oct. 1863.

[50]*O.R.*, XXX, Pt. 2, p. 53.

[51]Cleburne to Hill, Sept. 30, 1863, in Daniel Harvey Hill Papers, North Carolina Department of Archives and History, Raleigh.

[52]Cleburne, "Battle of Chickamauga," 3-6.

[53]*O.R.*, XXX, Pt. 2, p. 143.

[54]"By mistake, Rosecrans ordered T. J. Wood's Division to move from the right to the center of the Federal line about the same time that Hood and Longstreet launched the attack from the Confederate left. Eight Southern brigades, including the Texas Brigade [from the Army of Northern Virginia], poured through the half-mile gap left in Rosecrans' line by the withdrawal of Wood's Division." — Harold B. Simpson, *Hood's Texas Brigade: Lee's Grenadier Guard* (Waco, 1970), 324.

[55]Charles A. Dana, "Reminiscences of Men and Events of the Civil War," *McClure's Magazine*, X (1898), 353.

[56]W. W. Carnes, "Chickamauga," *S.H.S.P.*, XIV (1886), 403.

[57]Cleburne, "Battle of Chickamauga," 6-7. Col. R. Q. Mills later became a United States Senator from Texas.

[58]Cleburne, "Battle of Chickamauga," 7-8.

[59]*Ibid.*, 8-10. Twenty-one-year-old John Hollis Bankhead, captain of Co. K, 16th Alabama, Cleburne's division, was wounded while leading his company in a furious charge. When the dry sedge field where he lay caught fire, he managed to crawl to safety carrying a totally incapacitated private on his back. — Undated typewritten MS, p. 4, probably by Marie Bankhead Owen, in 16th Alabama Infantry Regiment (compiled data), Ala. Arch. and Hist. Captain Bankhead later was a United States Senator from Alabama. One of his sons, John Hollis Bankhead 2d, also was a United States Senator; and another son, William Brockman Bankhead, was Speaker of the House of Representatives and father of the actress Tallulah Bankhead.

The following names of members of Cleburne's division were inscribed in the Roll of Honor (see Chap. VIII, note 26) for their part in the battle of Chickamauga: *Alabama — 16th Regiment of Infantry:* Priv. George W. Tims, *k* Co. A; Priv. William A. Watts, *k* Co. B; Priv. William Hill, Co. C; Priv. Thomas Garner, *k* Co. D; Priv. Joshua Lewis, Co. E; Priv. John McMicken, *k* Co. F; Priv. James P. Young, *k* Co. G; Priv. Hiram L. White (since dead), Co. H; Corpl. W. Calvin Roden, *k* Co. I; Priv. David S. Stewart, Co. K. *33rd Regiment of Infantry:* Capt. W. E. Dodson, Co. C; Capt. B. F. Hammett, Co. D; Priv. W. R. Mock, Co. A; Priv. J. D. Pevy, Co. C; Sergt. C. L. Sessions, *k* Co. D; Priv. P. H. S. Lewis, *k* Co. E; 3rd Sergt. Richard R. Bush, *k* Co. G; Corpl. Alexander R. Bell, Co. H; Priv. W. E. Hatten, Co. I; Priv. William Harris, Co. K. The other companies made no selection. *Semple's Battery:* Priv. Robert G. Chambliss. *Arkansas. — 1st Regiment of Infantry:* Col John W. Colquitt; Adjt. S. N. Greenwood, *k*; Capt. Samuel Shoup, Co. G; 1st Lieut. Louis Hillman, Co. H; 1st Lieut. James G. Wilson, Co. F; 1st Lieut. A. J. Pitner, Co. B; 1st Lieut. M. G. Harris, Co. C; 2nd Lieut. Augustus Ruffner, Co. D; Sergt. L. J. Perry, Co. A; Priv. Charles Trickett, Co. B; Priv. J. W. Bell, Co. C; Sergt. N. B. Marshall, Co. D; Priv. J. H. Callahan, Co. E; Sergt. F. S. Barnett, Co. F; Priv. Joseph Hubbard, Co. G; Priv. James Word, Co. H; Priv. James R. Griffin, Co. I; Sergt. M. L. Nobles, Co. K. *19th and 24th Regiments of Infantry (consolidated):* Priv. Jacob Nugent, Co. A; Priv. G. W. Green, Co. B; Priv. C. W. Jones, Co. C; Priv. J. B. Floyd, Co. D; Priv. J. T. Cooper, Co. E; Priv. William Holman, Co. F; Priv. Peter Simpson, Co. G; Priv. Thaddeus Glass, Co. H; Priv. T. J. Thompson, Co. I; Sergt. W. L. White, Co. K. *Mississippi. — 32rd Regiment of Infantry:* Priv. Smith Scroggins (since dead), Co. A; Priv. J. B. Milton, *k* Co. B; Priv. Samuel H. Stevenson, Co. C; Priv. J. W. Looney, *k* Co. D; Priv. Munroe W. Miller, *k* Co. E; Priv. J. M. Cooper, Co. F; Sergt. C. H. Reed, Co. G; Second Sergt. John Calvin Dean, Co. H; Priv. C. C. Campbell, *k* Co. I;

Sergt. T. W. Crabb, Co. K. *45th Regiment of Infantry*: Priv. John J. Mahaffey, Co. A; 4th Sergt. F. M. McGaughy, Co. B, Priv. Joel Swindle, Co. C; Priv. E. H. Templeton, Co. D; Priv. Newton M. Brown, *k* Co. E; Priv. Samuel McNeely, Co. F; Priv. George W. Young, Co. G; Priv. Odom Cox, *k* Co. K. *Hawkins' battalion of sharpshooters*: 2nd Lieut. R. V. Coleman, *k* Co. A; Priv. Robert Jackson Custer, Co. A; Corpl. J. R. Wallis, Co. B. *Tennessee. – 2nd Regiment of Infantry*: Col. W. D. Robison; Lieut. Col. W. J. Hale; Capt. James T. C. McKnight, *k* Co. A; Capt. William P. Bowers, *k* Co. D; 1st Lieut. A. B. Schell, Co. I; Sergt. John W. Stone (color bearer); Priv. James O. Islin, Co. A; Sergt. Joseph D. Sheppard, Co. B; Priv. Andrew J. Allen, Co. C; Corpl. William R. Lamb, Co. D; Priv. Wallace Whitsett, Co. E; Sergt. W. J. Tood, Co. F; 1st Sergt. Thomas E. Stone, Co. H; Priv. James B. Malone, Co. I; Priv. John H. Terry, Co. K. *5th Regiment of Infantry*: Priv. R. A. Burton, Co. A; Priv. E. G. Seaton, Co. B; Priv. W. J. Thornton, Co. C; Priv. R. A. Coley, Co. E; Sergt. James G. Moffatt, Co. F; 5th Sergt. Patrick Kennedy, Co. H; Priv. G. M. Comer, Co. I. *35th Regiment of Infantry*: Col. B. J. Hill; Maj. G. S. Deakins; 1st Lieut. Warner Lewis, Co. H; 2nd Lieut. Z. B. Hamrick, Co. B; 2nd Lieut. W. W. Masey, Co. E; Sergt. Joseph Hambles (color bearer); 1st Sergt. James P. Hardcastle, Co. A; Corpl. W. J. Carter, Co. A; Corpl. A. J. Womack, Co. A; Sergt. F. T. Vannerson, Co. B; Corpl. S. R. Wood, Co. C; Priv. G. W. Martin, Co. C; Priv. Jesse Mooneyham, Co. C; Sergt. A. J. Taylor, Co. D; 1st Sergt. J. W. Warren, Co. E; Priv. M. Ritchey, Co. E; Priv. James W. Seal, Co. E; Priv. Barney Tomney, Co. F; Priv. James Anderson Hicks, Co. F; Priv. John Kennedy, Co. F; Priv. B. B. Snipes, Co. G; Sergt. Reuben C. Garner, Co. G; Priv. T. W. Wilson, Co. G; Priv. T. M. Golston, Co. H; Priv. M. E. Deakins, Co. H; Priv. West Walker, Co. H; Priv. J. M. Davis, Co. L; Priv. Thomas Lemons, Co. L; Priv. J. M. Head, Co. L; *48th Regiment of Infantry*: Col. George H. Nixon; Lieut. Col. Thomas R. Hughs; Capt. Lewis Miller, Co. G; Capt. James C. Cooper, Co. E; 1st Lieut. C. B. Tracy, Co. K; 1st Lieut. James Jackson, Co. F; 2nd Lieut. G. W. Prior, Co. G; Priv. B. F. Martin, Co. E; Priv. William McClain, Co. E; Sergt. B. F. Whitaker, Co. F; Sergt. C. P. Acklin, Co. F; Priv. J. M. Harding, Co. G; Priv. M. D. Harwell, Co. G; Priv. H. B. West, Co. H; Priv. A. A. Pennington, Co. H; Sergt. W. L. Ivy, Co. I; Priv. J. R. Choat, Co. I; Priv. J. G. Fuller, Co. K; Priv. A. J. Williams, Co. K. *3rd and 5th Confederate Infantry*: Maj. R. J. Person; Capt. James H. Beard, *k* Co. E; Capt. George Moore, *k* Co. H; Sergt. John Callahan, Co. A; Sergt. William McNamara, Co. C; Sergt. Walter Laracy, Co. D; Sergt. T. F. Brennan, Co. E; Sergt. Edward Doyle, Co. F; Sergt. George Cook, Co. G; Corpl. R. H.

Coleman, Co. H; Priv. Frederick Taffe, Co. B; Priv. Jack Wright, Co. E; Sergt. E. L. Moore,. Co. F. *Calvert's Battery*: Priv. James McCortney; Priv. George McMillan. *Douglas' Battery*: Priv. Eli E. Douglas. *Texas. — 6th and 10th Regiments of Infantry and 15th Regiment of Cavalry, dismounted (consolidated)*: Priv. Henry H, Cox, 6th Regiment, Co. H; Priv. James D. Smith, 10th Regiment, Co. H; Priv. Robert Cosby, 15th Regiment, Co. H. *17th, 18th, 24th, and 25th Regiments of Cavalry, dismounted (consolidated)*: Priv. David L. Hall, 18th Regiment, Co. F; Sergt. W. R. Burleson, 18th Regiment, Co. G; Sergt. Julian J. Lacoure, 25th Regiment, Co. H. Other companies declined selecting. — *O.R.*, XXX, Pt. 2, pp. 533-35, 537, 539-42. *k* Killed in action.

[60]*O.R.*, XXX, Pt. 1, p. 254.

[61]Glenn Tucker, *Chickamauga: Bloody Battle in the West* (Indianapolis, 1961), 303-04, 377-80; Connelly, *Autumn of Glory*, 225, 228-29; *cf.* Wiliam W. Mackall, *A Son's Recollections of His Father* (New York, 1930), 178-79.

CHAPTER X

MISSIONARY RIDGE – RINGGOLD GAP
(November 23 – 27, 1863)

With this affair [Ringgold Gap] there is nothing in
history comparable, except the Pass of Thermopylae
and the Bridge of Lodi.
– *Capt. C. W. Frazer, "Fifth Confederate."*

On the night of September 21, 1863, Cleburne's division
marched from the Chickamauga battlefield toward Chattanooga and bivouacked at Red House Ford, which crossed the
Chickamauga five miles east of Rossville. The next day, the division moved to a site on the crest and eastern slope of Missionary
Ridge, some three miles from the north end; and encamped.
Units were thrown "in front of Chattanooga at the foot of
Missionary Ridge," where a line of battle was established. The
night of September 22, Cleburne's skirmishers moved nearer
Chattanooga, almost to the railroad station. Company captains
of the 35th and 48th Tennessee recorded, "a lively skirmish
with enemy on night 24th running them over a mile."[1]
Bragg decided to invest Chattanooga and attempt to starve
the Federals into surrender. He established an extensive line
of rifle pits designed to cut off Rosecrans' communications.
From the north end of Missionary Ridge the pits extended
along the western base of the ridge about six miles, thence
west across the valley south of the city, and on to the
western slope of Lookout Mountain. Most of the Confederate
army was stationed on or near Missionary Ridge. Thus began
the investment operation which involved much watching but
little fighting for the next two months. Cleburne's division
remained in its position three miles from the north end of the
Confederate line. The troops underwent numerous hardships,
with much exposure to rain and cold because of the shortage
of tents, blankets, and shoes, "some of the men having their
feet on the ground."[2]
Because of Bragg's mismanagement at Chickamauga and

237

his attempt to shift the blame to other generals, efforts were made by his division and corps commanders to have him relieved as commander of the Army of Tennessee. On October 9, President Davis arrived to investigate first hand the numerous complaints and apparent command problems in the Army. A meeting of the senior commanders was called at Bragg's headquarters. In the presence of Bragg, Davis asked every officer to give his opinion of the commanding General. Each officer expressed an adverse opinion and said, in effect, that a new commander for the Army of Tennessee was essential. Cleburne expressed views similar to those contained in his letter to Bragg after the battle of Murfreesboro, and declared that a change was absolutely necessary.[3] The results of Davis' visit were: Bragg was retained as commander, D. H. Hill was relieved of his command, Leonidas Polk was sent to Mississippi to take Hardee's command, Hardee was brought back to succeed Polk, and Forrest was promoted and sent to Mississippi.

Cleburne's division was augmented by the return of Liddell's brigade, which had been temporarily detached as already noted. In the battle of Chickamauga, Brig. Gen. St. John Liddell, serving in Walker's corps, had commanded a small division which included his brigade. Col. D. C. Govan, of Phillips County, Arkansas, 2nd Arkansas Regiment, Liddell's brigade, had commanded the brigade in the battle. Several changes were made in Cleburne's division. To succeed Deshler, Col. J. A. Smith, 5th Confederate Regiment, Polk's brigade, was promoted to the rank of Brigadier General in command of the Texas Brigade. Wood, who resigned his commission as commander of the Mississippi and Alabama Brigade, was succeeded by Col. M. P. Lowrey of the 32nd Mississippi Infantry.

Late in October, Cleburne's division moved about a mile southward along Missionary Ridge. The new location was between Shallow Ford Road, which crossed the ridge about four miles from the north end, and General Bragg's headquarters, on the crest of the ridge five miles from the north end.[4] In leisure moments, Cleburne and members of his staff enjoyed an unique game of checkers. They used a checkerboard drawn on the ground; and colored leaves, for the "men."[5] Cleburne also attended meetings of Masonic Lodge No. 106, in Ringgold, Georgia.[6]

While at Missionary Ridge, Cleburne and two other general officers recommended Col. J. H. Kelly for promotion to Brigadier General. Kelly had been one of Cleburne's outstanding regimental commanders in the battle of Murfreesboro and had performed in a meritorious manner in subsequent operations. Just prior to Chickamauga, the twenty-three-year-old Kelly had been assigned to Buckner's corps, where he handled a brigade competently. As of November 1863, he became the youngest general officer in the Confederate Army.[7]

On November 8, 1863, from his headquarters on Missionary Ridge, Cleburne wrote to Bragg's adjutant David Urquhart requesting a commission for a young Englishman on his staff. The letter read:

> A week or two since I forwarded to your Head Quarters an application for a commission for Mr. Byrne. I am very desirous to see the application successful. This young gentleman is eminently deserving. He left England to volunteer his services in our cause. He has been on my staff. I have found him a brave and gallant officer, highly intelligent, and devoted to our cause.
>
> I am the more anxious he should be appointed, because he sacrificed the opportunity of being commissioned in the British Service. He passed the examination required to entitle him to be placed on the list of possible appointees, before he left England, which he did upon a limited leave of absence. His *leave* has now expired, and, as he understands, he has forfeited his chance of being subjected in that service.
>
> I write you this for such ends as may be convenient, and I shall feel much gratified if by any use of it, you can advance the gentleman's interest.[8]

The reply Cleburne received from Richmond stated that the appointment could not be made as a division was allowed only two assistant adjutants-general. Cleburne already had two and there was no vacancy in any other division. The letter concluded, "The Department would be glad to reward Mr. Byrne for the Sacrifice he has made; but the restrictions of Law and usage forbid it at present. His papers have been placed on file."[9]

While Cleburne and his division still occupied a sector in the line of investment, sometime prior to November 12, Cleburne's youngest brother, Pvt. Chris Cleburne, Company I, 2nd Kentucky Cavalry, arrived on horseback. He was a survivor of Morgan's ill-starred raid into Indiana and Ohio. Pending a reorganization of Morgan's command, Chris became a member of Lucius Polk's infantry brigade, where he was known as "Kit." Benham and Buck wrote that Chris served "in the ranks"; but a Confederate quartermaster record dated December 3, 1863, reads, "Lt. C. Cleburne," and one of December 28, "C. Cleburne, Lt. Co.__, 1st Arks." Apparently he had no formal commission but served in the capacity of a lieutenant or at least was called by that rank.10

From the beginning of the investment the Federals had shown much activity. Late in October, Grant, now in overall command in the West, arrived in Chattanooga and George Thomas succeeded Rosecrans as commander of the besieged Army of the Cumberland. Parts of two corps from the Army of the Potomac under the command of "Fighting Joe" Hooker arrived by ˙rail from Virginia. On October 28, Hooker's force, having advanced from Bridgeport, broke the Confederate blockade in Wills Valley. Also, four divisions that had participated in the Vicksburg campaign, commanded by Sherman, were en route from Memphis to Chattanooga to reinforce Thomas.

Although Bragg was well advised of the Union legions massing against him, early in November he sent Longstreet with fifteen thousand men (including cavalry) — about one-third of the Confederate army — to drive Ambrose Burnside from Knoxville. Responding to Longstreet's call for more men, and erroneously supposing that Grant was moving troops to reinforce Burnside, Bragg on November 22 ordered Cleburne to Knoxville with additional forces. However, he wrote Longstreet, "From the great strength of the enemy here you will see the importance of the return of General Cleburne's forces as soon as possible."11

2

Taking up the account in Cleburne's report of the battle of Missionary Ridge, dictated by him with Buck as amanuensis:

On the morning of the 23rd November, 1863, I was with my division at Chickamauga Station, on the Western and Atlantic Railroad, attending to the transportation of Buckner's and my own division by rail to Loudon, E. Tenn., where, with both divisions, I was ordered to report to Lieutenant-General Longstreet, then besieging Knoxville.

I had sent off all of Buckner's division except [A. W.] Reynolds' brigade, when I received the following order from army headquarters, viz:

"The general commanding desires that you will halt such portions of your command as have not yet left Chickamauga; such as may have left halt at Charleston [thirty miles northeast of Chattanooga]. Do not, however, separate brigades; if parts of brigades have gone, let the remaining portion of the brigade go, but halt at Charleston."

In compliance with the above, I sent forward the remainder of Johnson's brigade, but took a portion of Reynolds' brigade off the cars as it was about to start. I also telegraphed to Brig. Gen. Bushrod Johnson, commanding Buckner's division, directing him to halt the division at Charleston.

I immediately after received the following dispatch from army headquarters, viz:

"Order Johnson's troops at Charleston back here. Move up rapidly with your whole force."

I dispatched General Johnson accordingly.

In a few minutes after I received the following, viz:

"We are heavily engaged. Move up rapidly to these headquarters.

BRAXTON BRAGG."

Instructing Brigadier-General Polk to bring up the division, I galloped forward to headquarters for further instructions. I was ordered to rest for the night immediately behind Missionary Ridge, and placed my division accordingly. Returning to General Bragg's headquarters, he informed me that my division would act as reserve for the army, and would report directly to him. I ordered Reynolds' brigade, which I brought back with me from Chickamauga, to be reported directly to General Bragg, and had no further control of it.

During the night our line along the western front of Missionary Ridge was abandoned, and at early dawn I commenced to construct a new line of defense along the top of the ridge from the Shallow Ford road to General Bragg's headquarters. Before this was completed General Bragg informed me that the enemy had crossed the Tennessee River, both above and below the mouth of the Chickamauga, and directed me to send a brigade and battery to the East Tennessee and Georgia Railroad bridge over the Chickamauga to guard that point. I sent Brigadier-General Polk's command

and Semple's battery.[12]

Govan, commanding Liddell's brigade, the latter absent on leave, reminisced: "The day preceding the battle we stood on Missionary Ridge and saw the deployment of Gen. Grant's immense army, . . . a spectacle well calculated to test the nerves of the soldiers; but our veterans never wavered."[13]
Continuing with Cleburne's graphic report:

> About 2 P. M. on the 24th November, I received orders to proceed with the remaining three brigades and the batteries of my division to the right [toward the north end] of Missionary Ridge, near the point where the tunnel of the East Tennessee and Georgia Railroad passes through Missionary Ridge, where I would find an officer of General Hardee's staff, who would show me my position. At the same time General Bragg informed me that the enemy had already a division in line opposite the position I was intended to occupy; that he was rapidly crossing another, and had nearly completed a pontoon bridge over the Tennessee opposite my position. He also told me I must preserve the railroad bridge in my rear, where Brigadier-General Polk was stationed, at all hazards. Galloping forward ahead of my command, I found Major [D. H.] Poole, of General Hardee's staff, at the tunnel, who informed me he had been left by General Hardee to show me my position.
>
> I will attempt here a description of the ground. The right of Missionary Ridge, to which I was ordered, runs nearly north and south, parallel to the Tennessee River, which is about 1½ miles west of it. From the tunnel north along the ridge it is about a mile to the Chickamauga River, which bounds the ridge on that side, flowing thence westwardly into the Tennessee River. To simplify the description, the two rivers and the ridge may be said to form three sides of a square. The Tennessee Valley, between the rivers and the ridge, is mostly level, with a continuation of cleared fields bordering the ridge, but immediately in front of the center of my position, about 1,200 yards north and 600 yards west of the railroad tunnel, was a high detached ridge, which in a military point of view dominated over every point within cannon range.
>
> After passing through the tunnel the railroad runs in a northeasterly direction to the Chickamauga, which it crossed on the bridge Brigadier-General Polk was guarding. From the east side of the main ridge there projected two spurs, one, on the north boundary, with its precipitous north side washed by the Chickamauga; the other, jutting out just north of the tunnel, did not run directly back, but northeasterly for 1,000

yards, forming an acute angle with the parent ridge. Opposite the right of this spur, the main ridge was intersected by a little valley, through which came a road from the Tennessee Valley, where the enemy now was. The highest point on my line, and the point of chief interest in the battle on the right, and which I shall designate in this report as Tunnel Hill, was situated on the main ridge 250 yards north of the tunnel. The position pointed out for my command by Major Poole was to occupy, with one brigade, the detached ridge in the Tennessee Valley, and with the remainder of my command to stretch from the top of Tunnel Hill to the right of Walker's division, three- -quarters of a mile south of the tunnel.

I sent Major Poole to inform General Hardee that I had but three brigades, and could not cover so long a line. The head of my division, Smith's (Texas) brigade, was now at hand, and at the same moment reported to me from the detached ridge. Private Henry Smith, of the signal corps of my division, informed me he was just from that point; that the enemy was advancing on it in line of battle. I ordered Smith to move his brigade rapidly and try to get possession of it before the enemy had gained a foothold, but if he found the enemy in possession to fall back on the main ridge. General Smith moved into the valley, but was fired on from the top of the detached ridge as he approached its foot. Smith was too late. The enemy had crowned the ridge. He therefore marched by his right flank on to the main or Missionary Ridge, and formed on its top, his two left regiments facing the detached ridge, his right regiment thrown back in an easterly direction to protect his flanks. Smith had scarcely thrown out skirmishers before he was briskly attacked by the skirmishers of the enemy.[14]

Realizing that the Federals might make an immediate assault, Cleburne rapidly rode over the site he was to hold, carefully examining the ground and the approaches. He quickly set about placing the rest of his division.[15] His official report continued:

> In the meantime, I had placed Lowrey's brigade in position south of the tunnel and was about placing Govan's brigade on his left so as to complete my connection with Walker's division, when my attention was attracted to the fighting on my right. It was evident the enemy was endeavoring to turn my right flank and get possession of the main ridge between my right and the Chickamauga. If he succeeded, my connection with Brigadier-General Polk and my line of retreat by the bridge he was guarding was cut, and the safety of the whole

army was endangered. Instead of placing Govan's brigade on the main ridge, I placed him on that spur in rear of it which jutted out just north of the tunnel and covered the valley and road before described, which led over the main ridge from the direction of the enemy. Govan rapidly threw skirmishers across this road and between it and the Chickamauga.

Lieutenant-General Hardee was soon on the ground in person. He approved my dispositions, directed the destruction of a bridge which crossed the Chickamauga close in rear of my right flank, and ordered two regiments of Lowrey's brigade and some artillery into position in rear of my right flank. Between the left of Smith's brigade and Walker's division, a distance of near a mile, there was now but two regiments of Lowrey's brigade, and it so remained all night and until 7 A. M. next day.

It was now dark; the fighting had ceased in front of Smith's; he had maintained his position. Hearing of the disaster at Lookout,[16] I supposed our army would fall back beyond the Chickamauga, and accordingly had sent my ordnance and artillery across that river, with the exception of the two pieces of cannon planted beyond my right flank. I sent Captain Buck, my assistant adjutant-general, to head-quarters of the army so as to receive any orders that might be given as quickly as possible. About midnight he returned with the information that it was determined to await the enemy's attack on Missionary Ridge. I now ordered my artillery and ordnance to join me at daylight, sent to my train for the axes belonging to the division in order to throw up some defenses, and rode out myself to make a moonlight survey of the ground and line of retreat. I found a hill on the north bank of the Chickamauga, between my right and the railroad bridge, guarded by General Polk, which completely commanded my line of retreat.[17]

Cleburne's military skill is demonstrated in his placement of troops and artillery:

I ordered Brigadier-General Polk to occupy this hill at once with two regiments of infantry and a section of artillery. Discovering the facility which it afforded for turning me on the extreme right, I determined to immediately throw a line across the other east spur of Missionary Ridge, which jutted out from the north point of the ridge, and was washed by the Chickamauga. I placed the two regiments of Lowrey's brigade, left near the tunnel, on this line. In the meantime, Smith had thrown up some defenses in his front, but at my suggestion he now abandoned them and took up position as follows, viz, his

left resting on the crest of the main ridge about 150 yards
north of the tunnel, and running north along the crest for the
length of one regiment, the Sixth, Tenth, and Fifteenth Texas
(consolidated), Col. R. Q. Mills commanding. The right of this
regiment rested close under the crest of Tunnel Hill. On the
top of Tunnel Hill a space was left clear of infantry, and
Swett's battery of four Napoleon guns, commanded by Lieut.
H. Shannon, was placed on it so as to sweep north in the
direction of Smith's old position, northwest of the detached
ridge, or west into the Tennessee Valley as occasion might
require. At a point about 60 yards northeast of the right of
Mills' regiment, Smith's line recommenced, but instead of
continuing north, it now ran but slightly north of east down
the side of the hill for the length of two regiments, the
Seventh Texas, Col. H. B. Granbury commanding, and the
Seventeenth, Eighteenth, Twenty-fourth, and Twenty-fifth
Dismounted Cavalry (consolidated), Maj. W. A. Taylor commanding. This formation made the angle on the apex of
Tunnel Hill, where Swett's battery was planted, the weak
point in Smith's line, but it secured Smith's flank by throwing
his extreme right back within 200 yards of Govan's left,
bringing the latter officer's line nearly at right angles to his
north front, thus enabling each line to assist the other if
attacked. At a favorable point on Govan's line, selected by
General Hardee, I placed Douglas' battery, commanded by
Lieut. John N. Bingham, so as to enfilade any line attempting
to charge Smith's north front. Lowrey's position, across the
spur before mentioned, was en echelon about 200 paces in
front of Govan. I ordered the whole of his brigade to occupy
this position, and completed my line from Tunnel Hill to
[the] Chickamauga. Lowrey had no artillery, the spur being
too steep to admit of its being brought up. Calvert's battery,
commanded by Lieut. Thomas J. Key, I placed directly over
the tunnel, and between the tunnel and left of Smith's brigade
were placed three regiments of Brown's brigade, of Stevenson's
division. I was determined to construct a slight work in front
of my line. I was prevented for some time by an eclipse of the
moon, which rendered the morning very dark, but at length,
distributing our few axes, we went to work.[18]

Cleburne gave a modest account of his division's remarkable achievement:

> The day broke hazy, so that it was some time before the
> enemy could discover our operations. As soon as he did, he
> commenced a heavy fire on General Smith's working party,
> and prevented us from erecting any work whatever in front of

the battery on the top of Tunnel Hill. Up to 10:30 A. M. the enemy contented himself with severe skirmishing, and a heavy artillery fire from batteries erected by him during the night on the detached hill. About this hour he drove in Smith's skirmishers, and possessed himself of the breastworks which Smith had abandoned that morning. A heavy attack on the tunnel and on Smith's line was now imminent. General Hardee sent me directions to take my position at the tunnel, and to take charge of everything in that quarter and to the right of it. The enemy was now in sight, advancing in two long lines of battle, his right stretching far beyond my left, his left stretching beyond Smith's right, where farther view of it was prevented by the woods that covered and bordered the detached hill. For the full understanding of the fierce conflict that followed, it would be proper for me in this place to give a statement of the force of the enemy opposite my position as ascertained at a later hour from prisoners and other sources. It consisted of the divisions of Maj. Gen. Jef. C. Davis, three divisions of the army brought by Sherman from Vicksburg, and Howard's (Eleventh) corps, of the Army of the Potomac, all under the command of Major-General Sherman.

At 11 A. M. the first serious fight of the day commenced. It was heavy along Smith's whole line, and extended some distance south of the tunnel. The right of the enemy's line, exposed to the fire of several pieces of artillery planted over the tunnel, and met by a brigade sent by General Hardee to the foot of the ridge, swayed backward and forward for some time, but did not dare to advance nearer than 400 yards, and finally lay down, contenting itself with sending forward a large body of skirmishers and sending to the rear a much larger number of stragglers. The enemy's left, however, under shelter of Smith's abandoned work of the night before, and protected by the woods on that flank, and by the precipitous, heavily wooded sides of Tunnel Hill, advanced rapidly on Smith's line, and finally made a heavy charge on Swett's battery on the apex of the hill. The artillerymen stood bravely to their guns under a terrible cross-fire, and replied with canister at short range, but still the enemy advanced. When he had reached within 50 steps of the battery, Brigadier-General Smith charged him with the right of Mills' regiment and the left of the Seventh Texas, Smith's north front pouring into him from the breastworks a close volley at the same time. The enemy was routed and driven back to his cover behind the hill-side and abandoned work.[19]

Years later, a private in the Douglas' battery wrote that General Cleburne, on horseback, "was in the midst of the fight."[20] This was typical of Cleburne. The General's account continued:

> In this charge Brigadier-General Smith and Colonel Mills were both severely wounded at the head of their men. Col. H. B. Granbury, Seventh Texas, now assumed command of Smith's brigade. In less than half an hour the enemy made another desperate charge. He was met by the Texas men and artillery in front. Douglas' battery enfiladed him from Govan's hill, and Lowrey's extreme left regiment got a long-range volley on his flank. He was driven back in confusion as before.
>
> In these attacks Lieut. H. Shannon, commanding Swett's battery, was wounded. The command devolved on Lieut. Joseph Ashton; in a few minutes he was mortally wounded. The command then fell on Corpl. F. M. Williams. So many non-commissioned officers and men had been killed and disabled in the battery, Colonel Granbury was forced to make a detail from the infantry to work the guns. There was now a short lull in the battle during which, at the request of Colonel Granbury, I detailed the Second, Fifteenth, and Twenty-fourth Arkansas (consolidated), under Lieutenant-Colonel [E.] Warfield, from Govan's left, and posted them immediately in rear of the battery on top of the Tunnel Hill. I sent two of Swett's 12-pounders to report to Colonel Govan, as Douglas' guns were too light to be effective in their present position. I ordered Key's battery of four light field pieces to move up and replace the guns sent off, and put Lieutenant Key in command of all the artillery on Tunnel Hill.
>
> About 1 P. M. it was evident that another grand attack was soon to be made on my division. In a few minutes after it commenced. The enemy again lined Smith's abandoned works, and from them kept up a close, incessant fire on Smith's north front, and particularly on the artillery on top of the hill. Simultaneously a charge was made on the west face of Tunnel Hill. Warfield's regiment was thrown forward outside of the work to the crest of the hill, looking into the Tennessee Valley, to meet this charge. Key fired rapidly into the charging line as it crossed the open ground at the west foot of the ridge, but it was soon under shelter. At the steep the enemy's line now seemed to form into a heavy column on the march and rushed up the hill in the direction of the batteries. Warfield's fire stopped the head of the charging column just under the crest. Here the enemy lay down behind trees, logs, and projecting rocks, their first line not 25 yards from the guns, and opened fire. Tier after tier of the enemy, to the foot of the hill and in the valley beyond, supplied this fire and concentrated the whole on a space of not more than 40 yards,

till it seemed like one continuous sheet of hissing, flying lead. This terrific fire prevented Warfield's men from moving sufficiently forward to fire with effect down the hill, but otherwise it only swept over our heads. The cross-fire from Smith's abandoned work was, however, more fatal. It took Warfield in flank and was constantly disabling men near the top of the hill.

This desperate attack had now lasted more than half an hour. Key was depressing his guns to the utmost and firing shell and canister down the hill in the face of the enemy's fire. Discovering the impossibility of reaching the enemy by a direct fire, the officers of Warfield's regiment were pitching down heavy stones, apparently with effect.

General Hardee, from a hill south of the tunnel, seeing the stubbornness of the fight, had placed some pieces of artillery in position and was endeavoring to dislodge the enemy with a flank fire, but his right flank was protected by an intervening projection of the hill he was on and this fire was not effective. General Hardee also sent a brigade to move north along the west face of the ridge to strike the enemy in flank, but this brigade returned without accomplishing anything. At his point of the fight Colonel [J. T.] McConnell, commanding a Georgia regiment of [Alfred] Cumming's brigade, came up to the threatened point, and moved his regiment forward to where Warfield's men were fighting. McConnell was shot through the head, and his regiment fell back or was withdrawn. Brigadier-General Cumming, of Stevenson's division, now reported to me with the remainder of his brigade, and was posted in rear of the threatened point. Brigadier-General [George] Maney, of Walker's division, also reported to me with his brigade, and was posted in rear of Smith's line and parallel to it, with instructions to support the Texas brigade behind the works and the artillery at the angle.

The fight had lasted unceasingly for an hour and a half, and the enemy seemed to be constantly re-enforcing. The First and Twenty-seventh Tennessee, of Maney's brigade, Colonel [Hume R.] Field [Feild] commanding, was moved in front of the work, and placed on Warfield's right, the latter officer and his gallant regiment, still nobly holding their exposed position, although the regiment was diminished in numbers and almost out of ammunition. It was at this critical period of the day that Lieutenant-Colonel Warfield suggested to me that our men were wasting ammunition and becoming disheartened at the persistency of the enemy, and proposed a charge down upon them with the bayonet. Brigadier-General Cumming gallantly proposed to lead the charge with two of his regiments. I immediately consented, and directed General Cumming to prepare for the charge, and went to the left to see that a simultaneous charge was made on the enemy's right flank. I now ordered the left of Mills' (Texas) regiment, being the extreme left of my division, to make the charge on the enemy's flank the moment that Cumming charged them in front, and I remained at the breastwork myself to see the execution of the order.

In the meantime, General Cumming, having placed the Fifty-sixth Georgia in line for the charge, and supported it by placing the Thirty-sixth Georgia 10 paces in rear, moved forward to the charge; twice he was checked and had to reform. Warfield's (Arkansas) regiment with empty guns, and the gallant First and Twenty-seventh Tennessee prepared to share his next effort. At the command the whole rushed forward with a cheer, Lieutenant-Colonel [V. P.] Sanders, simultaneously leading the left of Mills' (Texas) regiment on the enemy's flank. The enemy, completely surprised, fled down the foot, the Texas troops on the left pursuing him beyond the foot and nearly across the open ground in front. Our charging columns returned with many prisoners and stand of colors; a fresh force of the enemy, attempting to follow us as we returned from this charge, was quickly met and routed by the Fiftieth Tennessee and with troops of my division. Immediately on his last repulse the enemy opened a rapid and revengeful artillery fire on Tunnel Hill from his batteries on the detached hill, and under cover of this fire he went to work felling trees and fortifying his position.[21]

Benham said: "Cleburne was very able and efficient in this battle. He was everywhere — he watched everything — he provided for everything. Once or twice he made sorties from his work — he had only a short line crossing the ridge — and charges from other parts of his position, leading or accompanying them in person." In the last charge, Cleburne placed himself at the head of the Texas brigade and led it, returning with the prisoners and flags.[22]

Cleburne's official account of Missionary Ridge continued:

It is but justice for me to state that the brunt of this long day's fight was borne by Smith's (Texas) brigade and the Second, Fifteenth, and Twenty-fourth Arkansas (consolidated), of Govan's brigade, together with Swett's and Key's batteries. The remainder of my division was only engaged in heavy skirmishing. The final charge was participated in and successful through the timely appearance and gallant assistance of the regiments of Cumming's and Maney's brigades before mentioned.

Out of the eight stand of colors shown by me to have been captured, four were presented to me by Mills' (Texas) regiment, two were presented by the Fifty-sixth and Thirty-sixth Georgia Regiments, of Cumming's brigade; one flag was presented by the First Tennessee, of Maney's brigade, and one by the Second, Fifteenth, and Twenty-fourth Arkansas (consolidated), of Govan's brigade; in all, eight colors, six of which I herewith transmit. Among them are the flags of the Twenty-seventh Pennsylvania and Ninety-third Illinois. About 500 prisoners were captured. At a critical moment of the battle I lost two of the bravest officers of my division — Brig. Gen. J. A. Smith, commanding the Texas brigade, and Col. R. Q. Mills, the same officer who commanded it in the battle of Chickamauga, after General Deshler fell. Including these gallant officers, other noble officers and men, some of whose names are handed down to history in the reports of brigade and regimental commanders.

I suffered the following losses in the three brigades of my division engaged, viz: 42 killed, 178 wounded, and 2 missing.

Colonel [Cyrus A.] Sugg, of the Fiftieth Tennessee Regiment, Maney's brigade, was dangerously wounded in the last charge. Colonel McConnell, of Cumming's brigade, and other gallant soldiers who fell in front of my works, I can but lament. I did not personally know them, but I saw and can bear witness to their gallant bearing and noble deaths.

The enemy must have suffered severely, the hill-side and the valley were thickly strewn with his dead, and if we can credit his published reports of casualties in this fight, he lost 1 major-general, John E. Smith, wounded; 3 brigadier-generals, [John M.] Corse, [Charles L.] Matthies, and Giles Smith, wounded, the latter mortally, and 1 colonel commanding brigade, Colonel [Green B.] Raum, mortally wounded.[23]

• • • • •

To Brigadier-Generals Smith, Cumming, and Maney, and Colonel Granbury, I return my thanks for the able manner in which they managed their commands. My thanks are also due to Brigadier-Generals Polk and Lowrey, and Colonel Govan, commanding brigade; although not actively engaged, they were rendering good service in holding important positions.

Swett's battery, under command of Lieut. H. Shannon, and Calvert's battery, commanded by Lieut. Thomas J. Key, were bravely fought and did great execution. Swett's battery was hotly engaged the whole day and lost some noble officers and men.

A section of [Overton W.] Barret's battery, under command of Lieut. Isaiah Lightner, in position where the road crosses the hill, did much toward driving back the right of the enemy's line in its attempted advance across the open fields.

Brig. Gen. John C. Brown's brigade, on my left flank, was engaged in heavy skirmishing most of the day.

Staff officers again cited by the General were Benham, J. K. Dixon, Buck, Mangum, and Hanly. Other staff members mentioned were Surg. D. A. Linthicum; and Capts. Charles S. Hill, ordnance officer, and C. H. Byrne, volunteer aide-de-camp, whose horses were shot under them. All of these staff officers, Cleburne said, "acted with their usual gallantry and discharged their duties with zeal and intelligence." "Messrs. Henry Smith and William Rucker, of the signal corps," the report concluded, "volunteered on my staff for the battle, and were very efficient."[24] In this battle Sherman commanded four divisions and a part of Howard's 11th Corps. The forces making the assaults were six brigades, and three regiments from Howard's corps. The Union casualties, including prisoners, were some 1,300. Sherman reported that his attacks drew "vast masses of the enemy" to his front.

The discomfited Sherman took issue with reports of his repulse, declaring, "Not so." General Hooker disagreed with Sherman and wrote Secretary of the Treasury Salmon P. Chase: "Sherman attacked [the enemy] in front and was repulsed, and only abandoned it after the fourth trial; . . . . All of Sherman's attacks were made long after I had carried Lookout [Mountain], ... This placed me on the direct line to cut off [the enemy's] retreat, while Sherman, had he been successful, could only have pushed him back over the only line he had to retreat on. This attack on the left . . . can only be considered in the light of a disaster."[25] Ironically, the north part of Missionary Ridge, where Cleburne defeated Sherman and saved the Confederate army from destruction, is now designated by the National Park Service as "Sherman's Reservation."

While cheers of victory from his men could still be heard up and down the line, Cleburne received a dispatch saying that the Confederate center was in danger.[26] His report continued:

Soon after the final defeat of the enemy in front of Smith's position, I received a dispatch from General Hardee to send to the center all the troops I could spare, as the enemy were pressing us in that quarter. I immediately ordered Generals Cumming and Maney, with their respective brigades, to report accordingly, and went myself to push them forward. Before I had gone far, however, a dispatch from General Hardee reached me, with the appalling news that the enemy had pierced our center, and were on Missionary Ridge, directing me to take command of my own, Walker's and Stevenson's divisions and form a line across the ridge, so as to meet an attack upon my flank, and take all other necessary measures for the safety of the right wing.[27]

Cleburne delivered the news to Benham in a whisper, but of course the heartbreaking information soon became generally known to his division.[28] In light of the intelligence received from Hardee, Cleburne said he "ordered Brigadier-General [S. R.] Gist, commanding Walker's division, to form it across the ridge; ordered all vehicles which could be spared, to cross the Chickamauga. Sent Brigadier-General Polk orders to dispatch a force to the Shallow Ford Bridge, and hold it at all hazards, and sent Govan's brigade to dispute the enemy's advance on the Shallow Ford Road."[29]

Meanwhile, Hooker's forces were moving north from Rossville Gap on top of Missionary Ridge; and on a road at the east base of the ridge, in rear of the lightly held Confederate line. Fearing that they were about to be surrounded by the enemy, most of the troops on the left and in the center of the Confederate line fled down the east slope of the ridge toward Chickamauga Creek, to escape death or capture.

Returning to Cleburne's report:

Soon after night was upon us, and General Hardee ordered an immediate retreat across the Chickamauga, and that Smith's (Texas) brigade should remain in position and bring up the rear. General Lowrey attacked and drove back the enemy's skirmishers in his front and then retreated. By 9 P.M. everything was across except the dead and a few stragglers lingering here and there under the shadow of the trees for the purpose of being captured, faint-hearted patriots succumbing to the hardships of the war and the imagined hopelessness of the hour. I now ordered Smith's brigade to move in retreat. Sadly, but not fearfully, this band of heroes left the hill they had held so well and followed the army across the Chicka-mauga.30

3

After firing the bridge over the Chickamauga, Cleburne's division, as rear guard, moved to Chickamauga Station. Arriving about midnight, the men "lay down" for a few hours' sleep. At dawn on the 26th, the broken and defeated main body of the Confederate army retreated toward Ringgold. Its destination was Dalton, Georgia, twenty-nine miles southeast of Chattanooga, on the railroad to Atlanta. In Govan's words, "Taking, as we always did, the post of honor, our division was ordered to retard the advance of the Federals, until our discomfited army could be rallied." The post of honor was shared with Joseph H. Lewis' Kentucky Brigade, known as the Orphan Brigade, which the day previous had been temporarily detached from Breckinridge's division to report to Cleburne. In addition to the responsibility as rear guard, the long line of wagons, ordnance trains, and artillery had to be protected. Govan's brigade was the rear of the division, while Cleburne rode in advance, hurrying up the trains. Progress was slow, wheels sank in the mud up to the hub and the trains bogged down frequently. The last of the column had just left Chickamauga Station when the Federals opened fire. Stalled teams, intermittent shelling, skirmishing, and some severe fighting reduced movement to a snail's pace. A caisson caught fire, halting the column until all of the shells therein had exploded. At one point, progress was so impeded that Cleburne moved a section of the stalled train to a field by the road in order to let the rear section move on to an area of low hills for protection. From this site the troops could fight to better advantage.

In the late afternoon the division reached Graysville, three and a half miles from Chickamauga Station. Past the town they marched to South Chickamauga Creek, adjacent to Gray's Mill. The creek generally flows in a northwesterly direction, roughly parallel to the railroad, but at the mill the flow is from east to west. It was about sundown when the troops crossed the creek. Cleburne's grave apprehension was of being attacked in the vicinity of Graysville by Hooker's command. He had intelligence that Hooker's forces were marching from Rossville in pursuit. Near Graysville, the road Hooker was traveling and that used by Cleburne were connected by three crossroads. To Cleburne's relief, all that occurred was an enemy cavalry attack south of Gray's Mill, which Govan easily repulsed. Afterwards it was learned that Hooker had been delayed at Red House Ford, where Confederates had destroyed the bridge. Without further combat, Cleburne's weary troops trudged on five miles farther until they reached South Chickamauga Creek opposite Ringgold, where the stream flows from south to north. By the time Cleburne's division had arrived here, the rest of the Army of Tennessee had forded the stream. The teams tugged the trains of Cleburne's division across the ford but the General had his troops remain on the east bank.[31]

Cleburne's withdrawal from Missionary Ridge to Ringgold and the fight at Ringgold Gap may properly be considered one military operation. Taking up the account in the opening of Cleburne's report of Ringgold Gap:

> On the retreat of the Army of Tennessee from Missionary Ridge, Tenn., to Ringgold, Ga., my division covered the retreat of Hardee's corps, arriving safely on the west bank of the East Chickamauga River [South Chickamauga Creek] at 10 P.M. on November 26. At this point the river had to be forded. It was nearly waist-deep and the night was freezing cold. I therefore determined to postpone crossing until the morning, and bivouacked on the hills near by.
>
> At 3 A.M. on the 27th, I received the following order, viz: "Major-General Cleburne:
>
> General: The general desires that you will take strong position in the gorge of the mountain and attempt to check pursuit of enemy. He must be punished until our trains and the rear of our troops get well advanced. The reports from the rear are meager and the general is not thoroughly advised of the state of things there. Will you be good enough to report fully?
>
> Respectfully,
> George Wm. Brent
> Assistant Adjutant-General."[32]

The officer from General Bragg first transmitted the message verbally, but Cleburne requested that it be put in writing. Cleburne knew that Hooker's forces were in pursuit, and thought it highly doubtful that a Confederate division of scarcely more than 4,000, totally unsupported, could hold back the masses which would be thrown against it. In case of disaster, he wanted a record of the order that he was to carry out.[33]

Cleburne next said in his report: "Leaving staff officers to conduct the troops across the river to the position designated, I went forward myself to examine the ground and form a plan for its defense."[34] Along the edge of the creek, where ice had formed, the troops took off their clothing below the waist. With their shirttails tucked under their belts, which were fastened under their armpits, and with their other clothing and cartridge boxes held high, they waded the creek. After crossing, they dressed near hot ashes and live coals, the remains of fires the troops preceding them had made from the worn rail fences nearby.[35]

Meanwhile, Cleburne made a hasty examination of the gap he was to occupy in a high ridge southeast of Ringgold.[36] He received a further message from Bragg, given to Buck at the commanding General's headquarters: "Tell General Cleburne to hold his position at all hazards, and keep back the enemy, until the artillery and transportation of the army is secure, the salvation of which depends upon him."[37]

In his report, Cleburne described the site and his placement of troops the next morning:

> The town of Ringgold, a place of 2,000 or 3,000 inhabitants, stands on a plain between the East Chickamauga River [South Chickamauga Creek] and the range of hills known as Taylor's Ridge. It is on the Western and Atlantic Railroad, about 20 miles southeast of Chattanooga. Taylor's Ridge, which rises up immediately back of the town, runs in a northerly and southerly direction. Opposite the town the ridge is intersected by a narrow gap, which admits the railroad, a wagon road, and a good sized creek [East Chickamauga Creek], a tributary of the Chickamauga. The creek hugs the southernmost or left-hand hill as you face Ringgold. The wagon and railroad run close to the creek. At its western mouth, next to Ringgold, the gap widens out to a breadth of

over 100 yards, leaving room for a patch of level wooded land
on each side of the roads. The gap is about half a mile through,
but the plain immediately in front of its east or rear mouth is
so cut up by the windings of the creek that three bridges, or
three fords, have to be crossed in the first half mile of road
leading from the gap to Dalton. It will be perceived at once
that this was a most dangerous position to be caught in if the
enemy should succeed in turning either flank.

The gap and the hills on either hand are thinly wooded,
except the base of the right-hand hill, along which, next to the
town, a heavy fringe of young timber extends from the gap
northward for 300 or 400 yards. Behind this fringe of trees I
placed two regiments of Smith's (Texas) brigade, Col. H. B.
Granbury, Seventh Texas, commanding; the Sixth, Tenth, and
Fifteenth Texas (consolidated), Capt. John R. Kennard commanding, on the left; the Seventeenth, Eighteenth, Twenty-
fourth, and Twenty-fifth Texas Dismounted Cavalry (consolidated), Maj. W. A. Taylor commanding, on the right; the
remaining regiment of the brigade, the Seventh Texas, Capt. C.
E. Talley commanding, I sent to the top of the right-hand hill,
with instructions to keep out of view, but watch well the right
flank of its brigade at the foot. On the precipitous hill to the
left of the gap and creek I placed the Sixteenth Alabama, Maj.
F. A. Ashford commanding, of Lowrey's (Alabama and
Mississippi) brigade, with instructions to conceal itself and
guard well the left flank. I also sent on the face of this hill
fronting Ringgold three companies of the Sixth and Seventh
Arkansas (consolidated), of Liddell's (Arkansas) brigade, under
charge of Lieutenant [James M.] Dulin, of General Liddell's
staff. For the defense of the gap itself, I disposed the rest of
the Arkansas brigade, under command of Col. D. C. Govan:
the Fifth and Thirteenth Arkansas (consolidated), Col. John E.
Murray commanding, I placed in a small ravine running across
the mouth of the gap from the right-hand hill to the railroad
embankment; the Eighth and Nineteenth Arkansas (consolidated), under command of Lieut. Col. A. S. Hutchison, 50
paces in rear and parallel to the former regiment; the Sixth and
Seventh Arkansas (consolidated), under command of Lieut.
Col Peter Synder, and the Second, Fifteenth, and Twenty-
Fourth Arkansas Regiments (consolidated), under Lieut. Col.
E. Warfield, at suitable distances in rear and covered as well as
the nature of the ground would permit, thus giving me four
short lines across the gap. From these regiments I sent a body
of skirmishers to occupy the patch of woods at the mouth of
the gap and left of the railroad and that portion of the bank of
the creek close to the mouth of the gap. In front of the mouth
of the gap, supported by Govan's foremost regiment in the
ravine, I placed a section of Semple's battery, two Napoleon

guns, commanded by Lieutenant Goldthwaite. I had screens of withered branches built up in front of these, so as to effectually conceal them from view, and made the artillerymen shelter themselves in the ravine close by. The remaining three regiments of Lowrey's brigade — consisting of the Thirty-second and Forty-fifth Mississippi Regiments (consolidated), under command of Col. A. B. Hardcastle; the Thirty-third Alabama, under command of Col. Samuel Adams, and the Forty-fifth Alabama, Lieut. Col. H. D. Lampley commanding — I placed in reserve in the center of the gap. The portion of Polk's (Tennessee and Arkansas) brigade with me — consisting of the First Arkansas, Col. J. W. Colquitt commanding; the Second Tennessee, Col. W. D. Robison commanding, and the Third and Fifth Confederate Regiments (consolidated), under Lieut. Col. J. C. Cole — I ordered to take position temporarily near the rear mouth of the gap with directions to observe my right flank and prevent the enemy from turning me in that quarter.[38]

Cleburne, on foot with his staff near Goldthwaite's two guns, awaited the assault by the enemy.[39]

His report of the brilliant defense of Ringgold Gap read:

> I had scarcely half an hour to make these dispositions, when I was informed the enemy's skrimishers were crossing the Chickamauga, driving our cavalry before them. Immediately after the cavalry retreated through the gap at a trot, and the valley in front was clear of our troops, but close in rear of the ridge our immense train was still in full view, struggling through the fords of the creek and the deeply cut up roads leading to Dalton, and my division, silent, but cool and ready, was the only barrier between it and the flushed and eager advance of the pursuing Federal army.
>
> Shortly after 8 A.M. [November 27] the enemy's skirmishers were in view, advancing. He opened fire, and under cover of it his lines of battle were placed and moved with the utmost decision and celerity against the ridge on the right of the gap. So quick and confident was this attack, the enemy must have been acting on a concerted plan, and must have had guides who knew well the nature of the country. As the first line moved toward the ridge its right flank became exposed at canister range to my artillery in the mouth of the gap. Five or six rapid discharges broke the right of this line to pieces and caused them to run for shelter under the railroad embankment.[40]

A private in the 13th Arkansas Regiment, supporting

Goldthwaite's two Napoleon guns and thus standing near General Cleburne, gave a more colorful account of the opening of the battle than that of the General. The private said that when the nearest line of Union troops was about fifty yards away, General Cleburne, watching them through field glasses, almost sprang into the air, clapped his knee, and shouted in a strong Irish accent, "NOW, *Lieutenant, give it to 'em*, NOW!" The first fearful blast full into the column was followed by volley after volley; and when the smoke cleared away, there were "patches of men scattered all over the field" and the rest were running "as fast as their legs could carry them."[41]

The General reported further:

Farther to his left, however, [the enemy] continued to advance, and made a heavy attack on the right-hand ridge. He continued to advance in the face of a deadly fire from Major Taylor's regiment, with the determination to turn the right flank of the Texas brigade. Major Taylor deployed skirmishers up the hill at right angles to his line of battle, and held him in check, while he informed Colonel Granbury of the state of affairs. Colonel Granbury sent two companies of his left regiment to re-enforce his right. With three companies of this own regiment Major Taylor charged down the hill upon the force attempting to turn him, and routed it, capturing between 60 and 100 prisoners and the colors of the Twenty-ninth Missouri Regiment.

In the meantime, I had ascertained that the enemy was moving another line of battle some distance beyond my present right with the view of ascending the ridge in that quarter. I instantly notified Brigadier-General Polk, stationed in the rear of the gap, to ascend the ridge and meet this attempt of the enemy. Luckily General Polk had already heard of this movement from a breathless straggler of our army who was fleeing before the enemy, and, anticipating my order, sent the First Arkansas up the hill and met the enemy's skirmishers within a few yards of the top. With the assistance of the Seventh Texas, after an obstinate fight, the enemy was driven down the hill. By this time large bodies of the enemy had crossed the Chickamauga, and it was evident that the main attack was about to be made upon the right. I ordered General Lowrey to move his command up the hill and assist General Polk in defending that position. Moving rapidly ahead of his command, General Lowrey found the First Arkansas again heavily engaged, but heroically holding its ground against great odds. Assuring the regiment that support was at hand, he brought up the Thirty-second and Forty-fifth Mississippi in double time, and threw them into the fight at the critical moment. The enemy gave way and went down the ridge in great confusion. Lowrey now brought up the two remaining regiments of his brigade and Polk up the two other regiments of his command. The enemy, constantly re-enforcing, made another powerful effort to crown the ridge still farther to the right.

A peculiarity of Taylor's Ridge is the wavy conformation of its north side. The enemy, moving up in a long line of battle, suddenly concentrated opposite one of the depressions in this wavy surface and rushed up it in heavy column. General Polk, with the assistance of General Lowrey, as quickly concentrated a double line opposite this point, at the same time placing the Second Tennessee in such a position as to command the flank of any force emerging from it. The attack was again defeated and the enemy hurled down the hill, with the loss of many killed on the spot, several prisoners, and the colors of the Seventy-sixth Ohio Regiment. The colors and most of the prisoners were captured by the First Arkansas.

In a fight where all fought nobly I feel it my duty to particularly compliment this regiment for its courage and constancy. In the battle the officers fought with pistols and with rocks, and so close was the fight that some of the enemy were knocked down with the latter missiles and captured. Apprehending another attack, General Polk rapidly threw up some slight defenses in his front.[42]

With reference to this critical phase of the struggle at Ringgold Gap, Lowrey afterward wrote:

The victory was ours and the enemy was gone down the hill in perfect confusion. A deafening shout of triumph went down our line, and General [Lucius] Polk, as if enwrapped in the glory of our success dashed up to me, and seizing me by the hand exclaimed "Just in time to save us, General!" The men, observing the rapture of their brigade commanders, again pierced the heavens with their shouts of triumph, greatly to the annoyance, no doubt, of the discomfited columns of the enemy. This was the most glorious triumph I ever witnessed on a battle field.[43]

Continuing with Cleburne's report:

But I must now return to the extreme left, which the

enemy attempted to turn. He sent what appeared to be a brigade of three regiments to the creek upon my left, and crossed over some companies of skirmishers. These were promptly met and stopped by a detachment from the Sixteenth Alabama, posted on the left-hand hill, and the main body was for some time held in check by Dulin's skirmishers, on the face of the left-hand hill, and the other skirmishers of Govan's brigade, on the creek bank and in the patch of woods to the left of the railroad. He got possession, however, of some houses and barns opposite this point, from which he annoyed me with a constant and well-directed fire of sharpshooters. At length, collecting in large numbers behind these houses, he made a charge on Govan's skirmishers on the left of the railroad. Lieutenant Goldthwaite quickly trained round his guns and swept them at quarter range with a load of canister and a solid shot. They ran back, leaving several dead and a stand of colors on the ground. Lieutenant Goldthwaite then shelled the houses, and greatly relieved us of the firing from that quarter. The stand of colors lay temptingly within 60 yards of my line, and some of the officers wanted to charge and get it, but as it promised no solid advantage to compensate for the loss of brave soldiers, I would not permit it.[44]

Throughout the fight, Govan's troops in the gap were subjected to heavy rifle fire. Cleburne remained at the entrance to the gap, watching every movement of the enemy. His men were inspired by his voice above the din of battle.[45]

Fortuitously, the enemy had been without its artillery, which arrived shortly before 1 P.M. One of the houses mentioned in the report, the Jobe house, is shown on the accompanying map of Ringgold Gap. The thick, brick walls provided excellent protection for the Federal sharpshooters. This house was razed in the 1950's.

General Cleburne's report of the defense of Ringgold Gap continued:

About 12 N. I received a dispatch from Lieutenant-General Hardee, to the effect that the train was now well advanced, and I might safely withdraw. On consultation with Generals Breckinridge and Wheeler, both of whom were present lending me their personal assistance, I determined to withdraw from Taylor's Ridge, and take up a new position on some wooded hills 1 mile in rear.

About 1 P. M. I rebuilt the screen in front of the artillery, which had been partially blown away, and then withdrew both pieces by hand without loss. By this time the enemy had concentrated a large portion of his army at Ringgold, and was doubtless preparing to throw an overwhelming force on my flanks. He opened a rapid artillery fire down the gap and on the crest of the ridge, but showed no disposition to advance in front. I now simultaneously withdrew the brigades, leaving a few skirmishers to hold the front, which they did without difficulty.

Soon after 2 P.M. I withdrew my skirmishers, fired the bridges in my rear, and proceeded to form line of battle in my new position. The enemy was visible on the ridge in about half an hour after I had withdrawn my skirmishers. He saw my new dispositions for defense, but showed no further inclination to attack, and ceased from all farther pursuit of our army.

I took into the fight: In Polk's brigade, 545; Lowrey's brigade, 1,330; Smith's (Texas) brigade, 1,266; Liddell's brigade, 1,016 effective men, making a total of 4,157 bayonets.

My loss was 20 killed, 190 wounded, and 11 missing. I am confident the enemy's loss was out of all proportion greater than mine.

The conduct of officers and men in this fight needs no comment; every man, as far as I know, did his whole duty.

To Brigadier-Generals Polk and Lowrey and Colonels Govan and Granbury, I must return my thanks. Four better officers are not in the service of the Confederacy.

Liuetenant Goldthwaite, of the artillery, proved himself a brave and skillful officer.[46]

Again citing staff officers J. K. Dixon, Buck, C. S. Hill, Linthicum, Mangum, Hanly, and Byrne, the General said that they "have my thanks for the efficient manner in which they discharged their responsible and dangerous duties"; and that Henry Smith and Rucker of the signal corps were "very efficient and useful." In concluding, Cleburne noted that "General Liddell was absent on leave, but hearing of the fight returned and rendered me all the assistance in his power. He selected and reformed the new line after we withdrew from our first position."[47]

In hand-to-hand fighting on the ridge, some of the enemy felled by stones were captured. After the battle, Cleburne was amused when one of the prisoners, an Irishman, met Chris Cleburne and declared, "Ah, you are the little divil who smashed me jaw with a rock!"[48]

Cleburne's troops remained undisturbed in line of battle on Dick's Ridge, where they had withdrawn. On the night of the 27th they moved three miles toward Dalton to the village of Tunnel Hill, Georgia, just west of a railroad tunnel through Tunnel Hill Ridge.[49] From here, General Cleburne penciled a note on rough paper to "Genl Braxton Bragg Comg A Tenn." The left edge is torn away; dots indicate the missing portion:

HdQrs Cleburnes Divsn
Tunnell Hill
27 Nov AD 1863

Genl
　　I held my position in front of east mouth of the gorge until it was quite dark and then marched here leaving large . . . fires burning and cavalry pickets in my works. I did . . . the enemy about dusk poured out from the gorge in the . . . of the road you told me to keep an eye on. I sent a picket . . . that road from here but there was no enemy as far as . . . where the road turns to this place. I have prisoners . . . and the 15th Army Corps. The enemies loss was . . . seems to have checked his ardor.

Respy
PR Cleburne
Maj Gen[50]

At Tunnel Hill the tired troops received their first regular ration in two days. The next morning, still undisturbed by the enemy, the division took up position in front of the village and above the tunnel.[51]

At Ringgold, Hooker commanded five divisions, five brigades from which were committed to action. In his report of the battle, Hooker said that he deemed it unwise to call up his other forces and deliver a general attack without his artillery. He claimed: "enemy killed and left on the field 130; We captured 230 prisoners; estimated . . . losses of the enemy at least three to our one." He further spoke of the Confederate "disaster at Ringgold."[52] Upon reading a copy of Hooker's report, Cleburne was indignant and requested Benham to prepare a summary of it. Respecting the Confederate casualties listed in Cleburne's report, Benham stated, ". . . all men who ever knew Cleburne will bear testimony that a more conscientiously truthful and accurate man was not to be met with."[53]

On February 9, 1864, a joint resolution, introduced by the Honorable Thomas B. Hanly of Helena, Arkansas, was adopted by the Confederate Congress, expressing appreciation to General Cleburne and his officers and men for their heroic defense of Ringgold Gap. The commendation "for distinguished service" read:

"Resolved, That the thanks of Congress are due, and are hereby tendered, to Maj. Gen. Patrick R. Cleburne, and the officers and men under his command, for the victory obtained by them over superior forces of the enemy at Ringgold Gap, in the State of Georgia, on the 27th day of November, 1863, by which the advance of the enemy was impeded, our wagon train and most of our artillery saved, and a large number of the enemy killed and wounded.

"Resolved, That the President be requested to communicate the foregoing resolution to Major-General Cleburne and his command."[54]

NOTES

CHAPTER X

[1]Buck, *Cleburne,* 157, 162; Record of Events, Co. A, 10th Texas Infantry, Sept. and Oct. 1863; Record of Events, Co. E, lst (Colquitt's) Arkansas Infantry, Sept. 1 to Nov. 1, 1863; Record of events, Cos. G, H, and I, 48th (Nixon's) Tennessee Infantry, Sept. and Oct. 1863; Record of Events, Co. D, 33rd Alabama Infantry, Sept. and Oct. 1863; Record of Events, Co. F, 35th (formerly 5th) Tennessee Infantry, Sept. and Oct. 1863.

[2]Record of Events, Co. G, 7th Texas Infantry, Sept. and Oct. 1863, M323/315, NA; *ibid.,* Co. A, Nov. and Dec. 1863.

[3]Buck, *Cleburne,* 158-59; *cf.* Horn, *Army of Tennessee,* 287-89. On Oct. 4, a secret meeting of the corps commanders was held to draft a petition to President Davis for the removal of Bragg and to recommend a successor. The petition unequivocally recommended removal of Bragg because "the condition of his health unfits him for the command of an army in the field." Twelve general officers, including Cleburne, subsequently signed the petition, which was not transmitted to Davis. However, Bragg and Davis learned of the document. Connelly, *Autumn of Glory,* 238-40, 248; Brent Diary, Oct. 4, 1863.

[4]*O.R.,* XXXI, Pt. 1, p. 222; Liddell, "Record," 30, 31; Preston, "Memoirs," 22.

[5]James W. Watterson, Jonesboro, Ga., conversation with authors, Aug. 25, 1965. Mr. Watterson told of being so informed by Dr. Minor Blackford, quoting his father, then on Cleburne's staff.

[6]John E. Conner, conversation with authors, Feb. 22, 1970.

[7]Maud McLure Kelly, "John Herbert Kelly: The Boy General of the Confederacy," *The Alabama Historical Quarterly,* IX (1947), 67-68; "John Herbert Kelly," in Ezra J. Warner, *Generals in Gray* (Baton Rouge, 1959), 168.

[8]Copy in files of John R. Peacock, High Point, N. C. See also, *The Collector,* LXIX (Sept. — Oct. 1956), 94.

[9]John W. Riely to Cleburne, Nov. 7, 1863, Ch. 1, Vol. 39, p. 10, M627/4, NA. Byrne remained with Cleburne's division through the Dalton to Atlanta campaign at least, and may have transferred eventually to another unit. An undated fragmentary record in National Archives shows that "Charles H. Byrne, volunteer aide-de-camp," was a captain in "Co. H, Tucker's Regt. " — Reference slip in CSR (Staff Officer) of Chas. H. Byrne, M331/44, NA.

[10]Benham, *Kennesaw Gazette,* IV (May 1, 1889), 2; *cf.* Buck,

Cleburne, 185; Voucher, "Received at Chickamauga, the Twelfth day of Nov. 1863," "Pay" and "Horse hire," "from Apl 30, 1863 to Oct. 31, 1863," in CSR, Christopher Cleburne; Manuscript No. 6722, Issues to Commissioned Officers, Cleburne's Div., Fourth Qr., 1863, RG 109, NA.

[11]*O.R.,* XXXI, Pt. 3, p. 736.

[12]*Ibid.,* Pt. 2, pp. 745-46; Major General Cleburne's Official Report of the Battle of Missionary Ridge," *Kennesaw Gazette,* III (May 15, 1888), 2.

[13]Govan to Poindexter Dunn, Dec. 16, 1878, in Fay Hempstead, *Historical Review of Arkansas* (Chicago, 1911), I, 244.

[14]*O.R.,* XXXI, Pt. 2, pp. 746-47.

[15]Benham, *Kennesaw Gazette,* IV (Apr. 15, 1889), 10-11.

[16]The loss of Lookout Mountain.

[17]*O.R.,* XXXI, Pt. 2, pp. 747-48.

[18]*Ibid.,* pp. 748-49.

[19]*Ibid.,* pp. 749-50.

[20]P. E. Hockersmith, "The Battle of Missionary Ridge," *Confederate Veteran,* VIII (1900), 320.

[21]*O.R.,* XXXI, Pt. 2, pp. 750-51.

[22]Benham, *Kennesaw Gazette,* IV (Apr. 15, 1889), 11; Buck, *Cleburne,* 171.

[23]Giles Smith and Raum were not mortally wounded.

[24]*O.R.,* XXXI, Pt. 2, pp. 752, 753.

[25]*Ibid.* pp. 575-76, 340.

[26]Benham, *Kennesaw Gazette,* IV (Apr. 15, 1889), 11; Hardee, "Major General Cleburne," 645-46.

[27]*O.R.,* XXXI, Pt. 2, p. 752.

[28]Benham, *Kennesaw Gazette* (Apr. 15, 1889), 11.

[29]*O.R.,* XXXI, Pt. 2, p. 752.

[30]*O.R.,* XXXI, Pt. 2, p. 753.

[31]Benham, *Kennesaw Gazette,* IV (May 1, 1889), 2; Govan to Dunn, Dec. 16, 1878, in Hempstead, *Historical Review of Arkansas,* I, 245; Buck, *Cleburne,* 174-76; Preston, "Memoirs," 23; A.D. Kirwan (ed.), *Johnny Green of the Orphan Brigade* (Lexington, 1956), 111-14; *O.R.,* XXXI, Pt. 2, p. 739.

[32]*O.R.,* XXXI, Pt. 2, pp. 753-54.

[33]Buck, *Cleburne,* 176.

[34]*O.R.,* XXXI, Pt. 2, p. 754.

[35]Preston, "Memoirs," 23.

[36]South of the gap, the ridge is known as Taylor's; its prolongation north of the gap, as Whiteoak Mountain. Cleburne referred to both the south and north side as Taylor's Ridge.

[37] Buck, *Cleburne*, 177.

[38] *O.R.*, XXXI, Pt. 2, pp. 754-55.

[39] Benham, *Kennesaw Gazette,* IV (May 1, 1889), 2.

[40] *O.R.*, XXXI, Pt. 2, p. 755.

[41] P.D. Stephenson, "Reminiscences of the Last Campaign of the Army of Tennessee, from May 1864 to January 1865," *S.H.S.P.*, XII (1884), 38-39.

[42] *O.R.*, XXXI, Pt. 2, pp. 755-56.

[43] M. P. Lowrey, "Gen. M. P. Lowrey," *Kennesaw Gazette*, III (Nov. 15, 1888), 3.

[44] *O.R.*, XXXI, Pt. 2, pp. 756-57.

[45] Buck, *Cleburne*, 182-83.

[46] *O.R.*, XXXI, Pt. 2, pp. 757-58.

[47] *Ibid.*

[48] Buck, Cleburne, 185.

[49] *Ibid.*, 184; Benham, *Kennesaw Gazette*, IV (May 1, 1889), 3; Preston, "Memoirs," 24.

[50] Cleburne to Bragg, Nov. 27, 1863 (MS in Bragg Papers, West. Res. Hist. Soc.).

[51] Buck, *Cleubrne,* 184; Preston, "Memoirs," 24.

[52] *O.R.*, XXXI, Pt. 2, pp. 323, 324.

[53] Benham, *Kennesaw Gazette*, IV (May 1, 1889), 3.

[54] *O.R.*, XXXI, Pt. 2, p. 758; "Journal of the Congress of the Confederate States of America, 1861-1865," *U.S. Senate Documents*, 58th Cong., 2d Sess., No. 234 (Washington, 1905), VI, 573.

CHAPTER XI

PROPOSAL FOR ENLISTING AND FREEING SLAVES

As between the loss of independence and the loss of slavery,
we assume that every patriot will freely give up the latter –
give up the negro slave rather than be a slave himself.
    – *P. R. Cleburne, Address to division and
    corps commanders, Army of Tennessee.*

At the end of November 1863, the Army of Tennessee, discouraged and debilitated, went into winter quarters at Dalton and vicinity. On November 30, General Bragg at his request was relieved of command of the army and General Hardee was placed in temporary command.[1]

Cleburne's division remained at Tunnel Hill, seven miles northwest of Dalton, in position, to block any attempt of the Federal army to advance south. Most of his command encamped southeast of the village, in a dominating position on the crest of Tunnel Hill Ridge. Some troops camped in the village, where the General had his headquarters, probably in one of the large frame houses.[2] Cleburne built strong breastworks, kept a regiment as an outpost a mile to the front both day and night, had numerous men on picket duty, and maintained an aggressive reconnaissance.[3] The troops of the division "built good comfortable winter quarters," consisting of log huts, with chimneys of split oak logs and clay, and entrances covered with "shelter tents" captured from the enemy. About every two weeks, a train ran from Dalton to Tunnel Hill, bringing supplies for the division — the only use made of the railroad between these points.[4]

Vacancies now existed in the command of the Texas and Arkansas Brigades, J. A. Smith having been incapacitated by his wounds and Liddell having been granted a transfer to the Trans-Mississippi Department. Cleburne recommended the promotion of Colonels Granbury and Govan to Brigadier General to fill these two positions;[5] both were commissioned two months later. The good judgment Cleburne displayed in choice of men for promotion, especially to Brigadier General, was a major factor in the brilliant record of his division.

During the winter respite from battle, Cleburne conducted a program for the military discipline of his troops. In a log cabin erected to use as a classroom, he instructed his officers in the art of war. Here, battle-scarred officers poured over Hardee's *Light Infantry Tactics* or the third volume of Scott's *Infantry Tactics*[6] in preparing for the day's lesson.[7]

In describing Cleburne's "system of daily recitations" and instruction, Hardee said:

> He himself heard the recitations of his brigade commanders, a quartette of lieutenants worthy of their captain — the stately Granberry [*sic*], as great of heart as of frame, a noble type of the Texan soldier — Govan, true and brave as he was courteous and gentle — Pope [*sic*], young, handsome, dashing and fearless, and — Lowry [*sic*], the parson soldier, who preached to his men in camp and fought with them in the field with equal earnestness and effect. These brigadiers heard the recitations of the regimental officers. The thorough instruction thus secured, first applied on the drill ground, and then tested in the field, gave the troops great efficiency in action.[8]

On December 27, Joseph E. Johnston, one of the Confederacy's ablest generals, assumed command of the Army of Tennessee. The entire army was pleased with this appointment. Hardee resumed the command of his corps, which was comprised of the divisions of Cleburne, Cheatham, and Walker.

2

By December, the worsened Confederate fortunes and the numerical strength of the Northern armies were matters of dire concern to the Southern soldiers. A less discernible menace, fully comprehended by Cleburne, was the divergent sources upon which the North could draw for recruits. Realizing that the situation demanded drastic action, Cleburne propounded the only plan adequate to meet the situation. His proposal was to make soldiers of a large body of slaves, and to guarantee freedom to all Negroes loyal to the South.

The idea of using slaves as soldiers had previously occurred to a number of Confederates but no substantial action had been taken to further such a measure. Early in

1863, Confederate representatives in Europe had discussed the advisability of the South countering Lincoln's emancipation proclamation by accepting Negroes in the Confederate army and granting them freedom. In September of the same year, a rumor circulated in London that the South would emancipate and make soldiers of 500,000 slaves. Referring to the rumor, Henry Hotze, able propagandist chief of the Confederacy in England, sent a secret letter to Secretary of State J. P. Benjamin stating that he favored the proposition, if required, and that, "I feel that I represent the views of the most loyal and most enthusiastic" Southern circles.[9]

There was no way that Cleburne could have known of the thinking of the Confederate representatives in Europe, and it is unlikely that he knew of the rumor in London. Perhaps he was aware of the opinion of some Southerners referred to in the diary of the English officer, Lieutenant Colonel Fremantle, following the latter's tour of the Confederacy from April to July 1863: ". . . if worst comes to worst, they can always fall back upon their Negroes as a last resort; but I do not think they contemplate such a necessity as likely to arise for a considerable time."[10] Also to be noted is a letter from Benjamin H. Micon of Tallassee, Alabama, to Secretary of State Benjamin, dated August 10, 1863, suggesting that Negro slaves be employed in the army (but not suggesting emancipation). In rejecting the idea on the ground of "very grave practical difficulties in the execution" of the "scheme," the Secretary referred to the "subject" as one "which has awakened attention in several quarters lately."[11]

The important fact is that Cleburne was the first person who had the courage and conviction publicly to press for enlisting Negroes in the Confederate army and granting emancipation for their serving as soldiers. Cleburne discussed his proposal, late in December, with several high ranking officers with whom he was closely associated. About half of the officers were willing to join Cleburne in signing a paper setting out his views.[12]

With characteristic forthrightness in word and action, Cleburne hoped his paper would influence public opinion to the realization that to attain Southern independence no sacrifice was too great, and that his plan would probably accomplish that objective. The next few days he spent all available time writing the manuscript, and when finished handed it to his aides Buck and Mangum for their opinions. They expressed the opinion that the proposition was radical and against all Southern tradition, and would be rejected by the army and the people. The aides tried to dissuade their friend and commander from advocating the proposal because it would damage him and destroy his prospects for promotion to Lieutenant General. They pointed out that a corps was then without a commander. Cleburne responded that in view of the grave crisis he was duty bound to present the proposal to the authorities regardless of the effect upon his career. Despite his devotion to his division, his convictions were so deep that he was willing to take command of a division of Negro troops. He went further to say that the worst that could happen would be his being court-martialed and cashiered, and in such event he would enlist as a private in his old regiment, the 15th Arkansas. When the manuscript was read to other members of the staff, Benham also disapproved of the proposal and asked for a copy in order to prepare a dissent.[13]

On January 2, 1864, the division and corps commanders of the Army of Tennessee were summoned to assemble that evening in Dalton, with no explanation of the purpose of the meeting. Cleburne rode horseback from Tunnel Hill to the headquarters of the commanding General, a residence at 314 Selvidge Street, which is still standing. At the request of General Johnston, General Hardee presided at the meeting, held in a large rear room. General Hardee announced that General Cleburne had prepared an important paper, which he would read.[14]

Cleburne then read the document, embodying an eloquent and forceful proposal that slaves be trained as soldiers, with a guarantee of freedom to them and all other Negroes who remained true to the Confederacy. Benefits expected from this course of action were: England and France would recognize and assist the Southern Confederacy; the North would cease to have Europeans as a source of recruitment; the Negro would no longer have an incentive to fight against the South; the people of the North would be deprived of a powerful motive for carrying on the war; the South would have armies numerically superior to those of the North, and could take the offensive and carry on a protracted struggle; independence, placed above every consideration of property, would clothe the South with new strength in battle. The General argued that if Negroes served as Southern soldiers, it would be essential to set free all slaves loyal to the Confederacy. He drew upon examples in history to support his position that the slaves would fight, succinctly disposed of other arguments against his proposal, and pleaded that action be taken upon his recommendation with all possible dispatch.[15]

Cleburne concluded his presentation by reading the names of the officers of his division who had signed the document; *viz.*, Generals Govan and Lowrey; Colonels Murray, Hardcastle, Colquitt, Snyder, Warfield, and G. F. Baucum (8th Arkansas); Majors Ashford, Richard J. Person (3rd and 5th Confederate), and G. S. Deakins (35th and 8th Tennessee); and Capt. J. H. Collett (commanding the 7th Texas). One signer, not of his command, was cavalry Gen. J. H. Kelly. Cleburne explained that he had been authorized to add the signatures of Generals Cheatham and Lucius E. Polk, who were away from the army.[16] The document in full is set out in the Appendix.

General Cleburne's plea, coming as a surprise to most of the officers present, produced much commotion; but failed to gain additional supporters. Generals Walker, Anderson, and Bate denounced the document; and Major Benham read his statement of dissent.[17] Because Generals Johnston, Stewart, and Stevenson were largely noncommital, General Cleburne had the impression that they were favorably disposed to his views; but subsequent correspondence shows that those generals did not approve of the document. The remaining two officers present, Generals Hardee and Hindman, who were already familiar with the proposal, favored it. Shortly afterward, Walker wrote that "agitation" of the propositions expressed in the paper "would ruin the efficacy of our Army and involve our cause in ruin and disgrace. . . ." Anderson declared that the propositions were "monstrous" and "revolting," and that open proposal of them would bring down "the universal indignation of the Southern people and the Southern soldiers upon the head of at least one of our bravest and most accomplished officers."[18]

To Cleburne's great disappointment, Johnston refused to submit the document to the War Department, on the ground that the matter was more political than military. When, therefore, Walker asked Cleburne for a copy to forward to the War Department in registering his protest against the memorial, Cleburne gladly supplied a copy, but signed only by himself, as the other signatures had been for the presentation at the meeting. Walker mailed this copy directly to President Davis.[19]

On January 13, President Davis replied to General Walker:

> I have received your letter with its enclosure informing me of the propositions submitted to a meeting of the general officers on the 2nd instant, and thank you for the information. Deeming it to be injurious to the public service that such subject should be mooted or even known to be entertained by persons possessed of confidence and respect of the people, I have concluded that the best policy under the circumstances will be to avoid all publicity, and the Secretary of War has therefore written to General Johnston requesting him to convey to those concerned my desire that it should be kept private. If it be kept out of the public journals its ill effect will be much lessened.[20]

In late January, General Cleburne spent several days in Mobile (this visit being treated of in the ensuing chapter). While in Mobile, unaware of the letter Davis had written to Walker, Cleburne "conversed with many of the wealthy men of Alabama on the subject of freeing the slaves and arming them to fight against the North"; and "many advocated the measure and believed that it would redound to the advantage of the South." En route to his command, while stopping overnight in Atlanta, Cleburne was visited in his hotel room by a member of the Confederate Congress from Tennessee, Col. A. S. Colyar. Cleburne discoursed at length upon the subject of enlisting and freeing Negroes. The next day, Colonel Colyar, in a letter to a relative in Cleburne's division, recorded his recollection of the General's remarks. The letter read in part:

> [General Cleburne said] That if we take this step now, we
> can mold the relations, for all time to come, between the
> white and colored races; and we can control the negroes, and
> that they will still be our laborers as much as they now are,
> and, to all intents and purposes, will be our servants, at less
> cost than now. His great argument is, that if the Yankees
> succeed in abolishing slavery, equality and amalgamation will
> finally take place.[21]

On January 31, the day after returning to Tunnel Hill,
General Cleburne received a dispatch from General Johnston
reporting on a letter from the Secretary of War respecting the
memorial. Johnston wrote:

> ...the Secretary of War ... expresses the earnest convic-
> tion of the President "that the dissemination or even promul-
> gation of such opinions under the present circumstances of the
> Confederacy, whether in the Army or among the people, can
> be productive only of discouragement, distraction, and dissen-
> sion. The agitation and controversy which must spring from
> the presentation of such views by officers high in the public
> confidence are to be deeply deprecated, and while no doubt or
> mistrust is for a moment entertained of the patriotic intents of
> the gallant author of the memorial, and such of his brother
> officers as may have favored his opinions, it is requested that
> you communicate to them, as well as all others present on the
> occasion, the opinions, as herein expressed, of the President,
> and urge on them the suppression, not only of the memorial
> itself, but likewise of all discussion and controversy respecting
> or growing out of it. . . .[22]

Cleburne promptly informed the officers who had signed the
paper of the views held by President Davis. He instructed an
aide to destroy all copies of the memorial except the one
which had been returned from Richmond. "After such an
opinion from the Commander-in-Chief of the Army and
highest officer of our Government, I feel it my duty," he
wrote Colonel Colyar, "to suppress the memorial and to
cease to advocate the measures mentioned."[23] He thereafter
made no reference to the subject.

However, before General Johnston received the communication from Richmond, varying reports of the memorial

had circulated among the troops and in civilian circles. On February 5, from Lowndesboro, Alabama, General Bragg, incensed about the proposal, in a letter to Gen. Marcus J. Wright, stated, "Great sensation is being produced . . . by the Emancipation project of Hardee, Cheatham, Cleburne & Co. It will kill them."[24] On February 14, cavalry Gen. Joseph Wheeler wrote Bragg, stating that the conspirators were Cheatham, Cleburne, and Hindman, and that even Hardee approved the proposal. Wheeler questioned Cleburne's loyalty, noting that he had been in the country only about ten years, and that in 1861 the citizens of Helena would have hanged Cleburne for making such a proposal.[25] In early March, Bragg, who had gone to Richmond as a "chief of staff" to the President, was still wrathful about what he characterized as "the Abolition party of the South." He wrote General Gist of the Army of Tennessee, "I should like to know as a matter of safety the secret history of the matter and the names of the backers."[26]

On February 1, John B. Hood, convalescing in Richmond from loss of a leg at Chickamauga, was appointed Lieutenant General to fill the vacancy existing in the command of a corps composed of Hindman's, Stevenson's, and Stewart's divisions. This appointment had been planned before Cleburne submitted his proposal. However, four and a half months later, on June 14, the revered Lieut. Gen. Leonidas Polk, whose corps had become part of the Army of Tennessee, was killed; and Maj. Gen. A. P. Stewart was promoted to Lieutenant General and assigned as commander of Polk's Corps. Stewart was an able general but this promotion no doubt would have gone to Cleburne had he not advocated the enlistment of slaves.[27] As already noted, Cleburne outranked Stewart, his appointment as Major General having antedated Stewart's by nearly six months. When Hardee was absent from the corps, Cleburne had served as corps commander and had been Stewart's superior officer. Cleburne exceeded Stewart in ability; and his record was more impressive and his prestige, greater.

3

For a number of months, Cleburne's proposition generally met with disfavor[28] but had the support of a small minority.[29] Continuing to be a subject of general discussion, it gained momentum; and by the fall of 1864 had the backing of some of the most influential Southern leaders. On September 26, Gov. Henry W. Allen of Louisiana, in a letter to the Secretary of War, unequivocally recommended enlistment of Negro soldiers: "I would free all able to bear arms, and put them in the field at once."[30] On October 17, at a convention in Augusta, Georgia, to consider "the present aspect of public affairs," Govs. William Smith of Virginia, Z. B. Vance of North Carolina, A. C. Magrath of South Carolina, Joseph E. Brown of Georgia, and Charles Clark of Mississippi, adopted a resolution reciting, "That the course of the enemy in appropriating our slaves who happen to fall into their hands to purposes of war, seems to justify a change of policy on our part." However, the five governors were unable to agree as to the change to be made, except for recommending that "such part of" the slaves be appropriated "to the public service as may be required."[31] Shortly thereafter, Secretary of State Benjamin became a strong advocate of the use of slaves as troops, with freedom as a reward; and pressed reluctant President Davis into recommending such measure to the Confederate Congress.[32] Governor Smith, in a message to the Virginia legislature on December 7, advocated arming slaves as soldiers even if the result were freeing those who fought.[33] By late winter, Cleburne's proposal had gained widespread public support among both civilians and soldiers.

Ten months after rejecting Cleburne's memorial, President Davis completely reversed his position and advocated legislation embodying the Arkansan's proposal. Davis wrote in *The Rise and Fall of the Confederate Government* that in November 1864, he urged "[his] views" for the

> need for the enrollment of negroes to take their place in the ranks. Strenuously I argued the question with members of Congress . . . . To a member of the Senate . . . I stated, as I had done to many others, the fact of having led negroes against a lawless body of armed white men, and the assurance which the experiment gave me that they might, under proper conditions, be relied on in battle, and finally used to him the expression . . .: "If the Confederacy falls, there should be written on its tombstone, 'Died of a theory.' "[34]

Primarily because of selfish slaveholding interests, the proposed legislation encountered strong opposition in the Confederate Congress. Finally in January 1865, a member of both the Virginia and Confederate Senate, Andrew Hunter, sought the views of Gen. Robert E. Lee, who the previous fall had recommended employing slaves as soldiers.[35]

General Lee, in his reply on January 11, unequivocally stated: "I think . . . we must decide whether slavery shall be extinguished by our enemies and the slaves be used against us, or use them ourselves . . . . My own opinion is that we should employ them without delay. I believe that with proper regulations they can be made efficient soldiers." Lee recommended immediate freedom to all slaves who enlisted, and at the end of the war freedom to the families of those who faithfully discharged their duties. Lee concluded: ". . . whatever measures are to be adopted should be adopted at once. Every day's delay increases the difficulty. Much time will be required to organize and discipline the men, and action may be deferred until it is too late." How like the words spoken by Cleburne a year earlier! General Lee, on February 18, again wrote a member of the Confederate House of Representatives, E. Barksdale, relative to the pending bill:

> . . .in my opinion, the negroes, under proper circumstances, will make efficient soldiers . . . . Under good officers, and good instructions, I do not see why they should not become soldiers. They possess all the physical qualifications, and their habits of obedience constitute a good foundation for discipline. They furnish a more promising material than many armies of which we read in history, ...[36]

After much debate, on March 13, 1865, a bill was adopted, essentially due to General Lee's influence, providing for the enlistment of Negroes as soldiers, and paving the way for their freedom. Thus, much of the proposal advocated by Cleburne was put into effect. The President was given a twofold authorization: (1) to ask slaveholders for Negroes to perform military service; and (2) to call on each state for her quota of 300,000 Negro troops. The Negroes would receive the same compensation as the other soldiers. In deference to states' rights, the act did not pledge emancipation of the slaves, but did provide that no slave would be accepted without "the approbation of his master by a written instrument conferring, as far as he may, the rights of a freedman."[37] It was "generally understood that any slaves who should fight in the Confederate armies would be made free by state action."[38]

The act of the Confederate legislators was deficient in that the Negro soldiers would be volunteers whose owners would be willing to release them. Even so, the legislation was effective. Immediately upon its enactment, letters started "pouring into the [War] department from men of military skill and character," asking authority to raise and command Negro troops. General Lee took measures for raising and organizing the colored troops.[39] Especially designated Confederate officers set about recruiting companies, battalions, and regiments of Negroes throughout the South. The recruitment was proceeding successfully when the Confederacy collapsed.[40] Only a few hours before General Lee evacuated Petersburg, he replied to a letter from President Davis concerning plans for raising Negro troops.[41]

Had adequate legislation been enacted without delay following Cleburne's proposal to use Negro troops, the Confederate States might have won their independence. As previously noted, one of the several benefits assigned by Cleburne from enrolling Negroes as soldiers was that the South would secure the means of carrying on a protracted struggle. General Grant in his *Memoirs* made two significant statements: "Anything that could have prolonged the war a year beyond the time that it did finally close, would probably have exhausted the North to such an extent that they might then have abandoned the contest and agreed to a separation." And, referring to the period July 1864: "The North was already growing weary, . . . the people governed, and could stop hostilities whenever they chose to stop supplies."[42]

General Cleburne's judgment that the slaves would have made effective soldiers is supported by the highest authority, Gen. Robert E. Lee. Those willing to fight for the Confederacy, with freedom as a reward, would have swelled the Confederate armies. More than 700,000 male slaves of proper age were available.[43] "That large numbers of the slaves would have fought with their masters, if given the chance, can not be doubted."[44] It is a reasonable conclusion that by adopting Cleburne's proposal in the spring of 1864, the Confederate States could have prolonged the war indefinitely and thereby have gained their independence. General Cleburne's thinking on this subject was far in advance of his countrymen.

NOTES

CHAPTER XI

[1]Soon thereafter Cleburne gave a dinner in honor of Hardee. — Liddell, "Record," 44. To Lieutenant Key and another of his artillerymen who visited him in his quarters on Dec. 9, Cleburne "was unusually communicative." Key recorded in his diary that General Cleburne's "criticisms on General Bragg and his military mis-management were quite severe." — Wirt Armistead Cate (ed.), *Two Soldiers: The Campaign Diaries of Thomas J. Key, C.S.A., December 7, 1863 – May 17, 1865, and Robert J. Campbell, U.S.A., January 1, 1864 – July 21, 1864* (Chapel Hill, N.C., 1938), 8-9, hereinafter cited as Cate (ed.), *Key Diary.*

[2]Joseph E. Johnston, *Narrative of Military Operations* (Bloomington, Ind., 1959), 276, 283; Cate (ed.), *Key Diary*, 23, 27, 31; Benham, *Kennesaw Gazette*, IV (May 1, 1889), 3.

[3]*O.R.*, LII, Pt. 2, p. 574; Preston, "Memoirs," 25; Record of Events, Co. E, 10th Texas Infantry, Nov. and Dec. 1863, and Jan. and Feb. 1864; Record of Events, Co. A, 1st (Colquitt's) Arkansas Infantry, Nov. 1 to Dec. 31, 1863; *ibid.*, Co. I, Jan. 1 to Mar. 1, 1864; W. W. Mackall to Cleburne, Feb. 11, 1864, MS in Communications to and from Cleburne's Division, January 31, 1863 — October 20, 1864 (Copied from books lent by Irving Buck) Chap. 2, Vol. 265, p. 43, RG 109, NA.

[4]Record of Events, Co. F, 32nd Mississippi Infantry, Nov. and Dec. 1863; Preston, "Memoirs," 24, 25.

[5]*E.g.*, recommendation of Cleburne, Dec. 10, 1863, for promotion of Granbury to Brigadier General, MS in CSR (Gen. Officer) of H. B. Granbury, M331/110, NA.

[6]Winfield Scott, *Infantry Tactics*, III (New York, 1854), a manual for evolutions of the line applicable to brigades.

[7]Hill, "Maj. Gen. Cleburne," 462; Buck, *Cleburne*, 187.

[8]Hardee, "Major General Cleburne," 646.

[9]Frank Lawrence Owsley, *King Cotton Diplomacy* (Chicago, 1959), 554-55.

[10]Lord (ed.), *Fremantle Diary*, 246.

[11]J. P. Benjamin to Benjamin H. Micon, Aug. 18, 1863, in C.S.A. State Department Records, 1861-1865, Vol. XXII, Library of Congress. On four occasions in 1861 and 1862, citizens wrote letters to governmental authorities or to a newspaper suggesting the possible use of slaves as soldiers. In Aug. 1863, the Alabama legislature enacted a resolution which recited that "the Government of the

United States has determined to put in the field negro soldiers"; and submitted "for the consideration of Congress the propriety ... of using ... a certain percentage of the male slave population ... to perform such services as Congress may ... direct." In the fall of 1863, several newspapers published in the deep South carried editorials favorable to the idea of enlisting Negroes as soldiers. Thus, a Mobile paper said, "If then, (and we would only employ them in case of clear necessity) negro soldiers are needed to beat the enemy and conquer independence and peace, there is no argument of doubtful expedience to counterbalance the superlative end." Only one editorial (in a Mississippi paper) advocated freeing slaves who should serve in the ranks. — Thomas Robson Hay, "The South and the Arming of the Slaves," *Mississippi Valley Historical Review*, VI (1919-20), 36-38; Bell Irvin Wiley, *Southern Negroes: 1861-1865* (New Haven, 1938), 149; *O.R.*, Ser. IV, Vol. II, p. 767; Mobile *Advertiser and Register*, Nov. 26, 1863, p. 2.

12Cate (ed.), *Key Diary*, 16-18. General Breckinridge thought that the time had not arrived for calling a Negro force into the army *(ibid.)*.

13Buck, *Cleburne*, 188-89; L. H. Mangum, Statement of, under heading, "General Cleburne on Freeing the Negroes," *Kennesaw Gazette*, III (June 1, 1888), 2; Benham, *Kennesaw Gazette*, IV (May 15, 1889), 6.

14W. H. T. Walker to Bragg, Mar. 8, 1864, in Bragg Papers, West. Res. Hist. Soc.; Patton Anderson to Leonidas Polk, Jan. 14, 1864, in *O.R.*, LII, Pt. 2, p. 598; Mangum, *Kennesaw Gazette*, III (June 1, 1888), 3; Mrs. Margaret Huff, who has resided in the Selvidge Street residence since 1886, when purchased by her father, conversation with authors, Oct. 30, 1967. The house, known as the Dr. James A. Black property, backed Selvidge Street but has since been turned to face that street.

15*O.R.*, LII, Pt. 2, pp. 586-92.

16Walker to Bragg, Mar. 8, 1864, in Bragg Papers, West. Res. Hist. Soc.

17After the war, when Benham wrote his biographical sketch of General Cleburne, his views had completely changed. In the sketch, Benham averred that if the General's proposal had been consummated soon, the "movement ... might, and doubtless would, have changed the destiny of ths southern people. The southern people were like the Roman denizens of Utica, all for the cause, but unwilling to emancipate and arm their slaves, as Cato wished them to do." — Benham, *Kennesaw Gazette*, IV (May 15, 1889), 6.

18A. S. Colyar to A. S. Marks, Jan. 30, 1864, in "General Cleburne's Views on Slavery," in Drake (ed.), *Annals of Army of Tennessee*, 51; J. E. Johnston to James A. Seddon, in *O.R.*, LII, Pt. 2, pp. 608-09;

Walker to Bragg, Mar. 8, 1864, in Bragg Papers, West. Res. Hist. Soc.; Cate (ed.), *Key Diary*, 16; Walker to Davis, Jan. 12, 1864, in *O.R.*, LII, Pt. 2, p. 595; Anderson to Polk, Jan. 14, 1864, in *O.R.*, LII, Pt. 2, pp. 598-99.

[19]Buck, *Cleburne*, 189-90; Walker to Davis, Jan 12, 1864, in *O.R.*, LII, Pt. 2, p. 595; Colyar to Marks, Jan. 30, 1864, in Drake (ed.), *Annals of Army of Tennessee*, 51.

[20]Davis to Walker, Jan. 13, 1864, in Bromfield L. Ridley, *Battles and Sketches of the Army of Tennessee* (Mexico, Mo., 1906), 290.

[21]Cate (ed.), *Key Diary* 32; Colyar to Marks, Jan. 30, 1864, in Drake (ed.), *Annals of Army of Tennessee*, 51.

[22]Joseph E. Johnston to Cleburne, Jan. 31, 1864, in *O.R.*, LII, Pt. 2, p. 608.

[23]Buck, *Cleburne*, 190; Colyar to Marks, Feb. 5, 1864, in Drake (ed.), *Annals of Army of Tennessee*, 52. During the Atlanta campaign, the copy returned from Richmond was destroyed when the Federals captured a desk where it was kept. The contents of the document were not revealed until twenty years later, following the death of Benham in California. Among his effects was the copy with the signatures of the other officers which had been given him for use in preparing his dissent. This copy was printed in the *Official Records.*—Buck, *Cleburne*, 190.

[24]Bragg to Marcus J. Wright, Feb. 5, 1864, in Marcus J. Wright Papers, Uni. N.C.

[25]Connelly, *Autumn of Glory*, 320.

[26]Walker to Bragg Mar. 8, 1864, in Bragg Papers, West. Res. Hist. Soc.

[27]See, *e.g.*, E. T. Sykes, "Walthall's Brigade," *Publications of the Mississippi Historical Society*, Cent. Ser., I (1916), 550, 558-59.

[28]Hardee, "Major General Cleburne," 647. The majority of the planters were averse to the plan. — See *e.g.*, Edward Younger (ed.), *Inside the Confederate Government: The Diary of Robert Garlick Hill Kean, Head of the Bureau of War* (New York, 1957), 177. Also, "the rank anf file of the southern army" opposed the measure; "they represented the class upon whose heels the enfranchised negro would inevitably tread." — Polk, *Leonidas Polk*, II, 340. Slavery was "a guarantee of white supremacy and civilization."—Ulrich Bonnell Phillips, *The Course of the South to Secession* (Reprint; Gloucester, 1958), 152-55. To make soldiers out of slaves "seemed bizarre and grotesque and wholly at variance with the very essence and character of Southern civilization." — E. Merton Coulter, *The Confederate States of America: 1861-1865* (Baton Rouge, 1950), 267-68.

[29]*E.g.*, entry Dec. 30, 1864, in diary of Key (now Captain), two days after Cleburne told him of the proposal: "Captain Charles Swett

... said ... to close the war and give us liberty he was ready to free his negroes, as he now did not value them above a 'dime each.' ... The idea of abolishing the institution at first startles everyone, but when it is viewed as the means of giving us victory or closing the war, every person with whom I have conversed readily concurs that liberty and peace are the paramount questions and is willing to sacrifice everything to obtain them." — Cate (ed.), *Key Diary*, 18-19. See also James Cooper Nisbet, *4 Years on the Firing Line* (Reprint; Jackson, Tenn., 1963), 172-73.

[30]Henry W. Allen to James A. Sedden, Sept. 26, 1864, in Sykes, "Walthall's Brigade," 557-58.

[31]"Journal of the Congress of the Confederate States of America, 1861-1865," *U.S. Senate Documents*, 58th Cong., 2d Sess., No. 234 (Washington, 1905), VII, 257-58; John Witherspoon DuBose, *General Joseph Wheeler and The Army of Tennessee* (New York, 1912), 259. The following month, the Governor of Mississippi made his own position clear: "Whatever may be the public opinion on this subject, I hesitate not to declare mine, that, with competent officers and firm discipline, [Negroes] can be made effective soldiers; and that the experiment should now be made. . . . I do not, however, favor the granting of freedom to slaves, ... These views I expressed to our delegation in Congress in November last, ..."— Governor's Message, Feb. 20, 1865, in J. J. Shannon & Co. (print.), *Journal of the Senate of the State of Mississippi, Called Session at Columbus, February and March 1865* (Meridian, 1865), 12-13.

[32]Pierce Butler, *Judahh P. Benjamin* (Philadelphia, 1906), 348-49.

[33]Richmond *Daily Examiner* Dec. 9, 1864, p. 3.

[34]Jefferson Davis, *The Rise and Fall of the Confederate Government* (New York, 1958), I, 518.

[35]Andrew Hunter to R. E. Lee, Jan. 7, 1865 in *O.R.*, Ser. IV, Vol. III, p. 1008; James Morton Callahan, *Diplomatic History of the Southern Confederacy* (Reprint; New York, 1964), 245.

[36]Lee to Hunter, Jan. 11, 1865, in *O.R.*, Ser. IV, Vol. III, p. 1013; Lee to E. Barksdale, Feb. 18, 1865, in J. B. Jones, *A Rebel War Clerk's Diary*, ed. Howard Swiggett (New York, 1935), II, 432.

[37]*O.R.*, Ser. IV, Vol. III, p 1161. On Mar. 6, the Virginia Legislature had enacted a law making it lawful for slaves to be organized as soldiers and "to bear arms . . . as other soldiers in the Army," but not providing for emancipation. — *Ibid.*, XLVI, Pt. 3, p. 1315.

[38]Coulter, *Confederate States*, 268.

[39]Jones, *Rebel War Clerk's Diary*, II, 451; *O.R.*, XLVI, Pt. 3, pp. 1339, 1356-57.

[40]*Ibid.*, Ser. IV, Vol III, pp. 1193-94; Dubose, *General Wheeler*,

258, (n), Nisbet, *4 Years on Firing Line*, 175; Coulter, *Confederate States*, 268.

[41]Douglas Southall Freeman, *R. E. Lee* (New York, 1940), IV, 56.

[42] U. S. Grant, *Personal Memoirs of U. S. Grant* (New York, 1886), II, 167, 345.

[43]"There are in the South six hundred and eighty thousand black men of fighting age, and capable of being made fighting men." — Excerpt from speech of Secretary of State Benjamin, Feb. 9, 1865, Richmond *Daily Examiner*, Feb. 10, 1865, p. 2. During the interim of thirteen months between this statement and Cleburne's memorial, much territory had been lost to the Northern arms, with accompanying loss of slaves.

[44]Henry, *Confederacy*, 440. See also Richard Taylor, *Destruction and Reconstruction: Personal Experiences of the Late War*, ed. Richard B. Harwell (New York, 1955), 256-57; John B. Gordon, *Reminiscences of the Civil War* (New York, 1904), 383; DuBose, *General Wheeler*, 256, 258; Nash, *Gen. Pat Cleburne*, 192-93; C. W. Raines (ed.), *Six Decades in Texas or Memoirs of Francis Richard Lubbock* (Austin, 1900), 560-61; *O.R.*, Ser. IV, Vol. III, pp. 1010-11, 1193. Harold B. Simpson, authority on Hood's Texas Brigade, says that in that military organization many slaves accompanied their masters to the front; were exposed to action; and although they had opportunities to escape, remained loyal to the end. A few of the former slaves even joined Hood's Texas Brigade Association, an organization of surviving veterans of the brigade formed after the war.

CHAPTER XII

INTERLUDES IN ALABAMA
(January—April 1864)

Rumor says [General Cleburne] lost his heart
with a young lady in Mobile.
—*From letter, Captain Buck to his sister, February 9, 1864.*

In January 1864, while the division was in winter camp at Tunnel Hill, Georgia, General Cleburne was asked to serve as best man at the wedding of his close friend General Hardee. The winter cessation in fighting enabled Hardee to be away, and permitted Cleburne to take his first leave except the forty-eight hours he had used in the winter of 1861. General Hardee, a widower of forty-eight, was marrying Miss Mary Foreman Lewis, aged twenty-six, of Marengo County, Alabama.[1] Cleburne took along his favorite orderly, J. A. Sepp. An Austrian who went through the Crimean war and Napoleon III's Solferino campaign, Sepp had enlisted in the Confederate Army from Arkansas.[2]

En route, the two generals stayed overnight with Cleburne's old friend, Dr. Charles E. Nash, who was in charge of the Confederate Marine Hospital at Selma. A stag dinner honoring the distinguished visitors was given by Comdr. Ebenezer Farrand, senior officer at the Selma shipyard on the Alabama River. Other guests were Dr. Nash and naval officers serving under Commander Farrand in the building of the *Tennessee,* a formidable Confederate ironclad. During the dinner, anecdotes and reminiscenses were enjoyed. Cleburne related a humorous incident at the expense of Hardee, who countered by asking Dr. Nash to tell a good story on Cleburne. "Yes, sir," Dr. Nash replied, "I can give you a good horse joke on him." Cleburne protested, "Don't tell that! I can ride now!" At the group's insistence, Dr. Nash told of Cleburne being pitched into a swamp when attempting to ride a racehorse. No one enjoyed the story more than Cleburne. While at Selma, Cleburne "promised" little Mary Nash that he would catch a live Yankee and send him to her in a cage. Shortly after returning to his division, Cleburne sent to Mary a sword which had belonged to a Federal officer, explaining that he did not catch the Yankee but got his sword.[3]

The wedding was a festive occasion on January 13 in the commodious residence of Bleak House plantation,[4] the home of the bride's brother, Major Ivey Foreman Lewis. Bleak House plantation was several miles east of Demopolis. The Confederate officers in full-dress uniforms added splendor and romance—the tall, handsome Hardee at the side of his beautiful brunette bride; Cleburne, resplendent with his sword and belt presented by the 15th Arkansas Regiment. Others present were Capt. Thomas J. Hardee, nephew and a staff officer of the bridegroom; Col. T. R. Roy, Hardee's chief of staff; Brig. Gen. Z. C. Deas of the Army of Tennessee; and Lieut. Robert Tarleton, from Fort Morgan in Mobile Bay. The Reverend Mr. Beckwith, Bishop of Georgia, Confederate chaplain and friend of General Hardee, officiated. The bride was given in marriage by her brother, Major Lewis, commander of the Jeff Davis (Cavalry) Legion of the Army of of Northern Virginia.[5]

When General Cleburne was presented to the maid of honor, Miss Susan Tarleton of Mobile, he realized immediately that she was the girl he would like to marry.[6] The charming, witty, and vivacious Miss Tarleton was the twenty-four-year-old sister of Lieut. Robert Tarleton.[7]

Probably the day following the wedding, as was customary among the gentry, the bridal party and some of the guests set out on the wedding trip by steamboat, with Mobile their destination. Among the ladies of the party were Miss Susan Tarleton, her sister Grace, and two of their close friends who were sisters—Sallie and Amelia Lightfoot. Among the men were General Cleburne; Henry Goldthwaite of Mobile, whose marriage to Grace Tarleton followed in a short time; and Robert Tarleton, who married Sallie Lightfoot ten months later.[8]

Henry Goldthwaite was a first cousin of Lieut. R. W.

Goldthwaite of Montgomery County, Alabama, whom General Cleburne had cited for bravery at Chickamauga and Ringgold Gap. Robert Tarleton, a Princeton graduate, had been a friend of Cleburne's aide Lieutenant Mangum during their college days. Sallie and Amelia Lightfoot were granddaughters of Jack Ferrill Ross, a banker who was the first territorial and state treasurer of Alabama. The sisters lived with their uncle, Dr. Philip Lewis Lightfoot, on his plantation Morven, north of Demopolis.[9]

From a wharf at the north edge of Demopolis, the luxurious steamboat[10] glided into the beautiful Tombigbee River with its low evergreen bank on the west and the high white bluff on the east. The steamer was probably flying a full set of colors, with the stars and bars of the Confederacy floating from the rear. Luxurious living quarters were located on the second deck, with staterooms on either side of a wide center hallway which was used for dining and dancing. The men's quarters were in the forward half; and the aft portion, with handsome carpets, grand piano, and gilded mirrors, was reserved for the ladies. Gay melodies on the calliope announced the steamboat as it approached landings.[11] Cleburne welcomed the respite from rugged army life and enjoyed the gaiety during the twenty-four-hour trip from Demopolis to Mobile down the Tombigbee.[12] Especially was he pleased in having the opportunity to become better acquainted with Miss Susan. Also, a friendship developed between Cleburne and the Lightfoot sisters.

General Cleburne remained in the picturesque city of Mobile for about eleven days. From the Battle House Hotel,[13] he could walk along broad, magnolia lined streets to the Tarleton residence, where he was a frequent visitor. Miss Susan was the eldest daughter of George W. Tarleton, a prosperous businessman and head of a firm of cotton factors. A native of New Hampshire, he was from a prominent colonial family. He did not further the Northern war effort, but was at heart a Yankee sympathizer. Mrs. Tarleton, a Brack of Montgomery County, Alabama, and all the Tarleton children were Southern to the core.[14]

The Tarleton residence, a spacious two-story brick dwelling on the southwest corner at the intersection of St.

Louis and Claiborne Streets, is still standing. In 1864 at the rear there was a garden enclosed with a high brick wall. One can imagine Cleburne facetiously telling Miss Susan that after he changed her name he would correct the spelling of "that street" on the east side of the house.

Cleburne spent much time with Miss Susan, met her family and friends, and enjoyed gatherings when she played the piano and accompanied her friends in group singing.[15] Miss Susan was proud to be courted by a dashing young general; and they likely attended services at her church, the historic Christ Episcopal Church.[16]

On January 22, 1864, in the Mobile daily paper appeared an editorial tribute to "Gen. Pat R. Cleburne," which began as follows:

> This gallant Irishman, says a writer in the Columbia South Carolinian, seems to have been the real hero in the late fight at Chattanooga. It is amazing that so little is known of one who has been twice so severely wounded in battle, and who has so often been distinguished for skill as well as heroism. As modest and unassuming as a girl, he has shunned the crowd of parasites and puffers, unfortunately too often found around headquarters. Hence, while columns are devoted to the exploits of tenth-rate men, but little has been said about this extraordinary man.

The editorial mentioned some of the General's military accomplishments, and concluded: "The distinguished subject of the foregoing sketch is now in our city. He is a soldier whom every true Confederate should delight to know."[17]

On Saturday afternoon, January 23, a "grand review" of the Confederate forces at Mobile was staged in honor of General Cleburne. The forces at this important port, under the command of Maj. Gen. Dabney H. Maury,[18] consisted of several thousand infantry, also artillery and cavalry. Carriages and pedestrians thronged Government Street for the review and ceremonies, which lasted two and a half hours. Ladies with "graceful forms and pleasing smiles" embellished the "beautiful promenade." The reviewing generals, Cleburne and Maury, escorted by staff officers, rode past the long line of troops. Each regiment came to "a present arms" as the generals passed. "The Arkansas chieftain," according to the Mobile paper, was "the cynosure of all observers."

The paper then described the General:

> The leader of the reviewing party was a tall and rather slender officer, with erect form but slightly bowed shoulders, a finely shaped head, with features prominent and striking—the firm set lip, betokening resolution and will, braced by a black moustache, and the long chin bearing a goatee *a la Empereur*. The hair of the head was black, tinged with a sprinkling of gray, and worn cut close to the head, in military style. The appearance of the hero of Ringgold Gap is striking and not easily forgotten.[19]

A week later, General Cleburne was back at Tunnel Hill, Georgia, with his division. Buck, in a letter to his sister Lucie, wrote: "Gen. Cleburne ... says he had a wonderful time. Rumor says he lost his heart with a young lady in Mobile. He has been in a heavenly mood and talks about another leave, already."[20]

Cleburne wrote to Dr. Nash about being in love with Miss Susan and requested his friend's assistance. He mentioned helping the doctor in winning Mrs. Nash. Dr. Nash promptly initiated a pleasant correspondence with Miss Tarleton concerning the General, which continued until Cleburne's death. Undoubtedly the doctor used glowing phrases concerning his friend similar to those in his *Biographical Sketch of Gen. Pat Cleburne:* a man of "marked ability"; "brave and fearless"; "a sterling type of the very best manhood, intelligence and public spirit"; "a born leader of men"; "a true friend, wise in counsel, of pure patriotism and unsullied honor"; "fidelity and perserverance" were "the rule of his life"; "his big heart took in sympathy enough to divide with the weak and distressed"; he possessed "great breadth of character and fixedness of will," "magnanimity of soul rarely equalled" and "never surpassed," and "the high merit of a moral man."[21]

2

Christopher Cleburne probably left the Army of Tennessee to rejoin Morgan's command about the time the General returned from Mobile. Morgan had escaped from a Northern prison; and on January 13, 1864, issued a proclamation, published in a Richmond paper, for his men to assemble at Decatur, Georgia.

On his return to Tunnel Hill, Cleburne found a gift of a pair of gauntlets from Miss Rowe Webster of Beech Grove, Tennessee, with a note complimenting his "many deeds of gallantry." Miss Webster, who was "refuging" in LaFayette, Alabama, said she was pining to return to her "native home"; and asked, "When shall we redeem Tennessee?" On January 31, 1864, Cleburne replied:

> Dear Miss Webster:
>   I write to return you many thanks for your kind remembrance of myself. I have received the comfortable pair of gauntlets you have sent me and I assure you they will be well appreciated. To my noble Division and not to myself belong the praises for the deeds of gallantry you mention. Whatever we have done, however, has been more than repaid by the generous appreciation of our countrymen. I assure you I feel the same ardent longing to again recover the magnificent forests and green vallies of Middle Tennessee that you do, and live in the hope that God will restore it to our arms. I cannot predict when that time will be, and yet I feel that it is certainly in the future. We may have to make greater sacrifices—*to use all the means that God has given us*—but when once our people, or the greater body of them, sincerely value independence above *every other earthly consideration,* then I will regard our success as an accomplished fact.
>
> Your friend,
P R Cleburne[22]

For several months Buck had importuned his chief for a picture to send to his family in Virginia. Cleburne had some photographs made while in Mobile and brought back one for his aide. Buck proudly wrote his sister: "Enclosed is General Cleburne's photograph with his autograph under it. Am sorry it is not better, for it does not do him justice. Do not let it fall into the hands of the Yankees, should they make a raid on Bel Air. I wish you to tell me what you think of the General."[23]

Cleburne gave immediate attention to the problem of the imminent expiration of enlistment terms of his three-year men. Federal gunboats patrolling the Mississippi had practically severed communication with the Trans-Mississippi area and his Arkansas and Texas troops had not heard from their families for a year or more. They had received reports of ravages of their homeland by the invading enemy. "No husband could know," said Hardee, "that his wife was not homeless—no father that his children were not starving. Every instinct that appeals most powerfully and most sacredly to manhood, called upon these men to return to their homes as soon as they could do so honourably." Nevertheless, because of the high morale in his division, the greater portion of Cleburne's men voluntarily reenlisted for the duration of the war. Cleburne cast aside the role of a commander and as a comrade talked with his troops who had not reenlisted, placing the cause of Southern independence above all other considerations. Inspired by their leader's exalted sense of duty and patriotism, the entire division reenlisted for the duration.[24]

When General Hardee returned to Dalton, his bride and daughters came with him to remain until fighting began. Within a few days after their arrival, Mrs. Hardee invited General Cleburne and Captain Buck to have breakfast with the family.[25]

As preparation for the spring campaign continued, a shipment from England of long-range Whitworth rifles came through the blockade; also received was a shipment of long-range Kerr rifles made in an arsenal at Macon, Georgia. Cleburne's division received thirty Whitworth and sixteen Kerr rifles, the largest allotment made to any division. With great care, Cleburne organized a corps of forty-six sharpshooters and chose as their commander Lieut. (later Capt.) A. B. Schell of the 2nd Tennessee Infantry. Part of Schell's right thumb had been shot off at the battle of Perryville. This corps of sharpshooters was perhaps the most skilled in the entire Confederate Army.[26]

On February 1, Gen. Kirby Smith, commander of the Department of the Trans Mississippi, wrote the War Department requesting a new commander for the District of Arkansas. Cleburne was one of three major generals whom Smith listed as suitable for the command. "An active, energetic successor, who can win the confidence of the people and excite the enthusiasm of his troops, is wanted."[27]

Realizing Cleburne's value to the Army of Tennessee, the War Department did not transfer him.

During the winter, the soldiers frequently received clothing and other items from ladies in Georgia. More of these gifts were designated for Cleburne's division than any other. The ladies realized the division consisted mostly of men whose families were in enemy occupied territory, and also appreciated the division's accomplishment at Ringgold Gap.[28]

3

On February 17, orders came from Richmond for Johnston to dispatch the infantry of the three divisions of Hardee's corps (including Cleburne's division) to the relief of Gen. Leonidas Polk in Alabama. During the winter, Sherman and his army had been sent from Chattanooga to Vicksburg, Thomas being placed in command at Chattanooga. Early in February, Sherman and 20,000 infantry had moved eastward from Vicksburg. Polk, opposing with an infantry force of only 9,000, had fallen back; and by February 12, Sherman was in Meridian, Mississippi. At Sherman's order, Gen. William Sooy Smith, with an infantry brigade and 7,000 cavalry, had left Memphis to join Sherman at Meridian.

Johnston began dispatching forces by railroad through Atlanta, to Demopolis, Leonidas Polk's headquarters. Each night from February 19 to 22, units of Cleburne's division cooked two day's rations and secretly left Tunnel Hill; marching to Dalton where they boarded the cars for Demopolis.[29] Whether Sherman's objective was Selma, Montgomery, or Mobile is unknown, because his plans went askew. On February 21, Forrest, with 2,500 cavalry, met Smith's forces near Okolona, Mississippi; and drove them back to Memphis. Sherman then abandoned his campaign and started back to Vicksburg.

Polk, after learning of Sherman's retreat on February 24, ordered Hardee's corps to return to Dalton. Some of Cleburne's division had then reached Montgomery; and others were at West Point, on the Georgia-Alabama state line. One regiment had arrived at Dalton but had not boarded the cars. Cleburne's troops at Montgomery and West Point reversed their direction, arriving in Atlanta the night of the

24th and the following day.[30]

Cleburne's division was needed at Dalton in repelling an attack by Thomas. General Grant had heard that Johnston had sent reinforcements to Leonidas Polk in Mississippi and to Longstreet in Chattanooga. Therefore, on February 14, Grant had ordered Thomas to move against Johnston, "the object being to gain possession of Dalton and as far south of that as possible."[31] Because of the terrain and the Confederate defenses, Thomas had a formidable task. Dalton lies in a valley east of Rocky Face, a high, precipitous ridge running north and south. The ridge is fourteen miles in length, Dalton being three miles from the middle point. Two gaps through the ridge provide access to the town. Three miles northwest of Dalton, through Mill Creek Gap, ran the Western & Atlantic Railroad. The lower pass, Dug Gap, is three and a half miles southwest of Dalton. North of Mill Creek Gap, Johnston had constructed a line of field works eastward from Rocky Face Ridge across Crow Valley.

On the 22nd, just as the last of Cleburne's regiments, the 32nd Mississippi, was about to entrain at Dalton, word was received that Thomas' forces of four divisions had moved into Ringgold and the upper end of Crow Valley. The 32nd Mississippi was ordered to remain at Dalton. During the next two days the Federals moved southward. The 32nd Mississippi marched to Mill Creek Gap but did not become engaged.[32] On the 25th, the Confederates were successful in two heavy skirmishes—at Mill Creek Gap, and in Crow Valley. A regiment of Federal cavalry, however, occupied Dug Gap, with instructions "to hold it as long as possible."[33]

In Atlanta the morning of the 25th, Cleburne, expecting to go into battle, secured a two days' supply of rations and arranged for it to be cooked by ladies of the city. Orders detained Cleburne and his command in Atlanta until the afternoon. Part of the division reached Dalton that night; and the rest, on the 26th and 27th. Granbury's brigade arrived first and was ordered by Cleburne to march to Dug Gap and retake the gap at dawn the next morning. Granbury placed half of his brigade on the crest of the ridge, and the other half at the entrance to the gap. The Federals hastily abandoned the position and withdrew quite a distance from the pass, much to the amusement of the Texans.[34]

Cleburne's division encamped for a few days near Dug Gap; and then moved to the banks of Mill Creek near the Middle Spring Place Road, the extreme right of the army, about three miles east of Dalton. The troops dug entrenchments and again prepared huts for winter quarters, where they remained for more than two months. During this stay east of Dalton, the commander of Company K, 7th Texas Infantry, recorded, "The health and morale of the company very fine indeed."[35]

4

Progress of General Cleburne's romance is reported in letters from Miss Susan's twenty-five-year-old brother Robert Tarleton. Robert wrote to his fiancee, Miss Sallie Lightfoot, from Fort Morgan on February 22, 1864; "I have nothing to report in the case of Sue and the General. She sent him a letter on Friday, but whether it was the first or the second I don't know—she would not let me see it—but I know it cost her an immense deal of trouble to write it." From Mobile on March 2 Robert again wrote: "Poor Sue is like the 'last rose of summer.' You would be an inestimable boon to her and besides she needs you to advise her about Gen'l. C. She is in some perplexity and you know you would be of much assistance to her in it."[36]

On March 3, Captain Buck wrote his sister Lucie from the headquarters of Cleburne's division near Dalton: "General Cleburne expects to start on a twelve days leave this evening to visit his sweetheart, he has scarcely been back a month, this is very suggestive is it not? Would not be surprised at another wedding soon."[37]

Cleburne, on leave, reached Mobile on March 6 accompanied by Lieutenant Mangum. Subsequent events were reported by Robert Tarleton from Fort Morgan on March 11 in a letter to Miss Sallie:

> Yesterday was a day to remember . . . . I had a visit from Henry Goldthwaite. He was accompanied by a Lieut. Mangum, an old college friend of mine and an aid to General Cleburne . . . . You have already guessed (pardon the word)—if you do not know it officially—that Genl. Patrick is in town. He has been there several days and has been pressing his suit with

vigor and Henry tells me, with complete success.

Robert seized upon this development as affording him an opportunity to see his beloved. His letter continues:

> Of course I am pleased if Sue is, but what especially delights me about the affair is the prospect, sudden, unexpected, glorious, which it opens of my getting a furlough in the course of a month. I sent the most affectionate message by Henry to old Pat. Told him that I longed to give him a fraternal embrace and that a furlough of twenty days early in April would make me his for life. I likewise sent a message to Sue to the same effect and respectfully solicited her influence. I think this is a very promising flank movement which must succeed unless something unforeseen occurs.38

The General, himself, in a gay letter to Miss Sallie, announced the news of his engagement:

> Battle House, Mobile, Ala.,
> 11th March 1864.
>
> Miss Sallie Lightfoot
> Dear Miss Sallie
> I cannot think of leaving Mobile, the scene of so many happy memories of yourself and sister, without writing you the news. I arrived here last Sunday. I took advantage of the lull after the little storm at Dalton to come down and learn my fate from Miss Sue. After keeping me in cruel suspense for six weeks she has at length consented to be mine and we are engaged. I need not say how *miserable* this has made me. From all I saw when we parted, I have little doubt but that you can without a very great stretch of memory recall what the feelings of an accepted lover are when the fair one has relented, when the heartless little conqueror shows that she is all heart by descending from her tall triumphal car, lifting her wounded captive from the mud and placing him palpitating with a thousand new emotions by her side. "Well (I imagine you saying), he is in the car—what next?" Or as the great novel writer says, "What will he do with it?" (By the way, tell Miss Amelia at her suggestion I read this book and I believe was more pleased with it than with any book of the kind I ever read. There are more healthful and clearly expressed rules of life in it than in half the novels I ever read put together.) But to answer your supposed question, I must ask you to revert to your own experience again. You can imagine yourself the magnanimous vanquisher and some brave young fellow of our

acquaintance the resuscitated captive. You still hold the reigns
in your own hands. Alas! What can the poor captive do but go
about in the flowery fetters wherever you *[sic]* will directs—
over the uneven long doubtful road between acceptance and
matrimony, weeks as long as months, months as long as years,
must be traveled over in a dangerous conveyance which may
upset and break the accepted's heart if not his neck at any
moment; and this must continue until he succeeds in coaxing
or snatching the reins from his bethrothed's hands. Once he
can accomplish this he will answer your question by driving as
straight and swift as an arrow to the altar and transforming
Miss Sallie into a meek, obedient, exemplary, happy wife; and
himself into such a pattern of a lord and master.

Dalton, Ga., 19th March.
I neglected to mail this in Mobile and have since returned
to Dalton. I found all your friends well and happy in Mobile.
Lt. T. very anxious to get a furlough of twenty days for next
month. I am going to write to some of my friends to help him
in the matter.... I found Miss Amelia's letter awaiting me
when I returned. I owe her many thanks for it. Give her my
sincere regards and tell her I will wait a few days before
answering it to see if I can't get some news to tell her. And
now, Miss Sallie, I shall expect to hear all your secrets and
some happy day to be able to call myself more than your
sincere friend,

P R Cleburne[39]

Robert Tarleton continued to keep Miss Sallie posted. In
a letter on March 18 he said: "Haven't heard anything from
my furlough yet.... [Sue] did send me one enigmatic
message to the effect that she would manage it for me if she
could—as if she were expected to do anything except give
Patrick his orders." Three weeks later he wrote:

Of Sue and the General I have nothing to report. Things
are getting on swimmingly. She is certainly quite happy and
likes him very much indeed. I have not seen any of his letters
yet but intend to make her show me some when I come up
again. Mother says the correspondence is a severe tax upon
Sue's energy. She says the General complains of the brevity of
her letters and says she takes all sorts of advantages of him by
writing very large and leaving large intervals between the
lines.[40]

Cleburne's intervention to obtain a furlough for his prospective brother-in-law brought results. The Confederate service record of Lieut. Robert Tarleton shows that in April 1864 he was granted a twenty day leave by order of General Maury.[41]

5

Soon after Cleburne returned to duty, the Rev. J. J. Hutchinson, a missionary to the army, conducted a service for Cleburne's division, assisted by Gen. M. P. Lowrey. In relating his war experiences, the Reverend Mr. Hutchinson recalled, "General Cleburne, the hero of many battlefields, treated me with much attention and kindness. . . ."[42]

In late March, a four-inch snowfall provided a pleasant diversion for the troops. A large-scale snowball battle that lasted all day, raged between Govan's and Polk's brigades. Cleburne commanded Polk's brigade during the snowball exchange because of the latter's illness. In their enthusiasm, some of the soldiers seized cannon, caissons, and horses; and dashed into the snowball battle. Cleburne was captured by Govan's forces, who promptly recalled the practice of some officers having a straggler carry a fence rail as punishment. The jovial captors shouted, "Arrest that soldier and make him carry a fence rail!" Cleburne was "paroled," but soon reentered the battle when Polk's brigade began having reverses. In a short time Polk's brigade was routed and Cleburne was chased to his quarters. The climax came when the General was threatened with "court-martial" on the charge of violating his parole, and ducking in icy Mill Creek was being considered as punishment. However, the victors relented when the General pleaded that this was his first and only violation.[43]

Just a few weeks earlier, Buck had written to his sister, "The troops are as much devoted to General Cleburne, as Stonewall Jackson's men were to him." Another veteran of the Army of Tennessee later mentioned that "Genl. Cleburne was greatly beloved by the officers of the Army and notably by Genl. Johnston."[44]

NOTES

CHAPTER XII

[1]Buck, *Cleburne,* 186-87; Alice V. D. Pierrepont, *Reuben Vaughan Kidd, Soldier of the Confederacy* (Petersburg, Va., 1947), 109; John Witherspoon DuBose, "Chronicles of the Canebrake, 1817-60," *The Alabama Historical Quarterly,* IX (1947), 543-44.

[2]CSR of J. A. Sepp, M317/90, NA; Benham, *Kennesaw Gazette,* IV (Sept. 1, 1889), 2; Hardee to his wife, June 24, 1864, in Hardee Papers, Ala. Arch. and Hist.

[3]Mobile *Daily Advertiser and Register,* Jan. 14, 1864, p. 2; Nash, *Gen. Pat Cleburne,* 110-11, 114-16; Reynolds (ed.), *Publications of Arkansas Historical Association,* I, 271; J. Thomas Scharf, *History of the Confederate States Navy* (New York, 1887), 550, 553, 555.

[4]Irving Buck to his sister Lucie, Jan. 23, 1864, microfilm copy in Buck Papers. The fine residence on Bleak House plantation was built by Ivey Foreman Lewis in the late 1850's. In it were famous paintings and copies purchased by Mr. Lewis during a European trip with his wife and sister.—Pierrepont, *Reuben Vaughan Kidd,* 108; DuBose, "Chronicles of the Canebrake," 534-55. The land that comprised the plantation is now in Hale County.

[5]Pierrepont, *Reuben Vaughan Kidd,* 109; DuBose, "Chronicles of the Canebrake," 543-44; Hughes, *General Hardee,* 117, 186, 188; Robert Tarleton to Sallie Lightfoot, Feb. 22, Mar. 24, 1864, in Tarleton Family Collection, Yale University Library; Robert Tarleton file record, Princeton University.

[6]Mangum, *Kennesaw Gazette,* II (June 15, 1887), 3; Nash, *Gen. Pat Cleburne,* 111-12; Robert Tarleton to Sallie Lightfoot, Mar. 11, 1864, in Tarleton Family Collection.

[7]Miss Ruth Dargan Huger, distant relative of Susan Tarleton through the Brack family, Mobile, conversation with authors, Aug. 19, 1961; Mrs. Bedford Moore, grandniece of Susan Tarleton, Charlottesville, Va., conversation with authors, Feb. 24, 1962; Robert M. Tarleton, nephew of Susan Tarleton, to Hay, Jan. 4, 1942, in Hay Collection.

[8]Mrs. A. R. Colvin, daughter of Robert Tarleton and Sarah Bernard (Sallie) Lightfoot, his wife, Statement of, undated, in Tarleton Family Collection; Robert Tarleton to Sallie Lightfoot, Apr. 5, 1864, in Tarleton Family Collection; Winston Smith to authors, Oct. 23, 1962; Marriage Book C-1, p. 575, Official Records of Greene County, Ala.; Mrs. F. L. DuValle, grandniece of Robert Tarleton, to authors, Feb. 19, Feb. 24, 1964. The romance resulting in the marriages of Robert Tarleton and Sallie Lightfoot, and of Grace

Tarleton and Henry Goldthwaite, had their inception in the trip to and in the brief stay at the wedding. In the letter to Miss Sallie of Mar. 11, 1864 (note 6, *supra*), Robert Tarleton informed her that Miss Susan and General Cleburne had become engaged; and went on to say, "So ends the grand three act drama 'Bleak House' . . . . The atmosphere of 'Bleak House' is certainly fatal, warranted to kill the strongest subject in ten days."

9W. Brewer, *Alabama* (Montgomery, 1872), 451-52; Peter A. Brannon, Dir., Ala. Arch. and Hist., to authors, Feb. 14, 1962; Mrs. Zara Jones Powers, Memorandum of, Oct. 8, 1940, in Tarleton Family Collection; Mrs. Colvin, Statement of., *ibid.*

10The wedding party doubtless traveled on one of the fine steam vessels used by the planters of the Black Belt. There were three such vessels: the *St. Nicholas*, the *Magnolia*, and the *Cherokee.*—Bert Neville to Winston Smith, Oct. 1963 (Tape recording in possession of Winston Smith).

11Tape recording, note 10, *supra;* James Fleetwood Foster, *Ante-Bellum Floating Palaces of the Alabama River,* ed. Bert Neville (Selma, 1960), 15-16, 19, 23, 24; "A Winter in the South," *Harper's New Monthly Magazine,* XVIII (1858), 12.

12Winston Smith to authors, Nov. 30, 1964 (estimate based on data furnished by Bert Neville, considering season of the year).

13General and Mrs. Hardee also went to the Battle House.—DuBose, "Chronicles of the Canebrake," 541.

14*Mobile City Directory,* 1866, p. 70; "History of Tarleton Family" (MS compiled Dec. 3, 1855, owned by Robert Tarleton), in possession of Mrs. F. L. DuValle, Mobile; Miss Huger and Mrs. DeValle, conversations with authors, Aug. 19, 1961.

15*Cf.* Robert Tarleton to Sallie Lightfoot, Feb. 18, 1864, in Tarleton Family Collection.

16As to Christ Church being Miss Tarleton's church, see funeral notice of Mrs. Susan Cole (née Susan Tarleton) in Mobile *Daily Register,* July 1, 1868, p. 1.

17Mobile *Daily Advertiser and Register,* Jan. 22, 1864, p. 2.

18General Maury, a Virginian and West Pointer, had a distinguished record as a young soldier in the Mexican War and as an officer in the Confederacy. He served as colonel and chief of staff to General Van Dorn in the Trans-Mississippi, and was made Brigadier General following the battle of Pea Ridge, Arkansas. Commissioned Major General in November 1862, after fighting at Iuka and Corinth, he assumed command at Mobile, which he skillfully defended.

19Mobile *Daily Advertiser and Register,* Jan. 23, 1864, p. 2; *ibid.,* Jan. 24, 1864, p. 3.

[20]Irving Buck to his sister Lucie, Feb. 9, 1864, microfilm copy in Buck Papers.

[21]Nash, *Gen. Pat Cleburne,* 10, 34-35, 74-75, 111, 159, 196, 199-200.

[22]"The Late Gen. Cleburne. — A Reminiscence," Mobile *Army Argus and Crisis,* Feb. 4, 1865; Cleburne to Miss Rowe Webster, Jan. 31, 1864, in Miscellaneous Files, Tennessee Historical Society Collections, Tenn. Lib. and Arch.

[23]Irving Buck to his sister Lucie, Feb. 9, 1864, microfilm copy in Buck Papers.

[24]Hardee, "Major General Cleburne," 646-47; Irving Buck to his sister Lucie, Jan. 23, Feb. 9, 1864, microfilm copies in Buck Papers. "All [the company] reenlisted for 99 years or the war."—Record of Events, Co. E, 10th Texas Infantry, Jan. and Feb. 1864. "All men and 3 officers of this Company have reenlisted for the War."—Record of Events, Co. A, 32nd Mississippi Infantry, Jan. and Feb. 1864. "The company Reenlisted for the war the 9 day of February 1864."—Record of Events, Co. C, 32nd Mississippi Infantry, Mar. and Apr. 1864.

[25]Irving Buck to his sister Lucie, Feb. 9, 1864, microfilm copy in Buck Papers.

[26]Frank H. Smith, "Interview with Capt. Schell," 219; Buck, *Cleburne,* 201; Drake, "General Cleburne," 246; Benham, *Kennesaw Gazette,* IV (Sept. 15, 1899), 4; James W. Blackmore, "Co. 'I,' 2nd Regiment Tennessee Infantry" (MS in possession of Mrs. Alex W. Hewitt, Dallas, Texas).

[27]*O.R.,* XXXIV, Pt. 2, p. 935; see also *ibid.,* pp. 869-70.

[28]Irving Buck to his sister Lucie, Mar. 3, 1864, microfilm copy in Buck Papers; Record of Events, Co. K, 7th Texas Infantry, Jan. and Feb. 1864.

[29]*O.R.,* XXXII, Pt. 2, p. 792; Record of Events, Cos. B and F, 15th (Cleburne's—Polk's—Josey's) Arkansas Infantry, Jan. and Feb. 1864; Record of Events, Cos. B and C, 35th (formerly 5th) Tennessee Infantry, Jan. and Feb. 1864; Record of Events, Co. H, 48th (Nixon's) Tennessee Infantry, Jan. and Feb. 1864; Record of Events, Co. K, 7th Texas Infantry Jan. and Feb. 1864.

[30]Company Records of Events cited note 29, *supra.*

[31]*O.R.,* XXXII, Pt. 1, p. 9.

[32]Record of Events, Cos. E, F, and H, 32nd Mississippi Infantry, Jan. and Feb. 1864.

[33]*O.R.,* XXXII, Pt. 1, p. 10.

[34]Buck, *Cleburne,* 202; Joseph E. Johnston, *Narrative,* 284-85; *O.R.,* XXXII, Pt. 1, p. 457.

[35]Simpson (ed.), *Bugle Softly Blows,* 48; Record of Events, Co. G,

15th (Cleburne's—Polk's—Josey's) Arkansas Infantry, Dec. 31, 1863 to Feb. 29, 1864; Buck, *Cleburne,* 203; Record of Events, Co. K, 7th Texas Infantry, Jan. and Feb. 1864.

[36]Robert Tarleton to Sallie Lightfoot, Feb. 22, 1864, Mar. 2, 1864, in Tarleton Family Collection.

[37]Irving Buck to his sister Lucie, Mar. 3, 1864, microfilm copy in Buck Papers.

[38]Robert Tarleton to Sallie Lightfoot, Mar. 11, 1864, in Tarleton Family Collection.

[39]Cleburne to Sallie Lightfoot, Mar. 11, Mar. 19, 1864, in Tarleton Family Collection.

[40]Robert Tarleton to Sallie Lightfoot, Mar. 18, Apr. 6, 1864, in Tarleton Family Collection.

[41]CSR of Robert Tarleton, M311/55, NA.

[42]J. William Jones, "The Morale of the Confederate Armies," in Evans (ed.), *Confederate Military History,* XII, 183; Preston, "Memoirs," 26.

[43]S. R. Watkins, "Snow Battle at Dalton," *Confederate Veteran,* I (1893), 261; Buck, *Cleburne,* 203. During this same snowfall, two other snow battles took place. One was between Walker's division of Georgians and Cheatham's division of Tennesseans.—George W. Gordon, "The Famous Snowball Battle in the Confederate Army at Dalton, Ga., 1864," in Ben LaBree (ed.), *Camp Fires of the Confederacy* (Louisville, 1898), 48-53; Melancthom Smith Journal of the Dalton and Atlanta Campaign (MS in Cheatham Papers), 1. The other battle was between battery companies. —Cate (ed.), *Key Diary,* 64-65. Earlier that winter, there were other large-scale snowball battles between units of Confederate soldiers.

[44]Irving Buck to his sister Lucie, Feb. 9, 1864, microfilm copy in Buck Papers; Young to Hay, May 29, 1918, in Hay Collection. ". . . the soldiers whom he commanded loved him to a man, and trusted him implicitly."—Mangum, *Kennesaw Gazette,* II (June 15, 1887), 3.

CHAPTER XIII

DALTON TO THE ETOWAH
(May 7 — 19, 1864)

Why Was Snake Creek Gap Left Unguarded?
—Wilbur G. Kurtz

Joseph E. Johnston, during the first four months of 1864, prepared the army for active campaigning, which was a certainty when the heavy rains ceased. Through Johnston's efforts, the men were well supplied and better equipped and Dalton was strongly fortified. Later, Sherman spoke of "the terrible door of death that Johnston had prepared for them in the Buzzard Roost."[1] Rocky Face Ridge, studded with field works, was almost inaccessible except at the gaps. Mill Creek, running through Mill Creek Gap, by the damming of railroad culverts had been made into a moat. The Confederates had confidence in General Johnston and more than 5,000 absentees had returned, increasing the army to 45,000. The morale of the troops was high although they were outnumbered more than two to one, Sherman's three "armies," commanded by George H. Thomas, James B. McPherson, and J. M. Schofield, totalled over 100,000.

Cleburne's division drilled when weather permitted, had rifle practice often and artillery practice occasionally, and once engaged in a sham battle using blank cartridges. Friendly competition, encouraged by Cleburne, existed among his four brigades, each striving to be the best. Once the entire army, drawn up in long lines, was reviewed by Johnston, Hardee, Cleburne, and other general officers, who rode past. Accompanying Hardee were his wife and daughters.[2]

While waiting for Sherman to commence his attack, Cleburne seized on an opportunity to strike at the Federals. William Gibbs Allen, adjutant in the 5th Tennessee Cavalry, years later recounted:

> Fifteenth of April, 1864 [I was ordered] to report with
> one hundred men to General Pat Cleburne at the top of Rocky
> Face Mountain at sunrise next morning. When I reached the
> Gap, I found a single man in the road. He had on a hunting
> shirt. I had never seen General Cleburne. I asked him where I
> could find General Cleburne. "Yes," he said, "I am General
> Cleburne. What orders have you?" I told him. He threw his
> hunting shirt back and I saw his stars. He turned to the west
> and said, "Do you see that smoke down in Dogwood Valley?"
> He told me to go down the mountain and charge into their
> camps. I said, "General, how many Yankees is down there?"
> He answered, "A brigade." I said, "I can do nothing with a
> brigade. I have only one hundred men." He said, "You can
> charge them and scatter them; and when they turn on you,
> you can out run them."
> I started. When I struck their vidette we raised the Rebel
> yell. They were at breakfast. They sure did scatter. They had a
> fine breakfast and I had trouble to hold a guard in line. Soon
> they rallied and chased us up the side of the mountain,
> wounding two men and several horses. When I reached the top
> of the mountain, the General said, "You scattered them! They
> went!" "Get close," the General said, "File right" And it
> seemed to me a thousand or more gun shots rang out, and
> many of the Yankees were killed and wounded.[3]

On May 5, Johnston having received reports that the
Federals were advancing in force, positioned his army to
meet the enemy. He formed the main infantry line of battle
across Mill Creek Gap, thence north on the crest of Rocky
Face for about a mile, thence east in a line of field works
across Crow Valley. Crow Valley and low parallel ridges to
the east provided routes to Dalton, which in Cleburne's
judgment were defensible. Cleburne's division was placed
immediately in front of Dalton, behind Mill Creek, facing
north toward Cleveland.[4]

On May 7, Sherman drove past Tunnel Hill and formed a
line opposite Johnston's forces. The next day, he attacked
the main Confederate line and the troops posted in Dug Gap.
In a subsequent report to Hardee, Cleburne related the
operations of his division:

> On the 7th of May, 1864, the enemy advanced, with heavy
> masses of infantry and other arms, toward Rocky Face

Gap, ... It was understood he was also advancing upon the
Cleveland road. My division at this time was intrenched upon
Mill Creek, ... The next day, the 8th of May I was ordered
to go with dispatch to Dug Gap, a pass in Rocky Face Ridge,
five miles southwest of Dalton, then being heavily attacked by
Hooker's corps. I was to take Lowrey's and Granbury's
brigades. I arrived there after a rapid march, which was
rendered very severe by the extreme heat of the summer and
the steep acclivity of the ridge, about an hour before sundown.
Reaching the gap (Dug Gap) in person, while my command
was still at the foot of the ridge, I found the First and Second
Arkansas Cavalry, dismounted, and [J. Warren] Grigsby's
brigade of Kentucky cavalry holding the position. They had
gallantly repulsed every assault. The fight was still going on,
and some anxiety was felt (you yourself were present) lest the
overwhelming numbers of the enemy might carry the position
before my command could ascend the hill.[5]

To speed the arrival of his men, Cleburne mounted
Granbury's brigade on horses which Grigsby's cavalrymen
had left at the foot of the ridge. The horses, each carrying
two men, climbed the abrupt scarp of the gap faster than the
riders could have walked. The rest of Cleburne's command
ascended on foot.[6]

The report continued:

The Arkansans and Kentuckians held [the position] firmly . . . until I placed Lowrey and Granbury in position, which
was done by night-fall. With night the enemy remitted his
attack, and everything was quiet. On the morning of the 9th
my pickets were advanced to the extreme base of the ridge on
its west face. Many of the enemy's dead were found and some
wounded, who were brought in and cared for . . . . A great
many small-arms were collected and brought in also. The
enemy did not attack during the day. His forces were plainly
in view in the valley. Their numbers, however, could not be
estimated, as the valley had only a small portion of cleared
land. Some prisoners were taken during the day.[7]

Despite the repulse of the Federals at Dug Gap and points
on the main line, Sherman succeeded in a strategic move.
Taking advantage of the terrain of the region, he upset the
Confederates' plan to defend Dalton. Seven miles below
Dalton, Rocky Face feathers out; but the rough terrain

continues in a series of high, rugged ridges. Between the two easternmost ridges is Snake Creek Gap, a narrow valley about four miles long. Through this gap tiny Snake Creek flows southward to the Oostanaula River. The lower end of Snake Creek Gap, twelve miles south of Dalton, was five miles northwest of Resaca. The latter town was on the railroad and the north bank of the Oostanaula River.

McPherson's army (the 15th and part of the 16th Corps), under Sherman's orders, on May 5 left Chattanooga and headed south for Snake Creek Gap. Encamping near Chickamauga battlefield, McPherson reached the western side of Taylor's Ridge the evening of May 7. South of Ringgold, Taylor's Ridge is broken by three gaps, the southernmost, Ship's Gap, being east of LaFayette. Four and a quarter miles north of Ship's Gap is Gordon's Springs Gap, with Nickajack Gap still farther north. On the morning of the 8th, the 16th Corps had crossed Taylor's Ridge at Ship's Gap; and the 15th Corps, at Gordon's Springs Gap. The Federals then marched through the hamlet of Villanow, a few miles from the upper end of Snake Creek Gap; and occupied that gap, unopposed.[8]

At dawn on the 9th, the advance of McPherson's army had issued from the eastern end of Snake Creek Gap and encountered Grigsby's brigade, just then arrived after a night ride from Dug Gap. McPherson drove Grigsby's horsemen toward Resaca and struck at two Confederate infantry regiments in the town. One regiment had been guarding the railroad bridge across the Oostanaula; and the other was the van of Leonidas Polk's command coming from Mississippi to reinforce Johnston.[9]

Because of McPherson's surprise appearance from Snake Creek Gap, Cleburne's and two other divisions were ordered about 1 A.M. on the 10th to move immediately toward Resaca. On the march from Dug Gap, Cleburne narrowly escaped being captured when he and two members of his staff were riding a half mile in front of his troops. A scouting party of McPherson's army crossed the road just behind Cleburne and captured two Confederate cavalrymen. After marching within a mile of Resaca and waiting two hours, Cleburne received orders to return to Dug Gap, because of a change in the enemy movements. He reached Dug Gap about sundown.[10]

In Cleburne's report to Hardee, written three months later, he denounced the gross neglect in leaving Snake Creek Gap unguarded and lamented the consequences:

> My division was now together [at Dug Gap]. Receiving orders during the night I marched on the morning of the 11th, starting at 7 o'clock, upon the Sugar Valley[11] road in the direction of Resaca. This move was rendered necessary by the untoward circumstances of Snake Creek Gap not being adequately occupied to resist the heavy force thrown against it, under the sagacious and enterprising McPherson. How this gap, which opened upon our rear and line of communication, from which it was distant at Resaca only five miles, was neglected I cannot imagine. General [W. W.] Mackall, Johnston's chief of staff, told me it was the result of a flagrant disobedience of orders, by whom he did not say. Certainly the commanding general never could have failed to appreciate its importance. Its loss exposed us in the outset of the campaign to a terrible danger, and on the left forced us to retreat from a position where, if he adhered to his attack, we might have detained the enemy for months, destroying vast numbers of his men, perhaps prolonged the campaign until the wet season would have rendered operations in the field impracticable. As it was, if McPherson had hotly pressed his advantage, Sherman supporting him strongly with the bulk of his army, it is impossible to say what the enemy might not have achieved — more than probable a complete victory. But McPherson faltered and hung back, indeed after penetrating within a mile of Resaca he actually returned, because, as I understood, he was not supported, and feared if we turned back suddenly upon him from Dalton he would be cut off, as doubtless would have been the result.[12]

On May 11, Johnston hastened additional troops of Leonidas Polk's command from Rome, Georgia, to Resaca. By that afternoon, it was evident that Sherman was moving the main body of his army along the west side of Rocky Face toward Snake Creek Gap. Hence Johnston was compelled to give up his position at Dalton and fall back to Resaca.

No official inquiry was made, or charges preferred, respecting the fatal error of neglecting Snake Creek Gap and its approaches. Singularly, Cleburne's is the only report of the Dalton operations which states or implies that Snake

Creek Gap, the "key to the fields," was left unguarded because of dereliction in duty. Nor does any other report or account denote surprise or chagrin because the Federal seizure of Snake Creek Gap made Dalton untenable. Apparently some of the generals chose to consign the matter "to limbo."[13]

In speaking of "a flagrant disobedience of orders," General Mackall apparently was referring to the cavalry commander, General Wheeler. The directives in question were these: (1) Dalton, May 5, Mackall to Wheeler: "General Johnston wishes you to take measures to acquire the most accurate information of the present position of the enemy this side and to the [west] of Taylor's Ridge." (2) Dalton, May 5, Mackall to Wheeler: "The general understands that your picket-lines hold Taylor's Ridge." (3) Dalton, May 7, 7 A.M., Mackall to Wheeler: "If driven into Mill Creek Gap, General Johnston wishes you to leave a body of cavalry in the valley west and south of the gap, in observation of the enemy. This body will report by way of the gap five miles below Dalton on the Villanow road to these headquarters."[14]

According to "Memoranda of Fights" by Wheeler, dated June 1, 1864, his three brigades picketed "the front and flank of our army, extending from Ship's Gap, on our left, to the Connasauga River, on our right."[15] But in disobedience particularly of the second of the above directives, Wheeler, by May 7, had removed his pickets from Ship's Gap for the fighting to the north. Furthermore, certainly on May 7 and 8, Wheeler failed to maintain reconnaissance west of Taylor's Ridge. At 5 P.M. on May 7, a Federal general in McPherson's army dispatched the following message to Sherman from the west side of Taylor's Ridge, near Gordon's Springs Gap: "No indications of a large force in this valley. Have had scouts up as far as Valley Head, who saw nor heard of nothing except guerillas." Simultaneously with sending this message, McPherson pushed ahead a brigade 2,000 strong to seize Ship's Gap.[16] Reaching the gap at 9 P.M., the brigade, "Saw only twenty of the enemy; they were on the Alabama road, none in the gap." One Federal regiment occupied Ship's Gap, and the rest of the brigade camped that night on the west side of

Taylor's Ridge.[17] Another Federal report, dated May 8, recited, ". . . there is not and has not been an enemy at LaFayette; it has been patrolled by 400 men; . . . ."[18]

Further evidence shows that Wheeler did not maintain scout patrols as directed, either west or east of Taylor's Ridge. Early on May 7, Hooker's 20th Corps, advancing on Dalton, pushed back Wheeler's pickets at Gordon's Springs Gap and crossed this gap. By 11 A.M. Hooker had driven Wheeler from Tunnel Hill and into Mill Creek Gap.[19] Thereafter Wheeler apparently had no scouts at Gordon's Springs Gap; or, as above indicated, at Ship's Gap. Also, he failed to carry out the direction to have a body of cavalry patrol the valley between Rocky Face and Taylor's Ridge. There is no record of any report by Wheeler that Union forces were at Gordon's Springs Gap or Ship's Gap on May 7 or the following morning. Nor is there any record that Wheeler reported McPherson's army moving from these gaps toward the Snake Creek corridor. Furthermore there is no record indicating that on May 7 Confederate cavalry scouted Taylor's Ridge or valleys on either side of the ridge.

After receipt of a peremptory order from Johnston before daybreak on May 8, Wheeler finally dispatched W. C. P. Breckinridge's cavalry regiment across Rocky Face at Dug Gap. Johnston's order was to send "a good regiment of cavalry . . . into the valley south and west of Mill Creek Gap."[20] At 10:15 A.M., Breckinridge sent a message to Mackall that a body of Union cavalry were on the Dalton and Villanow road. Three hours later, he sent another dispatch to Mackall that Federal cavalry, supported by a body of infantry, were moving toward Villanow. These forces were Judson Kilpatrick's cavalry and an infrantry brigade of the 20th Corps marching from Gordon's Springs Gap to join McPherson's army at Villanow.[21] Breckinridge's scouting was too late to discover McPherson's army. He was barred from patrolling as far south as Villanow because of the presence of Federal cavalry and infantry. Also, his scouts were prematurely called in when he had to assist in defending Dug Gap.

Breckinridge's initial message, which reached Johnston at noon, was the first word that the Confederate commander had received that Federals were moving in the direction of Villanow. Johnston immediately enjoined the commander of the regiments at Resaca to watch toward Villanow and Lafayette. Until the afternoon of May 9 Johnston was unaware that Snake Creek Gap was occupied by Federal infantry.[22] That Wheeler did not inform headquarters of the movement of McPherson's army from the gaps in Taylor's Ridge toward Snake Creek Gap is further evidenced by Mackall's inquiry to him on May 11: "Did the system of scouts established by you just before the advance of the enemy include the valley between Taylor's Ridge and Rocky Face?"[23]

Wilbur G. Kurtz, in his unpublished monograph, "Why Was Snake Creek Gap Left Unguarded?", mentioned that in addition to Wheeler's derelictions, Johnston, himself, had little or no knowledge of the strategic implications of Snake Creek Gap. Johnston had envisaged the possibility of a longer move by McPherson to the Confederate left by way of Rome and Kingston, Georgia.[24] Fed. Gen. Jacob D. Cox, in a postwar account stated:

> It is uncertain whether Johnston believed Snake Creek Gap to be a practicable route for a large column. It is hard to realize now how little accurate knowledge either party had of the topography of the country. Maps worthy the name there were none, and the Confederate staff seems to have been greatly inferior to that of the United States Army in working up such material as they had. . . . the opinion, which was the common one in Sherman's army at the time, [was] that Johnston rested securely in the belief that his position could only be turned by a much longer detour, and one involving many more contingencies for his opponent.[25]

Alfred H. Burne commented: "Johnston's conduct of the operations had been flawless — if we except the failure to hold Snake Creek Gap, about which there is some dispute: . . . ."[26]

2

On May 11, as part of Johnston's movement toward Resaca, Cleburne's division marched on the Sugar Valley

Road to a point ten miles from Dalton. Cleburne's report
continued:

> Determining upon a line of battle I camped for the night. At 7
> next morning, the 12th, the cavalry skirmishers in advance of
> me on the Sugar Valley road were driven in. Making my
> dispositions as promptly as possible, and more in detail than I
> had been able to do the evening before, I threw up
> breast-works and awaited the enemy, who was reported
> advancing in line of battle. He did not attack, however.[27]

At 2:30 P.M. on the 12th, from "Sugar Valley Road,"
Cleburne sent the following dispatch to Leonidas Polk at
Resaca, which the latter relayed by telegram to Johnston's
headquarters in Dalton:

> Private Walker and another of 7th Texas Regt just returned
> from Scout. Report that the Enemy were fortifying at
> Villanow last night. They are massing very heavily in Snake
> Creek Gap a great deal of artillery passed down in to the Gap
> by a Road Through the Woods. They moved in two columns.
> This he saw yesterday. Their talk is that they are going to
> Resaca, Calhoun, and Atlanta. This morning their Infantry was
> in line, and they could hear the artillery bugles sounding.[28]

To thwart the Federals and fight for the railroad at
Resaca, Johnston formed his army in a double line that faced
the Federals coming from Snake Creek Gap. The Confederate
line, which ran along a ridge west of Resaca, began at the
Oostenaula and extended northward; thence northeasterly
across the railroad to the Connasauga River.

In Cleburne's words: "On the 13th I marched to Resaca
and went into position on the crest of the ridge looking into
a valley several hundred yards wide formed by [Camp] Creek,
which at this point was parallel with the railroad, and about a
mile to the west of it. Here I covered myself with rifle-pits —
Bate on my right, Cheatham on my left."[29] Cleburne did not
report the reconnaissance he made soon after sunrise on the
14th, which his staff considered "a hazardous and imprudent
thing to do." Although the wooded ridge on the other side of
the valley might have concealed enemy troops, Cleburne
went alone on foot deep into the valley as far as the creek to

reconnoiter the ground in his front.[30]

A little later in the morning (Cleburne's official report continued),

> the enemy came into position on the ridge, opposite to me, and opened a heavy fusilade. In the course of the afternoon he made several attempts to charge, but uniformly they were unhappy failures. In front of Brigadier-General Govan, one of his officers, supposed to be a general officer, was heard to address his troops, endeavoring to incite them to the charge. He told them amongst other things that they were the men who had taken Missionary Ridge, and that they could take this. But his eloquence was of no avail. His men came but a few paces into the open ground of the valley, when they retired precipitately under our fire. Toward evening the enemy's fire slackened into a few dropping shots.
>
> Heavy musketry on my front early in the 15th gradually slackening until it was confined principally to sharpshooters, who were, however, quite troublesome.[31]

In this battle, Cleburne's corps of sharpshooters played an important part. They repeatedly silenced Union batteries eight hundred yards away, and almost annihilated a line of Federal skirmishers who had sought shelter in an area of deadened trees.[32]

Direct assaults were proving too costly for Sherman,[33] so the shrewd Union commander began a series of flanking movements with part of his army. Although Johnston's command had been increased to nearly 55,000 with the arrival at Resaca of two divisions of Polk's corps, it was still greatly outnumbered, almost two to one. Hence, Sherman could leave a large force at Resaca to threaten Johnston's front while employing his right wing to turn the Confederate left. Sherman's flanking force crossed the Oostenaula three and a half miles northwest of Calhoun, a town on the railroad five miles below Resaca. The flanking movement threatened the railroad — Johnston's life line to Atlanta.

Because of the disparity of forces, this, and subsequent out-flanking movements left the Confederate commander little recourse but to withdraw. General Johnston, in his *Narrative*, succinctly summarized his actions and plans, in the face of the superior numbers against him:

I ... thought it our policy to stand on the defensive, to spare the blood of our soldiers by fighting under cover habitually, and to attack only when bad position or division of the enemy's forces might give us advantages counterbalancing that of superior numbers. So we held every position occupied until our communications were strongly threatened; then fell back only far enough to secure them, watching for opportunities to attack ... and hoping to reduce the odds against us by partial engagements. A material reduction of the Federal army might also be reasonably expected before the end of June, by the expiration of the terms of service of the regiments that had not reenlisted. I was confident, too, that the Administration would see the expediency of employing Forrest and his cavalry to break the enemy's railroad communications, by which he could have been defeated.[34]

Pursuant to Johnston's policy, Cleburne's division, along with the rest of the army, withdrew from Resaca. Cleburne said in his report:

About 10 P.M. on the 15th, leaving my skirmishers in position, I withdrew from the works and crossed the Oostenaula River by the trestle bridge west of the railroad bridge. Halted at midnight within a few miles of Calhoun. About sunrise I proceeded to Calhoun with my division, and went into line, my left resting on the road leading to an unfinished bridge, my right stretching toward the railroad where it enters the town from the north. About 11 A.M. I was ordered to move to my left and rear to meet a force detached from the left of the position occupied by a body of the enemy lying on the left bank of the river, and held in check by Major-General [W. H. T.] Walker, commanding his own and [W. B.] Bate's divisions. This detachment was either directed against Calhoun or was seeking to get around Walker's right. I immediately threw forward Polk's brigade, formed Granbury's brigade as a second line behind him, and placed Govan's brigade in echelon on [Lucius] Polk's right. Lowrey's brigade, I disposed on a hill in the angle between [Oothcaloga] Creek and the river. I also placed four rifle pieces on the hill so as to enfilade the main body of the enemy in front of Walker. My escort was directed to observe the road from Resaca to Calhoun. Polk became briskly engaged with the enemy's skirmishers after advancing but a short distance. The rifle pieces on the hill opened upon the enemy's right, enfilading his line. This fire seemed to throw him into great confusion. It was entirely unexpected. It would doubtless have proved very destructive, but, unfortunately, before I had had time to fire more than a very few rounds a dispatch was sent me from my pickets that the enemy was coming upon Calhoun, driving Wheeler, with his cavalry, steadily before him. Receiving orders in view of the exposure of my rear to this force I withdrew my brigade and passed the creek. This was about 5 P.M. Here I found Major-General Walker in position. Placing Granbury on a small wooded hill on the bank of the creek, which commanded the approach to the bridge and ford over the creek, with Polk on his right along the creek bottom, I threw up rifle-pits and upon the hill epaulements for a battery. Govan and Lowrey were sent some two miles or more upon the Adairsville road. Skirmishers were thrown well out on the Calhoun side of the creek, and a strong force placed so as to hold a position (on that side of the creek) which it was feared the enemy, now swinging to the right and feeling for Polk, who had withdrawn from their front, might occupy. This position would have given the enemy command of Walker's flank and rear. The enemy did not come up.[35]

Johnston planned to make a stand eight miles to the south, just north of Adairsville. At this site an engineer's map showed the valley of Oothcaloga Creek to be narrow enough for the army to span it and hold the heights on each side. Cleburne continued his account:

Soon after night I received orders to march toward Adairsville. Leaving Granbury in position to draw in his pickets when all had got away, and join me, I moved at 1 A.M. May 17. I arrived at Adairsville about daylight (17th), halting about two miles north of the town. About 3 P.M. the enemy appeared in some considerable force on the railroad, from Calhoun. Cheatham was placed in position on the crest of a ridge immediately confronting the enemy, his line crossing the railroad at right angles. My division was drawn up on the left of the road in two lines, in Cheatham's rear, about 800 yards distant — Polk and Granbury in the first line, Govan and Lowrey in the second. An open field, traversed by a creek with swampy margins, intervened between me and Cheatham; along my left ran a considerable creek. Much attention was paid to my left flank. It was strengthened by rifle-pits, as also were my two lines. Skirmishers were disposed along the creek on my left, stretching down to Cheatham's left. A regiment of Lowrey's was thrown across the creek to my left for further protection to that flank. This force (regiment) afterward gave place to Bate. The enemy attacked Cheatham, but my division was not engaged.[36]

At this juncture, Cleburne received a message under a flag of truce from Gen. T. W. Sweeny, commander of the division opposing him. Sweeney, also a native of County Cork, Ireland, proposed to Cleburne that at the close of the war they together raise a Fenian army and liberate Ireland. Cleburne replied that he thought that after the war they both would have had enough fighting to last them the rest of their lives.[37]

The valley of the Oothcaloga proved to be much wider than depicted on the map, and unsuitable for a defensive position. Hence Johnston decided to move the army to the vicinity of Cassville, located off the railroad, nine miles southeast of Adairsville. To expedite the withdrawal he used two routes. Leonidas Polk's and Hood's corps traveled on the direct road from Adairsville to Cassville; and Hardee's corps, on a road running due south from Adairsville nine miles to Kingston, then on a road running westward five and a half miles to Cassville. The railroad paralleled the road Hardee used from Adairsville to Kingston. From Kingston the railroad ran southeasterly to Cass Station, four and a half miles southeast of Cassville. Cleburne's report to Hardee continued:

> Soon after night [on the 17th] I attended, at your summons, at your headquarters, and received orders to retire. Cheatham was to lead; Bate to follow in half an hour; Walker in another half hour, and I to bring up the rear as soon as I could get to the road. Skirmishers were to be left in position until the corps had got away. By some misunderstanding these skirmishers were withdrawn at 2 o'clock, and came in before my command had filed into the road, thus leaving nothing between me and the enemy. Fortunately, however, an impenetrable fog enveloped the army and covered our movements. I reached Kingston during the early part of the 18th, and halted for some hours. Moving again, I marched until about 4 P.M. with three of my brigades to within two miles of Cassville. [Lucius] Polk was left in Kingston as a rear guard. The next morning, May 19, I went into position. Polk had come up. My line crossed the railroad [near Cass Station] at right angles. I held the left, Walker next on my right.[38]

313

Confederate prospects were brightening. The rest of Leonidas Polk's forces — W. H. Jackson's cavalry and S. G. French's division — had arrived from Mississippi, increasing the strength of the army to some 64,000. Furthermore, Johnston hopefully expected that Federal forces, in following him to Cassville, would also divide at Adairsville. In such event Johnston planned to strike that portion of Sherman's army moving on the Adairsville-to-Cassville road while the rest of the Federal infantry was nearing Kingston.[39]

As early as May 17, Sherman had a preconceived idea that Johnston in withdrawing from Adairsville would march to Kingston, staying close to the railroad. For the next two days, he subconsciously twisted the facts to conform to his fixed idea. The Federal commander ordered his scattered forces, moving south in four columns under McPherson, Thomas, Hooker, and Schofield, to converge on Kingston.[40] When Sherman arrived at Adairsville the morning of May 18, he saw (to use his words) "the plain, well-marked trail of the enemy" on the road to Kingston.[41] The thought did not occur to him that the tracks which he saw on the Kingston road were left by only part of Johnston's army and that the rest of the army had taken the Cassville road.

Because the roads leading to Kingston were "not suited to one concentric movement," quoting Sherman, the Union army had to remain scattered "even at the hazard of beginning battle with but a part of our forces."[42] McPherson's column, on the west, entered Adairsville early on May 18; and proceeded toward Kingston on roads west of the railroad. Early that evening McPherson reached Woodland, four miles northwest of Kingston.[43] At 7 o'clock the next morning, May 19, he "[moved] forward on Kingston . . . in fighting trim, ready to deploy for battle.[44] Thomas' column, upon reaching Adairsville at 10 A.M. on May 18, set out in "pursuit" of Johnston on the road to Kingston and the adjacent railroad. Having camped three and a half miles north of Kingston, early on May 19 Thomas, accompanied by Sherman, moved on Kingston, arriving about 8 A.M.[45] Sherman, Thomas, and McPherson were surprised to find no Confederate army to attack.

Clinging to his erroneous assumption that all of Johnston's army had moved from Adairsville to Kingston, Sherman then decided that the Confederate army had withdrawn across the Etowah River, south of Kingston.[46] He held to this idea despite the fact that three large, covered bridges over the river were still intact.[47]

On the 18th, Hooker's corps, the third Federal column, had followed to the east and rear of Thomas on the march toward Kingston. Hooker reached the vicinity of Adairsville the evening of May 18 and camped about two miles south of the town. At daylight on the 19th, pursuant to the plan to concentrate on Kingston, Hooker's front column set out on the road from Adairsville to Cassville. His purpose was to "feel for the railroad" between Kingston and Cassville, and to connect with Thomas on the right. At 7:30, after marching about two miles, Hooker's forces left the main road and went due south. Throughout the march they were harassed by vigilant Confederate skirmishers. The fourth column, commanded by Schofield, was far behind Hooker — several hours in point of time.[48]

About 8 A.M. on May 19, Johnston's scouts reported sighting a Federal column three miles north of Kingston on the road from Adairsville. Scouts also reported seeing a Federal column on the road from Adairsville to Cassville. Not realizing that Sherman was unaware of the location of the Confederate army, Johnston thought that both enemy columns were headed for Cassville. Immediately he gave orders for an attack on the column coming straight from Adairsville, directing Hood to strike the left flank; and Polk, the front.[49] The Confederate army, with its communications secure, was delighted with the prospect of meeting the advancing Federals. However, Hood, believing that a unit of Federal cavalry to his right was a large enemy force, took a defensive position instead of making the flank attack on Hooker. Hence, the opportunity to assail a separate part of Sherman's army to advantage was lost.[50]

At Kingston, Sherman ordered Thomas to "put the head of his column four miles east of the town," where he would be joined by Hooker. Later in the day, Sherman directed Thomas to move on the Kingston-to-Cassville road and "press down" on what Sherman believed was a single Confederate division.[51] That afternoon, between 3 and 4 o'clock, Sherman received a message from Thomas that he had found the Confederate army, drawn up in line of battle. Thus, more than twenty-four hours had elapsed after the Confederate army reached Cassville before Sherman learned of its whereabouts.

After hastily ordering McPherson at Kingston to advance toward Cassville, Sherman "rode forward rapidly" to Thomas.[52] Expecting the enemy to attack, Johnston planned for his army to make a stand on, and adjacent to, a ridge south of Cassville. Johnston said of the position, that he remembered it "as the best that I saw occupied during the war."[53]

Continuing with Cleburne's report to his corps commander Hardee:

> About 3 P.M. [on May 19], attending with the other major-generals at your quarters, I received orders to send ambulances and ordnance trains to the rear of Cass Station, which was done. This was preparatory to withdrawing the whole line of the corps, a delicate operation in the presence of the enemy, ... The withdrawal was successfully accomplished, however, the enemy not venturing to press.[54]

Federal General Thomas, who was a witness to Hardee's withdrawal, later said, "I watched from a hill, Hardee's corps retire, by brigades-en-echelon. The precision of their movements was a beautiful exhibition of military tactics."[55]

"A new line was taken up a mile or so farther back," Cleburne continued, "my part of which I proceeded to fortify most industriously."[56] But Hood, supported by Leonidas Polk, insisted that this stand should not be made. They contended that the Confederate line was vulnerable to enfilade fire, rendering their positions untenable. Johnston yielded, and instead of fighting ordered a retreat below the Etowah River, eight miles to the rear. Johnston later wrote that this was a step "I have regretted ever since."[57] Cleburne, as well as the rest of the army, was much surprised and greatly disappointed at the turn of events.[58] Continuing Cleburne's account: "At an advanced hour in the night [of the 19th] I received orders to move. Sending my ordnance

train and the artillery serving with me, under Major Hotchkiss, in advance across the Etowah River by the bridge near
the railroad crossing, under the guidance of my senior staff
officer, I moved with the rest of the corps by [Douthit's]
Bridge to Willford's Mill, on Pumpkin Vine Creek."[59]

NOTES

CHAPTER XIII

[1]M. A. DeWolfe Howe (ed.), *Home Letters of General Sherman* (New York, 1909), 292.

[2]Preston, "Memoirs," 26, 30; Record of Events, Co. C, 10th Texas Infantry, Jan. and Feb. 1864.

[3]Questionnaire of William Gibbs Allen, veteran of 5th Tennessee Cavalry, Jan. 1922 (Tenn. Lib. and Arch.), 34-35.

[4]Joseph E. Johnston, *Narrative*, 304.

[5]*O.R.*, XXXVIII, Pt. 3, pp. 720-21.

[6]Austin Peay, "The Battle of Dug Gap, Ga.," *Confederate Veteran*, XXIX (1921), 182; Buck, *Cleburne*, 207.

[7]*O.R.*, XXXVIII, Pt. 3, p. 721.

[8]*Ibid.*, Pt. 1, p. 63; *ibid.*, Pt. 3, pp. 30, 90, 375, 397; *ibid.*, Pt. 4, pp. 66, 85.

[9]*Ibid.*, Pt. 4, pp. 103-04; W. C. P. Breckinridge, "The Opening of the Atlanta Campaign," in *Battles and Leaders*, IV, 279-80; Peay, "Battle of Dug Gap," 182; Nisbet, *4 Years on Firing Line*, 179-82.

[10]*O.R.*, XXXVIII, Pt. 3, p. 721; Joseph E. Johnston, *Narrative*, 307-08; Buck, *Cleburne*, 209.

[11]A hamlet five miles southwest of Resaca.

[12]*O.R.*, XXXVIII, Pt. 3, p. 721.

[13]Wilbur G. Kurtz, "Why Was Snake Creek Gap Left Unguarded?" (Typescript lent by Mr. Kurtz to authors in 1964, now in possession of Atlanta Historical Society).

[14]*O.R.*, XXXVIII, Pt. 4, pp. 664, 672.

[15]*Ibid.*, Pt. 3, pp. 943-44.

[16]*Ibid.*, Pt. 4, p. 67.

[17]*Ibid.*, Pt. 3, p. 375; *ibid.*, Pt. 4, p. 67.

[18]*Ibid.*, p. 85.

[19]*Ibid.*, pp. 58, 59; *ibid.*, Pt. 3, p. 944.

[20]*Ibid.*, Pt. 4, p. 673.

[21]*Ibid.*, pp. 58, 77, 93, 677-78; *ibid.*, Pt. 3, p. 30.

[22]*Ibid.*, Pt. 3, p. 614; *ibid.*, Pt. 4, p. 679.

[23]*Ibid.*, Pt. 4, p. 692.

[24]Kurtz, "Snake Creek Gap."

[25]Jacob D. Cox, "Atlanta," in *The Army in the Civil War* (New York, 1885), IX, 31-32. See also Thomas B. Van Horne, *The Life of Major-General George H. Thomas* (New York, 1882), 210, 220.

[26]Alfred H. Burne, *Lee, Grant and Sherman* (New York, 1939), 81.

[27]*O.R.*, XXXVIII, Pt. 3, pp. 721-22.

[28]Cleburne to L. Polk, May 12, 1864, quoted in telegram, L. Polk to Joseph E. Johnston, May 12, 1864 (MS in Huntington Library); *O.R.*, XXXVIII, Pt. 4, p. 703.

[29]*O.R.*, XXXVIII, Pt. 4, p. 722.

[30]Buck, *Cleburne*, 211.

[31]*O.R.*, XXXVIII, Pt. 3, p. 722.

[32]Drake, "General Cleburne," 246.

[33]"A man who assisted to disinter dead at Resaca, after the war, reported finding one hundred and seventy Confederate and seventeen hundred and ninety Federal dead." — W. J. Hardee, "Memoranda of Operations of my Corps, while under the command of General J. E. Johnston, in the Dalton and Atlanta, and North Carolina Campaigns," in Joseph E. Johnston, *Narrative*, 579.

[34]Joseph E. Johnston, *Narrative*, 318.

[35]*O.R.*, XXXVIII, Pt. 3, pp. 722-23.

[36]*Ibid.*, p. 723.

[37]Buck, *Cleburne*, 213, *O.R.*, XXXVIII, Pt. 1, p. 107. In 1866, Sweeny was a leader in the Fenian invasion of Canada. — Ella Lonn, *Foreigners in the Union Army and Navy* (Baton Rouge, 1951), 205.

[38]*O.R.*, XXXVIII, Pt. 3, p. 723.

[39]Joseph E. Johnston, *Narrative*, 320.

[40]*O.R.*, XXXVIII, Pt. 4, pp. 219, 232, 233, 242, 244.

[41]*Ibid.*, pp. 232, 234, 237.

[42]*Ibid.*, p. 242.

[43]*Ibid.*, pp. 227, 244.

[44]*Ibid.*, p. 260.

[45]*Ibid.*, p. 232; *ibid.*, Pt. 1, p. 142; *ibid.*, Pt. 4, pp. 219, 251.

[46]*Ibid.*, Pt. 4, p. 248.

[47]*Ibid.*, pp. 249, 250, 255, 257-58, 260.

[48]*Ibid.*, pp. 233, 239, 251-56. Schofield did not come up on Hooker's left until dark, May 19, in front of Cassville. — *Ibid.*, pp. 256-57.

[49]Joseph E. Johnston, *Narrative*, 320-21; *O.R.*, XXXVIII, Pt. 3, p. 615.

[50]Henry, *Confederacy*, 383; *O.R.*, XXXVIII, Pt. 2, pp. 751-52.

[51]*O.R.*, XXXVIII, Pt. 4, pp. 255, 249.

[52]*Cf.* William T. Sherman, *Memoirs of General William T. Sherman* (New York, 1913), II, 37-38. In his *Memoirs*, Sherman said that he received Thomas' message "about noon," but he was in error in his recollection. At 3 P.M., Thomas sent an earlier message to Sherman, from which it is clear that Thomas did not then realize that the Confederate army was in the vicinity of Cassville; but merely "one division ... and perhaps more," which he felt, with Hooker's and Schofield's help, he could "capture." — *O.R.*, XXXVIII, Pt. 4, p. 250. Hardee's corps withdrew sometime after 3 P.M., and Sherman

did not reach Thomas until after this withdrawal. — *Ibid.*, Pt. 3, p. 723; Sherman, *Memoirs*, II, 38.

[53]*O.R.*, XXXVIII, Pt. 3, p. 616; Joseph E. Johnston, *Narrative*, 322.
[54]*O.R.*, XXXVIII, Pt. 3, p. 723.
[55]George H. Thomas to Sherman, date not shown, in Nisbet, *4 Years on Firing Line*, 194.
[56]*O.R.*, XXXVIII, Pt. 3, p. 723.
[57]*Ibid.*, p. 616; Henry, *Confederacy*, 383.
[58]Buck, *Cleburne*, 215-16.
[59]*O.R.*, XXXVIII, Pt. 3, pp. 723-24.

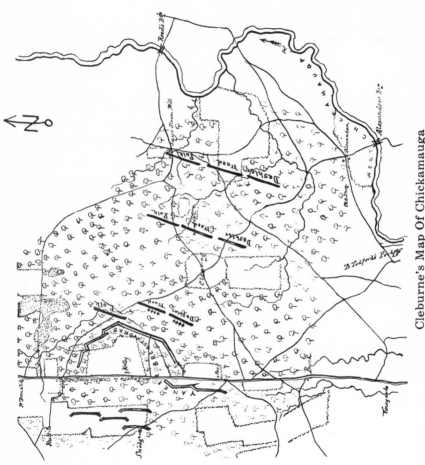

Cleburne's Map Of Chickamauga

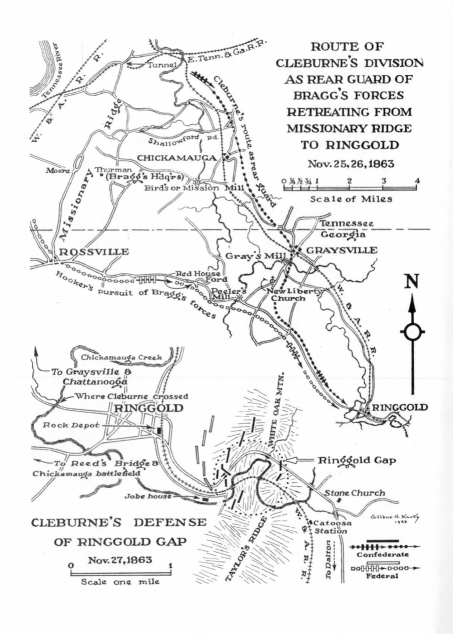

ROUTE OF
CLEBURNE'S DIVISION
AS REAR GUARD OF
BRAGG'S FORCES
RETREATING FROM
MISSIONARY RIDGE
TO RINGGOLD

Nov. 25, 26, 1863

Scale of Miles

0 ¼ ½ ¾ 1   2   3   4

Tennessee River

W. & A. R. R.

R. R.

E. Tenn. & Ga. R. R.

Tunnel

Ridge

Cleburne's route as rear guard

Shallowford Rd.

CHICKAMAUGA

Moore

Thurman
(Bragg's Hdqrs)

Bird's or Mission Mill

Missionary

Ridge

Tennessee
Georgia

ROSSVILLE

Gray's Mill

GRAYSVILLE

Red House
Ford

Hooker's pursuit of Bragg's forces

Peeler's
Mill

New Liberty
Church

W. & A. R. R.

N

RINGGOLD

Chickamauga Creek

To Graysville &
Chattanooga

Where Cleburne crossed

RINGGOLD

Rock Depot

To Reed's Bridge &
Chickamauga battlefield

Jobe house

WHITE OAK MTN.

Ringgold Gap

Stone Church

Wilbur G. Kurtz
1907

CLEBURNE'S DEFENSE
OF RINGGOLD GAP

Nov. 27, 1863

0   1
Scale one mile

TAYLOR'S RIDGE

W. & A. R. R.

Catoosa
Station

To Dalton

Confederate

Federal

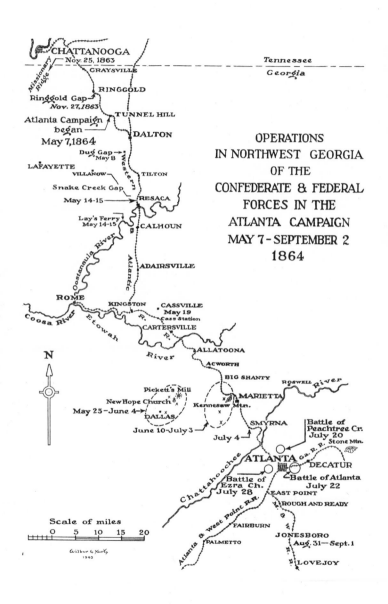

CHATTANOOGA
Nov. 25, 1863
GRAYSVILLE

Tennessee
Georgia

Missionary Ridge

RINGGOLD

Ringgold Gap
Nov. 27, 1863

Atlanta Campaign
began
May 7, 1864

TUNNEL HILL

DALTON

Dug Gap
May 8

LAFAYETTE

VILLANOW

TILTON

Snake Creek Gap

May 14-15

RESACA

Lay's Ferry
May 14-15

CALHOUN

Oostanaula River

Western

Atlantic

ADAIRSVILLE

OPERATIONS
IN NORTHWEST GEORGIA
OF THE
CONFEDERATE & FEDERAL
FORCES IN THE
ATLANTA CAMPAIGN
MAY 7-SEPTEMBER 2
1864

ROME

KINGSTON

CASSVILLE
May 19
Cass Station

CARTERSVILLE

Coosa River

Etowah

R.

R.

ALLATOONA

River

ACWORTH

N

BIG SHANTY

ROSWELL River

Pickett's Mill

New Hope Church

MARIETTA

May 25-June 4

Kennesaw Mtn.

DALLAS

SMYRNA

June 10-July 3

July 4

Battle of
Peachtree Cr.
July 20

Stone Mtn.

Chattahoochee

ATLANTA

Ga. R. R.

DECATUR

Battle of
Ezra Ch.
July 28

Battle of Atlanta
July 22

EAST POINT

ROUGH AND READY

Scale of miles

0   5   10   15   20

Atlanta & West Point R.R.

FAIRBURN

PALMETTO

JONESBORO
Aug. 31—Sept. 1

LOVEJOY

Wilbur G. Kurtz
1963

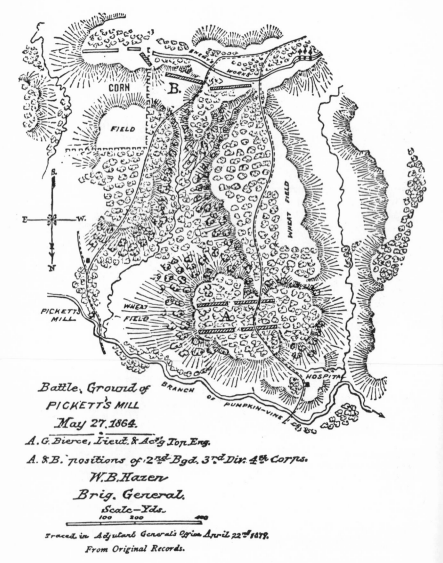

Battle Ground of
PICKETT'S MILL
May 27. 1864.
A. G. Bierce, Lieut. & Act'g Top. Eng.
A. & B. positions of 2nd Bgd. 3rd Div. 4th Corps.
W. B. Hazen
Brig. General.
Scale—Yds.
100   200   400
Traced in Adjutant General's Office April 22 1879.
From Original Records.

From W.B. Hazen (U.S.A.) *A Narrative of Military Service* (Boston, 1885), Showing Positions of One of the Eight Union Attacking Brigades.

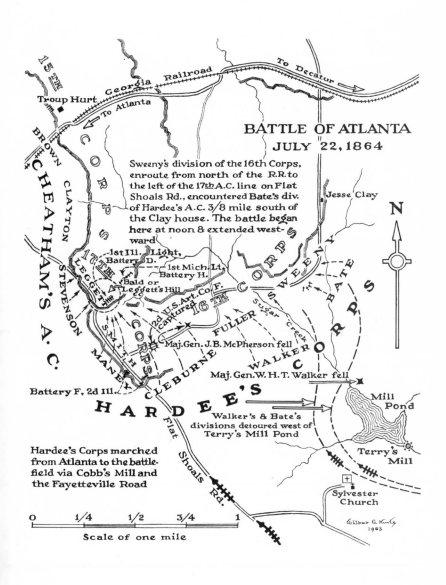

BATTLE OF ATLANTA
JULY 22, 1864

Sweeny's division of the 16th Corps, enroute from north of the R.R. to the left of the 17th A.C. line on Flat Shoals Rd., encountered Bate's div. of Hardee's A.C. 3/8 mile south of the Clay house. The battle began here at noon & extended westward

Jesse Clay

N

15 TH

Troup Hurt

Georgia Railroad

To Atlanta

To Decatur

BROWN

CHEATHAM'S A. C.

CLAYTON

STEVENSON

CORPS

17TH

LEGGETT

CORPS

1st Ill. Light, Battery D.
1st Mich. Lt. Battery H.
Bald or Leggett's Hill
2d U.S. Art. Co. F. Captured

MANEY

SMITHS

CLEBURNE

CORPS

16 TH

FULLER

CORPS

Sugar Creek

SWEENY

BATE

CORPS

WALKER'S

CORPS

Maj. Gen. J.B. McPherson fell

Maj. Gen. W. H. T. Walker fell

Battery F, 2d Ill.

H A R D E E'S

Flat Shoals Rd.

Walker's & Bate's divisions detoured west of Terry's Mill Pond

Mill Pond

Terry's Mill

Hardee's Corps marched from Atlanta to the battle-field via Cobb's Mill and the Fayetteville Road

Sylvester Church

0   1/4   1/2   3/4   1

Scale of one mile

Wilbur G. Kurtz
1963

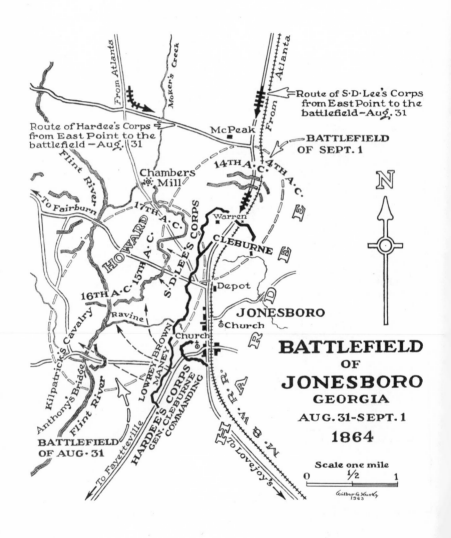

From Atlanta

Moker's Creek

From Atlanta

Route of S·D·Lee's Corps
from East Point to the
battlefield – Aug. 31

Route of Hardee's Corps
from East Point to the
battlefield – Aug. 31

McPeak

BATTLEFIELD
OF SEPT. 1

Flint River

Chambers
Mill

14TH A.C.

4TH A.C.

N

To Fairburn

17TH A.C.

S·D·LEE'S CORPS

Warren

CLEBURNE

HOWARD

15TH A·C·

Depot

16TH A·C·

JONESBORO

Church

Ravine

Kilpatrick's Cavalry

Church

Church

BATTLEFIELD
OF

Anthony's Bridge

LOWREY BROWN
MANEY

JONESBORO

Flint River

HARDEE'S CORPS
GEN. CLEBURNE
COMMANDING

GEORGIA

AUG. 31–SEPT. 1

1864

BATTLEFIELD
OF AUG. 31

To Fayetteville

To Lovejoy's

Scale one mile

0   ½   1

Wilbur G. Kurtz
1965

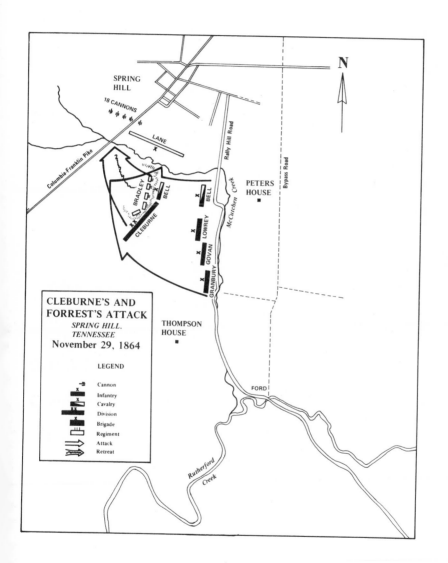

N

SPRING
HILL

18 CANNONS

Columbia-Franklin Pike

LANE

Rally Hill Road

Bypass Road

McCutcheon Creek

PETERS
HOUSE

BRADLEY

BELL

CLEBURNE

BELL

LOWREY

GOVAN

GRANBURY

CLEBURNE'S AND
FORREST'S ATTACK
SPRING HILL,
TENNESSEE
November 29, 1864

THOMPSON
HOUSE

FORD

Rutherford
Creek

LEGEND

Cannon
Infantry
Cavalry
Division
Brigade
Regiment
Attack
Retreat

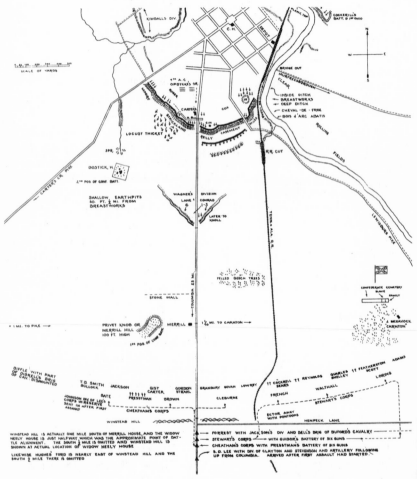

Portion Of Monroe F. Cockrell's Map Of Franklin

CHAPTER XIV

THE ETOWAH TO ATLANTA
(May 20 - July 15, 1864)

> Now at New Hope—no hope at all
> I see for us today;
> No man can scale a burning wall—
> Pat Cleburne's in the way.
>   *—Jos. M. Brown, "Pat Cleburne in the Way."*

Cleburne's division and the rest of Hardee's corps remained for three days on heights about three miles south of the Etowah and two miles east of Allatoona. When the Confederate cavalry reported that Sherman had crossed the river ten miles to the west, the corps set out to search for the Federal right flank. Tedious marching and countermarching through considerable stretches of Paulding County was recorded by Cleburne:

> Here [on Pumpkin Vine Creek] I remained until Monday, the 23rd day of May, [1864,] when I moved by Dyer's Tan-yard and Tanner's to the Dallas [-Marietta] road, six miles distant, and camped for the night. On the 24th, next day, I moved, via New Hope Church, to Powder Springs. On the 25th, at 3 A.M., I marched to Lyster's [Lester's farmhouse], retracing so far my steps of the day before. At Lyster's I turned to the right, and went a mile or so through the woods, making my headquarters at Darby's [farmhouse].[1]

Johnston, learning that the enemy was entrenched just east of Dallas, formed his army with Hood's corps on the right, making its center at New Hope Church (Primitive Baptist) about five miles northeast of Dallas. Hood's corps was strengthened by the arrival of William A. Quarles' brigade of 2,200 men.

Cleburne's report to Hardee continued:

321

I remained [at Darby's] under orders to be ready to move at a moment's notice, until about dark, when I received orders to move to New Hope Church, where Hood had been fighting for several hours. The night was intensely dark; it was impossible to distinguish the road. Being soon impeded by the rear of Walker's column I bivouacked and sent to you for instructions, in view of my embarrassment by the darkness and choked-up roads. About 10:30 P.M., I received orders to bivouac until 4 A.M. and then move to Maulding [Mauldin] on the Dallas-Atlanta road. I reached Maulding next morning (26th) at 6:30. Later in the day I moved to the right of the army to support Hindman. I got into position before sundown.[2]

Mauldin was a farmhouse at the left of Johnston's line. Johnston sent Cleburne from the farmhouse to the extreme right, past Hindman, because Sherman was moving forces in that direction with the object of turning the Confederates' right flank and seizing the Western & Atlantic Railroad, which was several miles in their rear. Johnston waited until Sherman committed himself to this movement before placing troops to defend against it. Premature dispositions by Johnston would have permitted Sherman to go around the Confederate left flank and achieve the same purpose.[3] Cleburne was temporarily reporting to Hood, who was in command of the right wing.

On May 27, near Widow Pickett's mill, three and a half miles northeast of New Hope Church, ensued the battle of Pickett's Mill (sometimes called the battle of New Hope Church). Pickett's Mill was "Pat Cleburne's great fight" in Georgia, as Ringgold Gap was "Cleburne's great stand" in Georgia. Benham of Cleburne's staff referred to Pickett's Mill as "the most beautiful and artistic fight" he ever witnessed.[4] The inspired genius of Cleburne brilliantly and skillfully managed to hold a narrow front in the tangled forest and prevented a turning of the Confederate right. He thereby saved the right wing of the army and kept Sherman from cutting Johnston's communications with Atlanta.

Cleburne's battle report written on May 30, three days after the engagement, is a "classic" of the Atlanta campaign:

. . . .
About 2 or 3 o'clock P.M. on the afternoon of the 26th, I arrived with my Division on the extreme right of the then line

of the Army, when I was sent to support Major General Hindman. At that point our line, the general bearing of which was north and south, retired for a few yards to the East. In continuation of this retiring line I placed Polk's brigade (of my Division) in and diagonally across it, upon a ridge en echelon by Battalion to avoid an artillery enfilade from a neighboring position held by the enemy. Resting on Polk's right was placed Hotchkiss' Artillery, consisting of four Napoleons, four Parrott guns, and four howitzers. Supporting Hotchkiss on the right was one Regiment of Govan's of my Division. The remainder of my Division was disposed in rear as a second line in support of Hindman's right Brigades and my first line. Entrenchments were thrown up in the afternoon and night of the 26th and in the morning of the 27th. The position was in the main covered with trees and undergrowth, which served as a screen along our lines, concealed us, and were left standing as far as practicable for that purpose.

On the morning of the 27th, at about 7 o'clock, Govan was sent to the north front on a reconnaissance, with directions to swing to the left in his advance. From time to time, while engaged in this reconnaissance, Govan sent me word that the enemy was moving to the right—his own left.[5]

By carefully observing the terrain over which the enemy would have to approach, Cleburne made preparations to direct the fire of his artillery into the thick woods to his front. With equal scrutiny he also studied the ground immediately behind the actual line selected for combat. Finding that troops could not be moved speedily to the line and from one place to another because of the vine-tangled and heavily wooded terrain, he cut paths running from each brigade to its rear and to the adjoining brigade, making sure that he would be ready for every contingency.[6] Cleburne continued with his battle report:

At eleven o'clock A.M., upon my order to that effect, Govan came in, leaving his skirmishers about three-quarters of a mile in front. I at once placed him on the right of Polk, where he covered himself in rifle-pits. About 4 o'clock P.M., hearing that the enemy's infantry in line of battle were pressing the cavalry on my right—they had already driven in my skirmish-ers—I placed Granbury on Govan's right. He had but just gotten into position, and a dismounted cavalry force, in line behind a few disconnected heaps of stones loosely piled together, had passed behind him, when the enemy advanced. He showed himself first, having driven back my skirmishers, in the edge of an open field in front of Govan, about 400 yards across, where he halted and opened fire.

From the point on the ridge where Govan's right and Granbury's left met, there made off a spur, which, at about a hundred yards from it, turned sharply to the northeast, running then in a direction almost parallel with it and maintaining about an equal elevation. Between this spur and the parent ridge, beginning in front of Granbury's left, was a deep ravine, the side of which next to Granbury was very steep, with occasional benches of rock, up to a line within 30 or 40 yards of Granbury's men, where it flattened into a natural glacis. This glacis was covered with well grown trees, and in most places with thick undergrowth. Here was the brunt of the battle—the enemy advancing along this front in numerous and constantly reinforced lines. His men displayed a courage worthy of an honorable cause—pressing in steady throngs within a few paces of our men, frequently exclaiming, "Ah! damn you, we have caught you without your logs now." Granbury's men, needing no logs, were awaiting them, and throughout awaited them with calm determination, and as they appeared upon the slope, slaughtered them with deliberate aim. The piles of his dead on this front, pronounced by the officers of this Army who have seen most service to be greater than they had ever seen before, were a silent but sufficient eulogy upon Granbury and his noble Texans. In the great execution here done upon the enemy, Govan, with his two right Regiments, disdaining the enemy in his own front, who were somewhat removed, and Key with two pieces of Artillery ran up by hand upon my order to a convenient breach made in our breastworks, materially aided Granbury by a right-oblique fire which enfiladed the masses in his front.

In front of a prolongation of Granbury's line and abutting upon his right was a field about three hundred yards square. The enemy, driving back some cavalry, at this point advanced completely across the field and passed some forty or fifty yards in its rear. Here, however, they were confronted by the 8th and 19th Arkansas, Consolidated, commanded by Colonel [George F.] Baucum, hastily sent by Govan upon Granbury's request and representation of the exigency. In a sweeping charge Baucum drove the enemy from the ridge in his front, and with irresistible impetuosity forced him across the field and back into the woods from which he had at first advanced. Here he fixed himself and kept up a heavy fire, aided by a deadly enfilade from the bottom of the ravine in front of Granbury. When Baucum was about to charge, [M. P.]

Lowrey, of my Division, who had been hastened up from his distant position upwards of a mile and a half from my right as finally established, came into line, throwing his regiments in successively, as they unmasked themselves by their flank march. His arrival was most opportune as the enemy was beginning to pour around Baucum's right. Colonel [Samuel] Adams, with the 33d Ala., which was the first of Lowrey's regiments to form into line, took position on Baucum's right and advanced with him—his seven left Companies being in the field with Baucum, and his other four in the woods to the right. Baucum and Adams, finding themselves suffering from the enemy's direct and oblique fire, withdrew, passing over the open space of the field behind them. The right companies of Adams, which were in the woods, retired to a spur which rises from the easterly edge of the field about two hundred yards from its southerly edge, where Baucum's and Adams' left companies rested. Here they halted—Captain [William E.] Dodson with fine judgment perceiving the importance of the position—it would have given the enemy an enfilading fire upon Granbury, which would have dislodged him—and making his company the basis of alignment for the remainder of Lowrey now coming into position. This retrograde movement across the field was not attended with loss as might have been expected—the enemy not advancing as it was made. It was mistaken, however, for a repulse, and some of my staff officers, hearing that my line had broken hastened forward, [William A.] Quarles' Brigade of [A. P.] Stewart's Division, just then providently *[sic]* sent up by General Hood to re-establish it. Lowrey, being under the same impression, detached his two right Regiments (which had not been engaged) under Colonels [W. H. H.] Tison and [A. B.] Hardcastle, and had them quickly formed in support of Baucum and Adams. The error, however, was soon discovered, and my line being ascertained to remain in its integrity, Quarles' Brigade was conducted to the rear of Lowrey and formed as a second line. The 4th Louisiana, Colonel [S. E.] Hunter, finding itself opposite an interval between the two regiments of Lowrey's line (caused by Baucum's resting closer upon Granbury on his return from the advance, than he had done at first), under the immediate superintendence of General Quarles, advanced into the field, halted and delivered a very effective fire upon the enemy in his front. After some minutes, Quarles withdrew this Regiment, and formed it behind the field, where they continued their fire across it. Genl. Quarles and his Brigade have my thanks.

During these movements, the battle continued to rage on Granbury's front, and was met with unflagging spirit.

About the time of Quarles getting into position night came

325

on, when the combat lulled. For some hours afterwards a desultory dropping fire, with short, vehement bursts of musketry, continued—the enemy lying in great numbers immediately in front of portions of my line, and so near it that their footsteps could be distinctly heard. About 10 o'clock P.M. I ordered Granbury and Lowrey to push forward skirmishers and scouts to learn the state of things in their respective fronts.

Granbury, finding it impossible to advance his skirmishers until he had cleared his front of the enemy lying up against it, with my consent charged with his whole line. [E. C.] Walthall, with his Brigade from Hindman's Division, whom I sent to his support, taking his place in the line as he stepped out of it. The Texans—their bayonets fixed—plunged into the darkness with a terrific yell—and with one bound were upon the enemy; but they met with no resistance. Surprised and panic-striken, many fled, escaping in the darkness, others surrendered and were brought into our lines. It needed but the brilliancy of this night attack to add lustre to the achievements of Granbury and his Brigade in the afternoon. I am deeply indebted to them both.

My thanks are also due to Genel Lowrey for the coolness and skill which he exhibited in forming his line. His successive formation was the precise answer to the enemy's movement in extending his left to turn our right. Time was of the essense of things, and his movement was the quickest. His line was formed under heavy fire, on ground unknown to him and of the most difficult character; and the stern firmness with which he and his men and Baucum's regiment drove off the enemy and resisted his renewed attacks without doubt saved the right of the Army, as Granbury had already done before.

During the progress of the battle much service was rendered by the rifle battery and two remaining howitzers of Key's battery, in position on Polk's right. They were trained in enfilade upon the enemy's reserves massed behind the hill in front of the spur we occupied. I regretted I did not have more guns for this service. I had sent the Napoleon guns to the right, where they were unable to find positions and so were useless.

During these operations Polk was not engaged, but it was a source of strength and confidence to the rest of the Division to know that he had charge of the weakest and most delicate part of our line.

Cleburne once again acknowledged "the industry, zeal and activity" of staff officers Benham, J. K. Dixon, Buck, Mangum, Hanly, Jetton, and volunteer aide Byrne; and another staff officer, Capt. Robert McFarland. He said that his ordnance, under C. S. Hill, his medical department, under Linthicum, and his artillery, under Hotchkiss, were "well administered." The General closed his report with a reference to losses suffered in the sharp engagement:

> My casualties in this battle were few. I had 85 killed, 363 wounded, carrying into the engagement 4,683 muskets. The enemy's losses were very heavy. The lowest estimate which can be made of his dead is 500. We captured 160 prisoners, who were sent to Army HdQrs, exclusive of 72 of his wounded carried to my Field Hospital. He could not have lost in all less than 3,000 killed and wounded. I took upwards of 1,200 small arms.
>
> This battle was fought at a place known as the "Pickett Settlement," and about two miles northeast of New Hope Church.[7]

The estimate furnished Cleburne of the number of Federals killed was inaccurate, as the Union dead lying before his line, "counted by many persons," was seven hundred.[8] A veteran of Cleburne's division recalled, "Pat Cleburne was the forked lightning's flash that followed Joe Johnston."[9] Unfortunately, this was the last battle report written by General Cleburne.

The Federal force at Pickett's Mill, under the command of Gen. O. O. Howard, consisted of Thomas J. Wood's division of the 4th Army Corps and Richard W. Johnson's division of the 14th Army Corps. Federal reports show that Howard pushed forward eight solid lines of battle against Cleburne.[10] Federal Gen. W. B. Hazen, commanding the leading brigade, described the engagement as "the most fierce, bloody, and persistent assault by our troops in the Atlanta campaign, and the Confederates . . . were victorious
. . . .
. . . The whole fight was terrific and the slaughter immense."[11]

Many of the Federals fell within ten feet of Cleburne's line. According to one Texan in the fray, the enemy came so close that when some of the dead and wounded fell forward, their guns struck Granbury's men.[12] Lieut. Thomas J. Stokes, another member of Granbury's brigade, writing to his sister about the battle said:

> The fighting of our men, to those who admire warfare, was magnificent. You could see a pleasant smile playing upon the countenances of many of the men, as they would cry out to the Yankees, "Come on, we are demoralized!"
> ...Major [John R.] Kennard ... was, as usual, encouraging the men by his battle cry of "put your trust in God, men, for He is with us," but concluded to talk to the Yankees awhile, sang out to them, "Come on, we are demoralized," when the Major was pretty severely wounded in the head, though not seriously, when raising himself up, he said:
> "Boys, I told them a lie, and I believe that is the reason I got shot."
> The fighting was very close and desperate and lasted until after dark. About 11 o'clock at night, three regiments of our brigade charged the enemy, our regiment among them. We went over ravines, rocks, and almost precipices, running the enemy entirely off the field. We captured many prisoners, and all of their dead and many of their wounded fell into our hands. This charge was a desperate and reckless thing, and if the enemy had made any resistance they could have cut us all to pieces.[13]

On May 29, two days after the battle of Pickett's Mill, Cleburne's division rejoined Hardee's corps and took position next to Bate's division, on the extreme left of the army. Because of the proximity of the opposing lines, each side maintained a constant vigil. Shortly after midnight, Cleburne's troops were suddenly awakened by heavy musketry and cannonade coming from the Union line facing Bate. Expecting a night attack, Cleburne's and Bate's troops instantly prepared to repel the assault. The Federals' furious fusilade lasted until nearly morning but no follow-up attack took place. Later it was learned that the Yankees had started firing because of a false report that the Confederates were making a charge. The accepted explanation as to the origin of the false report is interesting. One of Bate's pickets fired at a lightning bug, mistaken for the flash of an enemy musket. The ball whizzed over the head of a Yankee picket, who fired back thinking an attack had begun. Firing spread rapidly, both sides shooting at muskets and lightning bugs, apparently unable to determine which was which. The Yankee pickets reported that the "rebels" were making a night attack, and the batteries opened fire.[14]

On May 30, Sherman started sideslipping toward the railroad, extending his entrenched line to the northeast about a mile each day. On June 1, Johnston countered by ordering Cleburne to the extreme right of the Confederate line. The rest of Hardee's corps soon followed, and the Confederates kept pace as the Federal line was extended.[15]

Cleburne's constant concern for the welfare of his men is illustrated by his communication to Hardee's chief of staff on May 31:

> I last night received a note directing Division Commanders to send "a wagon at once" to Corps Hdqurs for the purpose of obtaining a supply of tools. I immediately sent to the Lieutenant commanding my Pioneer Company and ordered him to get his wagon and go after these articles. He (the Lieutenant) returned this morning and reports after a nights work and several trips on foot, between Corps Hdqurs. and Major [Stephen W.] Presstman's, he was informed by the latter, that I would be notified when the tools could be obtained. I respectfully call the attention of the Lieutenant General Commanding to the facts of this case, and ask if it is right, that those who had been working as constantly as my Pioneers have lately, should be kept tramping all night, only to ascertain, what might have been known in the beginning by the exercise of a little attention and care.[16]

2

On June 4, when Johnston was certain that the Federals were heading for the Western & Atlantic Railroad, he ordered the army to march southeastward, to a position where communications to Atlanta would be protected. Despite having been quite ill for several days, Cleburne set out with his divisions at 1:30 A.M. on June 5. Hardee said that the marching was "the hardest . . . I have ever known troops to encounter . . ., through mud and rain and darkness." The new Confederate line, beginning at Lost Mountain, skirted the north side of Kennesaw Mountain and crossed the railroad. Cleburne's division was put in the line on the northwestern edge of Kennesaw Mountain, near Gilgal Church.[17] The Federal army, increased by the 10,000 men of Francis P.

Blair Jr.'s command, on June 8 reached the railroad near Ackworth, north of the Confederate army. Johnston formed his army to cover the roads leading southward from the vicinity of Ackworth, Cleburne remaining near Gilgal Church.

By June 12, being "free from disease" but "not so strong as before," Cleburne had fully resumed his duties. On June 13, accompanied by an aide, he rode north of the Confederate line on a reconnaissance to the top of Pine Mountain to view the enemy in the valley on the other side. Confederate artillerymen, posted behind logs near the crest of the mountain, warned Cleburne that a Federal battery of Parrott rifled guns a half mile away had the area within range. When the General peered over the logs, two shells whistled past his head. "Let's get out of this," Cleburne said to his aide, "I have seldom known one to go where he had no business but that he got hurt."[18]

Two days later, on June 15, Hooker's corps of Thomas' army advanced toward that sector of the Confederate position which included Cleburne's front; and after heavy skirmishing, established a position within 100 yards of Johnston's main line. Immediately thereafter Cleburne and a small band of his men made a night charge which years later was described by a Texan who participated in the attack:

> Just think ... of that dark night charge Pat Cleburne made with us and almost caught Hooker and Thomas, but where their solid line of battle fired at us not over ten yards away! I thought all but myself were killed; but no one was hurt, as old Pat told us they would overshoot us. They wheeled to run, and running over each other became demoralized. General Cleburne told us that they would and that they would call for their commands, and he ordered us to answer them like quails answer their lost, saying that they would come to us the same way, and so they did, as well as I recollect.[19]

On the night of June 16, Johnston shifted Hardee's corps southward. Cleburne's new position was on a ridge, two and a half miles southeast of Gilgal Church, just east of Mud Creek and facing west toward Darby's farm. His troops set about constructing rifle pits atop the ridge with embrasures for batteries. Federals, now moved up to Darby's farm, shelled

330

Cleburne's troops, who fired back; and a fierce cannonade ensued.[20] While gallantly working his guns, a promising young officer, Lieut. Isaac Lightner, of Barret's Battery, fell, mortally wounded, both feet blown off by a solid shot. When being borne from the field, he met "his beloved General Cleburne." "General," he asked, saluting gaily, "have I not won promotion today?"[21] Another version is that the young officer exclaimed, "Ah! my General! We gave it to them—we are giving it to them yet, but they have finished me. I am gone. I have always done my duty, General, and you must put me in your report—put me in your report." General Cleburne expressed hope of the brave officer's recovery and promised to mention him in the battle report. In his sketch of Cleburne, staff officer Benham recounted this incident and explained: ". . . the General never had an opportunity to make that report. As well as I can, I do it for him."[22]

An even more serious casualty occurred in Cleburne's command when, late in the afternoon of June 17, Gen. Lucius Polk's horse was shot from under him. The same shell mangled the General's leg, permanently incapacitating him for further field service. Polk's brigade, which had been heavily engaged during the campaign, was so reduced in numbers that in a few weeks it was broken up and distributed to other brigades.[23]

During the night of June 18, as ordered by Johnston, Hardee's corps trudged eastward, toward Kennesaw Mountain. Torrential rains made the roads almost impassable and Noses Creek was out of its banks. The soldiers endured their hardships with "remarkable cheerfulness and without a murmur." As usual, their departure was not discovered by the enemy until several hours later.[24]

On the 19th, Johnston formed a new position and entrenched his line. The Confederate fortifications began two miles east of the Western & Atlantic Railroad and extended seven miles westward along the crest of Kennesaw Mountain, then curving to the southwest base of Little Kennesaw. Thence the line ran southward for three miles, across the Dallas Road and over a slight elevation now called Cheatham's Hill, terminating immediately north of a fork of Ward Creek. This three mile stretch was occupied by Hardee's

331

corps. Cheatham was at the south end, on his "hill," with Cleburne to his right. Cleburne's line extended on a ridge from the brow of this hill to the Dallas Road.[25] Immediately, heavy rains set in, making Ward Creek impassable and enabling the Federals (who had moved up) to extend an entrenched line three miles beyond the Confederate left. Hence Johnston transferred Hood's corps from near the railroad to a line extending south of Cheatham. Cleburne's and Cheatham's divisions were protected by strong breastworks with head logs but had only a single line of battle because of the distance covered.[26]

Cleburne had formed his part of the Confederate defense line with Lowrey on the south (left), Govan in the center, and Granbury on the north (right). The Federal line opposite Cleburne was on a ridge only 400 yards away. A shallow valley with a small ravine lay between the two armies. Lowrey's brigade faced open woods with dense undergrowth. In Govan's front lay a field, with felled timber scattered near the edge of the woods on his left. Cleburne's troops had collected blackjack saplings to continue the abatis. The sharp pointed ends of these saplings projecting from the ground interspersed with rails driven in the ground were so dense that, according to a private in Cleburne's division, "it would have been an uphill business for a rabbit to creep through."[27] Although the Federals shelled Johnston's line constantly no attack was made, but there was heavy skirmishing.

On June 22, Cleburne's best horse, Stonewall, a veteran of many battles, ran away. For several days the General placed the following advertisement in the Atlanta *Intelligencer* but to no avail:

LOST.

On Wednesday, the 22d of June, a dark bay horse, 16 hands high, white right hind foot, and star in forehead. Broke from the tree to which he was tied and ran, with a brush hanging to his halter, through Gen. Cheatham's troops and in the direction of Gen. Hindman's skirmishers, then engaged with the enemy (on the afternoon of the 22nd inst.) He is probably in Hood's Corps or Jackson's Cavalry Division. An ample reward will be paid for his delivery at my headquarters, or information which will lead to his restoration to me.

P. R. Cleburne,
Maj.—General.[28]

On the 23d, the enemy opened on Cleburne's front with the heaviest small arms and artillery firing of the campaign. Among those killed in this barrage was Cleburne's Austrian orderly, J. A. Sepp. He was standing beneath a tall tree near division headquarters 250 yards behind the lines, when a minié ball ricocheted from a limb fifty feet overhead and pierced his side. Cleburne was saddened by the loss of his favorite orderly.[29]

The evening of the 26th, a North Carolina light artillery battalion arrived to serve under Cleburne as the replacement for Hotchkiss' battalion, which had been assigned elsewhere. The North Carolinians, having seen only coast-guard service previously, with their new uniforms, guns, horses, and harness, created quite a contrast to Cleburne's battle-worn troops. At nightfall, anticipating an attack, Cleburne had some of his veterans assist the newcomers in digging embrasures and putting their guns in position. He had deep redoubts constructed for the eight or ten artillery pieces. The mouth of each cannon rested almost on the ground and was trained to sweep the field in front.[30] The division was now ready for further action and was to acquit itself well in the ensuing battle of Kennesaw Mountain.

Sherman at last had decided to make a general, frontal assault on the Confederate line. His battle plan was to attempt to break through, simultaneously, at two points considered vulnerable; and thus prevent one part of the Confederate line from reinforcing the other. One point of the Federal attack was more than a mile north of Cleburne's position; the second assault, however, was aimed at the southern end of Cleburne's command and Cheatham's entire division. In a special field order, Sherman announced that he would be on a hill, where he could observe the attacks and guide the operations by "telegraphic communication with all the army commanders."[31]

The 27th dawned hot, with a temperature that would rise to 100 degrees. At 8 o'clock Cleburne's men detected much activity behind the Federal line. Blue-coated troops marched, countermarched, and massed just behind their breastworks for an attack. Again, as at Pickett's Mill, General Howard commanded the troops opposite Cleburne. About 8:45 Howard's artillery opened with a deafening barrage. At 9 o'clock, Charles G. Harker's and G. D. Wagner's brigades of John Newton's division of Howard's corps, with fixed bayonets, in a "determined and powerful attack," scaled their works and advanced rapidly toward the left (southern) flank of Cleburne's division. The Federal brigades were in two closely massed columns, five lines deep, preceded by a strong line of skirmishers. Nathan Kimball's brigade of the same division moved in support.[32] Cleburne's men withheld their fire until the Federals were about 75 yards from the works. Aiming carefully and then firing and quickly reloading, they poured a sustained fire into the Union ranks. At the same time the artillery was sending canister and case shot into the closely massed formations.[33]

The Union commanders reported later that because of the dense undergrowth and the felled timber, their troops could not attain the momentum expected. More important, the commanders spoke of "well arranged batteries," the "deadly fire of artillery and musketry," "the murderous fire of the enemy's riflemen," and "the slashing and abatis made by the enemy." Sherman's advance terminated in the entanglements and the Union attack was a failure. Wagner's brigade retreated to the ravine and General Harker's command fell back after advancing close to Cleburne's works. Harker, who attempted a second advance with his brigade, was mortally wounded.[34]

In front of Govan, Federal dead and wounded lay thick in the ravine, near a grove of pine and blackjack. Shells from the Confederate artillery started fires in the grove; and flames spread rapidly across the ground, thickly covered with pine cones and needles. Flames were enveloping and the dense smoke was suffocating the wounded men, exposing them to horrible deaths. Lieut. Col. William H. Martin of Little Rock, commander of the 1st Arkansas Regiment, Cleburne's division, sprang upon the breastworks and waved a white handkerchief as a flag of truce. "Boys, this is butchery," he shouted, "Cease firing and help get out those men." The firing stopped. Confederates scaled the head logs and the Yankees came forward from their lines. Together, they rescued the maimed and wounded and then beat out the fires. Many of the Federals expressed their deep appreciation for Martin's gesture. Col. John I. Smith of the 31st Indiana Regiment took from his belt a brace of handsomely mounted pearl-handled pistols and presented them to Colonel Martin. "Accept them with my appreciation of the nobility of this deed," said Colonel Smith, "It deserves to be perpetuated to the deathless honor of every one of you concerned in it; and should you fight a thousand other battles, and win a thousand other victories, none will be so noble as this."[35]

After their mission of mercy, the troops returned to their positions and the fighting resumed. Kimball's Federal brigade, which had been held in reserve in the woods, and Wagner's brigade from the ravine valiantly charged Cleburne's works, but were driven back. The few Union soldiers who did reach the parapet were captured or killed. Two other Union brigades, held in reserve, were not commited to action, one being massed behind, and the other, before, the Federal fortifications. The latter sustained losses from Cleburne's artillery. After Cleburne's division had been engaged for only thirty minutes, exclusive of stoppages, Howard gave up and withdrew his forces.[36]

In front of Cleburne's line, 300 lay dead. The Federals reported General Howard's killed and wounded to be 754, Howard stating that his losses "were very heavy, particularly in valuable officers." Cleburne's loss was but two killed and nine wounded.[37] Sherman's assaults made a mile north of Cleburne and those against Cheatham's division also were repulsed with heavy casualties.

Two days later, on June 29, a truce was arranged to permit the burial of the Federal dead. A sergeant in an Ohio regiment that had attacked Cheatham's division gave this graphic account:

A general exchange of newspapers, coffee and tobacco [took place] while a jolly good feeling abounded everywhere. . . . Generals from both sides circulated freely between the lines,

335

.... Hindman, Cheatham and Maney were prominent. I was particularly interested in Pat Cleburne, ... He was tall, with a genial face and a good fighter, as we had a chance to know.[38]

After the termination of the truce, each side remained apprehensive of an assault because of the close proximity of the lines. On the night of the 30th, heavy fire of musketry and artillery broke out and Cleburne and his staff rushed forward on horseback from their headquarters. Activity near the enemy line had caused a false alarm among Cheatham's troops, who opened fire. Cleburne's riflemen and artillery joined in the firing, which lasted about thirty minutes. Unknown to the Confederates, a detachment of Federals moving to relieve troops in the line had caused the disturbance. A few days later, the Confederates were surprised to learn from a newspaper account that their fire had killed and wounded many Union soldiers, destroyed numerous mules, and caused "a grand stampede."[39]

Sherman, again employing his usual flanking tactics, started transferring a large part of his army to his right, already nearer Atlanta than the Confederate left. On the night of July 2 the Confederates were compelled to withdraw from the Kennesaw line. Each division moved silently on a designated road, lighted with small fires and hidden from the enemy by the forest. The withdrawal was so skillfully executed that all the Confederates had disappeared from their front before the Federals realized it. The Southerners entrenched at Smyrna Camp Ground, an elevation ten miles from Atlanta. In an attempt to delay Sherman, they formed two lines across the railroad with Cleburne's division occupying a position near the center. Another Federal flanking movement, however, forced the Confederates to withdraw after midnight, the morning of the 5th, to a line of intricate redoubts five miles in their rear, on the north bank of the Chattahoochee.[40]

This extensive and unique line of works had been devised by Gen. F. A. Shoup, chief of artillery of Johnston's army; and constructed under his supervision with slave labor. The defense line formed an arc north of the Chattahoochee a little over three miles long, with the ends resting on the river.

The Western & Atlantic Railroad bisected the arc about one quarter of a mile from where it struck the river on the north. In the rear, several pontoon bridges spanned the river. This "fort" was large enough for the entire Confederate army to camp within its confines. Redoubts eighty yards apart were built of heavy logs and connected by a stockade of logs firmly set in the ground. Shoup believed that with these fortifications the Confederates could repel assaults indefinitely. A single division could hold the fortifications, with the rest of the army free to move upon units of Sherman's forces on either side of the river.

Many of the Confederate troops, accustomed only to simple earthworks, scoffed at these strange fortifications. General Walker's men dismantled the stockades in their front, preferring to resort to "the faithful shovel." General Cleburne, however, climbed inside one of the redoubts; and from the top spoke to a group of soldiers below who were eager to hear the General's opinion. He praised the fortification, describing it as being entirely enclosed, with perpendicular sides protected by "face covers" against artillery and defended by cross fire from a half dozen other works within easy range. The soldiers agreed that they would be able to hold the redoubt against any attack; but even so, Cleburne had his men reenforce the stockade by logs covered with earth. Sherman described the Confederate works as "one of the strongest pieces of field-fortification I ever saw,"[41] and did not attack the redoubts. He achieved his purpose by another outflanking movement, causing the abandonment of Shoup's extensive works.

The Chattahoochee was fordable at several points. Schofield's command and one of McPherson's corps crossed and entrenched at two of these points on July 8 and 9. One crossing was about nine miles and the other, fifteen miles, northeast of the fortification. On the night of the 9th, Johnston withdrew across the Chattahoochee, using the pontoon bridges at the rear of the fort. After Cleburne's men crossed on one of these bridges, a detail of his infantry assisted the Engineer Corps in destroying it.[42]

The army now fell back to positions under construction about three miles north of Atlanta, Cleburne setting up headquarters in the residence of Archibald Whitehead.[43] Engineer-officers with Negro labor strengthened the entrenchments of Atlanta, while in welcome respite the rest of the army awaited Sherman and the battle for the city. In an order issued July 15, Cleburne paid the following tribute to forty men of the 48th Tennessee Regiment who were being transferred from his division after long service in Polk's brigade:

> As a battalion of sharpshooters its courage, skill, and endurance have been tested and proven in innumerable bloody skirmishes. The handful to which it is reduced attest [sic] how conspicuous a part it must have borne in building up the glorious reputation of the brigade and division which it is about to be separated from. Gen. Cleburne bids you a soldier's farewell, and trusts he may deserve and retain through life the good will and kind feelings which he bears to each surviving member of the Forty-eighth Tennessee.[44]

In the campaign from Dalton to Atlanta, Cleburne's men were under fire almost daily. The opposing armies were seldom out of sight of one another.[45] Goven later narrated: "It was a campaign that tried the endurance of the soldier to the utmost extent, and tried his soldierly qualities as in a crucible. We slept on our arms, lulled to sleep (if we slept at all) to the sound of the bullet, and awoke in the morning saluted by artillery."[46]

Cleburne worked closely with his famous corps of sharpshooters, having them report to him daily. The corps was engaged from daylight to dark sixty of the seventy days of the campaign, picking off victims each day. The enemy artillerymen feared the sharpshooters, whose firing meant "almost certain death ... at 900 yards." The Whitworth had a range of 1,400 yards and in one instance a Union soldier was killed at an estimated 1,600 yards. The corps, itself, lost twenty-five per cent killed and sixty per cent wounded; but vacancies were filled immediately from a list of expert marksmen, eager to be transferred to this elite unit.[47]

Reports of Federal commanders expressed respect for Cleburne's vigilance. Federal Gen. Daniel Butterfield, referring to Cleburne's men, wrote, "the enemy are vigilant and spiteful on my right." Another Federal general reported that his skirmishers could not move forward ten steps without drawing the fire of Cleburne's men, "who were very vigilant." A third Federal general recorded, "the enemy," Cleburne's division, "are very active and vigilant."[48]

Despite its retreat from Dalton, the Army of Tennessee was "in the highest feather and bore itself like a conquering host."[49] Although constantly outflanked, for 70 days it disputed the advance of Sherman's large army over a distance of 100 miles. The Union General was in somewhat of a precarious position; he was now a great distance from his base of supplies and in danger of having his line of communications cut. Johnston had always been the victor when his lines had been assaulted directly. The veteran Confederate army stood, intact, in formidable defenses of Atlanta, with faith in its general and confident of the ultimate success of the campaign.

3

Between battles and marches, Cleburne managed to write to Miss Susan. His close friend Mangum related:

> Letters which he wrote to his betrothed were sometimes read to the writer amidst some quiet camp scenes, and were often revelations, even to one who knew him well, as to the depth of his feelings. Devoid of all approach to sentimentality, they were full of a most sweet and tender passion. They detailed the author's thoughts and fancies in a style that was both elevated and beautiful, and in every line they were glowing with an affection that was exquisite in its pathos and tenderness.[50]

Correspondence from Miss Susan to Cleburne during the campaign was adverted to in her brother Robert's letters to Miss Sallie Lightfoot. Writing from Fort Morgan on June 3, 1864, Robert said of his sisters Susan and Grace:

> The dear creatures haven't deigned to write me a line since you were in Mobile . . . . In Sue's case, of course, I am prepared to make all allowances as she must be completely absorbed in paying her devotions to a more interesting correspondent, which I think very right and proper and to be commended to

all young ladies. I believe she writes twice a week—read and ponder.

And on July 21: "When I was in town I used Susie's writing desk and found it filled with rough drafts in pencil of her letters to the Gen'l. I wish I had kept one or two to show you."[51]

The last of June Miss Susan and her sister Grace visited Mrs. Hardee in La Grange, Georgia. In a letter to his wife, General Hardee referred to "Pat" and "Sue," saying, "He is a famous fellow and she may well be proud of him."[52]

NOTES

CHAPTER XIV

[1]*O.R.*, XXXVIII, Pt. 3, p. 724.

[2]*Ibid.*

[3]Benham, *Kennesaw Gazette,* IV (Aug. 1, 1889), 2.

[4]*Ibid.*

[5]Cleburne, "Report of Battle of 'Pickett Settlement,' May 27, 1864" (MS in Huntington Library), 1. This report, in Buck's handwriting as amanuensis (Buck, *Cleburne,* 220), bears Cleburne's signature. The same report appears in *O.R.*, XXXVIII, Pt. 3, pp. 724-26, except for a few editorial changes.

[6]Benham, *Kennesaw Gazette,* IV (Aug. 1, 1889), 2.

[7]Cleburne, "Battle of 'Pickett Settlement,' " 1-4.

[8]Johnston, *Narrative,* 331; *O.R.*, XXXVIII, Pt. 3, pp. 187, 706, 987; J. N. Wyatt to J. B. Cunningham, Aug. 10, 1864, in "Dalton-Atlanta Campaign," *Confederate Veteran,* V (1897), 520.

[9]J. M. Mallett, Address, Mar. 15, 1903, Cleburne, Tex., at celebration "Birthday of Pat Cleburne," quoted in (Cleburne) *Daily Enterprise,* Mar. 16, 1903, p. 1.

[10]*O.R.*, XXXVIII, Pt. 1, pp. 194, 377, 523, 594.

[11]W. B. Hazen, *A Narrative of Military Service* (Boston, 1885), 256, 258. On May 27, 1878, the fourteenth anniversary of the battle of Pickett's Mill, the survivors of the 23rd Kentucky Regiment (Federal) held a reunion at Newport, Ky. In an address, Capt. John Barnes recalled that the regiment had fought against the Army of Tennessee in all major engagements from the battle of Murfreesboro through the battle of Nashville, but that the battle of Pickett's Mill (the speaker called it New Hope Church) was "the most important event that embellishes the pages of the history of the Twenty-Third Kentucky Regiment. . . . We glance back fourteen years and what do we see? A handful of men, comparatively almost surrounded, almost within bayonet touch of the veterans of one of the most noted (and justly so) divisions of the Confederate Army—that of Pat. Cleburne. . . . Entering the engagement with less than one hundred men, the blood of fifty-nine of [the regiment's] heroes now consecrates the soil of New Hope battlefield"—Cincinnati *Commercial,* May 28, 1878, p. 5.

[12]W. W. Mackall to his wife, May 28, 1878, 1864, in William W. Mackall, *Son's Recollections,* 211; Joseph M'Clure, "Wounded Texan's Trip Home on Crutches," *Confederate Veteran,* XVII (1909), 162.

[13]Thomas J. Stokes to his sister, May 31, 1864, in Mary A. H. Gay, *Life in Dixie During the War* (Atlanta, 1892), 40-41.

[14]*O.R.*, XXXVIII, Pt. 3, pp. 706-07; Benham, *Kennesaw Gazette*, IV (Aug. 15, 1889), 2; Buck, *Cleburne*, 222; Kirwan (ed.), *Johnny Green*, 133-34; W. D. Pickett, "The Dead Angle," *Confederate Veteran*, XIV (1906), 459.

[15]Hardee to his wife, June 2, June 4, 1864, in Hardee Papers, Ala. Arch. and Hist.

[16]Cleburne to Roy, May 31, 1864, MS in Communications to and from Cleburne's Division, pp. 145-46. "Pioneers.—Soldiers equipped with axes, saws, and other instruments for clearing the way before an advancing army, or to entrench."—Lippincott (pub.), *U.S. Infantry Tactics*, 426.

[17]Hardee to his wife, June 4, June 5, 1864, in Hardee Papers, Ala. Arch. and Hist.; Buck, *Cleburne*, 222.

[18]Hardee to his wife, June 12, 1864, in Hardee Papers, Ala. Arch. and Hist; Buck, *Cleburne*, 222-23.

[19]*O.R.*, XXXVIII, Pt. 1, p. 149; M'Clure, "Texan's Trip Home," 162. "Sweet minor scatter calls" of quail reunite the members of a flock.—Neltje Blanchan, *The Bird Book* (New York, 1932), 415.

[20]Hardee to his wife, June 17, 1864, in Hardee Papers, Ala. Arch. and Hist.; Benham, *Kennesaw Gazette*, IV (Sept. 1, 1889), 2.

[21]"Lieut. Isaac Lightner," *Confederate Veteran*, IV (1896), 252.

[22]Benham, *Kennesaw Gazette*, IV (Sept. 1, 1889), 2.

[23]*Ibid.*; Cleburne to Kinloch Falconer, July 13, 1864, H-2452 (AIGO) 1864, M474/119, NA.

[24]Benham, *Kennesaw Gazette*, IV (Sept. 1, 1899), 2; W. W. Mackall to his wife, June 18, 1864, in William W. Mackall, *Son's Recollections*, 215; Hardee to his wife, June 18, June 19, 1864, in Hardee Papers, Ala. Arch. and Hist.

[25]Joseph E. Johnston, *Narrative*, 338-39; Cheatham's Journal of Military Operations around Atlanta (MS in Cheatham Papers), 5.

[26]T. G. Dabney, "Fight at Dead Angle, in Georgia," *Confederate Veteran*, XIV (1906), 312; Buck, *Cleburne*, 224; Joseph E. Johnston, *Narrative*, 339; Benham, *Kennesaw Gazette*, VI (Sept. 1, 1889), 2; W. T. Barnes, "An Incident of Kenesaw [sic] Mountain," *Confederate Veteran*, XXX (1922), 48-49; cf., Pickett, "The Dead Angle," 458.

[27]Pickett, "The Dead Angle," 458; *O. R.*, XXXVIII, Pt. 1, pp. 296, 304, 329, 336; cf., J. B. Work, *Map of Kennesaw Mountain battlefield at points of assault by Davis' division, 14th Corps, and Newton's division, 4th Corps, on Cheatham's and Cleburne's divisions* (Chicago, 1902), in possession of National Park Service, Kennesaw Mountain National Battlefield Park; *O. R.*, XXXVIII, Pt.

1, p. 199; Barnes, "Incident of Kenesaw *[sic]* Mountain," 49.

[28]Benham, *Kennesaw Gazette,* IV (Sept. 1, 1899), 2; advertisement in Atlanta *Daily Intelligencer,* June 29, 1864, and several later issues, quoted in *Kennesaw Gazette,* IV (Sept. 1, 1899), 3.

[29]Benham, *Kennessaw Gazette,* IV (Sept. 1, 1889), 2; Hardee to his wife, June 24, 1864, in Hardee Papers, Ala. Arch. and Hist.

[30]Barnes, "Incident of Kenesaw *[sic]* Mountain," 49.

[31]*O.R.,* XXXVIII, Pt. 4, p. 588.

[32]*O. R.,* XXXVIII, Pt. 1, pp. 199, 295, 304, 335; Joseph E. Johnston, *Narrative,* 342-43; Hardee, "Memoranda of Operations under Johnston," 580.

[33]*O.R.,* XXXVIII, Pt. 1, pp. 296, 304; Barnes, "Incident of Kenesaw *[sic]* Mountain," 49; Benham, *Kennesaw Gazette,* IV (Sept. 1, 1889), 2; W. J. Milner, "Lieut. Gen. William Joseph Hardee," *Confederate Veteran,* XXII (1914), 363; Buck, *Cleburne,* 224-25; *cf.,* Wyatt to Cunningham, Aug. 10, 1864, in "Dalton-Atlanta Campaign," 520; *O. R.,* XXXVIII, Pt. 4, p. 709.

[34]*O. R.,* XXXVIII, Pt. 1, pp. 199, 296, 304, 329, 335-36.

[35]Barnes, "Incident of Kenesaw *[sic]* Mountain," 49; Samuel G. French, *Two Wars: an Autobiography* (Nashville, 1901), 211; F. W. Bush, "Arkansans' Work on Kennesaw Mountain," *Confederate Veteran,* XIX (1911), 206; Milner, "Lieut. Gen. Hardee," 363; Buck, *Cleburne,* 225.

[36]*O. R.,* XXXVIII, Pt. 1, pp. 199, 224, 296, 304; Joseph E. Johnston, *Narrative,* 343; Benham, *Kennesaw Gazette,* IV (Sept. 1, 1899), 2; Oliver O. Howard, "The Struggle for Atlanta," in *Battles and Leaders,* IV, 311.

[37]Hardee, "Memoranda of Operations under Johnston," 580; *O. R.,* XXXVIII, Pt. 1, p. 199.

[38]Joseph E. Johnston, *Narrative,* 344; Nixon B. Stewart, *Dan. McCook's Regiment, 52nd O. V. I.* (Alliance, Ohio, 1900), 127.

[39]Cheatham Journal, 6; Dabney, "Fight at Dead Angle," 312, Pickett, "The Dead Angle," 459; Benham, *Kennesaw Gazette,* IV (Sept. 1, 1899), 2.

[40]Joseph E. Johnston, *Narrative,* 345-56; Benham, *Kennesaw Gazette,* IV (Sept. 1, 1899), 2; *ibid.,* (Sept. 15, 1899), 4-5; Stewart, *Dan. McCook's Regiment,* 129.

[41]F. A. Shoup, "Works at Chattahoochee River," *Confederate Veteran,* III (1895), 262-64; Sherman, *Memoirs,* II, 66.

[42]Roy to Cleburne, July 9, 1864, MS in Communications to and from Cleburne's Division, p. 200.

[43]Benham, *Kennesaw Gazette,* IV (Sept. 15, 1899), 5; Wilbur G. Kurtz, *Map of Atlanta . . . showing the field and fortified lines of the Confederate forces,* pub. Atlanta Chamber of Commerce (Atlanta, 1938).

[44]"Forty-eighth Tennessee Regiment," *Confederate Veteran*, II (1894), 239, 273; Cleburne to Falconer, July 13, 1864, H-2452 (AIGO) 1864, M474/119, NA.

[45]Frazer, "Fifth Confederate," 151; Joseph E. Johnston, *Narrative*, 345-46, 351.

[46]Govan to Dunn, Dec. 16, 1878, in Hempstead, *Historical Review of Arkansas*, I, 245.

[47]A. B. Schell, "A Partial Report of the Part I Played in the War between the States," enclosed in letter Schell to James W. Blackmore, July 14, 1905 (MS in possession of Mrs. Alex W. Hewitt), 3; "William H. Heard," *Confederate Veteran*, XI (1903), 289; Benham, *Kennesaw Gazette*, IV (Sept. 15, 1899), 4; Drake, "General Cleburne," 246; Cleburne to Falconer, May 27, 1864, MS in Communications to and from Cleburne's Division, p. 143; Harley, *Confederate Veteran*, VII (1899), 307; Frank H. Smith, "Interview with Capt. Schell," 219. The commander of a squad of the Whitworth sharpshooters, Sergt. Walter L. Bragg, in 1887 became one of the original appointees to the Interstate Commerce Commission.

[48]"Cleburne's Vigilance," *Kennesaw Gazette*, IV (Jan. 1, 1899), 2.

[49]Ex-Gov. James D. Porter of Tennessee, veteran of Cheatham's division, to the Nashville *American,* date not shown, in "An 'Unseen Message' of President Davis's," *Confederate Veteran*, XIV (1906), 369; Buck, *Cleburne*, 227.

[50]Mangum, *Kennesaw Gazette*, II (June 15, 1887), 3.

[51]Robert Tarleton to Sallie Lightfoot, June 3, July 21, 1864, in Tarleton Family Collection.

[52]Hardee to his wife, June 25, 1864, in Hardee Papers, Ala. Arch. and Hist.

CHAPTER XV

BATTLES AROUND ATLANTA
(July 17-27, 1864)

...Claibom's division of Hardee's corps passed, and here I
wish to say that in all of my experience I never saw a more
graceful rider astride a horse, or a grander looking man than
Pat Claibom, or at least I thought so on that eventful morning
of July 22, 1864.
— *W. P. Archer, History of the Battle of Atlanta.*

Atlanta was a vital communications center, with four
railroads originating at the city. The Georgia Railroad
extended eastward, passing through Decatur, six miles from
Atlanta. The Macon & Western went southeastward; and the
Atlanta & West Point, southwestward. The Western &
Atlantic, along which the armies had been fighting, extended
to the northwest.

About three miles north of Atlanta Peach Tree Creek
flowed from east to west. This stream emptied into the
Chattahoochee River at a point just north of the Western &
Atlantic railroad bridge.

Atlanta was protected by an inner and an outer line of
defense. The inner line encircled the city just beyond the
corporate limits. The outer line began four miles northwest
of the city, running south of Peach Tree Creek eastward for
six miles, and then south for two miles, almost reaching the
Georgia Railroad.

All of Sherman's forces having crossed the Chattahoochee
at points seven to twenty-five miles northwest of Atlanta, on
July 17 the Union commander began a concerted movement
of his armies against the Atlanta area. James B. McPherson
started a wide sweep southeastward to destroy the Georgia
Railroad near Decatur. West of McPherson marched John
Schofield and west of him, George Thomas moved directly

toward Peach Tree Creek.

At this crucial time, as the Confederate Army prepared to defend the city against the onslaught of Sherman's army, a War Department order came from Richmond, at the behest of President Davis, relieving Johnston from the command of the Army of Tennessee and replacing him with John B. Hood. The tragic blunder of removing Johnston was compounded by naming Hood as his successor. "No officer or soldier who ever served under me," said Sherman, "will question the generalship of Joseph E. Johnston."[1] Hood had a tremendous combat record with the Army of Northern Virginia and was a bold fighter. However, when he took command of the Army of Tennessee, he was shattered physically and lacked the bodily stamina to command an army. His left arm had been mangled at Gettysburg and his right leg severed at Chickamauga. On his way to join the Army of Tennessee in February 1864, he had sustained further injuries in a train wreck. He also suffered from rheumatism.[2] Authorities at Richmond expected Hood to adopt vigorous offensive operations even though his troop strength was only half that of Sherman's.

The Federals rejoiced at the change. Johnston had always confronted them "with impregnable fortifications," said Federal General Cox afterward; ". . . no wish was so common or so often expressed as that he would only try our works as we were trying his. It was now known that this was likely to come, ..."[3] In the Army of Tennessee, Johnston had been a popular commander, and officers and privates alike were indignant and depressed by the news of his removal. Cleburne's strong and frank disapproval of the transfer of command from Johnston to Hood destroyed any chance of "the Stonewall of the West" heading Hood's old corps.[4] The assignment was temporarily given to Cheatham.

The battle of Peach Tree Creek was fought July 20. Johnston's plan, which Hood sought to follow, was to attack the Federals while they were divided in crossing the creek. During the afternoon and night of the 19th, large units of Thomas' army crossed over the stream. By noon the next day nearly all of his army had reached the south side of the creek, opposed only by a Confederate skirmish line. Hood did not attack when Thomas's forces were divided and delayed until 1 P.M. on the 20th to order the attack. Pressure from McPherson's Army of the Tennessee on the east forced the Confederates to shift their lines and delay their attack until 4 o'clock. By then, Thomas' forces, in selected positions, were entrenched and waiting. Too, the few remaining hours of daylight were insufficient for the large-scale Confederate operations which had been planned.

Two of Stewart's and two of Hardee's divisions made the attack. Stewart was partially successful but Hardee was repulsed. To the northeast of Atlanta, Wheeler's cavalry and Cheatham's infantry were trying to hold back McPherson. As Hardee was about to send Cleburne's and Maney's (Cheatham's successor) divisions of his corps against Thomas, Hood ordered him to send a division to the relief of Wheeler. Hardee sent Cleburne's division to assist the Confederate cavalryman, and was then unable to press his attack against Thomas. Hood consequently ordered the troops to withdraw, leaving Thomas the victor.

Simultaneously, Cleburne's division started marching on Peach Tree Creek Road south to Atlanta, passed through the city, and turned eastward. His troops bivouacked about midnight at the edge of Atlanta, alongside the Georgia Railroad. After two hours of sleep, they continued to march eastward, using the railroad right of way, and reached Wheeler's line before daybreak on the 21st, two and a quarter miles from the city.[5]

The afternoon before, Wheeler's cavalry had improvised a temporary defense line running southward from the terminus of the outer defense works. Crossing the railroad, the line continued southward three-quarters of a mile on a low ridge; and then up to the crest of Bald Hill. The east side of the hill was rather steep but on the north and south sides the rise was gentle. The crest of this barren elevation stretched from the north to the south for over a quarter of a mile.[6] Wheeler's line extended almost the full length of the crest. Federals, M. D. Leggett's and Giles Smith's divisions of Francis Blair's 17th Army Corps, were entrenched on high ground some six hundred yards east of the hill.[7]

Cleburne resolved to relieve as many of Wheeler's cavalry

as practicable, and to prevent McPherson's army from entering Atlanta.[8] Leaving one regiment north of the railroad, Cleburne placed the rest of his three brigades as far south as feasible. His southernmost troops, two regiments of less than 300 men, were on the northern edge of the crest of Bald Hill. These regiments were part of Granbury's Texas Brigade,[9] to which now belonged a portion of Lucius Polk's old command. In Granbury's absence due to illness, this brigade was commanded by Gen. J. A. Smith, who had returned to duty after several months' absence. The rest of the line on the crest of Bald Hill was held by three cavalry brigades, about 2,000 men, commanded by Wheeler.[10] Wheeler's orders were to extend the line south of the hill.

There ensued, in Cleburne's words, "the bitterest" day's fighting of his life.[11] The Confederate line, constructed by cavalry unaccustomed to "digging," was inadequate and defective. The light works, on poorly selected ground, were crooked and irregular, exposing troops to enfilade fire. At dawn, when Cleburne's men began straightening and strengthening the line, Federal artillery and skirmishers opened fire with telling effect. Improving the line proceeded slowly and with much difficulty.[12]

About 7 A.M., a powerful battery, some 800 yards northeast of Granbury's old brigade, now commanded by J. A. Smith, swept his line with amazing accuracy. A single shell passed along a trench on Bald Hill, destroying an entire company of eighteen men of the 18th Texas Cavalry Regiment (dismounted). Six men, sitting side by side in the trench, were beheaded; and twelve were severely wounded. Within a few minutes, the brigade suffered a loss of 40 killed and over 100 wounded.[13]

At 8 o'clock, the enemy launched a furious cannonading, which appeared to signal an attack against Cleburne's and Wheeler's entire front. As the artillery barrage continued against the Confederate left, a Federal brigade demonstrated just north of the hill. Simultaneously Leggett's Federal division of three brigades made an assault on the hill, springing forward from the woods near its eastern and southeastern base. When M. F. Force's brigade of this division, following a strong line of skirmishers, started ascending the hill in two

lines, Cleburne rushed Key's and Swett's batteries to points
on the Confederate line adjacent to the hill. Union soldiers
fell "in bunches" as the Federal column was enfiladed with
shell and cannister. But the Federal column closed up, and as
described in Key's diary, "the terrible assault from the
Yanks" followed. Cleburne's riflemen on the hill, having
quietly awaited the charge, fired with steady aim; and turned
the course of the Federal column from their front.[14]

Unfortunately the Confederate cavalry brigades on Bald
Hill failed to meet the crisis. The southernmost of these
brigades had no defense works on its flank and feared that it
would be surrounded. It gave way in confusion when Federal
infantrymen started to ascend the southeast side of the hill.
As Force's Federal brigade went over and through the
barricades held by the remaining Confederate cavalry, Wheeler's men fell back in disorder, thereby causing the Texas
regiment next to them to give way.[15]

However, this regiment, the 24th and 25th Dismounted
Cavalry (consolidated), quickly rallied and regained its place
in the line. This unit and some of the cavalry then joined two
regiments from Lowrey's and Govan's brigades dispatched by
Cleburne. In "a dreadful fight" they recovered 200 yards of
the works which Wheeler had lost.[16] During the engagement,
the rest of Cleburne's division was repelling an attack by
Giles Smith's division; and Cleburne could spare no additional reinforcements. However, in the woods behind his line
Cleburne placed sharpshooters, who poured an enfilading fire
into the extreme right of the Federal line on Bald Hill. "So
galling was the fire," a colonel in Force's brigade reported,
that "every man who attempted to rise was shot."[17] But
Federal General Leggett brought up big howitzers and
effectively shelled the woods. Thus, the Federals were able to
make secure their lodgment on Bald Hill, throwing up a line
of works facing Atlanta, with a refused line running
northeasterly to protect their flank. From this forward
position they proceeded to shell the city. The Federals also
extended their line on Bald Hill a half mile to the south,
along Flat Shoals Road on a continuation of the ridge.[18]

During the rest of the long, sweltering day, Cleburne's
division withstood constant pressure on its entire front and

repulsed partial assaults when the Federals probed for weak spots. As artillery swept their flanks and shelled the front of their meager works, the Confederates had no opportunity to advance or countercharge. They strove to improve their works as the hours wore on, while constantly on the alert to resist a major assault. The division suffered severely, being harrassed by constant rifle fire and sustaining some 300 casualties.[19]

When night came on July 21, Cleburne had achieved his objective of preventing McPherson from entering the inner works of Atlanta.[20] Despite the handicaps under which they fought, Cleburne's men had made their prowess felt. The Federals had sustained 728 casualties. General Blair, commander of the 17th Corps, reported the Confederates made "a stubborn resistance."[21] General McPherson's inspector-general later recounted that the Union army commander watched "with intense interest the sharp and brilliant contest between the Seventeenth Corps and the enemy, ..."[22]

2

Other important duties were awaiting Cleburne's men. Hood had conceived a plan of general attack in which Hardee's corps (including Cleburne's division) was to march that night by a long detour in a "Jacksonian" strategic move. At dawn the corps was to strike McPherson's left flank and rear. Cheatham and Stewart were to take up the attack, from right to left, and to drive McPherson down Peach Tree Creek before Sherman could bring up reinforcements.

After dark on July 21, in carrying out Hood's plan, Cheatham and Stewart withdrew from the outer defense lines on the northeast to the inner line encircling the city. About the same time, Hardee withdrew from his position on the outer line near Peach Tree Creek and marched toward Atlanta. There, to be joined by Cleburne, Hardee's corps was to proceed southward on the detour.

If feasible, at dark Cleburne was to start withdrawing to the inner defense line, leaving skirmishers behind, and thus provide a few hours rest for his tired men before meeting Hardee. However, contact with McPherson's army necessitated Cleburne keeping at least one brigade on his line until 10 P.M. Those troops who had left the line earlier bivouacked in the Atlanta entrenchments for about three hours but those who had been retained on the line until 10 o'clock rested only a single hour. Thirty minutes past midnight, the division joined Hardee on the McDonough Road in Atlanta, probably bringing up the rear of the corps.[23]

In order to conceal its movement, Hardee's corps marched southeastward on the McDonough Road for five and a quarter miles to the Fayetteville Road. The soldiers, weary from two days' fighting and lack of rest, made slow progress during the hot night marching over the dusty narrow road. Seasoned troops fell in their tracks from exhaustion. Further delay and confusion resulted from the Confederate cavalry, en route to Decatur, using the same road and cutting through the entire column.

Turning on the Fayetteville Road, the corps moved a mile and a quarter to Cobb's Mill, which was three miles below the southern terminus of McPherson's line. Cleburne's troops reached Cobb's Mill after daybreak on July 22 and rested for two hours. Each man was now given twenty additional rounds of ammunition, preparatory to the corps moving northward on the enemy's flank and rear.[24]

As the Confederate columns advanced northward from Cobb's Mill on the Fayetteville Road, a company of Georgia militia stepped aside to let them pass. Years later a soldier in this company recorded: "...Claiborn's division of Hardee's corps passed, and here I wish to say that in all of my experience I never saw a more graceful rider astride a horse, or a grander looking man than Pat Claiborn, or at least I thought so on that eventful morning of July 22, 1864."[25]

A mile and a quarter beyond Cobb's Mill, the Fayetteville Road crossed the Flat Shoals Road, which ran northwestward directly to the Federal line. At this junction, Hardee split his corps, ordering Cleburne and Maney to deploy their troops and move forward, paralleling the Flat Shoals Road. Hardee accompanied Walker's and Bate's columns on the Fayetteville Road; and after moving three-quarters of a mile, directed that they leave the road and march northwestward, in order to reach the rear of McPherson's army. In front of all four divisions of the corps lay a vast wilderness with dense and almost impenetrable undergrowth. Hardee and his division commanders, without the aid of a map, were forced to move the troops through the thickets in line of battle.[26]

Brief reference will first be made to the operations of Bates' and Walker's divisions, which became engaged before the divisions of Cleburne and Maney. When Bate's and Walker's divisions came to the open ground of Sugar Creek, they had the misfortune, by chance, to be confronted with Sweeny's division (of the 16th Corps of McPherson's army) on a hill about 500 yards away. Sweeny was moving from north of the Georgia Railroad to reinforce the left of the Federal line and had halted. Here, at noon, began the battle of Atlanta, with the firing of a Yankee bullet which killed General Walker as he reconnoitered. The divisions of Bate and Walker assaulted the Federal division and a brigade of John W. Fuller's division of the 16th Corps which had been rushed to Sweeny's right. Attacking through open fields, the two Confederate divisions were repulsed by the heavy artillery and musketry to the Federal forces. The Confederates stoutly renewed the attack but without success.[27]

Cleburne, in the meantime, had advanced at 11:00 A.M. in line of battle from the Fayetteville Road.[28] General Cleburne's order, as recounted by a captain in his division, was "to move forward, and turn neither to the right nor to left until we were within the enemy's breastworks."[29] Govan's Arkansas Brigade advanced in a northwesterly direction, paralleling the Flat Shoals Road. To Govan's right was J. A. Smith's Texas Brigade, with Lowrey's Alabama and Mississippi Brigade 500 yards behind the Texans. Maney's division followed 300 yards behind Lowrey.[30]

After the Confederates struggled a mile and three-quarters through woods and undergrowth, the sound of two Napoleon guns from the direction of the Flat Shoals Road announced that the Federals were near and aware of the Southerners' presence. Contrary to information furnished Hardee's corps, Govan's troops soon saw that the enemy's works, instead of terminating on the Flat Shoals Road, curved northeast in a "fishhook" of heavy earthworks. In Govan's words, the works were "designed to protect" the Federals "from the very movement we were then making."[31] One line of the breastworks in the fishhook was about 200 yards farther northeast.[32] Also, as the Confederates would learn, Giles Smith's Federal division had been shifted to occupy the line from Bald Hill southward and Leggett's division had been posted on the hill itself. North of Bald Hill, the Federal 15th Corps had moved westward to the line vacated by Cleburne.

The evening previous, astute McPherson had ordered his 17th Corps to "work industriously" during the night, "strengthening their position ... so as to make it impregnable against any rebel assault."[33] They had cleared a space 80 to 100 yards in front of the entrenchments, using the brush and small oaks to make "an almost impassable abatis."[34]

Govan's single line of battle, supported by the four guns of Key's battery, charged to the abatis. For twenty minutes, subjected to withering fire of artillery and minié balls, Govan's men pressed forward through the entanglements until the enemy ceased firing and shouted, "We surrender!" But when the scant number of Confederates became apparent as they approached the breastworks to receive the surrender, they were captured instead by the Federals. The fighting was renewed — the Federals charged and the Confederates countercharged.[35]

Meanwhile the right of Govan's brigade, east of the breastworks, in a surging onslaught, had scattered a Federal line and advanced through a broad, flat valley covered with thick blackjack trees. About 300 yards north of the fishhook, a unit of these Confederates came to a winding field road running westward to Flat Shoals Road. On this road, Govan's men intercepted and captured six pieces of artillery (Battery F, 2d U.S. Regular), which the 16th Corps was returning to the 17th Corps at the urgent demand of General G. M. Dodge. The Confederates promptly turned the guns on the Federals.[36]

Then Govan's troops, those who had flanked the breastworks, swinging to the west in a skillful maneuver, attacked both the main line of Union works and the fishhook from the rear. At the same time, the remainder of Govan's brigade assaulted the refused line from the front. The brigade carried and held the refused line and about 250 yards of the main line. They captured an entire Federal regiment and had the satisfaction of rescuing their comrades who had been captured a short time earlier. The tables were turned, and the Federal officers now surrendered their swords to the Confederate officers they had captured.[37] Federal Gen. John A. Logan reported: ". . .the enemy, by the rapidity of his assault and the heavy force with which it was made, swept away 2 guns and several hundred prisoners."[38] The Union soldiers who were able to escape fled northward, "crowds" of them panic-stricken.[39]

On Govan's right, Smith's Texans had advanced rapidly through the three-quarters-of-a-mile gap between the breastworks and the Federal 16th Corps. The line of Federals in front of Smith scattered in confusion, many being captured by the pursuing Texans and Tennesseans. As skirmishers of the 5th Confederate (Tennessee) Regiment, assigned to the Texas brigade, reached the field road, from the woods came a Federal general on horseback rapidly riding toward them, heading westward. He was followed by an orderly and four Federal officers. When called upon to halt, the General veered his horse to the right, throwing himself forward in the saddle, evidently hoping to reach the pine thicket close at hand. Instantly a volley came from the Confederate skirmishers; and the General, James B. McPherson, fell from his horse, mortally wounded.[40] "Much respected by the Confederates,"[41] General McPherson was the only commander of a Federal army killed during the war.

Smith's Texas Brigade and some of Govan's men after sharp fighting forced Fuller's Federal brigade to withdraw eastward. J. A. Smith then swept northwestward toward the main Federal line on Flat Shoals Road, and assailed the hastily formed lines of Federal infantry and the six artillery pieces of Samuel DeGolyer's battery.[42] The Texans, with "ungovernable enthusiasm," carried three subsidiary lines; and forced the Federal infantry and battery to retreat to Bald Hill.[43]

The Union main line atop Bald Hill had been straightened and strongly fortified the previous night. Near the south end of Leggett's Union division was stationed Edward McAllister's four-gun battery of big howitzers (commanded by

Charles S. Cooper), a position so formidable that it could be classed as a "fort." The Federals whom the Texans had driven to Bald Hill formed a line of fence rails covered by earth running eastward from the main line, the howitzers being in the apex of the angle thus made, and the six-gun battery distributed along the new line for a short distance to the east.[44]

General Smith dispatched a request to General Cleburne for reinforcements but none were available. Lowrey's brigade, beset by difficulties, was in the forest and thickets south of the battlefield. The Texas Brigade, unsupported, attacked the northern part of Leggett's main line, charging westward across a field and up the hill, on ground over which Leggett's division had charged the day before.[45] A Federal officer, commanding a section of a six-gun battery supporting Leggett, and, who witnessed the charge of the Texans, wrote:

> Pat Cleburne's Texans . . . [their] line well formed, . . . emerged from their concealment in the woods, and yelling as only the steer-drivers of Texas could yell, charged upon our division. . . . On came the Texans; but they were met by a continuous volley of musketry and shrapnel, shell and canister from our six-rifled Rodmans and Cooper's howitzers. It seemed as if no man of all the host who were attacking us could escape alive; and yet, still yelling, they persisted in their desperate undertaking.
>
> . . . Only as the breath of a passing breeze blew the smoke away could the movements of the enemy be discerned clearly; but his unearthly yell could be heard above the sound of muskets and cannon.[46]

Many of the Texans reached the Federal breastwork. Those who crossed it battled with bayonet and clubbed musket until killed, captured, or were compelled to withdraw. The survivors reformed and made a second attack. But when the cross-fire made their position untenable, Smith ordered them to fall back. A small portion of the command, not receiving this order, pushed on to the Federal entrenchments, where, after a struggle, they were forced to surrender. The remainder of the brigade withdrew to the woods to reform.[47]

About the same time that J. A. Smith was engaged, from

the southwest Maney's division moved on Giles Smith's Federal division. Maney's attack was supported by some of Govan's men.[48] Hardee had ordered Maney's attack, having received intelligence that Federals were approaching in heavy force to turn the Confederate left. To combat Maney's advance, most of the Federal division formed in lines extending westward from the breastworks, with the rest remaining in the woods. The opposing forces became engaged; but since the Federals showed no disposition to carry out a turning movement, Hardee withdrew Maney's troops.[49]

In the foregoing phase of the battle, Cleburne had requested and received a battery from another division of Hardee's corps to support Captain Key; and with a section of this battery Key drove the enemy from some of the works. Key recorded the action in his diary:

> After I moved the enemy from these works, some troops began driving them on the left, and I galloped back to Generals Cleburne and Hardee and informed them of what I had done and how we were driving them, remarking "Generals to the front," which caused a smile to play upon Cleburne's face. They sanctioned my suggestions, and in a few moments Cleburne and I were riding rapidly over the ground that I had gained with [William B.] Turner's [Mississippi] battery.[50]

During the battle of Atlanta, Hood remained at the James E. Williams house, two and a half miles west of the starting point of the engagement, and a mile west of the nearest Federal line. From the second floor of the house, he attempted to view the action through binoculars.[51] Finally, after the battle had been in progress for nearly three hours, Hood gave the order for Cheatham's corps to attack. Soon after 3:00 o'clock,[52] two of Cheatham's divisions advanced from the Atlanta fortifications and struck points on the line of the 15th Corps and Leggett's division.[53]

Learning of Cheatham's attack, Cleburne rushed an order to Lowrey, in the forest, 500 yards south of the battlefield, to "move rapidly to the front and charge the works; that no time must be lost." Earlier Lowrey had received an order from Cleburne "to move up rapidly," followed by an order from Hardee "to move rapidly to the support of General

Govan." Again changing direction of march, Lowrey straightened his line and moved forward.[54]

Cheatham's attack on the 15th Corps met with initial success but the Federals counterattacked strongly. Cheatham brought his reserve division into action at 4 P.M. but later was forced to withdraw. Stevenson's Confederate division, which had attacked Leggett, withdrew to the woods to reform.[55]

About 4 o'clock, Lowrey's brigade of Alabamans and Mississipians, "with great impetuosity," attacked the breastworks of Giles Smith's division in a charge across forty or fifty yards of open ground. They met heavy firing from this division and two regiments of Leggett's division. Many of Lowrey's men fell[56] but the rest pressed on and closed with the enemy. As described by Federal General Smith, "The flags of two opposing regiments would meet on the opposite sides of the same works, and would be flaunted by their respective bearers in each other's faces. Men were bayoneted across the works, and officers with their swords fought hand-to-hand with men with bayonets. . . . It lasted for nearly three-quarters of an hour, when [the Confederates] reluctantly retired."[57] In their gallant attempt to take the works, half of Lowrey's men making the assault were casualties.[58]

About 5:00 o'clock, Cleburne, with Govan's and J. A. Smith's brigades, Maney's division, and Lowrey directing George A. Mercer's brigade of Walker's division, attacked the Federals along Flat Shoals Road and Bald Hill. Cleburne's brigades advanced from the southeast; Maney's division, from the southwest; and Mercer's brigade, from the south. Mercer's brigade carried two sections of the enemy's line but became disorganized, and its officers were unable to form their commands under the close and deadly fire.[59] Cleburne's and Maney's troops rolled back Giles Smith's entire Federal division and about one-third of Leggett's division. The Federal line on the crest of the hill was forced eastward, at right angles to its original position.[60]

Private Watkins of Maney's division wrote a graphic description of the initial phase of this attack:

We advanced to the attack on Cleburne's immediate left. Cleburne himself was leading us in person, so that we would not fire upon his men, who were then inside the Yankee line. His sword was drawn. I heard him say, "Follow me, boys." He ran forward, and amid the blazing fires of the Yankee guns was soon on top of the enemy's works. He had on a bob-tail Confederate coat, which looked as if it had been cut out of a scrimp pattern. (You see, I remember the little things). We were but a few paces behind, following close upon him, and soon had captured their line of works. We were firing at the flying foe — astraddle of their lines of battle.[61]

Govan's brigade, east of the breastworks, went 500 yards through the wood and came to an open field, just south of Bald Hill. DeGolyer's and McAllister's Federal batteries on the hill and Federal infantry in refused lines commanded the field. Govan's brigade charged across the open field through galling flank fire; then swinging left, where the Federals were nearest, they carried the entrenchments. About the same time a force from Maney's division struck the other side of the entrenchment.[62]

After the war, Lt. Col. Gilbert D. Munson of Leggett's division, who witnessed the attack, recalled the intensity of the action:

. . . men of the Fourth Division [Giles Smith's division] were driven along their intrenchments into the Second Brigade [of Leggett's division], many continuing to [Leggett's] First Brigade. . . . Colonel Wm. Hall, of the Eleventh Iowa, rallied a lot of men at the right of the Second Brigade, and stood with them behind our fort on Leggett's Hill [i.e., Bald Hill]. General Giles A. Smith rallied his men on low ground east of and next to the fort. Such numbers of the Fourth Division crowded the Second Brigade, or swept by along its intrenchments, that it seemed the rest must be either killed or captured, especially when right behind came the rebel columns in good order, aligned east and west, striking our flank, and actually marching over a part of the Second Brigade's refused line of intrenchments, killing and capturing some of the men defending them. The rebel line being perpendicular to ours, our men gained the reverse side of fortifications still in our possession, and by a steady fire at close range broke and stopped their advance directly astride of the intrenchments, and enfiladed them as they passed by crowding obliquely to their right. A large force, however, confronted us, fell behind trees, and fought us there until driven off; but the greater part

of the column passed steadily on, going to the north between
our position and the Sixteenth Corps; and from the south-west
charged Leggett's Hill, swung up against his First and Third
Brigades and portions of the Fourth Division gathered there,
desperately wounded General [M. F.] Force and Adjutant-
General [J. B.] Walker, and by the very viciousness of attack
came near retaking the hill, but were finally driven back. As
this charging column passed by the Second Brigade, there
came another attack on it from the direction of Atlanta
(Stevenson's division], which the men met by again reversing
their front behind their intrenchments. . . . gradually a part of
the intrenchments held by the Twentieth Ohio was abandoned
— our men beaten back; and, availing themselves of this, the
enemy's sharpshooters crept along the abandoned earthworks,
gathered behind the traverses, and springing up fired over them
down along our line, thus enfilading us; and, finally, artillery
was brought up and swept our position with a destructive fire
of canister. . . .

I reported to General Leggett the awful situation of the
Second Brigade — almost surrounded, no refused flank, and
the enemy astride of their intrenchments and gradually
crowding them back. He said he had sent orders for the
Second Brigade to change front, and showed me the position
— a continuation of the refused line of the First Brigade, at
right angles to our first line of battle.[63]

When Leggett's 2nd Brigade took its new position
extending eastward from the crest of Bald Hill, Giles Smith's
division continued the line along a ridge. The Federals hastily
threw up tight rifle-pits of rails and dirt, "like rat holes in a
curve."[64] Another Federal brigade, of the 15th Corps,
moved down from the north and extended the line farther
eastward. Concerning the action to take this position, Federal
General Blair reported:

These dispositions of the two divisions were made under a
heavy fire of musketry and artillery from the advancing
enemy, ... They made a determined and resolute attack,
advancing up to our breast-works on the crest of the hill,
planted their flags side by side with ours, and fought
hand-to-hand until it grew so dark that nothing could be seen
but the flash of the guns, from the opposite side of the same
works.[65]

Although the brunt of the attack from the south was against

the hill, fighting extended down the line to the east. A charge by Smith's Texans and Maney's Tennesseans against this line was repulsed, the Confederates being swept with fire in their front and "a terrific cross-fire."[66]

After dark on the 22nd the attacks for the most part ceased.[67] But the Confederate riflemen maintained a sporadic fire from the woods and the advanced breastworks which they had captured, and the artillery of both sides continued firing. Lieutenant Colonel Munson in Leggett's division further stated: "Before, the fear was of being driven from our position; now, for a time, it looked as if we would be shot from it. The line of fire was picking our men out as they lay hugging the ground."[68] Gen. John A. Logan, who had taken temporary command of McPherson's army, reported the situation to Sherman: "I find one division of the Seventeenth Corps somewhat despondent, but think they will hold their position; have sent them three fresh regiments to support them in holding the hill...."[69] Soon after midnight, the troops of these regiments crawled on their hands and knees to the fort and the angle.[70] Govan's brigade held the most advanced position of the Confederates, in a line extending to the crest of the hill within twenty-five yards of the Federals.

Shortly after 2 A.M. on the 23rd, Govan withdrew as his exposed position could not be maintained after daylight; but the Confederates held most of the ground they had gained.[71] Thus the battle of Atlanta came to a close.

This battle, Hardee reported, was "one of the most desperate and bloody of the war, and ... won the only decided success achieved by the army at Atlanta."[72] In 1867 with particular reference to Giles Smith's Federal division, Lurton Dunham Ingersoll wrote in *Iowa and the Rebellion:* "The battle of Atlanta was a warfare of giants. In the impetuosity, splendid *abandon*, and reckless disregard of danger with which the rebel masses rushed against our lines of fire, of iron, and of cold steel, there had been no parallel during the war, ..."[73]

Cleburne's Arkansas troops had accomplished what Federal General Howard had said was impossible. Howard declared after attacking Cleburne at Kennesaw: "My experience is that a line of works thoroughly constructed, with the front well covered with abatis and other entanglements, well manned with infantry, whether with our own or that of the enemy, cannot be carried by direct assault."[74] Furthermore, pursuant to Hood's plan of general attack by the Army of Tennessee, Cleburne, with Maney's support, had carried the left wing of the Federal army in its breastworks. Attendant upon these achievements, Cleburne's men captured 1,600 prisoners, numerous wagons loaded with ammunition and entrenching tools, mules, artillery horses, several hundred stand of small-arms, eight pieces of artillery, and four stand of colors.[75]

Cleburne's losses in killed, wounded, and missing totaled 1,388, which was more than one-half of his men engaged in the battle.[76] The loss in officers was the heaviest the division had ever sustained — twenty-nine field officers, "of the flower of the army," out of a total of less than forty.[77] Confederate General Smith was again severely wounded.[78] Among those killed were Col. John E. Murray, commander of the 5th Arkansas Regiment; and Lieut. Col. Anderson Watkins of the 8th Arkansas. Colonel Murray died on the enemy's parapet; Colonel Watkins, near the parapet with sword in hand. Cleburne regarded Murray as his most promising officer and had he survived the battle, he would have become a brigadier, as Cleburne was soon to have a vacancy at brigade level. Lieutenant Colonel Watkins, an able officer, was the son of a judge in Little Rock. These two brave young officers from Arkansas, wrapped in one cloak, were buried in the same grave.[79]

Cleburne's phenomenal accomplishments and the sacrifice made by his men were largely in vain. The Confederates did not achieve their objective of driving McPherson's army back to the Chattahoochee. Hood's greatest mistake was in failing to carry out his expressed plan that Cheatham and Stewart would take up the action as soon as Hardee became engaged. True, the battle opened farther to the east than Hood had anticipated, but it was evident that Hardee's corps was meeting with strong opposition. By not ordering the two other corps forward, Hood failed to make a coordinated attack, which was essential to success. He delayed nearly three hours before ordering Cheatham to attack, and Stewart was never committed to action.[80]

On July 23, Captain Key wrote in his diary: "Generals Hardee and Cleburne were up consulting and appeared to be in hesitancy whether to give up the ground that we had gained in the battle. . . . about 10 o'clock a flag of truce was agreed upon to bring off the wounded and bury the dead. . . . in the evening skirmishes began again . . . ." On July 24 Key wrote, "Early this morning, with Generals Hardee and Cleburne, I rode down our newly extended lines, ..."[81]

Following the battle, the major units assigned to Walker, whose division had suffered terrible losses, were reassigned to other Confederate commands. On July 25, Mercer's brigade was assigned to Cleburne. Because of poor health, Mercer was relieved as brigade commander, thus creating a vacancy for Hardee and Cleburne to fill. Granbury meanwhile returned to the division and resumed command of the Texas Brigade.[82]

At dawn on July 27, the Confederates discovered that the Federals had withdrawn from the front of Hardee's corps during the night. This was the beginning of Sherman's departure from the area east of Atlanta. Cleburne's division now moved north of the Georgia Railroad and occupied a mile and a half of the east line of Atlanta's outer fortifications. On a knoll immediately to the rear of the fortifications, Cleburne set up headquarters despite intermittent shelling by the enemy. The large stone house, in a grove of tall oaks at the northwest corner of Chase Street (now Charles Allen Drive) and Pine Street, was the residence of the Gardners, who had "refuged."[83]

NOTES

CHAPTER XV

[1]William T. Sherman, "The Grand Strategy of the Last Year of the War," in *Battles and Leaders*, IV, 253.

[2]F. B. Chilton, *Hood's Texas Brigade: A History & a Confederate Scrap Book* (Houston, 1911), 244; J. P. Hood, *Advance and Retreat*, ed. Richard N. Current (Bloomington, Ind., 1959), 359.

[3]Cox, "Atlanta," 148.

[4]L. H. Mangum, Statement of under heading, "Gen. Pat Cleburne's Life and Death," St. Louis *Missouri Republican*, Sept. 12, 1885, p. 9; Mangum, *Kennesaw Gazette*, II (June 15, 1887), 3.

[5]*O.R.*, XXXVIII, Pt. 3, pp. 733, 748, 752; Buck, Cleburne, 232; Cate (ed.), *Key Diary*, 92.

[6]*O.R.*, XXXVIII, Pt. 3, pp. 543-44; Grenville M. Dodge, *The Battle of Atlanta and Other Campaigns, Addresses, etc.* (Denver, 1965), 40; Buck, *Cleburne*, 232. Wilbur G. Kurtz, who had studied the terrain before Bald Hill was obliterated by steam shovels, gave this description of the hill in conversation with authors, Aug. 17, 1965.

[7]M. F. Force to W. T. Sherman, Aug. 31, 1875, in Sherman, *Memoirs*, II, 526; *O.R.*, XXXVIII, Pt. 3, p. 543; Buck, *Cleburne*, 232.

[8]That McPherson was endeavoring to enter Atlanta, see William E. Strong, "The Death of General James B. McPherson," in Military Order of the Loyal Legion of the United States, *Military Essays and Recollections: Papers Read before the Commandery of the State of Illinois* (Chicago, 1891), I, 314; Gilbert D. Munson, "Battle of Atlanta," in Robert Hunter (ed.), *Papers Prepared for the Ohio Commandery of the Military Order of the Loyal Legion of the United States* (Cincinnati, 1890), III, 312-14.

[9]*O.R.*, XXXVIII, Pt. 3, pp. 750-53. The two regiments were the 17th and 18th Texas Cavalry (dismounted), consolidated; and the 24th and 25th Texas Cavalry (dismounted), consolidated.

[10]*O.R.*, XXXVIII, Pt. 3, p. 752; Cate (ed.), *Key Diary*, 93. The cavalry consisted of W. W. Allen's and Alfred Iverson, Jr.'s brigades of Wheeler's corps, which numbered 1,600 men on July 17; and S. W. Ferguson's brigade of Jackson's division. — *O.R.*, XXXVIII, Pt. 3, pp. 646, 673, 951-52.

[11]*O.R.*, XXXVIII, Pt. 3, p. 699.

[12]Benham, *Kennesaw Gazette*, IV (Oct. 1, 1889), 3; Buck, *Cleburne*, 232-33; *O.R.*, XXXVIII, Pt. 3, pp. 730, 733, 746, 748, 750-51.

[13]*O.R.*, XXXVIII, Pt. 3, p. 746; Benham, *Kennesaw Gazette*, IV (Oct. 1, 1889), 3.

[14]Cate (ed.), *Key Diary*, 93, 101; Munson, "Battle of Atlanta," 215-16;

O.R., XXXVIII, Pt. 3, pp. 20, 746, 751; Lurton Dunham Ingersoll, *Iowa and the Rebellion* (Philadelphia, 1867), 238-39; Strong, "Death of General McPherson," 314-15; Force to Sherman, Aug. 31, 1875, in Sherman, *Memoirs*, II, 526.

[15]Benham, *Kennesaw Gazette*, IV (Oct. 1, 1889), 3; *O.R.*, XXXVIII, Pt. 3, pp. 752, 952; Munson, "Battle of Atlanta, 216, 217; Strong, "Death of General McPherson," 315; Force to Sherman, Aug. 31, 1875, in Sherman, *Memoirs*, II, 526.

[16]*O.R.*, XXXVIII, Pt. 3, pp. 746, 753, 952; Cate (ed.), *Key Diary*, 93; Strong, "Death of General McPherson," 315.

[17]*O.R.*, XXXVIII, Pt. 3, pp. 543-44; Munson, "Battle of Atlanta," 217.

[18]Force to Sherman, Aug. 31, 1875, in Sherman, *Memoirs*, II, 527; *O.R.*, XXXVIII, Pt. 3, pp. 20, 22, 544.

[19]*O.R.*, XXXVIII, Pt. 3, pp. 734, 748-50; Hardee, "Major General Cleburne," 649; Buck, *Cleburne*, 233-34; Benham, *Kennesaw Gazette*, IV (Oct. 1, 1889), 3.

[20]*O.R.*, XXXVIII. Pt. 3, p. 699.

[21]*Ibid.*, p. 543.

[22]Strong, "Death of General McPherson," 316.

[23]*O.R.*, XXXVIII, Pt. 5, p. 899; *ibid.*, Pt. 3, pp. 734, 737, 750; T. B. Roy, "General Hardee and the Military Operations Around Atlanta," *S.H.S.P.*, VIII (1880), 357-58.

[24]Wilbur G. Kurtz, "The Death of Major General W. H. T. Walker, July 22, 1864," *Civil War History*, VI (1960), 176; Kurtz, *Map of Atlanta*; Roy, "General Hardee," 354-55, 365; *O.R.*, XXXVIII, Pt. 3, p. 737.

[25]W. P. Archer, *History of the Battle of Atlanta* (Knoxville, Ga., 1940), 8.

[26]*O.R.*, XXXVIII, Pt. 3, pp. 737, 747; Roy, "General Hardee," 360; Kurtz, "Death of Major General Walker," 176-77, 179.

[27]Wilbur G. Kurtz, *The Atlanta Cyclorama: The Story of the Famed Battle of Atlanta* (Atlanta, 1954), 9; *O.R.*, XXXVIII, Pt. 3, pp. 369, 545, 759; Kurtz, "Death of Major General Walker," 179; Roy, "General Hardee," 361.

[28]*O.R.*, XXXVIII, Pt. 3, pp. 737, 748.

[29]Richard Beard to William E. Strong, date not shown, in Strong, "Death of General McPherson," 336.

[30]*O.R.*, XXXVIII, Pt. 3, pp. 731, 737, 747.

[31]*Ibid.*, p. 738. McPherson anticipated that his left flank would be attacked by Hood that day. — Strong, "Death of General McPherson," 316-20.

[32]Calvin D. Cowles (comp.), *The Official Atlas of the Civil War (to Accompany the Official Records of the Union and Confederate Armies)* (Washington, 1891-95), plate LXI, map 3.

[33]*O.R.*, XXXVIII, Pt. 5, p. 220.

[34]*Ibid.*, Pt. 3, p. 738.

[35]Cate (ed.), *Key Diary*, 94; *O.R.*, XXXVIII, Pt. 3, pp. 581, 738.

[36]Strong, "Death of General McPherson," 316; *O.R.*, XXXVIII, Pt. 3, pp. 371, 385, 738; Richard S. Tuthill, "An Artilleryman's Recollections of The Battle of Atlanta," in Military Order of the Loyal Legion of the United States, *Military Essays and Recollections: Papers Read before the Commandery of the State of Illinois* (Chicago, 1891), I, 302.

[37]Tuthill, "Battle of Atlanta," 302; *O.R.*, XXXVIII, Pt. 3, pp. 582, 738-39; Govan to Dunn, Dec. 16, 1878, in Hempstead, *Historical Review of Arkansas*, I, 245-46; Wm. W. Belknap to Govan, Sept. 2, 1878, in Govan Papers.

[38]*O.R.*, XXXVIII, Pt. 3, pp. 23-24.

[39]*Ibid.*, p. 738; Munson, "Battle of Atlanta," 222; Tuthill, "Battle of Atlanta," 301-02.

[40]*O.R.*, XXXVIII, Pt. 3, pp. 747, 750; Strong, "Death of General McPherson," 319, 325-31; "Incidents of Gen. McPherson's Death," *Confederate Veteran*, XI (1903), 118-19; Govan to Belknap, Dec. 15, 1878, in "Crocker's Iowa Brigade," *The Veteran*, I (1882), 11; *cf.* Frazer, "Fifth Confederate," 151. Generals McPherson, Logan, and Blair, and staffs had just finished lunch three-quarters of a mile behind their main line when they heard the firing that signaled the beginning of the conflict. McPherson immediately gave orders to meet the crisis; and took position near the south end of the 16th Corps' line, where he witnessed the assaults by Walker's and Bate's divisions. Following the failure of these attacks, McPherson was en route to the left of Giles Smith's line when he met the Confederate skirmishers. — Strong, "Death of General McPherson," 320-25.

[41]Benham, *Kennesaw Gazette*, IV (Oct. 15, 1889), 2.

[42]*O.R.*, XXXVIII, Pt. 3, p. 370; Georgia Civil War Historical Marker, East Side Ave., south of McPherson Ave. (written by Wilbur G. Kurtz); Tuthill, "Battle of Atlanta," 302-03.

[43]*O.R.*, XXXVIII, Pt. 3, pp. 546, 747, 750.

[44]Force to Sherman, Aug. 31, 1875, in Sherman, *Memoirs*, II, 527; Munson, "Battle of Atlanta," 219, 223; *O.R.*, XXXVIII, Pt. 3, p. 23; Tuthill, "Battle of Atlanta," 298, 303-04.

[45]*O.R.*, XXXVIII, Pt. 3, pp. 23, 546, 564, 731, 747.

[46]Tuthill, "Battle of Atlanta," 304-05.

[47]*Ibid., O.R.*, XXXVIII, Pt. 3, pp. 564-65, 730, 732, 747, 750-53.

[48]*O.R.*, XXXVIII, Pt. 3, pp. 546, 582, 748-49.

[49]Benham, *Kennesaw Gazette*, IV (Oct. 15, 1889), 2; *O.R.*, XXXVIII, Pt. 3, pp. 546, 582.

[50]Cate (ed.), *Key Diary*, 96.

[51]Wilbur G. Kurtz, conversation with authors, Aug. 8, 1962. Mr. Kurtz

stated that he had interviewed, separately, two men who had seen Hood there.

[52]*Cf. O.R.*, XXXVIII, Pt. 3, pp. 25, 779, 787.

[53]*Ibid.*, pp. 25, 546, 565.

[54]*Ibid.*, pp. 731-32.

[55]*Ibid.*, pp. 25-26, 546-47, 819; Tuthill, "Battle of Atlanta," 306; Munson, "Battle of Atlanta," 225.

[56]*O.R.*, XXXVIII, Pt. 3, pp. 547, 732-33.

[57]*Ibid.*, pp. 582-83.

[58]*Ibid.*, p. 732.

[59]*Ibid.*, pp. 547, 583, 732, 739, 749-50, 752, 754, 759. Mercer had taken over Walker's command. — Kurtz, *Atlanta Cyclorama*, 9.

[60]*O.R.*, XXXVIII, Pt. 5, pp. 547-48, 759.

[61]Sam R. Watkins, *"Co. Aytch"* (Reprint; Jackson, Tenn., 1952), 177.

[62]*O.R.*, XXXVIII, Pt. 3, p. 739; Munson, "Battle of Atlanta," 228; Force to Sherman, Aug. 31, 1875, in Sherman, *Memoirs*, II, 527.

[63]Munson, "Battle of Atlanta," 222-26.

[64]*Ibid.*, 220, 226; *O.R.*, XXXVIII, Pt. 3, pp. 27, 583; Frank P. Blair to J. E. Austin, Feb. 1875, in Hood, *Advance and Retreat*, 189; Munson, "Battle of Atlanta," 230; Cate (ed.), *Key Diary*, 102.

[65]*O.R.*, XXXVIII, Pt. 3, p. 547.

[66]*Ibid.*, pp. 583, 731, 749, 750, 752; Munson, "Battle of Atlanta," 226-27.

[67]*O.R.*, XXXVIII, Pt. 3, p. 740.

[68]Munson, "Battle of Atlanta," 228.

[69]*O.R.*, XXXVIII, Pt. 5, p. 232.

[70]*Ibid.*, Pt. 3, p. 371; Dodge, *Battle of Atlanta*, 49; *cf.* Munson, "Battle of Atlanta," 228-29.

[71]*O.R.*, XXXVIII, Pt. 3, pp. 548, 740, 754; Buck, *Cleburne*, 241; Cate (ed.), *Key Diary*, 99.

[72]*O.R.*, XXXVIII, Pt. 3, p. 699.

[73]Ingersoll, *Iowa and the Rebellion*, 261.

[74]*O.R.*, XXXVIII, Pt. 1, p. 199; Hardee, "Major General Cleburne," 649.

[75]Benham, *Kennesaw Gazette*, IV (Oct. 15, 1889), 2; *O.R.*, XXXVIII, Pt. 3, pp. 735, 740, 747, 749, 750, 751-52; Cate (ed.), *Key Diary*, 98-99.

[76]*O.R.*, XXXVIII, Pt. 3, pp. 733, 741, 748. Govan had 772 men in the battle (*ibid.*, p. 741); Lowrey had about 1,156 in his charge (*ibid.*, pp. 732-33); J. A. Smith's report does not give his effective total, but 3 of his 6 regiments totaled only 361 effectives (*ibid.*, pp. 731, 749, 751).

[77]Benham, *Kennesaw Gazette*, IV (Oct. 15, 1889), 2; Buck, *Cleburne*, 243.

[78]*O.R.*, XXXVIII, Pt. 3, p. 747.

[79]*Ibid.*, p. 739; Benham, *Kennesaw Gazette*, IV (Oct. 15, 1889), 2; Cate (ed.), *Key Diary*, 98.

[80]Buck, *Cleburne*, 234, 241, 242; Roy, "General Hardee," 361; Hay, "Atlanta Campaign," 41-43; Kurtz, *Atlanta Cyclorama*, 10; Henry, *Confederacy*, 392; *O.R.*, XXXVIII, Pt. 3, pp. 872, 926.

[81]Cate (ed.), *Key Diary*, 98-99.

[82]*O.R.*, XXXVIII, Pt. 3, p. 759; Buck, *Cleburne*, 246, 247; Roy, "General Hardee," 367; "Hugh Weedon Mercer," in Warner, *Generals in Gray*, 217.

[83]Buck, *Cleburne*, 247; *O.R.*, XXXVIII, Pt. 3, pp. 734-35; Cate (ed.), *Key Diary*, 102-03; Kurtz to authors, Feb. 4, 1966; Kurtz, *Map of Atlanta* (where Charles Allen Drive is shown under a former name, Parkway Drive).

CHAPTER XVI

SIEGE OF ATLANTA – JONESBORO CAMPAIGN
(July 28 – September 8, 1864)

By night and day, a weary way
Of vigil and of fight, ...
— Francis Oray Ticknor, "Loyal (To General Cleburne)."

The siege of Atlanta comprised the period of twenty-eight days following the battle of Ezra Church, where the Confederates, attacking at a disadvantage, had met with a sanguinary defeat on July 28, 1864. The church was a little more than a mile west of the Confederate fortifications surrounding Atlanta. Here, Hood had thrown three divisions of Stephen D. Lee's and Stewart's corps against the flank of the Federal 15th Corps. Former cavalry commander Lee had succeeded Cheatham as the commander of Hood's old corps.

At the beginning of the siege of Atlanta, the Federal army lay in an arc three-quarters of a mile north, and a mile west, of the city's fortifications. From the west wall of the fortifications, a Confederate hastily built line of entrenchments extended southwestward for about four miles. The line was about two miles west of and roughly paralleled the railroads leading to Alabama and south Georgia. These two railroads used a common right of way from Atlanta to East Point, six miles southwest of the city. At East Point, the Atlanta & West Point Railway continued southwestward; and the Macon & Western veered south, passing through Jonesboro, fifteen miles below East Point.

On August 3, Cleburne's division, "relieved from the ditches," bivouacked on the southwest side of Atlanta, near Hood's headquarters on Ashby Street. Four days later, Cleburne's "gallant band of men" entrenched at the extreme left of the Confederate line, with no Union troops in their immediate front. Cleburne established headquarters in the rear of his division at Baugh's House on the Sandtown Road. He selected his picket-line and stationed batteries at points of vantage.[1]

On August 10, Cleburne was notified by a letter from Col. D. H. Smith, commander of John Morgan's cavalry division, that his brother Christopher had been killed three months earlier in the battle of Cloyd's Farm, near Dublin, Virginia. Colonel Smith had written immediately upon learning that his adjutant had failed to notify Cleburne. In the battle at Cloyd's Farm, 2,400 Confederates were defeated by 6,500 Federals. As the Confederates were retreating, 400 of Morgan's dismounted cavalry, including Christopher Cleburne, reached the field, about 2 miles north of Dublin, and rendered valuable service by retarding the Federal pursuit. Described by Colonel Smith as one of the most efficient and promising officers in the command, Captain Cleburne fell while "gallantly leading his company."

About six weeks before receiving Colonel Smith's letter, Cleburne heard that Chris had been killed in a raid by Morgan into Kentucky. Upon receipt of that news Cleburne expressed his grief to Hardee but evidently waited for official confirmation before notifying the family.[2] Enclosing Colonel Smith's letter, Cleburne wrote to his brother Robert:

Atlanta Georgia 10th Augt 64

Dear Robert

I have just received the sad news that Captain Chris Cleburne was killed in action at Dublin Depot on the East Ten & Va Rail Road. My informant states he was killed May 9th 1864 leading a charge. Chris's grave has been substantially enclosed, carefully sodded and marked with his name. It is at or near Dublin Depot and a head board erected over it contains not only his name but his Regiment, date of his death, and the inscription "Dulce et decorum est pro patria mori." [It is sweet and glorious to die for one's country.[3]] Some kind ladies of the neighborhood have promised to plant over it appropriate flowers and to make its care their grateful charge. I have written to find the particulars of his death. The moment I get them I will forward to you. This is not the time or place, Robert, to tell you all I feel about my young brother's death. I cannot say however that I was surprised to hear it. His ardent, fearless self-sacrificing nature made me anticipate such a result. He had just been promoted from Pt to Captain and this was his

first battle in that capacity. Give my love to all and believe me
Your brother
P R Cleburne[4]

On August 11, hearing that the Federals intended to attack the Confederate left and take the railroad leading into Atlanta, Hardee wrote his wife, "Cleburne occupies the extreme left, and I would like nothing better."[5] Sherman did not attack but began extending his lines from Ezra Church eastward and southward toward the Confederate line. Anticipating that the enemy would try to take East Point, Hood ordered Thomas M. Scott's brigade from W. W. Loring's division of Stewart's corps to report to Cleburne. This brigade and some pioneers assisted Cleburne's division in constructing a fishhook on their line, to the southeast about a mile below East Point.[6] Meanwhile, with a strong picket-line posted, scouts out, and reports from cavalry, Cleburne maintained an active vigil for an enemy attack on East Point, protecting his line by abatis and artillery. Despite these safeguards, he was apprehensive because his long line was held by so few men.[7] However, no fighting occurred except for light picket skirmishing and brief artillery firing.[8] On occasions when Hardee went to Atlanta or East Point, he placed Cleburne in temporary command of the corps.[9]

On August 20, Cleburne moved his headquarters to a house immediately southwest of East Point. The next day his scouts captured a Union lieutenant, an aide to Gen. J. D. Cox. When the young officer was brought to headquarters, Cleburne invited him to share his mess, "such as it was," before sending him to the prisoner's confine in the rear. During the night the Lieutenant was robbed of his hat, boots, and blanket. Upon learning of the theft, Cleburne ordered a search for the culprit and the stolen articles, which proved fruitless. He then sent one of his own hats and one of his two blankets to the Federal officer.[10]

The only inspection report extant of Cleburne's division as a separate unit was dated "East Point Ga August 25th 1864." The report stated: "The material of which this command is composed [is] of the very best. Mostly Young & active men — the first to enter the Confed. Service. The officers of Lowrey's, Govan's & Granbury's Brigades are intelligent, prompt, active and efficient, & perform all duties required of them well & with alacrity." The report mentioned the "recently attached" Mercer's brigade as "composed of good material" but most of its officers had had "very little experience in the Field." The report adverted to the "difficulties . . . in procuring clothing." It noted that, "The Military appearance of both officers & men, as well as their comfort would be greatly improved if *soap* could be *supplied*." There had been no soap for nearly a month.[11]

On August 26, Sherman terminated the siege by withdrawing his forces north and west of Atlanta for the purpose of capturing the railroads to Alabama and south Georgia. Thereby he would sever the western railway from the southern railway and cut off the Confederate army from both. Then Hood would be forced to evacuate the city and possibly surrender his army.

O. O. Howard, successor to McPherson as commander of the Army of the Tennessee, marched his three corps westward to the valley of the Chattahoochee. Then he swung southward via Sandtown nine miles west of East Point, heading for Shadnor Church and Fairburn on the West Point Railroad, nine and eleven miles southwest of East Point. In a shorter swing, Thomas with the 4th and 14th Corps of his Army of the Cumberland, followed Howard, heading for Red Oak, six and a half miles southwest of East Point. A sixth corps under John M. Schofield lagged behind as a rear guard. The one corps of Sherman's entire three armies not participating in these movements — the 20th of the Cumberland Army — marched 'back to the railroad bridge across the Chattahoochee to guard his supply lines.

The Confederate army no longer had a commander with the acumen to discern Sherman's purpose and to thwart it. Hood could have struck the enemy while in motion or could have placed Lee's and Stewart's corps in line west of Fairburn and Red Oak before the Federals reached the West Point Railroad.[12] Hood misconceived the situation, believing that Wheeler, then on an expedition in rear of Sherman's lines, had destroyed twenty-five miles of railroad between Marietta and the Tennessee border. He also thought that Sherman,

371

bereft of supplies, was about to cross the Chattahoochee at the railroad bridge and at Sandtown, in full retreat.[13] Actually, Wheeler had succeeded in destroying only about three miles of track and Sherman was not seriously affected. By August 17 the tracks were repaired and the trains were running again.

On the evening of the 28th, the Federal armies of Howard and Thomas reached the West Point Railway and spent the next day demolishing it between Fairburn and Red Oak. The morning of the 30th, these two armies set out for Jonesboro, thirteen and a half miles away, to seize and destroy the only remaining railroad entering Atlanta.

In spite of Hardee's insistence that the Macon & Western Railroad should be protected at Jonesboro against Sherman's legions, Hood did not recognize that peril and could not believe that the Federals would be there in force. Despite his awareness that the Yankees were near the West Point Railway at Shadnor Church and Fairburn, Hood on the 28th sent only two infantry brigades to Jonesboro. These brigades (Reynold's of Stewart's corps and the Kentucky Orphan Brigade of Bate's division), in Hood's language, were to cooperate with a cavalry brigade in "repelling raids."[14] On the 29th Hood did nothing further to protect Jonesboro, although he was informed by Hardee that certainly five, and perhaps six, Federal corps were on the West Point Railroad. Also on that date, Confederate cavalry scouts in the Jonesboro area knew that heavy enemy infantry forces, estimated at 40,000 men, were nearing the town.[15] As late as 1 P. M. on August 30, Hood's chief of staff telegraphed Hardee: "General Hood does not think the necessity will arise to send any more troops to Jonesborough to-day." Twenty minutes later, the same officer wired General William H. Jackson: "General Hood does not think there can be a large force advancing upon Jonesborough."[16]

Hood suspected that Sherman might be massing forces to attack the environs of Atlanta from the southwest. Hence, the afternoon of August 30, Cleburne was sent an order to move three miles to a ridge south of East Point, between the two railroads, and to begin temporary works as protection against a Union advance on the Macon Railroad. To

Cleburne's left, the rest of Bate's division (in command of John C. Brown), extended the line of Hardee's corps as far as Rough and Ready, a settlement on the Macon Road four and a half miles below East Point. When Hood's order reached Cleburne, he was dictating a reply to a letter just received from the ladies of Dublin, Virginia, concerning their care of Chris' grave. This unfinished letter was destroyed sometime later when the Yankees seized and burned his desk.[17]

On the 30th, a dispatch from Hardee at Rough and Ready reached Hood at 3:15 P. M., at his headquarters in Atlanta. Now, Hood was convinced that the enemy was moving upon Jonesboro but insisted that Sherman had sent only two corps. He immediately summoned Hardee and S. D. Lee for a conference in his headquarters at 9 o'clock that night. The conference resulted in Hardee being directed to command an expedition to Jonesboro consisting of Lee's corps and his own (commanded by Cleburne) to attack the Federals. Hardee went by train from Atlanta to Jonesboro while Cleburne marched the corps southward, the rear of the command getting in motion about 11:30 P. M. S. D. Lee apparently traveled by train and joined his corps at East Point.[18]

The corps commanded by Cleburne set out on a dirt road from East Point to Jonesboro. Below Rough and Ready, the railroad swung eastward in an arc, coming back in line with the dirt road at the outskirts of Jonesboro. Brown's division led, followed by Cleburne's division (commanded by Lowrey) and Maney's division. Following Maney was Anderson's division of Lee's corps. The weary troops, unconditioned for marching after spending weeks in the trenches, plodded along the dusty, unfamiliar road in heat and darkness.[19]

Three miles from Jonesboro, Brown, anxious about a reconnoitering party which had not returned, halted his division and rode forward to ascertain if the road was clear. Cleburne and his staff overtook Brown in time to receive a volley from enemy pickets posted on a bridge across Moker's Creek a short distance farther down the road. Immediately beyond the ridge a Federal contingent was entrenched.[20] Rather than risk a night battle with large Federal forces close at hand, Cleburne decided to have his corps and Anderson's division detour by a lane, a mile and a half to the east, leading into a road abutting on the railroad. Considerable delay ensued when Cleburne ordered the stretched-out line of tired soldiers to close up before entering the lane. Meanwhile the Confederates discovered that to their right, beyond a low wooded ridge, a large body of the Federals was marching for Jonesboro. Cleburne was gravely concerned because a pitched battle might have meant the loss of his artillery and trains. However, the Federals did not attack and the Confederates proceeded safely along the lane and the road skirting the railroad. The head of Cleburne's column reached Jonesboro just before dawn on August 31. Later in the morning, most of S. D. Lee's corps arrived, having traveled another route. Cleburne's and Lee's troops were a welcome sight to the small beleagured Confederate force guarding the town.[21]

2

The Macon Railroad ran through the center of Jonesboro, paralleling the main street. About a mile and a half to the west, parallel to the railroad, was the Flint River.

Early in the evening on the 30th, the 15th Corps of Howard's Federal army had crossed the Flint River; proceeded to the top of a ridge a half mile west of Jonesboro; and entrenched, facing east. Howard had stationed his 16th Corps just west of the river; and his 17th, within supporting distance. About the same time, the two corps of Thomas' army and Schofield's 23rd Corps were in position northwest of Jonesboro ready to advance on the railroad.

Early in the morning of the 31st, most of the Federal 16th Corps crossed the river and formed a line, facing south, from the stream to the south end of the 15th Corps. The Federal 17th Corps moved to the left of the 15th and faced northeast.

About 9 A. M. on the 31st, Cleburne stationed half of his command in line west of the railroad, facing the Federal 15th Corps; and placed the rest of his command southeast of the Federal 16th Corps. Early in the afternoon, he had the troops just west of the railroad join those southeast of the 16th Corps. Beginning a half mile southeast from the angle formed by the Federal 15th and 16th Corps, Cleburne's line extended southwesterly for three-quarters of a mile. Lee's corps took position just west of the railroad, facing the Federal 15th Corps and continuing the Confederate line a mile northward.[22] Three brigades of Lee's corps which had been on picket duty joined the line at 1:30 in the afternoon.

Hardee made these dispositions in carrying out Hood's order from Atlanta that he "must attack and drive the enemy across the river."[23] Since the Federals were in full control of the battlefield area when the Confederates arrived, Hardee and Cleburne had no opportunity to reconnoiter and examine the terrain, most of which was covered by timber or brush.[24] Although they did not know how near the river Howard's lower flank extended, Hardee's plan of assault called for Cleburne to advance in a wheel to the right and turn the enemy's flank. Lee would attack Howard's front when Cleburne "had hotly engaged the enemy at close range."[25]

About 3:30 o'clock, the corps commanded by Cleburne moved forward; his own division, under Lowrey's command, on the left; Brown's, on the right; and Maney's, in reserve. Lowrey came upon a brigade of dismounted Federal cavalry, posted behind rail barricades, 300 yards from the river, guarding a bridge.[26] The Union brigade opened on the Confederates with rifle fire and two batteries, one of which was on a hill west of the river. Granbury's and Lowrey's brigades charged through an open field and routed the Federals, Key's three batteries giving effective support. A Union cavalry officer later reported that Cleburne's division "furiously assaulted" the works.[27] A temporary stand was made by a few Federals behind a second line of barricades before following their comrades in retreat across the river.

In order to maintain the wheel to the right, Cleburne had directed that none of his forces cross the river. But a colonel in Granbury's brigade, exercising justifiable discretion, crossed the stream with a battalion to drive the Union battery from the hill, which was continuing to fire on the Confederates. In the exuberance of the pursuit, Lowrey's and Mercer's brigades followed the Texans, and did not stop until they had gained the Union position across the river. The Federal battery with its supports fled, but a half hour elapsed before the enthusiastic Confederates could be withdrawn and realigned on the east bank of the river.[28]

Meanwhile, Maney directed his division to move forward rapidly to take up the slack in the right wheel and close in on Brown's left. Cleburne rode up to Maney, approved the movement, and then galloped off to hasten Lowrey's main attack.[29] When Brown's regiments had driven north to a point about fifty yards from the enemy's main works, they fired their muskets and started a rush to "give the Yanks the cold steel." Regimental Sergt. Maj. Johnny Green, in the Orphan Brigade of Kentucky Confederates, related the following in his journal:

> . . . horrow of horrows! just as we have fired the volley at them & begin to rush on them we come to a deep gully ten feet wide & fully as deep. No one can jump this gully & at this close range it will be impossible to clamber up the other side of the gully & reform to rush on them with fixed bayonets. The shot & shell & minnie balls are decimating our ranks. Forward we rush. The order is given, "Jump into the ditch!" for there we will for a time be out of range of their guns & although the walls of this ditch are so precipitious that we cannot climb out on the other side & renew the assault upon them we are forced to take this shelter & then move out by the flank & withdraw to our former position.[30]

Some of Brown's units did not go into the ravine, which extended westward to the river, but withdrew 300 yards to a woods and reformed. Before learning of the ravine, Cleburne had sent a dispatch to Maney ordering him to swing his whole division to the right and "attack the enemy in flank or rear."[31] Because of the strength of the Union position and since one brigade of his division had not come up, Maney chose not to attempt to carry out the order. That night, Maney was relieved from command of the division and replaced by Brig. Gen. John C. Carter.[32]

Meanwhile, when S. D. Lee heard the rapid discharge of artillery and small arms exchanged between Lowrey and the Federal cavalry, he thought that Cleburne had attacked the main works. Lee's corps accordingly advanced against the "blazing front" of Howard's army to within sixty yards of the breastworks. Unable to hold its position, the corps was driven back with heavy losses. Lee's troops were not able to renew their attack and were threatened with a counterattack by Howard. Therefore, Hardee sent an order to Cleburne to make no further attempt to take the Union works and to send a division to support Lee. Cleburne ordered his (Hardee's) Corps to return to its starting position and sent Lowrey to report to Lee. En route Lowrey was halted by Hardee because the fighting had ceased.[33]

3

On the afternoon of August 31, just prior to the battle of Jonesboro, General Schofield's Federal corps began destruction of the Macon Railroad at Rough and Ready. Soon afterward, a corps of Thomas' army began destroying the railroad between Jonesboro and Rough and Ready, working southward.

When news of the seizure of the railroad reached Hood, he again misjudged the situation. Still unable to accept the fact that the Federals were in force at Jonesboro, and believing that Sherman had massed troops in the vicinity of East Point for an attack on Atlanta,[34] Hood dispatched a message to Hardee at 6 P. M. by courier, calling for reinforcements for the Atlanta garrison. After midnight, Hardee was surprised to receive the following message:

> General Hood directs that you return Lee's corps to this place. Let it march by 2 o'clock to-morrow morning [September 1] . . . . Please return Reynolds' brigade, and, if you think you can do so . . ., send back a brigade or so of your corps also. There are some indications that the enemy may make an attempt on Atlanta to-morrow.[35]

Reluctantly, Hardee dispatched Lee's corps as ordered, leaving him with only one small corps to resist six Federal corps, commanded by Sherman in person. In the emergency, Cleburne and Hardee worked together in commanding the corps, with Lowrey continuing to command Cleburne's division. Knowing that destruction of the railroad lines would force Hood to leave Atlanta, Hardee and Cleburne proposed to make a stand throughout the day of September 1, determined to bring about the safe retreat of Stewart's and Lee's corps.[36]

At 1:30 A.M. on September 1, Hardee deployed his corps to cover the space vacated by Lee and extended the line northward. The long Confederate defense line terminated more than a mile north of Jonesboro at a point 450 yards west of the railroad. Cleburne's division held the northern end of the line, with Govan on the right and Granbury on the left. After daylight, amid shelling and sharpshooting, Govan constructed a salient, bending from the end of the main line eastward and extending 150 yards toward the railroad.[37]

During the forenoon, Thomas' army had moved south toward Jonesboro and D. S. Stanley's (4th) corps had destroyed the railroad. Sherman, early in the afternoon, having learned of S. D. Lee's departure, ordered Thomas to smash the Confederate's one remaining corps. Jefferson C. Davis' (14th) corps, near at hand, was to turn the Confederate right flank, and Stanley's corps was to join the fight after it reached the field.

Hardee, on reconnaissance accompanied by cavalry, discovered that Davis was moving to turn his right flank. Cleburne and Hardee withdrew the Orphan Brigade along with three other brigades from the south portion of the main line, and rapidly moved them to connect with Govan. It was "absolutely necessary" for Lowrey to improvise a new line by moving his division to a better position on a ridge. Beginning at a point on the salient about 100 yards from the main line, the new line of crude works extended southeast across the railroad. The sharp angle where the new line took off from the salient was a particularly vulnerable point.[38]

Goven's right regiment moved from the salient to the new line, with the Orphan Brigade taking position between Govan and the railroad, and the three other brigades extending the refused line. The entire line was thinly manned, in a single rank, with Granbury's and Govan's troops a yard apart; and the men in the Orphan Brigade, two yards apart.[39] Unfortunately, the converging fire of the Union artillery prevented the Confederates from destroying the abandoned part of the salient, which later afforded shelter for the Federals.[40]

At 3 P.M. on September 1, the first division of Davis' corps, having arrived on the battlefield, advanced toward the salient. Govan's brigade of veterans, supported by Key's and

Swett's batteries, met the charge with deadly fire, compelling the enemy to retreat with heavy loss. The Orphan Brigade fired a volley and then attacked with bayonets, forcing the Yankees to fall back. The Federals, bringing to bear overwhelming power, moved up three additional batteries west and north of the main Confederate line. They made "a net-work of crossing fire" in the space behind the angle,[41] some of the shells falling in the refused line.[42]

Before making a second assault, Davis, under Sherman's eye, strengthened his force by adding a new division; and from a reserve division, replaced a brigade that had been "used up" by Govan.[43] At 4:45 P.M., solid lines of bluecoats, advancing from three positions, in a broad attack, charged the entire front of Govan's brigade and that of the Orphan Brigade, and part of Granbury's brigade.[44] Four Federal brigades alone converged on Govan's front.[45]

Heroically holding their ground, the Confederate infantry and artillery fired steadily upon the advancing enemy.[46] Benham described the action:

> Moving with volume and power, like succeeding waves, the masses of blue came on, confident, too, as the sea, but only to be broken in turn against the moveless palisade of our living front. Our imperfect works were of little use to us. But they still came, the will directing that mighty flood, constant to its purpose, moving it unremittingly on. It was more than man could do to resist it long; death had no appreciable effect upon those exhaustless masses. The ground was strewn with dead, its entire color changed, it was carpeted with blue.[47]

Benham said of the Orphan Brigade: "The little band of Kentuckians, now wasted by the wild ravages of war from a full brigade to a mere handful — they were not enough for a battalion — sustained the reputation of their proud and noble commonwealth .... Cleburne's Division will never forget who stood upon their flank that day."[48]

Finally, without time to reload their guns, the Confederate infantry fought with clubbed muskets and at the point of the bayonet. The batteries of Key and Swett, although the wheels of their gun carriages had been destroyed by Federal counter-battery fire, continued to operate until the Yankees were within ten steps of their guns. The enemy swarmed over the vulnerable angle; and advanced through timber down the rear of the main line, swinging west in the rear of Govan's brigade and east in the rear of the Orphan Brigade.

The gallant Govan, with 600 of his command, most of Key's and Swett's batteries with their 8 pieces of artillery, and part of the Orphan Brigade, were forced to surrender. The remainder of Govan's command and the Orphan Brigade fell back 150 yards to a new position.

After this flanking movement, Granbury immediately started to throw back his line perpendicular to the main line in an effort to stem the Federal advance. Hardee, arriving at the scene of action, rode into the line to rally Granbury's troops, thinking they had given way. Surrounded by heavy fire, Granbury demanded immediate vindication: "General, my men never fall back unless ordered back!" When Lowrey, coming on the scene, assured Granbury that his right would be protected, the Texan returned his men to their original position. The remaining part of Govan's brigade charged but was unable to recover the works taken by the Federals.

Shortly before the break in the Confederate line, Cleburne ordered up Brig. Gen. George W. Gordon's brigade of Carter's division from the southern part of the main line and dispatched Buck to find out where it was most needed. Struck in the leg by a minié ball, Buck returned to his chief still astride his horse. He explained that although he was wounded he would conduct the brigade to its position. However, the General sent Buck to the rear and took charge of the brigade himself. Cleburne rushed Gordon's brigade toward the Federals in the woods south of the captured works; and with the assistance of Govan's men who had not been captured, drove back the bluecoats, holding them in Govan's previously abandoned trenches.[49]

Cleburne then ordered additional batteries brought up and stopped the Federal onslaught with heavy artillery and infantry fire.[50] When Stanley's Federal corps arrived at the battle area, Confederate skirmish lines and man-made entanglements prevented his force from assaulting the refused line east of the railroad before darkness ended the fight.

In the battle of September 1, the Confederates exacted a

toll of 1,272 Federal casualties. General Hardee, referring to the battle in his sketch of Cleburne, said: "The odds were fearful, and the contest . . . was a very trying one; but the position was held against the attacks made upon it through the day . . . . Cleburne's services were highly valuable in the operations of this day."[51] Hardee, having gained his objective of delaying the Federal advance, during the night moved to Lovejoy Station, four miles south of Jonesboro; and escaped encirclement by Sherman's forces. Cleburne covered the retreat of the army.[52]

About midnight, explosions of ammunition and flames from burning ordnance told the tired troops that Hood was departing from Atlanta. Regarding the action at Jonesboro and the loss of Atlanta, Hardee expressed these sound conclusions:

> The fall of Atlanta does not date from the result of the battle of Jonesborough, but from General Hood's misconception of his adversary's plans.
>
> After the 30th of August General Hood's whole plan of operations was based upon the hypothesis that Sherman was moving only a detachment to Jonesborough, whereas in reality he was moving his army. He [Hood] divided his forces to attack a concentrated enemy. He in effect sent a detachment of his army to attack an enemy who was superior in numbers to his whole army.
>
> Had it been possible with two corps to dislodge three corps of the enemy from a chosen position on the 31st, I should still have had to meet three fresh corps on the following morning with my own corps alone, for be it remembered that Lee's corps was withdrawn by General Hood before he knew the result of the fight on the 31st.
>
> The fate of Atlanta was sealed from the moment when General Hood allowed an enemy superior in numbers to pass unmolested around his flank and plant himself firmly upon his only line of railroad. If, after the enemy reached Jonesborough, General Hood had attacked him with his whole army instead of with a part of it, he could not reasonably have expected to drive from that position an army before which his own had been for four months retiring in the open field.[53]

Early the morning of September 2, Hardee's corps constructed entrenchments north of Lovejoy. In the afternoon, Cleburne's division repulsed an attack on their line, a mile northeast of the settlement.[54] On September 3 and 4, Stewart's and S. D. Lee's corps joined Hardee's. Two days later, Sherman began withdrawing to his prize, Atlanta; and on September 8, Hardee's corps reoccupied Jonesboro. The armies maintained a truce from September 11 to 22 and prisoners were exchanged. The men of Govan's and the Orphan Brigades who had been captured on September 1, returned to their respective units.

On September 18, the Army of Tennessee began marching toward Palmetto, a town twenty miles west of Jonesboro. The army went into camp two days later, with Hood establishing his headquarters at Palmetto. Cleburne's division encamped five miles northeast of the town.[55]

On September 25, President Davis arrived in Palmetto, greatly concerned about the state of affairs. Adding to his problems was the bitterness existing between Hardee and Hood. Hardee had repeatedly requested release from serving under Hood but had remained at the insistence of the President. Hood had urged Davis to remove Hardee, blaming him for the army's misfortunes (except Ezra Church) since Hood had assumed command of the Army of Tennessee. He asked that Cheatham replace Hardee. Davis manifestly promised to comply with Hood's requests; and Cleburne, the logical successor to Hardee, was eliminated from consideration as commander of the corps. Knowing that Cleburne considered the removal of Johnston and the appointment of Hood as a "disaster" to the army and the Confederacy, the relationship between Hood and Cleburne was strained.[56] Davis was beginning to realize the wisdom of Cleburne's proposal for enlisting Negroes as soldiers. Embarrased by his mistake in rejecting the plan, Davis stubbornly refused to recognize Cleburne's ability by promotion to corps commander.

On September 28, the day after leaving Palmetto, Davis telegraphed formal instructions to Hood for Hardee's release and assignment to command the Department of South Carolina, Georgia, and Florida. Immediately, Cheatham was promoted to corps commander. Eliminating Hardee and Cleburne — the generals best fitted to command the corps — "was to cost Hood and his cause, dearly" in the Tennessee campaign that lay ahead.[57] Cleburne, "grieved and distressed" by Hardee's departure, said in substance, "that but for his division, which was now the only tie that bound him to that army, he would apply for service in Hardee's new command, even if he had to resign his commission as Major-General and accept a position on Hardee's staff."[58]

NOTES

CHAPTER XVI

[1]Cate (ed.), *Key Diary*, 111, 112, 114; *O.R.*, XXXVIII, Pt. 3, p. 720.

[2]D. Howard Smith to Cleburne, July 27, 1864, in possession of Charles Cleburne Jordan; *O.R.*, XXXVII, Pt. 1, pp. 66-68; Milton W. Humphries, "The Battle at Cloyd's Farm," *Confederate Veteran,* XVII (1909), 598-99; Hardee to his wife, June 24, 1864, in Hardee Papers, Ala. Arch. and Hist.

[3]Horace, *Odes* — Book III, Ode 2, line 13.

[4]Cleburne to his half brother Robert, Aug. 10, 1864, in possession of Charles Cleburne Jordan.

[5]Hardee to his wife, Aug. 12, 1864, in Hardee Papers, Ala. Arch. and Hist.

[6]*O.R.*, XXXVIII, Pt. 5, pp. 951, 957-58, 967, 973; Wilbur G. Kurtz, "The Jonesboro Campaign," paper read at Atlanta Civil War round table, June 18, 1957 (mimeo. copy, gift to authors by Mr. Kurtz), 1.

[7]Roy to Cleubrne, Aug. 2, 11, 17, and 19, 1864; L. Hoxton to Buck, Aug. 14, 1864; Shoup to Cleburne, Aug. 19, 1864 — MSS in Communications to and from Cleburne's Division, pp. 218, 232, 235, 242, 254, 258; *O.R.*, XXXVIII, Pt. 5, pp. 973, 982, 984-86; Cate (ed.), *Key Diary*, 116; Hardee to his wife, Aug. 18, 1862, in Hardee Papers, Ala. Arch. and Hist.

[8]Cate (ed.), *Key Diary*, 114, 117; *O.R.*, XXXVIII, Pt. 5, pp. 455, 954, 976.

[9]Replies to dispatches received by Hardee's corps, Aug. 16, 1864; Roy to Cleburne, Aug. 18, 1864 — MSS in Communications to and from Cleburne's Division, pp. 238, 240, 249.

[10]*O.R.*, XXXVIII, Pt. 5, p. 976; Buck, *Cleburne*, 249; Hardee, "Major General Cleburne," 651; Hardee to his wife, Aug. 21, 1864, in Hardee Papers, Ala. Arch. and Hist.

[11]Inspection Report of Cleburne's Division, Hardee's Corps, Aug. 25, 1864, 8-H-14, RG 109, NA.

[12]*O.R.*, XXXVIII, Pt. 3, p. 700; A. A. Hoehling, *Last Train from Atlanta* (New York, 1958), 507; Cox, "Atlanta," 198.

[13]*O.R.*, XXXVIII, Pt. 3, p. 700; Kurtz, "Jonesboro Campaign," 2.

[14]*O.R.*, XXXVIII, Pt. 5, p. 998.

[15]Hardee to his wife, Aug. 30, 1864, in Hardee Papers, Ala. Arch. and Hist.; Kirwan (ed.), *Johnny Green*, 153.

[16]*O.R.*, XXXVIII, Pt. 5, pp. 1000, 1005.

[17]Benham, *Kennesaw Gazette*, IV (Nov. 1, 1889), 2; Cate (ed.), *Key Diary*, 124; Kurtz, "Jonesboro Campaign," 5; Buck, *Cleburne*, 250.

[18]*O.R.*, XXXVIII, Pt. 3, pp. 700, 764; *ibid.*, Pt. 5, p. 1001; Kurtz, "Jonesboro Campaign," 4.

[19]*O.R.*, XXXVIII, Pt. 3, pp. 772-73; Benham, *Kennesaw Gazette*, IV (Nov. 1, 1889), 2; *cf.* Kirwan (ed.), *Johnny Green*, 152.

[20]Benham, *Kennesaw Gazette*, IV (Nov. 1, 1889), 2. Some of the Federal trenches can be seen today.

[21]Benham, *Kennesaw Gazette*, IV (Nov. 1, 1889), 2; Cate (ed.), *Key Diary*, 124 (Key was in the second brigade of Cleburne's column); Kirwan (ed.), *Johnny Green*, 154.

[22]*O.R.*, XXXVIII, Pt. 3, pp. 700, 708, 726-27, 735, 741-42, 743, 764, 773.

[23]*Ibid.*, Pt. 5, p. 1006.

[24]*E.g., ibid.*, Pt. 3, pp. 709-10.

[25]*Ibid.*, pp. 700, 709-10, 727, 764, 773.

[26]*Ibid.*, Pt. 2, p. 856; *ibid.*, Pt. 3, pp. 727, 744.

[27]*Ibid.*, Pt. 2, p. 888.

[28]*Ibid.*, pp. 881, 888; *ibid.*, Pt. 3, pp. 727-28, 735, 744, 755-56; Cate (ed.), *Key Diary*, 125; C. F. Kohlheim, "Soldiering in Georgia in 1864," *Confederate Veteran*, XIX (1911), 173.

[29]*O.R.*, XXXVIII, Pt. 3, p. 709.

[30]Kirwan (ed.), *Johnny Green*, 155.

[31]*O.R.*, XXXVIII, Pt. 3, p. 709.

[32]"General Earl Maney," in Warner, *Generals in Gray*, 210, 384, note 315.

[33]Kurtz, "Jonesboro Campaign," 6; *O.R.*, XXXVIII, Pt. 3, pp. 701, 711, 727, 735.

[34]Kurtz, "Jonesboro Campaign," 6.

[35]*O.R.*, XXXVIII, Pt. 3, pp. 701, 765; *ibid.*, Pt. 5, p. 1007.

[36]*O.R.*, XXXVIII, Pt. 3, pp. 701-02, 712, 728, 729, 745; Kirwan (ed.), *Johnny Green*, 157-58.

[37]*O.R.*, XXXVIII, Pt. 1, p. 756; *ibid.*, Pt. 3, pp. 728, 742.

[38]Benham, *Kennesaw Gazette*, IV (Nov. 1, 1889), 2; *O.R.*, XXXVIII, Pt. 3, pp. 712, 728-29; *ibid.*, Pt. 1, pp. 641, 756; Roy, "General Hardee," 373.

[39]*O.R.*, XXXVIII, Pt. 3, pp. 712, 728, 729, 742, 745; Stan C. Harley, "Flag of Sixth Arkansas — Cleburne's Flag," *Confederate Veteran*, V (1897), 518; W. S. Chapman, "Correct Date of Battle of Jonesboro," *Confederate Veteran*, XII (1904), 390; Kirwan (ed.), *Johnny Green*, 158, 159.

[40]*O.R.*, XXXVIII, Pt. 1, pp. 558, 751-52, 810 (referred to by the Federals as the "front" or "first" "line of works," and "the short projecting point of rifle-pit"); *ibid.*, Pt. 3, pp. 728-29, 742.

[41]Benham, *Kennesaw Gazette*, IV (Nov. 1, 1889), 2. See also *O.R.*, XXXVIII, Pt. 1, pp. 526, 641.

[42]*O.R.*, XXXVIII, Pt. 3, pp. 729, 742; Cate (ed.), *Key Diary*, 126; Kirwan (ed.), *Johnny Green*, 158.

[43]*O.R.*, XXXVIII, Pt. 1, p. 757.

[44]*Ibid.*, pp. 517, 642, 750, 751, 757, 810; *ibid.*, Pt. 3, pp. 729, 742, 745; Cate (ed.), *Key Diary*, 126; Kirwan (ed.), *Johnny Green*, 159.

[45]*O.R.*, XXXVIII, Pt. 1, p. 756; *cf., ibid.*, Pt. 1, pp. 517, 641-42.

[46]*O.R.*, XXXVIII, Pt. 3, p. 729; Cate (ed.), *Key Diary*, 126; Roy, "General Hardee," 373.

[47]Benham, *Kennesaw Gazette*, IV (Nov. 1, 1889) 2; see also Joseph Erwin, "Swett's Battery at Jonesboro," *Confederate Veteran*, XII (1904), 112.

[48]Benham, *Kennesaw Gazette*, IV (Nov. 1, 1889), 2.

[49]*O.R.*, XXXVIII, Pt. 1, p. 752; *ibid.*, Pt. 3, pp. 712, 729, 742-43, 745; Cate (ed.), *Key Diary*, 127; Kirwan (ed.), *Johnny Green*, 159-61; Buck, *Cleburne*, 254-55; Roy, "General Hardee," 373, 375; Cox, "Atlanta," 207. Cox gives 865 as the number of Confederates captured.

[50]Cate (ed.), *Key Diary*, 127; *O.R.*, XXXVIII, Pt. 1, p. 527.

[51]Hardee, "Major General Cleburne," 650.

[52]George W. Gordon, Oration, May 10, 1881, at dedication of Cleburne monument, Helena, in "General P. R. Cleburne," *S.H.S.P.*, XVIII (1890), 265.

[53]*O.R.*, XXXVIII, Pt. 3, pp. 702-03.

[54]*Ibid.*, pp. 702, 736-37; Benham, *Kennesaw Gazette*, IV (Nov. 1, 1889), 3; Lowrey, "Gen. Lowrey," 3; Buck, *Cleburne*, 258; Cate (ed.), *Key Diary*, 128-29.

[55]Buck, *Cleburne*, 258-59; Kirwan (ed.), *Johnny Green*, 165; Cate (ed.), *Key Diary*, 136-37.

[56]Mangum, *Missouri Republican.*

[57]Thomas Robson Hay, *Hood's Tennessee Campaign* (New York, 1929), 27.

[58]Roy, "General Hardee," 381, 383.

CHAPTER XVII

SPRING HILL
(November 29-30, 1864)

If this cause that is so dear to my heart is
doomed to fail, I pray heaven may let me fall
with it, while my face is toward the enemy and
my arm battling for that which I know to be right.
From Cleburne's address to his troops, October 2, 1864.

On September 29, 1864, Hood opened his fall campaign by ordering a march northward. His strategic plan was to destroy the Federal communications and force Sherman to pursue him, perhaps into Tennessee. Sherman, to meet the threat of Hood invading Tennessee, dispatched Thomas to Nashville to take command of spare troops in the west.

The movement of Hood's army brought disappointment to Cleburne and his fiancée, as revealed in a letter from Miss Susan Tarleton on October 3 to her friend Sallie Lightfoot at Morven:

> . . . yesterday . . . I received a letter from the Genl. which put an end to my writing for the day, and sent me off for a good cry. You must know he had been counting on a furlough for some time and expected to get it about the first of this month. Well! on the 28th when he went to apply, Hood informed him that the next day his Corps was to move across the Chattahoochee and take such a position in Sherman's rear as would break up his communication. This puts an end to his visit, and what grieves me more, is but the commencement of another long and arduous campaign. I don't know how I am going to get through it, the past one has nearly used me up; everyone is telling me how thin and badly I am looking. I believe I have had a regular fit of "the blues," and now I feel provoked with you, for being so much more fortunate than Amelia and myself. I think we have been badly used by fate and I want to quarrel with everyone that has been better

treated .... Well! "what can't be cured must be endured" so I suppose I can but wait patiently and keep up a brave heart. I do trust, however, Amelia will be more fortunate than myself, ...

"... If I thought you showed my letters to anyone but Amelia I would never write again. I wish I could see you both, it would be the next to seeing the Gen. ..."[1]

By the evening of October 2, Cleburne's division, the right column of the army, had reached Powder Springs, Georgia,[2] twelve miles southwest of Marietta. Before extinguishing lights, the division gathered around the General's tent and serenaded him. Cleburne responded with an address, which was summarized in later years by a veteran of a Florida regiment who was present:

> At Powder Springs we serenaded General Cleburne and he spoke to us at some length, explaining to us the purpose of the rear move — the forced march — the result, if it succeeded, the consequences if it failed. He urged every man to do his whole duty, to stand firm by the righteous cause they had espoused. He pictured to us Ireland in its downfallen and trampled condition and told us if we failed our condition would be much worse than that of Ireland's, as long as that spirit of hate and revenge lived in the North. In closing his address that night he turned his face towards the skies and with all the fervency of his soul he exclaimed, "If this cause that is so dear to my heart is doomed to fail, I pray heaven may let me fall with it, while my face is toward the enemy and my arm battling for that which I know to be right." It was one of the most stirring patriotic speeches I ever listened to."[3]

During the next two days, detachments of Stewart's corps demolished several miles of railroad just north of Kennesaw Mountain and captured a small garrison, while the main body of Hood's army moved to New Hope Church, "with quick steps and buoyant hearts."[4] As Sherman set out in pursuit, the three corps of the Army of Tennessee continued their rapid march northward, by separate roads. Near Rome, in order to move faster, Hood sent his reserve artillery and surplus wagons toward Gadsden, Alabama. The patriotic civilians of Georgia freely supplied the Confederate commissaries with harvested crops, and fat oxen driven in from the mountains and coves in the valleys. With shoes worn through from tramping over rocky roads, many of the soldiers wrapped their feet in strips of green cattle hide, with the hairy side inward.[5]

Reaching Resaca on October 12, the Confederate army moved northward along the Western & Atlantic Railroad tearing up the track as they went. The following day, the army surrounded the Federal garrison at Dalton. The Colonel in charge of the detachment refused Hood's written demand for surrender, but later appeared in person before the Confederate commander. When the demand was repeated, the Colonel surrendered the garrison of 750 men, mostly Negro soldiers. He later stated in his report that "the division of Cleburne, which was in the immediate rear of the rebel general . . . was over anxious" to fight.[6] Having demolished the railroad as far as Tunnel Hill, the Confederate army moved through Snake Creek Gap, thence generally south-westward, to Gadsden. They reached this town in northeast Alabama on October 20,. Since the start of the campaign the Army of Tennessee had marched about 230 miles, averaging more than 10 miles a day.

Sherman, following far behind, had consistently been outmarched by his light traveling adversary, and had been drawn far into northern Georgia. On October 21, Sherman reached Gaylesville, Alabama, thirty-two miles northeast of Gadsden. Convinced that further pursuit would merely play into the hands of his enemy, he resolved to remain at Gaylesville, watch Hood's movements, and further his plans to march to the sea.

Hood now planned to cross the Tennessee River at Guntersville, Alabama; and move on north to capture Nashville, a major Federal base, before large Federal forces could be concentrated in that key city. Then he would march into Kentucky, threaten Louisville and Cincinnati, and seek recruits. Hopefully, he would march eastward into Virginia to reinforce Lee or attack Grant in the rear.

On October 22, Hood started to Guntersville, the nearest point of crossing the Tennessee. Modifying his plan en route, he turned westward, making his tentative destination Tuscumbia, Alabama, which was near the river and about ninety miles downstream from Guntersville. When Hood reached

Decatur, forty miles east of Tuscumbia, he considered crossing the Tennessee at that point. On October 27 and 28, skirmishers from Cleburne's and Bate's divisions demonstrated against Federal fortifications at Decatur.[7] Because of the vigorous Union defense, Hood did not attempt a crossing and continued westward toward Tuscumbia, where he had planned to set up his supply base. Upon learning Hood's position, Sherman ordered two of his corps (Schofield's and D. S. Stanley's) to join Thomas at Nashville. He also ordered Gen. A. J. Smith with two divisions from Missouri to report to Thomas. On October 30, the Army of Tennessee reached Tuscumbia, only twenty miles from the Tennessee state line. About the same time, Sherman transferred his headquarters to Kingston, Georgia. The Federal army was extended along a line from Rome to Atlanta so that it could easily be moved north or south on the railroad, which recently had been made serviceable by employing a force of 1,500 men.

A serious delay ensued while Hood was considering his next move. If he went into Tennessee, would Sherman follow him, and what should he do if Sherman did not follow him? His great concern about Sherman lessened his vigor in meeting the second problem, which in part delayed his advance into the volunteer state. The Memphis & Charleston Railroad had not been repaired, and supplies had to be hauled by wagon from the railhead fifteen miles west of Tuscumbia.[8]

Sometime during this period of inactivity, Cleburne went on a trip which took him through Selma. From Tuscumbia he probably traveled on horseback to the nearest point on the Blue Mountain Railroad. Reference is made to this trip by Dr. Nash in his *Biographical Sketch of Gen. Pat Cleburne*: "As Cleburne passed through Selma, Ala., I had an opportunity of exchanging a few words with him, as he was waiting for his car to move off. When I asked him to give me his opinion of the move, he replied, 'We are going to carry the war into Africa, but I fear we will not be as successful as Scipio was.'"[9] Cleburne's destination and the purpose of his trip are unknown. He was on official business, as the army's record of leaves shows none granted to him during this period.[10]

Soon after Cleburne returned to Tuscumbia, the mother and sister of Gen. Lucius Polk called on him. These "Spartan women" had traveled from Columbia, Tennessee, to Florence, Alabama, with mail and some contraband articles for Confederate soldiers, including a pair of gauntlets for Cleburne. The ladies told how they had managed to pass through a Federal encampment adjacent to their residence, Buena Vista.[11]

On November 14, from Johnsonville, Tennessee, Forrest with his cavalry reported to serve with the Army of Tennessee; and was assigned to command all the army's cavalry, which now numbered nearly 6,000 men. Hood, by mid-November, had resolved his doubts in favor of proceeding with the Tennessee campaign. By November 15, most of the army, including Cleburne's division, had crossed over the river to Florence. At the same time, Sherman started on his "march to the sea." To retard Hood's advance until the Federal forces at Nashville could be properly augmented, Thomas sent Schofield, with most of his corps and all of Stanley's corps, to Pulaski, Tennessee. Pulaski was fifty miles northeast of Florence and thirty miles south of Columbia. Also, stationed near Florence were 4,300 Federal cavalry.

2

On November 19 the Confederate army finally was ready to start toward its first objective, Nashville, 115 miles to the north. Hood's immediate plan was to march rapidly north and defeat Schofield just south of Columbia. Forrest's cavalry cleared the way toward Columbia on the 19th, and the infantry commenced its advance north on the 21st in a snowstorm.

Cleburne took up the march with three brigades, numbering a little more than 3,000 men, leaving his fourth brigade and Key's battery on duty at Florence. The General rode his favorite horse, Red Pepper, a large bay steed.[12] As usual, the three corps of the army marched on different routes, Cleburne's division (in Cheatham's corps) going via Waynesboro and Mt. Pleasant. The troops trudged through snow, sleet, and rain, facing a cold wind, over rough roads worsened by freezes and thaws.

On November 21, Schofield began a withdrawal from

Pulaski to Columbia, on the south bank of the Duck River. A night march enabled him to reach Columbia on November 24, just in time to prevent Forrest's cavalry from seizing the river crossings. Schofield's troops built strong entrenchments adjacent to Columbia as the remainder of his corps arrived from Nashville. The Federal army now consisted of infantry and artillery totaling 23,000, plus 7,000 cavalry commanded by Gen. James H. Wilson. The banks of Duck River were thirty to fifty feet high except at fords, and Wilson placed his troops on the north side of the river to guard the crossings east and west of Columbia.

On Saturday afternoon, November 26, Cleburne approached Columbia on the Mt. Pleasant Road after riding all day in the rain. On the right of the road the General noticed, standing in a grove of tall, green magnolia trees, an ivy covered red brick Gothic church with a cemetery to the rear. Welcoming a respite in this restful setting and probably reminded of the Athnowen churchyard, his father's burial place, Cleburne alighted from his horse. He walked along reading the inscriptions on gravestones of the Polk family. This prominent Tennessee family had built the church, St. John's, on their plantation, Ashwood, and given it to the diocese. Impressed with the dignity and beauty of the surroundings, Cleburne commented to Captain Hill, his ordnance officer, "It would not be hard to die if one could be buried in such a beautiful spot."[13]

On the 27th, the Confederate army closed in on Columbia. Schofield abandoned the town that night and withdrew to a strong position one and a half miles to the north, on a ridge extending across the open end of a horseshoe bend of Duck River. Federal infantry dug in at the bridges; and the cavalry, stationed along the north bank of the river, fanned out eastward for over ten miles watching the fords and guarding Schofield's flank. The Confederate army occupied Columbia and vicinity south of the river. Cheatham's corps was east and southeast of the town, Cleburne's division probably being about two and a half miles southeast of town.[14]

Twelve miles north by northeast of Columbia lay the village of Spring Hill. This village was located on the turnpike leading to Franklin and then on to Nashville, through the rolling hills of Middle Tennessee. Aware of these facts, Hood conceived an excellent tactical plan. Hood's plan called for a heavy demonstration in front of the enemy by Gen. S. D. Lee; and a rapid march by the main body of the army around the Federal left flank, to block the pike at Spring Hill. He then proposed to attack Schofield between Spring Hill and Columbia; and with Lee driving from the south, to annihilate the Federal army in a pincers movement. Hood's victorious army would then proceed to Nashville. On the 28th, as the first move in carrying out the operation, Forrest's three divisions of cavalry in a skillful advance forced a crossing of Duck River at points several miles east of Columbia; and drove Wilson's cavalry to the north.[15]

On the 28th, Cleburne called his troops together and addressed them. According to one of the soldiers, this was the last talk Cleburne made to his men. Among other things, he said that they would succeed; and, in his rich Irish brogue, he vowed that he would never lay down his arms and that he would rather die than surrender.[16]

At break of dawn on the 29th, Cleburne's division, the vanguard of the infantry making the flanking movement, marched eastward through cedar brakes along a wagon road. Lowrey's brigade led, followed by Govan's and then Granbury's brigades. Next came the two other divisions of Cheatham's corps (Bate's and Brown's), Stewart's corps, and Edward Johnson's division of Lee's corps. The Confederate infantry flanking forces thus consisted of 7 fine divisions totalling 20,000 men. The remaining 2 divisions of Lee's corps demonstrated before Columbia to hold Schofield there.

On the previous evening Confederate troops had laid a pontoon bridge across the Duck River at Davis Ford, four and a half miles southeast of Columbia and almost due south of Spring Hill. By 7:30 A.M., Cleburne's entire division had crossed the bridge and was moving northward on a country road with General Hood riding in front.[17] In a straight line, the distance from Davis Ford to Spring Hill was a little over twelve miles. But by the hilly country road, with numerous bends conforming to property lines, the travel distance was seventeen and a quarter miles. Under adverse conditions, the

Confederates pressed forward at a rapid pace. During the years, soil had washed away, leaving limestone ledges in the narrow road; and recent heavy rains had left boggy mudholes between the ledges. Marching on this road, the troops were some four miles east of and parallel to the Columbia-Spring Hill Pike and were screened by woods. Unfortunately, Union cavalry patrols had sighted the Confederate column; aware of this the troops kept in readiness to meet an attack. After marching about six miles from Davis Ford, Brown's division moved up, and formed a column, 400 yards to the east, paralleling Cleburne's and Bate's column, to provide a second line of battle in event of an attack. Upon reaching open country, the soldiers left the road and marched across fields toward Spring Hill.[18]

The previous afternoon, preliminary to withdrawing his army to Franklin, General Schofield had placed in position his supply, hospital, and ammunition trains — some 800 vehicles — 4 miles north of Columbia on the turnpike leading to Spring Hill. He also had ordered General Stanley to move his two divisions to the broad, mecadamized pike. Near daylight on the 29th, Schofield received a message from Wilson that the Confederate infantry was building pontoon bridges and was "expecting every minute to march." In light of this intelligence, Schofield ordered Stanley to dispatch part of his command, the reserve artillery, and the trains and ambulances, to Spring Hill. A few hours later, at 10:45, learning through reconnoissance that a "considerable" Confederate force "at least" was north of Duck River, Schofield wrote Stanley: "I will try to hold the enemy until dark, and then draw back. ... tell [Wilson] to cover Franklin and Spring Hill and try not to let the enemy get between us."[19]

But on the morning of the 29th, Forrest and his cavalry pressed Wilson back to a point five miles east of Spring Hill, leading him to think that the objective of the Confederate cavalry was Nashville. As Wilson retreated to cover the approaches to Nashville, Forrest turned sharply westward and rode toward Spring Hill. At noon, two miles east of the village, the head of Forrest's column met enemy skirmishers. These troops were the advance of G. D. Wagner's division of Stanley's command, which was approaching the village. At the sound of firing, Stanley rushed his entire command northward in double-quick time; and upon reaching Spring Hill, sized up the situation immediately. He repulsed the van of Forrest's cavalry, and promptly deployed two of the three brigades of his leading division in an arc to the north and east of Spring Hill.

The Columbia Turnpike entered Spring Hill near the southwest corner of the village. One mile east of the turnpike and a little over a mile south of the center of Spring Hill, was a high wooded knoll. On this site commanding the approaches from the east and south, Stanley formed a battle position with L. P. Bradley's brigade, numbering 2,000 men. Facing southeasterly, four regiments of the brigade formed in four groups in a long line behind a barricade of fence rails. As a wing to cover the flank, two other regiments, facing southward, were barricaded behind a rail fence extending for 200 yards to the right rear of the first line.[20] On a ridge near the southwest corner of Spring Hill, west of the pike, Stanley posted eighteen guns fronting on Bradley's position. Skirmishes continued between the Federals and Forrest's cavalry until the arrival of Cleburne's division.

About 3 o'clock in the afternoon, of November 29, 1864, with battle flags waving in the autumn sun, Cleburne's division reached Rally Hill Road, at a ford across Rutherford Creek, a mile and three quarters southeast of Bradley's position. From the ford Rally Hill Road continued west about 300 yards, then turning north, ran past the eastern foot of the knoll. Cleburne's troops removed their shoes and socks, rolled up their "pants," waded across the broad, swollen stream, and then headed northward.[21] Hood gave orders to Cheatham; and turning to Cleburne, said, "General, go with General Cheatham, assist him in every way you can, and do as he directs."[22]

Hood had formulated a tactical plan which he communicated to Cheatham and Cleburne, but modified it about an hour later. His original plan was for Cleburne's division "to attack immediately at Spring Hill any Federal forces found in [its] front without waiting for the whole command to come up";[23] Bate's and Brown's divisions were to support Cleburne;[24] and a portion of Stewart's corps was to move northwestward to the turnpike and then sweep southward toward Columbia. The modified plan was not communicated to Cleburne and perhaps not to Cheatham. Instead of supporting Cleburne, Bate's division became the force to march to the pike and thence toward Columbia;[25] and Stewart's corps and Johnson's division were to remain south of Rutherford Creek, in line of battle, to intercept Schofield's entrapped forces should they seek escape across-country to Federal fortifications at Murfreesboro, some 35 miles to the east.[26]

Cleburne's division advanced rapidly on Rally Hill Road, waded across a small creek, a tributary of Rutherford Creek, and continued along the road to the foot of the knoll. Just left of the road Cleburne formed his three brigades en echelon, facing westward, in line of battle. This movement was supervised by Hood, Cheatham having remained at Rutherford Creek to press the crossing of the rest of the corps. At about 4 P.M., after some delay, Hood ordered Cleburne to move forward and take the Union works. Hood told Cleburne that Bate had formed on his left and that Brown was advancing to form on his right. Cleburne's command went forward to assault the position occupied by Bradley's force.[27]

Hood then rode about a half mile south on Rally Hill Road to a point just west of the road, where Bate had deployed his division in line of battle ready to move on Cleburne's left. During this ride Hood apparently decided on his modified tactical plan. In Cheatham's absence, Hood ordered Bate to cross the fields northwestward to the turnpike, seize it, and move south toward Columbia.[28]

About 4:15, Cleburne's three brigades — Lowrey's on the right, Govan's in the center, and Granbury's on the left, en echelon — reached Bradley's line. Lowrey's and Govan's brigades charged the right side and wing of the Federal line. At the same time, Tyree H. Bell's dismounted brigade of Forrest's cavalry, with only four rounds of ammunition per man, charged the front of the line. Generals Cleburne and Forrest directed the attack, riding side by side behind Govan's brigade with swords drawn.[29] Later, Forrest pronounced the advance as having been made "with a promptness and energy and gallantry which I have never seen excelled."[30]

The intrepid Federal General, Bradley, who was severely wounded in the engagement, reported, "we were . . . furiously attacked."[31] According to a captain in Bradley's command, when the men of Lowrey's and Govan's brigades were within rifle range, they "pulled down the rims of their old hats over their eyes, bent their heads to the storm of missles pouring upon them, [and] changed direction to their right on double-quick in a manner that excited our admiration, ..."[32] These two brigades of Cleburne's swept away part of the Union line at the point of the bayonet. When the left of the attacking Confederate brigades overlapped the Union right wing, the entire wing crumbled.[33] Most of the troops in the enemy's front line were ordered to fall back, to avoid capture. The Federal captain in Bradley's command later recounted that the fleeing Union troops,

> were called on with loud oaths, charging them with a Yankee canine descent, to halt and surrender; and, not heeding the call, some of the men were shot down with the muzzles of the muskets almost touching their bodies. . . . The attack was pressed with so much vigor that, in a few minutes after the [Federals] had opened fire, Bradley's entire brigade was in rapid retreat towards Spring Hill, with Cleburne in close pursuit and pouring in a hot fire.[34]

General Lowrey afterward related that one Federal regiment on his right remained in line after the rest of the brigade had fled. Continuing the account in Lowrey's words:

> Here I will introduce an interesting incident in General Cleburne's conduct. As I passed the enemy on my right the officers by great efforts kept their men in position, and from the cheering and waving of swords and hats which I observed, I thought they were going to charge me on my right flank. I saw Cleburne on the field, dashed up to him and told him that the enemy was about to charge me on my right flank. With his right hand raised as though he held a heavy whip to be brought down upon his horse, and in a tone that manifested unusual excitement, he exclaimed "I'll charge them!" And dashing back to Govan's brigade he brought them up and did make a successful charge, driving the enemy in confusion from his position.[35]

After fleeing down the northwest side of the knoll, some

of Bradley's men sought refuge behind the line of Federal Col. J. Q. Lane of Wagner's division, commanding a brigade that was thinly spread to a point a quarter of a mile east of the pike. The rest of Bradley's men fled across the turnpike for protection behind the big guns. Federal General Wagner had rushed two artillery pieces, guarded by a regiment, between Bradley's work and the Columbia Pike, to sweep the open fields in front of Bradley. But Granbury's brigade forced the regiment and guns to retreat to the edge of Spring Hill.[36] Cleburne's division, now somewhat scattered, continued the pursuit as eight or more of the large Federal guns opened "with a furious cannonade." The fire was too high to do much damage to the Confederates, but the sudden noise of the exploding shells arrested their forward movement. Two of the guns, from a new position on the pike, fired at Cleburne's men in flank, causing a number of them to seek protection in a small ravine.[37]

To recitify his lines, Cleburne ordered his aide, Mangum, to have Granbury form his brigade along a fence paralleling the turnpike in a position ready to move onto the pike about 200 yards away. While the General was speaking, a shell fragment struck his horse, Red Pepper, causing the mount to rear violently. "Are you hurt?" Mangum anxiously inquired. "No!" thundered Cleburne, his face grim with determination, "Go on and tell Granbury what I told you." Mangum delivered the order to Granbury, who formed his brigade as instructed; and Govan and Lowrey rectified their lines. During the pause in the fighting, Cleburne made a point to tell some of his men how proud he was of the accomplishment of the division.[38]

"Near sunset," as Cleburne was ready to advance again, Major Joseph Bostick, assistant inspector-general on Cheatham's staff, rode up with an order directing Cleburne to remain where he was and not to move on the pike until further orders. Cleburne complied and waited anxiously for the order to advance.[39] General Govan later declared: "Had we not been halted and instead made a determined advance, we could in 20 minutes have captured or destroyed Stanley, together with 800 wagons and his artillery, and have planted our army firmly on the pike."[40] Mangum afterward said,

"The arrest of his movement on the turnpike was a bitter disappointment to General Cleburne, and he expressed himself very forcibly in regard to the failure [of Bate] that caused it."[41] Cleburne, not knowing that Hood had modified the plan, was unaware that Bate's orders had been changed.

3

To follow the sequence of events as reported by various officers, it should be noted that on November 20, 1864, by the time standard used in Middle Tennessee, the sun set at 4:46 o'clock at Srping Hill.[42] For an hour after sunset there was some visibility, with complete darkness by 6:17.

After Hood directed the initial movements of Cleburne and Bate, instead of continuing personal command of his forces, he left the carrying out of his orders entirely to Cheatham. About dark, Hood repaired to the Absalom Thompson house, a quarter of a mile north of Rutherford Creek and slightly west of Rally Hill Road. Making this large brick residence his headquarters, Hood remained there the rest of the evening and all night.

Now to gain further perspective about the attack on Spring Hill: The Federal commander, Stanley, had so skillfully disposed the artillery and his single division that Cheatham was bluffed into thinking that a much larger force of Federals occupied the village. He was convinced that to take the village, it would be necessary for Cleburne to have the support of both Bate and Brown. Cheatham was apparently unaware of Hood's order for Bate to move southward on the pike toward Columbia: Cheatham planned for Brown to resume the assault as soon as his division was in line of battle, and for Cleburne and Bate to take up the attack successively.

Brown's division followed Bate's division in fording Rutherford Creek. By advancing three of his four brigades in double-quick time, Brown was able to reach a point on Rally Hill Road just north of the knoll by about 4:30.[43] Cheatham ordered him to form a line of battle extending westward and to attack the Federal position, stating, "I will go and direct the other commanders along the line to advance as soon as they hear your guns." Cheatham then rode off with his staff and ordered Cleburne to attack on hearing Brown's guns. Not hearing the signal that the battle had begun, Cheatham kept asking impatiently, "Why don't we hear Brown's guns?";[44] and rode back to Brown's division. Cleburne's division stood in line of battle, set to move forward at the sound of the guns.[45]

General Brown later explained why he did not attack:

> I formed my line as speedily as worn out troops could move, and, after throwing forward a skirmish line, advanced four hundred or five hundred yards, when I discovered a line of the enemy thrown out of Spring Hill, across and threatening my right flank, . . . leaving me without any protection on my right flank or support in the rear. I had neither artillery nor cavalry, and was left in a position where I must meet with inevitable disaster if I advanced on Spring Hill. A hasty consultation with my brigade commanders resulted in a determination to suspend the advance and confer with the corps commander. . . . in a very few minutes [General Cheatham was] upon the field and fully approved of what had been done, ...[46]

Without notifying Cleburne, Cheatham then rode off to report the situation to General Hood.[47]

Actually the Federal infantry on Brown's right consisted of merely one regiment and one company.[48] But either Colonel Lane's clever placement of the troops, or an optical illusion, deceived the astute Brown, his brigadiers on the field, and Cheatham, into believing that a considerable force stood ready to hit Brown's flank and rear.

General Brown waited for further orders. According to two captains in his division, he "remained quietly in his position in front of Spring Hill for a long time," until "late in the afternoon." Then the captains did some reconnoitering, went to the rear, and met General Brown when "the day was nearly spent." They asked why an attack was not made, and Brown replied, "I don't know; I have no orders." Likewise, to Gen. J. R. Chalmers who rode up when it was still light, Brown again explained: "I have no orders."[49] When "nearly dark,"[50] Brown's fourth brigade (Gist's) reached the field, and was placed on the right flank. Even after dark an attack on Stanley's command would have been feasible, according to a captain in Forrest's cavalry: "It was . . . a starlight night,

. . . the battle would have been largely in a corn-field and an open piece of woodland."[51] But no orders came, and Brown continued to wait.[52]

It was "getting dark" when General Bate approached the Columbia Turnpike, having moved in line of battle almost two miles across the fields from Rally Hill Road. Bate was still acting under Hood's instructions to take the pike and sweep southward. When Bate's skirmishers were 100 yards from the turnpike, they saw Union troops and wagons coming north on the pike, going toward Spring Hill. The skirmishers fired into the head of the enemy column several times, driving it from the road and creating confusion.[53] These troops were Thomas. H. Ruger's division and W. C. Whitaker's brigade (of Nathan Kimball's division), commanded by Schofield himself. They had left the fortifications north of Columbia at 3 P.M.—the van of the forces to be withdrawn from Duck River.

While hastening to bring his main line into position to strike the Federal column in the flank, Bate received an order from Cheatham, by messenger, to halt and join his right to Cleburne's left. Reluctant to obey the order, Bate dispatched Maj. John B. Pirtle with a message to Cheatham that he "occupied a good position" from which to defeat the enemy. Pirtle found Cheatham at the Thompson house with General Hood and delivered the message. Cheatham responded with a peremptory order, spoken in Hood's presence, for Bate to move to his right and connect with Cleburne or else report under arrest to General Hood. Hence, Bate withdrew his division from contact with the Federals and moved northeast toward Cleburne's left, while Ruger and Whitaker, unmolested, continued their march to Spring Hill. Bate, however, sent a further message to Cheatham that the enemy on the pike was threatening his left.[54]

Additional exercises in futility under Hood's and Cheatham's generalship appear from Stewart's statements. Stewart was not permitted to cross Rutherford Creek until "between sunset and dark." He later said that riding in advance of his column, about dusk, a half mile north of the creek,[55]

> . . . I saw General Hood on the side of the road by a small fire, with a single orderly as his ·attendant. As soon as I got in

> speaking distance of Hood he began to inveigh against
> Cheatham for not obeying his order to attack Spring Hill. It
> was on my tongue to ask Hood why he had not himself seen
> that his order was obeyed, but I thought it would sound
> disrespectful.[56]

Stewart continued the account: "The commanding general
gave me a young man of the neighborhood as a guide, and
told me to move on and place my right across the pike
beyond [north of] Spring Hill, 'your left,' he added,
'extending down this way.'"[57]

At a bend in Rally Hill Road, the guide pointed out a
seldom used road which by-passed Spring Hill and ran into
the pike a mile and a half north of the village. Stewart and
the guide took this road, the head of the column following.
Soon, about 9 P.M., Stewart came upon Forrest's headquarters; and the two generals held a short consultation.[58] At this
juncture, one of Cheatham's staff officers rode up with an
order from Hood for Stewart to go into position on Brown's
right. The staff officer explained that he and General Brown
had been over the ground by daylight, and for this reason
General Hood had sent him to place General Stewart in
position. Stewart then went back to Rally Hill Road, and
moved his column on toward Spring Hill.

Stewart's account continued:

> Arriving near the line of Brown's division, General Brown
> explained his position, ... It was evident that if my
> command were marched up and formed on his right, it being
> now a late hour, it would require all night to accomplish it,
> .... Feeling satisfied there was a mistake, I directed the
> troops to be bivouacked while I rode back to find the
> commanding general to explain my situation and get further
> instructions.[59]

Forrest accompanied Stewart to Hood's headquarters.
When they arrived at 11 P.M., the commanding General of
the army had been in bed asleep for over two hours.[60]
Stewart related in his report that he asked General Hood if
he,

> had changed his mind as to what he wished me to do. He

replied that he had not, "But," said he, "the fact is, General Cheatham has been here and represented that there ought to be somebody on Brown's right." I explained to him that in the uncertainty I was in I had directed the troops, who had been marching rapidly since daylight, and it was now 11 P.M., to be placed in bivouac, and had come to report. He remarked, in substance, that it wasn't material; to let the men rest; and directed me to move before daylight in the morning, taking the advance toward Franklin.[61]

Hood's own report was similar to Stewart's in significant respects:

... I did not at dark abandon the hope of dealing the enemy a heavy blow. Accordingly, Lieutenant-General Stewart was furnished a guide and ordered to move his corps beyond Cheatham's and place it across the road beyond Spring Hill. Shortly after this General Cheatham came to my headquarters, and when I informed him of Stewart's movement, he said that Stewart ought to form on his right. ... one of Cheatham's staff officers was sent to show Stewart where his (Cheatham's) right rested.[62]

It is thus evident that dark had fallen before Cheatham reached Hood's headquarters to report the Union flanking force on Brown's right.[63] There is no explanation as to why Cheatham used so much time in getting to Hood's headquarters. Nor is there an explanation as to why Hood waited until at least 8:30 that night before starting the staff officer to Stewart with the instructions issued as a result of the information received from Cheatham. Brown stated: "I received no further orders that evening or during the night to advance or change my position."[64] Brown, therefore, took no action.

4

Returning to the progress of events in the early evening: Cleburne's division remained set for an attack until nightfall, waiting for the signal which did not come. Cleburne then permitted the hungry, tired men of Lowrey's and Govan's brigades to relax their vigil. They bivouacked in line of battle facing the village, on the knoll from which they had driven Bradley. Granbury's brigade was thrown forward to a position about ninety yards from the turnpike, and ordered to lie down in line of battle behind a fence paralleling the pike. About 6:45 P.M., Granbury's men heard troops marching on the pike. The advance element of the Federal division and brigade under Schofield which had been fired on earlier by Bate's skirmishers was now continuing on toward Spring Hill.[65]

Cleburne, restrained by the order to await the signal to attack, was compelled to permit the Federal column to pass by without interference. A member of a Tennessee regiment later recorded, "Cleburne was eager to strike the blow, and when he saw that he was denied the privilege he was deeply moved."[66]

At 7:30, after the Federal column had passed, Cleburne drew back Granbury's brigade and placed it, facing the pike, as a retired extension of the left of his other brigades. Throughout the night as they slept, Cleburne's division remained under arms, in line of battle.[67] In the darkness Bate had difficulty locating Cleburne's left, but by 8 o'clock his troops faced the pike as an extension of Granbury's line. Later they bivouacked there for the night, "the men sleeping on their arms in line of battle."[68] At 10 P.M. Edward Johnson's division, temporarily under Cheatham,[69] formed as an extension of Bate's line. Thus, the "twinkling camp-fires" of Cheatham's command stretched for a distance of nearly two miles paralleling the turnpike. Johnson's division, "under arms in line of battle and the guns loaded . . . waited hour after hour for the order to come to charge the enemy, ..."[70]

During this period, Schofield's main force of three divisions, withdrawing from Duck River, "silently and fearfully" moved north along the pike past the Confederates, undistrubed.[71] General Schofield regarded the situation as "extremely perilous";[72] and Brig. Gen. Thomas J. Wood of his army reported, "The effect of a night attack on a column en route would have been, beyond doubt, most disastrous."[73]

The head of these three Federal divisions began passing Cleburne's troops about 10:45 P.M.[74] Cleburne sent a courier to Hood with the message, "The enemy is passing in my front"; but Hood took no action.[75] Bate, with the aid of two couriers as guides, galloped to Hood's headquarters.

Arriving well after 11 P.M., he found the commanding General in conference with Forrest.[76] After Forrest left, Bate was invited into Hood's bedroom; and reported that Schofield's army was passing along the pike and that under Cheatham's orders he and Cleburne were powerless to act. Hood, after several moments of contemplation, said, "You and General Cleburne had better obey orders, as your lieutenant general may have some move we know not of."[77] Hood also said to Bate, "It makes no difference now, or it is all right anyhow, for General Forrest, as you see, has just left and informed me that he holds the turnpike with a portion of his forces north of Spring Hill, and will stop the enemy if he tries to pass toward Franklin, and so in the morning we will have a surrender without a fight. We can sleep quiet tonight."[78] Actually, Forest had informed Hood that Cheatham's corps had not blocked the turnpike; and Hood had seemed surprised, declaring that he had expressly ordered its seizure. Hood had then asked Forrest if he could throw his cavalry upon the pike north of Spring Hill in time to check the Union retreat; and Forrest had replied that all of his command were without ammunition except W. H. Jackson's small division, but that he would do the best he could in the emergency.[79]

Upon Bate's return to his division, he and Cleburne had a discussion. Cleburne, realizing that the opportunity for one of the greatest victories of the war was being wasted, proposed: "Bate, suppose you and I report to General Hood under arrest and leave our divisions under the commands of our brigadiers, and before we can get back they will have whipped the Yankee army."[80] Upon further consideration, Cleburne and Bate decided against taking this extreme action.

After Forrest's return to his command, he ordered Jackson to intercept Schofield's army on the way to Franklin. Jackson struck the Federal wagon trains and troops four miles north of Spring Hill, doing some damage and blocking the pike for some thirty minutes. But the small body of cavalry, no match for the Union infantry, was forced to withdraw. It was 2 A.M. before the rear of Schofield's marching divisions passed Cleburne and entered Spring Hill.[81] By daybreak, Schofield's advance had reached Franklin, fourteen miles north of Spring Hill.

405

5

Most of the troops of Hood's army felt that both the commanding General and General Cheatham were responsible for permitting Schofield's army to excape, "but the principal fault is at the door of General Cheatham."[82] This appraisal appears to be correct. Either Hood failed to notify Cheatham that he had ordered Bate to sweep south on the Columbia Pike, or Hood dispatched a message to Cheatham which was not delivered, or Cheatham did not comprehend it if delivered. Obviously someone blundered.

Irrespective of this blunder, the conclusion is obvious that Cheatham was culpable in several respects. Upon learning of the flanking force on Brown's right, why did not Cheatham direct that the attack be made as soon as Gist's brigade arrived, instead of waiting for a whole corps (Stewart's) to protect against a flank attack? Why did Cheatham permit so much time to elapse before reporting to Hood the presence of the flanking force? During the hour from 6 to 7 P.M. when Federal troops were passing by Bate's and Cleburne's divisions, why did not Cheatham order Bate and Cleburne to attack the Federal column? If the answer to this question be that Cheatham was unaware that the column was on the pike, then why was he, the corps commander, in such ignorance, particularly in view of Bate's messages to him? During the three and a half hours from 10:30 P.M. when Schofield's main forces began passing Johnson's division, until 2 A.M. when the rear of the column passed Cleburne's division, why did not Cheatham order Johnson, Bate, and Cleburne to attack these forces? Again, if the answer is that Cheatham was unaware of the continuous movement of these troops along the pike, why was he without this knowledge?

Perhaps the explanation of Cheatham's blunders is that he was intoxicated, as he was on the field the first day of the battle of Murfreesboro.[83] Also, there is evidence that he absented himself from his command and was entertained at the Peters' cottage, located a mile and a quarter northeast of the Thompson house. Federal cavalry General Wilson, in his book *Under the Old Flag*, stated that when he returned to the Spring Hill area a few weeks after the engagement, "I received what seemed to be reliable information that Cheatham, for a part of the night at least, was absent from his headquarters in the company of ladies at a nearby country house . . . ."[84] The "very handsome" Mrs. Peters and other women had been popular with some of the Confederate officers previously stationed at Spring Hill. Mrs. Peters' husband had left home eighteen months earlier after killing Confederate General Van Dorn because of the relationship between his wife and the General.[85]

Hood, as well as Cheatham, was at fault. Hood was a picture of inaction as his bold plan, skillfully executed up to the late afternoon of that ill-fated day, fizzled out. When Cheatham failed him, Hood did not ride to the front to direct the attack against Spring Hill and the seizure of the pike. Nor did he employ alternatives to see that his orders were executed, such as assigning Cleburne to command Cheatham's corps. Hood sought to retrieve the situation by ordering Stewart to block the pike north of Spring Hill, but permitted Cheatham to persuade him to retract the order. Later when Schofield's main force was passing by, Hood did not override Cheatham's orders and command Johnson, Bate, and Cleburne to attack the column in flank. However, in Hood's case there were mitigating circumstances. His physical disabilities resulted in his leaning inordinately on Cheatham. He had been up since 3 o'clock the morning of the 29th,[86] and the pain in the stump of his leg was further aggravated by the long hard ride. Because of physical handicaps, pain, and complete exhaustion he was in a state of collapse.

A successful Confederate attack at Spring Hill, resulting in the destruction of Schofield's army, would have radically changed the current of the war in the west.

NOTES

CHAPTER XVII

[1]Susan Tarleton to Sallie Lightfoot, Oct. 3, 1864, in Tarleton Family Collection.

[2]*O. R.,* XXXIX, Pt. 3, p. 782.

[3]John L. McKinnon, *History of Walton County* (Atlanta, 1911), 299-300.

[4]*Ibid.* The Confederate's only setback was sustained by French's division of Stewart's corps at Allatoona. French's forceful assaults on the redoubts were stoutly defended; and before gaining complete success, he was compelled to withdraw to avoid capture by Sherman's army. Killed in a charge on the redoubts when leading his regiment, the 45th Mississippi, was Col. William H. Clark, grandfather of Honorable Tom C. Clark, Associate Justice of the Supreme Court of the United States, retired.

[5]Mobile *Advertiser and Register,* Oct. 30, 1864, p. 2; H. K. Nelson, "Tennessee, a Grave or a Free Home," *Confederate Veteran,* XV (1907), 508; McKinnon, *History of Walton County,* 300.

[6]*O.R.,* XXXIX, Pt. 1, pp. 718-20.

[7]*O.R.,* XXXIX, Pt. 1, p. 827; Hay, *Hood's Tennessee Campaign,* 56.

[8]Hay, *Hood's Tennessee Campaign,* 61-66; Robert Selph Henry, *"First with the Most" Forrest* (Indianapolis, 1944), 383-84.

[9]Nash, *Gen. Pat Cleburne,* 159-60.

[10]Special Field Orders and Special Orders, Army of Tennessee, July 1874 — April 1865, Ch. II, Vol. 349, RG 109, NA.

[11]Mrs. Polk was the widow of William Julius Polk, and her daughter was Mrs. Joseph Branch. Mary Polk Branch, *Memoirs of a Southern Woman* (Chicago, 1912), 7, 16, 21-22, 29.

[12]Mangum, *Kennesaw Gazette,* II (June 15, 1887), 3; Cate (ed.), *Key Diary,* 153; Buck, *Cleburne,* 280.

[13]*O. R.,* XLV, Pt. 1, p. 730; Mangum, *Missouri Republican; cf.,* Buck, *Cleburne,* 280.

[14]Cleburne, accompanied by two junior officers, visited the home of Hugh Bradshaw, two and a half miles southeast of Columbia, and it is to be inferred that his division was stationed near this location. — Reminiscenses of Mrs. James Taylor Peters, formerly Mrs. Hugh Bradshaw (MS in possession of her grandson, Benjamin D. Hill, Jr., Washington, D. C.), Aug. 19, 1912.

[15]J. P. Young, "Hood's Failure at Spring Hill," *Confederate Veteran,* XVI (1908), 25; Henry, *Forrest,* 387-88.

[16]Preston, "Memoirs," 32.

[17]*O. R.*, XLV, Pt. 1, p. 742; Hood, *Advance and Retreat*, 283-84; Govan to George A. Williams, June 1906, in Buck, *Cleburne*, 272.

[18]Hood, *Advance and Retreat*, 284; Lowrey, "Gen. Lowrey," 3; *O. R.*, XLV, Pt. 1, pp. 736, 742; W. D. Gale to his wife, Jan. 14, 1865, in "Hood's Campaign in Tennessee," *Confederate Veteran*, II (1894), 4; John C. Brown to B. F. Cheatham, Oct. 24, 1881, accompanying B. F. Cheatham, "The Lost Opportunity at Spring Hill, Tenn.," *S. H. S. P.*, IX (1881), 537.

[19]*O. R.*, XLV, Pt. 1, pp. 113, 1141, 1143.

[20]*Ibid.*, pp. 113, 268-69; John K. Shellenberger, *The Battle of Spring Hill, Tennessee: November 29, 1864* (Cleveland, 1913), 27.

[21]Cheatham, "Lost Opportunity," 524; Young, "Hood's Failure," 31; Preston, "Memoirs," 32; *cf. O. R.*, XLV, Pt. 1, p. 742.

[22]Hood, *Advance and Retreat*, 284-85.

[23]Govan to Williams, June 1906, in Buck, *Cleburne*, 272.

[24]Mangum, *Kennesaw Gazette*, II (June 15, 1887), 3; Brown to Cheatham, Oct. 24, 1881, accompanying Cheatham, "Lost Opportunity," 537-38.

[25]*O. R.*, XLV, Pt. 1, p. 742.

[26]*Ibid.*, p. 712; Alexander P. Stewart to W. O. Dodd, Feb. 8, 1881, accompanying Cheatham, "Lost Opportunity," 535; Shellenberger, *Battle of Spring Hill*, 26-27.

[27]*O. R.*, XLV, Pt. 1, p. 753; Govan to Young, May 5, 1897, typescript in Hay Collection; Mangum, *Missouri Republican*.

[28]*O. R.*, XLV, Pt. 1, p. 742.

[29]Young, "Hood's Failure," 31; *O. R.*, XLV, Pt. 1, p. 753; Govan to Young, May 5, 1897, typescript in Hay Collection.

[30]*O. R.*, XLV, Pt. 1, p. 753.

[31]*Ibid.*, p. 269.

[32]Shellenberger, *Battle of Spring Hill*, 28.

[33]Govan to Young, May 5, 1897, typescript in Hay Collection.

[34]Shellenberger, *Battle of Spring Hill*, 29.

[35]Lowrey, "Gen. Lowrey," 3.

[36]*O. R.*, XLV, Pt. 1, pp. 114, 230, 255, 336; Shellenberger, *Battle of Spring Hill*, 27, 29-30; Govan to Williams, June 1906, in Buck, *Cleburne*, 272; Young, "Hood's Failure," 31-32.

[37]Govan to Williams, June 1906, in Buck, *Cleburne*, 272; Mangum, *Missouri Republican*; Shellenberger, *Battle of Spring Hill*, 30; *O. R.*, XLV, Pt. 1, p. 114. Cleburne's loss in the engagement was four killed, forty-five wounded. — Mangum, *Missouri Republican*, 9. Bradley's loss was 17 killed, 114 wounded, 67 captured and missing. — *O. R.*, XLV, Pt. 1, p. 269.

[38]"Forty-fifth Regiment Alabama Infantry" (Undated and unsigned MS in Compiled Data, 45th Alabama Infantry Regiment, Ala. Arch.

and Hist.), 3.

[39]Mangum, *Missouri Republican*; Mangum, *Kennesaw Gazette*, II (June 15, 1887), 3; Govan to Williams, June 1906, in Buck, *Cleburne*, 272-73; Buck, *Cleburne*, 266-67.

[40]Govan to Williams, June 1906, in Buck, *Cleburne*, 273; Shellenberger, *Battle of Spring Hill*, 47.

[41]Mangum, *Kennesaw Gazette*, II (June 15, 1887), 3.

[42]The time standard adopted in Middle Tennessee was based on local time at Nashville. By this time standard, the sun set at 4:45 o'clock on Nov. 29, 1862, at Nashville. — Bang, Walker & Co. (pub.), *Cumberland Almanac for 1862* (Nashville, 1861), 14. The sun set one minute later at Spring Hill than at Nashville. — Computation by Naval Observatory, Washington, D. C. (The time of sunset at Nashville on November 29, 1862, as given by the *Cumberland Almanac for 1862, i.e.,* 4:45, correlates closely with local civil time of sunset at Nashville on that date as computed in 1967 by the Naval Observatory — 4:46. The difference of one minute in the two computations may perhaps be due to a slight variation in the longitude used.)

[43]Brown to Cheatham, Oct. 24, 1881, accompanying Cheatham, "Lost Opportunity," 537. "Before sundown [Brown's] Division arrived at Spring Hill a little before sunset, ... Regiments and brigades were put in line of battle, ... The Federals were in plain view between us and the setting sun." — S. A. Cunningham, "Events Leading to the Battle," *Confederate Veteran,* XVIII (1910), 17.

[44]Young, "Hood's Failure," 33, 35.

[45]Govan to Williams, June 1906, in Buck, *Cleburne*, 276.

[46]Brown to Cheatham, Oct. 24, 1881, accompanying Cheatham, "Lost Opportunity," 538. Brown's asserting that detection of the Federal flanking force, after Cheatham had directed him to attack, caused his deferring the attack, is corroborated by his staff officer. — Young, "Hood's Failure," 35. The recollection of Major Vaulx of Cheatham's staff differs somewhat from that of Brown. According to Vaulx, when Cheatham was on his way to Brown to learn why the latter had not attacked, he met an aide coming from Brown to report the reason; and Cheatham and the aide went to Hood's headquarters to apprise the commanding General of "the situation on the right." Vaulx, however, corroborates Brown in the essential fact that, after learning the facts, Cheatham acquiesced in the deferment of the attack and departed for Hood's headquarters to report the Federal flanking force and receive instructions. — *Ibid.*, 33-34.

[47]Brown to Cheatham, Oct. 24, 1881, accompanying Cheatham, "Lost Opportunity," 538.

[48]*O. R.*, XLV, Pt. 1, p. 255.

[49]Young, "Hood's Failure," 34-35.

[50]Frank Stovall Roberts, "Spring Hill-Franklin-Nashville, 1864," *Confederate Veteran*, XXVII (1919), 58; *O.R.*, XLV, Pt. 1, p. 736.

[51]W. O. Dodd, "Reminiscences of Hood's Tennessee Campaign," *S. H. S. P.*, IX (1881), 521.

[52]Brown to Cheatham, Oct. 24, 1881, accompanying Cheatham "Lost Opportunity," 538.

[53]*O. R.*, XLV, Pt. 1, pp. 393, 742; Young, "Hood's Failure," 37; William B. Bate to Cheatham, Nov. 29, 1881, accompanying Cheatham, "Lost Opportunity," 541.

[54]*O. R.*, XLV, Pt. 1, p. 742; John P. Hickman, Statement of (quoting Bate) under heading, "Hood's Failure at Spring Hill," *Confederate Veteran*, XXII (1914), 14-15; John B. Pirtle, Address, Louisville, Feb. 1, 1881, to Southern Historical Society, Feb. 1, 1881, reported in *Cincinnati Commercial*, (Extra Sheet), 4, quoting Louisville *Courier-Journal*.

[55]*O. R.*, XLV, Pt. 1, p. 712.

[56]T. G. Dabney, "When Hood Superseded Johnston," *Confederate Veteran*, XXII (1914), 407. See also Stewart to Dodd, Feb. 8, 1881, accompanying Cheatham, "Lost Opportunity," 535; Young, "Hood's Failure," 39.

[57]*O. R.*, XLV, Pt. 1, p. 712.

[58]*Ibid.;* Young, "Hood's Failure," 39; Thomas Jordan and J. P. Pryor, *The Campaigns of Lieut.-Gen. N. B. Forrest and of Forrest's Cavalry* (New Orleans, 1868), 622.

[59]*O. R.*, XLV, Pt. 1, pp. 712-13.

[60]Young, "Hood's Failure," 39. "There was a house near by my headquarters, and about 9 P. M. [November 29, 1864] I walked over to it. In the drawing room I found Gen. James R. Chalmers and other cavalry officers . . . . Occasionally we heard some picket firing toward the north . . . . Cheatham's Corps went into bivouac near the pike, and so in comparative silence the long night wore away. Hood slept. The head and the eyes and ears of the army, all dead from sleeping." — French, *Two Wars*, 291.

[61]*O. R.*, XLV, Pt. 1, p. 713.

[62]*Ibid.*, pp. 652-53. Hood's and Cheatham's accounts of the fiasco at Spring Hill are cited herein sparingly and only where corroborated by other evidence. These attempts at self-justification omit material facts, and contain distortions and misstatements.

[63]It is true that Brown said (Brown to Cheatham, Oct. 24, 1881, accompanying Cheatham, "Lost Opportunity," 538) that a little while after Cheatham left him, "General Hood . . . directed that the attack should be delayed until the arrival of Generals Stewart and Gist, ..." Manifestly Brown was not referring to an order sent him

by Hood, but merely to what someone told him afterward.

[64]Brown to Cheatham, Oct. 24, 1881, accompanying Cheatham, "Lost Opportunity," 538.

[65]Govan to Young, May 5, 1897, typescript in Hay Collection; Jacob D. Cox, *The Battle of Franklin, Tennessee* (New York, 1897), 34; Young, "Hood's Failure," 37-38. The head of Ruger's division arrived at Spring Hill at 7 P. M. — *O. R.*, XLV, Pt. 1, p. 114.

[66]Thomas A. Head, *Campaigns and Battles of the Sixteenth Regiment, Tennessee Volunteers, in the War Between the States* (Nashville, 1885), 372.

[67]*O. R.*, XLV, Pt. 1, p. 742; Mangum, *Missouri Republican.*

[68]*O. R.*, XLV, Pt. 1, pp. 114, 742. See also Bate to Cheatham, Nov. 29, 1881, accompanying Cheatham, "Lost Opportunity," 541.

[69]Cheatham, "Lost Opportunity," 526.

[70]Young, "Hood's Failure," 38.

[71]Henry Stone, "The Battle of Franklin, Tennessee," in Theodore F. Dwight (ed.), *Papers of the Military Historical Society of Massachusetts* (Boston, 1908), VII, 463.

[72]*O. R.*, XLV, Pt. 1, p. 1138.

[73]*Ibid.*, p. 123.

[74]*Cf.* Young, "Hood's Failure," 38-39.

[75]Hempstead, *Historical Review of Arkansas*, I, 241.

[76]Hickman, "Hood's Failure," 14-15; Bate to Cheatham, Nov. 29, 1881, accompanying Cheatham, "Lost Opportunity," 541.

[77]Hickman, "Hood's Failure," 15.

[78]Bate to Cheatham, Nov. 29, 1881, accompanying Cheatham, "Lost Opportunity," 541.

[79]Jordan and Pryor, *Lieut. Gen. Forrest*, 623.

[80]Hickman, "Hood's Failure," 15.

[81]J. N. Beach, "From the Union Side at Franklin," *Confederate Veteran*, II (1894), 239.

[82]Dodd, "Hood's Tennessee Campaign," 521, 524.

[83]In December 1863, from Dalton, Georgia, General Bragg wrote President Davis: "You must make other changes here, or our success is hopeless. Breckinridge was totally unfit for any duty from the 23d to the 27th — during all our trials — from drunkenness. The same cause prevented our complete triumph at Murfreesborough .... General Hardee will assure you that Cheatham is equally dangerous." — Bragg to Davis, Dec. 1, 1863, in *O. R.*, LII, Pt. 2, p. 745. After the war, Bragg wrote Major Sykes: "In the Battle of Murfreesboro, Cheatham was so drunk on the field all the first day, that a staff officer had to hold him on his horse." — Bragg to E. T. Sykes, Feb. 8, 1873, in Polk, *Leonidas Polk*, II, 312. Further evidence of Cheatham's drunkenness at Murfreesboro is contained in a letter

written in 1927 to the State Librarian of Tennessee by John Johnston, a Confederate veteran. The letter stated: "... at the beginning of that battle [Murfreesboro] while his troops were standing in line waiting for orders to move, Gen. Cheatham rode out in front and in attempting to wave his hat to make an appeal to his 'Tennesseans,' rolled off his horse and fell to the ground as limp and helpless as a bag of meal — to the great humiliation and mortification of his troops. This was told to me by a personal friend, a lieutenant in Company K, Sixth Tennessee Infantry, who was present and witnessed it." — John Johnston to John Trotwood Moore, June 9, 1927, unidentified newspaper clipping in Scrapbk., U. D. C., Helena. At the outset of the war, Johnston enlisted as a private in Co. K, 6th Tennessee Infantry, Cheatham's brigade. He resigned because of illness; but recovered and joined Forrest's cavalry, serving until the war closed. Johnston became a prominent lawyer in Memphis and an elder in the Southern Presbyterian Church. — William T. Adlerson (ed.), "The Civil War Reminiscences of John Johnston, 1861-1865," *Tennessee Historical Quarterly*, XIII (1954), 65. See also Connelly, *Autumn of Glory*, 84.

84James Harrison Wilson, *Under the Old Flag* (New York, 1912), II, 44. According to a Federal veteran, "current [gossip] in our camp," founded on "the statements of Confederate officers at General Stanley's headquarters," was that Hood "[failed] to strike us at Spring Hill" because "General Cheatham was spending the evening with Mrs. Peters," and "could not be found" to make the attack "until the favorable moment had passed forever." — J. N. B., West Jefferson, Ohio, to Editor of the *Commercial*, Feb. 1881, quoted in, "The Campaign of Hood in Tennessee," Cincinnati *Commercial*, Feb. 22, 1881, p. 7.

85Robert G. Hartje, *Van Dorn: The Life and Times of a Confederate General* (Nashville, 1967), 309-19; E. Miller (ed.), *A Soldier's Honor* (New York, 1902), 249; Alderson (ed.), "Reminiscences of John Johnston," *Tennessee Historical Quarterly*, XIV (1955), 73.

86The Rt. Rev. Charles Todd Quintard, D. D., Diary (MS in Archives Department, Jesse Ball duPont Library, University of the South, Sewanee), Nov. 29, 1864.

CHAPTER XVIII

FRANKLIN
(November 30, 1864)

Well, Govan, if we are to die, let us die like men.
— *P. R. Cleburne, just before the charge at Franklin.*

At daylight the next morning, November 30, 1864, the Army of Tennessee headed north on the Columbia Turnpike in pursuit of Schofield's forces. Hood, "wrathy as a rattle-snake,"[1] blamed not only Cheatham, but Cleburne, Bate, and Brown for the escape of the Federals at Spring Hill the night before. Stewart's corps led the march northward. Cheatham's corps followed with Brown's division first, Cleburne's second, and Bate's division, third. S. D. Lee's corps brought up the rear. Because of Red Pepper's injury and the unfitness of his spare horse for service, Cleburne rode a brown mare belonging to one of his escorts, Lieut. Tip Stanton. The General was wearing a new gray uniform and his cherished old gray cap, a gift from some ladies. The heavy gold braid covering the cap was so faded that the original richness was hardly discernible.[2]

General Brown later wrote:

> On the march to Franklin General Cleburne, with whom I had long enjoyed very close personal relations, sent a message to the head of my column requesting an interview. Allowing my column to pass on, I awaited his arrival. When he came up we rode apart from the column through the fields, and he told me with much feeling that he had heard that the Commanding General was endeavoring to place upon him the responsibility of allowing the enemy to pass our position on the night previous. I replied to him that I had heard nothing on that subject, and that I hoped he was mistaken. He said, "No, I think not; my information comes through a very reliable channel," and said that he could not afford to rest under such an imputation, and

414

that he should certainly have the matter investigated to the fullest extent, so soon as we were away from the immediate presence of the enemy. General Cleburne was quite angry, and evidently was deeply hurt, under the conviction that the Commander-in-Chief had censured him. I asked General Cleburne who was responsible for the escape of the enemy during the afternoon and night previous. In reply to that inquiry he indulged in some criticisms of a command occupying a position on the left, and concluded by saying that "of course the responsibility rests with the Commander-in-chief, as he was upon the field during the afternoon and was fully advised during the night of the movement of the enemy." The conversation at this point was abruptly terminated by the arrival of orders for both of us from [Cheatham or Hood]. As he left he said, "We will resume this conversation at the first convenient moment, ..."[3]

There was never an opportunity for resuming the conversation.

Turning now to the Federal army: Schofield had been unable to get his trains and artillery across the Harpeth River as the "country bridge" northeast of Franklin, leading to Nashville, had been partially destroyed by fire.[4] At daylight on the 30th, a Federal engineer battalion began improvising a crossing on the ruins of the bridge and improving an adjacent ford. The Harpeth River makes a horseshoe bend around Franklin with the open end to the southwest. To protect their position against the Confederates until the wagon trains could be withdrawn, the Federal advance troops entrenched a convex line across the open end of the horseshoe, a little over a half mile south of the town.

Roads from the south converged on Franklin as spokes in a wheel — from the southeast, the Lewisburg Pike (west of and parallel to the Harpeth River); from the south, the Columbia Pike; and from the southwest, Carter's Creek Pike. Approaching the town, these roads crossed a gently rolling open plain of green pastures and a few scattered trees and houses.

By noon, the Federals had strong defenses for three-quarters of a mile, from the Harpeth River to Carter's Creek Pike. (This part of the line was subsequently attacked by the Confederates.[5]) The center of the Union defenses intersected the Columbia Pike on a low knoll. The Federals left this road open for passage of their wagons and artillery, but built a retrenchment across the road a few rods in rear.

From a point a little over a hundred yards east of the Columbia Pike, and continuing 200 yards west of it, the breastworks stood four feet above ground level. In front of these breastworks was a ditch four feet wide and three feet deep. (Elsewhere on the line, the breastworks were two and a half feet above ground level.)[6]

East of the Columbia Pike, the parapet swung southeastward, encompassing a large cotton gin located eighty yards from the pike. The angle made the length of the breastworks from the pike to the gin 100 yards. Two epaulements five feet high, with strong embrasures, were constructed in the breastworks, one just east of the pike and the second just east of the gin. The first had a battery of four guns and the second had two guns. Other guns were elsewhere on the line. In a shallow ditch behind the breastworks, stood two ranks of defenders; and fifty yards in their rear, was a second line of infantry.

Northeast of Franklin, on the north bank of the Harpeth, was Fort Granger, an earthwork constructed a year earlier. A Union battery of long-range rifles, crossing the ford, occupied the fort and commanded the field in front of the breastworks. This artillery had sufficient reach to fire as effectively as the guns in the line. General Schofield moved to the fort, leaving General Cox in command of the Federal defenses south of the river.

Before reaching the wide plain, the Columbia Pike crossed a range of hills through a gap two miles south of the Federal breastworks. On the east edge of the range was Breezy Hill, a relatively low elevation a quarter of a mile wide, just east of the Columbia Pike. Immediately west of the pike was high, rounded, Winstead Hill. From this hill, the range swung in an arc northwestward for a mile and a half to Carter's Creek Pike. The Federals deployed a division on Breezy Hill and across the gap, with one regiment on Winstead Hill.

About noon, with the van of Stewart's corps, Hood arrived at a point on the Columbia Pike a mile south of Winstead Hill. Previously, he no doubt had ridden to a site on the range of hills, and inspected the Federal line of works immediately south of Franklin. Of his own volition, he resolved to make a frontal attack on the enemy's breast-works.

Hood ordered Stewart to turn the flank of the enemy force on Breezy Hill by marching a mile and a quarter east to the Lewisburg Pike, and then north. As this movement began, Forrest rode up after reconnoitering.[7] When informed by Hood that a direct assault was to be made, the famous Confederate cavalry leader protested. "General Hood," he declared, "if you will give me one strong division of infantry with my cavalry, I will agree to flank the Federals from their works within two hours' time." Hood replied by directing Forrest to employ his cavalry in cooperation with the infantry's direct attack on the fortifications.[8]

At 1 P.M., its flank having been turned by Stewart, the Federal divison on the range of hills withdrew, placing one brigade and a section of artillery on Merrill Hill.[9] This hill, a mile north and 400 yards west of the Columbia Pike, was a knob 100 feet high.

Pursuant to Hood's plan of battle, Stewart's corps, concealed by woods, formed in a line extending west from the Lewisburg Pike, about a mile and a quarter southeast of the Federal breastworks.[10] Brown's division, arriving "at 1 or 2 P.M.,"[11] was kept under cover near the southern crest of Winstead Hill.[12] Forrest, as ordered by Hood, divided his none-too-large cavalry force. He sent Chalmer's division to the extreme west side of the field; and formed Jackson's division, dismounted, on the right of Stewart's corps, filling the 500-yard space between the Lewisburg Pike and Harpeth River. Forrest remained ready to ford the Harpeth with his third divison.

Cleburne arrived at Winstead Hill ahead of his command and rode to the crest. Not having his field glasses with him, he borrowed a pair; and studied the enemy's defenses for a long time. He simply remarked, "They are very formidable." Sitting on a tree stump, he wrote rapidly for several minutes in his current diary, a pocket notebook, doubtless describing the fortifications and terrain. While waiting for the head of his column, Cleburne and a member of his staff (as on other occasions) drew a checkerboard on the ground and played several games, using colored leaves for "men."[13] When his division arrived, it was halted just south of Winstead Hill.[14]

Hood, as his army was massing before Franklin, held a brief council of war at his pre-battle headquarters in the Harrison house, a brick mansion a short distance south of the hill. Cleburne, as well as some of the other generals present, opposed a frontal assault "as involving a terrible and useless waste of life," and recommended a flanking movement.[15] But their arguments were of no avail. Hood was intent upon destroying Schofield's army before it could concentrate with Thomas' forces at Nashville, eighteen miles north of Franklin. "If we take Franklin," declaimed Hood, "we will take Nashville, which is the key to the independence of the Southern Confederacy."[16] The commanding General was blind to the fact that a frontal attack was not the way to accomplish this objective.

Meanwhile, between 2:30 and 3:00 o'clock on November 30, the Federal brigade and artillery on Merrill Hill had withdrawn to a slight rise a half mile south of the Union main line.[17] With fence rails and earth, these forces and another Federal brigade hastily formed a lunette extending for about 300 yards on each side of the Columbia Pike. Behind this front line — between it and the Union main line — lay an open field. Soon after the Federals withdrew from Merrill Hill, Confederate sharpshooters of Brown's division posted themselves on that site.

After the consultation at his headquarters, Hood, along with Cleburne and other commanders, rode to the top of Winstead Hill. They were joined by Brown, who had not been present at the council of war. Brown later reported that "[Hood] stated in substance: 'The country around Franklin for many miles is open and exposed to the full view of the Federal army, and I cannot mask the movements of my troops so as to turn either flank of the enemy, and if I attempt it he will withdraw and precede me into Nashville. While his immediate center is very strong, his flanks are weak.'" Then Hood explained his battle dispositions: Stewart's corps, massed in the woods on the east, would attack on that side. Cleburne and Brown would attack in the center. Under cover of the range of hills, Bate would move northwestward before Cleburne and Brown advanced, in order to attack concurrently with them. Bate would connect with Brown's left, and with the right of Chalmer's cavalry division, which would be posted on the extreme Confederate left.[18]

Turning to Cleburne, Hood then said: "General, form your division on the right of the pike with your left resting on the same. General Brown will form on your left with his right resting on the pike. You will connect with Stewart on your right." After instructions as to the manner of forming the division, Hood continued: "Give orders to your men not to fire a gun until you drive the Federals from the first line of works in your front. Then press them and shoot them in the backs while running to the main line. Then fix bayonets, charge, go over the breastworks, and break the enemy's line at all hazards." General Cleburne merely answered, "General, I will take the works or fall in the attempt."[19]

It is a matter of conjecture whether Hood's determination to make a frontal attack resulted from misappraisal of the situation or anger because of the Federal army's escape at Spring Hill. Such an attack was unsound, and violated basic principles of war and allied tactical principles. First, a frontal assault would negate the initial superior mass of Hood's attacking troops. Second, such an assault would give the Federals mass superiority with accurate fire power from behind the fortifications supported by emplaced artillery. To order the charge without a preliminary artillery barrage was all the more unsound.

The flanking attack, with the rest of Hood's army making a strong demonstration, would have been the course to pursue. Hood's objections to a flanking movement were invalid. Had Schofield attempted to retreat to Nashville, the Federal General would have been confronted with the problem of protecting his wagon trains, artillery, and lines of communication. Even in open country, he could not have prevented Forrest's cavalry and Confederate infantry from hitting his flank and cutting the railroad and the Nashville Turnpike.

Manifestly, Hood should not have given the orders to

storm the breastworks. But a rule of Cleburne's life was that orders must be obeyed. His advice against the direct attack having been rejected, Cleburne obeyed and did his best to make the faulty plan work. From Winstead Hill Cleburne rode to the top of Breezy Hill, where he summoned his brigade commanders in council. He directed them to form their brigades on the east side of the pike, with the foremost troops just below the crest of Breezy Hill.[20]

General Govan gave an account of Cleburne on the eve of the battle:

> He seemed greatly depressed and fully realized, as did every officer present, the desperate nature of the assault we were about to make. He informed us that by the direction of Gen. Hood he had called us together to impress upon us the importance of carrying the works of the enemy at all hazards; that we were to move forward at the sound of the bugle, moving on the flank until we came under fire, then change front, form into line, fix bayonets and take the works at the point of the bayonet .... We were further directed to have our field officers assemble, then our company officers, and issue to them similar orders.[21]

Govan recalled that "looking over and beyond the bare common over which we had to move, you could see behind the heavy earthworks the bristling bayonets of the enemy, and glitter of Napoleon guns, as they peeped through the embrasures, ..."[22] As Govan saluted and turned to leave, he said, "Well, General, few of us will ever return to Arkansas to tell the story of this battle." Cleburne replied, "Well, Govan, if we are to die, let us die like men."[23]

While his brigadiers were forming their brigades, Cleburne rode forward to the crest of Merrill Hill, which commanded a full view of the main Federal works a mile away. Borrowing the long telescope from a sharpshooter's Whitworth rifle, Cleburne placed it on a stump, and carefully viewed the field. "They have three lines of works," he remarked; and after sweeping the field again as if to make certain, added, "And they are all completed." He returned the telescope, thanked the sharpshooter, and "with kindling eye and rapid movement," mounted his horse and galloped back to his division.[24]

Cleburne's and Brown's divisions moved forward. Having descended the north side of Breezy Hill, Cleburne's brigades were drawn up in "double columns at half distance" — Govan and Granbury in front, Lowrey in the rear. As his troops carried out an order to load, General Cleburne rode along the first line, cautioning them to save ammunition and to "use the bayonet." About 4 P.M., came the command "Forward."[25]

The charge at Franklin of Cleburne's and Brown's divisions and the three divisions of Stewart's corps was called by historian J. P. Young in 1892, "the great martial drama of American history," with Cleburne "the central figure" in it.[26] While army bands played "The Bonnie Blue Flag" and "Dixie," over 15,000 Confederate infantry advanced in splendid array. Great clouds of smoke came from the bursting shells as generals, staff officers, and couriers rode in front of and between the lines.

In advance of the main line, a battalion of Brown's sharpshooters halted until the main force could come up. One of the sharpshooters recorded: "From our position, a little elevated, we could see the entire line to our right, and it was a grand sight to see General Cleburne's division moving up to the charge with a line as steady and evenly dressed as if on parade."[27] During the advance, Generals Cleburne and Brown "met several times upon the turnpike road and conferred and acted in harmony in the movement."[28]

The advance line of the Federal infantry should have retired slowly to the main Union works, having accomplished its mission as outposts. The artillery in this line did withdraw to the main Federal line after firing a few shots. But the two Union advance infantry brigades vainly tried to hold their position against the sweeping gray tide.

Gen. George W. Gordon, commander of the right brigade of Brown's division, was separated from Cleburne's division only by the Columbia Turnpike. In 1891, at the unveiling of a memorial shaft at General Cleburne's grave in Helena, Arkansas, General Gordon, describing the attack at Franklin, drew upon personal experience:

> . . .the array of columns . . ., with a front of two miles or more in length, [moving] steadily . . . with flying banners, beating

drums and bristling guns, . . . presented a scene of the most imposing grandeur and magnificence. When we had arrived within about four hundred paces of the enemy's advanced line of entrenchments our columns were halted and deployed into two lines of battle preparatory to the charge. This advanced position of the enemy . . . was immediately in front of Cleburne's left and [Brown's] right. When all was ready the "charge"was ordered. With a wild shout we dashed forward upon this line. The enemy delivered one volley at our rushing ranks and precipitately fled for refuge to his main and rear line. At this juncture the shout was raised, "Go into the works with them." This cry was taken up and vociferated from a thousand throats as we rushed on after the flying forces we had routed — killing some in our running fire and capturing others who were slow of foot — sustaining but small losses ourselves, until we arrived within about one hundred paces of their main line and stronghold, when it seemed to me that hell itself had exploded in our faces. The enemy had thus long reserved their fire for the safety of their routed comrades who were flying to them for protection, and who were just in front of and mingled with the pursuing Confederates. When it became no longer safe for themselves to reserve their fire, they opened upon us (regardless of their own men who were mingled with us) such a hailstorm of shot and shell, musketry and canister that the very atmosphere was hideous with the shrieks of the messengers of death. The booming of cannon, the bursting of bombs, the rattle of musketry, the shrieking of shells, the whizzing of bullets, the shouting of hosts and the falling of men in their struggle for victory, all made a scene of surpassing terror and awful grandeur.[29]

Cleburne's command dashed forward into the fiery storm coming from the main works. The General followed his division into the midst of the battle, as was his custom, for better direction of troop movements. Mangum, while executing an order to locate a battery, received a message through Captain Hanly to report to the General at once. Mangum found Cleburne near the center of his division, immediately behind the line of battle. "It is too late," Cleburne said, "Go on with Granbury." Then turning his horse to the right, the General rode swiftly toward the center of Govan's brigade, which was making a mad rush for the enemy's works.[30]

At this point, Cleburne's galloping horse was killed from under him, about eighty yards from the works. An escort, nineteen-year-old James C. Brandon, a lanky Mississippian, immediately dismounted and gave his bay horse to the General. While Cleburne was in the act of mounting, this second horse was killed.[31] Govan, who was nearby, later recounted that General Cleburne, sword in hand, then "moved forward on foot, waving his cap; and I lost sight of him in smoke and din of battle . . . ."[32] A few seconds later — probably by an expert rifleman, trained to pick off leaders — Cleburne was killed, a minié ball striking just below his heart.[33] "Greater love has no man than this, that a man lay down his life for his friends"[34] — and his country. Monroe F. Cockrell wrote, "Cleburne never wavered and went down in death. He is recognized as a soldier who stood the test and won immortality."[35]

2

Unaware that their leader had fallen, Cleburne's superbly trained division converged upon the main Union line. Fighting with fiery vigor, the Federals had already repulsed a gallant attack by Stewart's corps.[36] Cleburne's division "came up just in time to receive a heavy right oblique fire" from several regiments of the Federals on the main line in Stewart's front.[37] The two nearest Union regiments were armed mostly with breech-loading rifles. In front of Cleburne's division, the four-gun battery at the pike and the two guns near the gin house opened a sustained fire, while the infantry fired from the main line and the cotton gin.[38] An orderly of an Illinois regiment, standing a few paces east of the gin, declared, "I never saw men put in such a hellish position as Cleburne's division was in for a few minutes at Franklin. The wonder is that any of them escaped death or capture."[39] General Granbury in a strong clear voice commanded: "Forward men, forward! Never let it be said that Texans lag in the fight!" A moment later he was dead, struck in the head by a bullet.[40]

Despite the terrible slaughter, Cleburne's "heavy assaulting columns," as told by Federal Gen. J. W. Reilly, commanding that part of the line, "follow[ed] closely and determinedly" on the heels of the fleeing Yankees from the Federal outpost.[41] As Confederate color-bearers planted their battleflags upon the enemy's breastworks, several hundred of Cleburne's troops charged over the works and some surged through the opening left in the fortifications at the pike. Driving back the Federals at the breastworks, Cleburne's division seized the four cannons adjacent to the pike and about 110 yards of the main line; gained the outside of the main works at a point east of the cotton gin; and killed, wounded and captured about 250 of the enemy.[42]

A Union regiment in reserve east of the gin rushed forward. Its Captain later reported: ". . . I found a sufficient extent of the line abandoned into which to throw my whole regiment. . . . a number of [Confederates] had gained the top and fired down into our ranks; even bayonets and clubbed muskets were used. After a severe struggle we gave the enemy a check, ..."[43]

Adjacent to the Columbia Pike, Cleburne's men turned the captured artillery on the Federals, but could not fire the guns since frightened horses had run away with the ammunition chests containing the primers.[44] Cleburne's veterans also attempted to capture the two artillery pieces near the cotton gin. As reported by a Federal officer: "The enemy tried hard to force a passage at the right embrasure of the battery. They several times got into the embrasure, pushing their guns through and fired upon the cannoneers. They were so unpleasantly close that we had to resort to the use of sponge staves, axes, and picks to drive them back."[45]

The second Union line, reinforced by reserves, charged forward four deep, and a hand-to-hand conflict ensued inside the works. Other Federals poured a heavy fire into those Confederates who had gained the works, two of the Union companies being armed with revolving rifles. Federal General Cox wrote, "Human courage could not endure the fire."[46] Some of these Confederates escaped to the outside ditch and the rest were killed or captured.[47]

Outside the fortifications, the soldiers who were left of Govan's and Granbury's brigades lodged up against the works and fought on despite fearful losses.[48] Lowrey, whose brigade comprised the rear column of Hood's division, later said:

> I brought up my brigade and under the most destructive fire I ever witnessed, I threw my brigade into the outside ditch of

his massive works, and my men fought the enemy across the parapet. Up to this time, about half my men had fallen, and the balance could not scale the works. It would have been certain death or capture to every one of them. I went on my horse to within thirty feet of the works, where I had my horse wounded, and when I saw that nothing more could be done, I went to the rear, and began the work of gathering up the fragments of our division.[49]

A Union captain recounted: "Along Reilly's line, it was a desperate, hand-to-hand conflict. Sometimes, it seemed that the masses of the assailants would overwhelm all opposition. The struggle was across and over the breastworks. The standards of both armies were upon them at the same time. Muskets flashed in men's faces. Officers fought with the men, musket in hand."[50]

Fighting with Cleburne's men were Gen. George W. Gordon and a few of his troops who had become separated from their brigade. "For some time," Gordon said, "we fought them across the breastworks, both sides lying low and putting their guns under the head-logs upon the works, firing rapidly and at random, and not exposing any part of the body except the hand that fired the gun." But enfilading fire in the section of the ditch occupied by Gordon and those immediately around him became so heavy that Gordon and some of his and Cleburne's men were forced to surrender.[51]

Writing to his wife two weeks after the battle, Govan said that when his brigade advanced to the main line of entrenchments, "here commenced the most desperate fight I ever witnessed which lasted until near midnight. Our men occupying one side of the breastworks, the Yankees the other, ..."[52]

3

Briefly turning to events elsewhere on the field: Soon after the battle began, Forrest's dismounted cavalry division, advancing on Stewart's right, drove the Federal cavalry across the Harpeth. East of the river, Forrest's mounted regiments engaged Federal cavalry and infantry. Stewart attacked the main Federal line again and again but was unable to penetrate it. A little more than 100 yards east of the Columbia Pike,

Brig. Gen. John Adams, of Stewart's corps, with his horse, died upon the works, the mount straddling the parapet; and Adams' body falling at the outer base of the works. Brig. Gen. Francis M. Cockrell, also of Stewart's command, thrice wounded, was pulled over the breastworks by Federal soldiers after falling an arm's length away. Brig. Gens. William A. Quarles and Thomas M. Scott, of Stewart's corps, also were wounded severely.

West of the Columbia Pike, Brown's division seized about 150 yards of the main Federal line and 4 guns. Parts of two of his brigades went over the breastworks and advanced some distance within the works. A valiant countercharge by Federal reserves drove these Confederates back; but Brown's division held about seventy-five yards of the outside of the parapet until the battle ended. Of Brown's division, Gist and Otho F. Strahl, brigadiers, were killed; J. C. Carter, a brigadier, mortally wounded; and Brown, badly wounded. Bate attacked later than Brown, Hood having underestimated the distance Bate would have to travel. Because of the formidable opposition and exposure of his left, Bate did not press his attack.

About dark, Hood threw in Johnson's division to help the center. In a courageous attack, this division also was decimated. Brig. Gen. Arthur M. Manigault from South Carolina, a brigade commander in Johnson's division, was severely wounded. The Federals, leaving their dead and wounded on the field, withdrew across the river about midnight, headed for Nashville.

Hood's losses were appalling. In addition to the unprecedented loss of general officers, many colonels and other field and company officers were among the casualties. Approximately 6,000 Confederates were killed and wounded. These figures attest to the morale and esprit of the Confederate troops, and the vigor with which they assaulted.[53] Cleburne's command sustained the greatest loss of any division, fifty-two percent.[54] The battle of Franklin made inevitable the defeat of the Army of Tennessee at Nashville sixteen days later and hastened the doom of the Confederacy.

NOTES

CHAPTER XVIII

[1]Young, "Hood's Failure," 36.

[2]Mangum, *Missouri Republican*; Buck, *Cleburne*, 289, 292; Young to Hay, June 10, 1918, in Hay Collection.

[3]Brown to Cheatham, Oct. 24, 1881, accompanying Cheatham, "Lost Opportunity," 538-39.

[4]Cox, *Battle of Franklin*, 50.

[5]The Confederates did not learn until the next day that the line from Carter's Creek Pike west to the Harpeth River was mere light barricades.

[6]J. P. Young, "Franklin," Memphis *Evening Scimitar*, Dec. 17, 1892, p. 9, *inter alia* quoting "Statement of S. A. Carter," an occupant of the Carter house during the battle, and "Statement of Thomas Kearns" of Cleburne's division, dates not shown.

[7]D. W. Sanders, "Hood's Tennessee Campaign," *Southern Bivouac*, N.S., I (1885-86), 7-8; *O.R.*, XLV, Pt. 1, p. 708; Jordan and Pryor, *Lieut. Gen. Forrest*, 625.

[8]John Allan Wyeth, *Life of Lieutenant-General Nathan Bedford Forrest* (New York, 1899), 544.

[9]Cox, *Battle of Franklin*, 69-70.

[10]*O.R.*, XLV, Pt. 1, p. 720; James H. M'Neilly, "Franklin-Incidents of the Battle," *Confederate Veteran*, XXVI (1918), 117; John L. Collins, "Gallant Mike Farrell," *ibid.*, XXXIV (1926), 373.

[11]*O.R.*, XLV, Pt. 1, p. 731.

[12]*Ibid.*, p. 736; George W. Gordon, Address, Nov. 30, 1899, in "Confederate Monument at Franklin," *Confederate Veteran*, VIII (1900), 6.

[13]Buck, *Cleburne*, 280-81.

[14]*O.R.*, XLV, Pt. 1, p. 736.

[15]Mangum, *Kennesaw Gazette*, II (June 15, 1887), 3. See also Govan to Buck, Sept. 3, 1907, in Buck, *Cleburne*, 290.

[16]Govan to Buck, Sept. 3, 1907, in Buck, *Cleburne*, 290.

[17]Cox, *Battle of Franklin*, 76.

[18]Brown, Report to Cheatham, date not shown, in James D. Porter, "Tennessee," in Evans (ed.), *Confederate Military History*, VIII, 156.

[19]Mangum, *Kennesaw Gazette*, II (June 15, 1887), 3.

[20]George W. Gordon, *S.H.S.P.*, XVIII, 266; George W. Gordon, *Confederate Veteran*, VIII, 7; *cf.* W. A. Washburn, "Cleburne's Division at Franklin," *Ibid.*, XIII (1905), 27.

[21]Typed excerpt from letter, Govan to Young, date not shown,

transmitted by letter, Young to Hay, May 5, 1921, in Hay Collection.

[22]Govan to Dunn, Dec. 16, 1878, in Hempstead, *Historical Review of Arkansas*, I, 246.

[23]Typed excerpt from letter, Govan to Young, cited note 21, *supra.*

[24]Isaac N. Shannon, "Sharpshooters with Hood's Army," *Confederate Veteran*, XV (1907), 124-25.

[25]George W. Gordon, *S.H.S.P.,* XVIII, 266; *O.R.*, XLV, Pt. 1, p. 336; Mangum, *Kennesaw Gazette*, II (June 15, 1887), 3; Washburn, "Cleburne's Division," 27.

[26]Young, Memphis *Evening Scimitar*, 10.

[27]Roberts, "Spring Hill-Franklin-Nashville," 59.

[28]Brown, Report to Cheatham, in Porter, "Tennessee," in Evans (ed.), *Confederate Military History*, XIII, 157.

[29]George W. Gordon, *S.H.S.P., XVIII*, 266-67.

[30]Mangum, *Kennesaw Gazette*, II (June 15, 1887), 3, 6.

[31]*Ibid.*, Mangum, Statement to Young, date not shown, in Young, Memphis *Evening Scimitar*, 10; CSR of J. C. Brandon, Capt. Buck's Co., Mississippi Cavalry, M269/72, NA.

[32]Govan to Young, Oct. 1, 1892, typescript in Hay Collection.

[33]Buck, *Cleburne,* 292. "Saw Gen Cleburn [sic] killed at Franklin with his sabra [sic] in his hand." — Questionnaire of J. E. Charlton, veteran of 5th Tennessee Infantry, received Apr. 13, 1922 (Tenn. Lib. and Arch.), 3. Brandon, seriously wounded, lay on the battlefield all night; and "not till he was found did he know that his beloved general lay dead within a stone's throw of him." — Mrs. James C. Brandon to George Moreland, date not shown, undated clipping from Memphis *Commercial Appeal*, in Scrapbk, U.D.C., Helena.

[34]John 15:13 (Rev. Standard Version).

[35]Cockrell to authors, July 1, 1962.

[36]Mangum, *Missouri Republican*. Stewart had encountered: destructive artillery fire from the rear of the main Federal line and from Fort Granger, down a railroad cut where a column of his men was moving; withering fire from the main line; an impenetrable palisade of Osage orange hedge in front of one of his brigades; and an abatis of thorny hedge branches elsewhere in his front.

[37]James Barr, "The Battle of Franklin," *Southern Bivouac*, N.S., I (1885-86), 315.

[38]Tillman H. Stevens, " 'Other Side' in Battle of Franklin," *Confederate Veteran*, XI (1903), 167; *O.R.*, XLV, Pt. 1, pp. 326, 334; E. Shapard, "At Spring Hill and Franklin Again," *Confederate Veteran*, XXIV (1916), 139; Jacob D. Cox, *Franklin and Nashville* (New

York, 1882), 89.

[39]Barr, "Battle of Franklin," 315.

[40]Mangum, *Kennesaw Gazette*, II (June 15, 1887), 6.

[41]*O.R.*, XLV, Pt. 1, p. 412.

[42]*Ibid.*, pp. 246, 326, 330, 334, 353, 415-16, 418, 419, 421; Cox, *Battle of Franklin*, 98, 104, 110, 113-14; Cox, *Franklin and Nashville*, 92; Thomas Speed, "The Battle of Franklin, Tennessee," in Robert Hunter (ed.), *Sketches of War History: 1861-1865: Papers Prepared for the Ohio Commandery of the Military Order of the Loyal Legion of the United States* (Cincinnati, 1890), 83, 84.

[43]*O.R.*, XLV, Pt. 1, p. 416.

[44]Cox, *Franklin and Nashville*, 90.

[45]*O.R.*, XLV, Pt. 1, p. 334.

[46]Cox, *Battle of Franklin*, 111.

[47]*O.R.*, XLV, Pt. 1, pp. 246, 412, 418, 419, 421; Cox, *Battle of Franklin*, 109-10, 111; Govan to Dunn, Dec. 16, 1878, in Hempstead, *Historical Review of Arkansas*, I, 246.

[48]*O.R.*, XLV, Pt. 1, p. 334.

[49]Lowrey, "Gen. Lowrey," 3.

[50]Speed, "Battle of Franklin," 80-81.

[51]George W. Gordon, *S.H.S.P.*, XVIII, 267-68. According to a Confederate account, "about fifty" troops in the ditch surrendered; and according to a Federal account, "about 300." — Washburn, "Cleburne's Division," 28; *O.R.*, XLV, Pt. 1, p. 422.

[52]Govan to his wife, Dec. 14, 1864, in Govan Papers.

[53]In 3 hours of heavy fighting by Hood's relatively small army, 1,750 of his men were killed — more than those killed in Federal Gen. A. E. Burnside's large army during 7 hours of fighting at Fredericksburg in December of 1862.

[54]George W. Gordon, *Confederate Veteran*, VIII, 9. Among the killed was Maj. A. T. Meek of the 2nd and 24th Arkansas Regiment, consolidated, Cleburne's division, one of four brothers who enlisted in the 2nd Arkansas. Two had been killed — J. M. Meek, at Chickamauga; and E. S. Meek, in the fighting around Atlanta. They were grandsons of Capt. James Meek, York County Militia, S. C., who fought in the battle of King's Mountain. Also killed at Franklin was Lieut. Thomas B. Moncrief, one of the remaining few who had enlisted in the Yell Rifles.

CHAPTER XIX

TRIBUTES TO PAT CLEBURNE

But in our hearts you live again,
The gentlest of the gallant brave,
And knightliest of the knightly train
Who died our Southern land to save.
— *Walter A. Clark, "Pat Cleburne's Truce at Kennesaw."*

There were eyes afar that watched your star
As it rose with the "Southern Cross,"
There were hearts that bled when its course was sped,
And Old Ireland felt your loss!
— *"Cleburne," Dublin (Ireland) Nation.*

Throughout the night, many of Cleburne's men remained in the ditch below the breastworks. The next day one of them said: "You see, we kept getting over, but they would reinforce and drive us out. Finally we said, 'let's . . . keep quiet till General Cleburne gives the word to charge so we'll all get over together' . . . we waited and waited and waited. And the boys kept crying for the word and wondered why it didn't come. But when it didn't come, I knew Pat Cleburne was *dead*; for if he had been living he would have given us that order."[1]

Parties which had been sent out during the night to search for Cleburne received erroneous information from an escaped Confederate prisoner that the General had been captured by the Federals. At dawn the next morning, a Confederate artillerist discovered General Cleburne's body forty or fifty yards in front of the breastworks and some one hundred yards east of the Columbia Pike. His boots, diary, watch, wallet, sword-belt, and pistol had been stolen from his body. At the edge of the breastworks, a Confederate chaplain and two members of the ambulance corps found the body of General Adams. The bodies of the two generals were taken by ambulance to Carnton, the residence of John W. Mc-Gavock, located just southeast of the battlefield.

Carnton, a two-story brick mansion with a broad two-story veranda across the rear, became a field hospital. While surgeons labored on the lower gallery, the house and yard were soon filled with wounded and dying men. The bodies of Generals Cleburne and Adams were placed on the lower gallery. The body of General Strahl had been carried to the house during the night, and after daylight that of General Granbury.[2] Thus the bodies of four generals lay side by side on the lower veranda.

The belief is prevalent that the bodies of all five generals who died during the conflict lay on this gallery the day following the battle. This popular conception is erroneous. General Gist died the night of November 30 in a field hospital on the opposite side of the battlefield from the McGavock house. The next morning his body was taken directly from the hospital to the residence of William White, which was nearby. The General's faithful body servant arranged for the burial of his master that day in the yard adjoining the White home.[3]

The four generals were on the porch at Carnton for only a brief period. By eleven o'clock on the morning following the battle (December 1) a horse-drawn wagon, carrying the bodies of General Strahl, Capt. James Johnston, and Lieut. John H. Marsh, was at least two-thirds of the twenty-six-mile distance to Columbia.[4] Mrs. John W. McGavock, with foresight took for safekeeping, the sword which General Cleburne had worn in battle, his cap, and a few personal effects. About seven weeks later, when the Federals returned to Franklin, Mrs. McGavock concealed these items and held them until they could be delivered to the General's friends.[5] His cap is now displayed in the Tennessee State Museum at Nashville.

The word of Cleburne's death spread swiftly through the Army of Tennessee. Hearts were heavy and tears were shed by hardened warriors. "'Cleburne has fallen,'" soldiers proclaimed in grief, "the good, the brave and generous Cleburne."[6] When meeting, troops would say, "Cleburne is killed!" hardly able to believe that such a calamity could befall the army.[7] Some of his men visited the McGavock house on the morning of December 1 for "a last look at the face of our beloved and matchless Pat Cleburne."[8]

Later in the day, the bodies of Generals Cleburne and Granbury and Col. R. B. Young, a regimental commander in Granbury's brigade, were transported to Columbia. Upon reaching Columbia, the bodies were placed in the parlor of Buena Vista, the residence of William Julius Polk. Clad in a gray uniform, General Cleburne lay in a walnut casket made by Elijah Neelley, a local cabinet maker.[9]

"In the sad watches of that dreary night," Miss Naomi Hays, a niece of President James K. Polk, composed a poem in tribute to General Cleburne, which she placed on his casket.[10] Before the funeral, one of Cleburne's aides removed the handkerchief from the General's face and substituted an embroidered one explaining, "This handkerchief was sent him from Mobile, and I think that he was engaged to the young lady."[11]

At 3 o'clock in the afternoon, December 2, members of the Polk family, including Gen. Lucius Polk, and staff officers gathered in the parlor for the funeral, conducted by Chaplain (later Bishop) Quintard. Under military escort, the bodies were taken to Rose Hill Cemetery a few blocks away. The three officers were interred near General Strahl and Lieutenant Marsh, whose burial had taken place a few hours earlier.[12]

The next day, December 3, Chaplain Quintard recorded in his diary:

> I could not content my mind with the resting place which had been chosen by the sexton for our gallant dead — in close proximity to the graves of soldiers — both white and black — of the Federal Army. . . . I know that in the grave all earthly distinctions cease. "There all are equal — side by side, the poor man and the son of pride, lie calm and still." But it is only so of the dead & it is becoming in the living to see that all honor is bestowed upon the earnest Christian and the devoted patriot.[13]

Chaplain Quintard immediately made arrangements for the bodies of Generals Cleburne, Granbury, and Strahl, Colonel Young and Lieutenant Marsh, to be disinterred and buried in St. John's churchyard at Ashwood. General Polk selected the grave sites.[14]

432

"The death of Cleburne cast a deep gloom over the army and the country. Eight millions of people, whose hearts had learned to thrill at his name, now mourned his loss, and felt there was none to take his place." — were the words of General Hardee.[15]

2

News of the battle of Franklin and General Cleburne's death was delayed in reaching Mobile. Federal raiding parties had cut telegraph wires and otherwise disrupted communication. Late in the afternoon of December 5, while in the garden of her family residence, Miss Susan Tarleton heard a newsboy shout, "Big battle near Franklin, Tennessee! General Cleburne killed! Read all about it." Miss Susan fainted and was in a state of shock for several days.[16] A letter soon came from Dr. Nash giving details of the General's death. Miss Susan's reply, Dr. Nash said, was "most pathetic and sorrowful."[17] The General's grief stricken fiancée went into "deep mourning."[18]

General Cleburne had instructed the members of his staff, that in the event of his death, his personal effects should be sent to Dr. Nash. Accordingly, Lieutenants Mangum and Hanly sent to Dr. Nash the uniform in which the General was killed and his "fine wearing apparel." Dr. Nash kept the uniform, which is now in the Confederate Museum in Richmond, Virginia; and forwarded the other items to Miss Tarleton.[19]

The staff members attempted to send to Dr. Nash Cleburne's two horses — Red Pepper and his fatigue horse. Dr. Nash wrote Miss Tarleton that he would send Red Pepper on to her and he would keep the other horse. Miss Tarleton replied asking Dr. Nash to keep Pepper in Selma at her expense, as the fall of Mobile was expected hourly. It developed that both horses were captured by the Federals and neither horse reached Dr. Nash. Mangum sent to Miss Tarleton the sword given to Cleburne by the 15th Arkansas Regiment and also the battle flag of the 29th Missouri Volunteers captured at Ringgold Gap. Subsequently, the General's sword belt was identified on a soldier and turned over to Mangum, who forwarded it to Miss Tarleton.[20]

In October 1867, Miss Tarleton married Capt. Hugh L.

Cole, a Confederate veteran. Captain Cole, a South Carolinian and a friend of her brother Robert at Princeton University, was practicing law in Mobile. Mrs. Cole died suddenly less than a year after her marriage. The funeral was at Christ Episcopal Church, with burial in the Tarleton family plot in New Cemetery (now Magnolia Cemetery).[21] The epitaph on her gravestone reads:

> A little while, and she was animate;
> A little while, and she is Death's pale bride;
> A little while, and holy, sanctified,
> She stands before God's thorne immaculate.

3

In 1870, a movement began in Phillips County to have General Cleburne's remains brought to Helena for final resting. The Ladies' Memorial Association of Phillips County raised the necessary funds, and delegated Dr. Grant and Lieutenant Mangum to make arrangements for the disinterment and transportation of the body from Tennessee.[22]

On April 26, 1870, Cleburne's body was taken from the churchyard at Ashwood, where each spring ladies of the neighborhood had bedecked the grave with flowers. The General's remains lay in state for about twenty-four hours in St. Peter's Episcopal Church in Columbia. Confederate veterans and prominent citizens, old and young, kept vigil during the night. The next day, all business houses in the town were closed. In the afternoon, a large procession of Masons marched to the church to escort the remains of their brother to the depot. One of the leaders was Capt. R. D. Smith, who had served on Cleburne's staff. The citizenry of Columbia joined in the procession, including Cleburne's friend, Gen. Lucius Polk.[23] The train, via Decatur, Alabama, and Corinth, Mississippi, arrived at Memphis on the afternoon of April 28.

All business in Memphis had been suspended for the day. Elaborate plans to honor the hero had been made by Confederate veterans, some of whom were former comrades of the General. A reception committee, composed of Gen. Patton Anderson and two officers of Cleburne's old command, were at the station. The Emmet Guards formed two

Christopher S. Cleburne,
Half Brother of General Cleburne
(1841-1864)

Grave of Capt. Christopher S. Cleburne, Near Dublin, Va.
Photograph Taken in 1962

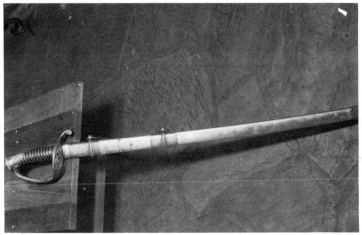

—*Courtesy Ralph V. Righton*

Sword Presented to General Cleburne
by 15th. Arkansas Infantry

—*Courtesy Texas Collection, Baylor University*

General Cleburne's Saddle

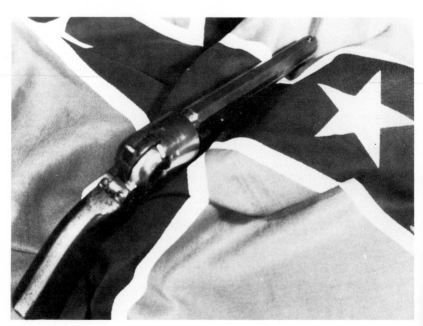

—*Courtesy U.D.C. Chapter No. 1971, Cleburne, Texas*

General Cleburne's Pistol

The Pat Cleburne Cemetery, Jonesboro, Ga.
Photograph Taken in 1965

Steamboat Pat Cleburne

—*Courtesy Col. Thomas E. Tappan*

Officers of Pat Cleburne Camp, U.C.V., No. 222 Waco, Texas
Circa 1900

—*Courtesy Mrs. C.M.T. Kirkman and the Phillips County Historical Society*

General Cleburne Grave and Monument, Confederate Hill,
Phillips County, Ark.

lines at the station entrance; and there were sixteen pallbearers, all Confederate veterans, several from Cleburne's
division. The casket was covered with a floral cross of ivy and
white roses.

A band, two military units, and the volunteer fire
department, preceded the horsedrawn hearse with the pallbearers marching on each side. In open carriages rode:
ex-President Davis, ex-Governor Harris, Generals Chalmers,
Cheatham, James F. Fagan, and Pillow, and Bishop Quintard.
General Fagan as a colonel had commanded the 1st Arkansas
Infantry at Shiloh. More than a hundred Confederate
veterans walked in the procession, followed by the Cleburne
Circle of the Fenian Brotherhood, two other Irish societies,
and the St. Andrew's Society. Also in the procession were
many citizens in carriages and on foot. In silent reverence,
the largest crowd ever before assembled in Memphis lined the
main streets to view the cortege. Bells tolled from churches
and fire-engine houses; flags throughout the city and on
steamboats were at half mast. The steamboat *George W.
Cheek* was waiting at the wharf, with the bier on the salon
deck, where the Emmet Guards took over as an escort for the
journey down the river. In the quiet twilight, from the bluff
and levee a large crowd watched the packet disappear around
the bend.[24] Thus, Memphis honored a great patriot who,
twenty years earlier, had traveled up the river, past that city,
an unknown newcomer from a foreign land.

All three Memphis newspapers were laudatory in apprais-
ing the honored chieftain. The leading newspaper, the *Daily
Appeal*, said:

> Gen. Pat Cleburne's name and deeds are familiar and dear
> to the people of the Valley of the Mississippi as those of
> Stonewall Jackson to dwellers in the mountains and lowlands
> of Virginia. Cleburne's deeds savored more of personal
> chivalric courage, and Jackson's of lofty, Christian heroism.
> The one, as regarded by the multitude, possessed the loftiest,
> sublimest courage of man; the other, that of a god. The one
> was sustained by his own proud, self-reliant manly spirit, as
> true as the blade he bore; the other, no less self-confident,
> leaned upon a Christian's faith, ... Jackson excited in the
> bosoms of his men a faith not unmixed with superstitious awe
> and reverence; while Cleburne's magnificent moral and intel-

lectual qualities appealed to the thoughtful self-reliance and pride of his followers. Cleburne made his men imitators of himself; Jackson made his, thorough devotees. Cleburne was feared, beloved and admired; while Jackson was regarded as something above and beyond ordinary men, ... There was a species of fanaticism developed by Jackson among his followers, even as Cleburne evoked, by his bearing and example, the loftiest sentiments, and appealed to the proudest incentives to honorable deeds.

Two such men have rarely lived in the same age, and that two such faultless soldiers should have risen in the armies of the same government at the same time, and each should have alike commanded the admiration of mankind, of accomplished soldiers and the undying love of their compatriots, is the chiefest wonder of the late mighty convulsion . . . .

. . . In campaigns or parts of campaigns conducted by Cleburne there was a . . . refined application of military science; . . . . Cleburne, by the excellence of his tactics, the variety and activity of his movements, and tireless toil, exhibited dazzling illustrations of wonderful military skill . . . . Jackson's "Valley Campaign," as it must long remain, is unrivaled. Of honors which it gave Jackson's name Cleburne won an equal share when he fell . . . .

When all the gravestones set up by the hand of grim-visaged war have been carved by the hand of art; . . . there are few . . . whose mausoleum shall . . . more effectively appeal to the admiration and gratitude of the people than the tablet of stone which may recite the grandest, sublimest, simplest story ever written — that of Pat Cleburne.[25]

When the *George W. Cheek* docked at Helena the next morning, on the wharf were a committee of five leading citizens and many friends and admirers of Cleburne. The pallbearers were General Tappan, Maj. W. E. Moore (former Chief Commissary, Army of Tennessee), and five veterans who had served under Cleburne. The Emmet Guards and the pallbearers led the procession up Rightor Street to St. John's Episcopal Church, past the drug store formerly owned by Nash & Cleburne. The Masonic Lodge officiated while the body lay in state at St. John's Church. Fifteen Masons "in full regalia of the ancient order" served,[26] most of whom were Confederate veterans, one having fought under Cleburne.

The grave site, in the Confederate Section of Evergreen (now Magnolia) Cemetery, was on a hilltop two miles from the church. The procession, stretching over half the distance, was led by a band in a solemn march. The fire company preceded the hearse flanked by the Masonic pallbearers; while in full regalia other Masons followed honoring their "illustrious brother." Then came many men and women from throughout the county, in carriages and on foot, with a group of young men on horseback bringing up the rear. The Masonic rites were conducted at the grave site according to "the beautiful moral teachings prescribed by the order to be read at a brother's grave."[27] The service closed with the band playing "Home, Sweet Home."[28]

4

Throughout the South people honored the memory of General Cleburne. In 1866, when Memorial Day was inaugurated by women of Columbus, Georgia, Cleburne was one of three Southern heroes mentioned. "We'll crown alike the honored resting place of the immortal Jackson in Virginia, Johnston at Shiloh, Cleburne in Tennessee, and the host of the gallant privates who adorned our ranks."[29] The United Confederate Veterans named twenty-six of their camps for Cleburne. This number was exceeded only by camps named for Stonewall Jackson, Joseph E. Johnston, and Robert E. Lee.[30]

"The snows of twenty winters have covered his modest grave," wrote Capt. C. W. Frazer of Memphis in 1884, "but now the mention of the name of Pat Cleburne brightens the eye and quickens the pulse of every man who had the fortune to fight under him."[31] Throughout life, men of his division were proud to be identified as "Pat Cleburne's boys."[32] Sixteen poems portray Cleburne's greatness and reveal the devotion of the people of the Confederacy.[33] Homage is paid to him in one poem written in the country of his birth.[34] In ten poems and a song, he shares tributes with other Confederate leaders.[35]

Cleburne's memory has been perpetuated in writings by friends and associates. Particular reference is made to the biographies and sketches by Avery, D. H. Hill, Hardee, Mangum, Benham, Edwin L. Drake, Nash, and Buck. In addition to citations given in previous chapters, quotations from two of these sources follow. General Hill wrote:

> Patrick R. Cleburne deserves a prominent place among the
> great heroes, who have illustrated Southern heroism and
> Southern history. His name brings a thrill of the heart to every
> true son of the South, just as his presence brought success
> wherever he moved on the field of battle. *"Cleburne is here!"*
> meant that "all was well."[36]

General Hardee, referring to Cleburne and his division,
declared: ". . . his fall was a greater loss to the cause he
espoused than that of any other Confederate leader,
after Stonewall Jackson." And, "Where this division
defended, no odds broke its lines; where it attacked,
no numbers resisted its onslaught, save only once;
— and there is the grave of Cleburne and his heroic
division."[37]

Other men who knew Cleburne in the war years paid
tribute to him, and foes attested to his prowess. When a
brigadier general, Cleburne's brigade, greatly feared by the
enemy, was known as "the Terrible."[38] Both Confederates
and Federals referred to his division as "Cleburne's famous
division."[39] Soldiers in the Army of Tennessee termed Cleburne "our hero, our ideal soldier,"[40] the "Knightly Cleburne,"[41] "Prex-Chevalier of the Army of Tennessee,"[42] "the
Bayard of the Army of Tennessee,"[43] "the Augereau of the
Army of Tennessee,"[44] "Bernadotte of the Western Army,"[45] "the lion hearted,"[46] "the Wizard of War,"[47] "the
Dessaix of the Confederate Army,"[48] and "the Ney of the
Southern Confederacy — 'the bravest of the brave.'"[49] The
most famous sobriquet gained by him during the war was
"the Stonewall Jackson of the West,"[50] by which he is
known to historians.

Brig. Gen. Randall L. Gibson of the Army of Tennessee
(later United States Senator from Louisiana) said of Cleburne:

> He was [a] complete . . . stranger . . . to physical or moral
> fear. He was always calm and thoroughly master of himself
> and his situation. No man, in my judgment, in either army could
> hold so many of his men around him when desperately

438

assailed. If he was ordered to advance and attack, he did it as
he would move upon the field for inspection. He would sit
unmoved on his horse and would see his division strike like a
bolt of thunder, and no member of his command could tell, by
reading his face, whether the battle was going well or ill.[51]

Confederate veteran Judge J. P. Young, an authority on the
battles in the Atlanta area and Hood's Tennessee campaign,
referred to Cleburne as "a great military mind and commander."[52]

In the twentieth century, historians John Hugh Reynolds,
T. R. Hay, Wilbur G. Kurtz, and John R. Peacock aided in
keeping Cleburne's memory green. In 1906, Reynolds, then
secretary of the Arkansas Historical Association, wrote: "Mr.
Cleburne was Arkansas' ablest general and indeed was one of
the great military leaders of the war. . . . our most distinguished soldier."[53] Careful study of Cleburne's amazing
military career justifies the conclusion that he made no
mistakes. Had Cleburne been given the opportunity to direct
an army, he may have well proved to be the best infantry
general in the Army of Tennessee.

In 1866, a veteran of the Army of Tennessee, Lieut.
Jerimiah Smith of the 22nd Alabama Infantry, suggested that
a new country in eastern Alabama be named for the General.
Cleburne County, through which passes the main highway
from Birmingham to Atlanta, is one of the most scenic
counties in Alabama.

In 1867, the pioneers of Johnson County, Texas, named
their county seat Cleburne. Many of the settlers were
Confederate soldiers who had served under the General.
Second Lieut. Matthew Graham, veteran of the 10th Texas
Infantry Regiment, Granbury's brigade, was a member of the
commission appointed to select a name for the town.
Cleburne, just a few miles south of Fort Worth, is now a
thriving city and has a population of nearly eighteen
thousand. In 1964, during the Civil War Centennial, the state
of Texas erected a monument on the courthouse grounds
explaining that the city is named for General Cleburne and
bearing a brief summary of his career. Three miles to the
southwest is Lake Pat Cleburne, which furnishes water for
the city; and sixteen miles west is Cleburne State Park.

In 1883, when the last county of Arkansas was formed, the citizens named it Cleburne. In the foothills of the beautiful Ozarks, where the meandering Little Red River becomes a large lake, Cleburne County is a popular resort.

Two communities now extinct bore the name of Cleburne: a station on the Western & Atlantic Railroad, four miles north of Atlanta; and a village in Maury County, Tennessee. Streets in the following cities and towns are named for General Cleburne: Fayetteville, and West Helena, Arkansas; Atlanta (Cleburne Avenue and Cleburne Terrace), and Marietta, Georgia; Spring Hill, Tennessee; and Cleburne, Dallas, Fort Worth, Houston, and Texarkana, Texas. In Franklin, Tennessee, there is a Cleburne Street, near the site of the breastworks, to which the town has now expanded.

In 1870, a new steam fire engine of the Little Rock Fire Department, drawn by six brown bays, was christened "The Pat Cleburne." A Mississippi River steamboat, launched by the Lee Line of Memphis, was named the *Pat Cleburne.* The citizens of Helena donated a fine portrait of the General to hang in the ballroom of the steamboat.

In historic Jonesboro, Georgia, The Pat Cleburne Cemetery is the burial ground of Confederates killed in that battle. In March 1918, the Arkansas Division of the United Daughters of the Confederacy endowed a bed in American Military Hospital No. 1 at Neuilly-sur-Seine, France, in honor of P. R. Cleburne. Presently two chapters of the United Daughters of the Confederacy and a camp of the Sons of Confederate Veterans bear the name of Cleburne.

A life-size figure of "Patrick Cleburne," clad in a Confederate general's uniform, is in the Civil War Section of the American Museum of Immigration. This museum, dedicated September 26, 1972, is located in the base of the Statue of Liberty, on Liberty Island in New York Harbor. His is the only figure of a general in that section. Also, a picture of him is in an adjoining display of photographs of nine Civil War officers who were immigrants.[54]

5

In 1866, the Probate Court of Phillips County, Arkansas, appointed a lawyer as administrator of General Cleburne's estate. The large land holdings accumulated by Cleburne were dissipated by the administrator; and the five surviving brothers and sisters, listed in the probate proceeding as his heirs, received nothing.[55]

Many years after Miss Tarleton's death, an in-law of her family discarded Cleburne's sword, unaware of its history and value. The present owner, a sword collector, purchased it from a dealer in Florida in 1960. On the scabbard is a plate stating that the sword was given to the General by his old regiment, the "Fifteenth Arkansas."

In 1900, General Cleburne's pistol was presented to the Pat Cleburne Camp of the United Confederate Veterans of Cleburne, Texas. The donor was Mr. Seakatz of New Braunfels, Texas. How he acquired possession of the pistol is unknown. When the veterans' camp became extinct, the pistol was placed in the custody of the Cleburne Chapter of the United. Daughters of the Confederacy. In 1945, the chapter presented the pistol to the Texas Army National Guard unit at Cleburne. In 1970 when the unit moved to another county, the pistol was placed in the custody of the Cleburne Chamber of Commerce and is on exhibit there. On the back strap of the silver-mounted pistol, an 1851 Colt cap and ball Navy sixshooter, is engraved, "P. R. Cleburne."

Also, about the turn of the century Cleburne's saddle was given to Baylor University at Waco, Texas. Records pertaining to the gift were lost many years ago, but the story goes that the saddle was brought back to Texas by a member of Cleburne's division who found it on the battleground of Franklin. It is now on exhibit in the Texas Collection of Baylor University. Many of the veterans living in Waco had served under Cleburne during the war, and when the camp of the United Confederate Veterans was organized there it was called the Pat R. Cleburne Camp.

6

In 1890 and 1891, the ladies of the Phillips County Memorial Association collected funds for the erection of a monument at the grave of the General. Chairman of the committee was Mrs. W. T. Moore, née Miss Naomi Hays, formerly of Columbia, Tennessee. Despite hard times, contributions came from Cleburne's friends and admirers throughout the South, including members of his command and other veterans of the Army of Tennessee. The General's brothers and sisters also contributed. Father P. E. O'Reilly, of the Catholic parish at Helena, lectured for the cause. The contributions included a bale of cotton, road carts, plows, crazy quilts, pigs, and sheep which were sold by the ladies of the Association. A Negro, born in slavery, sent $2.50, writing that General Cleburne's "Kindness to me when a little boy peddling apples upon the streets of Helena will never be forgotten."

Gen. Joseph E. Johnston had a replica of the Confederate seal molded in plaster, which was used in making an emblem for the Cleburne monument. A Union veteran, a Catholic priest of Cleveland, Ohio, an admirer of Cleburne, furnished Irish emblems for the monument and made an appeal for funds. Letters from contributors declared that Cleburne's name should be emblazoned on high for the emulation of future generations. Mrs. John T. Jones, president of the Association, died just as the goal was reached. A few hours before her death she wrote to Mrs. Moore, "You will imprint on the mind of our youth the grand attributes of Cleburne."

On Sunday, May 10, 1891, a large crowd including scores of veterans from distant points gathered for the unveiling of the monument. The colorful Chickasaw Guards of Memphis took part in the ceremony. Cleburne's brothers and sisters from Omaha, Nebraska, and Newport, Kentucky, were present. Following ceremonies at the opera house in Helena, the assemblage moved in a procession to the cemetery on Confederate Hill. General Tappan served as master of ceremonies and Father O'Reilly gave the invocation. The poem, "The Death of Cleburne," by Virginia Frazer Boyle, was read. The poet and her father, Captain Frazer, were present. Five young ladies, all daughters of Confederate veterans, unveiled the monument. The Ladies' Confederate Memorial Association of Memphis and the Fourth Alabama Veterans sent floral tributes.[56]

The monument stands on the summit of Confederate Hill, the highest surrounding Helena, 225 feet above the Mississippi. To this very hilltop Cleburne in his love of nature had often roamed.[57] The monument of Carrara marble, surmounted by an urn, is sixteen feet in height. On the front, beneath Cleburne's name, is the quotation: *"Dulce et decorum est pro patria mori."* On the three other sides are inscribed: Shiloh, Shelton House, Richmond, Ky., Chickamauga, Missionary Ridge, Ringgold Gap, and Franklin. On the base is inscribed a stanza from the poem by Naomi Hays:

> Rest thee, Cleburne; tears of sadness
>   Flow from hearts thou'st nobly won;
> Mem'ry ne'er will cease to cherish
>   Deeds of glory thou hast done.

In winter, when trees were bare, the tall marble shaft was visible from the Mississippi. Whenever men who had followed Cleburne traveled on the river past the monument, they stood at attention.

NOTES

CHAPTER XIX

[1] W. P. Johnston, *Gen. Albert Sidney Johnston*, 354.

[2] John McQuaide, Statement of, date not shown, in "Thomas R. Markham," *Confederate Veteran*, VII (1899), 272; Mangum, *Kennesaw Gazette*, II (June 15, 1887), 6; Buck, *Cleburne*, 292-93; Gertrude Whitehouse, "Gen. Cleburne's Pistol Recovered," (Cleburne, Tex.) *Yellow Jacket Yapper*, Sept. 22, 1944; Gale to his wife, Jan. 14, 1865, in "Hood's Campaign," 5; Thomas R. Markham, "Col. John McGavock," undated clipping from *Southwestern Presbyterian*, in Record Book of McGavock Confederate Cemetery, in possession of Mrs. Robert C. Bartlett, Franklin, Tenn.; Young to Hay, May 5, 1921, in Hay Collection; "Death of Gen. Strahl," *Confederate Veteran*, I (1893), 31; Mangum, *Missouri Republican*.

[3] An account of the death and burial of Gen. States Rights Gist, as given by his body servant, "Uncle Wiley" Howard, "a man of unusual ability and character. Intelligent, devoted, loyal, . . ." is contained in a Gist family scrapbook collected by Miss Margaret Adams Gist, published by Wilson Fee, *The Gist Family of South Carolina and Its Maryland Antecedents* (Charlottesville, 1934), 86-87. Uncle Wiley related that General Gist died in a field hospital the night of Nov. 30; that the next morning his body was taken from the hospital in an ambulance "to Mrs. White's — er nice lady; our hospital was betwixt her graveyard en de creek"; that General Gist was buried "in her yard, under er big cedar tree." Later, the body was removed to Trinity Churchyard, Columbia, S. C.

The two-story brick residence of William White was on the western edge of the battlefield, fronting on Boyd Mill Road, one and three-quarters miles west of the Carter house. — Miss Mildred Henderson, great granddaughter of William White, conversation with authors, Feb. 26, 1970. See deed, executed in 1877, to which B. F. White *et al.* were parties, partitioning "the lands of the late William White," Deed Record Book 8, page 54, Williamson County, Tenn. See also D. C. Beers & Co. (pub.), *Map of Williamson County, Tenn.* (Philadelphia, 1878). On this map B. F. White is depicted as the owner of the property in question. Hamilton Branch ran near this property.

The unreliability of rumor and general impressions in determining historical facts is illustrated by another version — that six bodies were on the McGavock veranda: Generals Cleburne, Adams, Strahl, Granbury, Gist, and Carter. — H. P. Figuers, "A Boy's Impressions of

Battle of Franklin," *Confederate Veteran,* XXIII (1915), 7. "On the McGavock piazza lay the cold and lifeless bodies of six Confederate generals, all slain in the battle. They were Gens. Cleburne of Arkansas, Granberry *[sic]* of Texas, Gist of South Carolina, Adams, Carter and Strahl of Tennessee." — Undated clipping from unidentified newspaper in McGavock Cemetery Record Book. General Carter, mortally wounded, was taken from the battlefield to the Harrison house, three miles south of Franklin, and died on Dec. 10. — Quintard Diary, Dec. 10, 1864.

[4]Under date of Dec. 1, 1864, Chaplain Quintard recorded in his diary: "At 10 o'clock started [from Columbia] ... for Franklin. After riding several miles towards Franklin I met Capt. [T. B.] Stepleton who was carrying the bodies of ... Gen'l Strahl, Lieut. John Marsh and Captain Jas. Johnston from the field of battle at Franklin." "Several miles" is a rather indefinite term, but the inference is justified that the chaplain at most had ridden only a third of the twenty-six-mile distance to Franklin when he met the wagon carrying General Strahl.

[5]Young to Hay, June 10, 1918, Apr. 19, 1921, in Hay Collection.

[6]Nash, *Gen. Pat Cleburne,* 197.

[7]Joseph Boyce, "Missourians in Battle of Franklin," *Confederate Veteran,* XXIV (1916), 103.

[8]William W. Gibson of Cleburne's division to Mrs. John W. McGavock in "The Women of Franklin," undated clipping from unidentified magazine, in McGavock Cemetery Record Book.

[9]Columbia (Tenn.) *Herald,* Apr. 29, 1870, p. 3; Columbia (Tenn.) *Daily Herald,* Jan. 15, 1908, p. 3.

[10]Mangum, *Kennesaw Gazette,* II (June 15, 1887), 6.

[11]Branch, *Memoirs of a Southern Woman,* 47.

[12]*Ibid.*; Mangum, *Kennesaw Gazette,* II (June 15, 1887), 6; Quintard Diary, Dec. 2, 1864.

[13]Quintard Diary, Dec. 3, 1864.

[14]*Ibid.,* Mangum, *Kennesaw Gazette,* II (June 15, 1887), 6.

[15]Hardee, "Major General Cleburne," 650.

[16]Mrs. Bedford Moore, conversation with authors, Feb. 24, 1962. See also Mobile *Evening News,* Dec. 5, 1864, p. 2.

[17]Nash, *Gen. Pat Cleburne,* 114.

[18]Mrs. Bedford Moore, conversation with authors, Feb. 24, 1962.

[19]Nash, *Gen. Pat Cleburne,* 113-14. "The military coat worn by General Patrick R. Cleburne when he was killed was given by Dr. Nash of Little Rock, Ark. to Mrs. Louise Miller Joblin in whose possession it remained until she placed it in this museum." — India W. Thomas, Director, The Confederate Museum, to authors, Aug. 16,

1962.

[20]Mangum, *Kennesaw Gazette,* II (June 15, 1887), 6; Mrs. Bedford Moore, conversation with authors, Feb. 24, 1962.

[21]Mobile *Daily Advertiser and Register,* Oct. 20, 1867; Robert Tarleton to Sallie Lightfoot, July 17, 1864, in Tarleton Family Collection; obituary, Hugh L. Cole, New York *Times,* Nov. 6, 1898, p. 7; Mobile *Daily Register,* July 1, 1868, p. 1; Records, Christ Episcopal Church, Mobile.

[22]Memphis *Daily Appeal,* Apr. 26, 1870, p. 2; Mangum, *Kennesaw Gazette,* II (June 15, 1887), 6; Memphis *Daily Avalanche,* Apr. 29, 1870, p. 3.

[23]Columbia (Tenn.) *Herald,* Apr. 29, 1870, p. 3.

[24]Memphis *Daily Avalanche,* Apr. 29, 1870, p. 3; Memphis *Public Ledger,* Apr. 28, 1870, p. 3; *ibid.,* Apr. 29, 1870, p. 1.

[25]Memphis *Daily Appeal,* Apr. 28, 1870, p. 2.

[26]Undated clipping from unidentified Helena newspaper in Scrapbk, U.D.C., Helena.

[27]*Ibid.*

[28]H. M. Grant to Editor, Helena *World,* June 29, 1891, in undated clipping from *World*; undated clippings from unidentified Helena newspapers in Scrapbk, U.D.C., Helena; Nash, *Gen. Pat Cleburne,* 199.

[29]Mary Carter Winter, "A Retrospect," *Confederate Veteran,* XXXVII (1929), 354-55; Ida Pace Purdue, *Papers Pertaining to Confederacy,* 34.

[30]The locations of camps named for Cleburne were: *Alabama.* — Dundee, Ensley. *Arkansas.* — Brinkley, Casa, Charleston, Dumas, Fayetteville, Fouke, Harrisburg, Mena, Piggott. *Florida.* — Springdale, Wauchula. *Indian Territory.* — Tecumseh, Tishomingo. *Kentucky.* — Owingsville. *Mississippi.* — Auguilla, Oxford, Rolling Fork. *Tennessee.* — Cookeville. *Texas.* — Cleburne, Hico, Navasota, Paradise, Waco. Location of Pat Cleburne Camp No. 1654 not ascertained.

[31]Frazer, "Fifth Confederate," 152.

[32]"Forty-fifth Regiment Alabama Infantry," 3; "Charles A. Leushuer," *Confederate Veteran,* XXI (1913), 248.

[33]Francis Orray Ticknor, "Loyal (To General Cleburne)," in Edwin Anderson Alderman, Joel Chandler Harris, and Charles William Kent (eds.), *Library of Southern Literature* (New Orleans, 1910), XII, 5365-66; M. A. Jennings, "Cleburne," in H. M. Wharton (comp.), *War Songs and Poems of the Southern Confederacy: 1861-1865* (Philadelphia, 1904), 114-15; "Oh No, He'll Not Need Them Again" (factually incorrect), *ibid.,* 49-50; Joseph M. Brown, "Pat Cleburne

in the Way," *Kennesaw Gazette,* II (May 15, 1887), 1; Naomi Hays, Lines written the night after Cleburne's death, *ibid.* (July 15, 1887), 3; P. L. M., "Lines on the Occasion of Gen. Pat Cleburne's Remains Passing through Memphis," Memphis *Daily Appeal,* Apr. 28, 1870, p. 4; John Trotwood Moore, "Cleburne's Banner," *Confederate Veteran,* V (1897), 569; Montgomery M. Folsom, "The Sword of Cleburne," *ibid.,* VIII (1900), 379; Walter A. Clark, "Pat Cleburne's Truce at Kennesaw," *ibid.,* XI (1903), 406-07; Milford Overley, "Cleburne at Ringgold Gap," *ibid.,* XX (1912), 542; Arthur Louis Peticobas, "Patrick Ronayne Cleburne," *ibid.,* XXXIX (1931), 25; Virginia A. Frazer, "Death of Cleburne," in Lindsley (ed.), *Military Annals of Tennessee,* 153-54; S. C. L., Luna Landing, Ark., "General Cleburne," undated clipping from unidentified newspaper in Scrapbook of Mrs. W. E. Moore, in Helena Library; three poems by Naomi Hays Moore (Mrs. W. E.), *viz.:* "Verse Written When Cleburne's Remains Were Brought to Helena" (MS, *ibid.*); "Pat Cleburne" (MS, *ibid.*); "Verse Dedicated to Portrait of Cleburne" (MS in Naomi Hays scrapbook in possession of Mrs. Moore Tappan, Helena).
[34]"Cleburne," undated clipping from Dublin (Ireland) *Nation,* in scrapbook of John E. Sherlock, in possession of Mr. Sherlock's daughter, Mrs. Charles N. Flitton, Arcadia, Calif.
[35]"Chickamauga — 'The Stream of Death,'" in William Gilmore Simms (ed.), *War Poetry of the South* (New York, 1867), 336; "Old-Time Confederates," *Confederate Veteran,* X (1902), 296; and XXVI (1918), 2 (different versions); I. M. Oliver, "The Battle of Franklin," *ibid.,* XVI (1908), 598; J. Lowrie Wilson, "The Southron's Farewell to Liberty," *ibid.,* XVIII (1910), 276-77; Virginia Frazer Boyle, Greeting to Our Heroes at Little Rock Reunion," *ibid.,* XIX (1911), cover page before p. 266; P. F. Brannan, "Confederate Comrades," *ibid.,* XIX (1911), 397; Dixon Merritt, "The Men at Chattanooga," *ibid.,* XXI (1913), 484; Poem about the Arkansas Confederate soldier, *ibid.,* XXIII (1915), 179; Fanny Downing, "Memorial Flowers," *ibid.,* XXIV (1916), 233; Arthur Louis Peticobas, "Chickamauga — September 19, 20, 1863," *ibid.,* XXXIII (1925), 330-32; Jacie Frazee Cappleman, "A Dirge to Our Southern Dead," undated clipping from unidentified newspaper, in Scrapbk, U.D.C., Helena.
[36]Hill, "Maj. Gen. Cleburne," 460.
[37]Hardee, "Major General Cleburne," 643, 650-51.
[38]Nash, *Gen. Pat Cleburne,* 205.
[39]Kohlheim, "Soldiering in Georgia," 173; "John H. Warren," *Confederate Veteran,* XV (1907), 374; *O.R.,* XXXVIII, Pt. 3, p. 571.
[40]McQuaide, Statement of, in "Markham," 272.
[41]James Dinkins, "The Battle of Franklin," New Orleans *Daily Picayune,* Nov. 30, 1902, 2nd Pt., p. 2.

[42]W. H. Rees, "Battle of New Hope Church," *Confederate Veteran*, XI (1903), 291; Buck, *Cleburne*, 297.

[43]Victor Montgomery, "The Sacrifice of the South," *Confederate Veteran*, XVIII (1910), 361.

[44]Ridley, *Battles and Sketches*, 220.

[45]W. J. McMurray, *History of the Twentieth Tennessee Regiment Volunteer Infantry, C.S.A.* (Nashville, 1904), 340.

[46]Fay Hempstead, *A Pictorial History of Arkansas* (St. Louis, 1890), 887.

[47]Nisbet, *4 Years on Firing Line*, 164.

[48]Undated clipping from Houston, Tex. *Pilot*, in Sherlock Scrapbook.

[49]Memphis *Daily Avalanche*, Apr. 29, 1870, p. 3.

[50]See, *e.g.*, War Correspondent "290," "The Battle of Ringgold," Atlanta *Daily Intellingencer*, Dec. 25, 1863, quoted in *Kennesaw Gazette*, I (Mar. 1886), 1.

[51]Typescript in Hay Collection.

[52]Young to Hay, May 26, 1921, in Hay Collection.

[53]Reynolds (ed.), *Publications of Arkansas Historical Association*, I, 238.

[54]The other eight photographs are: *Confederate Army* — Brig. Gen. Patrick T. Moore, 1st Sergt. Carl Rudolph Maximilian Pohle, drum major, 1st Regiment Virginia Volunteers; *Union Army* — Maj. Gens. Peter Joseph Osterhaus and Franz Sigel, Brig. Gens. Thomas Francis Meagher and Wladimir Krzyzanowski, and Cols. Hans Mattson and Alfred Nattie Duffie.

[55]File, Est. of P. R. Cleburne, Dec'd.

[56]New Orleans *Daily Picayune*, May 10, 1891, p. 10; *ibid.*, May 11, 1891, p. 1; Memphis *Appeal-Avalanche*, May 11, 1891, pp. 1, 2; clippings from unidentified Helena newspaper, May 10, 1891, Helena *World*, May 23, 1892, and unidentified newspapers, undated, in Scrapbook of Mrs. Moore; undated clippings from unidentified newspapers in Scrapbk, U.D.C., Helena.

[57]Mangum, *Kennesaw Gazette*, II (June 15, 1887), 6.

CHAPTER XX

EPILOGUE

The story has been told of how Patrick Ronayne and Christopher Cleburne fought and died for the Confederacy. But what of the other children and the widow of Dr. Joseph Cleburne, who also came to America?

Isabella Cleburne, a devoted "mother" to her children and stepchildren, died in Newport, Kentucky, in 1883. Her grave marker in the Cleburne family plot in Evergreen Cemetery, Newport, reads: "In Memory of OUR MOTHER, ISABELLA JANE Widow of the Late Joseph Cleburne MD."

William Cleburne was a pioneer surveyor in the westward expansion of railroads, with headquarters in Omaha, Nebraska. He was one of the first civil engineers with the Union Pacific Railroad, organized September 1862 as a "military necessity."[1] Until 1867 he was an assistant engineer in an exploring and surveying party for the construction of the railroad.

In 1873 William became Division Engineer, in charge of the construction and maintenance of roadbeds, tracks, bridges, and buildings. Late in the 1870's, he surveyed the Ogden-Salt Lake route of the Oregon Short Line Railway, a Union Pacific subsidiary. He remained Division Engineer for the Union Pacific in various locations until his retirement in 1887. In 1886, when the railroad was built through a small town in Pottawatomie County, Kansas, the citizens named the town Cleburne for the Division Engineer. The town vanished about 1962 when a lake was created by Tuttle Creek Dam.

In 1874, describing himself as "a novice" who wished "to attain a knowledge of botany," William collected, classified, and shipped to Yale University, from Wahsatch, Utah, specimens of several hundred plants indigenous to Northwestern states, which he had "gathered ... often in a great hurry." Yale named this collection for him.[2] For several years after retiring, William lectured in geology at Brownell Hall, an Episcopal school for girls near Omaha.

William acquired distinction in Masonry throughout Nebraska. He was residing in Omaha, the Territorial Capital of Nebraska, as early as 1857, when he became a member of the first Omaha lodge of Freemasonry, which was created that year. In 1890 he became a Thirty-third Degree Mason, and for the next five years was Deputy Inspector General for Nebraska of the Ancient and Accepted Scottish Rite of Freemasonry.

In 1905, following the death of his half brother Robert, William moved to Newport, Kentucky, and lived with his half sister Isabella and Robert's daughter, Isabella, until his death in December 1910. He was buried in Forest Lawn Cemetery, Omaha, with his wife, his sister Anne, and brother Joseph. William left no descendants.

After the deaths of her husband and infant daughter in 1860, Anne Cleburne Sherlock and her two sons, John E. and James L., continued living in the Newport-Cincinnati area. In 1877 they moved to Omaha to be near Anne's brother William. John became a civil engineer, and James a telegraph operator, with the Union Pacific Railroad. About 1888 John moved to Salt Lake City and built a flourishing business as owner of a knitting factory. James rose to Assistant Division Superintendent of the Union Pacific in Omaha. Anne was living in Omaha at the time of her death in July 1910.

Joseph Cleburne moved from LaPorte, Indiana, to Omaha and for many years worked for the Union Pacific. He died in Omaha in 1893 leaving two daughters, Minnie and Laura. Minnie married a Mr. Callahan, but had no issue. Laura married a Mr. Gigeric, and moved to Canada. They had five children but trace of the family has been lost.

Robert Stuart Cleburne worked as a machinist in Cincinnati and lived in Newport, Kentucky. In 1860 he was head of a household consisting of his mother, brother Christopher, and sister Isabella. Robert married about 1870; but his wife died in 1873, leaving a six-month's-old daughter, Isabella. He subsequently remarried but Isabella was his only child.

By 1877 Robert had become a mechanical engineer, and in 1879 was employed in that capacity at the famous Pike's

Opera House in Cincinnati. He remained in that position for the rest of his active life. In 1879 he became a member of Robert Burns Lodge No. 163, Free and Accepted Masons, in Newport; and was in good standing until his death in 1905. He owned the Cleburne "old home" in Newport, 620 Monroe Street.[3] His line of descent terminated at the death of his daughter, Isabella Cleburne Connelly, in 1959.

Isabella J. Cleburne, Patrick Ronayne's half sister, a music teacher in Newport, never married. Following the death of Robert's first wife, Isabella assumed the responsibility of rearing her infant niece, Isabella; and, in the latter's words, "was a mother to me."[4] Isabella cared for her elderly mother, and for her half brother William in his final illness. She died in 1916 and was buried in the family plot in Evergreen Cemetery with her mother and brother Robert.

The Cleburne family was proud of Patrick Ronayne. William and Anne collaborated with L. H. Mangum in his articles about General Cleburne in the *Arkansas Gazette* of May 30, 1886, and the *Kennesaw Gazette* of January 15, 1887. They also furnished basic facts to an Omaha newspaper for an article concerning their brother, which included the poem by Naomi Hays written the night after his death. Intermittently through the years, members of the Cleburne family corresponded with friends of the General and patriotic organizations in Helena. The family treasured and preserved letters written by Patrick Ronayne and mementoes of his military exploits.

In the Blue Ridge Mountains of Virginia, on the outskirts of the town of Dublin, near the spot where he fell, is buried the brave young Capt. Christopher Cleburne. His grave marker reads: "Died May 10, 1864 at the battle of Cloyd's Farm near Dublin, Va. in the 21st year of his age, CHRISTOPHER S. CLEBURNE 2d Kentucky Cavalry C. S. A. 'He rests in the State whose valor has given luster to the age, and his memory will not soon depart from his comrades who cherish it as that of a brave, chivalrous and true man.' " The landmark, known as "Cleburne's grave," enclosed by an iron fence, is located on the road to the Dublin airport. A lady in that area, who lived to be quite elderly, placed flowers at his grave every year on Confederate Decoration

Day. The grave is now cared for by the local chapter of the United Daughters of the Confederacy.

The only known descendants of General Cleburne's immediate family are those of Anne Cleburne Sherlock, through her two sons, John E. and James J. Sherlock:

John E. Sherlock (1854-1926), m. Dean Campbell, 1901. 1. Irene, b. 1902, m. Charles Flitton, 1948.

James J. Sherlock (1857-1935), m. Katherine Mahannal. 1. Anne (1884-1970).

Anne Sherlock, m. Charles J. Jordan, 1902. 1. James Sherlock Jordan (1903-1958); 2. Charles Cleburne Jordan, b. 1904; 3. Millicent Jordan.

James Sherlock Jordan, m. Eileen Donovan, 1944. 1. Timothy J., b. 1946; 2. Charles J., b. 1949; 3. John M., b. 1951.

Charles Cleburne Jordan, m. Margaret Lipovsky, 1936. 1. Donald Charles, b. 1937; 2. Barbara Ann, b. 1938.

Millicent Jordan, m. Jean Despujols, 1932; m. 2d, William Claire Martin, 1953. 1. Jeanne Millicent Despujols, b. 1933; 2. Jack B. Despujols, b. 1936; 3. Paulette Eugenie Despujols, b. 1941; 4. Anne Lenore Despujols, b. 1944.

Col. James Sherlock Jordan (1903-1958) was inspired by the life of his great, great uncle, General Cleburne. In the Korean Conflict, the Bronze Star medal was awarded Colonel Jordan for "superior leadership" and "ability," "complete disregard for personal hardship and devotion to duty."

NOTES

CHAPTER XX

[1]Grenville M. Dodge, *How We Built the Union Pacific* (Reprint; Denver, 1965), 10.
[2]William Cleburne to David C. Eaton, Apr. 4, May 6, 1874, in Yale University Library.
[3]Will of Robert S. Cleburne, Apr. 13, 1904, on file in office of Clerk, Campbell County, Newport, Ky.
[4]Isabella C. Connelly to Hay, Apr. 12, 1918, in Hay Collection.

APPENDIX

PROPOSAL TO MAKE SOLDIERS OF SLAVES AND GUARANTEE FREEDOM TO ALL LOYAL NEGROES. – ADDRESS BY P. R. CLEBURNE, JANUARY 2, 1864

COMMANDING GENERAL, THE CORPS, DIVISION, BRIGADE,
AND REGIMENTAL COMMANDERS
OF THE ARMY OF TENNESSEE:

GENERAL: Moved by the exigency in which our country is now placed, we take the liberty of laying before you, unofficially, our views on the present state of affairs. The subject is so grave, and our views so new, we feel it a duty both to you and the cause that before going further we should submit them for your judgment and receive your suggestions in regard to them. We therefore respectfully ask you to give us an expression of your views in the premises. We have now been fighting for nearly three years, have spilled much of our best blood, and lost, consumed, or thrown to the flames an amount of property equal in value to the specie currency of the world. Through some lack in our system the fruits of our struggles and sacrifices have invariably slipped away from us and left us nothing but long lists of dead and mangled. Instead of standing defiantly on the borders of our territory or harrassing those of the enemy, we are hemmed in to-day into less than two-thirds of it, and still the enemy menacingly confronts us at every point with superior forces. Our soldiers can see no end to this state of affairs except in our own exhaustion; hence, instead of rising to the occasion, they are sinking into a fatal apathy, growing weary of hardships and slaughters which promise no results. In this state of things it is easy to understand why there is a growing belief that some black catastrophe is not far ahead of us, and that unless some extraordinary change is soon made in our condition we must overtake it. The consequences of this condition are showing themselves more plainly every day; restlessness of morals spreading everywhere, manifesting itself in the army in a growing disregard for private rights; desertion spreading to a class of soldiers it never dared to tamper with before; military commissions sinking in the estimation of the soldier; our supplies failing; our fireside in ruins. If this state continues much longer we must be subjugated. Every man should endeavor to understand the meaning of subjugation before it is too late. We can give but a faint idea when we say it means the loss of all we now hold most sacred — slaves and all other personal property, lands, homesteads, liberty, justice, safety, pride, manhood. It means that the history of this heroic struggle will be written by the enemy; that our youth will be trained by Northern school teachers; will learn from Northern school books their version of the war; will be impressed by all the influences of history and education to regard our gallant dead as traitors, our maimed veterans as fit objects for derision. It means the crushing of Southern manhood, the hatred of our former slaves, who will, on a spy system, be our secret police. The conqueror's policy is to divide the conquered into factions and stir up animosity among them, and in training an

454

army of negroes the North no doubt holds this thought in perspective. We can see three great causes operating to destroy us: First, the inferiority of our armies to those of the enemy in point of numbers; second, the poverty of our single source of supply in comparison with his several sources; third, the fact that slavery, from being one of our chief sources of strength at the commencement of the war, has now become, in a military point of view, one of our chief sources of weakness.

The enemy already opposes us at every point with superior numbers, and is endeavoring to make the preponderance irresistible. President Davis, in his recent message, says the enemy "has recently ordered a large conscription and made a subsequent call for volunteers, to be followed, if ineffectual, by a still further draft." In addition, the President of the United States announces that "he has already in training an army of 100,000 negroes as good as any troops," and every fresh raid he makes and new slice of territory he wrests from us will add to this force. Every soldier in our army already knows and feels our numerical inferiority to the enemy. Want of men in the field has prevented him from reaping the fruits of his victories, and has prevented him from having the furlough he expected after the last reorganization; and when he turns from the wasting armies in the field to look at the source of supply, he finds nothing in the prospect to encourage him. Our single source of supply is that portion of our white men fit for duty and not now in the ranks. The enemy has three sources of supply: First, his own motley population; secondly, our slaves; and thirdly, Europeans whose hearts are fired into a crusade against us by fictitious pictures of the atrocities of slavery, and who meet no hindrance from their Governments in such enterprise, because these Governments are equally antagonistic to the institution. In touching the third cause, the fact that slavery has become a military weakness, we may rouse prejudice and passion, but the time has come when it would be madness not to look at our danger from every point of view, and to probe it to the bottom. Apart from the assistance that home and foreign prejudice against slavery has given to the North, slavery is a source of great strength to the enemy in a purely military point of view, by supplying him with an army from our granaries; but it is our most vulnerable point, a continued embarrassment, and in some respects an insidious weakness. Wherever slavery is once seriously disturbed, whether by the actual presence or the approach of the enemy, or even by a cavalry raid, the whites can no longer with safety to their property openly sympathize with our cause. The fear of their slaves is continually haunting them, and from silence and apprehension many of these soon learn to wish the war stopped on any terms. The next stage is to take the oath to save property, and they become dead to us, if not open enemies. To prevent raids we are forced to scatter our forces, and are not free to move and strike like the enemy; his vulnerable points are carefully selected and fortified depots. Ours are found in every point where there is a slave to set free. All along the lines slavery is comparatively valueless to us for labor, but of great and increasing worth to the enemy for information. It is an omnipresent spy system, pointing out our valuable men to the enemy, revealing our positions, purposes, and resources, and yet acting so safely and secretly that there is no means to guard against it. Even in the heart of our country, where our hold upon this secret espionage is firmest, it waits but the opening fire of the enemy's battle line to wake it, like a torpid serpent, into venemous activity.

In view of the state of affairs what does our country propose to do? In the words of President Davis, "no effort must be spared to add largely to our effective force as promptly as possible. The sources of supply are to be found in restoring to the army all who are improperly absent, putting an end to substitution, modifying the exemption law, restricting details, and placing in the ranks such of the able-bodied men now employed as wagoners, nurses, cooks, and other employes, as are doing service for which the negroes may be found competent." Most of the men improperly absent, together with many of the exempts and men having substitutes, are now without the Confederate lines and cannot be calculated on. If all the exempts capable of bearing arms were enrolled, it will give us the boys below eighteen, the men above forty-five, and those persons who are left at home to meet the wants of the country and the army, but this modification of the exemption law will remove from the fields and manufactories most of the skill that directed agriculture and mechanical labor, and, as stated by the President, "details will have to be made to meet the wants of the country," thus sending many of the men to be derived from this source back to their homes again. Independently of this, experience proves that striplings and men above conscript age break down and swell the sick lists more than they do the ranks. The portion now in our lines of the class who have substitutes is not on the whole a hopeful element, for the motives that created it must have been stronger than patriotism, and these motives added to what many of them will call breach of faith, will cause some to be not forthcoming, and others to be unwilling and discontented soldiers. The remaining sources mentioned by the President have been so closely pruned in the Army of Tennessee that they will be found not to yield largely. The supply from all these sources, together with what we now have in the field, will exhaust the white race, and though it should greatly exceed expectations and put us on an equality with the enemy, or even give us temporary advantages, still we have no reserve to meet unexpected disaster or to supply a protracted struggle.

Like past years, 1864 will diminish our ranks by the casualties of war, and what source of repair is there left us? We therefore see in the recommendation of the President only a temporary expedient, which at best will leave us twelve months hence in the same predicament we are in now. The President attempts to meet only one of the depressing causes mentioned; for the other two he has proposed no remedy. They remain to generate lack of confidence in our final success, and to keep us moving down hill as heretofore. Adequately to meet the causes which are now threatening ruin to our country, we propose, in addition to a modification of the President's plans, that we retain in service for the war all troops now in service, and that we immediately commence training a large reserve of the most courageous of our slaves, and further that we guarantee freedom within a reasonable time to every slave in the South who shall remain true to the Confederacy in this war. As between the loss of independence and the loss of slavery, we assume that every patriot will freely give up the latter — give up the negro slave rather than be a slave himself. If we are correct in this assumption it only remains to show how this great national sacrifice is, in all human probabilities, to change the current of success and sweep the invader from our country.

Our country has already some friends in England and France, and there are strong motives to induce these nations to recognize and assist us, but they cannot assist without helping slavery, and to do this would be in conflict with their policy for the last quarter of a century. England has paid hundreds of millions to emancipate her West India slaves and break up the slave trade. Could she now consistently spend her treasure to reinstate slavery in this country? But this barrier once removed, the sympathy and the interests of these and other nations will accord with our own, and we may expect from them both moral support and material aid. One thing is certain, as soon as the great sacrifice to independence is made and known in foreign countries there will be a complete change of front in our favor of the sympathies of the world. This measure will deprive the North of the moral and material aid which it now derives from the bitter prejudices with which foreigners view the institution, and its war, if continued, will henceforth be so despicable in their eyes that the source of recruiting will be dried up. It will leave the enemy's negro army no motive to fight for, and will exhaust the source from which it has been recruited. The idea that it is their special mission to war against slavery has held growing sway over the Northern people for many years, and has at length ripened into an armed and bloody crusade against it. This baleful superstition has so far supplied them with a courage and constancy not their own. It is the most powerful and honestly entertained plank in

457

their war platform. Knock this away and what is left? A bloody ambition for more territory, a pretended veneration for the Union, which one of their own most distinguished orators (Doctor Beecher[1] in his Liverpool speech) openly avowed was only used as a stimulus to stir up the anti-slavery crusade, and lastly the poisonous and selfish interests which are the fungus growth of war itself. Mankind may fancy it a great duty to destroy slavery, but what interest can mankind have in upholding this remainder of the Northern war platform? Their interests and feelings will be diametrically opposed to it. The measure we propose will strike dead all John Brown fanaticism, and will compel the enemy to draw off altogether, or in the eyes of the world to swallow the Declaration of Independence without the sauce and disguise of philanthropy. This delusion of fanaticism at an end, thousands of Northern people will have leisure to look at home and to see the gulf of despotism into which they themselves are rushing.

The measure will at one blow strip the enemy of foreign sympathy and assistance, and transfer them to the South; it will dry up two of his three sources of recruiting; it will take from his negro army the only motive it could have to fight against the South, and will probably cause much of it to desert over to us; it will deprive his cause of the powerful stimulus of fanaticism, and will enable him to see the rock on which his so-called friends are now piloting him. The immediate effect of the emancipation and enrollment of negroes on the military strength of the South would be: To enable us to have armies numerically superior to those of the North, and a reserve of any size we might think necessary; to take the offensive, move forward, and forage on the enemy. It would open to us in prospective another and almost untouched source of supply, and furnish us with the means of preventing temporary disaster, and carrying on a protracted struggle. It would instantly remove all the vulnerability, embarrassment, and inherent weakness which result from slavery. The approach of the enemy would no longer find every household surrounded by spies; the fear that sealed the master's lips and the avarice that has, in many cases, tempted him practically to desert us would alike be removed. There would be no recruits awaiting the enemy with open arms, no complete history of every neighborhood with ready guides, no fear of insurrection in the rear, or anxieties for the fate of loved ones when our armies moved forward. The chronic irritation of hope deferred would be joyfully ended with the negro, and the sympathies of his whole race would be due to his native South. It would restore confidence in an early termination of the war with all its inspiring consequences, and even if contrary to all expectations the enemy should succeed in overrunning the South, instead of finding a cheap, ready-made means of holding it down, he would find a common hatred and thirst for vengeance, which would break into acts at every favorable opportunity, would prevent him from settling on our lands, and render the South a very unprofitable conquest. It would remove forever all selfish taint from our cause and place independence above every question of property. The very magnitude of the sacrifice itself, such as no nation has ever voluntarily made before, would appall our enemies, destroy his spirit and his finances, and fill our hearts with a pride and singleness of purpose which would clothe us with new strength in battle. Apart from all other aspects of the question, the necessity for more fighting men is upon us. We can only get a sufficiency by making the negro share the danger and hardships of the war. If we arm and train him and make him fight for the country in her hour of dire distress, every consideration of principle and policy demand that we should set him and his whole race who side with us free. It is a first principle with mankind that he who offers his life in defense of the State should receive from her in return his freedom and his happiness, and we believe in acknowledgement of this principle. The Constitution of the Southern States has reserved to their respective governments the power to free slaves for meritorious services to the State. It is politic besides. For many years, ever since the agitation of the subject of slavery commenced, the negro has been dreaming of freedom, and his vivid imagination has surrounded that condition with so many gratifications that it has become the paradise of his hopes. To attain it he will tempt dangers and difficulties not exceeded by the bravest soldiers in the field. The hope of freedom is perhaps the only moral incentive that can be applied to him in his present condition. It would be preposterous then to expect him to fight against it with any degree of enthusiasm, therefore we must bind him to our cause by no doubtful bonds; we must leave no possible loop-hole for treachery to creep in. The slaves are dangerous now, but armed, trained, and collected in an army they would be a thousand fold more dangerous; therefore when we make soldiers of them we must make free men of them beyond all question, and thus enlist their sympathies also. We can do this more effectually than the North can now do, for we can give the negro not only his own freedom, but that of his wife and child, and can secure it to him in his old home. To do this, we must immediately make his marriage and parental relations sacred in the eyes of the law and forbid their sale. The past legislation of the South concedes that a large free middle class of negro blood, between the master and slave, must sooner or later destroy the institution. If, then, we touch the institution at all, we would do best to make the most of it, and by emancipating the whole race upon reasonable terms, and within such reasonable time as will prepare both races for the change, secure to ourselves all the advantages, and to our enemies all the disadvantages that can arise, both at home and abroad, from such a sacrifice. Satisfy the negro that if he faithfully adheres to our standard during the war he shall receive his freedom and that of his race. Give him as an earnest of our intentions such immediate immunities as will impress him with our sincerity and be in keeping with his new condition, enroll a portion of his class as soldiers of the Confederacy, and we change the race from a dreaded weakness to a position of strength.

Will the slaves fight? The helots of Sparta stood their masters good stead in battle. In the great sea fight of Lepanto where the Christians checked forever the spread of Mohammedanism over Europe, the galley slaves of portions of the fleet were promised freedom, and called on to fight at a critical moment of the battle. They fought well, and civilization owes much to those brave galley slaves. The negro slaves of Saint Domingo, fighting for freedom, defeated their white masters and the French troops sent against them. The negro slaves of Jamaica revolted, and under the name of Maroons held the mountains against their masters for 150 years, and the experience of this war has been so far that half-trained negroes have fought as bravely as many other half-trained Yankees. If, contrary to the training of a lifetime, they can be made to face and fight bravely against their former masters, how much more probable is it that with the allurement of a higher reward, and led by those masters, they would submit to discipline and face dangers.

We will briefly notice a few arguments against this course. It is said Republicanism cannot exist without the institution. Even were this true, we prefer any form of government of which the Southern people may have the moulding, to one forced upon us by a conqueror. It is said the white man cannot perform agricultural labor in the South. The experience of this army during the heat of summer from Bowling Green, Ky., to Tupelo, Miss., is that the white man is healthier when doing reasonable work in the open field than at any other time. It is said an army of negroes cannot be spared from the fields. A sufficient number of slaves is now administering to luxury alone to supply the place of all we need, and we believe it would be better to take half the able-bodied men off a plantation than to take the one master mind that economically regulated [regulates ?] its operations. Leave some of the skill at home and take some of the muscle to fight with. It is said slaves will not work after they are freed. We think necessity and a wise legislation will compel them to labor for a living. It is said it will cause terrible excitement and some disaffection from our cause. Excitement is far preferable to the apathy which now exists, and disaffection will not be among the fighting men. It is said slavery is all we are fighting for, and if we give it up we give up all. Even if this were true, which we deny, slavery is not all our enemies are fighting for. It is merely the pretense to establish sectional superiority and a more centralized form of government, and to deprive us of our rights and liberties.[2] We have now briefly proposed a plan which we believe will save our country. It may be imperfect, but in all human probability it would give us our independence. No objection ought to outweigh it which is not weightier than independence. If it is worthy of being put in practice it ought to be mooted quickly before the people, and urged earnestly by every man who believes in its efficacy. Negroes will require much training; training will require time, and there is danger that this concession to common sense may come too late.

P. R. CLEBURNE, major-general, commanding division;

D. C. GOVAN, brigadier-general;

JOHN E. MURRAY, colonel Fifth Arkansas;

G. F. BAUCUM, colonel Eight Arkansas;

PETER SNYDER, lieutenant-colonel, commanding Sixth and Seventh Arkansas;

E. WARFIELD, lieutenant-colonel, Second Arkansas;

M. P. LOWREY, brigadier-general;

A. B. HARDCASTLE, colonel Thirty-second and Forty-Fifth Mississippi;

F. A. ASHFORD, major Sixteenth Alabama;

JOHN W. COLQUITT, colonel First Arkansas;

RICH. J. PERSON, major Third and Fifth Confederate;

G. S. DEAKINS, major Thirty-Fifth and Eighth Tennessee;

J. H. COLLETT, captain, commanding Seventh Texas;

J. H. KELLY, brigadier-general, commanding Cavalry Division.

FOOTNOTES TO APPENDIX

[1]Henry Ward Beecher.
[2]This sentence, previously quoted, p 67, *supra*, is requoted in context.

BIBLIOGRAPHY

PRIMARY SOURCES

OFFICIAL DOCUMENTS AND RECORDS

Public Record Office, London

Records of Her Majesty's 41st Regiment of Foot, January 1, 1846 – September 30, 1849.

Dublin, Ireland

County Cork Ordnance Survey, 1845, National Library of Ireland.
Lease, dated April 16, 1836, between John Hawkes and Joseph Cleburne, Registry of Deeds.
Marriage settlement, dated September 13, 1823, made by Patrick Ronayne of Anne Brook, Registry of Deeds.
Surveyors House Book, dated July 22, 1848, as supplemented August 20, 1851, Public Record Office of Ireland.

Library of Congress

"Journal of the Congress of the Confederate States of America, 1861-1865," *U.S. Senate Documents*, 58th Cong., 2d Sess., No. 234 (Washington, 1905), VI, VII.
Journal of the Senate of the State of Mississippi, Called Session at Columbus, February and March, 1865 (Meridian, 1865).
The War of the Rebellion: A Compilation of the Official Records of the Union and Confederate Armies (Washington, 1880-1901), 70 vols. in 128 parts (cited in footnotes as *O.R.*); and accompanying *Atlas*.

National Archives Building

Circular dated July 21, 1863, Headquarters Hill's Corps, Army of Tennessee, By command of Cleburne, to A. P. Stewart, Record Group 109 (cited hereinafter as RG__).
Cleburne, P. R., Report of Military Operations, September 27, 1861 (MS in War Department Collection of Confederate Records, Miscellaneous Papers of Officers, 1862-64, RG 109.
Cleburne, Report of Military Operations, September 30, 1862 (MS in Miscellaneous Papers of Officers, RG 109).
Communications to and from Cleburne's Division, January 31, 1863 – October 20, 1864 (Copied from books lent by Irving Buck), Chap. 2,

Vol. 265, RG 109.

Compiled Service Records of Cleburne and numerous other Confederate soldiers, RG 109.

15th (Cleburne's — Polk's — Josey's) Arkansas Infantry, Muster and Pay Rolls, 1861-65, RG 109; and Descriptive List of "Yell Rifles" filed therewith.

General Orders No. 83, Richmond, June 13, 1863, RG 109.

T. C. Hindman Papers, RG 109.

Inspection Report of Cleburne's Division, Hardee's Corps, August 25, 1864, 8-H-14, RG 109.

Letters Received by the Confederate Adjutant and Inspector General, 1861-1865, RG 109 (cited in footnotes as AIGO).

List of Organization, July 3, 1861, from record, Co. E, 15th (Cleburne's — Polk's — Josey's) Arkansas Infantry, RG 109.

Manuscript No. 6722, Issues to Commissioned Officers, Cleburne's Division, Fourth Qr., 1863, RG 109.

Passenger List and Cargo Manifest, *Barque Bridgetown*, Arrived December 26, 1849, Port of New Orleans, RG 36.

Polk, L., to N. B. Forrest, September 19 (1:30 A.M.), 1862, Ch. II, Vol. 13, RG 109.

Records of the Appointment of Postmaster in Phillips County, Ark., Record of the Post Office Department, XIV, RG 28.

Records of Events from Muster Rolls of Field and Staff and all companies in the following Confederate regiments for the periods specified: *Alabama.* — 33rd Alabama Infantry, January 1863 — December 1863. *Arkansas.* — 1st (Colquitt's) Arkansas Infantry, October 31, 1862 — August 31, 1864; 15th (Cleburne's — Polk's — Josey's) Arkansas Infantry, January 1, 1862 — August 1864; 24th Arkansas Infantry, June 30, 1863 — December 31, 1863. *Mississippi.* — 32nd Mississippi Infantry, March 1863 — April 1864. *Tennessee.* — 2nd (Robison's) Tennessee Infantry, September 1862 — April 1864; 2nd (Walker's) Tennessee Infantry, July 17, July 19, July 23, 1863; 12th Tennessee Infantry, September and October 1862; 13th Tennessee Infantry, May 2, May 5, May 6, 1863; 23rd Tennessee Infantry, May 1862 — October 1862; 24th Tennessee Infantry, December 31, 1861 — April 1863; 35th (formerly 5th) Tennessee Infantry, February 28, 1862 — April 1864; 47th Tennessee Infantry, July 1862 — October 1862; 48th (Nixon's) Tennessee Infantry, January 1863 — February 1864; 154th Tennessee Infantry, May 5, 1863. *Texas.* — 7th Texas Infantry, September 1863 — February 1864; 10th Texas Infantry, December 31, 1862 — April 1864; 18th Texas Cavalry, July 1, 1862 — October 1863.

Riely, John W., to Cleburne, November 7, 1863, Ch. I, Vol. 39, RG 109.

Special Field Orders and Special Orders, Army of Tennessee, July 1874
    — April 1865, Ch. II, Vol. 349, RG 109.
U.S. Census Schedules, 1850, 1860, La Porte County, Ind.; *ibid.*, 1850,
    1860, Phillips County, Ark.; *ibid.*, 1860, Campbell County, Ky., RG
    29.
Voucher, Joseph F. Duffer (MS in Citizens' File, RG 109).

Arkansas History Commission, Little Rock

Order, Cleburne to Capt. Earle, Crittenden Rangers, July 4, 1861.
Schedule IV, U.S. Census Schedules, 1850, Phillips County, Ark.
Tax List, Phillips County, Ark., 1850-51.

Courthouse, Phillips County, Arkansas

Circuit Court Record Book "13."
County Court Record, October Term 1861, Vol. "G."
Deed Record Books, 1850-1861.
File, Estate of Patrick R. Cleburne, Dec'd, Probate File No. C-2-104.
Marriage Transcript Record Book, Vol. 1.
Nicholas Rightor, Surveyor, A Map of the Town of Helena, 1820
    (copied from original by L. R. Parmelee, Civil Engineer, in 1924).

The Western Reserve Historical Society, Cleveland

Cleburne to Braxton Bragg, January 13, 1863 (MS in Braxton Bragg
    Papers).
Cleburne to Bragg, November 27, 1863 (MS in Bragg Papers).
Cleburne, Report of Military Operations, September 26, 1862 (MS in
    William P. Palmer Collection).
Cleburne, Report of Military Operations, October 1, 1862 (MS in Bragg
    Papers).
Ten communications between officers in the Army of Tennessee other
    than Cleburne (MSS in Bragg Papers).

Tennessee State Library and Archives, Nashville

Cheatham's Journal of Military Operations around Atlanta (MS in
    Benjamin Franklin Cheatham Papers).
Cleburne, "Report of Battle of Chickamauga" (MS in Cheatham
    Papers).
Melancthom Smith Journal of the Dalton and Atlanta Campaign (MS in
    Cheatham Papers).

Henry E. Huntington Library and Art Gallery

Buckner, S. B., "Report of the Battle of Perryville," dated November 6, 1862 (MS). (HM — SB 265.)
Cleburne, "Report of Battle of 'Pickett Settlement,' May 27, 1864" (MS). (HM — JO 472.)
Polk, L., to Joseph E. Johnston, May 12, 1864 (MS). (HM — JO 250.)

Other Locations

Cleburne to D. H. Hill, September 30, 1863, in Daniel Harvey Hill Papers, North Carolina Department of Archives and History, Raleigh.
Cleburne to Hill, October 15, 1863, in D. H. Hill Papers, Virginia State Library, Richmond.
Cleburne, Report of Military Operations, September 28, 1862 (MS in Historical Society of Pennsylvania, Philadelphia, hereinafter cited as Hist. Soc. Pa.).
Deed Record Book 8, in Courthouse, Williamson County, Tenn.
Holland, James W., Superintendent, Shiloh National Military Park, memorandum for the Director, September 15, 1945, photostat in papers of Monroe F. Cockrell, Evanston.
Marriage Book C-1, in Courthouse, Greene County, Ala.
Will of Robert S. Cleburne, April 13, 1904, in office of Clerk, Campbell County, Newport, Ky.

BOOKS, MONOGRAPHS

Archer, W. P. *History of the Battle of Atlanta* (Knoxville, Ga., 1940).
Atkinson, J. R. (ed.). *The Civil War Letters of Captain Elliot H. Fletcher of Mill Bayou, Mississippi County, Arkansas: July to December 1861* (Little Rock, 1963).
Avery, I. W. "Patrick Ronayne Cleburne," *Kennesaw Gazette*, II (May 15, 1887).
Benham, Calhoun. "Major-Gen. P. R. Cleburne," *Kennesaw Gazette*, IV (1889).
Branch, Mary Polk. *Memoirs of a Southern Woman* (Chicago, 1912).
Breckinridge, W. C. P. "The Opening of the Atlanta Campaign," in Robert U. Johnson and Clarence O. Buell (eds.), *Battles and Leaders of the Civil War* (New York, 1887), III.
Buck, Irving A. *Cleburne and His Command* (Reprint; Jackson, Tenn., 1959).
Buell, Don Carlos. "East Tennessee and the Campaign of Perryville," in *Battles and Leaders*, III.

Cate, Wirt Armistead (ed.). *Two Soldiers: The Campaign Diaries of Thomas J. Key, C.S.A., December 7, 1863-May 17, 1865, and Robert J. Campbell, U.S.A., January 1, 1864-July 21, 1864* (Chapel Hill, N. C.).

Chilton, F. B. *Hood's Texas Brigade: A History & a Confederate Scrap Book* (Houston, 1911).

Cox, Jacob D. "Atlanta," in *The Army in the Civil War* (New York, 1886), IX.

─────────. *The Battle of Franklin, Tennessee* (New York, 1897).

─────────. *Franklin and Nashville* (New York, 1882).

Davis, Jefferson. *The Rise and Fall of the Confederate Government* (New York, 1958), I.

Dodge, Grenville M. *The Battle of Atlanta and Other Campaigns, Addresses, etc.* (Denver, 1965).

─────────. *How We Built the Union Pacific* (Reprint; Denver, 1965).

Drake, Edwin L. "General Patrick R. Cleburne," in Drake (ed.), *The Annals of the Army of Tennessee and Early Western History* (Nashville, 1878), I.

Duke, Basil W. *A History of Morgan's Cavalry* (Reprint; Bloomington, Ind., 1960).

─────────. *Reminiscences of General Basil W. Duke, C.S.A.* (New York, 1911).

Frazer, C. W. "Fifth Confederate," in John Berrien Lindsley (ed.), *The Military Annals of Tennessee* (Confederate), Nashville, 1886.

French, Samuel G. *Two Wars: an Autobiography* (Nashville, 1901).

Gay, Mary A. H. *Life in Dixie During the War* (Atlanta, 1892).

Gordon, John B. *Reminiscences of the Civil War* (New York, 1904).

Grant, U. S. *Personal Memoirs of U. S. Grant* (New York, 1886).

Hammond, Paul F. "Campaign of General E. Kirby Smith in Kentucky in 1862," *Southern Historical Society Papers*, X (cited hereinafter as *S.H.S.P.*).

Hardee, W. J. "Biographic Sketch of Major General P. R. Cleburne," in John Francis Maguire, *The Irish in America* (New York, 1873).

─────────. "Memoranda of Operations of my Corps, while under the command of General J. E. Johnston, in the Dalton and Atlanta, and North Carolina Campaigns," in Joseph E. Johnson, *Narrative of Military Operations* (Bloomington, Ind., 1959).

Hazen, W. B. *A Narrative of Military Service* (Boston, 1885).

Head, Thomas A. *Campaigns and Battles of the Sixteenth Regiment, Tennessee Volunteers, in the War Between the States* (Nashville, 1885).

Hill, D. H. "A Sketch of Maj. Gen. P. R. Cleburne," in Hill (ed.), *The Land We Love*, II (1867).

Hill, Daniel H. "Chickamauga — The Great Battle of the West," in

Battles and Leaders, III.

Hood, J. B. *Advance and Retreat*, ed. Richard N. Current (Bloomington, Ind., 1959).

Howard, Oliver A. "The Struggle for Atlanta," in *Battles and Leaders*, IV.

Howe, M. A. DeWolfe (ed.). *Home Letters of General Sherman* (New York, 1909).

Johnston, Joseph E. *Narrative of Military Operations.*

Johnson & Yerkes (print.). *Journal of both Sessions of the Convention of the State of Arkansas, Which Were Begun and Held in the Capitol, in the City of Little Rock* (Little Rock, 1861).

──────────. *Proceedings of the M: W: Grand Lodge of Free and Accepted Masons of the State of Arkansas: Held at Little Rock, November 6th, 1854* (Little Rock, 1854).

Jones, J. B. *A Rebel War Clerk's Diary*, ed. Howard Swiggett (New York, 1935), II.

Jordan, Thomas and Pryor, J. P. *The Campaigns of Lieut.-Gen. N. B. Forrest and of Forrest's Cavalry* (New Orleans, 1868).

Kirwan, A. D. (ed.). *Johnny Green of the Orphan Brigade* (Lexington, 1956).

Kniffin, G. C. "The Battle of Stone's River," in *Battles and Leaders*, III.

Lowrey, M. P. "Gen. M. P. Lowrey," *Kennesaw Gazette*, III (Nov. 15, 1888).

Mangum, L. H. "General P. R. Cleburne," *Kennesaw Gazette*, II (May 15, 1887).

──────────. "General Patrick Cleburne," Little Rock *Arkansas Gazette*, May 30, 1886.

──────────. Statement of under heading, "General Cleburne on Freeing the Negroes," *Kennesaw Gazette*, III (June 1, 1888).

──────────. Statement of under heading, "Gen. Pat Cleburne's Life and Death," St. Louis *Missouri Republican*, Sept. 12, 1885.

McKinnon, John L. *History of Walton County* (Atlanta, 1911).

McMurray, W. J. *History of the Twentieth Tennessee Regiment Volunteer Infantry, C.S.A.* (Nashville, 1904).

Miller, E. (ed.). *A Soldier's Honor* (New York, 1902).

Morrison, James L., Jr. (ed.). "The Memoirs of Henry Heth," *Civil War History*, VIII (1962).

Munson, Gilbert D. "Battle of Atlanta," in Robert Hunter (ed.), *Papers Prepared for the Ohio Commandery of the Military Order of the Loyal Legion of the United States* (Cincinnati, 1890), III.

Nash, Charles Edward. *Biographical Sketches of Gen. Pat Cleburne and Gen. T. C. Hindman* (Little Rock, 1898).

Nisbet, James Cooper. *4 Years on the Firing Line* (Reprint; Jackson, Tenn., 1963).

Noll, Arthur Howard (ed.). *Doctor Quintard, Chaplain C.S.A. and Second Bishop of Tennessee* (Sewanee, Tenn., 1905).

Raines, C. W. (ed.). *Six Decades in Texas or Memoirs of Francis Richard Lubbock* (Austin, 1900).

Roy, T. B. "General Hardee and the Military Operations around Atlanta," *S.H.S.P.*, VIII (1880).

Shellenberger, John K. *The Battle of Spring Hill, Tennessee: November 29, 1864* (Cleveland, 1913).

Sherman, William T. *Memoirs of General William T. Sherman* (New York, 1913), II.

——————. "The Grand Strategy of the Last Year of the War," in *Battles and Leaders*, IV.

Simpson, Harold B. (ed.). *The Bugle Softly Blows* (Waco, 1965).

Speed, Thomas. "The Battle of Franklin, Tennessee," in Robert Hunter (ed.), *Sketches of War History: 1861-1865: Papers Prepared for the Ohio Commandery of the Military Order of the Loyal Legion of the United States* (Cincinnati, 1890).

Stewart, Nixon B. *Dan McCook's Regiment, 52nd O.V.I.* (Alliance, Ohio, 1900).

Stone, Henry. "The Battle of Franklin, Tennessee," in Theodore F. Dwight (ed.), *Papers of the Military Historical Society of Massachusetts* (Boston, 1908), VII.

Strong, William E. "The Death of General James B. McPherson," in Military Order of the Loyal Legion of the United States, *Military Essays and Recollections: Papers Read before the Commandery of the State of Illinois* (Chicago, 1891), I.

Taylor, Richard. *Destruction and Reconstruction: Personal Experiences of the Late War*, ed. Richard B. Harwell (New York, 1904).

Tuthill, Richard S. "An Artilleryman's Recollections of The Battle of Atlanta," in Military Order of the Loyal Legion of the United States, *Military Essays and Recollections: Papers Read before the Commandery of the State of Illinois* (Chicago, 1891), I.

Watkins, Sam R. *"Co. Aytch"* (Reprint; Jackson, Tenn., 1952).

Wheeler, Joseph. "Bragg's Invasion of Kentucky," in *Battles and Leaders*, III.

Wilson, James Harrison. *Under the Old Flag* (New York, 1912), II.

Wright, Marcus J. *Diary of Brigadier-General Marcus J. Wright, C.S.A., April 23, 1861-February 26, 1863* (n.p., n.d.).

Young, J. P. "Hood's Failure at Spring Hill," *Confederate Veteran*, XVI (1908).

Younger, Edward (ed.). *Inside the Confederate Government: The Diary of Robert Garlick Hill Kean, Head of the Bureau of War* (New York, 1957).

468

ARTICLES, ADDRESSES

Alderson, William T. (ed.). "The Civil War Reminiscences of John Johnston, 1861-1865," *Tennessee Historical Quarterly*, XIII (1954).

Barnes, W. T. "An Incident of Kenesaw *[sic]* Mountain," *Confederate Veteran*, XXX (1922).

Barr, James. "The Battle of Franklin," *Southern Bivouac*, N.S., I (1885-86).

Beach, J. N. "From the Union Side at Franklin," *Confederate Veteran*, II (1894).

Berry, J. M. "The Quiet Humor of Gen. Pat Cleburne," *Confederate Veteran*, XII (1904).

Boyce, Joseph. "Missourians in Battle of Franklin," *Confederate Veteran*, XXIV (1916).

Brown, A. H. "Reminiscences of a Private Soldier," *Confederate Veteran*, XVII (1909).

Brown, W. C. "How Confederates Treated a Federal," *Confederate Veteran*, XIII (1905).

Carnes, W. W. "Chickamauga," *S.H.S.P.*, XIV (1886).

Chapman, W. S. "Correct Date of Battle of Jonesboro," *Confederate Veteran*, XII (1904).

Cheatham, B. F. "The Lost Opportunity at Spring Hill, Tenn.," *S.H.S.P.*, IX (1881).

Cheney, H. J. "Reminiscences of War Incidents," *Confederate Veteran*, XVIII (1910).

Collins, John L. "Gallant Mike Farrell," *Confederate Veteran*, XXXIV (1926).

"Concerning Re-Enlistmant at Dalton," *Confederate Veteran*, IX (1901).

Cunningham, S. A. "Events Leading to the Battle," *Confederate Veteran*, XVIII (1910).

Dabney, T. G. "Fight at Dead Angle, in Georgia," *Confederate Veteran*, XIV (1906).

———————. "When Hood Superseded Johnston," *Confederate Veteran*, XXII (1914).

Dana, Charles A. "Reminiscences of Men and Events of the Civil War," *McClure's Magazine*, X (1898).

"Death of Gen. Strahl," *Confederate Veteran*, I (1893).

Dinkins, James. "The Battle of Franklin," New Orleans *Daily Picayune*, November 30, 1902.

Dodd, W. O. "Reminiscences of Hood's Tennessee Campaign," *S.H.S.P.*, IX (1881).

Erwin, Joseph. "Swett's Battery at Jonesboro," *Confederate Veteran*, XII (1904).

Figuers, H. P. "A Boy's Impressions of Battle of Franklin," *Confederate Veteran*, XXIII (1915).

Gordon, George W. Address, November 30, 1899, in "Confederate Monument at Franklin," *Confederate Veteran*, VIII (1900).

──────────. Oration, May 10, 1891, at dedication of Cleburne monument, Helena, in "General P. R. Cleburne," *S.H.S.P.*, XVIII (1890).

Harley, Stan C. *Confederate Veteran*, VII (1899).

──────────. "Flag of Sixth Arkansas — Cleburne's Flag," *Confederate Veteran*, V (1897).

Henry, Pat. "Regimental Losses," *Confederate Veteran*, XXIII (1915).

Hockersmith, P. E. "The Battle of Missionary Ridge," *Confederate Veteran*, VIII, (1900).

Jones, James A. "About the Battle of Shiloh," *Confederate Veteran*, VII (1899).

Kohlheim, C. F. "Soldiering in Georgia in 1864," *Confederate Veteran*, XIX (1911).

Mallett, J. M. Address, Mar. 15, 1903, Cleburne, Tex., at celebration "Birthday of Pat Cleburne," quoted in (Cleburne) *Daily Enterprise*, March 16, 1903.

M'Clure, Joseph. "Wounded Texan's Trip Home on Crutches," *Confederate Veteran*, XVII (1909).

McQuaide, John, "Thomas R. Markham," *Confederate Veteran*, II (1899).

M'Daniel, J. R. "A Story of Shiloh," Nashville *American*, Apr. 6, 1908.

Milner, W. J. "Lieut. Gen. William Joseph Hardee," *Confederate Veteran*, XXII (1914).

M'Neilly, James H. "Franklin — Incidents of the Battle," *Confederate Veteran*, XXVI (1918).

Nelson, H. K. "Tennessee, a Grave or a Free Home," *Confederate Veteran*, XV (1907).

Ora. "Our Army Correspondence" (from Tullahoma, Tenn.), Mobile *Advertiser and Register*, January 21, 1863.

Peay, Austin. "The Battle of Dug Gap, Ga.," *Confederate Veteran*, XXIX (1921).

Peebles, T. H. "From Participant in Battle of Shiloh," *Confederate Veteran*, XVI (1908).

Pickett, W. D. "The Dead Angle," *Confederate Veteran*, XIV (1906).

Pilsbury, W. K. "The Fifth Georgia at Chickamauga," *Confederate Veteran*, III (1895).

Pirtle, John B. Address, February 1, 1881, Louisville, to Southern Historical Society, quoted in Louisville *Courier-Journal*.

Plummer, O. T. Address, about 1896, Cleburne, Tex., at memorial service honoring General Cleburne, quoted in undated and unidentified newspaper clipping in "Scrap Book" in Cleburne Public Library.

Rees, W. H. "Battle of New Hope Church," *Confederate Veteran*, XI (1903).

Roberts, Frank Stovall. "Spring Hill — Franklin — Nashville, 1864," *Confederate Veteran*, XXVII (1919).

Sanders, D. W. "Hood's Tennessee Campaign," *Southern Bivouac*, N.S., I (1885-86).

Shannon, Isaac N. "Sharpshooters with Hood's Army," *Confederate Veteran*, XV (1907).

Shapard, E. "At Spring Hill and Franklin Again," *Confederate Veteran*, XXIV (1916).

Shoup, F. A. "Works at Chattahoochee River," *Confederate Veteran*, III (1895).

Stephenson, P. D. "Reminiscences of the Last Campaign of the Army of Tennessee, from May 1864 to January 1865," *S.H.S.P.*, XII (1884).

Stevens, Tillman H. " 'Other Side' in Battle of Franklin," *Confederate Veteran*, XI (1903).

Sykes, E. T. "Walthall's Brigade," *Publications of the Mississippi Historical Society*, Cent. Ser., I (1916).

Washburn, W. A. "Cleburne's Division at Franklin," *Confederate Veteran*, XIII (1905).

Watkins, S. R. "Snow Battle at Dalton," *Confederate Veteran*, I (1893).

Webster, Miss R. C. "Some Reminiscences," *Confederate Veteran*, VII (1899).

Wheeler, J. A. "Cleburne's Brigade at Shiloh," *Confederate Veteran*, II (1894).

──────. "Letters from Veterans," *Confederate Veteran*, II (1894).

Wilson, S. F. Address, 1905, at unveiling of monument honoring 2nd Tennessee Regiment, in "The Confederate Monument at Shiloh," *Confederate Veteran*, XIII (1905).

Yeatman, W. E. Address to Confederate veterans, Knoxville, Tenn., quoted in Knoxville *Sentinel*, date not shown, clipping in Scrapbook belonging to Seven Generals Chapter, United Daughters of the Confederacy, Helena, Ark. (in Helena and Phillips County Public Library and Museum). (The Scrapbook is cited hereinafter as Scrapbk, U.D.C., Helena; and the Library and Museum, as Helena Library.)

Young, J. P. "Franklin," Memphis *Evening Scimitar*, December 17, 1892.

471

MANUSCRIPT COLLECTIONS, LETTERS, DIARIES, MEMOIRS, RECORDS OF INSTITUTIONS, FAMILY RECORD BOOK, MISCELLANEOUS PAPERS

"Apprentices Book," Apothecaries' Hall, Dublin, Ireland.

Blackmore, James W. "Co. 'I,' 2nd Regiment Tennessee Infantry" (MS in possession of Mrs. Alex W. Hewitt, Dallas).

George J. Blakemore Diary (MS in Tennessee State Library and Archives, hereinafter cited as Tenn. Lib. and Arch.)

Braxton Bragg Papers, The Western Reserve Historical Society, Cleveland (hereinafter cited as West. Res. Hist. Soc.)

Irving A. Buck Papers, Southern Historical Collection, The University of North Carolina Library (hereinafter cited as Uni. N.C.).

Burke Boykin & Company (print.). *Constitution of the Comrades of the Southern Cross: Adopted August 28th, 1863* (Macon, Ga., 1863), Uni. N.C.

Claiborne, Thomas. "The Campaign of 1862 into Kentucky of Gen'l Braxton Bragg" (MS in Thomas Claiborne Letters and Reminiscences, 1849-1929, Uni. N.C.).

Cleburne family *Record Book* of marriages, births, and deaths, in possession of Charles Cleburne Jordan, Minneapolis.

Cleburne, P. R., Letters in possession of Charles Cleburne Jordan.

Cleburne to Miss Rowe Webster, January 31, 1864, in Miscellaneous Files, Tennessee Historical Society Collections, Tenn. Lib. and Arch.

Cleburne's Book of Common Prayer, Helena Library.

Cleburne, William, to Patrick R. Cashman, July 8, 1849, in possession of Mrs. Otto Duemler, Fresno, Calif.

Cleburne, William, to David C. Eaton, April 4, May 6, 1874, in Yale University Library.

Daniel C. Govan Papers, Uni. N.C.

William J. Hardee Correspondence: 1861-1862, Library of Congress.

William Joseph Hardee Papers, Alabama Department of Archives and History, Montgomery (hereinafter cited as Ala. Arch. and Hist.).

Harlow, William F. "James Madison Hudson: Confederate Soldier." Unpublished master's thesis, Department of History, West Texas State University, 1964.

Thomas Robson Hay Collection of P. R. Cleburne Material, Locust Valley, New York.

"Headquarters of Confederate Generals Stationed in Corinth during 1862," compiled about 1920 by Corinth Chapter, United Daughters of the Confederacy (MS in possession of Mrs. Fred E. Rogers, Corinth).

Josiah Stoddard Johnston Papers, The Filson Club, Inc., Louisville.

Legal Pleading drafted by Cleburne, "Demurrer to Plea," (MS in Hist. Soc. Pa.).

Liddell, St. John. "Record of the Civil War" (MS in Govan Papers).

Martin, Will T., to Bragg, undated, in University of Texas Library.

William P. Palmer Collection, West. Res. Hist. Soc.

Peters, Mrs. James Taylor, "Reminiscences of" (MS in possession of Benjamin D. Hill, Jr., Washington).

Preston, W. E. "Memoirs of the War" (Undated MS in Compiled Data, 33rd Alabama Infantry Regiment, Ala. Arch. and Hist.).

"Prospectus" of the Spedding school, dated October 1840, in possession of John N. Bank, Cobh, County Cork, Ire.

The Rt. Rev. Charles Todd Quintard, D.D., Diary (MS in Archives Department, Jesse Ball duPont Library, University of the South, Sewanee).

Questionnaires of Confederate veterans, Tenn. Lib. and Arch.

Records, Cemetery of Spring Grove, Cincinnati.

Records, Christ Episcopal Church, Mobile.

Records, Parish Church of Cliburn, Westmorland County, England.

Records, Royal College of Surgeons of England, London.

Records, St. John's Episcopal Church, Helena.

Records, Trinity College, Dublin.

Schell, A. B. "A Partial Report of the Part I Played in the War between the States," enclosed in letter Schell to James W. Blackmore, July 14, 1905 (MS in possession of Mrs. Alex W. Hewitt).

Edmund Kirby Smith Papers, Uni. N.C.

Tarleton Family Collection, Yale University library.

Tarleton, Robert, file record, Princeton University.

J. J. Thornton Scrapbook, The Mississippi Department of Archives and History, Jackson.

Work, J. G. *Map of Kennesaw Mountain battlefield at point of assault on Cleburne's division, etc.* (Chicago, 1902), in possession of National Park Service, Kennesaw Mountain National Battlefield Park.

Marcus J. Wright Papers, Uni. N.C.

Yandell, D. W., to William Preston Johnston, November 8, 1862, in Mrs. Mason Barret Collection of Albert Sidney and William Preston Johnston Papers, Tulane University Library.

SECONDARY SOURCES

GOVERNMENT PUBLICATIONS

DeBow, J. D. B., Superintendent of Census (comp.). *The Seventh Census of the United States: 1850.*

Kennedy, Joseph C. G., Superintendent of Census (comp.). *Population of the United States in 1860: Compiled from the Original Returns of the Eighth Census* (Washington, 1864).

Military Secretary's Office, The, U.S. War Department, *Memorandum Relative to The General Officers Appointed by the President in the Armies of the Confederate States, 1861-1865: Compiled from Official Records* (Washington, 1905).

Reed, D. W. (comp.). *The Battle of Shiloh and the Organizations Engaged* (Washington, 1909).

BOOKS, MONOGRAPHS

Alderman, Edwin Anderson; Harris, Joel Chandler; and Kent, Charles William (eds.). *Library of Southern Literature* (New Orleans, 1910).

Beard, Charles A. and Mary F. *The Rise of American Civilization.* (New York, 1931).

Brewer, W. *Alabama* (Montgomery, 1872).

Burne, Alfred H. *Lee, Grant and Sherman* (New York, 1939).

Butler, Pierce. *Judah P. Benjamin* (Philadelphia, 1906).

Callahan, James Morton. *Diplomatic History of the Southern Confederacy* (Reprint; New York, 1964).

Chambers, William and Robert (eds.). *Chamber's Information for the People* (Philadelphia, 1857).

Cincinnati Directories, 1850, 1851-52, 1857, 1860, 1869.

Connelly, Thomas Lawrence. *Army of the Heartland: The Army of Tennessee, 1861-1862* (Baton Rouge, 1967).

——————. *Autumn of Glory: The Army of Tennessee, 1862-1865* (Baton Rouge, 1971).

Coulter, E. Merton. *The Confederate States of America: 1861-1865* (Baton Rouge, 1950).

Cumberland Almanac for 1862 (Nashville, 1861).

Curwen, John F. *A Pedigree of the Family of Curwen of Workington and Kindred Branches* (Kendal, Eng., 1904 ?).

Dowdey, Clifford. *The Land They Fought For* (Garden City, N. Y., 1955).

DuBose, John Witherspoon. *General Joseph Wheeler and The Army of Tennessee* (New York, 1912).

E. C. R. "Some Desmond Incidents and Notes on the Ronayne Family," *Journal of the Cork Historical & Archaeological Society*, XXIII, 2nd Ser. (1917).

Edwards, Anthony. *Cork Rembrancer* (Cork, Ire., 1792).

Eisenshiml, Otto. *The Story of Shiloh* (Chicago, 1946).

Fee, Wilson. *The Gist Family of South Carolina and Its Maryland Antecedents* (Charlottesville, 1934).

Foster, James Fleetwood. *Ante-Bellum Floating Palaces of the Alabama River*, ed. Bert Neville (Selma, 1960).

Freeman, Douglas Southall. *R. E. Lee* (New York, 1940).

The Goodspeed Publishing Co. (pub.). *Biographical and Historical Memoirs of Eastern Arkansas* (Chicago, 1890).

Hallum, John. *Biographical and Pictorial History of Arkansas* (Albany, 1887), I.

Harrell, John M. "Arkansas," in Clement A. Evans (ed.), *Confederate Military History* (Atlanta, 1899), X.

Hartje, Robert G. *Van Dorn: The Life and Times of a Confederate General* (Nashville, 1967).

Hay, Thomas Robson. *Hood's Tennessee Campaign* (New York, 1929).

Hempstead, Fay. *A Pictorial History of Arkansas* (St. Louis, 1890).

——————. *Historical Review of Arkansas* (Chicago, 1911), I.

Henry, Robert Selph. *"First with the Most" Forrest* (Indianapolis, 1944).

——————. *The Story of the Confederacy* (New York, 1936).

Hoehling, A. A. *Last Train from Atlanta* (New York, 1958).

Horace, *Odes* — Book III.

Horn, Stanley F. *The Army of Tennessee* (Norman, Okla., 1959).

Hughes, Mary B. *Hearthstones: The Story of Historic Rutherford County Homes* (Murfreesboro, Tenn., 1942).

Hughes, Nathaniel Cheairs, Jr. *General William J. Hardee: Old Reliable* (Baton Rouge, 1965).

Ingersoll, Lurton Dunham. *Iowa and the Rebellion* (Philadelphia, 1867).

Johnston, Mary. *Cease Firing* (Boston, 1912).

Johnston, William Preston. *The Life of Gen. Albert Sidney Johnston* (New York, 1878).

Knight, F. W. "General Patrick Ronayne Cleburne," *Journal of the Cork Historical & Archaeological Society*, XXI, 2nd Ser. (1915).

Knight, Frederick W. "Notes on the Family of Ronayne or Ronan, of Cos. Cork and Waterford," *Journal of the Cork Historical & Archaeological Society*, XXIII, 2nd Ser. (1916); *ibid.*, XXIII 2nd Ser. (1917).

Kurtz, Wilbur G. *The Atlanta Cyclorama: The Story of the Famed Battle of Atlanta* (Atlanta, 1954).

LaBree, Ben (ed.). *Camp Fires of the Confederacy* (Louisville, 1898).

Lewis, Samuel. *A Topographical Dictionary of Ireland* (London, 1837), I.

Lindsley, John Berrien (ed.). *The Military Annals of Tennessee (Confederate)*, (Nashville, 1886).

Lippincott, J. B. & Co. (pub.). *United States Infantry Tactics, for the Instruction, Exercise, and Manoeuvres of the United States Infantry*

(Philadelphia, 1862).

Lonn, Ella. *Foreigners in the Union Army and Navy* (Baton Rouge, 1951).

Lord, Walter (ed.). *The Fremantle Diary* (Boston, 1954).

Mackall, William W. *A Son's Recollections of His Father* (New York, 1930).

Maguire, John Francis. *The Irish in America* (New York, 1873).

Miller, Francis Trevelyan (ed.). *The Photographic History of the Civil War* (New York, 1912).

Mobile City Directory, 1866.

Nichols, John Gough (ed.). *The Annals of Youghal* (Youghal, Ire., 1847).

O'Brien, R. Barry (ed.). *Two Centuries of Irish History: 1691-1870* (London, 1907).

O'Hart, John. *Irish Pedigrees* (New York, 1915), II.

Owsley, Frank Lawrence. *King Cotton Diplomacy* (Chicago, 1959).

────────. *Plain Folk of the Old South* (Baton Rouge, 1949).

────────. "The Irrepressible Conflict," in Twelve Southerners, *I'll Take My Stand: The South and the Agrarian Tradition* (Reprint; New York, 1951).

Parks, Joseph Howard. *General Edmund Kirby Smith, C.S.A.* (Baton Rouge, 1962).

Phillips, Ulrich Bonnell. *The Course of the South to Secession* (Reprint; Gloucester, 1958).

Pierrepont, Alice V. C. *Reuben Vaughan Kidd, Soldier of the Confederacy* (Petersburg, Va., 1947).

Polk, William M. *Leonidas Polk: Bishop and General* (New York, 1915), II.

Porter, James D. "Tennessee," in Evans (ed.), *Confederate Military History*, VIII.

Pratt, John. *Pratt Family Records* (Millom, Eng., 1931).

Purdue, Ida Pace, *Papers Pertaining to the Confederacy* (Athens, Ga., 1961).

Ransom, John Crowe. "Reconstructed but Unregenerate," in *I'll Take My Stand*.

Reynolds, John Hugh. *Makers of Arkansas History* (New York, 1918).

Reynolds, John Hugh (ed.). *Publications of the Arkansas Historical Association* (Fayetteville, Ark., 1906), I.

Richard, J. Fraise. *The Florence Nightingale of the Southern Army* (New York, 1914).

Ridley, Bromfield L. *Battles and Sketches of the Army of Tennessee* (Mexico, Mo., 1906).

Roe, George Mortimer (ed.). *Cincinnati: The Queen City of the West* (Cincinnati, 1895).

Royal Commission on Historical Monuments, England. *An Inventory of the Historical Monuments in Westmoreland* (London, 1936).

Scharf, J. Thomas. *History of the Confederate States Navy* (New York, 1887).

School of Musketry, Hythe (comp.). *Regulations for conducting Musketry Instruction in the Army* (London, bet. 1855 and 1860).

Scott, Winfield. *Infantry Tactics* (New York, 1854), III.

Seitz, Don C. *Braxton Bragg: General of the Confederacy* (Columbia, S. C., 1924).

Simpson, Harold B. *Hood's Texas Brigade: Lee's Grenadier Guard* (Waco, 1970).

Sims, William Gilmore (ed.). *War Poetry of the South* (New York, 1867).

Slater, Isaac (comp.). *Slater's National Commercial Directory of Ireland* (Manchester, Eng., 1846).

Smith, Frank H. "Interview with Capt. A. Buck Schell, January 16, 1907," in Maury County Historical Society (comp.), *Frank H. Smith's History of Maury County, Tennessee* (Columbia, Tenn., 1969).

Spedding, John Carlisle D. *The Spedding Family* (Dublin, 1909).

Stickles, Arndt M. *Simon Bolivar Buckner: Borderland Knight* (Chapel Hill, 1940).

Taylor, Michael Waistell. *The Old Manorial Halls of Westmoreland & Cumberland: Publications of the Cumberland and Westmoreland Antiquarian and Archaeological Society* (Kendal, Eng., 1892), VIII.

Tucker, Glenn. *Chickamauga: Bloody Battle in the West* (Indianapolis, 1961).

United Confederate Veterans, By Authority of the, *The Flags of the Confederate States of America* (Baltimore, 1907).

Van Horne, Thomas B. *The Life of Major-General George H. Thomas* (New York, 1882).

Warner, Ezra L. *Generals in Gray* (Baton Rouge, 1959).

Wharton, H. M. (comp.). *War Songs and Poems of the Southern Confederacy: 1861-1865* (Philadelphia, 1904).

Whitehorne, A. C. *The History of the Welch Regiment* (Cardiff, Wales, 1932).

Wiley, Bell Irvin. *Southern Negroes: 1861-1865* (New Haven, 1938).

Williams, T. Harry. *P. G. T. Beauregard: Napoleon in Gray* (Baton Rouge, 1955).

Windele, J. *Historical and Descriptive Notices of the City of Cork and Its Vicinity* (Cork, Ire., 1839).

Wyeth, John Allan. *Life of Lieutenant-General Nathan Bedford Forrest* (New York, 1899).

ARTICLES, PERIODICALS

"An 'Unseen Message' of President Davis's," *Confederate Veteran*, XIV (1906).

"Athnowen," in Lewis, *Topographical Dictionary of Ireland*, I.

"Attention, Whitworth Sharpshooters," *Confederate Veteran*, I (1893).

"A Winter in the South," *Harper's New Monthly Magazine* XVIII (1858).

"Ballincollig," in Lewis, *Topographical Dictionary of Ireland*, I.

Bush, F. W. "Arkansas' Work on Kennesaw Mountain," *Confederate Veteran*, XIX (1911).

"Charles A. Leushuer," *Confederate Veteran*, XXI (1913).

Confederate Veteran, Nashville, 1893-1932, 40 vols.

"Crocker's Iowa Brigade," *The Veteran*, I (1882).

"Dalton-Atlanta Campaign," *Confederate Veteran*, V (1897).

DuBose, John Witherspoon. "Chronicles of the Canebrake, 1817-60," *The Alabama Historical Quarterly*, IX (1947).

"Facts about 'the Cleburne Flag,' " *Confederate Veteran*, XVII (1909).

"Forty-eighth Tennessee Regiment" *Confederate Veteran*, II (1894).

"General Cleburne's Views on Slavery," in Drake (ed.), *Annals of Army of Tennessee*, I.

"Gen. Pat R. Cleburne," Mobile *Daily Advertiser and Register*, January 22, 1864.

Godfrey, Michael. "The Price of Glory Extracted from War Office Records," (British) *Army Quarterly and Defence Journal*, LXXXVII (1963).

─────────. "300 Years of the Marines," (London) *Daily Telegraph and Morning Post*, April 24, 1964.

Hay, Thomas Robson, "The South and the Arming of the Slaves," *Mississippi Valley Historical Review*, VI (1919-20).

Hickman, John P. "Hood's Failure at Spring Hill," *Confederate Veteran*, XXII (1914).

Hindman, Biscoe, "General Pat. Cleburne," *S.H.S.P.*, XXXI (1903).

"Hood's Campaign in Tennessee," *Confederate Veteran*, II (1894).

Humphries, Milton W. "The Battle at Cloyd's Farm," *Confederate Veteran*, XVII (1909).

"Incidents of Gen. M'Pherson's Death," *Confederate Veteran*, XI (1903).

"John H. Warren," *Confederate Veteran*, XV (1907).

Jones, J. William, "The Morale of the Confederate Armies," in Evans (ed.), *Confederate Military History*, XII.

Kelly, Maud McLure. "John Herbert Kelly: The Boy General of the Confederacy," *The Alabama Historical Quarterly*, IX (1947).

The Kennesaw Gazette, Atlanta, 1886-1890, 5 vols.

Kurtz, Wilbur G. "The Death of Major General W. H. T. Walker, July 22, 1864," *Civil War History*, VI (1960).

Montgomery, Victor. "The Sacrifice of the South," *Confederate Veteran*, XVIII (1910).

Moreland, George M. "Pat Cleburne," Memphis *Commercial Appeal*, February 6, 1927.

Odenheimer, Cordella Powell, "From the President General," *Confederate Veteran*, XXIV (1916).

Pike, Albert. "A Shooting Match," in Octavius Coke (ed.), *The Scrapbook of Arkansas Literature* (Little Rock, 1939).

Randle, W. F. "Pat Cleburne's Early Career," *Confederate Veteran*, XIX (1911).

Ridley, B. L. "The Fifth and Sixteenth Tennessee," *Confederate Veteran*, VIII (1900).

Ross, Margaret, "Chronicles of Arkansas," Little Rock *Arkansas Gazette*, January 29, 1961; *ibid.*, February 5, 1961.

"Surgeons of the Confederacy: Dr. W. M. Gentry of Tennessee," *Confederate Veteran*, XL (1932).

"The Late Gen. Cleburne. — A Reminiscence," Mobile *Army Argus and Crisis*, February 4, 1865.

"To the Memory of John A. Cathey and John R. Loftin," *Confederate Veteran*, III (1895).

Whitehouse, Gertrude. "Gen. Cleburne's Pistol Recovered," (Cleburne, Tex.) *Yellow Jacket Yapper*, September 22, 1944.

"William H. Heard," *Confederate Veteran*, XI (1903).

Winter, Mary Carter. "A Retrospect," *Confederate Veteran*, XXXVII (1929).

Worley, Ted R. "Helena on the Mississippi," *Arkansas Historical Quarterly*, XIII (1954).

"W. T. Barnes," *Confederate Veteran*, XXVI (1918).

MANUSCRIPTS, SCRAPBOOKS, MISCELLANEOUS MATERIAL

Cleburne, Poem "To Miss Y" (Photostat in Arkansas History Commission).

Cockrell, Monroe F. *Notes and Articles by Monroe F. Cockrell for His Maps of the War between the States* (Evanston, 1950). (MSS in Library of Congress).

D. C. Beers & Co. (pub.). *Map of Williamson County, Tenn.* (Philadelphia, 1878).

"History of Tarleton Family" (MS compiled December 3, 1855, in possession of Mrs. F. L. DuValle, Mobile).

Kurtz, Wilbur G. *Map of Atlanta . . . showing the field and fortified lines of the Confederate forces*, pub. Atlanta Chamber of Commerce (Atlanta, 1938).

_____. "The Jonesboro Campaign," paper read at meeting of Atlanta Civil War Round Table, June 18, 1957 (Mimeo. copy, gift to authors by Mr. Kurtz).

_____. "Why Was Snake Creek Gap Left Unguarded?" (Typescript lent by Mr. Kurtz to authors in 1964, now in possession of Atlanta Historical Society).

McGavock Cemetery Record Book.

Owen, Marie Bankhead, MS re Capt. John Hollis Bankhead, in 16th Alabama Infantry Regiment (compiled data), Ala. Arch. and Hist.

Scrapbook Belonging to Seven Generals Chapter, United Daughters of the Confederacy, Helena, Ark., now in Helena Library.

"Scrap Book" in Cleburne (Tex.) Public Library.

Scrapbook of John E. Sherlock, in possession of Mrs. Charles N. Flitton, Arcadia, Calif.

Scrapbook of Mrs. W. E. Moore, in Helena Library.

Scrapbook of Mrs. W. E. (Naomi Hays) Moore, in possession of Mrs. Moore Tappan, Helena.

Thomas Robson Hay Collection of P. R. Cleburne Material.

Widders, J. D. H., (Librarian, Royal College of Surgeons of Ireland, Dublin), "A Note on the Apothecaries' Hall," dated Dec. 1964 (MS in possession of Dr. Denis Wilson, Cork City, Ire.).

NEWSPAPERS

In the preparation of this biography, all Helena, Ark., newspapers known to be extant, for the period 1850-1860, have been searched, as well as the Centennial Edition, Helena *World*, August 16, 1956. Also, newspapers published in the following cities have been examined for special periods: Cincinnati, Columbia (Tennessee), Little Rock, Memphis, Mobile, New Orleans, and Richmond. Particular issues are cited in the footnotes.

CORRESPONDENCE WITH AUTHORS

Letters to the authors from the following persons are cited in the footnotes: Dr. Peter A. Brannon, Director, Alabama Department of Archives and History; Monroe F. Cockrell; Mrs. F. L. DuValle; Anne Sherlock (Mrs. Charles J.) Jordan; Wilbur G. Kurtz; John Noel Ronayne Macnamara; Frank Moloney, Town Clerk of Youghal, Ire.; W. O'Sullivan, Keeper of MSS, Trinity College, Dublin; Dr. Winston Smith; and Miss India W. Thomas, Director, The Confederate Museum, Richmond. The letters are in the possession of the authors.

INDEX

PART I – CLEBURNE, PATRICK RONAYNE, "PAT"

PART II – MILITARY UNITS
Confederate

494

498

ERRATA

Page	Line	Correction
vii	12	"Cleburn's" should be "Cleburne's"
11	20	"convalscing" should be "convalescing"
41	25	"shoop" should be "whoop"
42	37	"of" at end of line should be "or"
43	7	Insert "the" after "bow"
43	12	"page 40" should be "pages 13-14"
59	42	"Cleburn" should be "Cleburne"
61	3	"Dermurrer" should be "Demurrer"
89	39	Insert "the" before "2nd"
141	28	"would be" should be "was"
144	9	"sympahizers" should be "sympathizers"
144	12	"Caliborne's" should be "Claiborne's"
146	7	"tow" should be "two"
215	5	"thier" should be "there"
218	5	Insert "the" after "on"
226	25	"sholder" should be "shoulder"
227	38	"H. W. Kinsey" should be "W. H. Kinsey"
246	45	Delete "the" before "Douglas' "
257	23	"skrimishers" should be "skirmishers"
261	27	"Liuetenant" should be "Lieutenant"
266	20	"Cleubrne" should be "Cleburne"
281	33	"anf" should be "and"
329	33	"divisions" should be "division"
352	18	"to" should be "of"
356	7	"woods" should be "works"
384	17	"Cleubrne" should be "Cleburne"
399	10	"Srping Hill" should be "Spring Hill"
406	4	"excape" should be "escape"
417	19	Insert "of Winstead Hill" after "north"
434	11	"thorne" should be "throne"
436	20	"wonderfil" should be "wonderful"
439	23	"country" should be "county"
440	9	Insert "Texarkana," after "Fayetteville,"

MISSOURI RIVER
St. Louis

ST. LOUIS & IRON MT. R.R.

I L L I N O I S

M I S S O U R

CURRE

Ft. Henry

MEMPHIS RIVER

TENNESSEE RIVER

WHITE RIVER

E N N

BI

Poc

Wa

Savannah
Pittsburg La

hiloh
huych
Michie's
Monterey
Farmington

A R K A N S

WHITE RIVER

Little Rock

A R K A N S A S RIVER

wyn

Napoleon

M I S S I S S I P P I

MOBILE &

THEATER OF OPERATIONS

PROXIMATE SCALE - MILES
10 20 30 40

-Van F. Pruitt-